STUDY GUIDE
for use with
McConnell and Brue
MACROECONOMICS

Seventeenth Edition

WILLIAM B. WALSTAD
PROFESSOR OF ECONOMICS
UNIVERSITY OF NEBRASKA–LINCOLN

McGraw-Hill
Irwin

Boston Burr Ridge, IL Dubuque, IA Madison, WI New York
San Francisco St. Louis Bangkok Bogotá Caracas Kuala Lumpur
Lisbon London Madrid Mexico City Milan Montreal New Delhi
Santiago Seoul Singapore Sydney Taipei Toronto

McGraw-Hill
Irwin

Study Guide for use with
Macroeconomics, Seventeenth Edition
Campbell R. McConnell, Stanley L. Brue, and William B. Walstad

Published by McGraw-Hill/Irwin, a business unit of The McGraw-Hill Companies, Inc., 1221 Avenue of the Americas, New York, NY 10020. Copyright © 2008 by The McGraw-Hill Companies, Inc.
All rights reserved.

1 2 3 4 5 6 7 8 9 0 QPD/QPD 0 9 8 7 6

ISBN 978-0-07-327320-4
MHID 0-07-327320-1

www.mhhe.com

About the Author

William B. Walstad is a professor of economics at the University of Nebraska–Lincoln, where he directs the National Center for Research in Economic Education and has been honored with a Distinguished Teaching Award. Professor Walstad also has been recognized with the Henry H. Villard Research Award for his published research in economic education by the National Association of Economic Educators and National Council on Economic Education. He is an associate editor of the *Journal of Economic Education* and was the previous chair of the Committee on Economic Education of the American Economic Association. He is a coeditor and contributor to *Teaching Undergraduate Economics: A Handbook for Instructors* (McGraw-Hill). He serves as the principal investigator for a National Science Foundation project for economics faculty members on interactive teaching and learning. Professor Walstad received his Ph.D. degree from the University of Minnesota.

To
Tammie, Laura, Kristin, Eileen, Clara, and Martha

Contents

How to Use the Study Guide to Learn Economics

This *Study Guide* should help you read and understand Campbell R. McConnell and Stanley L. Brue's textbook, *Macroeconomics*, seventeenth edition. If used properly, a study guide can be a great aid to you for what is probably your first course in economics.

No one pretends that the study of economics is easy, but it can be made easier with this *Study Guide*. Of course, it will not do your work for you, and its use is no substitute for reading the text. You must first be willing to read the text and work at learning if you wish to understand economics.

Many students, however, do read their text and work hard on their economics course and still fail to learn the subject. This problem occurs because economics is a new subject for those students. They want to learn economics but do not know how to do that because they have no previous experience with the subject. Here is where the *Study Guide* can help students. Let's first see what the *Study Guide* contains and then learn how to use it.

■ WHAT THE *STUDY GUIDE* IS

This *Study Guide* contains 19 chapters to support your learning of each of the 19 textbook chapters in *Macroeconomics*. There are also two more *Study Guide* chapters that fully support the two **Bonus Web Chapters** for *Macroeconomics*. In addition, the *Study Guide* has a **glossary**. This *Study Guide* should give you a complete set of resources to advance your learning of the principles of economics.

Each *Study Guide* chapter has 11 sections to give you complete coverage of the textbook material in each chapter. The first five sections help you **understand** the economics content in each chapter.

1. An *introduction* explains what is in the chapter of the text and how it is related to material in earlier and later chapters. It points out topics to which you should give special attention and reemphasizes difficult or important principles and facts.

2. A *checklist* tells you the things you should be able to do when you have finished the chapter.

3. A *chapter outline* shows how the chapter is organized and summarizes briefly the essential points made in the chapter, including the Last Word.

4. Selected *hints and tips* for each chapter help you identify key points and make connections with any previous discussion of a topic.

5. A list of the *important terms* points out what you must be able to define to understand the material in the chapter. Each term is bolded and italicized in the chapter outline so you can easily find it. Each term is also defined in the glossary at the end of the *Study Guide*.

The next six sections of the *Study Guide* allow you to **self-test** your understanding of the chapter material.

6. *Fill-in questions* (short-answer and list questions) help you learn and remember the important generalizations and facts in the chapter.

7. *True–false questions* test your understanding of the material in the chapter.

8. *Multiple-choice questions* also give you a chance to check your knowledge of the chapter content and prepare for this type of course examination.

9. *Problems* help you learn and understand economic concepts by requiring different skills—drawing a graph, completing a table, or finding relationships—to solve the problems.

10. *Short answer* and *essay questions* can be used as a self-test, to identify important questions in the chapter, and to prepare for examinations.

11. *Answers* to fill-in questions, true–false questions, multiple-choice questions, and problems are found at the end of each chapter. References to the specific pages in the textbook for each true–false, multiple-choice, and short answer or essay question are also provided.

■ HOW TO STUDY AND LEARN WITH THE HELP OF THE *STUDY GUIDE*

1. *Read and outline.* For the best results, quickly read the introduction, outline, list of terms, and checklist in the *Study Guide* before you read the chapter in *Macroeconomics*. Then read the chapter in the text slowly, keeping one eye on the *Study Guide* outline and the list of terms. Highlight the chapter as you read it by identifying the *major and minor* points and by placing *Study Guide* outline numbers or letters (such as I or A or 1 or a) in the margins. When you have completed the chapter, you will have the chapter highlighted, and the *Study Guide* outline will serve as a handy set of notes on the chapter.

2. *Review and reread.* After you have read the chapter in the text once, return to the introduction, outline, and list of terms in the *Study Guide*. Reread the introduction and outline. Does everything there make sense? If not, go back to the text and reread the topics that you do not remember well or that still confuse you. Look at the outline. Try to recall each of the minor topics that were contained in the text under each of the major points in the outline. When you come to the list of terms, go over them one by one. *Define or explain each to yourself and then look for the definition of the term either in the text chapter or in the glossary.* Compare your own definition or explanation with that in the *text or glossary*. The quick way to find the definition of a term in the text is to look in the text index for the page(s) in which that term or concept is mentioned. Make any necessary correction or change in your own definition or explanation.

3. *Test and check answers.* When you have done the above reading and review, you will have a good idea of what is in the text chapter. Now complete the self-test sections of the *Study Guide* to check your understanding.

In doing the self-test, start with the *fill-in, true–false, multiple-choice,* and *problems* sections. Tackle each of these four sections one at a time, using the following procedures: (1) Answer as many self-test items as you can without looking in the text or in the answer section of the *Study Guide*; (2) check the text for whatever help you need in answering the items; and (3) consult the answer section of the *Study Guide* for the correct answers and reread any section of the text for which you missed items.

The self-test items in these four sections are not equally difficult. Some will be easy to answer, and others will be harder. Do not expect to get them all correct the first time. Some are designed to pinpoint material of importance that you will probably miss the first time you read the text, and answering them will get you to read the text again with more insight and understanding.

The *short answer and essay questions* cover the major points in the chapter. For some of the easier questions, all you may do is mentally outline your answer. For the more difficult questions, you may want to write out a brief outline of the answer or a full answer. Do not avoid the difficult questions just because they are more work. Answering these questions is often the most valuable work you can do toward acquiring an understanding of economic relationships and principles.

Although no answers are given in the *Study Guide* to the short answer and essay questions, the answer section does list text page references for each question. You are *strongly* encouraged to read those text pages for an explanation of the question or for better insight into the question content.

4. *Double check.* Before you turn to the next chapter in the text and *Study Guide*, return to the checklist. If you cannot honestly check off each item in the list, you have not learned what the authors of the text and of this *Study Guide* hoped you would learn.

■ BONUS WEB CHAPTERS FOR *MACROECONOMICS*

The *Study Guide* fully supports the two Web-based chapters in *Macroeconomics*. These chapters are (1) Financial Economics (Chapter 14W); and (2) The Economics of Developing Countries (Chapter 16W). They are available at **www.mcconnell17.com**.

The *Study Guide* includes full content and self-test materials for these two chapters.

■ GLOSSARY

All the important terms and concepts in *Macroeconomics* are defined and described in the glossary. It is included in the *Study Guide* for easy reference when you see a term or concept you do not know. It will also aid your work on self-test items in the *Study Guide*.

■ SOME FINAL WORDS

Perhaps the method of using the *Study Guide* outlined above seems like a lot of work. It is! Study and learning require work on your part. This fact is one you must accept if you are to learn economics.

After you have used the *Study Guide* to study one or two chapters, you will find that some sections are more valuable to you than others. Let your own experience determine how you will use the material. But do not discontinue use of the *Study Guide* after one or two chapters merely because you are not sure whether it is helping you. *Stick with it.*

■ ACKNOWLEDGMENTS

Special thanks are due to Sharon Nemeth for her hard work in preparing the print and electronic versions of this *Study Guide*. I am also indebted to Stan Brue and Campbell McConnell for their ongoing support during the development of this *Study Guide*. While I am most grateful for all these contributions, I alone am responsible for any errors or omissions. You are welcome to send me comments or suggestions.

William B. Walstad

Limits, Alternatives, and Choices

Chapter 1 introduces you to economics—the social science that studies how individuals, institutions, and society make the optimal, or best, choices under conditions of scarcity. The first section of the chapter describes the three key features of the **economic perspective.** This perspective first recognizes that all choices involve costs and that those costs must be involved in an economic decision. The economic perspective also incorporates the view that to achieve a goal, people make decisions that reflect their purposeful self-interest. The third feature considers that people compare marginal benefits with marginal costs when making decisions and will choose the situation where the marginal benefit is greater than the marginal cost. You will develop a better understanding of these features as you read about the economic issues in this book.

Economics relies heavily on the **scientific method** to develop theories and principles to explain the likely effects from human events and behavior. It involves gathering data, testing hypotheses, and developing theories and principles. In essence, economic theories and principles (and related terms such as laws and models) are generalizations about how the economic world works.

Economists develop economic theories and principles at two levels. **Macroeconomics** focuses on the whole economy or large segments of it. Studies at this level investigate such issues as how to increase economic growth, control inflation, and maintain full employment. **Microeconomics** targets specific units in the economy. Studies at this level research such questions as how prices and output are determined for particular products and how consumers react to price changes. Studies at either level have elements of **positive economics,** which investigates facts or cause-and-effect relationships, or **normative economics,** which incorporates subjective views of what ought to be or what policies should be used to address an economic issue.

Several sections of the text are devoted to a discussion of the **economizing problem** from individual or societal perspectives. This problem arises from a fundamental conflict between economic wants and economics resources: (1) Individuals and society have *unlimited* economic wants; (2) the economic means or resources to satisfy those wants are *limited.* This economic problem forces individuals and societies to make a choice. And any time a choice is made, there is an opportunity cost—the next best alternative that was not chosen.

The economizing problem for individuals is illustrated with a microeconomic model that uses a **budget line** that shows graphically the meaning of many concepts defined in the chapter—scarcity, choice, tradeoffs, opportunity cost, and optimal allocation. The economizing problem for society is illustrated with a macroeconomic model that uses a **production possibilities curve.** It also shows graphically the economic concepts just listed, and in addition it can be used to describe macroeconomic conditions related to unemployment, economic growth, and trade. The production possibilities model can also be applied to many real economic situations, such as the economics of war, as you will learn from the text.

■ CHECKLIST

When you have studied this chapter you should be able to

☐ Write a formal definition of economics.

☐ Describe the three key features of the economic perspective.

☐ Give applications of the economic perspective.

☐ Identify the elements of the scientific method.

☐ Distinguish among hypotheses, theories, principles, laws, and models.

☐ Discuss how economic principles are generalizations and abstractions.

☐ Explain the "other-things-equal" (*ceteris paribus*) assumption and its use in economics.

☐ Distinguish between macroeconomics and microeconomics.

☐ Give examples of positive and normative economics.

☐ Explain the economizing problem for an individual (from a microeconomic perspective).

☐ Describe the concept of a budget line for the individual.

☐ Explain how to measure the slope of a budget line and determine the location of the budget line.

☐ Describe the economizing problem for society.

☐ Define the four types of economic resources for society.

☐ State the four assumptions made when a production possibilities table or curve is constructed.

☐ Construct a production possibilities curve when you are given the appropriate data.

☐ Define opportunity cost and utilize a production possibilities curve to explain the concept.

☐ Show how the law of increasing opportunity costs is reflected in the shape of the production possibilities curve.

☐ Explain the economic rationale for the law of increasing opportunity costs.

☐ Use marginal analysis to define optimal allocation.

☐ Explain how optimal allocation determines the optimal point on a production possibilities curve.

☐ Use a production possibilities curve to illustrate unemployment.

☐ Use the production possibilities curve to illustrate economic growth.

☐ Explain how international trade affects a nation's production possibilities curve.

☐ Give other applications of the production possibilities model.

☐ Identify the five pitfalls to sound economic reasoning (Last Word).

■ **CHAPTER OUTLINE**

1. *Economics* studies how individuals, institutions, and society make the optimal, or best, choices under conditions of **scarcity,** in which economic wants are *unlimited* and the means or resources to satisfy those wants are *limited.*

2. The *economic perspective* has three interrelated features.

    a. It recognizes that scarcity requires choice and that making a choice has an *opportunity cost*—giving up the next best alternative to the choice that was made.

    b. It views people as purposeful decision makers who base choices on their self-interests.

    c. It uses *marginal analysis* to assess how the marginal costs of a decision compare with the marginal benefits.

3. Economics relies on the *scientific method* for analysis.

    a. Several terms are used in economic analysis that are related to this method.

    (1) *Hypotheses* are propositions that are tested and used to develop economic *theories.*

    (2) A highly tested and reliable economic theory is called an *economic principle* or *law.* Theories, principles, and laws are meaningful statements about economic behavior or the economy that can be used to predict the likely outcome of an action or event.

    (3) *Models* are created when several economic laws or principles are used to explain or describe reality.

    b. There are several other aspects of economic principles.

    (1) Each principle or theory is a generalization that shows a tendency or average effect.

    (2) The *other-things-equal assumption* (*ceteris paribus*) is used to limit the influence of other factors in making a generalization.

    (3) Many economic models can be illustrated graphically and are simplified representations of economic reality.

4. Economic analysis is conducted at two levels, and for each level there can be elements of positive or normative economics.

    a. *Macroeconomics* looks at the entire economy or its major *aggregates* or sectors, such as households, businesses, and government.

    b. *Microeconomics* studies the economic behavior of individuals, particular markets, firms, and industries.

    c. *Positive economics* focuses on facts and is concerned with what is, or the scientific analysis of economic behavior.

    d. *Normative economics* suggests what ought to be and answers policy questions on the basis of value judgments. Most disagreements among economists involve normative economics.

5. Individuals face an *economizing problem* because economic wants are greater than the economic means to satisfy those wants. This can be illustrated with a microeconomic model with several features.

    a. Individuals have limited income to spend.

    b. Individuals have virtually unlimited wants for goods and services.

    c. The economizing problem for the individual can be illustrated with a budget line and two products (DVDs and books). The *budget line* shows graphically the combinations of the two products a consumer can purchase with his or her money income.

    (1) All combinations of the two products on or inside the budget line are *attainable* by the consumer; all combinations beyond the budget line are *unattainable.*

    (2) To obtain more DVDs the consumer has to give up some books, so there is a *tradeoff;* if to get a second DVD the consumer must give up two books, the *opportunity* cost of the additional DVD is two books.

    (3) Limited income forces individuals to evaluate the marginal cost and marginal benefit of a choice to maximize their satisfaction.

    (4) Changes in money income shift the budget line: An increase in income shifts the line to the right; a decrease in income shifts the line to the left.

6. Society also faces an economizing problem due to scarcity.

    a. *Economic resources* are scarce natural, human, or manufactured inputs used to produce goods and services.

    b. Economic resources are sometimes called *factors of production* and are classified into four categories:

    (1) *land,* or natural resources.

    (2) *labor,* or the contributed time and abilities of people who are producing goods and services.

    (3) *capital* (or capital goods), or the machines, tools, and equipment used to make other goods and services; economists refer to the purchase of such capital goods as *investment.*

    (4) *entrepreneurial ability,* or the special human talents of individuals who combine the other factors of production.

7. A macroeconomic model of production possibilities illustrates the economizing problem for society. The four assumptions usually made when such a production possibilities model is used are: (1) There is full employment of available resources; (2) the quantity and quality of resources are fixed; (3) the state of technology does not change; and (4) there are two types of goods being produced (*consumer goods* and *capital goods*).

a. The production possibilities table indicates the alternative combinations of goods an economy is capable of producing when it has achieved full employment and optimal allocation. The table illustrates the fundamental choice every economy must make: what quantity of each product it must sacrifice to obtain more of another.

b. The data in the production possibilities table can be plotted on a graph to obtain a *production possibilities curve.* Each point on the curve shows some maximum output of the two goods.

c. The opportunity cost of producing an additional unit of one good is the amount of the other good that is sacrificed. The *law of increasing opportunity costs* states that the opportunity cost of producing one more unit of a good (the marginal opportunity cost) increases as more of the good is produced.

(1) The production possibilities curve is bowed out from the origin because of the law of increasing opportunity costs.

(2) The reason the opportunity cost of producing an additional unit of a good increases as more of that good is produced is because resources are not completely adaptable to alternative uses.

d. Optimal allocation means that resources are devoted to the best mix of goods to maximize satisfaction in society. This optimal mix is determined by assessing marginal costs and benefits.

(1) The marginal-cost curve for a good increases because of the law of increasing opportunity costs; the marginal-benefit curve decreases because the consumption of a good yields less and less satisfaction.

(2) When the marginal benefit is greater than the marginal cost, there is an incentive to produce more of the good, but when the marginal cost is greater than the marginal benefit, there is an incentive to produce less of the good.

(3) Optimal or efficient allocation is achieved when the marginal cost of a product equals the marginal benefit of that product.

8. Different outcomes will occur when assumptions underlying the production possibilities model are relaxed.

a. Unemployment. When the economy is operating at a point inside the production possibilities curve, it means that resources are not fully employed.

b. *Economic growth.* The production possibilities curve shifts outward from economic growth because resources are no longer fixed and technology improves.

(1) Expansion in the quantity and quality of resources contributes to economic growth and shifts the production possibilities curve outward.

(2) Advancement in technology contributes to economic growth and also shifts the production possibilities curve outward.

(3) The combination of capital goods and consumer goods an economy chooses to produce in the present can determine the position of the production possibilities curve in the future. Greater production of capital goods relative to consumer goods in the present shifts the production possibilities curve farther outward in the future because that economy is devoting more of its resources to investment than to consumption.

c. Trade. When there is international specialization and trade, a nation can obtain more goods and services than is indicated by the production possibilities curve for a domestic economy. The effect on production possibilities is similar to that of an increase in economic growth.

9. (Last Word). Sound reasoning about economic issues requires the avoidance of five pitfalls.

a. *Bias* is a preconceived belief or opinion that is not warranted by the facts.

b. *Loaded terminology* is the use of terms in a way that appeals to emotion and leads to a nonobjective analysis of the issues.

c. The *fallacy of composition* is the assumption that what is true of the part is necessarily true of the whole.

d. The *post hoc fallacy* ("after this, therefore because of this") is the mistaken belief that when one event precedes another, the first event is the cause of the second.

e. *Confusing correlation with causation* means that two factors may be related, but that does not mean that one factor caused the other.

■ **HINTS AND TIPS**

1. The **economic perspective** presented in the first section of the chapter has three features related to decision making: scarcity and the necessity of choice, purposeful self-interest in decision making, and marginal analysis of the costs and benefits of decisions. Although these features may seem strange at first, they are central to the economic thinking used to examine decisions and problems throughout the book.

2. The chapter introduces two pairs of terms: **microeconomics** and **macroeconomics** and **positive economics** and **normative economics.** Make sure you understand what each pair means and how they are related to each other.

3. The **budget line** shows the consumer what it is possible to purchase in the two-good world, given an income. Make sure you understand what a budget line is. To test your understanding, practice with different income levels and prices. For example, assume you had an income of $100 to spend for two goods (A and B). Good A costs $10, and Good B costs $5. Draw a budget line to show the possible combinations of A and B that you could purchase.

4. The **production possibilities curve** is a simple and useful economic model for an economy. Practice your understanding of it by using it to explain the following economic concepts: scarcity, choice, opportunity cost, the law of increasing opportunity costs, full employment, optimal allocation, unemployment, and economic growth.

5. Opportunity cost is always measured in terms of a foregone alternative. From a production possibilities table, you can easily calculate how many units of one product you forgo when you get another unit of a product.

■ IMPORTANT TERMS

Note: See Glossary in the back of the book for definitions of terms.

economics
economic perspective
opportunity cost
utility
marginal analysis
scientific method
economic principle
"other-things-equal"
  assumption
  (*ceteris paribus*)
macroeconomics
aggregate
microeconomics
positive economics
normative economics
economizing problem

budget line
economic resources
factors of production
land
labor
capital
investment
entrepreneurial ability
consumer goods
capital goods
production
  possibilities curve
law of increasing
  opportunity costs
economic growth

SELF-TEST

■ FILL-IN QUESTIONS

1. The economic perspective recognizes that (resources, scarcity) _____ require(s) choice and that choice has an opportunity (benefit, cost) _____. "There is no s5g as a free lunch" in economics because scarce resources have (unlimited, alternative) _____ uses.

2. The economic perspective also assumes that people base choices on their self-interest and that they are (random, purposeful) _____. It also is based on comparisons of the (extreme, marginal) _____ costs and benefits of an economic decision.

3. Economics relies on the (model, scientific) _____ method. Statements about economic behavior that enable the prediction of the likely effects of certain actions are economic (facts, theories) _____. The most well-tested of these that have strong predictive accuracy are called economic (hypotheses, principles) _____, or sometimes they are called (laws, actions) _____. Simplified representations of economic behavior or how an economy works are called (policies, models) _____.

4. Economic principles are often expressed as tendencies or what is typical and are (fallacies, generalizations) _____ about people's economic behavior. When studying a relationship between two economic variables, economists assume that other variables or factors (do, do not) _____ change, or in other words they are using the (utility, other-things-equal) _____ assumption.

5. The study of the total output of the economy or the general level of prices is the subject of (microeconomics, macroeconomics) _____, and the study of output in a particular industry or of a particular product is the subject of _____.

6. The collection of specific units that are being added and treated as if they were one unit is an (assumption, aggregate) _____.

7. Two different types of statements can be made about economic topics. A (positive, normative) _____ statement explains what is by offering a scientific proposition about economic behavior that is based on economic theory and facts, whereas a _____ statement includes a value judgment about an economic policy or the economy that suggests what ought to be. Many of the reported disagreements among economists involve (positive, normative) _____ statements.

8. The economizing problem arises because individuals' and society's economic wants are (limited, unlimited) _____ and the economic means or resources to satisfy those wants are _____.

9. A schedule or curve that shows the various combinations of two products a consumer can (buy, sell) _____ with a money income is called a (budget, marginal-cost) _____ line.

10. All combinations of goods inside a budget line are (attainable, unattainable) _____, and all combinations of goods outside the budget line are _____.

11. When a consumer's income increases, the budget line shifts to the (left, right) _____, while a decrease in income shifts the budget line to the _____.

12. The four types of economic resources are

a. _____

b. _____

c. _____

d. _____

13. When a production possibilities table or curve is constructed, four assumptions are made:

a. _____

b. _____

c. _____

d. _____

14. Goods that satisfy economic wants directly are (consumer, capital goods) _____, and goods that do so indirectly by helping produce other goods are _____ goods. Assume an economy can produce two basic types of goods: consumer and capital goods. If the economy wants to produce more consumer goods, the capital goods the economy must give up are the opportunity (benefit, cost) _____ of producing those additional consumer goods.

15. The law of increasing opportunity costs explains why the production possibilities curve is (convex, concave) _____ from the origin. The economic rationale for the law is that economic resources (are, are not) _____ completely adaptable to alternative uses.

16. Optimal allocation of resources to production occurs when the marginal costs of the productive output are (greater than, less than, equal to) _____ the marginal benefits.

17. Following is a production possibilities curve for capital goods and consumer goods.

a. If the economy moves from point **A** to point **B,** it will produce (more, fewer) _____ capital goods and (more, fewer) _____ consumer goods.
b. If the economy is producing at point **X,** some resources in the economy are either (not available, unemployed) _____ or (underemployed, overemployed) _____.
c. If the economy moves from point **X** to point **B,** (more, fewer) _____ capital goods and (more, fewer) _____ consumer goods will be produced.
d. If the economy is to produce at point **Y,** there must be (unemployment, economic growth) _____.

18. Economic growth will shift a nation's production possibilities curve (inward, outward) _____, and it occurs because of a resource supply (decrease, increase) _____ or because of a technological (decline, advance) _____.

19. An economy can produce goods for the present such as (consumer, capital) _____ goods and goods for the future such as _____ goods. If an economy produces more goods for the future, this is likely to lead to a (greater, smaller) _____ shift outward in the production possibilities curve over time compared with the case where the economy produces more goods for the present.

20. International specialization and trade enable a nation to obtain (more, less) _____ of output than is possible with the output limits imposed by domestic production possibilities. The gains in output for an economy from greater international specialization and trade are similar to those that occur because of resource (increases, decreases) _____ or a technological (decline, advance) _____.

■ **TRUE–FALSE QUESTIONS**

Circle T if the statement is true, F if it is false.

1. Economics is the social science that studies how individuals, institutions, and society make choices under conditions of scarcity. **T F**

2. From the economic perspective, "there is no such thing as a free lunch." **T F**

3. The economic perspective views individuals or institutions as making purposeful choices based on the marginal analysis of the costs and benefits of decisions. **T F**

4. The scientific method involves the observation of real-world data, the formulation of hypotheses based on the data, and the testing of those hypotheses to develop theories. **T F**

5. A well-tested or widely accepted economic theory is often called an economic principle or law. **T F**

6. The "other-things-equal" or *ceteris paribus* assumption is made to simplify the reasoning process. **T F**

7. Macroeconomic analysis is concerned with the economic activity of specific firms or industries. **T F**

8. Microeconomic analysis is concerned with the performance of the economy as a whole or its major aggregates. **T F**

9. The statement that "the legal minimum wage should be raised to give working people a decent income" is an example of a normative statement. **T F**

10. A person is using positive economics when that person makes value judgments about how the economy should work.   **T F**

11. The conflict between the scarce economic wants of individuals or societies and the limited economic means and resources of individuals or societies gives rise to the economizing problem.   **T F**

12. The budget line shows all combinations of two products that the consumer can purchase, given money income and the prices of the products.   **T F**

13. A consumer is unable to purchase any of the combinations of two products which lie below (or to the left) of that consumer's budget line.   **T F**

14. An increase in the money income of a consumer shifts the budget line to the right.   **T F**

15. The factors of production are land, labor, capital, and entrepreneurial ability.   **T F**

16. From the economist's perspective, investment refers to money income.   **T F**

17. Given full employment and optimal allocation, it is not possible for an economy capable of producing just two goods to increase its production of both at any one point in time.   **T F**

18. The opportunity cost of producing more consumer goods is the other goods and services the economy is unable to produce because it has decided to produce these additional consumer goods.   **T F**

19. The opportunity cost of producing a good tends to increase as more of it is produced because resources less suitable to its production must be employed. **T F**

20. Drawing a production possibilities curve bowed out from the origin is a graphical way of showing the law of increasing opportunity costs.   **T F**

21. The economic rationale for the law of increasing opportunity costs is that economic resources are fully adaptable to alternative uses.   **T F**

22. Optimal allocation is determined by assessing the marginal costs and benefits of the output from the allocation of resources to production.   **T F**

23. Economic growth means an increase in the production of goods and services and is shown by a movement of the production possibilities curve outward and to the right. **T F**

24. The more capital goods an economy produces today, the greater will be the total output of all goods it can produce in the future, other things being equal.   **T F**

25. International specialization and trade permit an economy to overcome the limits imposed by domestic production possibilities and have the same effect on the economy as having more and better resources.   **T F**

■ **MULTIPLE-CHOICE QUESTIONS**

Circle the letter that corresponds to the best answer.

1. What statement would best complete a short definition of economics? "Economics studies
  (a) how businesses produce goods and services."
  (b) the equitable distribution of society's income and wealth."
  (c) the printing and circulation of money throughout the economy."
  (d) how individuals, institutions, and society make optimal choices under conditions of scarcity."

2. The idea in economics that "there is no such thing as a free lunch" means that
  (a) the marginal benefit of such a lunch is greater than its marginal cost
  (b) businesses cannot increase their market share by offering free lunches
  (c) scarce resources have alternative uses or opportunity costs
  (d) consumers are irrational when they ask for a free lunch

3. The opportunity cost of a new public stadium is the
  (a) money cost of hiring guards and staff for the new stadium
  (b) cost of constructing the new stadium in a future year
  (c) change in the real estate tax rate to pay off the new stadium
  (d) other goods and services that must be sacrificed to construct the new stadium

4. From the economic perspective, when a business decides to employ more workers, the business decision maker most likely has concluded that the marginal
  (a) costs of employing more workers have decreased
  (b) benefits of employing more workers have increased
  (c) benefits of employing more workers are greater than the marginal costs
  (d) costs of employing more workers are not opportunity costs for the business because more workers are needed to increase production

5. The combination of economic theories or principles into a simplified representation of reality is referred to as an economic:
  (a) fact
  (b) model
  (c) assumption
  (d) hypothesis

6. When we look at the whole economy or its major aggregates, our analysis will be at the level of
  (a) microeconomics
  (b) macroeconomics
  (c) positive economics
  (d) normative economics

7. Which would be studied in microeconomics?
  (a) the output of the entire U.S. economy
  (b) the general level of prices in the U.S. economy

(c) the output and price of wheat in the United States

(d) the total number of workers employed in the United States

8. Which is a normative economic statement?

(a) The consumer price index rose 1.2 percent last month.

(b) The unemployment rate of 6.8 percent is too high.

(c) The average rate of interest on loans is 4.6 percent.

(d) The economy grew at an annual rate of 3.6 percent.

9. Sandra states that "there is a high correlation between consumption and income." Arthur replies that the correlation occurs because "people consume too much of their income and don't save enough."

(a) Both Sandra's and Arthur's statements are positive.

(b) Both Sandra's and Arthur's statements are normative.

(c) Sandra's statement is positive and Arthur's statement is normative.

(d) Sandra's statement is normative and Arthur's statement is positive.

10. Assume that a consumer can buy only two goods, *A* and *B,* and has an income of $100. The price of *A* is $10, and the price of *B* is $20. The maximum amount of *A* the consumer is able to purchase is

(a) 5

(b) 10

(c) 20

(d) 30

11. Assume that a consumer can buy only two goods, *A* and *B,* and has an income of $100. The price of *A* is $10, and the price of B is $20. What is the slope of the budget line if *A* is measured horizontally and *B* is measured vertically?

(a) −0.5

(b) −1.0

(c) −2.0

(d) −4.0

12. Tools, machinery, or equipment that is used to produce other goods would be an example of

(a) public goods

(b) capital goods

(c) social goods

(d) consumer goods

13. An "innovator" is defined as an entrepreneur who

(a) makes basic policy decisions in a business firm

(b) combines factors of production to produce a good or service

(c) invents a new product or process for producing a product

(d) introduces new products on the market or employs a new method to produce a product

14. When a production possibilities schedule is written (or a production possibilities curve is drawn) in this chapter,

four assumptions are made. Which is one of those assumptions?

(a) The state of technology changes.

(b) More than two products are produced.

(c) The economy has full employment of available resources.

(d) The quantities of all resources available to the economy are variable, not fixed.

Answer Questions 15, 16, and 17 on the basis of the data given in the following production possibilities table.

	Production possibilities (alternatives)					
	A	B	C	D	E	F
Capital goods	100	95	85	70	50	0
Consumer goods	0	100	180	240	280	300

15. If the economy is producing at production alternative **D**, the opportunity cost of 40 more units of consumer goods is

(a) 5 units of capital goods

(b) 10 units of capital goods

(c) 15 units of capital goods

(d) 20 units of capital goods

16. In the table, the law of increasing opportunity costs is suggested by the fact that

(a) capital goods are relatively more scarce than consumer goods

(b) greater and greater quantities of consumer goods must be given up to get more capital goods

(c) smaller and smaller quantities of consumer goods must be given up to get more capital goods

(d) the production possibilities curve will eventually shift outward as the economy expands

17. The present choice of alternative **B** compared with alternative **D** would tend to promote

(a) increased consumption in the present

(b) decreased consumption in the future

(c) a greater increase in economic growth in the future

(d) a smaller increase in economic growth in the future

18. What is the economic rationale for the law of increasing opportunity costs?

(a) Optimal allocation and full employment of resources have not been achieved.

(b) Economic resources are not completely adaptable to alternative uses.

(c) Economic growth is being limited by the pace of technological advancement.

(d) An economy's present choice of output is determined by fixed technology and fixed resources.

19. The underallocation of resources by society to the production of a product means that the

(a) marginal benefit is greater than the marginal cost

(b) marginal benefit is less than the marginal cost

(c) opportunity cost of production is rising

(d) consumption of the product is falling

Answer Questions 20, 21, and 22 based on the following graph for an economy.

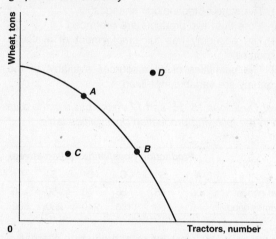

20. Unemployment and productive inefficiency would best be represented in the graph by point:
(a) *A*
(b) *B*
(c) *C*
(d) *D*

21. The choice of point *B* over point *A* as the optimal product mix for society would be based on .
(a) the state of technology
(b) full employment of resources
(c) the law of increasing opportunity costs
(d) a comparison of marginal costs and benefits

22. Economic growth could be represented by
(a) a movement from point *A* to point *B*
(b) a movement from point *B* to point *A*
(c) a shift in the production possibilities curve out to point *C*
(d) a shift in the production possibilities curve out to point *D*

23. If there is an increase in the resources available within the economy,
(a) the economy will be capable of producing fewer goods
(b) the economy will be capable of producing more goods
(c) the standard of living in the economy will decline
(d) the state of technology will deteriorate

24. Which situation would be most likely to shift the production possibilities curve for a nation in an outward direction?
(a) deterioration in product quality
(b) reductions in the supply of resources
(c) increases in technological advance
(d) rising levels of unemployment

25. You observe that more education is associated with more income and conclude that more income leads to more education. This would be an example of
(a) the post hoc fallacy
(b) the fallacy of composition
(c) confusing correlation and causation
(d) using the other-things-equal assumption

■ PROBLEMS

1. Use the appropriate number to match the terms with the phrase.

1. **economics**   4. **normative economics**
2. **macroeconomics**   5. **microeconomics**
3. **positive economics** 6. **marginal analysis**

a. The attempt to establish scientific statements about economic behavior; a concern with "what is" rather than "what ought to be." _____

b. Part of economics that involves value judgments about what the economy should be like or the way the economic world should be. _____

c. Social science that studies how individuals, institutions, and society make optimal choices under conditions of scarcity. _____

d. Part of economics concerned with the whole economy or its major sectors. _____

e. The comparison of additional benefits and additional costs. _____

f. Part of economics concerned with the economic behavior of individual units such as households, firms, and industries (particular markets). _____

2. *News report:* "The worldwide demand for wheat from the United States increased and caused the price of wheat in the United States to rise." This is a *specific* instance of a more *general* economic principle. Of which economic *generalization* is this a particular example?

_____

_____

3. Following is a list of economic statements. Indicate in the space to the right of each statement whether it is positive (**P**) or normative (**N**). Then, in the last four lines below, write two of your own examples of positive economic statements and two examples of normative economic statements.

a. New York City should control the rental price of apartments. _____

b. Consumer prices rose at an annual rate of 2% last year. _____

c. Most people who are unemployed are just too lazy to work. _____

d. Generally, if you lower the price of a product, people will buy more of that product. _____

e. The profits of drug companies are too large and ought to be used to conduct research on new medicines. _____

f. Government should do more to help the poor. _____

g. _____ __P__

h. _____ __P__

i. _____ __N__

j. _____ __N__

4. Following is a list of resources. Indicate in the space to the right of each whether the resource is land (**LD**), labor (**LR**), capital (**C**), entrepreneurial ability (**EA**), or some combination of these resources.

   a. Fishing grounds in the North Atlantic   _____

   b. A computer in a retail store   _____

   c. Uranium deposits in Canada   _____

   d. An irrigation ditch in Nebraska   _____

   e. Bill Gates in his work in starting Microsoft   _____

   f. The oxygen breathed by human beings   _____

   g. An IBM plant in Rochester, Minnesota   _____

   h. The food on the shelf of a grocery store   _____

   i. A machine in an auto plant   _____

   j. A person who creates new computer software and uses it to start a successful business   _____

   k. A carpenter building a house   _____

5. Following is a production possibilities table for two products: corn and cars. The table is constructed using the usual assumptions. Corn is measured in units of 100,000 bushels, and cars in units of 100,000.

Combination	Corn	Cars
A	0	7
B	7	6
C	13	5
D	18	4
E	22	3
F	25	2
G	27	1
H	28	0

   a. Follow the general rules for making graphs (see the appendix to Chapter 1); plot the data from the table on the graph below to obtain a production possibilities curve. Place corn on the vertical axis and cars on the horizontal axis.

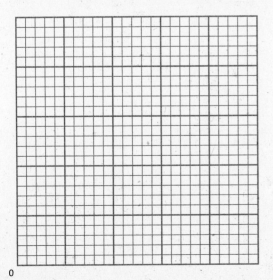

0

   b. Fill in the following table, showing the opportunity cost per unit of producing the 1st through the 7th car unit in terms of corn units.

Cars	Cost of production
1st	_____
2nd	_____
3rd	_____
4th	_____
5th	_____
6th	_____
7th	_____

   c. What is the *marginal* opportunity cost of the 3rd car unit in terms of units of corn? _____

   d. What is the *total* opportunity cost of producing 6 car units in terms of units of corn? _____

■ **SHORT ANSWER AND ESSAY QUESTIONS**

  1. What are the three interrelated features of the economic perspective?

  2. What is the economic meaning of the statement "there is no such thing as a free lunch"?

  3. What are the differences and similarities between hypotheses, theories, principles, laws, and models?

  4. Why do economists use the "other-things-equal" assumption?

  5. Why are economic principles necessarily generalized and abstract?

  6. Explain the difference between macroeconomics and microeconomics.

  7. What are some current examples of positive economic statements and normative economic statements?

  8. Explain what the term "economizing problem" means for an individual and for society.

  9. What is a budget line for an individual? How can it be used to illustrate tradeoffs and opportunity costs?

10. What are the four economic resources? How is each resource defined?

11. What four assumptions are made in drawing a production possibilities curve or schedule?

12. What is the law of increasing opportunity costs? Why do costs increase?

13. What determines the optimal product mix for society's production possibilities?

14. How can unemployment be illustrated with the production possibilities curve?

15. What will be the effect of increasing resource supplies on production possibilities?

16. Describe how technological advances will affect the production possibilities curve.

17. Explain the tradeoff between goods for the present and goods for the future and the effect of this tradeoff on economic growth.

18. What qualification does international specialization and trade make for the interpretation of production possibilities?

19. Explain how the production possibilities curve can be used to explain the economics of war.

20. Explain each of the five pitfalls to sound economic reasoning.

ANSWERS

Chapter 1 Limits, Alternatives, and Choices

FILL-IN QUESTIONS

1. scarcity, cost, alternative
2. purposeful, marginal
3. scientific, theories, principles, laws, models
4. generalizations, do not, other-things-equal (or *ceteris paribus*)
5. macroeconomics, microeconomics
6. aggregate
7. positive, normative, normative
8. unlimited, limited
9. buy, budget
10. attainable, unattainable
11. right, left
12. *a.* land or natural resources; *b.* labor; *c.* capital; *d.* entrepreneurial ability
13. *a.* there is full employment and optimal allocation; *b.* the available supplies of the factors of production are fixed; *c.* technology does not change during the course of the analysis; *d.* the economy produces only two products (any order for *a–d*)
14. consumer, capital, cost
15. concave, are not
16. equal to
17. *a.* fewer, more; *b.* unemployed, underemployed; *c.* more, more; *d.* economic growth
18. outward, increase, advance
19. consumer, capital, greater
20. more, increases, advance

TRUE–FALSE QUESTIONS

1. T, p. 4	10. F, p. 7	19. T, pp. 12–13
2. T, p. 4	11. T, pp. 7, 10	20. T, p. 13
3. T, pp. 4–5	12. T, p. 8	21. F, p. 13
4. T, pp. 5–6	13. F, pp. 8–9	22. T, p. 13
5. T, p. 6	14. T, p. 10	23. T, p. 15
6. T, p. 6	15. T, p. 10	24. T, pp. 16–18
7. F, pp. 6–7	16. F, p. 10	25. T, p. 18
8. F, p. 7	17. T, pp. 11–12	
9. T, p. 7	18. T, p. 11	

MULTIPLE-CHOICE QUESTIONS

1. d, p. 4	10. b, p. 8	19. a, pp. 13–14
2. c, p. 4	11. a, p. 8	20. c, pp. 14–15
3. d, p. 4	12. b, p. 10	21. d, pp. 13–14
4. c, p. 5	13. d, p. 10	22. d, pp. 15–16
5. b, pp. 5–6	14. c, p. 11	23. b, p. 15
6. b, p. 6	15. d, pp. 11–12	24. c, pp. 15–16
7. c, pp. 6–7	16. b, pp. 12–13	25. c, p. 17
8. b, p. 7	17. c, pp. 16–18	
9. c, p. 7	18. b, p. 13	

PROBLEMS

1. *a.* 3; *b.* 4; *c.* 1; *d.* 2; *e.* 6; *f.* 5
2. An increase in the demand for an economic good will cause the price of that good to rise.
3. *a.* N; *b.* P; *c.* N; *d.* P; *e.* N; *f.* N
4. *a.* LD; *b.* C; *c.* LD; *d.* C; *e.* EA; *f.* LD; *g.* C; *h.* C; *i.* C; *j.* EA; *k.* LR
5. *b.* 1, 2, 3, 4, 5, 6, 7 units of corn; *c.* 3; *d.* 21

SHORT ANSWER AND ESSAY QUESTIONS

1. pp. 4–5	8. pp. 7,10	15. p. 15
2. p. 4	9. p. 8	16. pp. 15–16
3. pp. 5–6	10. p. 10	17. pp. 16–18
4. p. 6	11. p. 10	18. p. 18
5. p. 6	12. pp. 12–13	19. p. 14
6. pp. 6–7	13. p. 13	20. pp. 16–17
7. p. 7	14. pp. 14–15	

APPENDIX TO CHAPTER 1

Graphs and Their Meaning

This appendix introduces graphing in economics. Graphs help illustrate and simplify the economic theories and models presented throughout this book. The old saying that "a picture is worth 1000 words" applies to economics; graphs are the way that economists "picture" relationships between economic variables.

You must master the basics of graphing if these "pictures" are to be of any help to you. This appendix explains how to achieve that mastery. It shows you how to construct a graph from a table with data of two variables, such as income and consumption.

Economists usually, but not always, place the **independent variable** (income) on the horizontal axis and the **dependent variable** (consumption) on the vertical axis of the graph. Once the data points are plotted and a line is drawn to connect the plotted points, you can determine whether there is a **direct** or an **inverse relationship** between the variables. Identifying direct and inverse relationships between variables is an essential skill used repeatedly in this book.

Information from data in graphs and tables can be written in an equation. This involves determining the **slope** and **intercept** from a straight line in a graph or data in a table. Using values for the slope and intercept, you can write a **linear equation** that will enable you to calculate what the dependent variable would be for a given level of the independent variable.

Some graphs used in the book are *nonlinear*. With **nonlinear curves**, the slope of the line is no longer constant throughout but varies as one moves along the curve. This slope can be estimated at a point by determining the slope of a straight line that is drawn tangent to the curve at that point. Similar calculations can be made for other points to see how the slope changes along the curve.

■ APPENDIX CHECKLIST

When you have studied this appendix you should be able to

☐ Explain why economists use graphs.
☐ Construct a graph of two variables by using the numerical data from a table.
☐ Make a table with two variables from data on a graph.
☐ Distinguish between a direct and an inverse relationship when given data on two variables.
☐ Identify dependent and independent variables in economic examples and graphs.

☐ Describe how economists use the other-things-equal (*ceteris paribus*) assumption in graphing two variables.
☐ Calculate the slope of a straight line between two points when given the tabular data and indicate whether the slope is positive or negative.
☐ Describe how slopes are affected by the choice of the units of measurement for either variable.
☐ Explain how slopes are related to marginal analysis.
☐ Graph infinite or zero slopes and explain their meaning.
☐ Determine the vertical intercept for a straight line in a graph with two variables.
☐ Write a linear equation using the slope of a line and the vertical intercept; when given a value for the independent variable, determine a value for the dependent variable.
☐ Estimate the slope of a nonlinear curve at a point by using a line that is tangent to the curve at that point.

■ APPENDIX OUTLINE

1. Graphs illustrate the relationship between variables and give economists and students another way, in addition to verbal explanation, to understand economic phenomena. Graphs are aids in describing economic theories and models.

2. The construction of a simple graph involves plotting the numerical data of two variables from a table.
  a. Each graph has a *horizontal axis* and a *vertical axis* that can be labeled for each variable and then scaled for the range of the data points that will be measured on the axis.
  b. Data points are plotted on the graph by drawing perpendiculars from the scaled points on the two axes to the place on the graph where the perpendiculars intersect.
  c. A line or curve can then be drawn to connect the points plotted on the graph. If the graph is a straight line, it is *linear*.

3. A graph provides information about relationships between variables.
  a. An upward-sloping line to the right on a graph indicates that there is a positive or *direct relationship* between two variables: An increase in one is associated with an increase in the other; a decrease in one is associated with a decrease in the other.
  b. A downward-sloping line to the right means that there is a negative or *inverse relationship* between

the two variables: An increase in one is associated with a decrease in the other; a decrease in one is associated with an increase in the other.

4. Economists are often concerned with determining cause and effect in economic events.

    a. A *dependent variable* changes (increases or decreases) because of a change in another variable.

    b. An *independent variable* produces or "causes" the change in the dependent variable.

    c. In a graph, mathematicians place an independent variable on the horizontal axis and a dependent variable on the vertical axis; economists are more arbitrary in the placement of the dependent or independent variable on an axis.

5. Economic graphs are simplifications of economic relationships. When graphs are plotted, usually an implicit assumption is made that all other factors are being held constant. This "other-things-equal" or *ceteris paribus* assumption is used to simplify the analysis so that the study can focus on the two variables of interest.

6. The *slope of a straight line* in a two-variable graph is the ratio of the vertical change to the horizontal change between two points.

    a. A *positive* slope indicates that the relationship between the two variables is *direct*.

    b. A *negative* slope indicates that there is an *inverse* relationship between the two variables.

    c. Slopes are affected by the *measurement units* for either variable.

    d. Slopes measure *marginal* changes.

    e. Slopes can be *infinite* (line parallel to vertical axis) or zero (line parallel to horizontal axis).

7. The *vertical intercept* of a straight line in a two-variable graph is the point where the line intersects the vertical axis of the graph.

8. The slope and intercept of a straight line can be expressed in the form of a **linear equation**, which is written as $y = a + bx$. Once the values for the intercept (*a*) and the slope (*b*) are calculated, then given any value of the independent variable (*x*), the value of the dependent variable (*y*) can be determined.

9. The slope of a straight line is constant, but the slope of a nonlinear curve changes throughout. To estimate the slope of a *nonlinear curve* at a point, the slope of a line *tangent* to the curve at that point is calculated.

■ **HINTS AND TIPS**

1. This appendix will help you understand the graphs and problems presented throughout the book. Do not skip reading the appendix or working on the self-test questions and problems in this *Study Guide*. The time you invest now will pay off in improved understanding in later chapters. Graphing is a basic skill for economic analysis.

2. Positive and negative relationships in graphs often confuse students. To overcome this confusion, draw a two-variable graph with a positive slope and another two-

variable graph with a negative slope. In each graph, show what happens to the value of one variable when there is a change in the value of the other variable.

3. A straight line in a two-variable graph can be expressed in an equation. Make sure you know how to interpret each part of the linear equation.

■ **IMPORTANT TERMS**

horizontal axis	independent variable
vertical axis	slope of a straight line
direct (positive) relationship	vertical intercept
inverse (negative) relationship	nonlinear curve
dependent variable	tangent

SELF-TEST

■ **FILL-IN QUESTIONS**

1. The relationship between two economic variables can be visualized with the aid of a two-dimensional (graph, matrix) _____, which has (a horizontal, an inverse) _____ axis and a (vertical, direct) _____ axis.

2. Customarily, the (dependent, independent) _____ variable is placed on the horizontal axis and the _____ variable is placed on the vertical axis. The _____ variable is said to change because of a change in the _____ variable.

3. The vertical and horizontal (scales, ranges) _____ of the graph are calibrated to reflect the _____ of values in the table of data points on which the graph is based.

4. The graph of a straight line that slopes downward to the right indicates that there is (a direct, an inverse) _____ relationship between the two variables. A graph of a straight line that slopes upward to the right tells us that the relationship is (direct, inverse) _____. When the value of one variable increases and the value of the other variable increases, then the relationship is _____; when the value of one increases and the other decreases, the relationship is _____.

5. In interpreting an economic graph, the "cause" or the "source" is the (dependent, independent) _____ variable and the "effect" or "outcome" is the _____ variable.

6. Other variables, beyond the two in a two-dimensional graph, that might affect the economic relationship are assumed to be (changing, held constant) _____. This assumption is also referred to as the "other-things-equal" assumption or as (*post hoc, ceteris paribus*) _____.

7. The slope of a straight line between two points is defined as the ratio of the (vertical, horizontal) _____ change to the _____ change.

8. When two variables move in the same direction, the slope will be (negative, positive) _____; when the variables move in opposite directions, the slope will be _____.

9. The slope of a line will be affected by the (units of measurement, vertical intercept) _____.

10. The concept of a slope is important to economists because it reflects the influence of a (marginal, total) _____ change in one variable on another variable.

11. A graph of a line with an infinite slope is (horizontal, vertical) _____, while a graph of a line with a zero slope is _____.

12. The point at which the slope of the line meets the vertical axis is called the vertical (tangent, intercept) _____.

13. We can express the graph of a straight line with a linear equation that can be written as $y = a + bx$.

   a. *a* is the (slope, intercept) _____, and *b* is the _____.

   b. *y* is the (dependent, independent) _____ variable, and *x* is the _____ variable.

   c. If *a* were 2, *b* were 4, and *x* were 5, then *y* would be _____. If the value of x changed to 7, then *y* would be _____. If the value of *x* changed to 3, then *y* would be _____.

14. The slope of a (straight line, nonlinear curve) _____ is constant throughout; the slope of a _____ varies from point to point.

15. An estimate of the slope of a nonlinear curve at a certain point can be made by calculating the slope of a straight line that is (tangent, perpendicular) _____ to the point on the curve.

■ **TRUE–FALSE QUESTIONS**

Circle T if the statement is true, F if it is false.

1. Economists design graphs to confuse people.
T   F

2. If the straight line on a two-variable graph slopes downward to the right, then there is a positive relationship between the two variables.
T   F

3. A variable that changes as a consequence of a change in another variable is considered a dependent variable.
T   F

4. Economists always put the independent variable on the horizontal axis and the dependent variable on the vertical axis of a two-variable graph.
T   F

5. *Ceteris paribus* means that other variables are changing at the same time.
T   F

6. In the ratio for the calculation of the slope of a straight line, the vertical change is in the numerator and the horizontal change is in the denominator.
T   F

7. If the slope of the linear relationship between consumption and income is .90, then it tells us that for every $1 increase in income there will be a $.90 increase in consumption.
T   F

8. The slope of a straight line in a two-variable graph will *not* be affected by the choice of the units for either variable.
T   F

9. The slopes of lines measure marginal changes.
T   F

10. Assume in a graph that price is on the vertical axis and quantity is on the horizontal axis. The absence of a relationship between price and quantity would be a straight line parallel to the horizontal axis.
T   F

11. A line with an infinite slope in a two-variable graph is parallel to the horizontal axis.
T   F

12. In a two-variable graph, income is graphed on the vertical axis and the quantity of snow is graphed on the horizontal axis. If income was independent of the quantity of snow, then this independence would be represented by a line parallel to the horizontal axis.
T   F

13. If a linear equation is $y = 10 + 5x$, the vertical intercept is 5.
T   F

14. When a line is tangent to a nonlinear curve, then it intersects the curve at a particular point.
T   F

15. If the slope of a straight line on a two-variable (*x, y*) graph were .5 and the vertical intercept were 5, then a value of 10 for *x* would mean that *y* is also 10.
T   F

16. A slope of –4 for a straight line in a two-variable graph indicates that there is an inverse relationship between the two variables.
T   F

17. If *x* is an independent variable and *y* is a dependent variable, then a change in *y* results in a change in *x*.
T   F

18. An upward slope for a straight line that is tangent to a nonlinear curve indicates that the slope of the nonlinear curve at that point is positive.
T   F

19. If one pair of *x, y* points was (13, 10) and the other pair was (8, 20), then the slope of the straight line between the two sets of points in the two-variable graph, with x on the horizontal axis and y on the vertical axis, would be 2. **T F**

20. When the value of x is 2, a value of 10 for y would be calculated from a linear equation of $y = -2 + 6x$. **T F**

■ MULTIPLE-CHOICE QUESTIONS

Circle the letter that corresponds to the best answer.

1. If an increase in one variable is associated with a decrease in another variable, then we can conclude that the variables are
(a) nonlinear
(b) directly related
(c) inversely related
(d) positively related

2. The ratio of the vertical change to the horizontal change between two points of a straight line is the
(a) slope
(b) vertical intercept
(c) horizontal intercept
(d) point of tangency

3. There are two sets of x, y points on a straight line in a two-variable graph, with y on the vertical axis and x on the horizontal axis. If one set of points was (0, 5) and the other set was (5, 20), the linear equation for the line would be
(a) $y = 5x$
(b) $y = 5 + 3x$
(c) $y = 5 + 15x$
(d) $y = 5 + .33x$

4. In a two-variable graph of data on the price and quantity of a product, economists place
(a) price on the horizontal axis because it is the independent variable and quantity on the vertical axis because it is the dependent variable
(a) price on the vertical axis because it is the dependent variable and quantity on the horizontal axis because it is the independent variable
(c) price on the vertical axis even though it is the independent variable and quantity on the horizontal axis even though it is the dependent variable
(d) price on the horizontal axis even though it is the dependent variable and quantity on the vertical axis even though it is the independent variable

5. In a two-dimensional graph of the relationship between two economic variables, an assumption is usually made that
(a) both variables are linear
(b) both variables are nonlinear
(c) other variables are held constant
(d) other variables are permitted to change

6. If the slope of a straight line is zero, then the straight line is
(a) vertical
(b) horizontal
(c) upward sloping
(d) downward sloping

Questions 7, 8, 9, and 10 are based on the following four data sets. In each set, the independent variable is in the left column and the dependent variable is in the right column.

(1)		(2)		(3)		(4)	
A	**B**	**C**	**D**	**E**	**F**	**G**	**H**
0	1	0	12	4	5	0	4
3	2	5	8	6	10	1	3
6	3	10	4	8	15	2	2
9	4	15	0	10	20	3	1

7. There is an inverse relationship between the independent and dependent variables in data sets
(a) 1 and 4
(b) 2 and 3
(c) 1 and 3
(d) 2 and 4

8. The vertical intercept is 4 in data set
(a) 1
(b) 2
(c) 3
(d) 4

9. The linear equation for data set 1 is
(a) $B = 3A$
(b) $B = 1 + 3A$
(c) $B = 1 + .33A$
(d) $A = 1 + .33B$

10. The linear equation for data set 2 is
(a) $C = 12 - 1.25D$
(b) $D = 12 + 1.25C$
(c) $D = 12 - .80C$
(d) $C = 12 - .80D$

Answer Questions 11, 12, 13, and 14 on the basis of the following diagram.

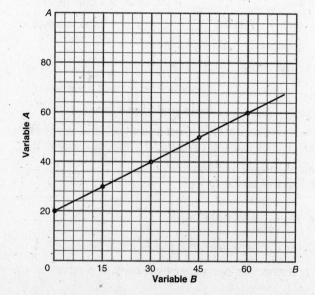

11. The variables **A** and **B** are
(a) positively related
(b) negatively related
(c) indirectly related
(d) nonlinear

12. The slope of the line is
(a) .33
(b) .67
(c) 1.50
(d) 3.00

13. The vertical intercept is
(a) 80
(b) 60
(c) 40
(d) 20

14. The linear equation for the slope of the line is
(a) $A = 20 + .33B$
(b) $B = 20 + .33A$
(c) $A = 20 + .67B$
(d) $B = 20 + .67A$

Answer Questions 15, 16, and 17 on the basis of the following diagram.

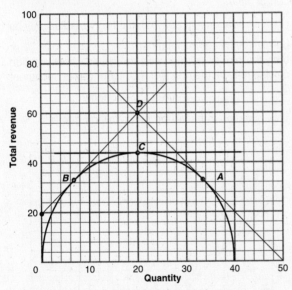

15. The slope of the line tangent to the curve at point **A** is
(a) 2
(b) −2
(c) −1.5
(d) −0.5

16. The slope of the line tangent to the curve at point **B** is
(a) −2
(b) 2
(c) 3
(d) 0.5

17. The slope of the line tangent to the curve at point **C** is
(a) −1
(b) 1
(c) 0
(d) undefined

18. Assume that the relationship between concert ticket prices and attendance is expressed in the equation $P = 25 - 1.25Q$, where **P** equals ticket price and **Q** equals concert attendance in thousands of people. On the basis of this equation, it can be said that
(a) more people will attend the concert when the price is high compared to when the price is low
(b) if 12,000 people attended the concert, then the ticket price was $10
(c) if 18,000 people attended the concert, then entry into the concert was free
(d) an increase in ticket price by $5 reduces concert attendance by 1000 people

19. If you know that the equation relating consumption (**C**) to income (**Y**) is $C = \$7500 + .2Y$, then
(a) consumption is inversely related to income
(b) consumption is the independent variable and income is the dependent variable
(c) if income is $15,000, then consumption is $10,500
(d) if consumption is $30,000, then income is $10,000

20. If the dependent variable changes by 22 units when the independent variable changes by 12 units, then the slope of the line is
(a) 0.56
(b) 1.83
(c) 2.00
(d) 3.27

■ **PROBLEMS**

1. Following are three tables for making graphs. On the graphs, plot the economic relationships contained in each table. Be sure to label each axis of the graph and indicate the unit measurement and scale used on each axis.

a. Use the table at the top of the next page to graph national income on the horizontal axis and consumption expenditures on the vertical axis below; connect the seven points and label the curve "Consumption." The relationship between income and consumption is (a direct, an inverse) _____ one, and the consumption

curve is (an up-, a down-) _____ sloping curve.

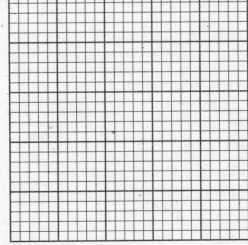

National income, billions of dollars	Consumption expenditures, billions of dollars
$ 600	$ 600
700	640
800	780
900	870
1000	960
1100	1050
1200	1140

b. Use the next table to graph investment expenditures on the horizontal axis and the rate of interest on the vertical axis; connect the seven points and label the curve "Investment." The relationship between the rate of interest and investment expenditures is (a direct, an inverse) _____ one, and the investment curve is (an up-, a down-) _____ sloping curve.

Rate of interest, %	Investment expenditures, billions of dollars
8	$220
7	280
6	330
5	370
4	400
3	420
2	430

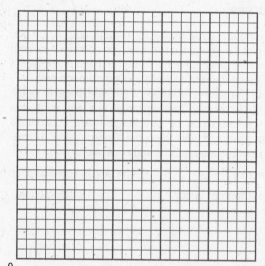

c. Use the next table to graph average salary on the horizontal axis and wine consumption on the vertical axis; connect the seven points.

Average salary, U.S. college professors	Annual per capita wine consumption in liters
$62,000	11.5
63,000	11.6
64,000	11.7
65,000	11.8
66,000	11.9
67,000	22.0
68,000	22.1

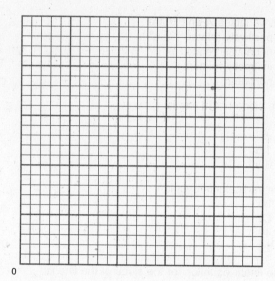

(1) The average salary of a college professor and wine consumption (are, are not) _____ *correlated*. The higher average salary (is, is not) _____ the *cause* of the greater consumption of wine.

(2) The relationship between the two variables may be purely (coincidental, planned) _____, or both the higher salaries and the greater consumption of wine may be the result of the higher (taxes, incomes) _____ in the U.S. economy.

2. This question is based on the following graph.

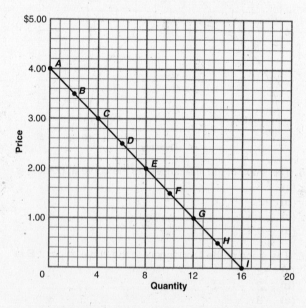

a. Construct a table for points **A–I** from the data shown in the graph.

b. According to economists, price is the (independent, dependent) _____ variable and quantity is the _____ variable.

c. Write a linear equation that summarizes the data.

3. The following three sets of data each show the relationship between an independent variable and a dependent variable. For each set, the independent variable is in the left column and the dependent variable is in the right column.

(1)		(2)		(3)	
A	**B**	**C**	**D**	**E**	**F**
0	10	0	100	0	20
10	30	10	75	50	40
20	50	20	50	100	60
30	70	30	25	150	80
40	90	40	0	200	100

a. Write an equation that summarizes the data for each of the sets (1), (2), and (3).

b. State whether each data set shows a positive or an inverse relationship between the two variables.

c. Plot data sets 1 and 2 on the following graph. Use the same horizontal scale for both sets of independent variables and the same vertical scale for both sets of dependent variables.

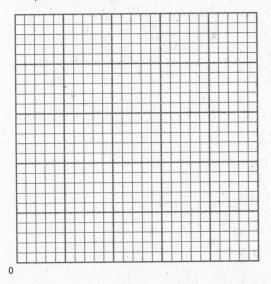

0

4. This problem is based on the following graph.

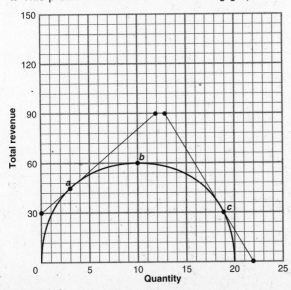

a. The slope of the straight line through point **a** is?

b. The slope of the straight line through point **b** is?

c. The slope of the straight line through point **c** is?

■ **SHORT ANSWER AND ESSAY QUESTIONS**

1. Why do economists use graphs in their work?

2. Give two examples of a graph that illustrates the relationship between two economic variables.

3. What does the slope tell you about a straight line? How would you interpret a slope of 4? A slope of −2? A slope of .5? A slope of −.25?

4. If the vertical intercept increases in value but the slope of a straight line stays the same, what happens to the graph of the line? If the vertical intercept decreases in value, what will happen to the line?

5. How do you interpret a vertical line on a two-variable graph? How do you interpret a horizontal line?

6. When you know that the price and quantity of a product are inversely related, what does this tell you about the slope of a line where price is on the vertical axis and quantity is on the horizontal axis? What do you know about the slope when the two variables are positively related?

7. Which variable is the dependent and which is the independent in the following economic statement: "A decrease in business taxes had a positive effect on investment spending."

8. How do you tell the difference between a dependent and an independent variable when examining economic relationships?

9. Why is an assumption made that all other variables are held constant when we construct a two-variable graph of the price and quantity of a product?

10. How do mathematicians and economists differ at times in how they construct two-dimensional graphs? Give an example.

11. How is the slope of a straight line in a two-variable graph affected by the choice of the units for either variable? Explain and give an example.

12. What is the relationship between the slopes of lines and marginal analysis?

13. Describe a case in which a straight line in a two-variable graph would have an infinite slope and a case in which the slope of a line would be zero.

14. If you know that the equation relating consumption (*C*) to income (*Y*) is $C = 10{,}000 + 5Y$, then what would consumption be when income is $5000? Construct an income-consumption table for five different levels of income.

15. How do the slopes of a straight line and a nonlinear curve differ? How do you estimate the slope of a nonlinear curve?

ANSWERS

Appendix to Chapter 1 Graphs and Their Meaning

FILL-IN QUESTIONS

1. graph, a horizontal, vertical
2. independent, dependent, dependent, independent
3. scales, ranges
4. an inverse, direct, direct, inverse
5. independent, dependent
6. held constant, *ceteris paribus*
7. vertical, horizontal
8. positive, negative
9. units of measurement
10. marginal
11. vertical, horizontal
12. intercept
13. *a.* intercept, slope; *b.* dependent, independent; *c.* 22, 30, 14
14. straight line, nonlinear curve
15. tangent

TRUE–FALSE QUESTIONS

1. F, p. 21	8. F, p. 23	15. T, p. 24
2. F, p. 22	9. T, p. 23	16. T, p. 23
3. T, p. 22	10. T, p. 24	17. F, p. 24
4. F, p. 22	11. F, p. 24	18. T, p. 25
5. F, p. 23	12. T, p. 24	19. F, p. 24
6. T, p. 23	13. F, p. 24	20. T, p. 24
7. T, p. 23	14. F, p. 25	

MULTIPLE-CHOICE QUESTIONS

1. c, p. 22	8. d, p. 24	15. b, p. 25
2. a, p. 23	9. c, p. 24	16. b, p. 25
3. b, p. 24	10. c, p. 24	17. c, p. 25
4. c, p. 22	11. a, p. 22	18. b, p. 24
5. c, p. 23	12. b, p. 23	19. c, p. 24
6. b, p. 24	13. d, p. 24	20. b, p. 23
7. d, p. 22	14. c, p. 24	

PROBLEMS

1. *a.* a direct, an up-; *b.* an inverse, a down-; *c.* (1) are, is not; (2) coincidental, incomes (standard of living, or similar answer)
2. *a.* table below; *b.* independent, dependent; *c.* $P = 4.00 - .25Q$

Point	Price	Quantity
A	$4.00	0
B	3.50	2
C	3.00	4
D	2.50	6
E	2.00	8
F	1.50	10
G	1.00	12
H	.50	14
I	.00	16

3. *a.* (1) $B = 10 + 2A$; (2) $D = 100 - 2.5C$; (3) $F = 20 + .4E$; *b.* (1) positive; (2) inverse; (3) positive
4. *a.* 5; *b.* 0; *c.* −10

SHORT ANSWER AND ESSAY QUESTIONS

1. p. 21	5. p. 24	9. p. 23	13. p. 24
2. pp. 21-22	6. p. 23	10. p. 22	14. p. 24
3. p. 23	7. p. 22	11. p. 23	15. p. 25
4. p. 24	8. p. 22	12. p. 23	

CHAPTER 2

The Market System and the Circular Flow

Every economy needs to develop an **economic system** to respond to the economizing problem of limited resources and unlimited wants. The two basic types of systems are the **command system** and the **market system.** In the command system, there is extensive public ownership of resources and the use of central planning for most economic decision making in the economy. In the market system, there is extensive private ownership of resources and the use of markets and prices to coordinate and direct economic activity.

A major purpose of Chapter 2 is to explain the main characteristics of the market system because it is the one used in most nations. The first part of this section describes the **ideological** and **institutional** characteristics of the market system. In this system, most of the resources are owned as private property by citizens, who are free to use them as they wish in their own self-interest. Prices and markets express the self-interests of resource owners, consumers, and business firms. Competition regulates self-interest—to prevent the self-interest of any person or any group from working to the disadvantage of the economy and to make self-interests work for the benefit of the entire economy. Government plays an active, but limited, role in a market economy.

Three other characteristics are found in a market economy: the employment of large amounts of **capital goods,** the development of **specialization,** and the **use of money.** Economies use capital goods and engage in specialization because this is a more efficient use of their resources; it results in larger total output and the greater satisfaction of wants. When workers, business firms, and regions within an economy specialize, they become dependent on each other for the goods and services they do not produce for themselves and they must engage in trade. Trade is made more convenient when money is used as a medium of exchange.

The chapter also explains in detail how the market system works. There are **Five Fundamental Questions** that any economic system must answer in its attempt to use its scarce resources to satisfy its material wants. The five questions or problems are: (1) What goods and services will be produced? (2) How will the goods and services be produced? (3) Who will get the goods and services? (4) How will the system accommodate change? (5) How will the system promote progress?

The explanation of how the market system finds answers to the Five Fundamental Questions is only an approximation—a simplified explanation—of the methods actually employed by the U.S. economy and other market economies. Yet this explanation is realistic enough to be truthful and general enough to be understandable. If the aims of this chapter are accomplished, you can begin to understand the market system and the methods our economy uses to solve the economizing problem presented in Chapter 1.

Although central planning served as a powerful form of economic decision making in command systems such as the Soviet Union and China (before its market reform), it had two serious problems. The first problem was one of **coordination,** which resulted in production bottlenecks and managers and bureaucrats missing production targets. Central planning also created an **incentive problem** because it sent out incorrect and inadequate signals for directing the efficient allocation of an economy's resources and gave workers little reason to work hard. The lack of incentives killed entrepreneurship and stifled innovation and technological advance.

The chapter ends with a description of the **circular flow model** (or **diagram**). In a market economy, there is a resource market and a product market that connect households and businesses. There is also a flow of money and flows of goods and services and resources that indicate that households and businesses have dual roles as buyers and sellers depending on whether they are operating in the product market or the resource market.

■ CHECKLIST

When you have studied this chapter you should be able to

☐ Compare and contrast the command system and the market system.
☐ Identify the nine important characteristics of the market system.
☐ Describe the role of private property rights in the market system.
☐ Distinguish between freedom of enterprise and freedom of choice.
☐ Explain why self-interest is a driving force in the market system.
☐ Identify two features of competition in the market system.
☐ Explain the roles of markets and prices in the market system.
☐ Describe how the market system relies on technology and capital.
☐ Discuss how two types of specialization improve efficiency in the market system.

☐ Describe the advantages of money over barter for the exchange of goods and services in the market system.

☐ Describe the size and role of government in the market system.

☐ List the Five Fundamental Questions to answer about the operation of a market economy.

☐ Explain how a market system determines what goods and services will be produced and the role of consumer sovereignty and dollar votes.

☐ Explain how goods and services will be produced in a market system.

☐ Find the least costly combination of resources needed for production when given the technological data and the prices of the resources.

☐ Explain how a market system determines who will get the goods and services it produces.

☐ Describe the guiding function of prices in accommodating change in the market system.

☐ Explain how the market system promotes progress by fostering technological advances and capital accumulation.

☐ State how the "invisible hand" in the market system tends to promote public or social interests.

☐ List three virtues of the market system.

☐ Compare how a command economy coordinates economic activity with how a market economy coordinates economic activity.

☐ Explain the problems with incentives in a command economy.

☐ Draw the circular flow model, correctly labeling the two markets and the real and money flows between the two sectors in this simplified economy.

☐ What role does private property play in helping a market economy find the most productive combination of resources? (Last Word)

■ **CHAPTER OUTLINE**

1. An *economic system* is a set of institutions and a coordinating mechanism to respond to the economizing problem for an economy.

    a. The **command system** (also called *socialism* or *communism*) is based primarily on extensive public ownership of resources and the use of central planning for most economic decision making. There used to be many examples of command economies (Soviet Union), but today there are few (Cuba, North Korea). Most former socialistic nations have been or are being transformed into capitalistic and market-oriented economies.

    b. The **market system** (*capitalism*) has extensive private ownership of resources and uses markets and prices to coordinate and direct economic activity. In pure (*laissez-faire*) capitalism there is a limited government role in the economy. In a capitalist economy such as the United States, government plays a large role, but the two characteristics of the market system—private property and markets—dominate.

2. The market system has the following nine characteristics.

    a. Private individuals and organizations own and control their property resources by means of the institution of **private property.**

    b. These individuals and organizations possess both the **freedom of enterprise** and the **freedom of choice.**

    c. These economic units are motivated largely by **self-interest.**

    d. **Competition** is based on the independent actions of buyers and sellers, who have the freedom to enter or leave markets. This competition spreads economic power and limits its potential abuse.

    e. **Markets** and prices are used to communicate and coordinate the decisions of buyers and sellers.

    f. The **market system** employs complicated and advanced methods of production, new technology, and large amounts of capital equipment to produce goods and services efficiently.

    g. It is a highly specialized economy. Human and geographic **specializations** increase the productive efficiency of the economy.

    h. It uses **money** extensively to facilitate trade and specialization. Money functions as a **medium of exchange** that is more efficient to use than **barter** for trading goods.

    i. Government has an active but limited role.

3. The system of prices and markets and households' and business firms' choices furnish the market economy with answers to **Five Fundamental Questions.**

    a. *What goods and services will be produced?* In a market economy, there is **consumer sovereignty** because consumers are in command and express their wishes for goods and services through **dollar votes.** The demands of consumers for products and the desires of business firms to maximize their profits determine what and how much of each product is produced and its price.

    b. *How will the goods and services be produced?* The desires of business firms to maximize profits by keeping their costs of production as low as possible guide them to use the most efficient techniques of production and determine their demands for various resources; competition forces them to use the most efficient techniques and ensures that only the most efficient will be able to stay in business.

    c. *Who will get the goods and services?* With resource prices determined, the money income of each household is determined, and with product prices determined, the quantity of goods and services those money incomes will buy is determined.

    d. *How will the system accommodate change?* The market system is able to accommodate itself to changes in consumer tastes, technology, and resource supplies. The desires of business firms for maximum profits and competition lead the economy to make the appropriate adjustments in the way it uses its resources.

    e. *How will the system promote progress?* Competition and the desire to increase profits promote better techniques of production and capital accumulation.

    (1) The market system encourages technological advance because it can help increase revenue or decrease costs for businesses, thus increasing profits. The use of new technology spreads rapidly because firms must stay innovative or they will fail. There can also be

creative destruction where new technology creates the market positions of firms adopting the new technology and destroys the market positions of firms using the old technology.

(2) Business owners will take their profit income and use it to make more capital goods that improve production and increase profits.

4. Competition in the economy compels firms seeking to promote their own interests to promote (as though led by an ***"invisible hand"***) the best interests of society as a whole.

   a. Competition results in an allocation of resources appropriate to consumer wants, production by the most efficient means, and the lowest possible prices.

   b. Three noteworthy merits of the market system are

   (1) The *efficient* use of resources

   (2) The *incentive* the system provides for productive activity

   (3) The personal *freedom* allowed participants as consumers, producers, workers, or investors.

5. The demise of command systems occurred largely because of two basic problems with a centrally planned economy.

   a. The *coordination problem* involved the difficulty of coordinating the economy's many interdependent segments and avoiding the chain reaction that would result from a bottleneck in any one of the segments. This coordination problem became even more difficult as the economy grew larger and more complex and more economic decisions had to be made in the production process. There were also inadequate measures of economic performance to determine the degree of success or failure of enterprises or to give clear signals to the economy.

   b. The *incentive problem* arose because in a command economy incentives are ineffective for encouraging economic initiatives and work and for directing the most efficient use of productive resources. In a market economy, profits and losses signal what firms should produce, how they should produce, and how productive resources should be allocated to best meet the wants of a nation. Central planning in command economies also lacked entrepreneurship and stifled innovation, both of which are important forces for achieving long-term economic growth. Individual workers lacked much motivation to work hard because pay was limited and there were few consumer goods to buy or they were of low quality.

6. The ***circular flow model*** or ***diagram*** is a device used to clarify the relationships between households and business firms in a market economy. In the ***resource market,*** households sell and firms buy resources, and in the ***product market,*** firms sell and households buy products. Households use the incomes they obtain from selling resources to purchase the goods and services produced by the firms, and in the economy there is a real flow of resources and products and a money flow of incomes and expenditures.

7. (Last Word). There are tens of billions of ways in which resources could be arranged in a market economy, but most combinations would be useless. The reason that a market economy produces the few combinations from the total possible that are productive and serve human goals is private property. With it, people have an incentive to make the best use of their resources and find the most rewarding combination.

■ **HINTS AND TIPS**

1. This chapter describes nine characteristics and institutions of a market system. After reading the section, check your understanding by listing the nine points and writing a short explanation of each one.

2. The section on the *Five Fundamental Questions* is both the most important and the most difficult part of the chapter. Detailed answers to the five questions are given in this section of the chapter. If you examine each one individually and in the order in which it is presented, you will more easily understand how the market system works. (Actually, the market system finds the answers simultaneously, but make your learning easier for now by considering them one by one.)

3. Be sure to understand the *importance* and *role* of each of the following in the operation of the market system: (1) the guiding function of prices, (2) the profit motive of business firms, (3) the entry into and exodus of firms from industries, (4) the meaning of competition, and (5) consumer sovereignty.

■ **IMPORTANT TERMS**

economic system	medium of exchange
command system	barter
market system	money
private property	consumer sovereignty
freedom of enterprise	dollar votes
freedom of choice	creative destruction
self-interest	"invisible hand"
competition	circular flow diagram
market	resource market
specialization	product market
division of labor	

SELF-TEST

■ **FILL-IN QUESTIONS**

1. The institutional arrangements and coordinating mechanisms used to respond to the economic problem are called (*laissez-faire,* an economic system) _____.

2. In a command economy, property resources are primarily (publicly, privately) _____ owned. The coordinating device(s) in this economic system (is central planning, are markets and prices) _____.

3. In capitalism, property resources are primarily (publicly, privately) _____ owned. The means used to direct and coordinate economic activity (is central planning, are markets and prices) _____.

4. The ownership of property resources by private individuals and organizations is the institution of private (resources, property) _____. The freedom of private businesses to obtain resources and use them to produce goods and services is the freedom of (choice, enterprise) _____, while the freedom to dispose of property or money as a person sees fit is the freedom of _____.

5. Self-interest means that each economic unit attempts to do what is best for itself, but this might lead to an abuse of power in a market economy if it were not directed and constrained by (government, competition) _____. Self-interest and competition (are, are not) _____ the same thing in a market economy.

6. Broadly defined, competition is present if two conditions prevail; these two conditions are

   a. _____
     _____
   b. _____
     _____

7. In a capitalist economy, individual buyers communicate their demands and individual sellers communicate their supplies in the system of (markets, prices) _____, and the outcomes from economic decisions are a set of product and resource _____ that are determined by demand and supply.

8. In market economies, money functions chiefly as a medium of (commerce, exchange) _____. Barter between two individuals will take place only if there is a coincidence of (resources, wants) _____.

9. In a market system, government is active but is assigned (a limited, an extensive) _____ role.

10. List the Five Fundamental Questions every economy must answer.

   a. _____
   b. _____
   c. _____
   d. _____
   e. _____

11. Consumers vote with their dollars for the production of a good or service when they (sell, buy) _____ it, and because of this, consumers are said to be (dependent, sovereign) _____ in a market economy. The buying decisions of consumers (restrain, expand) _____ the possible choices of firms in regard to what they produce, and so they make what is profitable.

12. Firms are interested in obtaining the largest economic profits possible, and so they try to produce a product in the (most, least) _____ costly way. The most efficient production techniques depend on the available (income, technology) _____ and the (prices, quotas) _____ of needed resources.

13. The market system determines how the total output of the economy will be distributed among its households by determining the (incomes, expenditures) _____ of each household and by determining the (prices, quality) _____ of each good and service produced.

14. In market economies, change is almost continuous in consumer (preferences, resources) _____, in the supplies of _____, and in technology. To make the appropriate adjustments to these changes, a market economy allows price to perform its (monopoly, guiding) _____ function.

15. The market system fosters technological change. The incentive for a firm to be the first to use a new and improved technique of production or to produce a new and better product is a greater economic (profit, loss) _____, and the incentive for other firms to follow its lead is the avoidance of _____.

16. Technological advance will require additional (capital, consumer) _____ goods, and so the entrepreneur uses profit obtained from the sale of (capital, consumer) _____ goods to acquire _____ goods.

17. A market system promotes (unity, disunity) _____ between private and public interests. Firms and resource suppliers seem to be guided by (a visible, an invisible) _____ hand to allocate the economy's resources efficiently. The two *economic* arguments for a market system are that it promotes (public, efficient) _____ use of resources and that it uses (incentives, government) _____ to direct economic activity. The major *noneconomic* argument for the market system is that it allows for personal (wealth, freedom) _____.

18. Coordination and decision making in a market economy are (centralized, decentralized) _____, but in a command economy they are _____. The market system tends to produce a reasonably (efficient, inefficient) _____ allocation of resources, but in command economies this is _____ and results in production bottlenecks. As a command economy grows over time, the coordination problem becomes (more, less) _____ complex and indicators of economic performance are (adequate, inadequate) _____ for determining the success or failure of economic activities.

19. Another problem with command economies is that economic incentives are (effective, ineffective) _____ for encouraging work or for giving signals to planners for efficient allocation of resources in the economy. Command economies do not have the (production targets, entrepreneurship) _____ important for technological advance, and because there was no business competition, innovation (fostered, lagged) _____.

20. In the circular flow model,
   a. Households are buyers and businesses are sellers in (product, resource) _____ markets, and businesses are buyers and households are sellers in _____ markets.
   b. The flow of economic resources and finished goods and services is the (money, real) _____ flow, and the flow of income and expenditures is the _____ flow.

■ TRUE–FALSE QUESTIONS

Circle T if the statement is true, F if it is false.

1. A command economy is characterized by the private ownership of resources and the use of markets and prices to coordinate and direct economic activity. **T F**

2. In a market system, the government owns most of the property resources (land and capital). **T F**

3. Pure capitalism is also called *laissez-faire* capitalism. **T F**

4. Property rights encourage investment, innovation, exchange, maintenance of property, and economic growth. **T F**

5. The freedom of business firms to produce a particular consumer good is always limited by the desires of consumers for that good. **T F**

6. The pursuit of economic self-interest is the same thing as competition. **T F**

7. When a market is competitive, the individual sellers of a product are unable to reduce the supply of the product and control its prices. **T F**

8. The market system is an organizing mechanism and also a communication network. **T F**

9. Increasing the amount of specialization in an economy generally leads to the more efficient use of its resources. **T F**

10. One way human specialization can be achieved is through a division of labor in productive activity. **T F**

11. Money is a device for facilitating the exchange of goods and services. **T F**

12. "Coincidence of wants" means that two persons want to acquire the same good or service. **T F**

13. Shells may serve as money if sellers are generally willing to accept them as money. **T F**

14. One of the Five Fundamental Questions is who will control the output. **T F**

15. Industries in which economic profits are earned by the firms in the industry will attract the entry of new firms. **T F**

16. Consumers are sovereign in a market economy and register their economic wants with "dollar votes." **T F**

17. Economic efficiency requires that a given output of a good or service be produced in the least costly way. **T F**

18. If the market price of resource A decreases, firms will tend to employ smaller quantities of resource A. **T F**

19. The incentive that the market system provides to induce technological improvement is the opportunity for economic profits. **T F**

20. Creative destruction is the hypothesis that the creation of new products and production methods simultaneously destroys the market power of existing monopolies and businesses. **T F**

21. The tendency for individuals pursuing their own self-interests to bring about results that are in the best interest of society as a whole is often called the "invisible hand." **T F**

22. A basic economic argument for the market system is that it promotes an efficient use of resources. **T F**

23. A command economy is significantly affected by missed production targets. **T F**

24. Profit is the key indicator of success and failure in a command economy. **T F**

25. In the circular flow model, there is a *real flow* of economic resources and finished goods and services and a *money flow* of income and consumption expenditures. **T F**

■ MULTIPLE-CHOICE QUESTIONS

Circle the letter that corresponds to the best answer.

1. The private ownership of property resources and the use of markets and prices to direct and coordinate economic activity are characteristic of
(a) socialism
(b) communism
(c) a market economy
(d) a command economy

2. Which is one of the main characteristics of the market system?
(a) central economic planning
(b) limits on freedom of choice
(c) the right to own private property
(d) an expanded role for government in the economy

3. In the market system, freedom of enterprise means that
(a) government is free to direct the actions of businesses
(b) businesses are free to produce products that consumers want
(c) consumers are free to buy goods and services that they want
(d) resources are distributed freely to businesses that want them

4. The maximization of profit tends to be the driving force in the economic decision making of
(a) workers
(b) consumers
(c) legislators
(d) entrepreneurs

5. How do consumers typically express self-interest?
(a) by minimizing their economic losses
(b) by maximizing their economic profits
(c) by seeking the lowest price for a product
(d) by seeking jobs with the highest wages and benefits

6. Which is a characteristic of competition as economists see it?
(a) a few sellers of all products
(b) the widespread diffusion of economic power
(c) a small number of buyers in product markets
(d) the relatively difficult entry into and exit from industries by producers

7. To decide how to use its scarce resources to satisfy economic wants, a market economy primarily relies on
(a) prices
(b) planning
(c) monopoly power
(d) production targets

8. The market system is a method of
(a) making economic decisions by central planning
(b) communicating and coordinating economic decisions
(c) promoting specialization, but not division of labor
(d) allocating money, but not economic profits or losses

9. When workers specialize in various tasks to produce a commodity, the situation is referred to as
(a) division of labor
(b) freedom of choice
(c) capital accumulation
(d) a coincidence of wants

10. In what way does human specialization contribute to an economy's output?
(a) It is a process of creative destruction.
(b) It serves as consumer sovereignty.
(c) It acts like an "invisible hand."
(d) It fosters learning by doing.

11. Which is a prerequisite of specialization?
(a) market restraints on freedom
(b) having a convenient means of exchanging goods
(c) letting government create a plan for the economy
(d) deciding who will get the goods and services in an economy

12. In the market system, the role of government is best described as
(a) limited
(b) extensive
(c) significant
(d) nonexistent

13. Which would necessarily result, sooner or later, from a decrease in consumer demand for a product?
(a) a decrease in the profits of firms in the industry
(b) an increase in the output of the industry
(c) an increase in the supply of the product
(d) an increase in the prices of resources employed by the firms in the industry

14. The demand for resources is
(a) increased when the price of resources falls
(b) most influenced by the size of government in a capitalist economy
(c) derived from the demand for the products made with the resources
(d) decreased when the product that the resources produce becomes popular

Answer Questions 15, 16, and 17 on the basis of the following information.

Suppose 50 units of product X can be produced by employing just labor and capital in the four ways shown below. Assume the prices of labor and capital are $5 and $4, respectively.

	A	B	C	D
Labor	1	2	3	4
Capital	5	3	2	1

15. Which technique is economically most efficient in producing product X?
(a) A
(b) B
(c) C
(d) D

16. If the price of product X is $1, the firm will realize
(a) an economic profit of $28
(b) an economic profit of $27
(c) an economic profit of $26
(d) an economic profit of $25

17. Now assume that the price of labor falls to $3 and the price of capital rises to $5. Which technique is economically most efficient in producing product X?
(a) A
(b) B
(c) C
(d) D

18. Which is the primary factor determining the share of the total output of the economy received by a household?
(a) the tastes of the household
(b) the medium of exchange used by the household
(c) the prices at which the household sells its resources
(d) ethical considerations in the operation of a market economy

19. If an increase in the demand for a product and a rise in its price cause an increase in the quantity supplied, price is successfully performing its
(a) guiding function
(b) circular flow role
(c) division-of-labor role
(d) medium-of-exchange function

20. In the market system, if one firm introduces a new and better method of production that enhances the firm's economic profits, other firms will be forced to adopt the new method to
(a) increase circular flow
(b) follow rules for capital accumulation
(c) avoid economic losses or bankruptcy
(d) specialize and divide the labor in an efficient way

21. The advent of personal computers and word processing software that eliminated the market for electric typewriters would be an example of
(a) specialization
(b) derived demand
(c) the "invisible hand"
(d) creative destruction

22. The chief economic virtue of the competitive market system is that it
(a) allows extensive personal freedom
(b) promotes the efficient use of resources
(c) provides an equitable distribution of income
(d) eliminates the need for decision making

23. In the system of central planning, the outputs of some industries became the inputs for other industries, but a failure of one industry to meet its production target would cause
(a) widespread unemployment
(b) inflation in wholesale and retail prices
(c) profit declines and potential bankruptcy of firms
(d) a chain reaction of production problems and bottlenecks

24. The two kinds of markets found in the circular flow model are
(a) real and money markets
(b) real and socialist markets
(c) money and command markets
(d) product and resource markets

25. In the circular flow model, businesses
(a) buy products and resources
(b) sell products and resources
(c) buy products and sell resources
(d) sell products and buy resources

■ **PROBLEMS**

1. Use the appropriate number to match the term with the phrase.

1. invisible hand	4. consumer sovereignty
2. coincidence of wants	5. creative destruction
3. division of labor	6. specialization

a. Using the resources of an individual, a firm, a region, or a nation to produce one (or a few) goods and services. _____

b. The tendency of firms and resource suppliers seeking to further their own self-interest while also promoting the interests of society in a market economy. _____

c. The situation where new products and production methods eliminate the market position of firms doing business using existing products or older production methods. _____

d. Splitting the work required to produce a product into a number of different tasks that are performed by different workers. _____

e. A situation in which the product the first trader wants to sell is the same as the product the second trader wants to buy and the product the second trader wants to sell is the same as the product the first trader wants to buy. _____

f. Determination by consumers of the types and quantities of goods and services that will be produced in a market economy. _____

2. Assume that a firm can produce product A, product B, *or* product C with the resources it currently employs. These resources cost the firm a total of $50 per week. Assume, for the purposes of the problem, that the firm's employment of resources cannot be changed. Their market prices and the quantities of A, B, and C these resources will produce per week are given below. Compute the firm's profit when it produces A, B, or C, and enter those profits in the table below.

Product	Market price	Output	Economic profit
A	$7.00	8	$_____
B	4.50	10	_____
C	.25	240	_____

a. Which product will the firm produce? _____

b. If the price of A rose to $8, the firm would _____

_____

(Hint: You will have to recompute the firm's profit from the production of A.)

c. If the firm were producing A and selling it at a price of $8, what would tend to happen to the number of firms producing A?

_____

3. Suppose a firm can produce 100 units of product X by combining labor, land, capital, and entrepreneurial ability in three different ways. If it can hire labor at $2 per unit, land at $3 per unit, capital at $5 per unit, and entrepreneurship at $10 per unit, and if the amounts of the resources required by the three methods of producing 100 units of product X are as indicated in the table, answer the following questions.

Resource	Method		
	1	2	3
Labor	8	13	10
Land	4	3	3
Capital	4	2	4
Entrepreneurship	1	1	1

a. Which method is the least expensive way of producing 100 units of X? _____

b. If X sells for 70 cents per unit, what is the economic profit of the firm? $_____

c. If the price of labor should rise from $2 to $3 per unit and if the price of X is 70 cents,

(1) the firm's use of

labor would change from _____ to _____

land would change from _____ to _____

capital would change from _____ to _____
entrepreneurship would not change

(2) The firm's economic profit would change from

$_____ to $_____

4. In the circular flow diagram below, the upper pair of flows (**a** and **b**) represents the resource market and the lower pair (**c** and **d**) represents the product market.

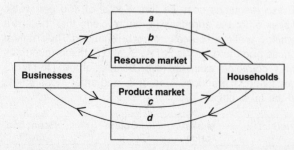

Supply labels or explanations for each of the four flows:

a. _____

b. _____

c. _____

d. _____

■ **SHORT ANSWER AND ESSAY QUESTIONS**

1. The command system and the market system differ in two important ways. Compare and contrast the two economic systems.

2. Explain the major characteristics—institutions and assumptions—embodied in a market system.

3. What do each of the following seek if they pursue their own self-interest: consumers, resource owners, and business firms?

4. Explain what economists mean by competition. For a market to be competitive, why is it important that there be buyers and sellers and easy entry and exit?

5. How does an economy benefit from specialization and the division of labor?

6. Give an example of how specialization can benefit two separate and diversely endowed geographic regions.

7. What is money? What important function does it perform? Explain how money performs this function and how it overcomes the disadvantages associated with barter.

8. In what way do the desires of entrepreneurs to obtain economic profits and avoid losses make consumer sovereignty effective?

9. Why is the ability of firms to enter industries that are prosperous important to the effective functioning of competition?

10. Explain in detail how an increase in the consumer demand for a product will result in more of the product being produced and more resources being allocated to its production.

11. Describe the production factor for businesses that determines what combinations of resources and technologies will be used to produce goods and services.

12. Who will get the output from a market economy? Explain.

13. How can the market system adapt to change? How is this done?

14. How do prices communicate information and guide and direct production in a market economy?

15. Explain how the market system provides a strong incentive for technological advance and creative destruction.

16. Who "votes" for the production of capital goods, why do they "vote" for capital goods production, and where do they obtain the dollars needed to cast those "votes"?

17. "An invisible hand operates to identify private and public interests." What are private interests, and what is the public interest? What is it that leads the economy to operate as if it were directed by an invisible hand?

18. Describe three virtues of the market system.

19. Explain the two major economic problems with command economies and then explain why market economies avoid such problems.

20. In the circular flow model, what are the two markets? What roles do households play and what roles do businesses play in each market?

ANSWERS

Chapter 2 The Market System and the Circular Flow

FILL-IN QUESTIONS

1. an economic system
2. publicly, is central planning
3. privately, are markets and prices
4. property, enterprise, choice
5. competition, are not
6. *a.* independently acting buyers and sellers operating in markets; *b.* freedom of buyers and sellers to enter or leave these markets
7. markets, prices
8. exchange, wants
9. a limited
10. *a.* What goods and services will be produced? *b.* How will the goods and services be produced? *c.* Who will get the goods and services? *d.* How will the system accommodate change? *e.* How will the system promote progress?
11. buy, sovereign, restrain
12. least, technology, prices
13. incomes, prices
14. preferences, resources, guiding
15. profit, losses
16. capital, consumer, capital
17. unity, an invisible, efficient, incentives, freedom
18. decentralized, centralized, efficient, inefficient, more, inadequate
19. ineffective, entrepreneurship, lagged
20. *a.* product, resource; *b.* real, money

TRUE–FALSE QUESTIONS

1. F, p. 29	10. T, p. 32	19. T, pp. 36–37
2. F, p. 29	11. T, p. 32	20. T, p. 37
3. T, p. 29	12. F, p. 32	21. T, p. 37
4. T, pp. 29–30	13. T, p. 32	22. T, p. 37
5. T, p. 30	14. F, p. 34	23. T, p. 38
6. F, pp. 30–31	15. T, p. 34	24. F, p. 38
7. T, p. 31	16. T, p. 34	25. T, pp. 39–41
8. T, p. 31	17. T, p. 35	
9. T, p. 32	18. F, p. 35	

MULTIPLE-CHOICE QUESTIONS

1. c, p. 29	10. d, p. 32	19. a, p. 36
2. c, pp. 29–30	11. b, p. 32	20. c, p. 36
3. b, p. 30	12. a, p. 33	21. d, p. 37
4. d, pp. 30–31	13. a, p. 33	22. b, p. 37
5. c, pp. 30–31	14. c, pp. 34–35	23. d, p. 38
6. b, p. 31	15. b, p. 35	24. d, pp. 39–41
7. a, p. 31	16. a, p. 35	25. d, pp. 39–41
8. b, p. 31	17. d, p. 35	
9. a, p. 32	18. c, pp. 35–36	

PROBLEMS

1. *a.* 6; *b.* 1; *c.* 5; *d.* 3; *e.* 2; *f.* 4
2. $6, −$5, $10; *a.* C; *b.* produce A and have an economic profit of $14; *c.* it would increase
3. *a.* method 2; *b.* 15; *c.* (1) 13, 8; 3, 4; 2, 4; (2) 15, 4
4. *a.* money income payments (wages, rent, interest, and profit); *b.* services or resources (land, labor, capital, and entrepreneurial ability); *c.* goods and services; d. expenditures for goods and services

SHORT ANSWER AND ESSAY QUESTIONS

1. p. 29	8. p. 34	15. pp. 36–37
2. pp. 29–33	9. pp. 34–35	16. p. 37
3. pp. 30–31	10. pp. 34–35	17. p. 37
4. p. 31	11. p. 35	18. p. 37
5. p. 32	12. pp. 35–36	19. p. 38
6. pp. 32–33	13. p. 36	20. pp. 39–41
7. pp. 32–33	14. p. 36	

CHAPTER 3

Demand, Supply, and Market Equilibrium

Chapter 3 introduces you to the most fundamental tools of economic analysis: demand and supply. Demand and supply are simply "boxes" or categories into which all the forces and factors that affect the price and quantity of a good bought and sold in a competitive market are placed. Demand and supply determine price and quantity exchanged. It is necessary to understand *why* and *how* they do this.

Many students never learn to *define* demand and supply. They never learn (1) what an increase or decrease in demand or supply means, (2) the important distinctions between "demand" and "quantity demanded" and between "supply" and "quantity supplied," and (3) the equally important distinctions between a change in demand and a change in quantity demanded and between a change in supply and a change in quantity supplied.

Once students learn these things, however, it is no great trick to comprehend the so-called laws of demand and supply. The equilibrium price—that is, the price that will tend to prevail in the market as long as demand and supply do not change—is simply the price at which **quantity demanded** and **quantity supplied** are equal. The quantity bought and sold in the market (the equilibrium quantity) is the quantity demanded and supplied at the equilibrium price. If you can determine the equilibrium price and quantity under one set of demand and supply conditions, you can determine them under any other set.

This chapter includes a brief examination of the factors that determine demand and supply and the ways in which changes in those determinants affect and cause changes in demand and supply. A graphic method is used in this analysis to illustrate demand and supply, equilibrium price and quantity, changes in demand and supply, and the resulting changes in equilibrium price and quantity. The **demand curve** and the **supply curve** are graphic representations of the same data contained in the schedules of demand and supply.

The application section at the end of the chapter explains government-set prices. When the government sets a legal price in a competitive market, it creates a **price ceiling** or **price floor**. This prevents supply and demand from determining the equilibrium price and quantity of a product that will be provided by a competitive market. As you will learn, the economic consequence of a price ceiling is a persistent shortage of the product. An example of a price ceiling would be price controls on apartment rents. A price floor will result in a persistent surplus of a product, and the example given is price supports for an agricultural product.

You will use demand and supply over and over. It will turn out to be as important to you in economics as jet propulsion is to the pilot of an airplane: You can't get off the ground without it.

■ **CHECKLIST**

When you have studied this chapter you should be able to

☐ Define demand and state the law of demand.
☐ Give three explanations for the inverse relationship between price and quantity demanded.
☐ Graph the demand curve when you are given a demand schedule.
☐ Explain the difference between individual demand and market demand.
☐ List the five major determinants of demand and explain how each one shifts the demand curve.
☐ Define normal goods, inferior goods, substitute goods, and complementary goods.
☐ Distinguish between change in demand and change in the quantity demanded.
☐ Define supply and state the law of supply.
☐ Graph the supply curve when you are given a supply schedule.
☐ List the major determinants of supply and explain how each one shifts the supply curve.
☐ Distinguish between change in supply and change in the quantity supplied.
☐ Describe how the equilibrium price and quantity are determined in a competitive market.
☐ Define surplus and shortage.
☐ Determine, when you are given the demand for and the supply of a good, the equilibrium price and the equilibrium quantity.
☐ Explain the meaning of the rationing function of prices.
☐ Distinguish between productive efficiency and allocative efficiency.
☐ Predict the effects of changes in demand on equilibrium price and quantity.
☐ Predict the effects of changes in supply on equilibrium price and quantity.
☐ Predict the effects of changes in both demand and supply on equilibrium price and quantity.
☐ Explain the economic effects of a government-set price ceiling on product price and quantity in a competitive market.

☐ Describe the economic consequences of a government-set price floor on product price and quantity.

■ CHAPTER OUTLINE

1. A market is any institution or mechanism that brings together buyers ("demanders") and sellers ("suppliers") of a particular good or service. This chapter assumes that markets are highly competitive.

2. *Demand* is a schedule of prices and the quantities that buyers would purchase at each of those prices during a selected period.

   a. The *law of demand* states that there is an inverse or negative relationship between price and quantity demanded. Other things equal, as price increases, buyers will purchase smaller quantities, and as price decreases, they will purchase larger quantities. There are three explanations for the law of demand:

   (1) *Diminishing marginal utility.* After a point, consumers get less satisfaction or benefit from consuming more and more units.

   (2) *Income effect.* A higher price for a good decreases the purchasing power of consumers' incomes so that they can't buy as much of the good.

   (3) *Substitution effect.* A higher price for a good encourages consumers to search for cheaper substitutes and thus buy less of it.

   b. The *demand curve* has a downward slope and is a graphic representation of the law of demand.

   c. Market demand for a good is a summation of all the demands of all consumers of that good at each price. Although price has the most important influence on quantity demanded, other factors can influence demand. These factors, called *determinants of demand,* are consumer tastes (preferences), the number of buyers in the market, consumers' income, the prices of related goods, and consumer expectations.

   d. An increase or decrease in the entire demand schedule and the demand curve (a change in demand) results from a change in one or more of the determinants of demand. For a particular good,

   (1) an increase in *consumer tastes or preferences* increases its demand;

   (2) an increase in *the number of buyers* increases its demand;

   (3) *consumers' income* increases its demand if it is a *normal good* (one where income and demand are positively related), but an increase in consumers' income decreases its demand if it is an *inferior good* (one where income and demand are negatively related);

   (4) an increase in *the price of a related good* will increase its demand if the related good is a *substitute good* (one that can be used in place of another), but an increase in the price of a related good will decrease its demand if the related good is a *complementary good* (one that is used with another good);

   (5) an increase in *consumer expectations* of a future price increase or a future rise in income will increase its current demand.

   e. A *change in demand* means that the entire demand curve or schedule has changed because of a change in one of these determinants of demand, but a *change in the quantity demanded* means that there has been a movement along an existing demand curve or schedule because of a change in price.

3. *Supply* is a schedule of prices and the quantities that sellers will sell at each of those prices during some period of time.

   a. The *law of supply* shows a positive relationship between price and quantity supplied. Other things equal, as the price of the good increases, larger quantities will be offered for sale, and as the price of the good decreases, smaller quantities will be offered for sale.

   b. The *supply curve* is a graphic representation of supply and the law of supply; it has an upward slope, indicating the positive relationship between price and quantity supplied.

   c. The market supply of a good is the sum of the supplies of all sellers or producers of the good at each price.

   d. Although price has the most important influence on the quantity supplied, other factors can influence supply. Those factors, called *determinants of supply,* are changes in (1) resource prices; (2) technology; (3) taxes and subsidies; (4) prices of other good; (5) price expectation; and (6) the number of sellers in a market.

   e. A *change in supply* is an increase or decrease in the entire supply schedule and the supply curve. It is the result of a change in one or more of the determinants of supply that affect the cost of production. For a particular good,

   (1) a decrease in *resource prices* increases its supply;

   (2) an improvement in technology increases its supply;

   (3) a decrease in *taxes or* an increase in *subsidies* increases its supply;

   (4) a decrease in *the price of another good* that could be produced leads to an increase in the supply of the particular good;

   (5) an increase in *producer expectations* of higher prices for the good may increase or decrease its supply.

   f. A *change in supply* means that the entire supply curve or schedule has changed because of a change in one of these determinants of supply, but a *change in the quantity supplied* means that there has been a movement along an existing supply curve or schedule because of a change in price.

4. The *market* or *equilibrium price* of a product is that price at which quantity demanded and quantity supplied are equal; the quantity exchanged in the market (the equilibrium quantity) is equal to the quantity demanded and supplied at the equilibrium price.

   a. If the price of a product is above the market equilibrium price, there will be a *surplus* or *excess supply.* In this case, the quantity demanded is less than the quantity supplied at that price.

b. If the price of a product is below the market equilibrium price, there will be a **shortage** or *excess demand.* In this case, the quantity demanded is greater than the quantity supplied at that price.

c. The rationing function of prices is the elimination of surpluses and shortages of a product.

d. Competitive markets produce **productive efficiency,** in which the goods and services society desires are being produced in the least costly way. They also create **allocative efficiency,** in which resources are devoted to the production of the goods and services society values most highly.

e. Changes in supply and demand result in changes in the equilibrium price and quantity. The simplest cases are ones where demand changes and supply remains constant or where supply changes and demand remains constant. More complex cases involve simultaneous changes in supply and demand.

(1) *Demand changes.* An increase in demand, with supply remaining the same, will increase the equilibrium price and quantity; a decrease in demand, with supply remaining the same, will decrease the equilibrium price and quantity.

(2) *Supply changes.* An increase in supply, with demand staying the same, will decrease the equilibrium price and increase the equilibrium quantity; a decrease in supply, with demand staying the same, will increase the equilibrium price and decrease the equilibrium quantity.

(3) *Complex cases.* These four cases involve changes in demand and supply: Both increase; both decrease; one increases and one decreases; and one decreases and one increases. For the possible effects on the equilibrium price and quantity in the four complex cases, see #4 in the "Hints and Tips" section.

5. Supply and demand analysis has many important applications to **government-set prices.**

a. A **price ceiling** set by government prevents price from performing its rationing function in a market system. It creates a shortage (quantity demanded is greater than quantity supplied) at the government-set price.

(1) Another rationing method must be found, and so government often steps in and establishes one. But all rationing systems have problems because they exclude someone.

(2) A government-set price creates an illegal *black market* for those who want to buy and sell above the government-set price.

(3) One example of a legal price ceiling that creates a shortage would be the rent control established in some cities to restrain the rental price of apartments.

b. A **price floor** is a minimum price set by government for the sale of a product or resource. It creates a surplus (quantity supplied is greater than quantity demanded) at the fixed price. The surplus may induce the government to increase demand or decrease supply to eliminate the surplus. The use of price floors has often been applied to agricultural products such as wheat.

6. (Last Word). Supply and demand analysis can be used to understand the shortage of organs for transplants. The demand curve for such organs is downsloping, and the supply is fixed (vertical) and to the left of the zero price on the demand curve. Transplanted organs have a zero price. At that price the quantity demanded is much greater than the quantity supplied, creating a shortage that is rationed with a waiting list. A competitive market for organs would increase the price of organs and make them more available for transplantation (make the supply curve upsloping), but there are moral and cost objections to this change.

■ HINTS AND TIPS

1. This chapter is the most important one in the book. Make sure you spend extra time on it and master the material. If you do, your long-term payoff will be a much better understanding of the applications in later chapters.

2. One mistake students often make is to confuse **change in demand** with **change in quantity demanded.** A change in demand causes the entire demand curve to *shift*, whereas a change in quantity demanded is simply a *movement* along an existing demand curve.

3. It is strongly recommended that you draw supply and demand graphs as you work on supply and demand problems so that you can see a picture of what happens when demand shifts, supply shifts, or both demand and supply shift.

4. Make a chart and related graphs that show the eight possible outcomes from changes in demand and supply. Figure 3.7 in the text illustrates the *four single shift* outcomes:

(1) $D\uparrow$: $P\uparrow$, $Q\uparrow$ (3) $S\uparrow$: $P\downarrow$, $Q\uparrow$
(2) $D\downarrow$: $P\downarrow$, $Q\downarrow$ (4) $S\downarrow$: $P\uparrow$, $Q\downarrow$

Four shift combinations are described in Table 3.7 of the text. Make a figure to illustrate each combination.

(1) $S\uparrow$, $D\downarrow$: $P\downarrow$, Q?   (3) $S\uparrow$, $D\uparrow$: P?, $Q\uparrow$
(2) $S\downarrow$, $D\uparrow$: $P\uparrow$, Q?   (4) $S\downarrow$, $D\downarrow$: P?, $Q\downarrow$

5. Make sure you understand the "other-things-equal" assumption described in the Consider This box on salsa and coffee beans. It will help you understand why the law of demand is not violated even if the price and quantity of a product increase over time.

6. Practice always helps in understanding graphs. Without looking at the textbook, draw a supply and demand graph with a **price ceiling** below the equilibrium price and show the resulting shortage in the market for a product. Then draw a supply and demand graph with a **price floor** above the equilibrium price and show the resulting surplus. Explain to yourself what the graphs show. Check your graphs and your explanations by referring to textbook Figures 3.8 and 3.9 and the related explanations.

■ IMPORTANT TERMS

demand	law of demand
demand schedule	diminishing marginal utility

income effect

substitution effect

demand curve

determinants of demand

normal goods

inferior goods

substitute good

complementary good

change in demand

change in quantity demanded

supply

supply schedule

law of supply

supply curve

determinants of supply

change in supply

change in quantity supplied

equilibrium price

equilibrium quantity

surplus

shortage

price ceiling

price floor

SELF-TEST

■ FILL-IN QUESTIONS

1. A market is the institution or mechanism that brings together buyers or (demanders, suppliers) _____ and sellers or _____ of a particular good or service.

2. The relationship between price and quantity in the demand schedule is (a direct, an inverse) _____ relationship; in the supply schedule the relationship is _____ one.

3. The added satisfaction or pleasure a consumer obtains from additional units of a product decreases as the consumer's consumption of that product increases. This phenomenon is called diminishing marginal (equilibrium, utility) _____.

4. A consumer tends to buy more of a product as its price falls because
a. The purchasing power of the consumer is increased and the consumer tends to buy more of this product (and of other products); this is called the (income, substitution) _____ effect;
b. The product becomes less expensive relative to similar products and the consumer tends to buy more of the original product and less of the similar products, which is called the _____ effect.

5. When demand or supply is graphed, price is placed on the (horizontal, vertical) _____ axis and quantity on the _____ axis.

6. The change from an individual to a market demand schedule involves (adding, multiplying) _____ the quantities demanded by each consumer at the various possible (incomes, prices) _____.

7. When the price of one product and the demand for another product are directly related, the two products are called (substitutes, complements) _____;

however, when the price of one product and the demand for another product are inversely related, the two products are called _____.

8. When a consumer demand schedule or curve is drawn, it is assumed that five factors that determine demand are fixed and constant. These five determinants of consumer demand are

a. _____

b. _____

c. _____

d. _____

e. _____

9. A decrease in demand means that consumers will buy (larger, smaller) _____ quantities at every price or will pay (more, less) _____ for the same quantities.

10. A change in income or in the price of another product will result in a change in the (demand for, quantity demanded of) _____ the given product, and a change in the price of the given product will result in a change in the _____ the given product.

11. An increase in supply means that producers will make and be willing to sell (larger, smaller) _____ quantities at every price or will accept (more, less) _____ for the same quantities.

12. A change in resource prices or the prices of other goods that could be produced will result in a change in the (supply, quantity supplied) _____ of the given product, but a change in the price of the given product will result in a change in the _____.

13. The fundamental factors that determine the supply of any commodity in the product market are

a. _____

b. _____

c. _____

d. _____

e. _____

f. _____

14. The equilibrium price of a product is the price at which quantity demanded is (greater than, equal to) _____ quantity supplied, and there (is, is not) _____ a surplus or a shortage at that price.

15. If quantity demanded is greater than quantity supplied, price is (above, below) _____ the equilibrium price, and the (shortage, surplus) _____ will cause the price to (rise, fall) _____. If quantity demanded is less than the quantity supplied, price is (above, below) _____ the equilibrium price, and the (shortage, surplus) _____ will cause the price to (rise, fall) _____.

16. In the space next to **a–h,** indicate the effect [*increase* (+), *decrease* (−), or *indeterminate* (?)] on equilibrium price (**P**) and equilibrium quantity (**Q**) of each of these changes in demand and/or supply.

	P	**Q**
a. Increase in demand, supply constant	____	____
b. Increase in supply, demand constant	____	____
c. Decrease in demand, supply constant	____	____
d. Decrease in supply, demand constant	____	____
e. Increase in demand, increase in supply	____	____
f. Increase in demand, decrease in supply	____	____
g. Decrease in demand, decrease in supply	____	____
h. Decrease in demand, increase in supply	____	____

17. If supply and demand establish a price for a good so that there is no shortage or surplus of the product, then price is successfully performing its (utility, rationing) _____ function. The price that is set is a market-(changing, clearing) _____ price.

18. A competitive market produces two types of efficiency: Goods and services will be produced in the least costly way, and so there will be (allocative, productive) _____ efficiency, and resources will be devoted to the production of the mix of goods and services society most wants, or there will be _____ efficiency.

19. A price ceiling is the (minimum, maximum) _____ legal price a seller may charge for a product or service, whereas a price floor is the _____ legal price set by government.

20. If a price ceiling is below the market equilibrium price, a (surplus, shortage) _____ will arise in a competitive market, and if a price floor is above the market equilibrium price, a (surplus, shortage) _____ will arise in a competitive market.

■ **TRUE–FALSE QUESTIONS**

Circle T if the statement is true, F if it is false.

1. A market is any arrangement that brings together the buyers and sellers of a particular good or service. **T F**

2. Demand is the amount of a good or service that a buyer will purchase at a particular price. **T F**

3. The law of demand states that as price increases, other things being equal, the quantity of the product demanded increases. **T F**

4. The law of diminishing marginal utility is one explanation of why there is an inverse relationship between price and quantity demanded. **T F**

5. The substitution effect suggests that, at a lower price, you have the incentive to substitute the more expensive product for similar products which are relatively less expensive. **T F**

6. There is no difference between individual demand schedules and the market demand schedule for a product. **T F**

7. In graphing supply and demand schedules, supply is put on the horizontal axis and demand on the vertical axis. **T F**

8. If price falls, there will be an increase in demand. **T F**

9. If consumer tastes or preferences for a product decrease, the demand for the product will tend to decrease. **T F**

10. An increase in income will tend to increase the demand for a product. **T F**

11. When two products are substitute goods, the price of one and the demand for the other tend to move in the same direction. **T F**

12. If two goods are complementary, an increase in the price of one will tend to increase the demand for the other. **T F**

13. A change in the quantity demanded means that there has been a change in demand. **T F**

14. Supply is a schedule that shows the amounts of a product a producer can make in a limited period. **T F**

15. An increase in resource prices will tend to decrease supply. **T F**

16. A government subsidy for the production of a product will tend to decrease supply. **T F**

17. An increase in the prices of other goods that could be made by producers will tend to decrease the supply of the current good that the producer is making. **T F**

18. A change in supply means that there is a movement along an existing supply curve. **T F**

19. A surplus indicates that the quantity demanded is less than the quantity supplied at that price. **T F**

20. If the market price of a product is below its equilibrium price, the market price will tend to rise because demand will decrease and supply will increase. **T F**

21. The rationing function of prices is the elimination of shortages and surpluses. **T F**

22. Allocative efficiency means that goods and services are being produced by society in the least costly way. **T F**

23. If the supply of a product increases and demand decreases, the equilibrium price and quantity will increase.
T F

24. If the demand for a product increases and the supply of the product decreases, the equilibrium price will increase and the equilibrium quantity will be indeterminate. **T F**

25. A price ceiling set by government below the competitive market price of a product will result in a surplus.
T F

■ MULTIPLE-CHOICE QUESTIONS

Circle the letter that corresponds to the best answer.

1. A schedule that shows the various amounts of a product consumers are willing and able to purchase at each price in a series of possible prices during a specified period of time is called
(a) supply
(b) demand
(c) quantity supplied
(d) quantity demanded

2. The reason for the law of demand can best be explained in terms of
(a) supply
(b) complementary goods
(c) the rationing function of prices
(d) diminishing marginal utility

3. Assume that the price of video game players falls. What most likely will happen to the equilibrium price and quantity of video games, assuming this market is competitive?
(a) Price will increase; quantity will decrease.
(b) Price will decrease; quantity will increase.
(c) Price will decrease; quantity will decrease.
(d) Price will increase; quantity will increase.

4. Given the following individuals' demand schedules for product X, and assuming these are the only three consumers of X, which set of prices and output levels below will be on the market demand curve for this product?

Price X	Consumer 1 Q_{dx}	Consumer 2 Q_{dx}	Consumer 3 Q_{dx}
$5	1	2	0
4	2	4	0
3	3	6	1
2	4	8	2
1	5	10	3

(a) ($5, 2); ($1, 10)
(b) ($5, 3); ($1, 18)
(c) ($4, 6); ($2, 12)
(d) ($4, 0); ($1, 3)

5. Which change will decrease the demand for a product?
(a) a favorable change in consumer tastes
(b) an increase in the price of a substitute good
(c) a decrease in the price of a complementary good
(d) a decrease in the number of buyers

6. The income of a consumer decreases, and the consumer's demand for a particular good increases. It can be concluded that the good is
(a) normal
(b) inferior
(c) a substitute
(d) a complement

7. Which of the following could cause a decrease in consumer demand for product X?
(a) a decrease in consumer income
(b) an increase in the prices of goods that are good substitutes for product X
(c) an increase in the price that consumers expect will prevail for product X in the future
(d) a decrease in the supply of product X

8. If two goods are substitutes for each other, an increase in the price of one will necessarily
(a) decrease the demand for the other
(b) increase the demand for the other
(c) decrease the quantity demanded of the other
(d) increase the quantity demanded of the other

9. If two products, A and B, are complements, then
(a) an increase in the price of A will decrease the demand for B
(b) an increase in the price of A will increase the demand for B
(c) an increase in the price of A will have no significant effect on the price of B
(d) a decrease in the price of A will decrease the demand for B

10. If two products, X and Y, are independent goods, then
(a) an increase in the price of X will significantly increase the demand for Y
(b) an increase in the price of Y will significantly increase the demand for X
(c) an increase in the price of Y will have no significant effect on the demand for X
(d) a decrease in the price of X will significantly increase the demand for Y

11. The law of supply states that, other things being constant, as price increases,
(a) supply increases
(b) supply decreases
(c) quantity supplied increases
(d) quantity supplied decreases

12. If the supply curve moves from S_1 to S_2 on the graph below, there has been
- **(a)** an increase in supply
- **(b)** a decrease in supply
- **(c)** an increase in quantity supplied
- **(d)** a decrease in quantity supplied

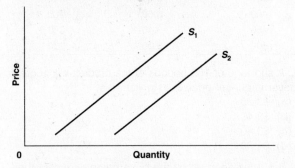

13. A decrease in the supply of a product most likely would be caused by
- **(a)** an increase in business taxes
- **(b)** an increase in consumer incomes
- **(c)** a decrease in resource costs for production
- **(d)** a decrease in the price of a complementary good

14. If the quantity supplied of a product is greater than the quantity demanded for that product, then
- **(a)** there is a shortage of the product
- **(b)** there is a surplus of the product
- **(c)** the product is a normal good
- **(d)** the product is an inferior good

15. If the price of a product is below the equilibrium price, the result will be
- **(a)** a surplus of the good
- **(b)** a shortage of the good
- **(c)** a decrease in the supply of the good
- **(d)** an increase in the demand for the good

16. Which would be the best example of allocative efficiency? When society devoted resources to the production of
- **(a)** slide rules instead of handheld calculators
- **(b)** horse-drawn carriages instead of automobiles
- **(c)** computers with word processors instead of type-writers
- **(d)** long-playing records instead of compact discs

Answer Questions 17, 18, and 19 on the basis of the data in the following table. Consider the following supply and demand schedules for bushels of corn.

Price	Quantity demanded	Quantity supplied
$20	395	200
22	375	250
24	350	290
26	320	320
28	280	345
30	235	365

17. The equilibrium price in this market is
- **(a)** $22
- **(b)** $24

- **(c)** $26
- **(d)** $28

18. An increase in the cost of labor lowers the quantity supplied by 65 bushels at each price. The new equilibrium price would be
- **(a)** $22
- **(b)** $24
- **(c)** $26
- **(d)** $28

19. If the quantity demanded at each price increases by 130 bushels, then th e new equilibrium quantity will be
- **(a)** 290
- **(b)** 320
- **(c)** 345
- **(d)** 365

20. A decrease in supply and a decrease in demand will
- **(a)** increase price and decrease the quantity exchanged
- **(b)** decrease price and increase the quantity exchanged
- **(c)** increase price and affect the quantity exchanged in an indeterminate way
- **(d)** affect price in an indeterminate way and decrease the quantity exchanged

21. An increase in demand and a decrease in supply will
- **(a)** increase price and increase the quantity exchanged
- **(b)** decrease price and decrease the quantity exchanged
- **(c)** increase price and the effect on quantity exchanged will be indeterminate
- **(d)** decrease price and the effect on quantity exchanged will be indeterminate

22. An increase in supply and an increase in demand will
- **(a)** increase price and increase the quantity exchanged
- **(b)** decrease price and increase the quantity exchanged
- **(c)** affect price in an indeterminate way and decrease the quantity exchanged
- **(d)** affect price in an indeterminate way and increase the quantity exchanged

23. A cold spell in Florida devastates the orange crop. As a result, California oranges command a higher price. Which of the following statements best explains the situation?
- **(a)** The supply of Florida oranges decreases, causing the supply of California oranges to increase and their price to increase.
- **(b)** The supply of Florida oranges decreases, causing their price to increase and the demand for California oranges to increase.
- **(c)** The supply of Florida oranges decreases, causing the supply of California oranges to decrease and their price to increase.
- **(d)** The demand for Florida oranges decreases, causing a greater demand for California oranges and an increase in their price.

*Answer Questions 24, 25, 26, and 27 based on the fol-
lowing graph showing the market supply and demand for
a product.*

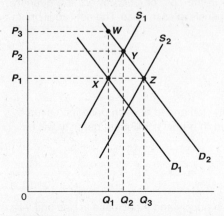

24. Assume that the market is initially in equilibrium where D_1
and S_1 intersect. If there is an increase in the number of buyers, then the new equilibrium most likely would be at point
   (a) **W**
   (b) **X**
   (c) **Y**
   (d) **Z**

25. Assume that the equilibrium price and quantity in the
market are P_2 and Q_2. Which factor would cause the equilibrium price and quantity to shift to P_1 and Q_3?
   (a) an increase in product price
   (b) an increase in demand
   (c) an increase in supply
   (d) a decrease in quantity

26. What would cause a shift in the equilibrium price and
quantity from point **Z** to point **X**?
   (a) a decrease in production costs and more favorable
   consumer tastes for the product
   (b) an increase in the number of suppliers and an
   increase in consumer incomes
   (c) an increase in production costs and a decrease in
   consumer incomes
   (d) an improvement in production technology and a
   decrease in the price of a substitute good

27. Assume that the market is initially in equilibrium where
D_1 and S_1 intersect. If consumer incomes increased and
the technology for making the product improved, the new
equilibrium most likely would be at
   (a) P_1 and Q_1
   (b) P_2 and Q_2
   (c) P_1 and Q_3
   (d) P_3 and Q_1

28. The demand curve with its inverse relationship
between price and quantity demanded is based on the
assumption of
   (a) other-things-equal
   (b) complementary goods
   (c) increasing marginal utility
   (d) changing consumer expectations

*Questions 29 and 30 relate to the following table, which
shows a hypothetical supply and demand schedule for
a product.*

Quantity demanded (pounds)	Price (per pound)	Quantity supplied (pounds)
200	$4.40	800
250	4.20	700
300	4.00	600
350	3.80	500
400	3.60	400
450	3.40	300
500	3.20	200

29. A shortage of 150 pounds of the product will occur if
a government-set price is established at
   (a) $3.20
   (b) $3.40
   (c) $3.80
   (d) $4.00

30. If a price floor set by the government is established
at $4.20, there will be a
   (a) surplus of 300 pounds
   (b) shortage of 300 pounds
   (c) surplus of 450 pounds
   (d) shortage of 450 pounds

■ **PROBLEMS**

1. Using the demand schedule at the top of the next
column, plot the demand curve on the graph below the
schedule. Label the axes and indicate for each axis the
units being used to measure price and quantity.

Price	Quantity demanded 1000 bushels of soybeans
$7.20	10
7.00	15
6.80	20
6.60	25
6.40	30
6.20	35

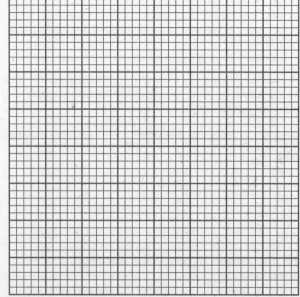

0

a. Plot the following supply schedule on the same graph.

Price	Quantity demanded 1000 bushels of soybeans
$7.20	40
7.00	35
6.80	30
6.60	25
6.40	20
6.20	15

b. The equilibrium price of soybeans will be $_____.
c. How many thousand bushels of soybeans will be exchanged at this price? _____
d. Indicate clearly on the graph the equilibrium price and quantity by drawing lines from the intersection of the supply and demand curves to the price and quantity axes.
e. If the Federal government supported a price of $7.00 per bushel, there would be a (shortage, surplus) _____ of _____ bushels of soybeans.

2. The demand schedules of three individuals (Ellie, Sam, and Lynn) for loaves of bread are shown in the following table. Assuming there are only three buyers of bread, determine and graph the total or market demand schedule for bread.

Price	Quantity demanded, loaves of bread			Total
	Ellie	Sam	Lynn	
$1.50	1	4	0	_____
1.40	3	5	1	_____
1.30	6	6	5	_____
1.20	10	7	10	_____
1.10	15	8	16	_____

3. Following is a demand schedule for bushels of apples. In columns 3 and 4 insert any new figures for quantity that represent in column 3 an increase in demand and in column 4 a decrease in demand.

(1) Price	(2) Quantity demanded	(3) Demand increases	(4) Demand decreases
$6.00	400	_____	_____
5.90	500	_____	_____
5.80	600	_____	_____
5.70	700	_____	_____
5.60	800	_____	_____
5.50	900	_____	_____

4. Assume that O'Rourke has, when his income is $100 per week, the demand schedule for good A shown in columns 1 and 2 of the following table and the demand schedule for good B shown in columns 4 and 5. Assume that the prices of A and B are $.80 and $5, respectively.

Demand for A (per week)			Demand for B (per week)		
(1)	(2)	(3)	(4)	(5)	(6)
Price	Quantity demanded	Quantity demanded	Price	Quantity demanded	Quantity demanded
$.90	10	0	$5.00	4	7
.85	20	10	4.50	5	8
.80	30	20	4.00	6	9
.75	40	30	3.50	7	10
.70	50	40	3.00	8	11
.65	60	50	2.50	9	12
.60	70	60	2.00	10	13

a. How much A will O'Rourke buy? _____
How much B? _____
b. Suppose that as a consequence of a $10 increase in O'Rourke's weekly income, the quantities demanded of A become those shown in column 3 and the quantities demanded of B become those shown in column 6.

(1) How much A will he now buy? _____
How much B? _____

(2) Good A is (normal, inferior) _____.

(3) Good B is _____.

5. The market demand for good X is shown in columns 1 and 2 of the following table. Assume the price of X to be $2 and constant.

(1) Price	(2) Quantity demanded	(3) Demand increases	(4) Demand decreases
$2.40	1600	1500	1700
2.30	1650	1550	1750
2.20	1750	1650	1850
2.10	1900	1800	2000
2.00	2100	2000	2200
1.90	2350	2250	2450
1.80	2650	2550	2750

a. If as the price of good Y rises from $1.25 to $1.35, the quantities demanded of good X become those shown in column 3, it can be concluded that X and Y are (substitute, complementary) _____ goods.
b. If as the price of good Y rises from $1.25 to $1.35, the quantities of good X become those shown in column 4, it can be concluded that X and Y are _____ goods.

6. The existing demand and supply schedules are given in columns 1, 2, and 3 of the following table.

Demand and Supply Schedules			New Demand and Supply Schedules		
(1)	(2)	(3)	(4)	(5)	(6)
Price	Quantity demanded	Quantity supplied	Price	Quantity demanded	Quantity supplied
$5.00	10	50	$5.00	_____	_____
4.00	20	40	4.00	_____	_____
3.00	30	30	3.00	_____	_____
2.00	40	20	2.00	_____	_____
1.00	50	10	1.00	_____	_____

a. Now the demand *increases* by 10 units at each price and supply *decreases* by 10 units. Enter the new amounts for quantity demanded and quantity supplied in columns 5 and 6.

b. What was the old equilibrium price? _____

What will be the new equilibrium price? _____

c. What was the old equilibrium quantity? _____

What will be the new equilibrium quantity? _____

7. In a local market for hamburger on a given date, each of 300 identical sellers of hamburger has the following supply schedule.

(1) Price	(2) Quantity supplied—one seller, lbs	(3) Quantity supplied—all sellers, lbs
$2.05	150	_____
2.00	110	_____
1.95	75	_____
1.90	45	_____
1.85	20	_____
1.80	0	_____

a. In column 3 construct the market supply schedule for hamburger.

b. Following is the market demand schedule for hamburger on the same date and in the same local market as that given above.

Price	Quantity demanded, lbs
$2.05	28,000
2.00	31,000
1.95	36,000
1.90	42,000
1.85	49,000
1.80	57,000

If the Federal government set a price on hamburger of $1.90 a pound, the result would be a (shortage,

surplus) _____ of _____ pounds of hamburger in this market.

8. Each of the following events would tend to increase or decrease either the demand for or the supply of computer games and, as a result, would increase or decrease the price of these games. In the first blank, indicate the effect on demand or supply (increase, decrease); in the second blank, indicate the effect on price (increase, decrease). Assume that the market for computer games is a competitive one.

a. It becomes known that an electronics store is going to have a sale on these games 3 months from now.

_____; _____

b. The workers who produce the games go on strike for over 2 months. _____;

_____

c. The workers in the industry receive a $2 an hour wage increase. _____; _____

d. The average price of movie tickets (a substitute for games) increases. _____;

_____

e. The price of business software, a product also supplied by the computer software producers, rises.

_____; _____

f. It is announced by a private research institute that children who play computer games also improve their grades in school. _____; _____

g. Because of the use of mass-production techniques, the amount of labor necessary to produce a game decreases. _____; _____

h. The price of computers decreases. _____

_____; _____

i. The average consumer believes that a shortage of games is developing in the economy.

_____; _____

j. The Federal government imposes a $5 tax per game on the manufacturers of computer games.

_____; _____

■ **SHORT ANSWER AND ESSAY QUESTIONS**

1. Define demand and the law of demand.

2. Use the concept of diminishing marginal utility to explain why the quantity demanded of a product will tend to rise when the price of the product falls.

3. In past decades, the price of coffee in the United States rose significantly as a result of bad weather in coffee-producing regions. Use the concepts of the income effect and the substitution effect to explain why the quantity of coffee demanded in the United States significantly decreased.

4. What is the difference between individual demand and market demand? What is the relationship between these two types of demand?

5. Explain the difference between an increase in demand and an increase in the quantity demanded.

6. What are the factors that cause a change in demand? Use supply and demand graphs to illustrate what happens to price and quantity when demand increases.

7. How are inferior and normal (or superior) goods defined? What is the relationship between these goods and changes in income?

8. Why does the effect of a change in the price of related goods depend on whether a good is a substitute or a complement? What are substitutes and complements?

9. A newspaper reports that "blue jeans have become even more popular and are now the standard clothing that people wear for both play and work." How will this change affect the demand for blue jeans? What will happen to the price and quantity of blue jeans sold in the market? Explain and use a supply and demand graph to illustrate your answer.

10. Compare and contrast the supply schedule with the demand schedule.

11. Supply does not remain constant for long because the factors that determine supply change. What are those factors? How do changes in them affect supply?

12. Explain the difference between an increase in supply and an increase in the quantity supplied.

13. Describe and illustrate with a supply and demand graph the effect of an increase in supply on price and quantity. Do the same for a decrease in supply.

14. The U.S. Congress passes a law that raises the excise tax on gasoline by $1 per gallon. What effect will this change have on the demand and supply of gasoline? What will happen to gasoline prices and quantity? Explain and use a supply and demand graph to illustrate your answer.

15. Given the demand for and the supply of a commodity, what price will be the equilibrium price of this commodity? Explain why this price will tend to prevail in the market and why higher (lower) prices, if they do exist temporarily, will tend to fall (rise).

16. What is the relationship between the price of a product and a shortage of that product? What is the relationship between the price of a product and a surplus of that product?

17. Explain why competition implies both productive efficiency and allocative efficiency.

18. Analyze the following quotation and explain the fallacies contained in it: "An increase in demand will cause price to rise; with a rise in price, supply will increase and the increase in supply will push price down. Therefore, an increase in demand results in little change in price because supply will increase also."

19. What are the consequences of a price ceiling for a product if it is set below the equilibrium price? Illustrate your answer with a graph.

20. What are the economic problems with price floors? How have they been used by government?

ANSWERS

Chapter 3 Demand, Supply, and Market Equilibrium

FILL-IN QUESTIONS

1. demanders, suppliers
2. an inverse, a direct
3. utility
4. *a.* income; *b.* substitution
5. vertical, horizontal
6. adding, prices
7. substitutes, complements
8. *a.* the tastes or preferences of consumers; *b.* the number of consumers in the market; *c.* the money income of consumers;

d. the prices of related goods; *e.* consumer expectations with respect to future prices and income (any order for *a–e*)
9. smaller, less
10. demand for, quantity demanded of
11. larger, less
12. supply, quantity supplied
13. *a.* the technology of production; *b.* resource prices; *c.* taxes and subsidies; *d.* prices of other goods; *e.* producer expectations of price; *f.* the number of sellers in the market (any order for *a–f*)
14. equal to, is not
15. below, shortage, rise, above, surplus, fall
16. **a.** +, +; **b.** −, +; **c.** −, −; **d.** +, −; **e.** ?, +; **f.** +, ?; **g.** ?, −; **h.** −, ?
17. rationing, clearing
18. productive, allocative
19. maximum, minimum
20. shortage, surplus

TRUE–FALSE QUESTIONS

1. T, p. 45	**10.** T, p. 48	**19.** T, p. 54
2. F, p. 45	**11.** T, p. 49	**20.** F, pp. 53–54
3. F, p. 46	**12.** F, p. 49	**21.** T, p. 55
4. T, p. 46	**13.** F, pp. 49–50	**22.** F, p. 55
5. F, p. 46	**14.** F, p. 50	**23.** F, pp. 56–57
6. F, p. 47	**15.** T, pp. 51–52	**24.** T, pp. 56–57
7. F, pp. 46–47	**16.** F, p. 52	**25.** T, pp. 58–59
8. F, pp. 46, 49–50	**17.** T, p. 52	
9. T, p. 48	**18.** F, pp. 52–53	

MULTIPLE-CHOICE QUESTIONS

1. b, p. 45	**11.** c, p. 50	**21.** c, pp. 56–57
2. d, p. 46	**12.** a, pp. 51–52	**22.** d, pp. 56–57
3. d, pp. 46–47	**13.** a, pp. 51–52	**23.** b, pp. 56–57
4. b, pp. 46–47	**14.** b, pp. 53–55	**24.** c, pp. 56–57
5. d, pp. 48–49	**15.** b, pp. 53–55	**25.** c, pp. 56–57
6. b, p. 48	**16.** c, p. 55	**26.** c, pp. 56–57
7. a, p. 48	**17.** c, p. 53	**27.** c, pp. 56–57
8. b, p. 49	**18.** d, pp. 51,56–57	**28.** a, p. 58
9. a, p. 49	**19.** d, pp. 49–50; 56–57	**29.** b, pp. 58–59
10. c, p. 49	**20.** d, pp. 56–57	**30.** c, pp. 59–60

PROBLEMS

1. *a.* graph; *b.* 6.60; *c.* 25,000; *d.* graph; *e.* surplus, 20,000
2. Total: 5, 9, 17, 27, 39
3. Each quantity in column 3 is greater than in column 2, and each quantity in column 4 is less than in column 2.
4. *a.* 30, 4; *b.* (1) 20, 7; (2) inferior; (3) normal (superior)
5. a. complementary; *b.* substitute
6. a. column 5 (quantity demanded): 20, 30, 40, 50, 60; column 6 (quantity supplied): 40, 30, 20, 10, 0; *b.* $3.00, $4.00; *c.* 30, 30
7. *a.* 45,000; 33,000; 22,500; 13,500; 6,000; 0; *b.* shortage, 28,500
8. *a.* decrease demand, decrease price; *b.* decrease supply, increase price; *c.* decrease supply, increase price; *d.* increase demand, increase price; *e.* decrease supply, increase price; *f.* increase demand, increase price; *g.* increase supply, decrease price; *h.* increase demand, increase price; *i.* increase demand, increase price; *j.* decrease supply, increase price

SHORT ANSWER AND ESSAY QUESTIONS

1. pp. 45–46	**8.** p. 49	**15.** pp. 53–54
2. p. 46	**9.** pp. 48; 57	**16.** pp. 54–55
3. p. 46	**10.** pp. 45; 50–51	**17.** p. 55
4. pp. 46–47	**11.** pp. 51–52	**18.** pp. 56–57
5. pp. 49–50	**12.** pp. 52–53	**19.** pp. 58–59
6. pp. 48–49	**13.** pp. 52; 56–57	**20.** pp. 59–61
7. p. 48	**14.** pp. 52; 56–57	

CHAPTER 4

The U.S. Economy: Private and Public Sectors

The U.S. economy is divided into a private sector and a public sector. The first half of Chapter 4 discusses the private sector—the characteristics of millions of households and business firms. The second half of the chapter describes the public sector—the functions and financing of the Federal, state, and local governments. Learning about these two sectors will give you the basic facts and framework you need to understand the U.S. economy.

Chapter 4 begins with an examination of the **households** of the economy. Two different distributions of household income are examined. The way in which the total personal income received by all U.S. households is divided among the five types of earned income is called the *functional distribution of income*. The way in which the total personal income received by all households is distributed among the various income classes is called the *personal distribution of income*. Households dispose of the income they receive by spending money on *personal consumption expenditures*, paying *personal taxes*, and allocating funds to *personal saving*.

Businesses in the United States are also a focus of the chapter. It is apparent that what most characterizes U.S. businesses is the differences among firms in size and legal form, as well as in the products they produce. You should note the distinctions between a *sole proprietorship*, a *partnership*, and a *corporation*. You will also learn about the principal–agent problem with corporations that can arise from the separation of ownership (the principals) and management (the agents).

Chapter 4 also introduces you to the five basic functions performed by **government** in the U.S. economy. The chapter does not attempt to list all the specific ways in which government affects the behavior of the economy. Instead, it provides a general classification and description of the five functions that government performs.

The chapter also returns to the **circular flow model** first presented in Chapter 2. The model has been modified to include government along with the business and household sectors. This addition changes the real and monetary flows in the model.

The facts of **government finance** in the United States are presented in the final sections of Chapter 4. The organization of the discussion is relatively simple. First, the trends for taxes collected and expenditures made by all levels of government—Federal, state, and local—are examined. Second, an explanation is given for the major items on which the Federal government spends its income, the principal taxes it levies to obtain its income, and the relative importance of those taxes. Third, the chapter closes with a look at the major expenditures and taxes of the state and local governments.

■ CHECKLIST

When you have studied this chapter you should be able to

☐ Define and distinguish between a functional and a personal distribution of income.

☐ State the five sources of personal income in the functional distribution.

☐ List the three uses to which households put their personal incomes and state the relative size of each one.

☐ Distinguish among durable goods, nondurable goods, and services in personal consumption expenditures.

☐ Give definitions for a plant, a firm, and an industry.

☐ List the three legal forms of a business enterprise.

☐ Describe the advantages of corporations in terms of finance, risk and liability, and longevity.

☐ Explain the principal–agent problem as it applies to corporations.

☐ List the five economic functions of government in the United States.

☐ Give examples of how government provides the legal framework for the economy.

☐ Define monopoly and explain why government wishes to prevent monopoly and maintain competition in the economy.

☐ Explain why government redistributes income and list the three principal policies it uses for that purpose.

☐ Define negative externality and positive externality.

☐ Explain why a competitive market fails to allocate resources efficiently when there are external costs and benefits.

☐ List two actions government can take to reduce external costs.

☐ List three actions government can take to encourage external benefits.

☐ Give definitions of a public good and a quasi-public good.

☐ Explain how the government reallocates resources from the production of private goods to the production of public or quasi-public goods.

☐ Describe the stabilization role of government and the two main economic problems it is designed to address.

☐ Explain the qualifications to government's role in the economy.

☐ Draw the circular flow model to include businesses, households, and government.

☐ Explain the difference between government purchases and transfer payments and the effect of each on the composition of national output.

☐ Identify the four largest categories of Federal expenditures.

☐ List the three main sources of Federal tax revenues.

☐ Define and explain the differences between marginal and average tax rates.

☐ Identify the major expenditures by state and local governments.

☐ Describe how state and local governments raise tax revenue.

☐ Explain the problems facing the Social Security program and the solutions that have been proposed (Last Word).

■ CHAPTER OUTLINE

1. Households play a dual role in the economy. They supply the economy with resources, and they purchase the greatest share of the goods and services produced by the economy. They obtain their personal incomes in exchange for the resources they furnish the economy and from the transfer payments they receive from government.

   a. The *functional distribution of income* indicates the way in which total personal income was divided among the five sources of earned income in 2005: wages and salaries (71%); proprietors' income (9%); corporate profits (14%); interest (5%); and rents (1%).

   b. The *personal distribution of income* indicates the way in which total personal income is divided among households in different income classes. The 2004 data show an unequal distribution of income by five household classes (20% of households in each). The percentage of total personal income by class is as follows: lowest (3.4%); second (8.7%); middle (14.7%); fourth (23.2%); and highest (50.1%).

2. Households use their incomes to purchase consumer goods, pay taxes, and accumulate savings.

   a. *Personal taxes* constitute a deduction from a household's personal income; what remains after taxes can be either saved or spent. It accounted for 12% of household income in 2005.

   b. *Saving* is what a household does not spend of its after-tax income. It was negative in 2005.

   c. *Personal consumption expenditures* account for most of the disposition of household income (88% in 2005). This category is spent on **durable goods** (12%)—products with lives of 3 or more years, **nondurable goods** (29%)—products with lives of less than 3 years, and **services** (59%)—work or a product supplied by others for a consumer.

3. The **businesses** of the U.S. economy consist of three major types of entities. A **plant** is a physical structure that produces a product. A **business firm** is an organization that owns and operates plants. (Multiplant firms may be horizontally or vertically integrated, or they may be conglomerates.) An **industry** is a group of firms producing the same or similar goods or services.

4. There are three principal *legal forms* of business firms. The **sole proprietorship** is a business owned and operated by a single person. The **partnership** is a business owned and operated by two or more persons. The **corporation** is a legal entity that operates as a business. The dominant form of business is the corporation. Although they represent only 20% of U.S. business firms, corporations account for 84% of total sales or output value.

   a. Corporations have several advantages. They can raise substantial financial capital through the sale of **stocks** (equity financing), which represents a share of ownership in the corporation. They can also obtain funds through the sale of corporate **bonds** (debt financing), which is similar to a loan to a corporation from the bond buyer, and over time the corporation pays the bond buyer interest on the amount of the bond. Corporations also provide **limited liability** for their owners (the stockholders) because they are liable only for losses that would equal the value of their stock holdings and the stockholders cannot be sued as individuals. Corporations, as legal entities, have unlimited life independent of their current owners and managers, and thus they can make long-term plans for continued growth.

   b. Large corporations are a major feature of the U.S. economy, but their size creates the **principal–agent problem.** This problem arises from the separation of corporate ownership (by stockholders) and control (by corporate executives). This problem sometimes can be overcome by aligning the interests of executives with those of stockholders through stock payment plans.

5. Government performs five economic functions.

   a. The first of these functions is to provide the *legal framework and services* that contribute to the effective operation of the market economy.

   b. The second function of government is *to maintain competition* by controlling **monopoly** through regulation and antitrust laws. (A monopoly is where a single seller dominates an industry.)

   c. Government performs its third function when it *redistributes income* to reduce income inequality. The policies and programs it uses to achieve this objective are transfer payments, market interventions (changing market prices), and taxation.

   d. When government *reallocates resources,* it performs its fourth function; in doing so it addresses externality problems or provides public goods.

   (1) It reallocates resources to take into account negative or positive externalities or spillovers from market outcomes.

   (a) **Negative externalities** are production or consumption costs paid for by a third party without compensation. For example, when a corporation pollutes the environment while making a product and neither the corporation nor the consumer of the product pays for the cost of that pollution, the pollution cost is an external cost that is borne by a third party: the other members of society adversely affected by the pollution.

(b) Negative externalities can be discouraged either with legislation (prohibiting practices which create external costs) or by imposing taxes (and thus raising the cost of production).

(c) **Positive externalities** are outcomes that benefit third parties without those parties paying for the benefits. Health immunizations and education are examples of services that have external benefits to others who do not pay for the services.

(d) External benefits can be encouraged by subsidizing consumers or producers (or by having government provide the goods when the external benefits are large).

(2) Government provides **public goods.** These goods have the characteristics of *nonrivalry* (benefits are not reduced by consumption by others) and *nonexcludability* (people cannot be excluded from the benefits). Examples of such public goods would be national defense and street lighting.

(3) Government also provides **quasi-public goods** that have large external benefits. Although these goods (such as education) can be provided by the private market because people can be excluded from obtaining them if they do not pay, they will be underproduced or underconsumed if left to the private market alone. Government will provide access to these goods at a reduced cost to encourage their production or consumption and increase the external benefits.

(4) Government levies taxes and uses tax revenues to reallocate income and resources from private uses to public ones (for providing public and quasi-public goods).

e. The fifth function of government is **stabilization** of the economy by controlling inflation and reducing unemployment.

f. The economic role of government is conducted in the context of politics. This process can lead to imperfect and inefficient outcomes.

6. A **circular flow model** that includes the public sector as well as business firms and households in the private sector of the economy reveals that government purchases public goods from private businesses, collects taxes from and makes transfer payments to those firms, purchases labor services from households, collects taxes from and makes transfer payments to those households, and can alter the distribution of income, reallocate resources, and change the level of economic activity by affecting the real and monetary flows in the diagram.

7. Government finance is important in the economy. Total government spending consists of **government purchases** of goods and services and **transfer payments** (payments made to people for which no contribution is made by the people in return). The two types of spending have different effects on the economy. Government purchases are *exhaustive* because they directly use the economy's resources, whereas transfers

are *nonexhaustive*. Total government spending is equal to three-tenths (31%) of domestic output.

8. The expenditures and tax revenues for the Federal government are of several types.

a. *Federal Expenditures:* Most spending goes for pensions and income security (35%), national defense (20%), health care (21%), and interest on the public debt (7%).

b. *Federal Tax Revenues:* The major sources are **personal income taxes** (43%), **payroll taxes** (37%), and **corporate income taxes** (13%).

(1) The Federal personal income tax is progressive, which means it is one whose average rate rises as income increase.

(2) The **average tax rate** is the total tax paid divided by total taxable income.

(3) The **marginal tax rate** is the rate paid on additional income.

9. State and local governments have different sources of revenue and spend their funds on different types of public goods.

a. *State governments* depend largely on **sales and excise taxes** (48%) and also on personal income taxes (34%); they spend their revenues on education (35%), public welfare (28%), health care (7%), highways (7%), and public safety (4%).

b. *Local governments* rely heavily on **property taxes** (73%) and to some extent on sales and excise taxes (17%); they spend much of the revenue on education (44%), welfare and health care (12%), public safety (11%), housing, parks, sewerage (8%), and streets and highways (5%).

10. (Last Word). The Social Security program is financed by payments into the system from current workers, and those payments are made to current Social Security retirees. The program will experience financial problems in the future because the number of workers paying into the system is declining and the number of retirees receiving benefits is rising. Several options have been proposed to shore up the finances, such as cutting program benefits, extending the retirement age, raising taxes, and setting up individual retirement accounts.

■ **HINTS AND TIPS**

1. This chapter is a long one, so do not try to learn everything at once. Break the chapter into its three natural parts and work on each one separately. The first part describes features of the private sector. The second part explains the functions of government. The third part looks at government finance.

2. There are many descriptive statistics about the private and public sectors. Avoid memorizing those statistics. Instead, look for the trends and generalizations that the statistics illustrate about the private or public sector. For example, the discussion of government finance describes recent trends in government expenditures and taxes and indicates the relative importance of taxes and expenditures at each level of government.

■ IMPORTANT TERMS

functional distribution of income	monopoly
personal distribution of income	externality
	negative externalities
durable goods	positive externalities
nondurable goods	public goods
services	free-rider problem
plant	quasi-public goods
firm	government purchases
industry	transfer payments
sole proprietorship	personal income tax
partnership	marginal tax rate
corporation	average tax rate
stock	payroll taxes
bond	corporate income tax
limited liability	sales and excise taxes
principal–agent problem	property taxes

SELF-TEST

■ FILL-IN QUESTIONS

1. There are approximately 113 million (businesses, households) _____ in the United States. They play a dual role in the economy because they (sell, buy) _____ their resources and _____ most of the total output of the economy.

2. Data on the functional distribution of household income shows that the largest single source in the United States is (rents, wages and salaries) _____ and the smallest is _____.

3. Data on the personal distribution of household income in the United States show that about 3% of household income is received by the (poorest, richest) _____ 20% of households and about 50% of household income is received by the _____ 20% of households.

4. The total income of households is disposed of in three ways: personal _____, personal _____ _____, and personal _____.

5. If a product has an expected life of 3 years or more, it is a (durable, nondurable) _____ good, whereas if it has an expected life of less than 3 years, it is a _____ good.

6. There are millions of business (firms, industries) _____ in the United States. The legal form of the great majority of them is the (sole proprietorship, partnership, corporation) _____, but the legal form that produces about 84% of the sales of the U.S. economy is the _____.

7. Shares of ownership of corporations are called (stocks, bonds) _____, and promises by corporations to repay a loan, usually at a fixed rate of interest, are _____. The liabilities of corporations are (limited, unlimited) _____, and the life span for a corporation is _____.

8. The separation of ownership and control in a corporation may create a (free-rider, principal–agent) _____ problem. In this case, stockholders would be the (riders, principals, agents) _____ and managers would be the _____.

9. List the five economic functions of government.

   a. _____

   b. _____

   c. _____

   d. _____

   e. _____

10. To control monopoly, the U.S. government has created commissions to (tax, regulate) _____ natural monopolies, and in cases at the local level, government has become an (agent, owner) _____. Government has also enacted (trust, antitrust) _____ laws to maintain competition.

11. The market system, because it is an impersonal mechanism, results in an (equal, unequal) _____ distribution of income. To redistribute income from the upper- to the lower-income groups, the government has provided (transfer, tax) _____ payments, engaged in (military, market) _____ intervention, and used the (income, sales) _____ tax to raise much of its revenues.

12. Government frequently reallocates resources when it finds instances of (market, public) _____ failure. The two major cases of such failure occur when the competitive market system either

   a. _____; or

   b. _____

13. There is an externality whenever some of the costs of producing a product accrue to people other than the (seller, buyer) _____ or some of the benefits from consuming a product accrue to people other than the _____. Competitive markets bring about an efficient allocation of resources only if there are no (private, external) _____ costs or benefits in the consumption and production of a good or service.

a. What two things can government do to make the market reflect external costs?

(1) _____

(2) _____

b. What three things can government do to make the market reflect external benefits?

(1) _____

(2) _____

(3) _____

14. One characteristic of a public good is (rivalry, nonrivalry) _____, and the other characteristic is (excludability, nonexcludability) _____. A private firm will not find it profitable to produce a public good because there is a (free-rider, principal–agent) _____ problem.

15. To reallocate resources from the production of private goods to the production of public and quasi-public goods, government reduces the demand for private goods by (taxing, subsidizing) _____ consumers and then uses the (profits, tax revenue) _____ to buy public or quasi-public goods.

16. To stabilize the economy with less than full employment, government may try to increase total spending by (increasing, decreasing) _____ its expenditures for public goods and services, by (increasing, decreasing) _____ taxes, or by (raising, lowering) _____ interest rates. When there are inflationary pressures, the government may try to decrease total spending by (decreasing, increasing) _____ its expenditures for public goods and services, by _____ taxes, or by (raising, lowering) _____ interest rates.

17. An examination of government finance reveals that since 1960 government *purchases* of goods and services as a percentage of domestic output have (increased, decreased) _____, and government *transfer payments* as a percentage of domestic output have (increased, decreased) _____. Government purchases of goods and services are _____ because they absorb resources, and government transfer payments are (exhaustive, nonexhaustive) _____ because they do not absorb resources or create output.

18. The most important source of revenue for the Federal government is the (personal income, payroll) _____ tax; next in importance is the _____ tax. The largest category of Federal expenditures is for (national defense, pensions and income security) _____.

19. Federal income tax rates are progressive, which means that people with (lower, higher) _____ incomes pay a larger percentage of that income as taxes than do persons with _____ incomes. The tax rate paid on an additional unit of income is the (average, marginal) _____ tax rate, and the total tax paid divided by the total taxable income is the _____ tax rate.

20. Many state governments rely primarily on the (property, sales) _____ tax, and many local governments rely primarily on the _____ tax. The largest category of spending for both state and local governments is (education, public safety) _____.

■ **TRUE–FALSE QUESTIONS**

Circle T if the statement is true, F if it is false.

1. The personal distribution of income describes the manner in which society's total personal income is divided among wages and salaries, corporate profits, proprietors' income, interest, and rents.   **T F**

2. Dissaving means that personal consumption expenditures exceed after-tax income.   **T F**

3. A durable good is defined as a good that has an expected life of 3 years or more.   **T F**

4. A plant is defined as a group of firms under a single management.   **T F**

5. An industry is a group of firms that produce the same or nearly the same products.   **T F**

6. Limited liability refers to the fact that all members of a partnership are liable for the debts incurred by one another.   **T F**

7. The corporate form of organization is the one least used by firms in the United States.   **T F**

8. Whether a business firm should incorporate depends chiefly on the amount of money capital it must have to finance the enterprise.   **T F**

9. Bonds are shares of ownership in a corporation.   **T F**

10. When the interests of the principals are the same as those of agents, there is a free-rider problem.   **T F**

11. When the Federal government provides for a monetary system, it is doing so primarily to maintain competition. **T F**

12. Transfer payments are one means government uses to redistribute income. **T F**

13. If demand and supply reflected all the benefits and costs of producing a product, there would be efficient resource use. **T F**

14. When there are external costs, more resources are allocated to the production of the product and more is produced than is efficient. **T F**

15. One way for government to correct for external costs from a product is to increase its demand. **T F**

16. When there are external benefits from a product, there will be an overallocation of resources for its production. **T F**

17. One way for government to correct external benefits from a product is to subsidize consumers of the product. **T F**

18. Nonexcludability means government provides public goods so as to exclude private businesses from providing them. **T F**

19. Obtaining the benefits of private goods requires that they be purchased; obtaining benefits from public goods requires only that they be produced. **T F**

20. Government provides homeland defense services because these services have public benefits and because private producers of such services experience the free-rider problem. **T F**

21. When the Federal government takes actions to control unemployment or inflation, it is performing the allocative function of government. **T F**

22. Government purchases of goods and services are called nonexhaustive expenditures, and government transfer payments are called exhaustive expenditures. **T F**

23. When a government levies taxes and uses the tax revenue to make transfer payments, it shifts resources from the production of private goods to the production of public goods. **T F**

24. The chief source of revenue for the Federal government is the corporate income tax. **T F**

25. Property taxes account for the largest percentage of the total revenues of local governments. **T F**

■ **MULTIPLE-CHOICE QUESTIONS**

Circle the letter that corresponds to the best answer.

1. The functional distribution for the United States shows that the largest part of the nation's earned income is
   (a) wages and salaries
   (b) proprietors' income
   (c) corporate profits
   (d) interest and rents

2. The part of after-tax income which is not consumed is defined as
   (a) saving
   (b) capital investment
   (c) wages and salaries
   (d) nondurable goods expenditure

3. If personal consumption expenditures were 80% of income and personal taxes were 8% of income, personal savings would be
   (a) 8% of income
   (b) 10% of income
   (c) 12% of income
   (d) 88% of income

4. Consumer products that have expected lives of 3 years or more are
   (a) durable goods
   (b) nondurable goods
   (c) quasi-public goods
   (d) services

5. A firm owns and operates a farm growing wheat, a flour-milling plant, and a plant that bakes and sells bakery products. This firm would best be described as
   (a) a horizontally integrated firm
   (b) a vertically integrated firm
   (c) a conglomerate
   (d) a monopoly

6. Limited liability is associated with
   (a) sole proprietorships
   (b) partnerships
   (c) free-riders
   (d) corporations

7. Which form of business can most effectively raise money capital?
   (a) corporation
   (b) partnership
   (c) proprietorship
   (d) households

8. The separation of ownership and control in a corporation may create
   (a) a principal–agent problem
   (b) a free-rider problem
   (c) a monopoly
   (d) limited liability

9. One major means that government uses to deal with a monopoly is to
   (a) increase the demand for its product
   (b) decrease the supply of its product
   (c) stabilize incomes
   (d) regulate the firm

10. Government redistributes income through
   (a) limited liability
   (b) conglomerates
   (c) transfer payments
   (d) sole proprietorships

11. To redistribute income from high-income to low-income households, government might
   (a) increase transfer payments to high-income and decrease transfer payments to low-income households

(b) increase the taxes paid by high-income households and increase the transfer payments to low-income households

(c) increase the taxes paid by low-income households and decrease the taxes paid by high-income households

(d) decrease the taxes paid by high-income households and decrease the transfer payments to low-income households

12. Which is the best example of a good or service providing the economy with an external cost?
(a) a textbook
(b) an automobile
(c) a business suit
(d) an audit of a business firm's books

13. Which economic situation would result in overallocation of resources to the production of a good?
(a) a good with external benefits
(b) a good with external costs
(c) a good with free-rider problem
(d) a good with an inflation problem

14. How does government correct for external benefits?
(a) by taxing consumers
(b) by taxing producers
(c) by subsidizing producers
(d) by separating ownership from control

15. Which is characteristic of public goods?
(a) nonrivalry
(b) excludability
(c) limited liability
(d) external costs

16. There is a free-rider problem when people
(a) are willing to pay for what they want
(b) are not willing to pay for what they want
(c) benefit from a good without paying for its cost
(d) want to buy more than is available for purchase in the market

17. Quasi-public goods are goods and services
(a) that are indivisible
(b) that have large external costs
(c) that have large external benefits
(d) that would not be produced by private producers through the market system

18. In the circular flow model, government provides goods and services and receives net taxes from
(a) colleges and universities
(b) businesses and households
(c) resource and product markets
(d) foreign nations and corporations

19. Which accounts for the largest percentage of all Federal expenditures?
(a) health care
(b) national defense
(c) interest on the public debt
(d) pensions and income security

20. Which is the largest source of the tax revenues of the Federal government?
(a) payroll taxes

(b) property taxes
(c) sales and excise taxes
(d) personal income taxes

21. A progressive tax is one where people with
(a) lower incomes pay the same percentage of their income in taxes than people do with higher incomes
(b) lower incomes pay a larger percentage of their income in taxes than people do with higher incomes
(c) higher incomes pay a smaller percentage of their income in taxes than people do with higher incomes
(d) higher incomes pay a larger percentage of their income in taxes than people do with lower incomes

Questions 22 and 23 are based on the tax table below. [Note: Total tax is for the highest income in that tax bracket.]

Taxable income	Total tax
$ 0	$ 0
30,000	5,000
70,000	15,000
150,000	42,000

22. The marginal tax rate at the $70,000 level of taxable income is
(a) 16.6%
(b) 21.4%
(c) 25.0%
(d) 28.0%

23. The average tax rate at the $150,000 level of taxable income is
(a) 21.4%
(b) 28.0%
(c) 31.5%
(d) 33.8%

24. Which pair represents the chief source of income and the most important type of expenditure of *state* governments?
(a) personal income tax and expenditures for hospitals
(b) personal income tax and expenditures for highways
(c) sales and excise taxes and expenditures for education
(d) sales and excise taxes and expenditures for public safety

25. Which pair represents the chief source of income and the most important type of expenditure of local governments?
(a) property tax and expenditures for highways
(b) property tax and expenditures for education
(c) sales and excise taxes and expenditures for public welfare
(d) sales and excise taxes and expenditures for police, fire, safety, and general government

■ **PROBLEMS**

1. The following table shows the functional distribution of total income in the United States in a recent year.

	Billions of dollars
Wages and salaries	$7125
Proprietors' income	939
Corporate profits	1352
Interest	498
Rents	73
Total income	$9987

Of the total income about _____% were wages and salaries, and about _____% were corporate profits.

2. Following is a list of various government activities. Indicate in the space to the right of each into which of the five classes of government functions the activity falls. If it falls under more than one of the functions, indicate this.

a. Maintaining an army _____

b. Providing for a system of unemployment compensation

_____

c. Establishment of the Federal Reserve Banks

_____

d. Providing medical care for government employees

_____

e. Establishment of an Antitrust Division in the Department of Justice

_____

f. Making it a crime to sell stocks and bonds under false pretenses

_____

g. Providing low-cost lunches to schoolchildren

_____

h. Taxation of beer and wine

_____

i. Regulation of organized stock, bond, and commodity markets

_____

j. Setting tax *rates* higher for larger incomes than for smaller ones

_____

3. The following circular flow diagram includes business firms, households, and the government (the public sector). Also shown are the product and resource markets.

a. Supply a label or an explanation for each of the 12 flows in the model:

(1) _____

(2) _____

(3) _____

(4) _____

(5) _____

(6) _____

(7) _____

(8) _____

(9) _____

(10) _____

(11) _____

(12) _____

b. If government wished to

(1) expand output and employment in the economy, it would increase expenditure flows _____ or _____, decrease net tax flows _____ or _____, or do both;

(2) increase the production of public goods and decrease the production of private goods in the economy, it would increase flows _____ and _____ or _____;

(3) redistribute income from high-income to low-income households, it would (increase, decrease) _____ the net taxes (taxes minus transfers) paid by the former and _____ the net taxes paid by the latter in flow _____.

4. In the following table are several levels of taxable income and hypothetical marginal tax rates for each $1000 increase in income.

Taxable income	Marginal tax rate, %	Tax	Average tax rate, %
$1500		$300	20
2500	22	520	20.8
3500	25	____	____
4500	29	____	____
5500	34	____	____
6500	40	____	____

a. At the four income levels compute the tax and the average tax rate.

b. As the marginal tax rate

(1) increases, the average tax rate (increases, decreases, remains constant) _____.

(2) decreases, the average tax rate _____.

c. This tax is (progressive, regressive) _____ because the average tax rate increases as income (decreases, increases) _____.

■ SHORT ANSWER AND ESSAY QUESTIONS

1. Explain the difference between a functional and a personal distribution of income. List the five major categories for functional income and their relative sizes. Describe the difference between the poorest and richest categories in the personal distribution of income.

2. In what ways do households dispose of their income? How is it possible for a family's personal consumption expenditures to exceed its after-tax income?

3. What is the difference between a plant and a firm? Between a firm and an industry?

4. Define the three legal forms of business organization.

5. Explain the advantages of corporations in terms of financing, liability, and longevity.

6. Explain what "separation of ownership and control" of the modern corporation means. What problem does this separation create for stockholders and managers?

7. How does government provide a legal framework and services for the effective operation of the economy?

8. What does the government do to maintain competition?

9. Why does the market system provide some people with lower incomes than it provides others?

10. What is meant by an externality in general and by an external cost and an external benefit in particular?

11. How does the existence of positive and negative externalities affect the allocation of resources and the prices of products?

12. What methods does government use to reallocate resources to take account of negative and positive externalities?

13. Distinguish between a private and a public good. Include in your answer an explanation of rivalry, excludability, and the free-rider problem.

14. What basic method does government in the United States use to reallocate resources away from the production of private goods and toward the production of public and quasi-public goods?

15. What is the stability function of government? What are the two economic problems that this function addresses?

16. How does politics affect the five economic functions of government in practice?

17. In a circular flow diagram that includes not only business firms and households but also government (or the public sector), what are the four flows of money into or out of the government sector of the economy? Using this diagram, explain how government redistributes income, reallocates resources from the private to the public sector, and stabilizes the economy.

18. Government expenditures fall into two broad classes: expenditures for goods and services and transfer payments. Explain the difference between these and give examples of expenditures that fall into each of the two classes.

19. Explain precisely the difference between the marginal tax rate and the average tax rate.

20. Explain in detail the differences that exist among Federal, state, and local governments in regard to the taxes on which they primarily rely for their revenues and the major purposes for which they use those revenues.

ANSWERS

Chapter 4 The U.S. Economy: Private and Public Sectors

FILL-IN QUESTIONS

1. households, sell, buy
2. wages and salaries, rents
3. poorest, richest
4. consumption, saving, taxes (any order)
5. durable, nondurable
6. firms, sole proprietorship, corporation
7. stocks, bonds, unlimited, unlimited
8. principal–agent, principals, agents
9. *a.* provide a legal foundation; *b.* maintain competition; *c.* redistribute income; *d.* reallocate resources; *e.* stabilize the economy (any order for *a–e*)
10. regulate, owner, antitrust
11. unequal, transfer, market, income
12. market; *a.* produces the "wrong" amounts of certain goods and services; *b.* fails to allocate any resources to the production of certain goods and services whose production is economically justified
13. seller, buyer, external; *a.* (1) enact legislation, (2) pass special taxes; *b.* (1) subsidize consumers, (2) subsidize suppliers, (3) government financing or production of the product
14. nonrivalry, nonexcludability, free-rider
15. taxing, tax revenue
16. increasing, decreasing, lowering, decreasing, increasing, raising
17. decreased, increased, exhaustive, nonexhaustive
18. personal income, payroll, pensions and income security
19. higher, lower, marginal, average
20. sales, property, education

TRUE–FALSE QUESTIONS

1. F, pp. 66–67	**10.** F, pp. 69–70	**19.** T, p. 73
2. T, p. 67	**11.** F, p. 71	**20.** T, p. 73
3. T, pp. 67–68	**12.** T, p. 71	**21.** F, p. 74
4. F, p. 68	**13.** T, p. 72	**22.** F, p. 75
5. T, p. 68	**14.** T, p. 72	**23.** F, p. 75
6. F, p. 69	**15.** F, p. 72	**24.** F, pp. 77–78
7. F, p. 68	**16.** F, pp. 72–73	**25.** T, p. 80
8. T, p. 69	**17.** T, pp. 72–73	
9. F, p. 69	**18.** F, p. 73	

MULTIPLE-CHOICE QUESTIONS

1. a, p. 66	**10.** c, pp. 71–72	**19.** d, pp. 77–78
2. a, p. 67	**11.** b, pp. 71–72	**20.** d, pp. 77–78
3. c, p. 67	**12.** b, p. 72	**21.** d, pp. 78–79
4. a, p. 68	**13.** b, p. 72	**22.** c, p. 80
5. b, p. 68	**14.** c, p. 73	**23.** b, p. 80
6. d, p. 69	**15.** a, p. 73	**24.** c, pp. 78–79
7. a, pp. 68–69	**16.** c, p. 73	**25.** b, pp. 78–79
8. a, p. 69	**17.** c, p. 73	
9. d, p. 71	**18.** b, pp. 75–76	

SHORT ANSWER AND ESSAY QUESTIONS

1. pp. 66–67	**8.** p. 71	**15.** p. 74
2. pp. 67–68	**9.** pp. 71–72	**16.** pp. 74–75
3. p. 68	**10.** p. 72	**17.** pp. 75–76
4. p. 69	**11.** pp. 72–73	**18.** pp. 75–76
5. pp. 68–69	**12.** pp. 72–73	**19.** pp. 78–79
6. pp. 69–70	**13.** p. 73	**20.** pp. 77–80
7. p. 71	**14.** pp. 73–74	

PROBLEMS

1. 71, 14

2. *a.* reallocates resources; *b.* redistributes income; *c.* provides a legal foundation and stabilizes the economy; *d.* reallocates resources; *e.* maintains competition; *f.* provides a legal foundation and maintains competition; *g.* redistributes income; *h.* reallocates resources; *i.* provides a legal foundation; *j.* redistributes income

3. *a.* (1) businesses pay costs for resources that become money income for households; (2) households provide resources to businesses; (3) household expenditures become receipts for businesses; (4) businesses provide goods and services to households; (5) government spends money in product market; (6) government receives goods and services from product market; (7) government spends money in resource market; (8) government receives resources from resource market; (9) government provides goods and services to households; (10) government provides goods and services to businesses; (11) businesses pay net taxes to government; (12) households pay net taxes to government; *b.* (1) 5, 7 (either order), 11, 12 (either order); (2) 9, 10, 11 (any order); (3) increase, decrease, 12

4. *a.* tax: $770, 1060, 1400, 1800; average tax rate: 22%, 23.6%, 25.5%, 27.7%; *b.* (1) increases, (2) decreases; *c.* progressive, increases

CHAPTER 5

The United States in the Global Economy

The United States is linked to the global economy in many ways. As you will learn in the first section of Chapter 5, there are four types of **economic flows** among nations: trade; resource; information and technology; and financial.

The second section explains **why international trade is important** to the United States. In *relative* terms, other nations have exports and imports that are a larger percentage of their GDPs because they often have a small domestic market and a limited resource base. By contrast, the exports and imports of the United States account for a smaller percentage of its GDP because it has a larger domestic market and a more abundant resource base. In *absolute* terms, however, the United States is the world's largest trading nation. Most of the trade is with other industrially advanced nations such as Canada, Japan, and Germany. This volume of trade has grown over the years with expansion of the global economy, the rise of multinational corporations, and the emergence of new trading nations.

In the third section, you will learn about the principle of **comparative advantage,** which is the basis for all trade between individuals, regions, and nations. A nation, for example, will specialize in the production of a product for which it has a lower domestic opportunity cost and trade to obtain those products for which its domestic opportunity cost is higher. Thus, specialization and trade increase productivity within a nation and increase a nation's output and standard of living.

Trading in a global economy requires a **foreign exchange market** in which national currencies are exchanged, as you will discover in the fourth section. When the U.S. dollar price of another currency has increased, the value of the U.S. dollar has *depreciated* relative to the other currency. Conversely, when the U.S. dollar price of another currency has decreased, the value of the U.S. dollar has *appreciated* in value relative to the other currency.

Government can affect international trade in many ways, as you will learn in the fifth section. Governments can impose protective tariffs, import quotas, and nontariff barriers, or they can foster exports through subsidies. The reasons for the interventions are difficult to explain in light of the strong economic rationale for free trade based on the principle of comparative advantage. Nevertheless, public misunderstanding of the gains from trade, or political considerations designed to protect domestic industries, often lead to government policies that create trade barriers and distort the free flow of products between nations, thus increasing costs for society.

The sixth section discusses **multilateral agreements** among nations and the creation of **free-trade zones** that have been designed to reduce trade barriers and increase world trade. In the United States, the process of gradual tariff reduction began with the Reciprocal Trade Agreements Act of 1934. Since 1947, worldwide multilateral negotiations to reduce trade barriers have been conducted through the General Agreement on Tariffs and Trade (GATT). The Uruguay Round of GATT negotiations established the World Trade Organization (WTO) as GATT's successor. Trade negotiations under the WTO continue in the Doha Round that began in 2001.

The other major development has been the formation of free-trade zones. The European Union (EU), which was originally started in 1958 as the Common Market, is now a trading bloc of 25 European nations. A major accomplishment of the EU, in addition to the reduction of trade barriers among member nations, was the establishment of a common currency (the **euro**) that is used by 12 nations. The United States, Canada, and Mexico established a free-trade zone in 1993 through the North American Free Trade Agreement (NAFTA).

The final section of the chapter briefly explores the issue of the effects of **increased competition in the global economy.** Global competition has certainly changed production practices and employment in U.S. industry. Many U.S. firms have adapted to the changes by increasing productivity to reduce costs, improving product quality, and expanding export markets. Although some firms have failed and domestic jobs have been lost, the benefits of free trade to the economy in the form of lower prices, greater economic efficiency, and a wider variety of products far outweigh any losses.

■ **CHECKLIST**

When you have studied this chapter you should be able to

☐ Identify the four main categories of economic flows linking nations.

☐ Explain the importance of international trade to the U.S. economy in terms of volume, dependence, trade patterns, and financial linkages.

☐ Describe several factors that have facilitated the rapid growth of international trade since World War II.

☐ Identify the key participating nations in international trade.

☐ Explain the basic principle of comparative advantage based on an individual example.

☐ Compute the comparative costs of production from

production possibilities data when you are given an example with cost data for two countries.

☐ Determine which of two countries has a comparative advantage in an example.

☐ Indicate the range in which the terms of trade will be found in an example.

☐ Show the gains from specialization and trade in an example.

☐ Define the main characteristics of the foreign exchange market.

☐ Distinguish between the appreciation and depreciation of a currency.

☐ Identify four means by which governments interfere with free trade.

☐ Discuss two reasons why governments intervene in international trade.

☐ Give estimates of the cost to society from trade restrictions.

☐ List the major features of the Reciprocal Trade Agreements Act.

☐ State the three principles of the General Agreement on Tariffs and Trade (GATT).

☐ Identify the major provisions of the Uruguay Round of GATT.

☐ Describe the World Trade Organization (WTO).

☐ Describe the history and results of the European Union (EU).

☐ Explain what the euro is and the results from using it.

☐ Describe the North American Free Trade Agreement (NAFTA).

☐ Discuss the effects of global competition on U.S. firms, workers, and consumers.

☐ Describe how Fredric Bastiat satirized the proponents of protectionism (Last Word).

■ **CHAPTER OUTLINE**

1. Four main categories of **economic flows** link nations: goods and services flows, capital and labor flows, information and technology flows, and financial flows.

2. Trade is important and thus warrants special attention.
   a. Although the relative importance of international trade to the United States is less than it is for other nations, it is still vital.
   (1) Exports and imports are about 11–16% of U.S. GDP, and the United States is the largest trading nation in the world.
   (2) The U.S. economy depends on international trade for vital raw materials and a variety of finished products.
   (3) There are some patterns in U.S. trade: The United States has a trade deficit because its exports exceed its imports. Most trade is with industrially advanced nations, with Canada being the largest trade partner; overall imports exceed exports, but the trade deficits are greatest with China, Japan, and OPEC countries.
   (4) International trade must be financed, and in the case of the United States, large trade deficits have required the selling of business ownership (securities)

to companies in other nations.
   b. Factors facilitating trade since World War II include improvements in transportation and communications technology and a general decline in tariffs.
   c. There are many participants in international trade.
   (1) The United States, Japan, and the nations of western Europe are the major players in international trade, and they provide the headquarters for **multinational corporations** that have substantial production facilities in different nations.
   (2) Newer participants include many Asian economies—Hong Kong (now part of China), Singapore, South Korea, Taiwan, Malaysia, and Indonesia. China has also emerged as a major trading nation in this region. The collapse of communism in the former Soviet Union and the emergence of Russia and the nations of eastern Europe significantly changed trade patterns in that region, opened those nations to market forces, and increased international trade.

3. Specialization and international trade are advantageous because they increase the productivity of a nation's resources, increase total output, and increase incomes.

4. **Comparative advantage** explains the gains from trade and is directly related to opportunity cost. In essence, a nation has a comparative advantage in the production of a good when it can produce the good at a lower domestic opportunity cost than can a trading partner. A nation will specialize in the production of a product for which it is the low (opportunity) cost producer and trade for the other goods it wants.
   a. Suppose the world is composed of only two nations (the United States and Mexico), each of which is capable of producing two different goods (avocados and soybeans). The production possibilities table for each nation assumes a constant opportunity cost, and so a constant amount of one good must be given up to get more of another good. With different domestic opportunity cost ratios, each nation will have a comparative (cost) advantage in the production of one of the two goods.
   b. The ratio at which one product is traded for another—the **terms of trade**—lies between the opportunity cost ratios of the two nations.
   c. Each nation gains from this trade because specialization permits a greater total output from the same resources and a better allocation of the world's resources.

5. The **foreign exchange market** is where national currencies such as the European euro, Japanese yen, and U.S. dollar are traded for each other. The equilibrium prices for national currencies are called **exchange rates**. An exchange rate shows how much of a nation's currency is needed to purchase a unit of another nation's currency.
   a. In the dollar–yen market, the dollar price of a yen would be on the vertical axis and the quantity of yen would be on the horizontal axis. The intersection of the upsloping supply of yen curve and downsloping

demand for yen curve would determine the dollar price of a yen.

b. If U.S. demand for Japanese goods increased, more yen would be needed to pay for the goods, and so the demand for yen would increase. This change increases the dollar price of yen, which means there has been a *depreciation* of the U.S. dollar relative to the yen. Conversely, if Japanese demand for U.S. goods increased, more dollars would be needed to pay for the goods, and the supply of yen would increase. This change will decrease the dollar price of yen, which means there has been an *appreciation* of the U.S. dollar relative to the yen.

6. Governments often restrict trade in several ways, and that has consequences.

a. There are four ways by which governments restrict trade:

(1) placing *protective tariffs* (excise taxes or duties) on imported goods to protect domestic producers;

(2) setting *import quotas* to limit the quantity or value of goods that can be imported;

(3) imposing *nontariff barriers* such as burdensome and costly licensing or regulatory requirements;

(4) using export subsidies that are government payments to domestic producers of imported goods.

b. Governments intervene in trade for two basic reasons:

(1) The gains from trade are misunderstood. Exports are thought to be good because they increase domestic employment, and imports are thought to be bad because they reduce domestic employment. The gains from trade come from increased output resulting from specialization and exchange that require importing and exporting.

(2) Trade may be good for a nation as a whole, but certain groups or industries can be adversely affected by imports, and thus they seek political protection through trade restrictions.

c. Trade restrictions impose substantial costs. Domestic consumers pay higher prices for products on which trade restrictions are imposed, and so do domestic firms that use such products or other imported commodities in their production.

7. International trade policies have changed over the years with the development of **multilateral agreements** and **free-trade** zones. They are used to counter the destructive aspects of the trade wars that arose when nations imposed high tariffs. A classic example is the *Smoot-Hawley Tariff Act* of 1930 that caused other nations to impose equally high tariffs, caused a trade war, and reduced worldwide trade.

a. U.S. trade policy has been significantly affected by the *Reciprocal Trade Agreements Act* of 1934. Until 1934, the United States steadily increased tariff rates to protect private interest groups, but since the passage of the 1934 act, tariff rates have been substantially reduced. This act gave the president the authority to negotiate with foreign nations and included *most-favored-nation clauses.*

b. The *General Agreement on Tariffs and Trade*

(GATT) began in 1947. GATT provided equal treatment of all member nations and sought to reduce tariffs and eliminate import quotas through multilateral negotiations. The Uruguay Round of GATT negotiations started in 1986 and was completed in 1993. The major provisions, which were scheduled to be phased in through 2005, reduce tariffs on products, cut restrictive rules applying to services, phase out quotas on textiles and apparel, and decrease subsidies for agriculture.

c. The *World Trade Organization (WTO)* was the successor to GATT. It oversees trade agreements and provides a forum for trade negotiations, the latest of which is the *Doha Round* that was launched in 2001 in Doha, Qatar. The WTO works to expand trade and reduce protectionism, but the outcomes can be controversial.

d. The *European Union (EU)* is an example of a regional free-trade zone or *trade bloc* among 25 European nations.

(1) The EU abolished tariffs among member nations and developed common policies on various economic issues, such as the tariffs on goods to and from non-member nations. The EU has produced freer trade and increased economies of scale for production in its member nations, but such a trading bloc creates trade frictions with nonmember nations like the United States.

(2) Some 12 of the EU nations share a common currency—the *euro.* The chief advantages of such a currency are that it reduces transactions costs for exchanging goods and services in Euro Zone nations and allows consumers and businesses to comparison shop.

e. In 1993, the *North American Free Trade Agreement (NAFTA)* created a free-trade zone or trade bloc covering the United States, Mexico, and Canada. Critics of this agreement feared job losses and the potential for abuse by other nations using Mexico as a base for production, but the dire outcomes have not occurred. There has been increased trade among Canada, Mexico, and the United States because of the agreement.

8. Increased international trade has resulted in more global competition. Most U.S. firms have been able to meet the competitive challenge by lowering production costs, improving products, or using new technology. Some firms and industries have had difficulty remaining competitive and continue to lose market share and employment. Overall, increased trade has produced substantial benefits for U.S. consumers (lower prices and more products) and enabled the nation to make more efficient use of its scarce resources.

9. (Last Word). Frederic Bastiat (1801–1850) was a French economist who wrote a satirical letter to counter the proponents of protectionism. His "petition" to the French government called for blocking out the sun because it was providing too much competition for domestic candlestick makers, thus illustrating the logical absurdity of protectionist arguments.

■ HINTS AND TIPS

1. When the production possibilities schedules for two nations that trade two products have constant cost ratios, you can reduce the schedules to a 2 × 2 table. Put the two products in the two columns and the two nations in the two rows of the matrix. In each cell of the matrix put the *maximum* of each product that can be produced by that row's nation. Then, for each nation, divide the maximum amount of one product into the maximum amount of the other product to get the domestic opportunity cost of one product in terms of the other.

This point can be illustrated with an example from Problem 2 in this *Study Guide* chapter. Lilliput can produce a *maximum* of 40 pounds of apples or 20 pounds of bananas. Brobdingnag can produce a *maximum* of 75 pounds of apples or 25 pounds of bananas. The 2 × 2 matrix would look like this:

	Apples	Bananas
Lilliput	40	20
Brobdingnag	75	25

For Lilliput, the domestic opportunity cost of producing 1 pound of apples is .5 pound of bananas. In Brobdingnag, the domestic opportunity cost of producing 1 pound of apples is .33 pound of bananas. Brobdingnag is the lower (opportunity) cost producer of apples and will specialize in the production of that product. Lilliput is the lower (opportunity) cost producer of bananas, because producing 1 pound of bananas requires giving up 2 pounds of apples, whereas in Brobdingnag producing 1 pound of bananas requires giving up 3 pounds of apples.

2. Foreign exchange rates often confuse students because they can be expressed in two ways: the U.S. dollar price of a unit of foreign currency ($1.56 for 1 British pound) or the amount of foreign currency that can be purchased by one U.S. dollar ($1 can purchase .64 British pound). If you know the exchange rate in one way, you can easily calculate it the other way. Using the information from the first way, dividing $1.56 into 1 British pound gives you the British pound price for 1 U.S. dollar (1/1.56 = .64 of a British pound). Using information from the second way, dividing .64 of a British pound into 1 U.S. dollar gives you the dollar price of a British pound (1/.64 = 1.56). Both ways may be used, although one way may be used more often than the other. Rates for British pounds or Canadian dollars are usually expressed the first way, in terms of U.S. dollars. Rates for the Swiss franc, Japanese yen, and European euro are expressed the second way, per U.S. dollar.

■ IMPORTANT TERMS

multinational corporations	exchange rates
comparative advantage	depreciation
terms of trade	appreciation
foreign exchange market	protective tariffs

import quotas	World Trade Organization (WTO)
nontariff barriers	
export subsidies	Doha Round
Smoot-Hawley Tariff Act	European Union (EU)
Reciprocal Trade Agreements Act	trade bloc
	euro
most-favored-nation clauses	North American Free Trade Agreement (NAFTA)
General Agreement on Tariffs and Trade (GATT)	

SELF-TEST

■ FILL-IN QUESTIONS

1. List the four major economic flows among nations.

a. _____

b. _____

c. _____

d. _____

2. The importance of international trade varies by nation. Nations in which exports account for a relatively high percentage of GDP tend to have a (limited, diversified) _____ resource base and domestic market, whereas nations in which exports account for a lower percentage of GDP tend to have a _____ resource base and domestic market. An example of a higher exporting nation would be the (United States, Neth erlands) _____, and a lower exporting nation would be the _____.

3. In relative terms, the imports and exports of the United States amounted to about (11–16, 31–36) _____% of the economy's GDP in 2005. In absolute terms, the United States is the world's (smallest, largest) _____ trading nation.

4. The bulk of the trade of the United States is with (less-developed, industrially advanced)_____ nations. The largest trading partner for the United States is (Canada, Japan) _____. The United States has a large trade deficit with (Canada, Japan) _____.

5. Factors that have helped increase the growth of world trade since World War II include improvement in _____ and _____ technology and a general decline in _____.

6. The top participants in international trade include the _____, _____, and the nations of western Europe. These participants serve as the headquarters for most (national, multinational) _____ corporations and dominate world trade. The economies of Singapore, South Korea, and Taiwan have (increased, decreased) _____ their share of world trade in recent decades. Another major trading nation in Asia is (China, Thailand) _____.

7. Specialization and trade (increase, decrease) _____ the productivity of a nation's resources and _____ total output more than would be the case without them.

8. When one nation has a lower opportunity cost of producing a product relative to another nation, it has a (nontariff barrier, comparative advantage) _____. The amount of one product that must be given up to obtain 1 unit of another product is the (for eign exchange, opportunity cost) _____.

9. When the dollar price of foreign currency increases, there has been a(n) (appreciation, depreciation) _____ in value of the dollar. When the dollar price of foreign currency decreases, there has been a(n) _____ in the value of the dollar. For example, if the dollar price of a euro decreases from $1.00 = 1 euro to $0.90 = 1 euro, it means that there has been a(n) (appreciation, depreciation) _____ in the value of the dollar, but if the dollar price of a euro increases from $0.95 = 1 euro to $1.05 = 1 euro, it means that there has been a(n) _____ in the value of the dollar.

10. In the market for Japanese yen, an increase in the (demand for, supply of) _____ yen will decrease the dollar price of yen, whereas an increase in the _____ yen will increase the dollar price of yen. If the dollar price of the yen increases, Japanese goods imported into the United States will be (more, less) _____ expensive.

11. The major government policies that restrict trade include
    a. excise taxes or duties on imported goods that are called _____,
    b. limits on the quantities or total value of specific items that may be imported, referred to as _____,
    c. licensing requirements, unreasonable standards, and red tape for a product, which are _____,
    d. government payments to domestic producers of export goods, known as _____.

12. Governments may intervene in trade between nations because they mistakenly think of (exports, imports) _____ as helpful and _____ as harmful for a national economy. In fact, there are important gains from trade in the form of the extra output

obtained from abroad. Trade makes it possible to obtain (exports, imports) _____ at a lower cost than would be the case if they were produced using domestic resources, and the earnings from _____ help a nation pay for these lower cost (exports, imports) _____.

13. Another reason why governments interfere with free trade is based on (private, political) _____ considerations. Groups and industries seek protection from foreign competition through (GATT, tariffs) _____ and import (quotas, subsidies) _____ or other kinds of trade restrictions. The costs of trade protectionism are (clear to, hidden from) _____ consumers in the protected product, and so there is little opposition to demands for protectionism.

14. Tariffs and quotas (benefit, cost) _____ domestic firms in the protected industries but _____ domestic consumers in the form of (lower, higher) _____ prices than would be the case if there were free trade. They also (benefit, cost) _____ domestic firms that use the protected goods as inputs in their production processes.

15. Until 1934, the trend of tariff rates in the United States was (upward, downward) _____. The trend has been (upward, downward) _____ since the 1934 passage of the (Smoot-Hawley Tariff, Reciprocal Trade Agreements) _____ Act. This act empowered the president to lower (tariffs, quotas) _____ by up to 50% in return for a reduction in foreign restrictions on U.S. goods and incorporated (quotas, most-favored-nation) _____ clauses in U.S. trade agreements.

16. The three cardinal principles established in the General Agreement on Tariffs and Trade (GATT) of 1947 were
    a. _____
    b. _____
    c. _____

17. GATT negotiations have been conducted as (circles, rounds) "_____" that last many years. One of the major provisions of the eighth round (the Uruguay Round) was to create a successor to GATT that is called the (Reciprocal, World) _____ Trade Organization. The current ninth round of negotiations is the (Abba, Doha) _____ Round, and it continues to focus on (increasing, reducing) _____ tariffs and quotas and _____ agricultural subsidies.

18. An example of a free-trade zone or trade bloc is the (Western, European) _____ Union.

   a. The specific aims of the EU were the abolition of (capital and labor, tariffs and quotas) _____, the establishment of (common, different) _____ tariffs on goods imported from outside the EU, the (restricted, free) _____ movement of capital and labor within the EU, and common policies on other matters.

   b. The EU created (small, large) _____ markets and stimulated production that has allowed industries to achieve (higher, lower) _____ costs. The economic effects of the EU on nonmember nations such as the United States are mixed because economic growth in the EU causes U.S. exports to the EU to (decrease, increase) _____ while the tariff barriers cause U.S. exports to _____.

   c. The common currency of many of the member nations of the EU is called the (peso, euro) _____.

19. The North American Free Trade Agreement (NAFTA) formed a trade (barrier, bloc) _____ among the United States, Canada, and Mexico. This agreement will eliminate (terms of trade, tariffs) _____ among the nations. Critics in the United States said that it would (increase, decrease) _____ jobs, but the evidence shows a(n) _____ in jobs and total output since its passage.

20. Many U.S. firms can (monopolize, compete) _____ and be successful in the global economy; however, some firms that benefited from past trade protection may find it difficult to adjust to global (control, competition) _____ and may go out of business.

■ TRUE–FALSE QUESTIONS

Circle T if the statement is true, F if it is false.

1. For the United States, the volume of international trade has been increasing relatively but not absolutely.
   T F

2. The U.S. economy's share of world trade has decreased since 1950.   **T F**

3. The United States exports and imports goods and services with a dollar value greater than that of any other nation in the world.   **T F**

4. The United States is dependent on trade for certain commodities that cannot be obtained in domestic markets.   **T F**

5. Canada is the most important trading partner for the United States in terms of the volume of exports and imports.   **T F**

6. If a person, firm, or region has a comparative advantage in the production of a particular commodity, it should specialize in the production of that commodity.   **T F**

7. If one nation has a comparative advantage in the production of a commodity over another nation, it has a higher opportunity cost of production relative to the other nation.   **T F**

8. The economic effects of specialization and trade between nations are similar to increasing the quantity of resources or to achieving technological progress.   **T F**

9. The interaction of the demand for and supply of Japanese yen will establish the dollar price of Japanese yen.   **T F**

10. An increase in incomes in the United States would tend to cause the dollar price of the Japanese yen to fall. **T F**

11. When the dollar price of another nation's currency increases, there has been an appreciation in the value of the dollar.   **T F**

12. When the dollar depreciates relative to the value of the currencies of the trading partners of the United States, goods imported into the United States will tend to become more expensive.   **T F**

13. Export subsidies are government payments to reduce the price of a product to buyers from other nations.   **T F**

14. Nontariff barriers include excise taxes or duties placed on imported goods.   **T F**

15. Through world trade, an economy can reach a point beyond its domestic production possibilities curve. **T F**

16. One reason that trade restrictions get public support is that the alleged benefits of the restrictions are often immediate and clear-cut, but the adverse effects are often obscure and dispersed over the economy.   **T F**

17. Tariffs and quotas benefit domestic firms in the protected industries and also help domestic consumers by lowering the prices for those products.   **T F**

18. The Smoot-Hawley Tariff Act of 1930 reduced tariffs in the United States to the lowest level ever in an attempt to pull the nation out of the Great Depression.   **T F**

19. If the United States concludes a tariff agreement that lowers the tariff rates on goods imported from another nation, the lower tariff rates are then applied to those goods when they are imported from nations with most-favored-nation (MFN) status.   **T F**

20. The World Trade Organization (WTO) is the world's major advocate for trade protectionism.   **T F**

21. The members of the European Union (EU) have experienced freer trade since it was formed.   **T F**

22. The economic integration of nations creates larger markets for firms within the nations that integrate and makes it possible for those firms and their customers to benefit from the economies of large-scale (mass) production.   **T F**

23. The formation of the European Union (EU) may make it more difficult for U.S. firms to compete for European customers with firms located within the EU.   **T   F**

24. The 1993 North American Free Trade Agreement (NAFTA) includes all Central American nations.   **T   F**

25. Major U.S. firms are unable to compete in global markets without significant protection from foreign competition.   **T   F**

■ **MULTIPLE-CHOICE QUESTIONS**

Circle the letter that corresponds to the best answer.

1. Which nation is the world's leading trading nation in terms of absolute volumes of imports and exports?
  (a) Japan
  (b) China
  (c) Germany
  (d) United States

2. Which nation is our most important trading partner in terms of the quantity of trade volume?
  (a) Japan
  (b) Canada
  (c) Germany
  (d) United Kingdom

3. Which of the following is true?
  (a) Exports as a percentage of GDP are greatest in the United States.
  (b) The United States is almost totally dependent on other nations for aircraft, machine tools, and coal.
  (c) Most of the exports and imports trade of the United States is with industrially advanced nations.
  (d) The United States has a trade surplus with Japan.

4. A trade deficit occurs when
  (a) exports exceed imports
  (b) imports exceed exports
  (c) tariff costs exceed tariff benefits
  (d) tariff benefits exceed tariff costs

5. What is one way the United States finances its trade deficit?
  (a) by lending to foreigners
  (b) by selling real assets to foreigners
  (c) by purchasing real assets from foreigners
  (d) by passing protective tariffs on foreign products

6. Which factor has greatly facilitated international trade since World War II?
  (a) greater import quotas
  (b) expanded export subsidies
  (c) increased nontariff barriers
  (d) improved communications

7. Which industrializing nation would be considered one of the new participants in international trade?
  (a) Canada
  (b) Sweden
  (c) Japan
  (d) China

8. Why do nations specialize and engage in trade?
  (a) to protect multinational corporations
  (b) to increase output and income
  (c) to improve communications
  (d) to control other nations

Answer Questions 9, 10, 11, and 12 on the basis of the data given for two regions, Slobovia and Utopia, which have the following production possibilities tables.

SLOBOVIA PRODUCTION POSSIBILITIES TABLE

	Production alternatives					
Product	A	B	C	D	E	F
Cams	1500	1200	900	600	300	0
Widgets	0	100	200	300	400	500

UTOPIA PRODUCTION POSSIBILITIES TABLE

	Production alternatives				
Product	A	B	C	D	E
Cams	4000	3000	2000	1000	0
Widgets	0	200	400	600	800

9. In Slobovia, the comparative cost of
  (a) 1 cam is 3 widgets
  (b) 1 widget is .33 of a cam
  (c) 1 cam is .33 of a widget
  (d) 3 widgets is 1 cam

10. Which of the following statements is *not* true?
  (a) Slobovia should specialize in the production of widgets.
  (b) Slobovia has a comparative advantage in the production of widgets.
  (c) Utopia should specialize in the production of widgets.
  (d) Utopia has a comparative advantage in the production of cams.

11. The terms of trade will be
  (a) greater than 7 cams for 1 widget
  (b) between 7 cams for 1 widget and 5 cams for 1 widget
  (c) between 5 cams for 1 widget and 3 cams for 1 widget
  (d) less than 3 cams for 1 widget

12. Assume that if Slobovia did not specialize it would produce alternative C and that if Utopia did not specialize it would select alternative B. The gains from specialization are
  (a) 100 cams and 100 widgets
  (b) 200 cams and 200 widgets
  (c) 400 cams and 500 widgets
  (d) 500 cams and 400 widgets

13. If the dollar–yen exchange rate is $1 for 110 yen, then a Sony VCR priced at 27,500 yen would cost a U.S. consumer
  (a) $200
  (b) $250
  (c) $275
  (d) $300

14. If the equilibrium exchange rate changes so that the dollar price of Japanese yen increases,
  (a) the dollar has appreciated in value
  (b) the dollar has depreciated in value
  (c) U.S. citizens will be able to buy more Japanese goods
  (d) Japanese citizens will be able to buy fewer U.S. goods

15. A decrease in the U.S. demand for Japanese goods will
  (a) increase the demand for Japanese yen and increase the dollar price of yen
  (b) increase the demand for Japanese yen but decrease the dollar price of yen
  (c) decrease the demand for Japanese yen and decrease the dollar price of yen
  (d) decrease the demand for Japanese yen but increase the dollar price of yen

16. If the exchange rate for one U.S. dollar changes from 1.0 euro to 1.1 euros, there has been
  (a) an appreciation in the value of the euro
  (b) a depreciation in the value of the dollar
  (c) a depreciation in the value of the euro
  (d) an increase in the price of the euro

17. Which of the following is designed to restrict trade?
  (a) GATT
  (b) NAFTA
  (c) import quotas
  (d) multinational corporations

18. Why do governments often intervene in international trade?
  (a) to expand a nation's production possibilities
  (b) to improve the position of multinational corporations
  (c) to protect domestic industries from foreign competition
  (d) to increase revenue from tariff duties and excise taxes

19. Tariffs and quotas in a nation benefit domestic
  (a) consumers and foreign producers of the protected product
  (b) consumers and producers of the protected product
  (c) producers of the protected product, but harm domestic consumers of the product
  (d) producers and foreign producers of the product

20. Which one of the following specifically empowered the president of the United States to reduce tariff rates up to 50% if other nations would reduce their tariffs on American goods?
  (a) the Smoot-Hawley Tariff Act of 1930
  (b) the Reciprocal Trade Agreements Act of 1934
  (c) the General Agreement on Tariffs and Trade of 1947
  (d) the North American Free Trade Agreement of 1993

21. Which of the following is characteristic of the General Agreement on Tariffs and Trade? Nations signing the agreement were committed to

  (a) the expansion of import quotas
  (b) the establishment of a world customs union
  (c) the reciprocal increase in tariffs by negotiation
  (d) the nondiscriminatory treatment of all member nations

22. One important outcome from the Uruguay Round of GATT was
  (a) an increase in tariff barriers on services
  (b) establishment of the World Trade Organization
  (c) removal of voluntary export restraints in manufacturing
  (d) abolishment of patent, copyright, and trademark protection

23. One of the potential problems with the European Union is that
  (a) an unregulated free flow of labor and capital may reduce productivity
  (b) economies of large-scale production may increase consumer prices
  (c) tariffs may reduce trade with nonmember nations
  (d) governments may have difficulty covering the shortfall from the elimination of duties and taxes

24. An example of the formation of a trade bloc would be the
  (a) Smoot-Hawley Tariff Act
  (b) North American Free Trade Agreement
  (c) Reciprocal Trade Agreements Act
  (d) General Agreement on Tariffs and Trade

25. The increase in global competition has resulted in
  (a) greater inefficiency among U.S. producers
  (b) lower quality in the production of goods
  (c) the inability of most U.S. firms to compete
  (d) lower prices for many consumer goods and services

■ PROBLEMS

1. The following problem will help you understand the principle of comparative advantage and the benefits of specialization. A tailor named Hart has the production possibilities table for trousers and jackets as given. He chooses production alternative D.

HART'S PRODUCTION POSSIBILITIES TABLE

Product	A	B	C	D	E	F
			Production alternatives			
Trousers	75	60	45	30	15	0
Jackets	0	10	20	30	40	50

Another tailor, Schaffner, has the following production possibilities table and chooses production alternative E.

SCHAFFNER'S PRODUCTION POSSIBILITIES TABLE

Product	A	B	C	D	E	F	G
				Production alternatives			
Trousers	60	50	40	30	20	10	0
Jackets	0	5	10	15	20	25	30

a. To Hart,

(1) the cost of one pair of trousers is _____ jackets

(2) the cost of one jacket is _____ pairs of trousers

b. To Schaffner,

(1) the cost of one pair of trousers is _____ jackets

(2) the cost of one jacket is _____ pairs of trousers

c. If Hart and Schaffner were to form a partnership to make suits,

(1) _____ should specialize in the making of trousers because he can make a pair of trousers at the cost of _____ of a jacket, whereas it costs his partner _____ of a jacket to make a pair of trousers.

(2) _____ should specialize in the making of jackets because he can make a jacket at the cost of _____ pairs of trousers, whereas it costs his partner _____ pairs of trousers to make a jacket.

d. Without specialization, Hart and Schaffner were able to make 50 pairs of trousers and 50 jackets. If each specializes completely in the item in the production of which he has a comparative advantage, their combined production will be _____ pairs of trousers and _____ jackets. Thus, the gain from specialization is _____.

e. When Hart and Schaffner come to divide the income of the partnership between them, the manufacture of a pair of trousers should be treated as the equivalent of from _____ to _____ jackets (or a jacket should be treated as the equivalent of from _____ to _____ pairs of trousers).

2. The countries of Lilliput and Brobdingnag have the production possibilities tables for apples and bananas shown below.

Note that the costs of producing apples and bananas are constant in both countries.

LILLIPUT PRODUCTION POSSIBILITIES TABLE

	Production alternatives					
Product	A	B	C	D	E	F
Apples	40	32	24	16	8	0
Bananas	0	4	8	12	16	20

BROBDINGNAG PRODUCTION POSSIBILITIES TABLE

	Production alternatives					
Product	A	B	C	D	E	F
Apples	75	60	45	30	15	0
Bananas	0	5	10	15	20	25

a. In Lilliput the cost of producing

(1) 8 apples is _____ bananas

(2) 1 apple is _____ bananas

b. In Brobdingnag the cost of producing

(1) 15 apples is _____ bananas

(2) 1 apple is _____ bananas

c. In Lilliput the cost of producing

(1) 4 bananas is _____ apples

(2) 1 banana is _____ apples

d. In Brobdingnag the cost of producing

(1) 5 bananas is _____ apples

(2) 1 banana is _____ apples

e. The cost of producing 1 apple is lower in the country of _____, and the cost of producing 1 banana is lower in the country of _____.

f. Lilliput has a comparative advantage in the production of _____, and Brobdingnag has a comparative advantage in the production of _____.

g. The information in this problem is not sufficient to determine the exact terms of trade, but the terms of trade will be greater than _____ apples for 1 banana and less than _____ apples for 1 banana. Put another way, the terms of trade will be between _____ bananas for 1 apple and _____ bananas for 1 apple.

h. If neither nation could specialize, each would produce production alternative C. The combined production of apples in the two countries would be _____ apples, and the combined production of bananas would be _____ bananas.

(1) If each nation specializes in producing the fruit for which it has a comparative advantage, their combined production will be _____ apples and _____ bananas.

(2) Their gain from specialization will be _____ apples and _____ bananas.

3. Use the following table that shows 10 different currencies and how much of each currency can be purchased with a U.S. dollar.

		Currency per U.S. $		
Country	Currency	Year 1	Year 2	A or D
Brazil	Real	0.85	0.91	_____
Britain	Pound	0.65	0.59	_____
Canada	Dollar	1.41	1.51	_____
Switzerland	Franc	1.33	1.19	_____
Germany	Euro	1.58	1.69	_____
India	Rupee	31.39	34.55	_____
Japan	Yen	100.15	110.23	_____
Mexico	Peso	4.65	5.09	_____
Norway	Krone	6.88	6.49	_____
Thailand	Bhat	25.12	23.22	_____

a. In the far right column of the table, indicate whether the U.S. dollar has appreciated **(A)** or depreciated **(D)** from year 1 to year 2.

b. In year 1, a U.S. dollar would purchase _____ Swiss francs, but in year 2, it would purchase _____ Swiss francs. The U.S. dollar has (appreciated, depreciated) _____ against the Swiss franc from year 1 to year 2.

c. In year 1, a U.S. dollar would purchase _____ Japanese yen, but in year 2, it would purchase _____ Japanese yen. The U.S. dollar has (appreciated, depreciated) _____ against the Japanese yen from year 1 to year 2.

4. This problem asks you to calculate prices based on exchange rates. Use the data in the table for Problem 3 to answer the following items.

a. Using the exchange rates shown for year 1, what would be the U.S. dollar cost for the following products?

(1) Japanese television costing 30,000 yen.

$_____

(2) Swiss scarf costing 200 francs. $_____
(3) Thai artwork costing 3768 bhats. $_____
(4) German auto costing 79,000 euros. $_____
(5) Mexican silver bracelet costing 1376 pesos.

$_____

b. Using the exchange rates shown for year 2, what would be the U.S. dollar cost of the following products?

(1) Japanese television costing 30,000 yen.

$_____

(2) Swiss scarf costing 200 francs. $_____
(3) Thai artwork costing 3768 bhats. $_____
(4) German auto costing 79,000 euros. $_____
(5) Mexican silver bracelet costing 1376 pesos.

$_____

c. Indicate whether the U.S. dollar cost of each product in 4b has increased (+) or decreased (−) from year 1 to year 2. _____ _____ _____ _____ _____

d. What is the relationship between your answers in 4c to the ones you gave for the corresponding nations in 3a?

(1) When the U.S. dollar *appreciates* in value against a foreign currency, the U.S. dollar cost of a product from that nation will (increase, decrease) _____.

(2) When the U.S. dollar *depreciates* in value against a foreign currency, the U.S. dollar cost of a product from that nation will (increase, decrease) _____.

■ **SHORT ANSWER AND ESSAY QUESTIONS**

1. Describe the four major economic flows that link the United States to other nations.

2. In relative and absolute terms, how large is the volume of the international trade of the United States? What has happened to these figures over the last 40 or so years?

3. What are the principal exports and imports of the U.S. economy? What commodities used in the economy come almost entirely from abroad, and what American industries sell large percentages of their outputs abroad?

4. Which nations are the principal trading partners of the United States? How much of this trade is with the industrially advanced nations, and how much of it is with the developing nations of the world?

5. Give several factors that have facilitated trade since World War II.

6. Who are the major participants in international trade? Describe the relative influence of the key players.

7. Use an example of two individuals to describe the basic principle of comparative advantage.

8. What is meant by comparative cost and comparative advantage?

9. Explain how comparative advantage determines the terms of trade between nations.

10. What is the gain for a nation that results from specialization in the production of products for which it has a comparative advantage?

11. Describe the characteristics of a foreign exchange market and of exchange rates. Why is an exchange rate an unusual price?

12. Illustrate with a supply and demand graph how equilibrium is determined in a dollar–yen market. Be sure to label axes and curves.

13. Why might an appreciation in the value of the U.S. dollar relative to the Japanese yen depress the U.S. economy and stimulate the Japanese economy? Why might a government intervene in the foreign exchange market and try to increase or decrease the value of its currency?

14. What are the major trade impediments and subsidies? How do they restrict international trade?

15. Why do governments intervene in international trade and develop restrictive trade policies?

16. What is the cost to society from trade protectionism? Who benefits and who is hurt by trade protectionism?

17. What was the Smoot-Hawley Tariff Act of 1930? What international trade problems are illustrated by this act?

18. Explain the basic provisions of the Reciprocal Trade Agreements Act of 1934.

19. What were the cardinal principles contained in the General Agreement on Tariffs and Trade (GATT)? What were the basic provisions and important results of the Uruguay Round of GATT negotiations?

20. Describe the purpose of the World Trade Organization (WTO). Why is it controversial?

21. What is the European Union? What has the EU achieved?

22. Discuss the potential effects of the European Union on the trade of the United States.

23. What is the euro, and what have been its likely economic effects?

24. What is the North American Free Trade Agreement (NAFTA)? What do critics and defenders say about the agreement?

25. Evaluate the effects of increased global competition on U.S. firms, workers, and consumers.

ANSWERS

Chapter 5 The United States in the Global Economy

FILL-IN QUESTIONS

1. *a.* goods and services flows (trade flows); *b.* capital and labor flows (resource flows); *c.* information and technology flows; *d.* financial flows (any order for *a–d*)
2. limited, diversified, Netherlands, United States
3. 11–16, largest
4. industrially advanced, Canada, Japan
5. transportation, communications (either order), tariffs
6. United States, Japan (either order), multinational, increased, China
7. increase, increase
8. comparative advantage, opportunity cost
9. depreciation, appreciation, appreciation, depreciation
10. supply of, demand for, more
11. *a.* protective tariffs; *b.* import quotas; *c.* nontariff barriers; *d.* export subsidies
12. exports, imports, imports, exports, imports
13. political, tariffs, quotas, hidden from
14. benefit, cost, higher, cost
15. upward, downward, Reciprocal Trade Agreements, tariffs, most-favored-nation
16. *a.* equal, nondiscriminatory treatment of all member nations; *b.* reduction of tariffs by multilateral negotiations; *c.* elimination of import quotas
17. rounds, World, Doha, reducing, reducing
18. European; *a.* tariffs and quotas, common, free; *b.* large, lower, increase, decrease; *c.* euro
19. bloc, tariffs, decrease, increase
20. compete, competition

TRUE–FALSE QUESTIONS

1. F, pp. 85–86	**10.** F, p. 93	**19.** T, p. 97
2. T, p. 86	**11.** F, p. 93	**20.** F, p. 97
3. T, p. 86	**12.** T, p. 93	**21.** T, p. 98
4. T, pp. 86–87	**13.** T, p. 95	**22.** T, p. 98
5. T, p. 87	**14.** F, p. 95	**23.** T, p. 98
6. T, pp. 91–92	**15.** T, p. 95	**24.** F, p. 98
7. F, pp. 91–92	**16.** T, p. 95	**25.** F, p. 99
8. T, pp. 91–92	**17.** F, p. 95	
9. T, pp. 93	**18.** F, p. 96	

MULTIPLE-CHOICE QUESTIONS

1. d, p. 86	**10.** c, pp. 90–92	**19.** c, p. 95
2. b, p. 86	**11.** c, p. 91	**20.** b, p. 97
3. c, pp. 86–87	**12.** a, pp. 91–92	**21.** d, p. 97
4. b, p. 88	**13.** b, pp. 92–93	**22.** b, p. 97
5. b, p. 88	**14.** b, p. 93	**23.** c, p. 98
6. d, p. 88	**15.** c, p. 93	**24.** b, p. 98
7. d, p. 89	**16.** c, p. 93	**25.** d, p. 99
8. b, p. 89	**17.** c, p. 95	
9. c, pp. 90–92	**18.** c, p. 95	

PROBLEMS

1. a. (1) .67, (2) 1.5; *b.* (1) .5, (2) 2; *c.* (1) Schaffner, .5, .67; (2) Hart, 1.5, 2; *d.* 60, 50, 10 pairs of trousers; *e.* .5, .67, 1.5, 2
2. *a.* (1) 4, (2) .5; *b.* (1) 5, (2) .33; *c.* (1) 8, (2) 2; *d.* (1) 15, (2) 3; *e.* Brobdingnag, Lilliput; *f.* bananas, apples; *g.* 2, 3, .33, .5; *h.* 69, 18, (1) 75, 20, (2) 6, 2
3. *a.* A, D, A, D, A, A, A, A, D, D; *b.* 1.33, 1.19, depreciated; *c.* 100.15, 110.23, appreciated
4. *a.* (1) 299.55 (2) 150.38 (3) 150 (4) 50,000 (5) 295.91; *b.* (1) 272.16 (2) 168.07 (3) 162.27 (4) 46,745.56 (5) 270.33; *c.* (1) − (2) + (3) + (4) − (5) −; *d.* (1) decrease (2) increase

SHORT ANSWER AND ESSAY QUESTIONS

1. p. 85	**10.** pp. 91–92	**19.** p. 97
2. pp. 85–86	**11.** pp. 92–93	**20.** p. 97
3. pp. 85–86	**12.** p. 93	**21.** p. 98
4. pp. 86–87	**13.** p. 93	**22.** p. 98
5. p. 88	**14.** p. 95	**23.** p. 98
6. pp. 88–89	**15.** p. 95	**24.** p. 98
7. pp. 90–92	**16.** p. 96	**25.** p. 99
8. pp. 90–91	**17.** p. 96	
9. p. 91	**18.** p. 97	

CHAPTER 6

Measuring Domestic Output and National Income

The subject of Chapter 6 is **national income accounting.** The first measure you will learn about in the chapter is the **gross domestic product** (GDP). The GDP is an important economic statistic because it provides the best estimate of the total market value of all final goods and services produced by the economy in 1 year. You will also discover why GDP is a monetary measure that counts only the value of final goods and services and excludes nonproductive transactions such as secondhand sales.

National income accounting involves estimating output, or income, for the nation's society as a whole rather than for an individual business firm or family. Note that the terms **"output"** and **"income"** are interchangeable because the nation's domestic output and its income are identical. The value of the nation's output equals the total expenditures for that output, and those expenditures become the income of those who have produced that output. Consequently, there are two equally acceptable methods—expenditures and income—for determining GDP.

From an **expenditure** perspective, GDP is composed of four expenditure categories: personal consumption expenditures (C), gross private domestic investment (I_g), government purchases (G), and net exports (X_n). These expenditures become income for people or the government when they are paid out in the form of employee compensation, rents, interest, proprietors' income, corporate profits, and taxes on production and imports. GDP can be calculated from national income by making adjustments to account for net foreign factor income, a statistical discrepancy, and depreciation. In national income accounting, the amount spent to purchase this year's total output is equal to the money income derived from the production of this year's output.

The chapter also explains the relationship of GDP to other **national income** accounts. Those accounts include *net domestic product* (NDP), *national income* (NI) as derived from NDP, *personal income* (PI), and *disposable income* (DI). The relationship between GDP, NDP, NI, PI, and DI is shown in Table 6.4 in the text. The circular flow using the expenditures and income approaches to GDP is illustrated in Figure 6.3 in the text.

The next to last section of the chapter shows you how to calculate **real GDP** from **nominal GDP.** This adjustment is important because nominal GDP is measured in monetary units, and so if accurate comparisons are to be made for GDP over time, these monetary measures must be adjusted to take account of changes in the price level. A simple example is presented to show how a GDP price index is constructed. The index is then used to adjust *nominal GDP* to obtain *real GDP* and make correct GDP comparisons from one year to the next. The text also provides data for the U.S. economy so that you can see why the calculation of real GDP is necessary and how it is used.

The last section of the chapter looks at the **shortcomings of GDP** as a measure of total output and economic well-being. You will learn about economic factors that are excluded from GDP measurement—nonmarket or illegal transactions, changes in leisure and product quality, differences in the composition and distribution of output, and the environmental effects of GDP production—and how their exclusion can lead to an under- or overstatement of economic well-being. Although national income accounts are not perfect measures of all economic conditions, they are still reasonably accurate and useful indicators of the performance of the national economy.

Chapter 6 provides the essential background for Parts 2 and 3 of the text, which explain the history of and the factors that determine the level of domestic output and income in the economy. Chapter 6 is important because it explains the several methods used to measure the performance of the economy in a given year and to make the adjustments necessary to ensure accurate measurements of performance over time.

■ **CHECKLIST**

When you have studied this chapter you should be able to

☐ Identify three ways national income accounting can be used for economic decision making.

☐ Give a definition of the gross domestic product (GDP).

☐ Explain why GDP is a monetary measure.

☐ Describe how GDP measures value added and avoids multiple counting.

☐ Give examples of two types of nonproduction transactions that are excluded from GDP.

☐ Describe the relationship between the expenditures and income approaches to GDP accounting.

☐ List the three types of expenditures included in personal consumption expenditures (C).

☐ Identify three items included in gross private domestic investment (I_g).

☐ Explain why changes in inventories are an investment.

☐ Distinguish between gross and net investment.

☐ Discuss how differences in the amount of net investment affect the production capacity of the economy.

☐ List the two components included in government purchases (*G*).

☐ Describe the meaning and calculation of net exports (*X$_n$*).

☐ Compute GDP by using the expenditures approach when given national income accounting data.

☐ Identify the six income items that make up U.S. national income.

☐ List three things that can happen to corporate profits.

☐ Explain the inclusion of taxes on production and imports to national income accounts.

☐ Describe the effect of net foreign factor income on national income accounts.

☐ Define consumption of fixed capital and discuss how it affects national income accounts.

☐ Compute GDP by using the income approach when given national income accounting data.

☐ Define net domestic product (NDP).

☐ Show how to derive U.S. national income (NI) from net domestic product (NDP).

☐ Define personal income (PI) in national income accounts.

☐ Explain how to obtain disposable income (DI) from personal income (PI).

☐ Use Figure 6.3 in the text to describe the circular flow model for GDP.

☐ Distinguish between nominal and real GDP.

☐ Construct a price index when given the necessary price and quantity data.

☐ Obtain a price index when given data on nominal and real GDP.

☐ Discuss some real-world factors that affect the GDP price index.

☐ List seven shortcomings of GDP as a measure of total output and economic well-being.

☐ Identify some of the sources of data the Bureau of Economic Analysis uses to estimate consumption, investment, government purchases, and net exports (Last Word).

■ **CHAPTER OUTLINE**

1. *National income accounting* consists of concepts that enable those who use them to measure the economy's output, compare it with past outputs, explain its size and the reasons for changes in its size, and formulate policies designed to increase it.

2. The market value of all final goods and services produced in the economy during the year is measured by the *gross domestic product (GDP).*
   a. GDP is a *monetary measure* that is calculated in dollar terms rather than in terms of physical units of output.
   b. GDP includes only the value *final goods* and services (goods and services that will not be processed further during the *current* year) in its calculation. GDP excludes the value of *intermediate goods* (ones that are purchased for resale or further processing) because including both final goods and intermediate goods would result in *multiple counting* of the goods and overstate GDP. Another way to avoid multiple counting is to measure and add only the *value added* at each stage of the production process.
   c. Nonproduction transactions are not included in GDP.
   (1) Purely financial transactions such as public transfer payments, private transfer payments, and stock market transactions are simply exchanges of money or paper assets and do not create output.
   (2) Sales of secondhand or used goods are excluded because they were counted in past production and do not contribute to current production.
   d. Measurement of GDP can be accomplished by either the expenditures method or the income method, and the same result is obtained by the two methods.

3. Computation of the GDP by the *expenditures approach* requires the summation of the total amounts of the four types of spending for final goods and services.
   a. *Personal consumption expenditures* (*C*) are the expenditures of households for *durable goods* and *nondurable goods* and for *services*.
   b. *Gross private domestic investment* (*I$_g$*) is the sum of spending by business firms for machinery, equipment, and tools; spending by firms and households for new buildings; and changes in the inventories of business firms.
   (1) A change in inventories is included in investment because it is the part of the output of the economy that was not sold during the year.
   (2) Investment does not include expenditures for stocks or bonds or for secondhand capital goods.
   (3) Gross investment exceeds net investment by the value of the capital goods worn out during the year. An economy in which net investment is positive is one with an expanding production capacity.
   c. *Government purchases* (*G*) are the expenditures made by all governments in the economy for products produced by business firms and for resource services from households. They include expenditures the government makes for products and services to provide public services, plus spending for social capital (goods with a long lifetime such as highways).
   d. *Net exports* (*X$_n$*) in an economy equal the expenditures made by foreigners for goods and services produced in the economy less the expenditures made by the consumers, governments, and investors in the economy for goods and services produced in foreign nations.
   e. In equation form, *C + I$_g$ + G + X$_n$ = GDP.*

4. Computation of GDP by the *income approach* requires adding the income derived from the production and sales of final goods and services. The six income items are:

a. *Compensation of employees* (the sum of wages and salaries *and* wage and salary supplements).

b. *Rents* (the income received by property owners).

c. *Interest* (only the interest payments made by business firms are included, and interest payments made by government are excluded).

d. *Proprietors' income* (the profits or net income of unincorporated firms).

e. *Corporate profits* (they are allocated in the following three ways: as corporate income taxes, dividends paid to stockholders, and undistributed corporate profits retained by corporations).

f. *Taxes on production and imports* are added because they are initially income that later gets paid to government. They include general sales taxes, excise taxes, business property taxes, license fees, and custom duties.

g. The sum of all six categories equals national income, but to move from the national income to GDP, three adjustments must be made.

(1) Net foreign factor income is subtracted because it reflects income from all output regardless of the foreign or domestic source of the income. (Net foreign factor income is income earned by American-owned resources abroad minus income earned by foreign-owned resources in the United States.)

(2) A statistical discrepancy is added to national income to make the income approach match the expenditures approach.

(3) The **consumption of fixed capital** is added to national income to get to GDP because it is a cost of production that does not add to anyone's income. It covers depreciation of private capital goods and social capital goods such as roads and bridges.

5. Four other national accounts are important in evaluating the performance of the economy. Each has a distinct definition and can be computed by making additions to or deductions from another measure.

a. *Net domestic product (NDP)* is the annual output of final goods and services over and above the private and social capital goods worn out during the year. It is equal to the GDP minus depreciation (consumption of fixed capital).

b. *National income (NI)* is the total income *earned* by U.S. owners of land and capital and by U.S. suppliers of labor and entrepreneurial ability during the year *plus* taxes on production and imports. It equals NDP *minus* a statistical discrepancy and plus net foreign factor income.

c. *Personal income (PI)* is the total income *received*—whether it is earned or unearned—by the households of the economy before the payment of personal taxes. It is found by taking national income and *adding* transfer payments and then *subtracting* taxes on production and imports, Social Security contributions, corporate income taxes, and undistributed corporate profits.

d. *Disposable income (DI)* is the total income available to households after the payment of personal taxes. It is calculated by taking personal income and then *subtracting* personal taxes. It is also equal to personal consumption expenditures plus personal saving.

e. The relations among the five income-output measures are summarized in Table 6.4.

f. Figure 6.3 is a more realistic and complex circular flow diagram that shows the flows of expenditures and incomes among the households, business firms, and governments in the economy.

6. *Nominal GDP* is the total output of final goods and services produced by an economy in 1 year multiplied by the market prices when they were produced. Prices, however, change each year. To compare total output over time, nominal GDP is converted to *real GDP* to account for these price changes.

a. There are two methods for deriving *real GDP* from *nominal GDP*. The first method involves computing a **price index.**

(1) This index is a ratio of the price of a market basket in a given year to the price of the same market basket in a base year, with the ratio multiplied by 100.

(2) To obtain real GDP, divide nominal GDP by the price index expressed in hundredths.

b. In the second method, nominal GDP is broken down into prices and quantities for each year. Real GDP is found by using base-year prices and multiplying them by each year's physical quantities. The GDP price index for a particular year is the ratio of nominal to real GDP for that year.

c. In the real world, complex methods are used to calculate the GDP price index. The price index is useful for calculating real GDP. The price index number for a reference period is arbitrarily set at 100.

(1) For years when the price index is below 100, dividing nominal GDP by the price index (in hundredths) inflates nominal GDP to obtain real GDP.

(2) For years when the price index is greater than 100, dividing nominal GDP by the price index (in hundredths) deflates nominal GDP to obtain real GDP.

7. GDP has shortcomings as a measure of total output and economic well-being.

a. It excludes the value of final goods and services not bought and sold in the markets of the economy.

b. It excludes the amount of leisure the citizens of the economy are able to have.

c. It does not record the improvements in the quality of products that occur over the years.

d. It does not measure the market value of the final goods and services produced in the underground sector of the economy.

e. It does not record the pollution costs to the environment of producing final goods and services.

f. It does not measure changes in the composition and the distribution of the domestic output.

g. It does not measure noneconomic sources of well-being.

8. (Last Word). The Bureau of Economic Analysis (BEA) is a unit of the Department of Commerce that is responsible for compiling the national income and product accounts. It obtains data from multiple sources to estimate consumption, investment, government purchases, and net exports for the calculation of GDP.

■ HINTS AND TIPS

1. Read through the chapter several times. A careful reading will enable you to avoid the necessity of memorizing. Begin by making sure you know precisely what GDP means and what is included in and excluded from its measurement.

2. Accounting is essentially an adding-up process. This chapter explains in detail and lists the items that must be added to obtain GDP by the *expenditures approach* or the *income approach*. It is up to you to learn what to add on the expenditure side and what to add on the income side. Figure 6.1 is an important accounting reference for this task.

3. Changes in the price level have a significant effect on the measurement of GDP. Practice converting nominal GDP to real GDP by using a price index. Problems 4 and 5 in this *Study Guide* should help you understand nominal and real GDP and the conversion process.

4. GDP is a good measure of the market value of the output of final goods and services that are produced in an economy in 1 year; however, the measure is not perfect, and so you should be aware of its limitations, which are noted at the end of the chapter.

■ IMPORTANT TERMS

national income accounting

gross domestic product (GDP)

intermediate goods

final goods

multiple counting

value added

expenditures approach

income approach

personal consumption expenditures (C)

gross private domestic investment (I_g)

net private domestic investment

government purchases (G)

net exports (X_n)

taxes on production and imports

national income (NI)

consumption of fixed capital (depreciation)

net domestic product (NDP)

personal income (PI)

disposable income (DI)

nominal GDP

real GDP

price index

SELF-TEST

■ FILL-IN QUESTIONS

1. National income accounting is valuable because it provides a means of keeping track of the level of (unemployment, production) _____ in the economy and the course it has followed over the long run and the information needed to make public (policies, payments) _____ that will improve the performance of the economy.

2. Gross domestic product (GDP) measures the total (market, nonmarket) _____ value of all (intermediate, final) _____ goods and services produced in a country (in 1 year, over 2 years) _____.

3. GDP for a country includes goods and services produced (within, outside) _____ its geographic boundaries and (does, does not) _____ treat resources supplied by U.S. citizens differently from resources supplied by citizens of other countries.

4. GDP is a (monetary, nonmonetary) _____ measure that permits comparison of the (relative, absolute) _____ worth of goods and services.

5. In measuring GDP, only (intermediate, final) _____ goods and services are included; if _____ goods and services were included, the accountant would be (over-, under-) _____ stating GDP, or (single, multiple) _____ counting.

6. GDP accounting excludes (production, nonproduction) _____ transactions. These include (financial, nonfinancial) _____ transactions such as public or private transfer payments or the sale of securities and (first-, second-) _____ hand sales.

7. Personal consumption expenditures are the expenditures of households for goods such as automobiles, which are (durable, nondurable) _____, and goods such as food, which are _____, plus expenditures for (housing, services) _____.

8. Gross private domestic investment basically includes the final purchases of (capital, consumer) _____ goods by businesses, all (construction of new, sales of existing) _____ buildings and houses, and changes in (services, inventories) _____.

9. The difference between gross and net private domestic investment is equal to (depreciation, net exports) _____. If gross private domestic investment is greater than depreciation, net private domestic investment is (positive, negative) _____ and the production capacity of the economy is (declining, expanding) _____.

10. An economy's *net* exports equal its exports (minus, plus) _____ its imports. If exports are less than imports, net exports are (positive, negative) _____, but if exports are greater than imports, net exports are

_____.

11. Using the expenditure approach, the GDP equation equals ($NDP + NI + PI$, $C + I_g + G + X_n$) _____.

12. The compensation of employees in the system of social accounting consists of actual wages and salaries (plus, minus) _____ wage and salary supplements. Salary supplements are the payments employers make to Social Security or (public, private) _____ insurance programs and to _____ pension, health, and welfare funds.

13. Corporate profits are disposed of in three ways: corporate income (taxes, interest) _____, (depreciation, dividends) _____, and undistributed corporate (taxes, profits) _____.

14. Three adjustments are made to national income to obtain (GDP, DI) _____. Net foreign factor income is (added, subtracted) _____, a statistical discrepancy is _____, and the consumption of fixed capital is _____.

15. Gross domestic product overstates the economy's production because it fails to make allowance for (multiple counting, depreciation) _____ or the need to replace (consumer, capital) _____ goods. When the adjustment is made, the calculations produce (net domestic product, national income)

_____.

16. National income is equal to net domestic product (plus, minus) _____ net foreign factor income _____ a statistical discrepancy. Personal income equals national income (plus, minus) _____ transfer payments _____ the sum of taxes on production and imports, Social Security contributions, corporate income taxes, and undistributed corporate profits. Disposable income equals personal income (plus, minus) _____ personal taxes.

17. A GDP that reflects the prices prevailing when the output is produced is called unadjusted, or (nominal, real), _____ GDP, but a GDP figure that is deflated or inflated for price level changes is called adjusted, or _____, GDP.

18. To calculate a price index in a given year, the combined price of a market basket of goods and services in that year is (divided, multiplied) _____ by the combined price of the market basket in the base year. The result is then _____ by 100.

19. Real GDP is calculated by dividing (the price index, nominal GDP) _____ by _____. The price index expressed in hundredths is calculated by dividing (real, nominal) _____ GDP by _____ GDP.

20. For several reasons, GDP has shortcomings as a measure of total output or economic well-being.

   a. It does not include the (market, nonmarket) _____ transactions that result in the production of goods and services or the amount of (work, leisure) _____ of participants in the economy.
   b. It fails to record improvements in the (quantity, quality) _____ of the products produced or the changes in the (level, composition) _____ and distribution of the economy's total output.
   c. It does not take into account the undesirable effects of GDP production on the (government, environment) _____ or the goods and services produced in the (market, underground) _____ economy.

■ **TRUE–FALSE QUESTIONS**

Circle T if the statement is true, F if it is false.

1. National income accounting allows us to assess the performance of the economy and make policies to improve that performance. **T F**

2. Gross domestic product measures at their market values the total output of all goods and services produced in the economy during a year. **T F**

3. GDP is simply a count of the quantity of output and is not a monetary measure. **T F**

4. The total market value of the wine produced in the United States during a year is equal to the number of bottles of wine produced in that year multiplied by the (average) price at which a bottle sold during that year. **T F**

5. GDP includes the sale of intermediate goods and excludes the sale of final goods. **T F**

6. The total value added to a product and the value of the final product are equal. **T F**

7. Social Security payments and other public transfer payments are counted as part of GDP. **T F**

8. The sale of stocks and bonds is excluded from GDP. **T F**

9. In computing gross domestic product, private transfer payments are excluded because they do not represent payments for currently produced goods and services.
T F

10. The two approaches to the measurement of the gross domestic product yield identical results because one approach measures the total amount spent on the products produced by business firms during a year and the second approach measures the total income of business firms during the year.
T F

11. Personal consumption expenditures only include expenditures for durable and nondurable goods.
T F

12. The expenditure made by a household to have a new home built is a personal consumption expenditure.
T F

13. In national income accounting, any increase in the inventories of business firms is included in gross private domestic investment.
T F

14. If gross private domestic investment is greater than depreciation during a given year, the economy's production capacity has declined during that year.
T F

15. Government purchases include spending by all units of government on the finished products of business but exclude all direct purchases of resources such as labor.
T F

16. The net exports of an economy equal its exports of goods and services less its imports of goods and services.
T F

17. The income approach to GDP includes compensation of employees, rents, interest income, proprietors' income, corporate profits, and taxes on production and imports.
T F

18. Taxes on production and imports are the difference between gross private domestic investment and net private domestic investment.
T F

19. Net foreign factor income is the difference between the earnings of foreign-owned resources in the United States and the earnings from U.S.-supplied resources abroad.
T F

20. A GDP that has been deflated or inflated to reflect changes in the price level is called real GDP.
T F

21. To adjust nominal GDP for a given year to obtain real GDP, it is necessary to multiply nominal GDP by the price index (expressed in hundredths) for that year.
T F

22. If nominal GDP for an economy is $11,000 billion and the price index is 110, then real GDP is $10,000 billion.
T F

23. GDP is a precise measure of the economic well-being of society.
T F

24. The productive services of a homemaker are included in GDP.
T F

25. The external costs from pollution and other activities associated with the production of the GDP are deducted from total output.
T F

■ MULTIPLE-CHOICE QUESTIONS

Circle the letter that corresponds to the best answer.

1. Which is a primary use for national income accounting?
(a) It provides a basis for assessing the performance of the economy.
(b) It measures economic efficiency in specific industries.
(c) It estimates expenditures on nonproduction transactions.
(d) It analyzes the cost of pollution to the economy.

2. Gross domestic product (GDP) is defined as
(a) personal consumption expenditures and gross private domestic investment
(b) the sum of wage and salary compensation of employees, corporate profits, and interest income
(c) the market value of final goods and services produced within a country in 1 year
(d) the market value of all final and intermediate goods and services produced by the economy in 1 year

3. GDP provides an indication of society's valuation of the relative worth of goods and services because it
(a) provides an estimate of the value of secondhand sales
(b) gives increased weight to security transactions
(c) is an estimate of income received
(d) is a monetary measure

4. To include the value of the parts used in producing the automobiles turned out during a year in gross domestic product for that year would be an example of
(a) including a nonmarket transaction
(b) including a nonproduction transaction
(c) including a noninvestment transaction
(d) multiple counting

5. Which of the following is a public transfer payment?
(a) the Social Security benefits sent to a retired worker
(b) the sale of shares of stock in Microsoft Corporation
(c) the sale of a used (secondhand) toy house at a garage sale
(d) the birthday gift of a check for $50 sent by a grandmother to her grandchild

6. The sale in year 2 of an automobile produced in year 1 would not be included in the gross domestic product for year 2; doing so would involve
(a) including a nonmarket transaction
(b) including a nonproduction transaction
(c) including a noninvestment transaction
(d) public transfer payments

7. The service a babysitter performs when she stays at home with her baby brother while her parents are out and for which she receives no payment is not included in the gross domestic product because
(a) this is a nonmarket transaction
(b) this is a nonproduction transaction

(c) this is a noninvestment transaction

(d) multiple counting would be involved

8. According to national income accounting, money income derived from the production of this year's output is equal to

(a) corporate profits and the consumption of fixed capital

(b) the amount spent to purchase this year's total output

(c) the sum of interest income and the compensation of employees

(d) gross private domestic investment less the consumption of fixed capital

9. Which would be considered an investment according to economists?

(a) the purchase of newly issued shares of stock in Microsoft

(b) the construction of a new computer chip factory by Intel

(c) the resale of stock originally issued by the General Motors Corporation

(d) the sale of a retail department store building by Sears to JCPenney

10. A refrigerator was produced by its manufacturer in year 1, sold to a retailer in year 1, and sold by the retailer to a final consumer in year 2. The refrigerator was

(a) counted as consumption in year 1

(b) counted as savings in year 1

(c) counted as investment in year 1

(d) not included in the gross domestic product of year 1

11. The annual charge that estimates the amount of private capital equipment used up in each year's production is called

(a) investment

(b) depreciation

(c) value added

(d) multiple counting

12. If gross private domestic investment is greater than depreciation, the economy most likely is

(a) static

(b) declining

(c) expanding

(d) inflationary

13. GDP in an economy is $3452 billion. Consumer expenditures are $2343 billion, government purchases are $865 billion, and gross investment is $379 billion. Net exports are

(a) + $93 billion

(b) + $123 billion

(c) − $45 billion

(d) − $135 billion

14. What can happen to the allocation of corporate profits?

(a) It is paid to proprietors as income.

(b) It is paid to stockholders as dividends.

(c) It is paid to the government as interest income.

(d) It is retained by the corporation as rents.

15. The allowance for the private and social capital that has been used up or consumed in producing the year's GDP is

(a) net domestic product

(b) consumption of fixed capital

(c) undistributed corporate profits

(d) taxes on production and imports

Questions 16 through 22 use the national income accounting data given in the following table.

	Billions of dollars
Net private domestic investment	$ 32
Personal taxes	39
Transfer payments	19
Taxes on production and imports	8
Corporate income taxes	11
Personal consumption expenditures	217
Consumption of fixed capital	7
U.S. exports	15
Dividends	15
Government purchases	51
Net foreign factor income	0
Undistributed corporate profits	10
Social Security contributions	4
U.S. imports	17
Statistical discrepancy	0

16. Gross private domestic investment is equal to

(a) $32 billion

(b) $39 billion

(c) $45 billion

(d) $56 billion

17. Net exports are equal to

(a) − $2 billion

(b) $2 billion

(c) − $32 billion

(d) $32 billion

18. The gross domestic product is equal to

(a) $298 billion

(b) $302 billion

(c) $317 billion

(d) $305 billion

19. Corporate profits are equal to

(a) $15 billion

(b) $25 billion

(c) $26 billion

(d) $36 billion

20. The net domestic product is equal to

(a) $298 billion

(b) $302 billion

(c) $317 billion

(d) $321 billion

21. National income is equal to

(a) $245 billion

(b) $278 billion

(c) $298 billion
(d) $310 billion

22. Personal income is equal to
(a) $266 billion
(b) $284 billion
(c) $290 billion
(d) $315 billion

23. If both nominal gross domestic product and the level of prices are rising, it is evident that
(a) real GDP is constant
(b) real GDP is declining
(c) real GDP is rising but not as rapidly as prices
(d) no conclusion can be drawn concerning the real GDP of the economy on the basis of this information

24. Suppose nominal GDP rose from $500 billion to $600 billion while the GDP price index increased from 125 to 150. Real GDP
(a) was constant
(b) increased
(c) decreased
(d) cannot be calculated from these figures

25. In an economy, the total expenditure for a market basket of goods in year 1 (the base year) was $4000 billion. In year 2, the total expenditure for the same market basket of goods was $4500 billion. What was the GDP price index for the economy in year 2?
(a) .88
(b) 1.13
(c) 188
(d) 113

26. Nominal GDP is less than real GDP in an economy in year 1. In year 2, nominal GDP is equal to real GDP. In year 3, nominal GDP is slightly greater than real GDP. In year 4, nominal GDP is significantly greater than real GDP. Which year is most likely to be the base year that is being used to calculate the price index for this economy?
(a) 1
(b) 2
(c) 3
(d) 4

27. Nominal GDP was $3774 billion in year 1 and the GDP deflator was 108, and nominal GDP was $3989 in year 2 and the GDP deflator that year was 112. What was real GDP in years 1 and 2, respectively?
(a) $3494 billion and $3562 billion
(b) $3339 billion and $3695 billion
(c) $3595 billion and $3725 billion
(d) $3643 billion and $3854 billion

28. A price index one year was 145, and the next year it was 167. What is the approximate percentage change in the price level from one year to the next as measured by that index?

(a) 12%
(b) 13%
(c) 14%
(d) 15%

29. GDP accounting includes
(a) the goods and services produced in the underground economy
(b) expenditures for equipment to reduce the pollution of the environment
(c) the value of the leisure enjoyed by citizens
(d) the goods and services produced but not bought and sold in the markets of the economy

30. Which is a major reason why GDP is *not* an accurate index of society's economic well-being?
(a) It includes changes in the value of leisure.
(b) It excludes many improvements in product quality.
(c) It includes transactions from the underground economy.
(d) It excludes transactions from the buying and selling of stocks.

■ **PROBLEMS**

1. Following are national income accounting figures for the United States.

	Billions of dollars
Exports	$ 367
Dividends	60
Consumption of fixed capital	307
Compensation of employees	1722
Government purchases	577
Rents	33
Taxes on production and imports	255
Gross private domestic investment	437
Corporate income taxes	88
Transfer payments	320
Interest	201
Proprietors' income	132
Personal consumption expenditures	1810
Imports	338
Social Security contributions	148
Undistributed corporate profits	55
Personal taxes	372
Net foreign factor income	0
Statistical discrepancy	0

a. In the following table, use any of these figures to prepare an income statement for the economy similar to the one found in Table 6.3 in the text.

Receipts: Expenditures approach		Allocations: Income approach	
Item	Amount	Item	Amount
_____	$_____	_____	$_____
_____	$_____	_____	$_____
_____	$_____	_____	$_____
_____	$_____	_____	$_____
		_____	$_____
		_____	$_____
		_____	$_____
		National income	$_____
		_____	$_____
		_____	$_____
		_____	$_____
Gross domestic product	$_____	Gross domestic product	$_____

b. Use the other national accounts to find
(1) Net domestic product is $_____
(2) National income is $_____
(3) Personal income is $_____
(4) Disposable income is $_____

2. A farmer owns a plot of ground and sells the right to pump crude oil from his land to a crude oil producer. The crude oil producer agrees to pay the farmer $20 a barrel for every barrel pumped from the farmer's land.
  a. During one year 10,000 barrels are pumped.
  (1) The farmer receives a payment of $_____ from the crude oil producer.
  (2) The value added by the farmer is $_____.
  b. The crude oil producer sells the 10,000 barrels pumped to a petroleum refiner at a price of $25 a barrel.
  (1) The crude oil producer receives a payment of $_____ from the refiner.
  (2) The value added by the crude oil producer is $_____.
  c. The refiner employs a pipeline company to transport the crude oil from the farmer's land to the refinery and pays the pipeline company a fee of $1 a barrel for the oil transported.
  (1) The pipeline company receives a payment of $_____ from the refiner.
  (2) The value added by the company is $_____.
  d. From the 10,000 barrels of crude oil, the refiner produces 315,000 gallons of gasoline and various by-products that are sold to distributors and gasoline service stations at an average price of $1 per gallon.
  (1) The total payment received by the refiner from its customers is $_____.
  (2) The value added by the refiner is $_____.
  e. The distributors and service stations sell the 315,000 gallons of gasoline and by-products to consumers at an average price of $1.30 a gallon.
  (1) The total payment received by distributors and service stations is $_____.

(2) The value added by them is $_____.
f. The total value added by the farmer, crude oil producer, pipeline company, refiner, and distributors and service stations is $_____, and the market value of the gasoline and by-products (the final good) is $_____.

3. Following is a list of items which may or may not be included in the five income-output measures of the national income accounts (**GDP, NDP, NI, PI, DI**). Indicate in the space to the right of each which of the income-output measures includes this item; it is possible for the item to be included in none, one, two, three, four, or all of the measures. If the item is included in none of the measures, indicate why it is not included.

a. Interest on the national debt _____
b. The sale of a used computer _____
c. The production of shoes that are not sold by the manufacturer _____
d. The income of a dealer in illegal drugs

_____
e. The purchase of a share of common stock on the New York Stock Exchange

_____
f. The interest paid on the bonds of the General Motors Corporation _____
g. The labor performed by a homemaker

_____
h. The labor performed by a paid babysitter

_____
i. The monthly check received by a college student from her parents _____
j. The purchase of a new tractor by a farmer

_____
k. The labor performed by an assembly line worker in repapering his own kitchen

_____
l. The services of a lawyer

_____
m. The purchase of shoes from the manufacturer by a shoe retailer

_____
n. The monthly check received from the Social Security Administration by a college student whose parents have died _____
o. The rent a homeowner would receive if she did not live in her own home

_____

4. Following is hypothetical data for a market basket of goods in year 1 and year 2 for an economy.
  a. Compute the expenditures for year 1.

MARKET BASKET FOR YEAR 1 (BASE YEAR)

Products	Quantity	Price	Expenditures
Toys	3	$10	$_____
Pencils	5	2	$_____
Books	7	5	$_____
Total			$_____

b. Compute the expenditures for year 2.

MARKET BASKET FOR YEAR 2

Products	Quantity	Price	Expenditures
Toys	3	$11	$_____
Pencils	5	3	$_____
Books	7	6	$_____
Total			$_____

c. In the space below, show how you computed the GDP price index for year 2.

_____

5. The following table shows nominal GDP figures for 3 years and the price indices for each of the 3 years. (The GDP figures are in billions.)

Year	Nominal GDP	Price Index	Real GDP
1929	$104	121	$_____
1933	56	91	$_____
1939	91	100	$_____

a. Use the price indices to compute the real GDP in each year. (You may round your answers to the nearest billion dollars.) Write answers in the table.
b. Which of the 3 years appears to be the base year?

_____

c. Between
(1) 1929 and 1933 the economy experienced (inflation, deflation) _____.

(2) 1933 and 1939 it experienced _____.
d. The nominal GDP figure
(1) for 1929 was (deflated, inflated, neither)

_____.

(2) for 1933 was _____.

(3) for 1939 was _____.
e. The price level

(1) fell by _____ % from 1929 to 1933.

(2) rose by _____ % from 1933 to 1939.

■ **SHORT ANSWER AND ESSAY QUESTIONS**

1. Of what use is national income accounting to economists and policymakers?

2. What is the definition of GDP? How are the values of output produced at a U.S.-owned factory in the United States and a foreign-owned factory in the United States treated in GDP accounting?

3. Why is GDP a monetary measure?

4. How does GDP accounting avoid multiple counting and exaggeration of the value of GDP?

5. Why does GDP accounting exclude nonproduction transactions?

6. What are the two principal types of nonproduction transactions? List examples of each type.

7. What are the two sides to GDP accounting? What are the meanings of and the relationship between the two sides?

8. What would be included in personal consumption expenditures by households?

9. How is gross private domestic investment defined?

10. Is residential construction counted as investment or consumption? Explain.

11. Why is a change in inventories an investment?

12. How do you define an expanding production capacity using the concepts of gross private domestic investment and depreciation?

13. What do government purchases include and what do they exclude?

14. How are imports and exports handled in GDP accounting?

15. What are six income components of GDP that add up to national income? Define and explain the characteristics of each component.

16. What are the three adjustments made to the national income to get it to equal GDP? Define and explain the characteristics of each one.

17. Explain how to calculate net domestic product (NDP), national income (NI), personal income (PI), and disposable income (DI).

18. What is the difference between real and nominal GDP? Describe two methods economists use to determine real GDP. Illustrate each method with an example.

19. Describe the real-world relationship between nominal and real GDP in the United States. Explain why nominal GDP may be greater or less than real GDP depending on the year or period selected.

20. Why might GDP not be considered an accurate measure of total output and the economic well-being of society? Identify seven shortcomings of GDP.

ANSWERS

Chapter 6 Measuring Domestic Output and National Income

FILL-IN QUESTIONS

1. production, policies
2. market, final, in 1 year
3. within, does not
4. monetary, relative
5. final, intermediate, over-, multiple
6. nonproduction, financial, second-
7. durable, nondurable, services

8. capital, construction of new, inventories
9. depreciation, positive, expanding
10. minus, negative, positive
11. $C + I_g + G + X_n$
12. plus, public, private
13. taxes, dividends, profits
14. GDP, subtracted, added, added
15. depreciation, capital, net domestic product
16. plus, minus, plus, minus, minus
17. nominal, real
18. divided, multiplied
19. nominal GDP, the price index, nominal, real
20. *a.* nonmarket, leisure; *b.* quality, composition; *c.* environment, underground

TRUE–FALSE QUESTIONS

1. T, p. 106	**10.** F, p. 108	**19.** T, p. 112
2. F, p. 106	**11.** F, p. 108	**20.** T, pp. 116–117
3. F, p. 106	**12.** F, p. 108	**21.** F, pp. 116–117
4. T, p. 106	**13.** T, p. 107	**22.** T, pp. 116–117
5. F, p. 106	**14.** F, pp. 109–110	**23.** F, p. 118
6. T, pp. 106–107	**15.** F, pp. 109–110	**24.** F, p. 118
7. F, p. 107	**16.** T, p. 110	**25.** F, p. 119
8. T, p. 107	**17.** T, p. 111	
9. T, p. 107	**18.** F, p. 112	

MULTIPLE-CHOICE QUESTIONS

1. a, p. 106	**11.** b, p. 109	**21.** c, p. 113
2. c, p. 106	**12.** c, pp. 109–110	**22.** b, pp. 113–114
3. d, p. 106	**13.** d, p. 110	**23.** d, p. 116
4. d, pp. 106–107	**14.** b, p. 112	**24.** a, pp. 116–117
5. a, p. 107	**15.** b, pp. 112–113	**25.** d, pp. 116–117
6. b, p. 107	**16.** b, p. 109	**26.** b, pp. 117–118
7. a, pp. 107, 118	**17.** a, p. 110	**27.** a, pp. 116–117
8. b, p. 108	**18.** d, p. 110	**28.** d, p. 118
9. b, pp. 108–109	**19.** d, p. 112	**29.** b, p. 119
10. c, p. 109	**20.** a, p. 113	**30.** b, p. 119

PROBLEMS

1. *a.* See the following table; *b.* (1) 2546, (2) 2546, (3) 2320, (4) 1948

Receipts: Expenditures approach		Allocations: Income approach	
Item	**Amount**	**Item**	**Amount**
Personal consumption expenditures	$1810	Compensation of employees	$1722
		Rents	33
Gross private domestic investment	437	Interest	201
		Proprietors' income	132
Government purchases	577	Corporate income Taxes	88
		Dividends	60
Net exports	29	Undistributed corporate profit	55
		Taxes on production and imports	255
		National income	$2546
		Net foreign factor Income	0
		Statistical discrepancy	0
		Consumption of fixed capital	307
Gross domestic product	$2853	Gross domestic product	$2853

2. *a.* (1) 200,000, (2) 200,000; *b.* (1) 250,000, (2) 50,000; *c.* (1) 10,000, (2) 10,000; *d.* (1) 315,000, (2) 55,000; *e.* (1) 409,500, (2) 94,500; *f.* 409,500, 409,500

3. *a.* personal income and disposable income, a public transfer payment; *b.* none, a secondhand sale; *c.* all, represents investment (additions to inventories); *d.* none, illegal production and incomes are not included if not reported; *e.* none, a purely financial transaction; *f.* all; *g.* none, a nonmarket transaction; *h.* all if reported as income, none if not reported; *i.* none, a private transfer payment; *j.* all; *k.* none, a nonmarket transaction; *l.* all; *m.* all, represents additions to the inventory of the retailer; *n.* personal income and disposable income, a public transfer payment; *o.* all, estimate of rental value of owner-occupied homes is included in rents as if it were income and in personal consumption expenditures as if it were payment for a service

4. *a.* 30, 10, 35, 75; *b.* 33, 15, 42, 90; *c.* ($90/$75) 100 = 120

5. *a.* 86, 62, 91; *b.* 1939; *c.* (1) deflation, (2) inflation; *d.* (1) deflated, (2) inflated, (3) neither; *e.* (1) 24.8 (2) 9.9

SHORT ANSWER AND ESSAY QUESTIONS

1. p. 106	**8.** p. 108	**15.** pp. 111–112
2. p. 106	**9.** p. 109	**16.** pp. 112–113
3. p. 106	**10.** p. 109	**17.** pp. 113–114
4. p. 106	**11.** p. 109	**18.** pp. 116–117
5. p. 107	**12.** pp. 109–110	**19.** pp. 117–118
6. p. 107	**13.** pp. 109–110	**20.** pp. 118–119
7. p. 108	**14.** p. 110	

Introduction to Economic Growth and Instability

The economic health of a nation relies on **economic growth,** which reduces the burden of scarcity. Small differences in real growth rates result in large differences in the standards of living in nations. The first short section of this chapter introduces you to this important concept and identifies the two main sources of growth. It also presents data on the long-term growth record of the United States.

This record has been interrupted by periods of economic instability, a topic that is the major focus of the chapter. The second section of the chapter discusses the **business cycle:** the ups and downs in the employment of labor and the real output of the economy that occur over the years. What may not be immediately evident to you, but will become clear as you read this chapter, is that these alternating periods of prosperity and hard times have taken place over a long period in which the trends in real output, employment, and the standard of living have been upward. During this long history booms and busts have occurred quite irregularly; their duration and intensity have been so varied that it is better to think of them as economic instability rather than regular business cycles.

Two principal problems result from the instability of the economy. The first problem is described in the third section of the chapter. Here you will find an examination of the **unemployment** that accompanies a downturn in the level of economic activity in the economy. You will first learn how economists measure the unemployment rate in the economy and the problems they encounter. You will also discover that there are three different kinds of unemployment and that full employment means that less than 100% of the labor force is employed. You will also find out how unemployment imposes an economic cost on the economy and learn that this cost is unequally distributed among different groups in the society.

The second major problem that results from economic instability is **inflation.** It is examined in the fourth section of the chapter and also in the following two sections. Inflation is an increase in the general (or average) level of prices in an economy. It does not have a unique cause: It may result from increases in demand, from increases in costs, or from both sources.

Regardless of its cause, inflation may impose a real hardship on different groups in our society, as you will learn in the fifth section of the chapter. **Inflation arbitrarily redistributes real income and wealth** in the economy. Unanticipated inflation hurts those on fixed incomes, those

who save money, and those who lend money. If inflation is anticipated, some of its burden can be reduced, but that depends on whether a group can protect its income with cost-of-living or interest rate adjustments.

Finally, inflation has redistribution effects on the real output of the economy, as described in the last section of the chapter. **Cost-push inflation** and **demand-pull inflation** have different effects on output and employment that vary with the severity of the inflation. In the extreme, an economy can experience very high rates of inflation—**hyperinflation**—that can result in its breakdown.

Gaining an understanding of the basics of economic growth and the twin problems of unemployment and inflation is important because it prepares you for later chapters and the explanations of how the macroeconomy works.

■ **CHECKLIST**

When you have studied this chapter you should be able to

☐ Define economic growth in two different ways.
☐ Explain why economic growth is an important goal.
☐ Describe how different growth rates affect real domestic output over time.
☐ Identify the two main sources of economic growth and indicate their relative importance.
☐ Describe the growth record of the U.S. economy since 1950 and several qualifications to that record.
☐ Explain what the business cycle means.
☐ Describe the four phases of a generalized business cycle.
☐ Identify the immediate cause of cyclical changes in the levels of real output and employment.
☐ Explain differences in the way cyclical fluctuations affect industries that produce capital and consumer durable goods and how they affect those which produce consumer nondurable goods and services.
☐ Describe how the Bureau of Labor Statistics (BLS) measures the rate of unemployment and list the two criticisms of its survey data.
☐ Distinguish among frictional, structural, and cyclical types of unemployment and explain the causes of these three kinds of unemployment.
☐ Define full employment and the full-employment unemployment rate (the natural rate of unemployment).

☐ Identify the economic and noneconomic costs of unemployment.

☐ Define the GDP gap and state Okun's law.

☐ Discuss the unequal burdens of unemployment.

☐ Define inflation and the rate of inflation.

☐ Explain how inflation is measured with the Consumer Price Index.

☐ Make international comparisons of inflation rate and unemployment rate data.

☐ Define demand-pull inflation and explain its effects in ranges 1, 2, and 3 of a price level and real domestic output graph.

☐ Define cost-push inflation and its relation to per-unit production costs.

☐ Describe the complexities involved in distinguishing between demand-pull and cost-push inflation.

☐ Distinguish between real and nominal income and calculate real income when given data on nominal income and the price level.

☐ List groups that are hurt by and groups that are unaffected or benefit from unanticipated inflation.

☐ Describe how the redistributive effects of inflation are changed when it is anticipated.

☐ Explain the difference between the real and the nominal interest rates.

☐ Make three final points about the redistribution effects of inflation.

☐ Describe the effects of cost-push inflation on real output.

☐ Explain the contrasting views on the effects of demand-pull inflation on real output.

☐ Define hyperinflation and explain its effects on prices and real output.

☐ Explain the relationship, or lack of one, between the stock market and the macroeconomy (Last Word).

■ **CHAPTER OUTLINE**

1. *Economic growth* can be defined as an increase in real GDP over some time period. It can also be defined as an increase in *real GDP per capita* over some time period. The second definition takes into account the size of the population. With either definition, economic growth is calculated as a percentage rate of growth per year.

  a. Economic growth is important because it lessens the burden of scarcity; it provides the means of satisfying economic wants more fully and fulfilling new wants.

  b. One or two percentage point differences in the rate of growth result in substantial differences in annual increases in the economy's output. The approximate number of years required to double GDP can be calculated by the *rule of 70,* which involves dividing 70 by the annual percentage rate of growth.

  c. Economic growth can be increased by increasing the inputs of resources and increasing the *productivity* of those inputs. In the United States, about one-third of growth comes from more inputs and two-thirds comes from improved productivity.

  d. Over the last 50 years the U.S. economy has had an impressive record of economic growth. The growth

record may be understated because it does not take into account improvements in product quality or increases in leisure time. The effects of growth on the environment or quality of life can be negative *or* positive.

  e. The growth record of the United States over the last 50 years lagged behind that of other major nations, but in the last decade it has surged ahead of those nations.

2. Economic growth in the U.S. economy has been interrupted by periods of inflation, recession, or both.

  a. The *business cycle* means alternating periods of prosperity and recession. These recurrent periods of ups and downs in employment, output, and prices are irregular in their duration and intensity, but the typical pattern is *peak, recession, trough,* and *expansion* to another peak.

  b. Most economists think that changes in the levels of output and employment are largely the result of changes in the level of total spending in the economy.

  c. The business cycle affects almost the entire economy, but it does not affect all parts in the same way and to the same degree: The production of capital and consumer durable goods fluctuates more than does the production of consumer nondurable goods and services during the cycle because the purchase of capital and consumer durable goods can be postponed.

3. One of the twin problems arising from economic instability is **unemployment.**

  a. The *unemployment rate* is calculated by dividing the number of persons in the *labor force* who are unemployed by the total number of persons in the labor force. Unemployment data have been criticized for at least two reasons:

  (1) Part-time workers are considered fully employed.

  (2) *Discouraged workers* who have left the labor force are not counted as unemployed.

  b. Full employment does not mean that all workers in the labor force are employed and there is no unemployment; some unemployment is normal. There are at least three types of unemployment.

  (1) *Frictional unemployment* is due to workers searching for new jobs or waiting to take new jobs; this type of unemployment is generally desirable.

  (2) *Structural unemployment* is due to changes in technology and in the types of goods and services consumers wish to buy; these changes affect the total demand for labor in particular industries or regions.

  (3) *Cyclical unemployment* is due to insufficient total spending in the economy; this type of unemployment arises during the recession phase of the business cycle.

  c. "Full employment" is less than 100% because some frictional and structural unemployment is unavoidable. The *full-employment unemployment rate* or the *natural rate of unemployment (NRU)* is the sum of frictional and structural unemployment and is achieved when cyclical unemployment is zero (the real output of the economy is equal to its *potential output*). The natural rate is about 4 to 5% of the labor force. It is not automatically achieved and changes over time.

d. Unemployment has an economic cost.

(1) The *GDP gap* is a measure of that cost. It is the difference between actual and potential GDP. When the difference is negative, it means that the economy is underperforming relative to its potential. *Okun's law* predicts that for every 1% the actual unemployment rate exceeds the natural rate of unemployment, there is a negative GDP gap of about 2%.

(2) This cost is unequally distributed among different groups of workers in the labor force.

e. Unemployment also has noneconomic costs in the form of social and psychological problems.

f. Unemployment rates differ across nations because of differences in phases of the business cycle and natural rates of unemployment.

4. Over its history, the U.S. economy has experienced not only periods of unemployment but also periods of *inflation.*

a. Inflation is an increase in the general level of prices in the economy; a decline in the level of prices is deflation.

b. The primary measure of inflation in the United States is the *Consumer Price Index (CPI).* It compares the prices of a "market basket" of consumer goods in a particular year to the prices for that market basket in a base period to produce a price index. The rate of inflation from one year to the next is equal to the percentage change in the CPI between the current year and the preceding year. *The rule of 70* can be used to calculate the number of years it will take for the price level to double at any given rate of inflation.

c. The United States has experienced both inflation and deflation, but the past half-century has been a period of inflation. Other industrial nations also have experienced inflation.

d. There are at least two types of inflation. They may operate separately or simultaneously to raise the price level.

(1) *Demand-pull inflation* is the result of excess total spending in the economy.

(2) *Cost-push inflation* is the result of factors that raise *per-unit production costs.* This average cost is found by dividing the total cost of the resource inputs by the amount of output produced. With cost-push inflation, output and employment decline as the price level rises. The major source of this type of inflation has been supply shock from an increase in the prices of resource inputs.

e. It is difficult to distinguish between demand-pull and cost-push inflation in the real world.

5. Inflation arbitrarily redistributes real income and wealth. It benefits some groups and hurts other groups in the economy.

a. Whether someone benefits or is hurt by inflation is measured by what happens to real income. Inflation injures those whose real income falls and benefits those whose real income rises.

(1) *Real income* is determined by dividing *nominal income* by the price level expressed in hundredths.

(2) The percentage change in real income can be approximated by subtracting the percentage change in the price level from the percentage change in nominal income.

(3) The redistribution effects of inflation depend on whether the inflation is anticipated or unanticipated.

b. *Unanticipated inflation* hurts *fixed-income receivers, savers,* and *creditors* because it lowers the real value of their assets.

c. Unanticipated inflation may not affect or may help *flexible-income receivers.* For examples, some union workers get automatic *cost-of-living adjustments (COLAs)* in their pay when the CPI rises. It helps *debtors* because it lowers the real value of debts to be repaid.

d. When there is *anticipated inflation,* people can adjust their nominal incomes to reflect the expected rise in the price level, and the redistribution of income and wealth is lessened. To reduce the effects of inflation on a *nominal interest rate,* an inflation premium (the expected rate of inflation) is added to the *real interest rate.*

6. Inflation also has an effect on real output that varies by the type of inflation and its severity.

a. Cost-push inflation reduces real output, employment, and income.

b. Views of mild demand-pull inflation vary. It may reduce real output, or it may be a necessary by-product of economic growth.

c. Hyperinflation—extremely high rates of inflation—can lead to a breakdown of the economy by redistributing income and reducing real output and employment.

7. (Last Word). Do changes in the stock market affect the economy? The evidence indicates that changes in stock prices have only a weak effect on consumption and investment and the macroeconomy. Stock market bubbles where there is a large increase in stock prices that then decline rapidly can adversely affect the macroeconomy. Stock prices are a relatively good indicator of future business conditions because they are related to business profits.

■ **HINTS AND TIPS**

1. Some students get confused by the seemingly contradictory term **full-employment unemployment rate** and related unemployment concepts. Full employment does not mean that everyone who wants to work has a job; it means that the economy is achieving its potential output and has a natural rate of unemployment. Remember that there are three types of unemployment: frictional, structural, and cyclical. There will always be some unemployment arising from frictional reasons (e.g., people searching for jobs) and structural reasons (e.g., changes in industry demand), and these two types of unemployment are "natural" for an economy. When there is cyclical unemployment because of a downturn in the business cycle, the economy is not producing its potential output.

Thus, the full-employment unemployment rate means that there are no cyclical reasons causing unemployment, only frictional and structural reasons.

2. To verify your understanding of how to calculate the unemployment rate, GDP gap, or inflation rate, do Problems 3, 4, and 5 in this *Study Guide* chapter.

3. Inflation is a rise in the *general* level of prices, not just a rise in the prices of a few products. An increase in product price is caused by supply or demand factors. You now know why the prices for many products rise in an economy. The macroeconomic reasons given in Chapter 7 for the increase in the general level of prices are different from the microeconomic reasons for a price increase that you learned about in Chapter 3.

■ **IMPORTANT TERMS**

economic growth	potential output
real GDP per capita	GDP gap
rule of 70	Okun's law
productivity	inflation
business cycle	Consumer Price Index (CPI)
peak	demand-pull inflation
recession	cost-push inflation
trough	per-unit production costs
expansion	nominal income
labor force	real income
unemployment rate	anticipated inflation
discouraged workers	unanticipated inflation
frictional unemployment	cost-of-living adjustments (COLAs)
structural unemployment	real interest rate
cyclical unemployment	nominal interest rate
full-employment rate of unemployment	deflation
natural rate of unemployment (NRU)	hyperinflation

SELF-TEST

■ **FILL-IN QUESTIONS**

1. Economic growth is best measured either by an increase in (nominal, real) _____ GDP over a time period or by an increase in _____ GDP per capita over a time period.

2. A rise in real output per capita (increases, decreases) _____ the standard of living and _____ the burden of scarcity in the economy.

3. Assume an economy has a real GDP of $3600 billion. If the growth rate is 5%, real GDP will increase by ($360, $180) _____ billion next year, but if the rate of growth is only 3%, the annual increase in real

GDP will be ($54, $108) _____ billion. A two percentage point difference in the growth rate results in a ($72, $254) _____ billion difference in the annual increase in real GDP.

4. The two main ways in which society can increase its real output and income are by increasing inputs of (products, resources) _____ and by increasing the (consumption, productivity) _____ of those inputs.

5. Between 1950 and 2005, real GDP increased (threefold, sixfold) _____ and real GDP per capita increased more than _____. These figures do not fully account for (better, worse) _____ products and services and (more, less) _____ leisure.

6. The business cycle is a term that encompasses the recurrent ups, or (decreases, increases) _____, and downs, or _____, in the level of business activity in the economy. The order of the four phases of a typical business cycle are peak, (expansion, trough, recession) _____, _____, and _____.

7. Expansion and contraction of the economy affect to a greater extent the production of and employment in the consumer (durables, nondurables) _____ and (capital, consumer) _____ goods industries than they do (durable, nondurable) _____ goods and service industries.

8. The unemployment rate is found by dividing the number of (employed, unemployed) _____ persons by the (population, labor force) _____ and (multiplying, dividing) _____ by 100.

9. When workers are searching for new jobs or waiting to start new jobs, this type of unemployment is called (structural, frictional, cyclical) _____, and when workers are laid off because of changes in the consumer demand and technology in industries or regions, this unemployment is called _____; when workers are unemployed because of insufficient total spending in the economy, this type of unemployment is called _____.

10. The full-employment unemployment rate is called the (Okun, natural) _____ rate of unemployment. It is equal to the total of (frictional and structural, cyclical and frictional) _____ unemployment in the economy. It is realized when the (frictional, cyclical) _____ unemployment in the economy is equal to zero and when the actual output of the economy is (less than, equal to) _____ its potential output. When the economy achieves its natural rate of unemployment, the number of job seekers is (greater than, equal to) _____ the number of job vacancies.

11. The GDP gap is equal to the actual GDP (minus, plus) _____ the potential GDP. For every percentage point the unemployment rate rises above the natural rate, there will be a GDP gap of (2, 5) _____ %.

12. The burdens of unemployment are borne more heavily by (black, white) _____, (adult, teenage) _____, and (white-collar, blue-collar) _____ workers, and the percentage of the labor force unemployed for 15 or more weeks is much (higher, lower) _____ than the overall unemployment rate.

13. Inflation means (an increase, a decrease) _____ in the general level of (unemployment, prices) _____ in the economy. To calculate the rate of inflation from year 1 to year 2, subtract the price index for year 1 from year 2, then (multiply, divide) _____ the result by the price index for year 1, and _____ by 100.

14. To find the approximate number of years it takes the price level to double, (multiply, divide) _____ 70 by the percentage annual increase in the rate of inflation. This approximation is called (Okun's law, the rule of 70) _____.

15. The basic cause of demand-pull inflation is (an increase, a decrease) _____ in total spending beyond the full-employment output rate in the economy. Cost-push inflation is explained in terms of factors that raise per-unit (inflation, production) _____ costs. In practice, it is (easy, difficult) _____ to distinguish between the two types of inflation.

16. The amount of goods and services one's nominal income can buy is called (variable, real) _____ income. If one's nominal income rises by 10% and the price level increases by 7%, the percentage of increase in (variable, real) _____ income would be (1, 2, 3) _____. If nominal income was $60,000 and the price index, expressed in hundredths, was 1.06, then (variable, real) _____ income would be ($56,604, $63,600) _____.

17. Unanticipated inflation hurts those whose nominal incomes are relatively (fixed, flexible) _____, penalizes (savers, borrowers) _____, and hurts (creditors, debtors) _____.

18. The redistributive effects of inflation are less severe when it is (anticipated, unanticipated) _____.

Clauses in labor contracts that call for automatic adjustments of workers' incomes from the effects of inflation are called (unemployment benefits, cost-of-living) _____ adjustments.

19. The percentage increase in purchasing power that the lender receives from the borrower is the (real, nominal) _____ rate of interest; the percentage increase in money that the lender receives is the _____ rate of interest. If the nominal rate of interest is 8% and the real interest rate is 5%, then the inflation premium is (8, 5, 3) _____ %.

20. Cost-push inflation (increases, decreases) _____ real output. The output effects of demand-pull inflation are (more, less) _____ certain. Some economists argue that mild demand-pull inflation (increases, decreases) _____ real output, and others argue that it _____ real output. Economists generally agree that there may be an economic collapse from (hyperproduction, hyperinflation) _____.

■ **TRUE–FALSE QUESTIONS**

Circle T if the statement is true, F if it is false.

1. The more useful of the two definitions of economic growth for comparing living standards across economies is an increase in real GDP per capita. **T F**

2. Suppose two economies both have GDPs of $500 billion. If the GDPs grow at annual rates of 3% in the first economy and 5% in the second economy, the difference in their amounts of growth in one year is $10 billion. **T F**

3. Increased labor productivity has been more important than increased labor inputs in the growth of the U.S. economy. **T F**

4. Growth rate estimates generally attempt to take into account changes in the quality of goods produced and changes in the amount of leisure members of the economy enjoy. **T F**

5. The U.S. economy has always experienced steady economic growth, price stability, and full employment. **T F**

6. The business cycle is best defined as alternating periods of increases and decreases in the rate of inflation in the economy. **T F**

7. Business cycles tend to be of roughly equal duration and intensity. **T F**

8. The unemployment rate is equal to the number of people in the labor force divided by the number of people who are unemployed. **T F**

9. Frictional unemployment is not only inevitable but also partly desirable so that people can voluntarily move to better jobs. **T F**

10. The essential difference between frictionally and structurally unemployed workers is that the former *do not have* and the latter *do have* salable skills.　**T　F**

11. When the number of people seeking employment is less than the number of job vacancies in the economy, the actual rate of unemployment is less than the natural rate of unemployment, and the price level will tend to rise.　**T　F**

12. If unemployment in the economy is at its natural rate, the actual and potential outputs of the economy are equal.　**T　F**

13. An economy cannot produce an actual real GDP that exceeds its potential real GDP.　**T　F**

14. The economy's GDP gap is measured by subtracting its potential GDP from its actual GDP.　**T　F**

15. The economic cost of cyclical unemployment is the goods and services that are not produced.　**T　F**

16. Unemployment imposes equal burdens on different groups in the economy.　**T　F**

17. Inflation is defined as an increase in the total output of an economy.　**T　F**

18. From one year to the next, the Consumer Price Index rose from 154.5 to 160.5. The rate of inflation was therefore 6.6%.　**T　F**

19. If the price level increases by 10% each year, the price level will double every 10 years.　**T　F**

20. The essence of demand-pull inflation is "too much spending chasing too few goods."　**T　F**

21. Cost-push inflation explains rising prices in terms of factors that increase per-unit production cost.　**T　F**

22. A person's real income is the amount of goods and services that the person's nominal (or money) income will enable him or her to purchase.　**T　F**

23. Whether inflation is anticipated or unanticipated, the effects of inflation on the distribution of income are the same.　**T　F**

24. Borrowers are hurt by unanticipated inflation.　**T　F**

25. Hyperinflation may cause economic collapse in an economy by encouraging speculation, hoarding, and decisions based largely on inflationary expectations.　**T　F**

■ **MULTIPLE-CHOICE QUESTIONS**

Circle the letter that corresponds to the best answer.

1. Which is a benefit of real economic growth to a society?
 (a) The society is less able to satisfy new wants.
 (b) Everyone enjoys a greater nominal income.
 (c) The burden of scarcity increases.
 (d) The standard of living increases.

2. If the real output of an economy were to increase from $2000 billion to $2100 billion in 1 year, the rate of growth of real output during that year would be
 (a) 1%
 (b) 5%
 (c) 10%
 (d) 50%

3. Which is one of the four phases of a business cycle?
 (a) inflation
 (b) recession
 (c) unemployment
 (d) hyperinflation

4. Most economists believe that the immediate determinant of the levels of domestic output and employment is
 (a) the price level
 (b) the level of total spending
 (c) the size of the civilian labor force
 (d) the nation's stock of capital goods

5. Production and employment would be *least* affected by a severe recession in which type of industry?
 (a) nondurable consumer goods
 (b) durable consumer goods
 (c) capital goods
 (d) labor goods

6. The unemployment rate in an economy is 8%. The total population of the economy is 250 million, and the size of the civilian labor force is 150 million. The number of employed workers in this economy is
 (a) 12 million
 (b) 20 million
 (c) 138 million
 (d) 140 million

7. The labor force includes those who are
 (a) less than 16 years of age
 (b) in mental institutions
 (c) not seeking work
 (d) employed

8. The unemployment data collected by the Bureau of Labor Statistics have been criticized because
 (a) part-time workers are not counted in the number of workers employed
 (b) discouraged workers are not considered a part of the labor force
 (c) it covers frictional unemployment but not cyclical unemployment, which inflates unemployment figures
 (d) the underground economy may understate unemployment

9. A worker who loses a job at a petroleum refinery because consumers and business firms switch from the use of oil to the burning of coal is an example of
 (a) frictional unemployment
 (b) structural unemployment
 (c) cyclical unemployment
 (d) disguised unemployment

10. A worker who has quit one job and is taking 2 weeks off before reporting to a new job is an example of

(a) frictional unemployment
(b) structural unemployment
(c) cyclical unemployment
(d) disguised unemployment

11. Insufficient total spending in the economy results in
(a) frictional unemployment
(b) structural unemployment
(c) cyclical unemployment
(d) disguised unemployment

12. The full-employment unemployment rate in the economy has been achieved when
(a) frictional unemployment is zero
(b) structural unemployment is zero
(c) cyclical unemployment is zero
(d) the natural rate of unemployment is zero

13. Which has helped decrease the natural rate of unemployment in the United States since 1980?
(a) a smaller proportion of young workers in the labor force
(b) the increased size of benefits for the unemployed
(c) less competition in product and labor markets
(d) more workers covered by unemployment programs

14. Okun's law predicts that when the actual unemployment rate exceeds the natural rate of unemployment by two percentage points, there will be a negative GDP gap of about
(a) 2% of the potential GDP
(b) 3% of the potential GDP
(c) 4% of the potential GDP
(d) 5% of the potential GDP

15. If the negative GDP gap were equal to 6% of the potential GDP, the actual unemployment rate would exceed the natural rate of unemployment by
(a) two percentage points
(b) three percentage points
(c) four percentage points
(d) five percentage points

16. The burden of unemployment is *least* felt by
(a) white-collar workers
(b) African-Americans
(c) teenagers
(d) males

17. If the Consumer Price Index was 110 in one year and 117 in the next year, the rate of inflation from one year to the next was
(a) 3.5%
(b) 4.7%
(c) 6.4%
(d) 7.1%

18. The price of a good has doubled in about 14 years. The approximate annual percentage rate of increase in the price level over this period has been
(a) 2%
(b) 3%
(c) 4%
(d) 5%

19. Only two resources, capital and labor, are used in an economy to produce an output of 300 million units. If the total cost of capital resources is $150 million and the total cost of labor resources is $50 million, the per-unit production costs in this economy are
(a) $0.67 million
(b) $1.50 million
(c) $2.00 million
(d) $3.00 million

20. If a person's nominal income increases by 8% while the price level increases by 10%, the person's real income
(a) increases by 2%
(b) increases by 18%
(c) decreases by 18%
(d) decreases by 2%

21. If the average level of nominal income in a nation is $21,000 and the price level index is 154, the average real income is about
(a) $12,546
(b) $13,636
(c) $15,299
(d) $17,823

22. Who would be hurt by *unanticipated* inflation?
(a) those living on incomes with cost-of-living adjustments
(b) those who find prices rising less rapidly than their nominal incomes
(c) those who lent money at a fixed interest rate
(d) those who became debtors when prices were lower

23. With no inflation, a bank would be willing to lend a business firm $10 million at an annual interest rate of 8%. But if the rate of inflation was anticipated to be 6%, the bank would charge the firm an annual interest rate of
(a) 2%
(b) 6%
(c) 8%
(d) 14%

24. Which contributes to cost-push inflation?
(a) an increase in employment and output
(b) an increase in per-unit production costs
(c) a decrease in resource prices
(d) an increase in unemployment

25. If an economy has experienced an inflation rate of over 1000% per year for several years, this economic condition would best be described as
(a) a cost-of-living adjustment
(b) cost-push inflation
(c) hyperinflation
(d) GDP gap

■ **PROBLEMS**

1. Given the hypothetical data in the following table, calculate the annual rates of growth in real GDP and real per capita GDP over the period given. The numbers for real GDP are in billions.

Year	Real GDP	Annual growth in %	Real GDP per capita	Annual growth in %
1	$2416		$11,785	
2	2472	_____	11,950	_____
3	2563	_____	12,213	_____
4	2632	_____	12,421	_____
5	2724	_____	12,719	_____
6	2850	_____	12,948	_____

2. Suppose the real GDP and the population of an economy in 7 different years were those shown in the following table.

Year	Population, millions	Real GDP, billions of dollars	Per capita real GDP
1	30	$ 9	$300
2	60	24	_____
3	90	45	_____
4	120	66	_____
5	150	90	_____
6	180	99	_____
7	210	105	_____

a. How large would the real per capita GDP of the economy be in each of the other 6 years? Put your figures in the table.

b. What would have been the size of the optimum population of this economy? _____

c. What was the *amount* of growth in real GDP between year 1 and year 2? $ _____

d. What was the rate of growth in real GDP between year 3 and year 4? _____ %

3. The following table gives statistics on the labor force and total employment during year 1 and year 5. Make the computations necessary to complete the table. (Numbers of persons are in thousands.)

	Year 1	Year 5
Labor force	84,889	95,453
Employed	80,796	87,524
Unemployed	_____	_____
Unemployment rate	_____	_____

a. How is it possible that *both* employment and unemployment increased? _____

_____

b. In relative terms, if unemployment increases, employment will decrease. Why? _____

_____

c. Would you say that year 5 was a year of full employment?

_____

d. Why is the task of maintaining full employment over the years more than just a problem of finding jobs for those who happen to be unemployed at any given time? _____

_____

4. Suppose that in year 1 an economy is at full employment, has a potential and actual real GDP of $3000 billion, and has an unemployment rate of 5.5%.

a. Compute the GDP gap in year 1 and enter it in the table below.

Year	Actual GDP	Potential GDP	GDP gap
1	$3000.0	$3000	$_____
2	3724.0	3800	_____
3	3712.5	4125	_____

b. The actual and potential real GDPs in years 2 and 3 are also shown in the table. Compute and enter into the table the GDP gaps in those 2 years.

c. In year 2, the actual real GDP is _____% of the potential real GDP. (Hint: Divide the actual real GDP by the potential real GDP and multiply by 100.)

(1) The actual real GDP is _____% less than the potential real GDP.

(2) Using Okun's law, the unemployment rate will rise from 5.5% in year 1 and be _____% in year 2.

d. In year 3 the actual real GDP is _____% of the potential real GDP.

(1) The actual real GDP is _____% less than the potential real GDP.

(2) The unemployment rate, according to Okun's law, will be _____%.

5. The following table shows the price index in the economy at the end of four different years.

Year	Price index	Rate of inflation
1	100.00	
2	112.00	_____%
3	123.20	_____
4	129.36	_____

a. Compute and enter in the table the rates of inflation in years 2, 3, and 4.

b. Employing the rule of 70, how many years would it take for the price level to double at each of these three inflation rates? _____

c. If nominal income increased by 15% from year 1 to year 2, what was the approximate percentage change in real income? _____

d. If nominal income increased by 7% from year 2 to year 3, what was the approximate percentage change in real income? _____

e. If nominal income was $25,000 in year 2, what was real income that year? _____

f. If nominal income was $25,000 in year 3, what was real income that year? _____

g. If the nominal interest rate was 14% to borrow money from year 1 to year 2, what was the approximate real rate of interest over that period?_____

h. If the nominal interest rate was 8% to borrow money from year 3 to year 4, what was the approximate real rate of interest over that period? _____

6. Indicate in the space below each of the following the most likely effect—beneficial **(B)**, detrimental **(D)**, or indeterminate **(I)**—of unanticipated inflation on these persons:

a. A retired business executive who now lives each month by spending a part of the amount that was saved and deposited in a fixed-rate savings account for a long term. _____

b. A retired private-school teacher who lives on the dividends received from shares of stock owned. _____

c. A farmer who borrowed $500,000 from a bank at a fixed rate; the loan must be repaid in the next 10 years. _____

d. A retired couple whose sole source of income is the pension they receive from a former employer. _____

e. A widow whose income consists entirely of interest received from the corporate bonds she owns. _____

f. A public school teacher. _____

g. A member of a union who works for a firm that produces computers. _____

■ **SHORT ANSWER AND ESSAY QUESTIONS**

1. What two ways are used to measure economic growth? Why should the citizens of the United States be concerned with economic growth?

2. What is the relationship between real GDP produced in a year and the quantity of resource inputs and the productivity of those inputs?

3. Describe the growth record of the U.S. economy over the last half-century and in the last decade. Compare recent U.S. growth rates with those in other nations.

4. Define the business cycle. Why do some economists prefer the term "business fluctuations" to "business cycle"? Describe the four phases of a business cycle.

5. In the opinion of most economists, what is the immediate determinant or cause of fluctuations in the levels of output and employment in the economy?

6. Compare the manner in which the business cycle affects output and employment in the industries producing capital and durable goods with the way it affects industries producing nondurable goods and services. What causes these differences?

7. How is the unemployment rate measured in the United States? What criticisms have been made of the method the Bureau of Labor Statistics uses to determine the unemployment rate?

8. Distinguish among frictional, structural, and cyclical unemployment.

9. When is there full employment in the U.S. economy? (Answer in terms of the unemployment rate, the actual and potential output of the economy, and the markets for labor.)

10. What is the natural rate of unemployment? Will the economy always operate at the natural rate? Why is the natural rate subject to revision?

11. What is the economic cost of unemployment, and how is this cost measured? What is the quantitative relationship (called Okun's law) between the unemployment rate and the cost of unemployment?

12. What groups in the economy tend to bear the burdens of unemployment? How are women affected by unemployment, and how is the percentage of the labor force unemployed 15 or more weeks related to the unemployment rate in the economy?

13. How does the unemployment rate in the United States compare with the rates for other industrialized nations in recent years?

14. What is inflation, and how is the rate of inflation measured?

15. What has been the experience of the United States with inflation since the 1920s? How does the inflation rate in the United States compare with those of other industrialized nations in recent years?

16. Compare and contrast demand-pull and cost-push types of inflation.

17. What groups benefit from and what groups are hurt by inflation?

18. What is the difference between the effects of unanticipated inflation and the effects of anticipated inflation on the redistribution of real incomes in the economy?

19. What are the effects of cost-push and demand-pull inflation on real output? Are economists in agreement about these effects? Discuss.

20. Explain how the type and severity of inflation influence domestic output.

ANSWERS

Chapter 7 Introduction to Economic Growth and Instability

FILL-IN QUESTIONS

1. real, real
2. increases, decreases
3. $180, $108, $72

4. resources, productivity
5. sixfold, threefold, better, more
6. increases, decreases, recession, trough, expansion
7. durables, capital, nondurable
8. unemployed, labor force, multiplying
9. frictional, structural, cyclical
10. natural, frictional and structural, cyclical, equal to, equal to
11. minus, 2
12. black, teenage, blue-collar, lower
13. an increase, prices, divide, multiply
14. divide, the rule of 70
15. an increase, production, difficult
16. real, real, 3, real, $56,604
17. fixed, savers, creditors
18. anticipated, cost-of-living
19. real, nominal, 3
20. increases, less, increases, decreases, hyperinflation

TRUE–FALSE QUESTIONS

1. T, p.125	10. F, p. 130	19. F, p. 135
2. T, pp.125–126	11. T, pp. 130–131	20. T, p. 136
3. T, p. 126	12. T, pp. 130–131	21. T, p. 136
4. F, p. 126	13. F, p. 131	22. T, pp. 137–138
5. F, p. 126	14. T, p. 131	23. F, p. 139
6. F, p. 127	15. T, p. 131	24. F, p. 139
7. F, pp. 127–128	16. F, p. 133	25. T, p. 141
8. F, p. 129	17. F, p. 134	
9. T, p. 130	18. F, pp. 134–135	

MULTIPLE-CHOICE QUESTIONS

1. d, p. 125	10. a, p. 130	19. a, p. 136
2. b, p. 125	11. c, p. 130	20. d, pp. 137–138
3. b, p. 127	12. c, pp. 130–131	21. b, p. 138
4. b, p. 128	13. a, p. 131	22. c, pp. 138–139
5. a, p. 128	14. c, p. 131	23. d, p. 139–140
6. c, p. 129	15. b, p. 131	24. b, p. 140
7. d, p. 129	16. a, p. 132	25. c, p. 141
8. b, pp. 129–130	17. c, p. 135	
9. b, p. 130	18. d, p. 135	

PROBLEMS

1. *real GDP*: years 1–2 (2.3%); years 2–3 (3.7%); years 3–4 (2.7%); years 4–5 (3.5%); years 5–6 (4.6%); *real GDP per capita*: years 1–2 (1.4%); years 2–3 (2.2%); years 3–4 (1.7%); years 4–5 (2.4%); years 5–6 (1.8%)

2. *a.* 400, 500, 550, 600, 550, 500; *b.* 150 million; *c.* $15 billion; *d.* 46.7%

3. year 1: 4093, 4.8; year 5: 7929, 8.3; *a.* the labor force increased more than employment increased; *b.* because unemployment and employment in relative terms are percentages of the labor force and *always* add to 100%, and if one increases, the other must decrease; *c.* no economist would argue that the full-employment unemployment rate is as high as 8.3%, and year 5 was not a year of full employment; *d.* the number of people looking for work expands

4. *a.* 0; *b.* 76, 412.5; *c.* 98, (1) 2, (2) 6.5; *d.* 90, (1) 10, (2) 10.5

5. *a.* 12, 10, 5; *b.* 5.8, 7, 14; *c.* 3; *d.* –3; *e.* $22,321; *f.* $20,292; *g.* 2; *h.* 3

6. *a.* D; *b.* I; *c.* B; *d.* D; *e.* D; *f.* I; *g.* I

SHORT ANSWER AND ESSAY QUESTIONS

1. p. 125	8. p. 130	15. p. 135
2. p. 125	9. pp. 130–131	16. p. 136
3. p. 126	10. p. 131	17. p. 137
4. p. 127	11. p. 131	18. p. 139
5. p. 128	12. p. 133	19. pp. 140–141
6. p. 128	13. p. 134	20. p. 141
7. p. 129	14. p. 134	

Basic Macroeconomic Relationships

This chapter introduces you to three basic relationships in the economy: income and consumption, the interest rate and investment, and changes in spending and changes in output. The relationships between these economic "aggregates" are essential building blocks for understanding the macro models that will be presented in the next two chapters.

The first section of Chapter 8 describes the relationship involving the largest aggregate in the economy—**consumption.** An explanation of consumption, however, also entails a study of saving because saving is simply the part of disposable income that is not consumed. This section develops the consumption and saving schedules and describes their main characteristics. Other key concepts are also presented: average propensities to consume (APC) and save (APS), marginal propensities to consume (MPC) and save (MPS), and the nonincome determinants of consumption and saving.

Investment is the subject of the next section of the chapter. The purchase of capital goods depends on the rate of return that business firms expect to earn from an investment and on the real rate of interest they have to pay for the use of money. Because firms want to make profitable investments and avoid unprofitable ones, they undertake all investments that have an expected rate of return greater than (or equal to) the real rate of interest and do not undertake an investment when the expected rate of return is less than the real interest rate. This relationship between the real interest rate and the level of investment spending is an inverse one: the lower the interest rate, the greater the investment spending. It is illustrated by a downsloping **investment demand curve.** As you will learn, this curve can be shifted by five factors that can change the expected rate of return on investment. You will also learn that investment, unlike consumption, is quite volatile and is the most unstable component of total spending in the economy.

The third section of the chapter introduces you to the concept of the **multiplier.** It shows how an initial change in spending for consumption or investment changes real GDP by an amount that is larger than the initial stimulus. You will also learn about the rationale for the multiplier and find out how to interpret it. The multiplier can be derived from the marginal propensity to consume and the marginal propensity to save. You will have learned about these marginal propensities at the beginning of the chapter, and now they are put to use as you end the chapter.

■ **CHECKLIST**

When you have studied this chapter you should be able to

☐ Explain how consumption and saving are related to disposable income.
☐ Draw a graph to illustrate the relationship among consumption, saving, and disposable income.
☐ Construct a hypothetical consumption schedule.
☐ Construct a hypothetical saving schedule and identify the level of break-even income.
☐ Compute the four propensities (APC, APS, MPC, and MPS) when given the necessary data.
☐ State the relationship between the APC and the APS as income increases.
☐ Demonstrate that the MPC is the slope of the consumption schedule and the MPS is the slope of the saving schedule.
☐ Explain each of the four nonincome determinants of consumption and saving.
☐ Use a graph with real GDP on the horizontal axis to show shifts in consumption and saving schedules.
☐ Explain the difference between a change in the amount consumed (or saved) and a change in the consumption (or saving) schedule.
☐ Describe how a change in taxes shifts consumption and saving schedules.
☐ Explain how the expected rate of return affects investment decisions.
☐ Describe the influence of the real interest rate on an investment decision.
☐ Draw a graph of an investment demand curve for the business sector and explain what it shows.
☐ Explain how each of the five noninterest determinants of investment will shift the investment demand curve.
☐ Give four reasons why investment spending tends to be unstable.
☐ Define the multiplier effect in words, with a ratio, and using an equation.
☐ Make three clarifying points about the multiplier.
☐ Cite two facts on which the rationale for the multiplier is based.
☐ Discuss the relationship between the multiplier and the marginal propensities.
☐ Find the value of the multiplier when you are given the necessary information.
☐ Explain the significance of the multiplier.

☐ Discuss the reasons for the difference between the textbook example for the multiplier and the actual multiplier for the U.S. economy.

☐ Give a humorous example of the multiplier effect (Last Word).

■ CHAPTER OUTLINE

1. There is a positive or direct relationship between consumption and disposable income (after-tax income) because as disposable income increases, so does consumption. Saving is disposable income that is not spent for consumer goods. Disposable income is the most important determinant of both consumption and saving. The relationship among disposable income, consumption, and saving can be shown in a graph with consumption on the vertical axis and disposable income on the horizontal axis. The **45-degree line** on the graph would show where consumption would equal disposable income. If consumption is less than disposable income, the difference is saving.

   a. The **consumption schedule** shows the amounts that households plan to spend for consumer goods at various levels of income, given a price level.

   b. The **saving schedule** indicates the amounts households plan to save at different income levels, given a price level.

   c. The average propensity to consume (APC) and the average propensity to save (APS) and the marginal propensity to consume (MPC) and the marginal propensity to save (MPS) can be computed from the consumption and saving schedules.

   (1) The **average propensity to consume (APC)** and the **average propensity to save (APS)** are, respectively, the percentages of income spent for consumption and saved, and they sum to 1.

   (2) The **marginal propensity to consume (MPC)** and the **marginal propensity to save (MPS)** are, respectively, the percentages of additional income spent for consumption and saved, and they sum to 1.

   (3) The MPC is the slope of the consumption schedule and the MPS is the slope of the saving schedule when the two schedules are graphed.

   d. In addition to income, there are several important nonincome determinants of consumption and saving. Changes in *these nonincome determinants* will cause the consumption and saving schedules to change. An increase in spending will shift the consumption schedule upward, and a decrease in spending will shift it downward. Similarly, an increase in saving will shift the saving schedule upward, and a decrease in saving will shift if downward.

   (1) The amount of wealth affects the amount that households spend and save. If household wealth increases, people will spend more because they think they are wealthier (the **wealth effect**), and they will save less.

   (2) *Expectations* about the future affect spending and saving decisions. If prices are expected to rise in the future, people will spend more today and save less.

   (3) *Real interest rates* change spending and saving decisions. When real interest rates fall, households tend to consume more, borrow more, and save less.

   (4) The level of *household debt* influences consumption. Increasing debt will increase consumption, but if the debt level gets too high, it will decrease consumption, because households have to spend money to pay off loans.

   e. Several other considerations need to be noted:

   (1) Macroeconomists are more concerned with the effects of changes in consumption and saving on *real GDP*, and so it replaces disposable income on the horizontal axis of the consumption and saving schedules.

   (2) A change in the amount consumed (or saved) is a movement along the consumption (or saving) schedule, but a change in the consumption (or saving) that is due to a change in one of the nonincome determinants is a shift in the entire consumption (or saving) schedule.

   (3) Changes in wealth, expectations, and household debt shift consumption and saving schedules in opposite directions. An increase in one of these factors will decrease consumption and saving; a decrease in one of these factors will increase consumption and saving.

   (4) Changes in taxes shift the consumption and saving schedules in the same direction. An increase in taxes will reduce both consumption and saving; a decrease in taxes will increase both consumption and saving.

   (5) Both consumption and saving schedules tend to be stable over time unless they are changed by major tax increases or decreases. The stability arises from long-term planning and because some nonincome determinants cause shifts that offset each other.

2. The investment decision is a marginal-benefit and marginal-cost decision that depends on the expected rate of return (r) from the purchase of additional capital goods and the real rate of interest (i) that must be paid for borrowed funds.

   a. The **expected rate of return** is directly related to the net profits (revenues less operating costs) that are expected to result from an investment. It is the marginal benefit of investment for a business.

   b. The *real rate of interest* is the price paid for the use of money. It is the marginal cost of investment for a business. When the expected real rate of return is greater (less) than the real rate of interest, a business will (will not) invest because the investment will be profitable (unprofitable).

   c. For this reason, the lower (higher) the real rate of interest is, the greater (smaller) will be the level of investment spending in the economy; the **investment demand curve** shows this inverse relationship between the real rate of interest and the level of spending for capital goods. The amount of investment by the business sector is determined by the point where the marginal benefit of investment (r) equals the marginal cost (i).

   d. There are at least five noninterest determinants of investment demand, and a change in any of these determinants will shift the investment demand curve.

   (1) If the *acquisition, maintenance, and operating costs* for capital goods change, this change in costs will change investment demand. Rising costs decrease investment demand, and declining costs increase it.

   (2) Changes in *business taxes* are like a change in costs, and so they have an effect on investment demand similar to that of the previous item.

(3) *An increase in technological progress* will stimulate investment and increase investment demand.

(4) *The stock of existing capital goods* will influence investment decisions. If the economy is overstocked, there will be a decrease in investment demand, and if the economy is understocked, there will be an increase in investment demand.

(5) *Expectations* of the future are important. If expectations are positive because of more expected sales or profits, there is likely to be an increase in investment demand. Negative expectations will have the opposite effect on investment demand.

e. Unlike consumption and saving, investment is inherently unstable. Four factors explain this instability.

(1) *Capital goods are durable*, and so when they get replaced may depend on the optimism or pessimism of business owners. If owners are more optimistic about the future, they probably will spend more to obtain new capital goods.

(2) *Innovation is not regular,* which means that technological progress is highly variable and contributes to instability in investment spending decisions.

(3) *Profit expectations* influence the investment spending of businesses, but profits are highly variable.

(4) *Other expectations* concerning such factors as exchange rates, the state of the economy, and the stock market can create positive or negative expectations that change investment spending.

3. There is a direct relationship between changes in spending and changes in real GDP. The initial change in spending, however, results in an increase in real GDP that is greater than the initial change in spending. This outcome is called the *multiplier effect*. The **multiplier** is the ratio of the change in the real GDP to the initial change in spending. The initial change in spending typically comes from investment spending, but changes in consumption, net exports, or government spending can also have multiplier effects.

a. The multiplier effect occurs because a change in the dollars spent by one person alters the income of another person in the same direction, and because any change in the income of one person will change that person's consumption and saving in the same direction by a fraction of the change in income. For example, assuming a marginal propensity to consume (MPC) of .75, a change in investment spending of $5.00 will cause a change in consumption of $3.75. The change in consumption ($3.75) will become someone else's income in the second round. The process will continue through successive rounds, but the amount of income in each round will diminish by 25 percent because that is the amount saved from each change in income. After all the rounds are completed, the initial change of $5 in investment spending produces a total of $20 change because the multiplier was 4 (see Table 8.3 in the text).

b. There is a formula for calculating the multiplier. The multiplier is directly related to the marginal propensity to consume (MPC) and inversely related to the marginal propensity to save (MPS). The multiplier is equal to [1/(1 − MPC)]. It is also equal to [1/MPS]. The significance of the multiplier is that relatively small changes in the spending plans of business firms or households bring about large changes in the equilibrium real GDP.

c. The simple multiplier that has been described here differs from the actual multiplier for the economy. In the simple case, the only factor that reduced income in successive rounds was the fraction that went to savings. For the domestic economy, there are other leakages from consumption besides saving, such as spending on imports and payment of taxes. These factors reduce the value of the multiplier. For the U.S. economy the multiplier is estimated to be about 2.

4. (Last Word). Art Buchwald wrote a humorous story about the multiplier that illustrates the spiral effect on consumer spending from a reduction in income. A car salesman reserved a new car for a regular customer, but the customer can't buy the car because he is getting a divorce. The car salesman then tells his painter he can't afford to have his house painted. The house painter then decides to return a new television he bought from the store. And so the story continues from one person to another.

■ HINTS AND TIPS

1. An important graph in the chapter is the **consumption schedule** (see Key Graph 8.2). Know how to interpret it. There are two lines on the graph. The 45-degree reference line shows all points where disposable income equals consumption (there is no saving). The consumption schedule line shows the total amount of disposable income spent on consumption at each and every income level. Where the two lines *intersect*, all disposable income is spent (consumed). At all income levels to the right of the intersection, the consumption line lies below the 45-degree line, and not all disposable income is spent (there is saving). To the left of the intersection, the consumption line lies above the 45-degree line, and consumption exceeds disposable income (there is dissaving).

2. Always remember that **marginal propensities** sum to 1 (MPC + MPS = 1). The same is true for average propensities (APC + APS = 1). Thus, if you know the value of one marginal propensity (e.g., MPC), you can always figure out the other (e.g., 1 − MPC = MPS).

3. The **multiplier** effect is a key concept in this chapter and in the ones that follow, so make sure you understand how it works.

a. The multiplier is simply the ratio of the change in real GDP to the *initial* changes in spending. Multiplying the *initial* change in spending by the *multiplier* gives you the amount of change in real GDP.

b. The multiplier effect works in both positive and negative directions. An *initial* decrease in spending will result in a larger decrease in real GDP, and an *initial* increase in spending will create a larger increase in real GDP.

c. The multiplier is directly related to the marginal propensities. The multiplier equals 1/MPS. The multiplier also equals 1/(1 − MPC).

d. The main reason for the multiplier effect is that the *initial* change in income (spending) induces additional rounds of income (spending) that add progressively less in each round as some of the income (spending) gets saved because of the marginal propensity to save (see Table 8.3 in the text).

■ **IMPORTANT TERMS**

45-degree line

consumption schedule

saving schedule

break-even income

average propensity to consume (APC)

average propensity to save (APS)

marginal propensity to consume (MPC)

marginal propensity to save (MPS)

wealth effect

expected rate of return

investment demand curve

multiplier

SELF-TEST

■ **FILL-IN QUESTIONS**

1. The consumption schedule shows the various amounts that households plan to (save, consume) _____ at various levels of disposable income, and the saving schedule shows the various amounts that households plan to _____.

2. Both consumption and saving are (directly, indirectly) _____ related to the level of disposable income. At lower levels of disposable income, households tend to spend a (smaller, larger) _____ proportion of this income and save a _____ proportion, but at higher levels of disposable income, they tend to spend a (smaller, larger) _____ proportion of this income and save a _____ proportion. At the break-even income, consumption is (greater than, less than, equal to) _____ disposable income.

3. As disposable income falls, the average propensity to consume (APC) will (rise, fall) _____ and the average propensity to save (APS) will _____.

4. The sum of APC and APS is equal to (0, 1) _____. If the APC is .90, then the APS is (.10, 1) _____.

5. The marginal propensity to consume (MPC) is the change in (consumption, income) _____ divided by the change in _____.

6. The marginal propensity to save (MPS) is the change in (saving, income) _____ divided by the change in _____.

7. The sum of MPC and MPS is equal to (0, 1) _____. If the MPC is .75, then the MPS is (0, .25) _____.

8. The MPC is the numerical value of the slope of the (consumption, saving) _____ schedule, and the MPS is the numerical value of the slope of the _____ schedule.

9. The most important determinants of consumption spending, other than the level of income, are

a. _____

b. _____

c. _____

d. _____

10. An increase the consumption schedule means that the consumption schedule shifts (upward, downward) _____ and a decrease in the consumption schedule means that it will shift _____, and these shifts occur because of a change in one of the nonincome determinants. An increase in the amount consumed occurs because of an increase in (income, stability) _____.

11. The investment spending decision depends on the expected rate of (interest, return) _____ and the real rate of _____.

12. The expected rate of return is the marginal (cost, benefit) _____ of investment, and the real rate of return is the marginal _____ of investment.

13. If the expected rate of return on an investment is greater than the real rate of interest for the use of money, a business firm will (increase, decrease) _____ its investment spending, but if the expected rate of return is less than the real rate of interest, the firm will _____ its investment spending.

14. The relationship between the real rate of interest and the total amount of investment in the economy is (direct, inverse) _____ and is shown in the investment (supply, demand) _____ curve. This curve shows that if the real rate of interest rises, the quantity of investment will (increase, decrease) _____, but if the real rate of interest falls, the quantity of investment will _____.

15. Five noninterest determinants of investment demand are

a. _____

b. _____

c. _____

d. _____

e. _____

16. The demand for new capital goods tends to be unstable because of the (durability, nondurability) _____ of capital goods, the (regularity, irregularity) _____ of innovation, the (stability, variability) _____ of current and expected profits, and the _____ of expectations.

17. The multiplier is the change in real GDP (multiplied, divided) _____ by an initial change in spending. When the initial change in spending is _____ by the multiplier, the result equals the change in real GDP.

18. The multiplier means that an increase in initial spending may create a multiple (increase, decrease) _____ in real GDP, and also that a decrease in initial spending may create a multiple _____ in real GDP.

19. The multiplier has a value equal to 1 divided by the marginal propensity to (consume, save) _____, which is the same thing as 1 divided by the quantity of 1 minus the marginal propensity to _____.

20. The higher the value of the marginal propensity to consume, the (larger, smaller) _____ the value of the multiplier, but the larger the value of the marginal propensity to save, the _____ the value of the multiplier.

■ **TRUE–FALSE QUESTIONS**

Circle T if the statement is true, F if it is false.

1. Consumption equals disposable income plus saving. **T F**

2. The most significant determinant of the level of consumer spending is disposable income. **T F**

3. Historical data suggest that the level of consumption expenditures is directly related to the level of disposable income. **T F**

4. Consumption rises and saving falls when disposable income increases. **T F**

5. Empirical data suggest that households spend a larger proportion of a small disposable income than of a large disposable income. **T F**

6. The break-even income is the income level at which business begins to make a profit. **T F**

7. The average propensity to save is equal to the level of saving divided by the level of consumption. **T F**

8. The marginal propensity to consume is the change in consumption divided by the change in income. **T F**

9. The slope of the saving schedule is equal to the average propensity to save. **T F**

10. An increase in wealth will increase the consumption schedule (shift the consumption curve upward). **T F**

11. An increase in the taxes paid by consumers will decrease both the amount they spend for consumption and the amount they save. **T F**

12. Both the consumption schedule and the saving schedule tend to be relatively stable over time. **T F**

13. The real interest rate is the nominal interest rate minus the rate of inflation. **T F**

14. A business firm will purchase additional capital goods if the real rate of interest it must pay exceeds the expected rate of return from the investment. **T F**

15. An increase in the stock of capital goods on hand will decrease the investment-demand curve. **T F**

16. The relationship between the rate of interest and the level of investment spending is called the interest schedule. **T F**

17. Investment tends to be relatively stable over time. **T F**

18. The irregularity of innovations and the variability of business profits contribute to the instability of investment expenditures. **T F**

19. The multiplier is equal to the change in real GDP multiplied by the initial change in spending. **T F**

20. The initial change in spending for the multiplier is usually associated with investment spending because of investment's volatility. **T F**

21. The multiplier effect works only in a positive direction in changing GDP. **T F**

22. The multiplier is based on the idea that any change in income will cause both consumption and saving to vary in the same direction as a change in income and by a fraction of that change in income. **T F**

23. The higher the marginal propensity to consume, the larger the size of the multiplier. **T F**

24. When it is computed as 1/MPS, the multiplier reflects only the leakage of income into saving. **T F**

25. The value of the actual multiplier for the economy will usually be greater than the value of a textbook multiplier because the actual multiplier is based only on the marginal propensity to save. **T F**

MULTIPLE-CHOICE QUESTIONS

Circle the letter that corresponds to the best answer.

1. Saving equals
  (a) investment plus consumption
  (b) investment minus consumption
  (c) disposable income minus consumption
  (d) disposable income plus consumption

2. As disposable income decreases, *ceteris paribus*,
 (a) both consumption and saving increase
 (b) consumption increases and saving decreases
 (c) consumption decreases and saving increases
 (d) both consumption and saving decrease

3. Households tend to spend a larger portion of
 (a) a small disposable income than a large disposable income
 (b) a large disposable income than a small disposable income
 (c) their disposable income on saving when the rate of return is high
 (d) their saving than their disposable income when the rate of return is low

4. If consumption spending increases from $358 to $367 billion when disposable income increases from $412 to $427 billion, it can be concluded that the marginal propensity to consume is
 (a) 0.4
 (b) 0.6
 (c) 0.8
 (d) 0.9

5. If disposable income is $375 billion when the average propensity to consume is 0.8, it can be concluded that
 (a) the marginal propensity to consume is also 0.8
 (b) the marginal propensity to save is 0.2
 (c) consumption is $325 billion
 (d) saving is $75 billion

6. As the disposable income of the economy increases,
 (a) both the APC and the APS rise
 (b) the APC rises and the APS falls
 (c) the APC falls and the APS rises
 (d) both the APC and the APS fall

7. The slope of the consumption schedule or line for a given economy is the
 (a) marginal propensity to consume
 (b) average propensity to consume
 (c) marginal propensity to save
 (d) average propensity to save

Answer Questions 8 and 9 on the basis of the following graph.

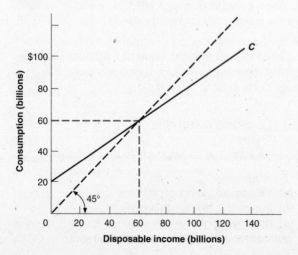

8. This graph indicates that
 (a) consumption decreases after the $60 billion level of disposable income
 (b) the marginal propensity to consume decreases after the $60 billion level of disposable income
 (c) consumption decreases as a percentage of disposable income as disposable income increases
 (d) consumption increases as disposable income decreases

9. If the relevant saving schedule were constructed, one would find that
 (a) the marginal propensity to save is negative up to the $60 billion level of disposable income
 (b) the marginal propensity to save increases after the $60 billion level of disposable income
 (c) saving is zero at the $60 billion level of disposable income
 (d) saving is $20 billion at the $0 level of disposable income

*Answer Questions 10, 11, and 12 on the basis of the following disposable income (**DI**) and consumption (**C**) schedules for a private, closed economy. All figures are in billions of dollars.*

DI	C
$ 0	$ 4
40	40
80	76
120	112
160	148
200	184

10. If plotted on a graph, the slope of the consumption schedule would be
 (a) 0.6
 (b) 0.7
 (c) 0.8
 (d) 0.9

11. At the $160 billion level of disposable income, the average propensity to save is
 (a) 0.015
 (b) 0.075
 (c) 0.335
 (d) 0.925

12. If consumption increases by $5 billion at each level of disposable income, then the marginal propensity to consume will
 (a) change, but the average propensity to consume will not change
 (b) change, and the average propensity to consume will change
 (c) not change, but the average propensity to consume will change
 (d) not change, and the average propensity to consume will not change

13. If the slope of a linear saving schedule decreases, then it can be concluded that the
(a) MPS has decreased
(b) MPC has decreased
(c) income has decreased
(d) income has increased

14. An increase in wealth shifts the consumption schedule
(a) downward and the saving schedule upward
(b) upward and the saving schedule downward
(c) downward and the saving schedule downward
(d) upward and the saving schedule upward

15. Expectations of a recession are likely to lead households to
(a) increase consumption and saving
(b) decrease consumption and saving
(c) decrease consumption and increase saving
(d) increase consumption and decrease saving

16. Higher real interest rates are likely to
(a) increase consumption and saving
(b) decrease consumption and saving
(c) decrease consumption and increase saving
(d) increase consumption and decrease saving

17. An increase in taxes shifts the consumption schedule
(a) downward and the saving schedule upward
(b) upward and the saving schedule downward
(c) downward and the saving schedule downward
(d) upward and the saving schedule upward

18. Which relationship is an inverse one?
(a) consumption and disposable income
(b) investment spending and the rate of interest
(c) saving and disposable income
(d) investment spending and GDP

19. A decrease in investment demand would be a consequence of a decline in
(a) the rate of interest
(b) the level of wages paid
(c) business taxes
(d) expected future sales

20. Which would increase investment demand?
(a) an increase in business taxes
(b) an increase in the cost of acquiring capital goods
(c) a decrease in the rate of technological change
(d) a decrease in the stock of capital goods on hand

21. Which best explains the variability of investment?
(a) the predictable useful life of capital goods
(b) constancy or regularities in business innovations
(c) instabilities in the level of profits
(d) business pessimism about the future

22. If there was a change in investment spending of $10 and the marginal propensity to save was .25, then real GDP would increase by
(a) $10
(b) $20
(c) $25
(d) $40

23. If the value of the marginal propensity to consume is 0.6 and real GDP falls by $25, this was caused by a decrease in initial spending of
(a) $10.00
(b) $15.00
(c) $16.67
(d) $20.00

24. If the marginal propensity to consume is 0.67 and initial spending increases by $25, real GDP will
(a) increase by $75
(b) decrease by $75
(c) increase by $25
(d) decrease by $25

25. If in an economy a $150 billion increase in investment spending creates $150 billion of new income in the first round of the multiplier process and $105 billion in the second round, the multiplier and the marginal propensity to consume will be, respectively,
(a) 5.00 and 0.80
(b) 4.00 and 0.75
(c) 3.33 and 0.70
(d) 2.50 and 0.40

PROBLEMS

1. The following table is a consumption schedule. Assume that taxes and transfer payments are zero and that all saving is personal saving.

(GDP = DI)	C	S	APC	APS
1500	$1540	$_____	1.027	−.027
1600	1620	_____	1.013	−.013
1700	1700	_____	_____	_____
1800	1780	_____	.989	.011
1900	1860	_____	.979	.021
2000	1940	_____	_____	_____
2100	2020	_____	.962	.038
2200	2100	_____	_____	_____

a. Compute saving at each of the eight levels of disposable income and the missing average propensities to consume and to save.
b. The break-even level of disposable income is

$ _____ .

c. As disposable income rises, the marginal propensity to consume remains constant. Between each two GDPs the MPC can be found by dividing $ _____

by $ _____ and is equal to _____ .
d. The marginal propensity to save also remains constant when the GDP rises. Between each two GDPs

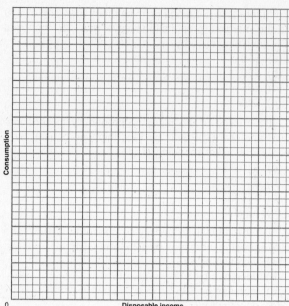

Consumption

0   Disposable income

the MPS is equal to $_____ divided by $_____,

or to _____.

e. Plot the consumption schedule, the saving schedule, and the 45-degree line on the graph above.

(1) The numerical value of the slope of the consumption schedule is _____, and the term that is used to describe it is the _____.

(2) If the relevant saving schedule were constructed, the numerical value of the slope of the saving schedule would be _____, and the term that is used to describe it would be the _____.

2. Indicate in the space to the right of each of the following events whether the event will tend to increase (+) or decrease (−) the saving schedule.

a. Development of consumer expectations that prices will be higher in the future   _____

b. Gradual shrinkage in the quantity of real assets owned by consumers   _____

c. Increase in the volume of consumer indebtedness   _____

d. Growing belief that disposable income will be lower in the future   _____

e. Expectations that there will be a current shortage of consumer goods   _____

f. Rise in the actual level of disposable income   _____

g. An increase in the financial assets owned by consumers   _____

h. Development of a belief by consumers that the Federal government can and will prevent recessions in the future   _____

3. The following schedule has eight different expected rates of return and the dollar amounts of the investment projects expected to have each of those return rates.

Expected rate of return	Investment projects (billions)
18%	$ 0
16	10
14	20
12	30
10	40
8	50
6	60
4	70

a. If the real rate of interest in the economy were 18%, business firms would plan to spend $_____ billion for investment, but if the real interest rate were 16%, they would plan to spend $_____ for investment.

b. Should the real interest rate be 14%, and they would still wish to make the investments they were willing to make at real interest rates of 18% and 16%, they would plan to spend an additional $_____ billion for investment, and their total investment would be $_____ billion.

c. If the real rate of interest were 12%, they would make all the investments they had planned to make at higher real interest rates plus an additional $_____ billion, and their total investment spending would be $_____ billion.

d. Complete the following table by computing the amount of planned investment at the four remaining real interest rates.

Real rate of interest	Amount of investment (billions)
18%	$ 0
16	10
14	20
12	60
10	_____
8	_____
6	_____
4	_____

e. Graph the schedule you completed on the following graph. Plot the real rate of interest on the vertical axis and the amount of investment planned at each real rate of interest on the horizontal axis.

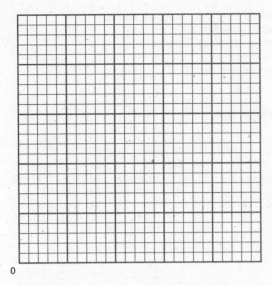

0

f. Both the graph and the table show that the relationship between the real rate of interest and the amount of investment spending in the economy is _____.
This means that when the real rate of interest
(1) increases, investment will (increase, decrease)

_____.

(2) decreases, investment will _____.
g. It also means that should we wish to

(1) increase investment, we would need to _____ the real rate of interest.

(2) decrease investment, we would have to _____ the real rate of interest.

h. This graph (or table) is the _____ curve.

4. Indicate in the space to the right of the following events whether the event would tend to increase (+) or decrease (−) investment spending.

a. Rising stock market prices _____

b. Development of expectations by business executives that business taxes will be higher in the future _____

c. Step-up in the rates at which new products and new production processes are being introduced _____

d. Business beliefs that wage rates may be lower in the future and labor and capital are complementary resources _____

e. An expectation of a recession _____

f. A belief that business is "too good" and the economy is due for a period of "slow" consumer demand _____

g. Rising costs in the construction industry _____

h. A rapid increase in the size of the economy's population _____

i. A recent period of a high level of investment spending, which has resulted in productive capacity in excess of the current demand for goods and services _____

5. Assume the marginal propensity to consume is 0.8 and the change in investment is $10. Complete the following table modeled after Table 8.3 in the textbook.

	Change in income	Change in consumption	Change in saving
Increase in gross Investment of $10	$ + 10	$____	$____
Second round	____	____	____
Third round	____	____	____
Fourth round	____	____	____
Fifth round	____	____	____
All other rounds	16.38	13.10	3.28
Totals			

■ SHORT ANSWER AND ESSAY QUESTIONS

1. What is the most important determinant of consumer spending and personal saving? What is the relationship between consumer spending and personal saving?

2. Use a graph to illustrate the historical relationship between consumption and disposable income in the U.S. economy. Explain why the slope of the consumption line will be less than the 45-degree reference line.

3. Describe the relationship between consumption and disposable income, called the consumption schedule. Draw a graph of this schedule.

4. Describe the relationship between saving and disposable income, called the saving schedule. Draw a graph of this schedule.

5. Define the two average propensities and the two marginal propensities.

6. Explain briefly how the average propensity to consume and the average propensity to save vary as disposable income varies. Why do APC and APS behave this way? What happens to consumption and saving as disposable income varies?

7. Why do the sum of the APC and the APS and the sum of the MPC and the MPS always equal exactly 1?

8. What is the relationship between MPC and MPS and the slopes of the consumption schedule and saving schedule?

9. Explain briefly and explicitly *how* changes in the five nonincome determinants will affect the consumption schedule and the saving schedule and *why* such changes will affect consumption and saving in the way you have indicated.

10. Why does taxation shift both the consumption and saving schedules in the same direction?

11. What is the difference between a change in the amount consumed and a change in the consumption schedule? Explain your answer using a graph.

12. Are consumption and saving schedules relatively stable? Explain.

13. Discuss the marginal cost and marginal benefit of an investment decision. How are the marginal cost and the marginal benefit of investment measured?

14. Draw an investment demand curve. Use it to explain why investment spending tends to rise when the real rate of interest falls, and vice versa.

15. Identify and explain how five noninterest determinants of investment spending can increase or decrease the amount of investment. Illustrate the changes with a graph.

16. Why does the level of investment spending tend to be highly unstable? State four reasons.

17. What is the multiplier effect? Give an equation and an example to show how it works.

18. State the rationale for the multiplier effect.

19. How is the multiplier effect related to the marginal propensities? Explain in words and equations.

20. How large is the actual multiplier effect? Explain the reasons for the difference between the textbook example of the multiplier and the actual multiplier for the economy.

ANSWERS

Chapter 8 Basic Macroeconomic Relationships

FILL-IN QUESTIONS

1. consume, save
2. directly, larger, smaller, smaller, larger, equal to
3. rise, fall
4. 1, .10
5. consumption, income
6. saving, income
7. 1, .25
8. consumption, saving
9. *a.* wealth; *b.* expectations; *c.* real interest rate; *d.* level of household debt (any order for *a–d*)
10. upward, downward, income
11. return, interest
12. benefit, cost
13. increase, decrease
14. inverse, demand, decrease, increase
15. *a.* the cost of acquiring, maintaining, and operating capital goods; *b.* business taxes; *c.* technological change; *d.* the stock of capital goods on hand; *e.* Expectations (any order *a-c*)
16. durability, irregularity, variability, variability
17. divided, multiplied
18. increase, decrease
19. save, consume
20. larger, smaller

TRUE–FALSE QUESTIONS

1. F, p. 147	**10.** T, p. 151	**19.** F, p. 158
2. T, pp. 147–148	**11.** T, p. 152	**20.** T, p. 158
3. T, p. 147	**12.** T, p. 152	**21.** F, pp. 158–159
4. F, pp. 148–149	**13.** T, p. 153	**22.** T, pp. 158–159
5. T, pp. 147–148	**14.** F, pp. 153–154	**23.** T, p. 161
6. F, pp. 148–149	**15.** T, p. 156	**24.** T, p. 161
7. F, p. 150	**16.** F, p. 155	**25.** F, pp. 161–162
8. T, p. 150	**17.** F, p. 157	
9. F, p. 151	**18.** T, pp. 157–158	

MULTIPLE-CHOICE QUESTIONS

1. c, p. 147	**10.** d, p. 151	**19.** d, pp. 156–157
2. d, p. 148	**11.** b, p. 150	**20.** d, p. 156
3. a, p. 148	**12.** c, pp. 150–151	**21.** c, pp. 157–158
4. b, p. 150	**13.** a, p. 151	**22.** d, pp. 158–159
5. d, p. 150	**14.** b, p. 151	**23.** a, pp. 158–159
6. c, p. 150	**15.** c, p. 151	**24.** b, pp. 158–159
7. a, p. 151	**16.** c, pp. 151–152	**25.** c, pp. 158–159
8. c, pp. 148–149	**17.** c, p. 152	
9. c, pp. 148–149	**18.** b, pp. 154–155	

PROBLEMS

1. *a.* S: −40, −20, 0, 20, 40, 60, 80, 100; APC: 1.000, 0.970, 0.955; APS: 0.000, 0.030, 0.045; *b.* 1700; *c.* 80, 100, .8; *d.* 20, 100, .20; *e.* (1) .8, MPC, (2) .2, MPS
2. *a.* −; *b.* +; *c.* −; *d.* +; *e.* −; *f.* none; *g.* −; *h.* −
3. *a.* 0, 10; *b.* 20, 30; *c.* 30, 60; *d.* 100, 150, 210, 280; *f.* inverse, (1) decrease, (2) increase; *g.* (1) lower, (2) raise; *h.* investment-demand
4. *a.* +; *b.* −; *c.* +; *d.* +; *e.* −; *f.* −; *g.* −; *h.* +; *i.* −
5. Change in income: 8.00, 6.40, 5.12, 4.10, 50; Change in consumption: 8.00, 6.40, 5.12, 4.10, 3.28, 40.00; Change in saving: 2.00, 1.60, 1.28, 1.02, 0.82, 10.00

SHORT ANSWER AND ESSAY QUESTIONS

1. p. 147	**8.** p. 151	**15.** p. 156
2. p. 147	**9.** pp. 151–152	**16.** pp. 157–158
3. pp. 148–149	**10.** p. 152	**17.** pp. 158–159
4. pp. 148–149	**11.** p. 152	**18.** pp. 159, 161
5. p. 150	**12.** p. 152	**19.** p. 161
6. p. 150	**13.** pp. 153–154	**20.** pp. 161–162
7. p. 150	**14.** pp. 153–155	

CHAPTER 9
The Aggregate Expenditures Model

This chapter develops the first macroeconomic model of the economy presented in the textbook—the **aggregate expenditures model.** You will find out what determines the demand for real domestic output (real GDP) and how an economy achieves an equilibrium level of output.

The chapter begins with some simplifying assumptions and then explains how the investment decisions of individual firms can be used to construct an **investment schedule.** The investment schedule is combined with the consumption schedule to form an aggregate expenditures schedule that shows the various amounts that will be spent in a private closed economy at each possible output or income level. These aggregate expenditures presented in tabular or graphical form can be used to find **equilibrium GDP** for this economy. It will be important for you to understand how equilibrium GDP is determined and why this level of output will be produced when you are given information about consumption and investment schedules.

Two other features of this simplified aggregate expenditures model are worth noting. Saving and *actual* investment are always equal because they are defined in exactly the same way: the output of the economy minus its consumption. **Saving** and **planned investment,** however, are equal only when real GDP is at its equilibrium level. When real GDP is *not* at its equilibrium level, saving and planned investment are *not* equal and there are **unplanned changes in inventories.** Equilibrium real GDP is achieved when saving and *planned* investment are equal and there are no unplanned changes in inventories.

From Chapter 9 you will also learn **what causes real GDP to rise and fall** as a result of changes in or additions to aggregate expenditures. The first change that will be discussed is the effect of a change in investment spending on equilibrium real GDP in a closed private economy. The initial change in investment will increase equilibrium real GDP by more than the initial investment stimulus because of the multiplier effect.

The method used to find the equilibrium real GDP in an open economy (one that exports and imports) is the same one used for a closed economy. The economy will tend to produce a real GDP that is equal to aggregate expenditures. The only difference is that now the aggregate expenditures include not only consumption and investment but also **net exports** (exports minus imports). An increase in net exports, like an increase in investment, will increase the equilibrium real GDP. A change in net exports also has a multiplier effect on real GDP just as a change in investment does.

The section titled "Adding the Public Sector" introduces **government taxing and spending** into the analysis of equilibrium real GDP. Government purchases of goods and services add to aggregate expenditures, and taxation reduces the disposable income of consumers, reducing both the amount of consumption and the amount of saving that will take place at any level of real GDP. You will need to know the level of real GDP that will be produced and why.

It is important to be aware that the equilibrium real GDP is not necessarily the real GDP at which full employment is achieved. Aggregate expenditures may be greater or less than the full-employment real GDP. If they are greater, there is an **inflationary expenditure gap.** If they are less, there is a **recessionary expenditure gap.** The chapter explains how to measure the size of each expenditure gap: the amount by which the aggregate expenditures schedule must change to bring the economy to its full-employment real GDP. Several historical examples are given to help you see the application of recessionary and inflationary expenditure gaps.

The aggregate expenditures model is a valuable tool for explaining such economic events as recession, inflation, and economic growth. **The model also has limitations.** The last section of the chapter describes the major shortcomings and explains how later chapters in the textbook will address them.

■ CHECKLIST

When you have studied this chapter you should be able to

☐ Describe the simplifying assumptions used in this chapter.
☐ Construct an investment schedule showing the relationship between planned investment and GDP.
☐ Combine the consumption and investment schedules to form an aggregate expenditures schedule to explain the equilibrium levels of output, income, and employment in a private closed economy.
☐ Explain why the economy will tend to produce its equilibrium GDP rather than a smaller or larger level of real GDP.
☐ Illustrate graphically equilibrium in an aggregate expenditure model with consumption and investment components.
☐ Explain the relationship between saving and planned investment at equilibrium GDP.

☐ State the conditions for changes in inventories at equilibrium GDP.

☐ Discuss why equilibrium real GDP changes when the aggregate expenditure schedule shifts upward as a result of an increase in investment spending.

☐ Use the concept of net exports to define aggregate expenditures in an open economy.

☐ Describe the net export schedule and its relationship to real GDP.

☐ Explain what the equilibrium real GDP in an open economy will be when net exports are positive and net exports are negative.

☐ Find the equilibrium real GDP in an open economy when given the tabular or graphical data.

☐ Give three examples of how circumstances or policies abroad can affect domestic GDP.

☐ List three simplifying assumptions that are used to add the public sector to the aggregate expenditures model.

☐ Find the equilibrium real GDP in an economy in which the government purchases goods and services when given the tabular or graphical data.

☐ Determine the effect on the equilibrium real GDP when lump-sum taxes are included in the aggregate expenditures model.

☐ Describe the conditions for leakages and injections and unplanned changes in inventories at the equilibrium level of GDP.

☐ Distinguish between the equilibrium real GDP and the full-employment real GDP.

☐ Find the recessionary and the inflationary expenditure gaps when you are given the relevant data.

☐ Apply the concepts of recessionary and inflationary expenditure gaps to two historical events in the United States.

☐ Explain five shortcomings of the aggregate expenditures model.

☐ Describe Say's law and Keynes's critique of it (Last Word).

■ **CHAPTER OUTLINE**

1. To simplify the explanation of the *aggregate expenditures model,* it is assumed that the economy is private and closed, which means there is no international trade or government spending (or taxes). It is also assumed that output or income measures are equal (real GDP = disposable income, DI); aggregate output and employment are directly related to aggregate expenditures; and the economy has excess production capacity and unemployed labor, so the price level is constant.

2. The investment decisions of businesses in an economy can be aggregated to form an *investment schedule* that shows the amounts business firms collectively intend to invest (their *planned investment*) at each possible level of GDP. A simplifying assumption is made that investment is independent of disposable income or real GDP.

3. In the aggregate expenditures model, the *equilibrium GDP* is the real GDP at which

a. aggregate expenditures (consumption plus planned investment) equal real GDP, or $C + I_g = GDP$;

b. in graphical terms, the *aggregate expenditures schedule* crosses the 45-degree line. The slope of this curve is equal to the marginal propensity to consume.

4. There are two other features of equilibrium GDP.

a. The *investment schedule* indicates what investors plan to do. Actual investment consists of both planned and unplanned investment (unplanned changes in inventories). At above equilibrium levels of GDP, *saving* is greater than *planned investment,* and there will be unintended or unplanned investment through increases in inventories. At below equilibrium levels of GDP, planned investment is greater than saving, and there will be unintended or unplanned disinvestment through a decrease in inventories.

b. Equilibrium is achieved when planned investment equals saving and there are no *unplanned changes in inventories.*

5. Changes in investment (or consumption) will cause the equilibrium real GDP to change in the same direction by an amount greater than the initial change in investment (or consumption). The reason for this greater change is the *multiplier effect.*

6. In an *open economy* there are *net exports* (X_n), which are defined as exports (X) minus imports (M).

a. The equilibrium real GDP in an open economy means real GDP is equal to consumption plus investment plus net exports.

b. The net export schedule will be positive or negative. The schedule is positive when exports are greater than imports; it is negative when imports are greater than exports.

c. Any increase in X_n will increase the equilibrium real GDP with a multiplier effect. A decrease in X_n will do the opposite.

d. In an open-economy model, circumstances and policies abroad can affect the real GDP in the United States.

(1) If there is an increase in real output and incomes in other nations that trade with the United States, the United States can sell more goods abroad, which increases net exports, and thus increase real GDP. A decline in the real output or incomes of other trading nations has the opposite effects.

(2) High tariffs or strict quotas can have an adverse effect on net exports and thus reduce real GDP. Lower tariffs or the elimination of quotas has the opposite effects.

(3) A depreciation in the value of the U.S. dollar will increase the purchasing power of foreign currency, and this change will increase U.S. exports. The result is an increase in net exports and real GDP. An appreciation in the value of the U.S. dollar has the opposite effects.

7. Changes in **government spending and tax rates** can affect equilibrium real GDP. This simplified analysis assumes that government purchases do not affect investment or consumption, that taxes are purely personal taxes, and that a fixed amount of taxes is collected regardless of the level of GDP.

a. Government purchases of goods and services add to the aggregate expenditures schedule and increase equilibrium real GDP; an increase in these purchases has a multiplier effect on equilibrium real GDP.

b. Taxes decrease consumption and the aggregate expenditures schedule by the amount of the tax times the **MPC.** They decrease saving by the amount of the tax times the **MPS.** An increase in taxes has a negative multiplier effect on the equilibrium real GDP.

(1) When government both taxes and purchases goods and services, the equilibrium GDP is the real GDP at which aggregate expenditures (*consumption + investment + net exports + government purchases of goods and services*) equals real GDP.

(2) From a leakages and injections perspective, the equilibrium GDP is the real GDP at which leakages (*saving + imports + taxes*) equals injections (*investment + exports + government purchases*).

(3) At equilibrium real GDP, there are no unplanned changes in inventories.

8. The **equilibrium level of real GDP** may turn out to be an equilibrium that is at less than full employment, at full employment, or at full employment with inflation.

a. If the equilibrium real GDP is less than the real GDP consistent with full-employment real GDP, there is a *recessionary expenditure gap.* Aggregate expenditures are less than what is needed to achieve full-employment real GDP. The size of the recessionary expenditure gap equals the amount by which the aggregate expenditures schedule must increase (shift upward) to increase the real GDP to its full-employment level.

b. The U.S. recession of 2001 is an example of a recessionary expenditure gap as investment spending declined, thus reducing aggregate expenditures.

c. If aggregate expenditures are *greater* than those consistent with full-employment real GDP, there is an *inflationary expenditure gap.* This expenditure gap results from excess spending and will increase the price level, creating demand-pull inflation. The size of the inflationary expenditure gap equals the amount by which the aggregate expenditures schedule must decrease (shift downward) if the economy is to achieve full-employment real GDP.

d. An example of the inflationary expenditure gap is the U.S. inflation in the late 1980s, during which the economy moved beyond its full-employment output and the price level rose.

e. The economy can achieve full-employment output with large negative net exports, as it did in 2005. Although economic theory suggests that the large negative net exports should reduce equilibrium real GDP below its potential, this result did not occur in the U.S. economy because it was offset by additional consumption, investment, and government spending during that period.

9. There are **five limitations** of the aggregate expenditures model: an inability to measure price-level changes or the rate of inflation; no explanation for why demand-pull inflation can occur before the economy reaches its full-employment level of output; no insights into why the economy can expand beyond its full-employment level of real GDP; no coverage of cost-push inflation; and it does not permit "self-correction."

10. (Last Word). Classical economists held the view that when there were deviations from full employment in the economy, it would eventually adjust and achieve equilibrium. This view was based on Say's law, which says that supply creates its own demand. It implies that the production of goods will create the income needed to purchase the produced goods. The events of the Great Depression led to doubts about this law, and it was challenged by John Maynard Keynes in his 1936 book *General Theory of Employment, Interest, and Money.* Keynes showed that supply may not create its own demand because not all income need be spent in the period in which it was earned, thus creating conditions for high levels of unemployment and economic decline.

■ **HINTS AND TIPS**

1. Do not confuse the **investment demand curve** for the business sector with the **investment schedule** for an economy. The former shows the inverse relationship between the real interest rate and the amount of total investment by the business sector, whereas the latter shows the collective investment intentions of business firms at each possible level of disposable income or real GDP.

2. The distinction between **actual investment, planned investment,** and **unplanned investment** is important for determining the equilibrium level of real GDP. Actual investment includes both planned and unplanned investment. At any level of real GDP, saving and actual investment will always be equal by definition, but saving and planned investment may not equal real GDP because there may be unplanned investment (unplanned changes in inventories). Only at the equilibrium level of real GDP will saving and planned investment be equal (there is no unplanned investment).

3. There is an important difference between **equilibrium** and **full-employment real GDP** in the aggregate expenditures model. Equilibrium means there is no tendency for the economy to change its output (or employment) level. Thus, an economy can experience a low level of output and high unemployment and still be at equilibrium. The *recessionary expenditure gap* shows how much aggregate expenditures need to increase, so that when this increase is multiplied by the multiplier, it will shift the economy to a higher equilibrium and to the full-employment level of real GDP. Remember that you multiply the needed increase in aggregate expenditures (the recessionary expenditure gap) by the multiplier to calculate the change in real GDP that moves the economy from below to full-employment equilibrium.

■ IMPORTANT TERMS

planned investment

investment schedule

aggregate expenditures schedule

equilibrium GDP

leakage

injection

unplanned changes in inventories

net exports

lump-sum tax

recessionary expenditure gap

inflationary expenditure gap

SELF-TEST

■ FILL-IN QUESTIONS

1. Some simplifying assumptions used in the first part of the chapter are that the economy is (an open, a closed) _____ economy, that the economy is (private, public) _____, that real GDP equals disposable (consumption, income) _____, and that an increase in aggregate expenditures will (increase, decrease) _____ real output and employment but not raise the price level.

2. A schedule showing the amounts business firms collectively intend to invest at each possible level of GDP is the (consumption, investment) _____ schedule. For this schedule, it is assumed that planned (saving, investment) _____ is independent of the level of current disposable income or real output.

3. Assuming a private and closed economy, the equilibrium level of real GDP is determined where aggregate expenditures are (greater than, less than, equal to) _____ real domestic output, consumption plus investment is _____ real domestic output, and the aggregate expenditures schedule or curve intersects the (90-degree, 45-degree) _____ line.

4. A leakage is (an addition to, a withdrawal from) _____ the income expenditure stream, whereas an injection is _____ the income expenditure stream. In this chapter, an example of a leakage is (investment, saving) _____ and an example of an injection is _____.

5. If aggregate expenditures are greater than the real domestic output, saving is (greater than, less than)

_____ planned investment, there are unplanned (increases, decreases) _____ in inventories, and real GDP will (rise, fall) _____.

6. If aggregate expenditures are less than the real domestic output, saving is (greater than, less than) _____ planned investment, there are unplanned (increases, decreases) _____ in inventories, and real GDP will (rise, fall) _____.

7. If aggregate expenditures are equal to the real domestic output, saving is (greater than, less than, equal to) _____ planned investment, unplanned changes in inventories are (negative, positive, zero) _____, and real GDP will neither rise nor fall.

8. An upshift in the aggregate expenditures schedule will (increase, decrease) _____ the equilibrium GDP. The upshift in the aggregate expenditures schedule can result from (an increase, a decrease) _____ in the consumption schedule or _____ in the investment schedule.

9. When investment spending increases, the equilibrium real GDP (increases, decreases) _____, and when investment spending decreases, the equilibrium real GDP _____. The changes in the equilibrium real GDP are (greater, less) _____ than the initial changes in investment spending because of the (lump-sum tax, multiplier) _____.

10. In an open economy, a nation's net exports are equal to its exports (plus, minus) _____ its imports. In this type of economy, aggregate expenditures are equal to consumption (plus, minus) _____ investment (plus, minus) _____ net exports.

11. What would be the effect, an increase (+) or a decrease (−), of each of the following on an open economy's equilibrium real GDP?

a. an increase in imports _____

b. an increase in exports _____

c. a decrease in imports _____

d. a decrease in exports _____

e. an increasing level of national income among trading partners _____

f. an increase in trade barriers imposed by trading partners _____

g. a depreciation in the value of the economy's currency _____

12. Increases in public spending will (decrease, increase) _____ the aggregate expenditures schedule and equilibrium real GDP, and decreases in public spending will _____ the aggregate expenditures schedule and equilibrium real GDP.

13. A tax yielding the same amount of tax revenue at each level of GDP is a (lump-sum, constant) _____ tax.

14. Taxes tend to reduce consumption at each level of real GDP by an amount equal to the taxes multiplied by the marginal propensity to (consume, save) _____; saving will decrease by an amount equal to the taxes multiplied by the marginal propensity to _____.

15. In an economy in which government both taxes and purchases goods and services, the equilibrium level of real GDP is the real GDP at which aggregate (output, expenditures) _____ equal(s) real domestic _____ and at which real GDP is equal to consumption (plus, minus) _____ investment (plus, minus) _____ net exports (plus, minus) _____ purchases of goods and services by government.

16. When the public sector is added to the model, the equation for the leakages and injections shows (consumption, investment) _____ plus (imports, exports) _____ plus purchases of goods and services by government equals (consumption, saving) _____ plus (exports, imports) _____ plus taxes.

17. A recessionary expenditure gap exists when equilibrium real GDP is (greater, less) _____ than the full-employment real GDP. To bring real GDP to the full-employment level, the aggregate expenditures schedule must (increase, decrease) _____ by an amount equal to the difference between the equilibrium and the full-employment real GDP (multiplied, divided) _____ by the multiplier.

18. The amount by which aggregate spending at the full-employment GDP exceeds the full-employment level of real GDP is (a recessionary, an inflationary) _____ expenditure gap. To eliminate this expenditure gap, the aggregate expenditures schedule must (increase, decrease) _____.

19. One limitation of the aggregate expenditures model is that it can explain (cost-push, demand-pull) _____ inflation but not _____ inflation. Another problem is that the model also includes no way of measuring the rate of (interest, inflation) _____ because there is no price level.

20. Three other limitations of the aggregate expenditures model are its inability to explain premature (demand-pull, cost-push) _____ inflation, how the economy can expand (to, beyond) _____ the full-employment level of output, and how the economy "self-(inflates," corrects") _____.

■ **TRUE–FALSE QUESTIONS**

Circle T if the statement is true, F if it is false.

1. The basic premise of the aggregate expenditures model is that the amount of goods and services produced and the level of employment depend directly on the level of total spending. **T F**

2. In the aggregate expenditures model of the economy, the price level is assumed to be constant. **T F**

3. The investment schedule is a schedule of planned investment rather than a schedule of actual investment. **T F**

4. The equilibrium level of GDP is the GDP level that corresponds to the intersection of the aggregate expenditures schedule and the 45-degree line. **T F**

5. At levels of GDP below equilibrium, the economy wants to spend at higher levels than the levels of GDP the economy is producing. **T F**

6. At levels of GDP below equilibrium, aggregate expenditures are less than GDP, which causes inventories to rise and production to fall. **T F**

7. Saving is an injection into and investment is a leakage from the income expenditures stream. **T F**

8. Saving and actual investment are always equal. **T F**

9. Saving at any level of real GDP equals planned investment plus unplanned changes in inventories. **T F**

10. The equilibrium level of GDP will change in response to changes in the investment schedule or the consumption schedule. **T F**

11. If there is a decrease in the investment schedule, there will be an upshift in the aggregate expenditures schedule. **T F**

12. Through the multiplier effect, an initial change in investment spending can cause a magnified change in domestic output and income. **T F**

13. The net exports of an economy equal the sum of its exports and imports of goods and services. **T F**

14. An increase in the volume of a nation's exports, other things being equal, will expand that nation's real GDP. **T F**

15. An increase in the imports of a nation will increase the exports of other nations.　**T F**

16. A falling level of real output and income among U.S. trading partners enables the United States to sell more goods abroad.　**T F**

17. An appreciation of the dollar will increase net exports.　**T F**

18. If the MPS were 0.3 and taxes were levied by the government so that consumers paid $20 in taxes at each level of real GDP, consumption expenditures at each level of real GDP would be $14 less.　**T F**

19. Equal changes in government spending and taxes do not have equivalent effects on real GDP.　**T F**

20. At equilibrium, the sum of leakages equals the sum of injections.　**T F**

21. The equilibrium real GDP is the real GDP at which there is full employment in the economy.　**T F**

22. The existence of a recessionary expenditure gap in the economy is characterized by the full employment of labor.　**T F**

23. An inflationary expenditure gap is the amount by which the economy's aggregate expenditures schedule must shift downward to eliminate demand-pull inflation and still achieve the full-employment GDP.　**T F**

24. The aggregate expenditures model is valuable because it indicates how much the price level will rise when aggregate expenditures are excessive relative to the economy's capacity.　**T F**

25. The aggregate expenditures model provides a good explanation for cost-push inflation.　**T F**

■ MULTIPLE-CHOICE QUESTIONS

Circle the letter that corresponds to the best answer.

1. The premise of the model in this chapter is that the amount of goods and services produced, and therefore the level of employment, depends
(a) directly on the rate of interest
(b) directly on the level of total expenditures
(c) inversely on the level of disposable income
(d) inversely on the quantity of resources available

2. If the economy is private and is closed to international trade and government neither taxes nor spends, real GDP equals
(a) saving
(b) consumption
(c) disposable income
(d) investment spending

Question 3 is based on the following consumption schedule.

Real GDP	C
$200	$200
240	228
280	256
320	284
360	312
400	340
440	368
480	396

3. If the investment schedule is $60 at each level of output, the equilibrium level of real GDP will be
(a) $320
(b) $360
(c) $400
(d) $440

4. If real GDP is $275 billion, consumption is $250 billion, and investment is $30 billion, real GDP
(a) will tend to decrease
(b) will tend to increase
(c) will tend to remain constant
(d) equals aggregate expenditures

5. On a graph, the equilibrium real GDP is found at the intersection of the 45-degree line and the
(a) saving curve
(b) consumption curve
(c) investment demand curve
(d) aggregate expenditures curve

6. Which is an injection of spending into the income expenditures stream?
(a) investment
(b) imports
(c) saving
(d) taxes

7. When the economy's real GDP exceeds its equilibrium real GDP,
(a) leakages equal injections
(b) planned investment exceeds saving
(c) there is unplanned investment in the economy
(d) aggregate expenditures exceed the real domestic output

8. If saving is greater than planned investment,
(a) saving will tend to increase
(b) businesses will be motivated to increase their investments
(c) real GDP will be greater than planned investment plus consumption
(d) aggregate expenditures will be greater than the real domestic output

9. At the equilibrium level of GDP,
(a) actual investment is zero
(b) unplanned changes in inventories are zero
(c) saving is greater than planned investment
(d) saving is less than planned investment

Answer Questions 10 and 11 on the basis of the following table for a private, closed economy. All figures are in billions of dollars.

Real rate of return	Investment	Consumption	GDP
10%	$ 0	$200	$200
8	50	250	300
6	100	300	400
4	150	350	500
2	200	400	600
0	250	450	700

10. If the real rate of interest is 4%, the equilibrium level of GDP will be
(a) $300 billion
(b) $400 billion
(c) $500 billion
(d) $600 billion

11. An *increase* in the real interest rate by 4% will
(a) increase the equilibrium level of GDP by $200 billion
(b) decrease the equilibrium level of GDP by $200 billion
(c) decrease the equilibrium level of GDP by $100 billion
(d) increase the equilibrium level of GDP by $100 billion

12. Compared with a closed economy, aggregate expenditures and GDP will
(a) increase when net exports are positive
(b) decrease when net exports are positive
(c) increase when net exports are negative
(d) decrease when net exports are zero

Use the data in the following table to answer Questions 13 and 14.

Real GDP	$C + I_g$	Net exports
$ 900	$ 913	$3
920	929	3
940	945	3
960	961	3
980	977	3
1000	993	3
1020	1009	3

13. The equilibrium real GDP is
(a) $960
(b) $980
(c) $1000
(d) $1020

14. If net exports are increased by $4 billion at each level of GDP, the equilibrium real GDP will be
(a) $960
(b) $980
(c) $1000
(d) $1020

15. An increase in the real GDP of an economy will, other things remaining constant,
(a) increase its imports and the real GDPs in other economies
(b) decrease its imports and the real GDPs in other economies
(c) increase its imports and decrease the real GDPs in other economies
(d) decrease its imports and increase the real GDPs in other economies

16. Other things remaining constant, which would increase an economy's real GDP and employment?
(a) an increase in the exchange rate for foreign currencies
(b) the imposition of tariffs on goods imported from abroad
(c) an appreciation of the dollar relative to foreign currencies
(d) an increase in the level of national income among the trading partners for this economy

17. The economy is operating at the full-employment level of output. A depreciation of the dollar most likely will result in
(a) a decrease in exports
(b) an increase in imports
(c) a decrease in real GDP
(d) an increase in the price level

Answer Questions 18 and 19 on the basis of the following diagram.

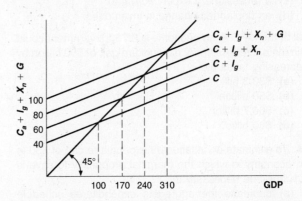

18. If this were an open economy without a government sector, the level of GDP would be
(a) $100
(b) $170
(c) $240
(d) $310

19. In this graph it is assumed that investment, net exports, and government expenditures
(a) vary directly with GDP
(b) vary inversely with GDP
(c) are independent of GDP
(d) are all negative

Questions 20 and 21 are based on the following consumption schedule.

Real GDP	C
$300	$290
310	298
320	306
330	314
340	322
350	330
360	338

20. If taxes were zero, government purchases of goods and services $10, planned investment $6, and net exports zero, equilibrium real GDP would be
(a) $310
(b) $320
(c) $330
(d) $340

21. If taxes were $5, government purchases of goods and services $10, planned investment $6, and net exports zero, equilibrium real GDP would be
(a) $300
(b) $310
(c) $320
(d) $330

22. The amount by which an economy's aggregate expenditures must shift upward to achieve full-employment GDP is
(a) an injection
(b) a lump-sum tax
(c) a recessionary expenditure gap
(d) an unplanned change in inventories

23. If the MPC in an economy is 0.75, government could eliminate a recessionary expenditure gap of $50 billion by decreasing taxes by
(a) $33.3 billion
(b) $50 billion
(c) $66.7 billion
(d) $80 billion

24. To eliminate an inflationary expenditure gap of $50 in an economy in which the marginal propensity to save is 0.1, it will be necessary to
(a) decrease the aggregate expenditures schedule by $50
(b) decrease the aggregate expenditures schedule by $5
(c) increase the aggregate expenditures schedule by $50
(d) increase the aggregate expenditures schedule by $5

25. One of the limitations of the aggregate expenditures model is that it
(a) fails to account for demand-pull inflation
(b) has no method for measuring the rate of inflation
(c) explains recessionary expenditure gaps but not inflationary expenditure gaps
(d) gives more weight to cost-push than to demand-pull inflation

■ PROBLEMS

1. Following are two schedules showing several GDPs and the level of investment spending (*I*) at each GDP. (All figures are in billions of dollars.)

Schedule number 1		Schedule number 2	
GDP	I	GDP	I
$1850	$90	$1850	$ 75
1900	90	1900	80
1950	90	1950	85
2000	90	2000	90
2050	90	2050	95
2100	90	2100	100
2150	95	2150	105

a. Each schedule is an _____ schedule.
b. When such a schedule is drawn up, it is assumed that the real rate of interest is _____.
c. In schedule
(1) number 1, GDP and *I* are (unrelated, directly related) _____.

(2) number 2, GDP and *I* are _____.

d. Should the real rate of interest rise, investment spending at each GDP would (increase, decrease) _____ and the curve relating GDP and investment spending would shift (upward, downward) _____.

2. The following table shows consumption and saving at various levels of real GDP. Assume the price level is constant, the economy is closed to international trade, and there is no government, no business savings, no depreciation, and no net foreign factor income earned in the United States.

Real GDP	C	S	I_g	$C + I_g$	UI
$1300	$1290	$10	$22	1312	−12
1310	1298	12	22	1320	−10
1320	1306	14	____	____	____
1330	1314	16	____	____	____
1340	1322	18	____	____	____
1350	1330	20	____	____	____
1360	1338	22	____	____	____
1370	1346	24	____	____	____
1380	1354	26	____	____	____
1390	1362	28	22	1384	+6
1400	1370	30	22	1392	+8

a. The next table is an investment demand schedule that shows the amounts investors plan to invest at different rates of interest. Assume the rate of interest is 6%. In the previous table, complete the gross investment, the consumption-plus-investment, and unplanned investment (*UI*) columns, showing unplanned increase in inventories with a + and unplanned decrease in inventories with a −.

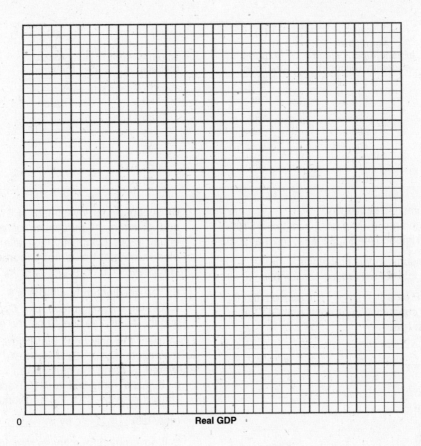

0   **Real GDP**

Interest rate	I_g
10%	$ 0
9	7
8	13
7	18
6	22
5	25

b. The equilibrium real GDP will be $ _____.

c. The value of the marginal propensity to consume in this problem is _____, and the value of the marginal propensity to save is _____.

d. The value of the simple multiplier is _____.

e. If the rate of interest fell from 6% to 5%, investment would (increase, decrease) _____ by $ _____ and the equilibrium real GDP would, as a result, (increase, decrease) _____ by $_____.

f. Suppose the rate of interest were to rise from 6% to 7%. Investment would _____ by $_____, and the equilibrium real GDP would _____ by $ _____.

g. Assuming the rate of interest is 6%, on the graph above, plot **C, C + I_g**, and the 45-degree line and indicate the equilibrium real GDP.

3. The second column of the schedule at the top of the next page shows what aggregate expenditures (consumption plus investment) would be at various levels of real domestic product in a closed economy.

a. If this economy became an open economy, the volume of exports would be a constant $90 billion (column 3), and the volume of imports would be a constant $86 billion (column 4). At each of the seven levels of real GDP (column 1), net exports would be $_____ billion (column 5).

b. Compute aggregate expenditures in this open economy at the seven real GDP levels and enter them in the table (column 6).

c. The equilibrium real GDP in this open economy would be _____ billion.

d. The value of the multiplier in this open economy is equal to _____.

e. A $10 billion increase in

(1) exports would (increase, decrease) _____ the equilibrium real GDP by $_____ billion.

(2) imports would (increase, decrease) _____ the equilibrium real GDP by $_____ billion.

(1) Possible levels of real GDP (billions)	(2) Aggregate expenditures, closed economy (billions)	(3) Exports (billions)	(4) Imports (billions)	(5) Net exports (billions)	(6) Aggregate expenditures, open economy (billions)
$ 750	$ 776	$90	$86	$____	$____
800	816	90	86	____	____
850	856	90	86	____	____
900	896	90	86	____	____
950	936	90	86	____	____
1000	976	90	86	____	____
1050	1016	90	86	____	____

4. Below are consumption schedules.

a. Assume government levies a lump-sum tax of $100. Also assume that imports are $5. Because the marginal

propensity to consume in this problem is _____, the imposition of this tax will reduce consumption at all

levels of real GDP by $_____. Complete the **$C_a$** column to show consumption at each real GDP after this tax has been levied.

Real GDP	C	C_a	$C + I_g + X_n + G$
$1500	$1250	$____	$____
1600	1340	____	____
1700	1430	____	____
1800	1520	____	____
1900	1610	____	____
2000	1700	____	____
2100	1790	____	____

b. Suppose that investment is $150, exports are $5, and government purchases of goods and services equal $200. Complete the (after-tax) consumption-plus-investment-plus-net-exports-plus-government-purchases column ($C_a + I_g + X_n + G$).

c. The equilibrium real GDP is $ _____.

d. On the following graph, plot C_a, $C_a + I_g + X_n + G$, and the 45-degree line. Show the equilibrium real GDP.

(To answer the questions that follow, it is *not* necessary to recompute C_a, or $C_a + I_g + X_n + G$. They can be answered by using the multipliers.)

e. If taxes remained at $100 and government purchases rose by $10, the equilibrium real GDP would

(rise, fall) _____ by $ _____.

f. If government purchases remained at $200 and the lump-sum tax increased by $10, the equilibrium real

GDP would _____ by $ _____.

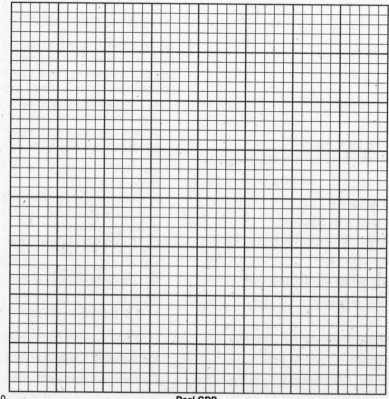

0   **Real GDP**

g. The combined effect of a $10 increase in government purchases *and* a $10 increase in taxes is to _____ real GDP by $ _____ .

5. Here is a consumption schedule for a closed economy. Assume that the level of real GDP at which full employment without inflation is achieved is $590.

Real GDP	C
$550	$520
560	526
570	532
580	538
590	544
600	550
610	556
620	562
630	568

a. The value of the multiplier is _____ .

b. If planned investment is $58, the equilibrium nominal GDP is $_____ and exceeds full-employment real GDP by $_____ . There is a(n) _____ expenditure gap of $_____ .

c. If planned investment is $38, the equilibrium real GDP is $_____ and is less than full-employment real GDP by $_____ . There is a(n) _____ expenditure gap of $_____ .

■ **SHORT ANSWER AND ESSAY QUESTIONS**

1. What does it mean that an economy is private and closed?

2. What assumptions are made in this chapter about production capacity, unemployment, and the price level?

3. What is the difference between an investment demand curve and an investment schedule?

4. Why is the equilibrium level of real GDP the level of real GDP at which domestic output equals aggregate expenditures? What will cause real GDP to rise if it is below this level, and what will cause it to fall if it is above this level?

5. Explain what is meant by a leakage and by an injection. Which leakage and which injection are considered in this chapter? Why is the equilibrium real GDP the real GDP at which the leakages equal the injections?

6. Why is it important to distinguish between planned and actual investment in explaining how a private, closed economy achieves its equilibrium level of real GDP?

7. Why does the equilibrium level of real GDP change?

8. How do exports and imports get included in the aggregate expenditures model?

9. What happens to the aggregate expenditures schedule when net exports increase or decrease?

10. Give some examples of international economic linkages affecting the domestic level of GDP.

11. Explain the simplifying assumptions used to include the public sector in the aggregate expenditures model.

12. Describe how government expenditures affect equilibrium GDP.

13. What effect will taxes have on the consumption schedule?

14. Explain why, with government taxing and spending, the equilibrium real GDP is the real GDP at which real GDP equals consumption plus investment plus net exports plus government purchases of goods and services.

15. Use leakages and injections to explain how changes in the different components of aggregate expenditures cause GDP to move to its equilibrium level.

16. Explain what is meant by a recessionary expenditure gap.

17. What economic conditions contributed to the recessionary expenditure gap in the U.S. economy in 2001?

18. What is an inflationary expenditure gap? Why is the U.S. inflation in the late 1980s an example of an inflationary expenditure gap?

19. Why did the large negative net exports in 2005 not cause a decline in the U.S. economy below its potential and substantial unemployment?

20. What are the limitations of the demand aggregate expenditures model in terms of measurement of the price level and treatment of demand-pull and cost-push inflation? Are there other limitations?

ANSWERS

Chapter 9 The Aggregate Expenditures Model

■ **FILL-IN QUESTIONS**

1. a closed, private, income, increase
2. investment, investment
3. equal to, equal to, 45-degree
4. a withdrawal from, an addition to, saving, investment
5. less than, decreases, rise
6. greater than, increases, fall
7. equal to, zero
8. increase, an increase, an increase
9. increases, decreases, greater, multiplier
10. minus, plus, plus
11. *a.* −; *b.* +; *c.* +; *d.* −; *e.* +; *f.* −; *g.* +

12. increase, decrease
13. lump-sum
14. consume, save
15. expenditures, output, plus, plus, plus
16. investment, exports, saving, imports
17. less, increase, divided
18. an inflationary, decrease
19. demand-pull, cost-push, inflation
20. demand-pull, beyond, corrects

TRUE–FALSE QUESTIONS

1. T, p.166	10. T, p. 172	19. T, p. 178
2. T, p. 167	11. F, p. 172	20. T, pp. 178–179
3. T, p. 167	12. T, p. 172	21. F, p. 179
4. T, pp. 168–169	13. F, p. 173	22. F, p. 179
5. T, p. 169	14. T, pp. 173–174	23. T, pp. 179–180
6. F, p. 169	15. T, p. 175	24. F, p. 183
7. F, p. 171	16. F, p. 175	25. F, p. 183
8. T, p. 171	17. F, p. 175	
9. T, p. 171	18. T, pp. 176–177	

MULTIPLE-CHOICE QUESTIONS

1. b, p. 166	10. c, pp. 167–168	19. c, pp. 176–177
2. c, p. 167	11. b, p. 172	20. c, pp. 176-177
3. c, pp. 168–170	12. a, p. 173	21. b, pp. 176–177
4. b, pp. 168–170	13. b, pp. 173–174	22. c, p. 179
5. d, pp. 168–170	14. c, pp. 173–174	23. c, p. 179
6. a, p. 171	15. a, p. 175	24. a, pp. 179–180
7. c, p. 171	16. d, p. 175	25. b, p. 183
8. c, p. 171	17. d, p. 175	
9. b, p. 171	18. c, p. 174	

PROBLEMS

1. *a.* investment; *b.* constant (given); *c.* (1) unrelated, (2) directly related; *d.* decrease, downward

2. *a.* I_g: 22, 22, 22, 22, 22, 22, 22; *C* + I_g: 1328, 1336, 1344, 1352, 1360, 1368, 1376; *UI:* −8, −6, −4, −2, 0, +2, +4; *b.* 1360; *c.* 0.8, 0.2; *d.* 5; *e.* increase, 3, increase, 15; *f.* decrease, 4, decrease, 20

3. *a.* $4 (and put $4 in each of the seven net exports values in the table); *b.* $780, 820, 860, 900, 940, 980, 1020; *c.* $900; *d.* 5; *e.* (1) increase, $50, (2) decrease, $50

4. *a.* 0.9, 90, C_a: 1160, 1250, 1340, 1430, 1520, 1610, 1700; *b.* $C_a + I_g + X_n + G$: 1510, 1600, 1690, 1780, 1870, 1960, 2050; *c.* 1600; *d.* plot graph; *e.* rise, 100; *f.* fall, 90; *g.* raise, 10

5. *a.* 2.5; *b.* 620, 30, inflationary, 12; *c.* 570, 20, recessionary, 8

SHORT ANSWER AND ESSAY QUESTIONS

1. p. 167	8. pp. 173–174	15. p. 179
2. p. 167	9. pp. 173–174	16. p. 179
3. p. 167	10. p. 175	17. pp. 180–181
4. pp. 168–170	11. pp. 175–176	18. pp. 179–180
5. p. 171	12. pp. 176–177	19. p. 181
6. p. 171	13. pp. 177–179	20. p. 183
7. p. 172	14. pp. 178–179	

CHAPTER 10

Aggregate Demand and Aggregate Supply

Chapter 10 introduces another macro model of the economy, one based on aggregate demand and aggregate supply. This model can be used to explain real domestic output and the level of prices at any point in time and to understand what causes output and the price level to change.

The **aggregate demand (AD) curve** is downsloping because of the real-balances, interest-rate, and foreign purchases effects that result from changes in the price level. With a downsloping aggregate demand curve, changes in the price level have an inverse effect on the level of spending by domestic consumers, businesses, government, and foreign buyers and thus on real domestic output, assuming *other things equal*. This change would be equivalent to a movement along an existing aggregate demand curve: A lower price level increases the quantity of real domestic output demanded, and a higher price level decreases the quantity of real domestic output demanded.

The aggregate demand curve can increase or decrease because of a change in one of the nonprice level **determinants of aggregate demand.** These determinants include changes affecting consumer, investment, government, and net export spending. You will learn that underlying each demand determinant are various factors that cause that determinant to change. The size of the change involves two components. For example, if one of these spending determinants increases, aggregate demand will increase. The change in aggregate demand involves an increase in initial spending plus a multiplier effect that results in a greater change in aggregate demand than the initial change.

The **aggregate supply (AS) curve** shows the relationship between the output of producers and the price level. In the long run, the aggregate supply curve is vertical because the price level does not change production at the full-employment level of output. In the short run, however, the upsloping shape of the aggregate supply curve reflects what happens to per-unit production costs as real domestic output increases or decreases.

You should remember that an assumption has been made that other things are equal when one moves along an aggregate supply curve. When other things change, the aggregate supply curve can shift. The **determinants of aggregate supply** include changes in input prices, changes in productivity, and changes in the legal and institutional environment for production. As with aggregate demand, you will learn that there are underlying factors that cause these supply determinants to change.

The intersection of the aggregate demand and aggregate supply curves determines **equilibrium real output** and the **equilibrium price level.** Assuming that the determinants of aggregate demand and aggregate supply do not change, there are pressures that tend to keep the economy at equilibrium. If a determinant changes, aggregate demand, aggregate supply, or both can shift.

When **aggregate demand increases,** this will lead to changes in equilibrium real output and the price level. If the economy is operating at full employment, the increase in AD may not have its full multiplier effect on the real GDP of the economy, and it will result in **demand-pull inflation.** There can also be a **decrease in aggregate demand,** but it may reduce output and not the price level. In this case, there can be downward price inflexibility for several reasons, as you will learn in this chapter.

Aggregate supply may increase or decrease. An increase in aggregate supply provides a double bonus for the economy because the price level falls and output and employment increase. Conversely, a decrease in aggregate supply doubly harms the economy because the price level increases and output and employment fall, and thus the economy experiences **cost-push inflation.**

The aggregate demand–aggregate supply model is an important framework for determining the equilibrium level of real domestic output and prices in an economy. This model will be used extensively throughout the next eight chapters to analyze how different parts of the economy function.

■ CHECKLIST

When you have studied this chapter you should be able to

☐ Define aggregate demand.
☐ Describe the characteristics of the aggregate demand curve.
☐ Use the real-balances, interest-rate, and foreign purchases effects to explain why the aggregate demand curve slopes downward.
☐ Use a graph to distinguish between a movement along a fixed aggregate demand curve and a shift in aggregate demand.
☐ Give an example of the effect of the multiplier on an increase in aggregate demand.
☐ Explain the four factors that can change the consumer spending determinant of aggregate demand.

☐ Explain the two factors that can change the investment spending determinant of aggregate demand.

☐ Explain what changes the government spending determinant of aggregate demand.

☐ Explain the two factors that can cause changes in the net export spending determinant of aggregate demand.

☐ Discuss how the four major spending determinants of aggregate demand (and their underlying factors) can increase or decrease aggregate demand.

☐ Define aggregate supply in both the long run and the short run.

☐ Explain why the aggregate supply curve in the long run is vertical.

☐ Explain why the aggregate supply curve in the short run is upsloping.

☐ Identify the three major spending determinants of aggregate supply.

☐ Describe three factors that change the input prices determinant of aggregate supply.

☐ Explain what changes the productivity determinant of aggregate supply.

☐ Identify two factors that change the legal-institutional environment determinant of aggregate supply.

☐ Explain how the three major determinants of aggregate supply (and their underlying factors) can increase or decrease aggregate supply.

☐ Explain why in equilibrium the economy will produce a particular combination of real output and the price level rather than another combination.

☐ Show the effects of an increase in aggregate demand on the real output and the price level and relate the changes to demand-pull inflation.

☐ Illustrate the effects of a decrease in aggregate demand on real output and the price level in the economy and relate the changes to recession and unemployment.

☐ Explain the meaning of the terms "deflation" and "disinflation."

☐ Give five reasons for downward inflexibility of changes in the price level when aggregate demand decreases.

☐ Explain the effects of a decrease in aggregate supply on real output and the price level and relate the changes to cost-push inflation.

☐ Describe the effects of an increase in aggregate supply on real output and the price level.

☐ Explain how increases in productivity reduce inflationary pressures by using an aggregate demand–aggregate supply graph.

☐ Explain why increases in oil prices have lost their strong effect on core inflation and the U.S. economy (Last Word).

■ CHAPTER OUTLINE

1. This chapter introduces the *aggregate demand–aggregate supply model* (AD–AS model). It explains why real domestic output *and* the price level fluctuate in the economy. The chapter begins by explaining the meaning and characteristics of aggregate demand.

   a. *Aggregate demand* is a curve that shows the total quantity of goods and services (real output) that will be purchased (demanded) at different price levels. With aggregate demand there is an inverse or negative relationship between the amount of real output demanded and the price level, and so the curve slopes downward.

   b. Three reasons account for the inverse relationship between real output and the price level and the downward slope of the aggregate demand curve.

   (1) *Real-balances effect:* An increase in the price level decreases the purchasing power of financial assets with a fixed money value, and because those who own such assets are now poorer, they spend less for goods and services. A decrease in the price level has the opposite effects.

   (2) *Interest-rate effect:* With the supply of money fixed, an increase in the price level increases the demand for money, increases interest rates, and as a result reduces expenditures (by consumers and business firms) that are sensitive to increased interest rates. A decrease in the price level has the opposite effects.

   (3) *Foreign purchases effect:* An increase in the price level (relative to foreign price levels) will reduce U.S. exports because U.S. products are now more expensive for foreigners and expand U.S. imports because foreign products are now less expensive for U.S. consumers. As a consequence, net exports will decrease, which means there will be a decrease in the quantity of goods and services demanded in the U.S. economy as the price level rises. A decrease in the price level (relative to foreign price levels) will have the opposite effects.

2. Spending by domestic consumers, businesses, government, and foreign buyers that is independent of changes in the price level constitutes the *determinants of aggregate demand.* The amount of changes in aggregate demand involves two components: the amount of the initial change in one of the determinants and a multiplier effect that multiplies the initial change. These determinants are also called aggregate demand shifts because a change in one of them, other things equal, will shift the entire aggregate demand curve. Figure 10.2 shows the shifts. What follows is a description of each of the four major determinants and the underlying factors.

   a. *Consumer spending* can increase or decrease AD. If the price level is constant and consumers decide to spend more, AD will increase; if consumers decide to spend less, AD will decrease. Four factors increase or decrease consumer spending.

   (1) *Consumer wealth:* If the real value of financial assets increases, consumers will feel wealthier and spend more, and AD increases. If the real value of financial assets falls, consumers will spend less and AD will decrease.

   (2) *Consumer expectations:* If consumers become more optimistic about the future, they probably will spend more and AD will increase. If consumers expect the future to be worse, they will decrease their spending and AD will decrease.

   (3) *Household debt:* If consumers have increased debt relative to a constant level, they may be forced to reduce their spending, thus decreasing AD. Conversely,

if debt decreases from a constant level, consumers may be able to borrow more money and increase their spending, thus increasing AD.

(4) *Personal taxes:* Cuts in personal taxes increase disposable income and the capacity for consumer spending, thus increasing AD. A rise in personal taxes decreases disposable income, consumer spending, and AD.

b. Investment spending can increase or decrease AD. If the price level is constant and businesses decide to spend more on investment, then AD will increase. If businesses decide to spend less on investment then AD will decrease. Three factors increase or decrease investment spending.

(1) *Real interest rates:* A decrease in real interest rates will increase the quantity of investment spending, thus increasing AD. An increase in real interest rates will decrease the quantity of investment spending, thus decreasing AD.

(2) *Expected returns:* If businesses expect higher returns on investments in the future, they probably will increase their investment spending today, and so AD will increase. If businesses expect lower returns on investments in the future, they will decrease their investment spending today, and AD will decrease. These expected returns are influenced by expectations about future business conditions, the state of technology, the degree of excess capacity (the amount of unused capital goods), and business taxes.

(a) More positive future expectations, more technological progress, less excess capacity, and lower taxes will increase investment spending and thus increase AD.

(b) Less positive future expectations, less technological progress, more excess capacity, and higher taxes will decrease investment spending and thus decrease AD.

c. Government spending has a direct effect on AD, assuming that tax collections and interest rates do not change as a result of that spending. More government spending tends to increase AD, and less government spending will decrease AD.

d. Net export spending can increase or decrease AD. If the price level is constant and net exports (exports minus imports) increase, then AD will increase. If net exports are negative, then AD will decrease. Two factors explain the increase or decrease in net export spending.

(1) *National income abroad:* An increase in the national income of other nations will increase the demand for all goods and services, including U.S. exports. If U.S. exports increase relative to U.S. imports, then net exports will increase, and so will AD. A decline in national incomes abroad will tend to reduce U.S. net exports and thus reduces AD.

(2) *Exchange rates:* A depreciation in the value of the U.S. dollar means that U.S. imports should decline because domestic purchasers cannot buy as many imports as they used to buy. U.S. exports should increase because foreigners have more purchasing power to buy U.S. products. These events increase net exports and thus increase AD. An appreciation in the value of the dollar will decrease net exports and thus decrease AD.

3. *Aggregate supply* is a curve that shows the total quantity of goods and services that will be produced (supplied) at different price levels.

a. In the **long run,** the aggregate supply curve is vertical at the full-employment level of output for the economy because the rise in wages and other inputs will match changes in the price level.

b. In the **short run,** the aggregate supply curve is upsloping because nominal wages and input prices adjust only slowly to changes in the price level. With this curve, an increase in the price level increases real output and a decrease in the price level reduces real output.

4. The ***determinants of aggregate supply*** that shift the curve include changes in the prices of inputs for production, changes in productivity, and changes in the legal and institutional environment in the economy, as outlined in Figure 10.5.

a. A change in **input prices** for resources used for production will change aggregate supply in the short run. Lower input prices increase AS, and higher input prices decrease AS. These input prices are for both domestic and imported resources, and they can be influenced by market power.

(1) *Domestic resource prices* include the prices for labor, capital, and natural resources used for production. If any of these input prices decreases, then AS will decrease because the per-unit cost of production will decrease. When the prices of these domestic factors of production increase, then AS will decrease.

(2) The *prices of imported resources* are the cost of paying for resources imported from other nations. If the value of the dollar appreciates, then it will cost less to pay for imported resources used for production. As a result, per-unit production costs will decrease, and AS will increase. Conversely, if the value of the dollar depreciates, then it will cost more to import resources, and so AS will decrease.

(3) A change in the degree of *market power* in resource markets can change resource prices and thus change AS. A more competitive market will tend to decrease resource prices and increase AS. A more monopolistic market will tend to drive up resource prices and decrease AS.

b. As ***productivity*** improves, per-unit production costs will fall and AS will increase. This outcome occurs because productivity (output divided by input) is the denominator for the formula for per-unit production costs (which is total input cost divided by productivity). As productivity declines, per-unit production costs will increase, and so AS will decrease.

c. Changes in the **legal and institutional environment** for business can affect per-unit production costs and thus AS.

(1) A decrease in *business taxes* is like a reduction in the per-unit cost of production, and so it will increase AS. The same effect occurs when there is an increase in *business subsidies.* The raising of taxes or the lowering of subsidies for business will increase per-unit production costs and decrease AS.

(2) A decrease in the amount of *government regulation* is similar to a decrease in the per-unit cost of production, and so it will increase AS. An increase in government regulation will raise costs and thus decrease AS.

5. The **equilibrium real output** and the **equilibrium price level** are at the intersection of the aggregate demand and aggregate supply curves. If the price level were below equilibrium, then producers would supply less real output than was demanded by purchasers. Competition among buyers would bid up the price level and producers would increase their output until an equilibrium price level and an equilibrium quantity were reached. If the price level were above equilibrium, then producers would supply more real output than was demanded by purchasers. Competition among sellers would lower the price level and producers would reduce their output until an equilibrium price level and an equilibrium quantity were reached. The aggregate demand and aggregate supply curves can also *shift to change equilibrium.*

  a. An **increase in aggregate demand** would result in an increase in both real domestic output and the price level. An increase in the price level beyond the full-employment level of output is associated with *demand-pull inflation.* A classic example occurred during the late 1960s because of a sizable increase in government spending for domestic programs and the war in Vietnam.

  b. A **decrease in aggregate demand** reduces real output and increases cyclical unemployment, but it may not decrease the price level. In 2001, there was a significant decline in investment spending that reduced aggregate demand and led to a fall in real output and a rise in cyclical unemployment. The rate of inflation fell (there was disinflation), but there was no decline in the price level (deflation). The reason the economy experiences a "GDP gap with no deflation" is that the *price level is inflexible downward.* The price level is largely influenced by labor costs, which account for most of the input prices for the production of many goods and services. There are at least five interrelated reasons for this downward inflexibility of the price level.

  (1) There is a fear of a starting a *price war* in which firms compete with each other on lowering prices regardless of the cost of production. Such a price war hurts business profits and makes firms reluctant to cut prices for fear of starting one.

  (2) Firms are reluctant to change input prices if there are costs related to changing the prices or announcing the change. Such **menu costs** increase the waiting time before businesses make any price changes.

  (3) If wages are determined largely by *long-term contracts,* wages cannot be changed in the short run.

  (4) *Morale, effort, and productivity* may be affected by changes in wage rates. If current wages are **efficiency wages** that maximize worker effort and morale, employers may be reluctant to lower wages because such changes reduce work effort and productivity.

  (5) The *minimum wage* puts a legal floor on wages for the least skilled workers in the economy.

  c. A **decrease in aggregate supply** means there will be a decrease in real domestic output (economic growth) and employment along with a rise in the price level, or *cost-push inflation.* This situation occurred in the mid-1970s when the price of oil substantially and significantly increased the cost of production for many goods and services and reduced productivity.

  d. An **increase in aggregate supply** arising from an increase in productivity has the beneficial effect of improving real domestic output and employment while maintaining a stable price level. Between 1996 and 2000, the economy experienced strong economic growth, full employment, and very low inflation. Those outcomes occurred because of an increase in aggregate demand in combination with an increase in aggregate supply from an increase in productivity resulting from technological change.

6. (Last Word). In the mid-1970s, sizable increases in the price of oil increased production costs and reduced productivity, thus decreasing aggregate supply. Those changes led to cost-push inflation, higher unemployment, and a decline in real output. More recent increases in oil prices during 2000 and in 2005 did not have the adverse effects on the U.S. economy that had been the case in the past. Although there were many reasons for this switch, perhaps the most important was that oil was not as significant a resource for production in the U.S. economy as it had been in the past. The U.S. economy was about 33 percent less sensitive to fluctuations in oil prices.

■ HINTS AND TIPS

1. Aggregate demand and aggregate supply are the tools used to explain what determines the economy's real output and price level. These tools, however, are **different from the demand and supply** used in Chapter 3 to explain what determines the output and price of a *particular* product. Instead of thinking about the quantity of a *particular* good or service demanded or supplied, it is necessary to think about the total or *aggregate* quantity of all final goods and services demanded (purchased) and supplied (produced). You will have no difficulty with the way demand and supply are used in this chapter once you switch from thinking about a *particular* good or service and its price to considering the *aggregate* of all final goods and services and their average price.

2. Make a chart showing each of the **determinants** of aggregate demand (see Figure 10.2) and aggregate supply (Figure 10.5). In the chart, state the direction of the change in each determinant and then state the likely resulting change in AD or AS. For example, if consumer wealth *increases,* then AD *increases.* Or if imported prices for resources *increase,* then AS *decreases.* This simple chart can help you see in one quick glance all the possible changes in determinants and their likely effects on AD or AS. Problem 2 in this *Study Guide* will give you an application for this chart.

3. Make sure you know the difference between a **movement** along an existing aggregate demand or supply curve and a **shift** in (increase or decrease in) an aggregate demand or supply curve. Figures 10.7 and 10.9 illustrate the distinction.

■ IMPORTANT TERMS

aggregate demand–
  aggregate supply
  (AD–AS) model

aggregate demand (AD)

real-balances effect

interest-rate effect

foreign purchases effect

determinants of aggregate
  demand

aggregate supply (AS)

long-run aggregate supply
  curve

short-run aggregate supply
  curve

determinants of aggregate
  supply

productivity

equilibrium price level

equilibrium real output

efficiency wages

menu costs

SELF-TEST

■ FILL-IN QUESTIONS

1. Aggregate demand and aggregate supply together determine the equilibrium real domestic (price, output) _____ and the equilibrium _____ level.

2. The aggregate demand curve shows the quantity of goods and services that will be (supplied, demanded) _____ or purchased at various price levels. For aggregate demand, the relationship between real output and the price level is (positive, negative) _____.

3. The aggregate demand curve slopes (upward, downward) _____ because of the (real-balances, consumption) _____ effect, the (profit, interest) _____-rate effect, and the (domestic, foreign) _____ purchases effect.

4. For the aggregate demand curve, an increase in the price level (increases, decreases) _____ the quantity of real domestic output demanded, whereas a decrease in the price level _____ the quantity of real domestic output demanded, assuming other things equal.

5. For the aggregate demand curve, when the price level changes, there is a (movement along, change in) _____ the curve. When the entire aggregate demand curve shifts, there is a change in (the quantity of real output demanded, aggregate demand) _____.

6. List the four factors that may change consumer spending and thus shift aggregate demand:

a. _____

b. _____

c. _____

d. _____

7. List two major factors that may change investment spending and thus shift aggregate demand:

a. _____

b. _____

8. If government spending increases, then aggregate demand is likely to (increase, decrease) _____, but if government spending decreases, it is likely to _____.

9. If there is an increase in national income abroad, then net exports spending is most likely to (increase, decrease) _____, and if there is a depreciation of the value of the U.S. dollar, then net exports are likely to _____. When net exports increase, aggregate demand will (increase, decrease) _____.

10. The aggregate supply curve shows the quantity of goods and services that will be (demanded, supplied) _____ or produced at various price levels. As the price level increases, real domestic output (increases, decreases) _____, and as the price level decreases, real domestic output _____. The relationship between the price level and real domestic output supplied is (positive, negative) _____.

11. The basic cause of a decrease in aggregate supply is the (increase, decrease) _____ in per-unit costs of producing goods and services, and the basic cause of an increase in aggregate supply is the _____ in per-unit costs of production, all other things equal.

12. Aggregate supply shifts may result from:
  a. a change in input prices caused by a change in

  (1) _____

  (2) _____

  (3) _____
  b. a change in (consumption, productivity)

  _____

  c. a change in the legal and institutional environment caused by a change in

  (1) _____

  (2) _____

13. The equilibrium real domestic output and price level are found at the (zero values, intersection) _____ of the aggregate demand and aggregate supply curves. At this price level, the aggregate quantity of goods and services demanded is (greater than, less than, equal to) _____ the aggregate quantity of goods and services supplied. And at this real domestic output, the prices producers are willing to (pay, accept) _____ are equal to the prices buyers are willing to _____.

14. If the price level is below equilibrium, the quantity of real domestic output supplied will be (greater than, less than) _____ the quantity of real domestic output demanded. As a result, competition among buyers eliminates the (surplus, shortage) _____ and bids up the price level.

15. If the price level is above equilibrium, the quantity of real domestic output supplied will be (greater than, less than) _____ the quantity of real domestic output demanded. As a result, competition among producers eliminates the (surplus, shortage) _____ and lowers the price level.

16. An increase in aggregate demand will (increase, decrease) _____ real domestic output and _____ the price level. If the economy is initially operating at its full-employment level of output and aggregate demand increases, it will produce (demand-pull, cost-push) _____ inflation.

17. If aggregate demand decreases, then real domestic output will (increase, decrease) _____. Such a change often produces economic conditions called (inflation, recession) _____, and unemployment (rises, falls) _____.

18. When aggregate demand decreases, the price level is often inflexible (upward, downward) _____. This inflexibility occurs because of wage (contracts, flexibility) _____, because workers are paid (efficiency, inefficiency) _____ wages, because there is a (maximum, minimum) _____ wage, because businesses experience menu (benefits, costs) _____, and because there is fear of (price, wage) _____ wars.

19. A decrease in aggregate supply will (increase, decrease) _____ real output and _____ the price level. Such a change in aggregate supply contributes to (demand-pull, cost-push) _____ inflation.

20. An increase in aggregate supply will (increase, decrease) _____ real domestic output and _____ the price level. If aggregate demand increased, the price level would (increase, decrease) _____, but a simultaneous increase in aggregate supply (reinforces, offsets) _____ this change and helps keep the price level stable.

■ TRUE–FALSE QUESTIONS

Circle T if the statement is true, F if it is false.

1. Aggregate demand reflects a positive relationship between the price level and the amount of real output demanded.   **T F**

2. The explanation for why the aggregate demand curve slopes downward is the same as the explanation for why the demand curve for a single product slopes downward.   **T F**

3. A fall in the price level increases the real value of financial assets with fixed money values and, as a result, increases spending by the holders of those assets. **T F**

4. Given a fixed supply of money, a rise in the price level increases the demand for money in the economy and drives interest rates downward.   **T F**

5. A rise in the price level of an economy (relative to foreign price levels) tends to increase that economy's exports and reduce its imports of goods and services.   **T F**

6. A movement along a fixed aggregate demand curve is the same as a shift in aggregate demand.   **T F**

7. Changes in aggregate demand involve a change in initial spending from one of the determinants and a multiplier effect on spending.   **T F**

8. A change in aggregate demand is caused by a change in the price level, *other things equal*.   **T F**

9. A fall in excess capacity, will increase the demand for new capital goods and therefore increase aggregate demand.   **T F**

10. The real-balances effect is one of the determinants of aggregate demand.   **T F**

11. A large decline in household debt will increase consumption spending and aggregate demand.   **T F**

12. Appreciation of the dollar relative to foreign currencies will tend to increase net exports and aggregate demand.   **T F**

13. The aggregate supply curve is vertical in the long run at the full-employment level of output.   **T F**

14. When the determinants of short-run aggregate supply change, they alter the per-unit production cost and thus aggregate supply.   **T F**

15. A change in the degree of market power or monopoly power held by sellers of resources can affect input prices and aggregate supply. **T F**

16. Productivity is a measure of real output per unit of input. **T F**

17. Per-unit production cost is determined by dividing total input cost by units of output. **T F**

18. At the equilibrium price level, the real domestic output purchased is equal to the real domestic output produced. **T F**

19. An increase in aggregate demand will increase both the price level and the real domestic output. **T F**

20. An increase in aggregate demand is associated with cost-push inflation. **T F**

21. The greater the increase in the price level that results from an increase in aggregate demand, the greater the increase in the equilibrium real GDP. **T F**

22. A significant decrease in aggregate demand can result in recession and cyclical unemployment. **T F**

23. Fear of price wars tends to make the price level more flexible rather than less flexible. **T F**

24. A decrease in aggregate supply decreases the equilibrium real domestic output and increases the price level, resulting in cost-push inflation. **T F**

25. An increase in aggregate supply driven by productivity increases can offset the inflationary pressures from an increase in aggregate demand. **T F**

■ MULTIPLE-CHOICE QUESTIONS

Circle the letter that corresponds to the best answer.

1. The aggregate demand curve is the relationship between the
(a) price level and what producers will supply
(b) price level and the real domestic output purchased
(c) price level and the real domestic output produced
(d) real domestic output purchased and the real domestic output produced

2. When the price level rises,
(a) the demand for money and interest rates rises
(b) spending that is sensitive to interest-rate changes increases
(c) holders of financial assets with fixed money values increase their spending
(d) holders of financial assets with fixed money values have more purchasing power

3. One explanation for the downward slope of the aggregate demand curve is that a change in the price level results in
(a) a multiplier effect
(b) an income effect
(c) a substitution effect
(d) a foreign purchases effect

4. A sharp decline in the real value of stock prices, which is independent of a change in the price level, would best be an example of
(a) the interest-rate effect
(b) the foreign purchases effect
(c) a change in household debt
(d) a change in the real value of consumer wealth

5. The aggregate demand curve will be increased by
(a) a decrease in the price level
(b) an increase in the price level
(c) a depreciation in the value of the U.S. dollar
(d) an increase in the excess capacity of factories

6. The aggregate supply curve is the relationship between the
(a) price level and the real domestic output purchased
(b) price level and the real domestic output produced
(c) price level producers are willing to accept and the price level purchasers are willing to pay
(d) real domestic output purchased and the real domestic output produced

7. In the long run, the aggregate supply curve is
(a) upsloping
(b) downsloping
(c) vertical
(d) horizontal

8. The short-run aggregate supply curve assumes that
(a) nominal wages respond to changes in the price level
(b) nominal wages do not respond to changes in the price level
(c) the economy is operating at full-employment output
(d) the economy is operating at less than full-employment output

9. If the prices of imported resources increase, then this event most likely will
(a) decrease aggregate supply
(b) increase aggregate supply
(c) increase aggregate demand
(d) decrease aggregate demand

Suppose that real domestic output in an economy is 50 units, the quantity of inputs is 10, and the price of each input is $2. Answer Questions 10, 11, 12, and 13 on the basis of this information.

10. The level of productivity in this economy is
(a) 5
(b) 4
(c) 3
(d) 2

11. The per-unit cost of production is
(a) $0.40
(b) $0.50
(c) $2.50
(d) $3.50

12. If productivity increased so that 60 units are now produced with the quantity of inputs still equal to 10, then per-unit production costs would .
  (a) remain unchanged and aggregate supply would remain unchanged
  (b) increase and aggregate supply would decrease
  (c) decrease and aggregate supply would increase
  (d) decrease and aggregate supply would decrease

13. All else equal, if the price of each input increases from $2 to $4, productivity will
  (a) decrease from $4 to $2 and aggregate supply will decrease
  (b) decrease from $5 to $3 and aggregate supply will decrease
  (c) decrease from $4 to $2 and aggregate supply will increase
  (d) remain unchanged and aggregate supply will decrease

14. If Congress passed much stricter laws to control the air pollution from businesses, this action would tend to
  (a) increase per-unit production costs and shift the aggregate supply curve to the right
  (b) increase per-unit production costs and shift the aggregate supply curve to the left
  (c) increase per-unit production costs and shift the aggregate demand curve to the left
  (d) decrease per-unit production costs and shift the aggregate supply curve to the left

15. An increase in business taxes will tend to
  (a) decrease aggregate demand but not change aggregate supply
  (b) decrease aggregate supply but not change aggregate demand
  (c) decrease aggregate demand and decrease aggregate supply
  (d) decrease aggregate supply and increase aggregate demand

16. If at a particular price level real domestic output from producers is less than real domestic output desired by buyers, there will be a
  (a) surplus and the price level will rise
  (b) surplus and the price level will fall
  (c) shortage and the price level will rise
  (d) shortage and the price level will fall

Answer Questions 17, 18, and 19 on the basis of the following aggregate demand–aggregate supply schedule for a hypothetical economy.

Real domestic output demanded (in billions)	Price level	Real domestic output supplied (in billions)
$1500	175	$4500
$2000	150	$4000
$2500	125	$3500
$3000	100	$3000
$3500	75	$2500
$4000	50	$2000

17. The equilibrium price level and quantity of real domestic output will be
  (a) 100 and $2500
  (b) 100 and $3000
  (c) 125 and $3500
  (d) 150 and $4000

18. If the quantity of real domestic output demanded increased by $2000 at each price level, the new equilibrium price level and quantity of real domestic output would be
  (a) 175 and $4000
  (b) 150 and $4000
  (c) 125 and $3500
  (d) 100 and $3000

19. Using the original data from the table, if the quantity of real domestic output demanded *increased* by $1500 and the quantity of real domestic output supplied *increased* by $500 at each price level, the new equilibrium price level and quantity of real domestic output would be
  (a) 175 and $4000
  (b) 150 and $4500
  (c) 125 and $4000
  (d) 100 and $3500

20. An increase in aggregate demand will increase
  (a) the price level and have no effect on real domestic output
  (b) the real domestic output and have no effect on the price level
  (c) the price level and decrease the real domestic output
  (d) both real output and the price level

21. In the aggregate demand–aggregate supply model, an increase in the price level will
  (a) increase the real value of wealth
  (b) increase the strength of the multiplier
  (c) decrease the strength of the multiplier
  (d) have no effect on the strength of the multiplier

22. Aggregate demand decreases and real output falls, but the price level remains the same. Which factor most likely contributes to downward price inflexibility?
  (a) an increase in aggregate supply
  (b) the foreign purchases effect
  (c) lower interest rates
  (d) efficiency wages

23. Fear of price wars, menu costs, and wage contracts are associated with
  (a) a price level that is inflexible upward
  (b) a price level that is inflexible downward
  (c) a domestic output that cannot be increased
  (d) a domestic output that cannot be decreased

24. If there were cost-push inflation,
  (a) both the real domestic output and the price level would decrease
  (b) the real domestic output would increase and rises in the price level would become smaller

(c) the real domestic output would decrease and the price level would rise

(d) both the real domestic output and rises in the price level would become greater

25. An increase in aggregate supply will

(a) increase the price level and real domestic output

(b) decrease the price level and real domestic output

(c) decrease the price level and increase real domestic output

(d) decrease the price level and have no effect on real domestic output

■ **PROBLEMS**

1. Following is an aggregate supply schedule.

Price level	Real domestic output supplied
250	2100
225	2000
200	1900
175	1700
150	1400
125	1000
100	900

a. Plot this aggregate supply schedule on the graph below.

b. The following table has three aggregate demand schedules.

Price level	Real domestic output demanded		
(1)	(2)	(3)	(4)
250	1400	1900	500
225	1500	2000	600
200	1600	2100	700
175	1700	2200	800
150	1800	2300	900
125	1900	2400	1000
100	2000	2500	1100

(1) On the graph, plot the aggregate demand curve shown in columns 1 and 2; label this curve **AD₁**. At this level of aggregate demand, the equilibrium real domestic output is _____, and the equilibrium price level is _____.

(2) On the same graph, plot the aggregate demand curve shown in columns 1 and 3; label this curve **AD₂**. The equilibrium real domestic output is _____, and the equilibrium price level is _____.

(3) On the same graph, plot the aggregate demand curve shown in columns 1 and 4; label it **AD₃**. The equilibrium real domestic output is _____, and the equilibrium price level is _____.

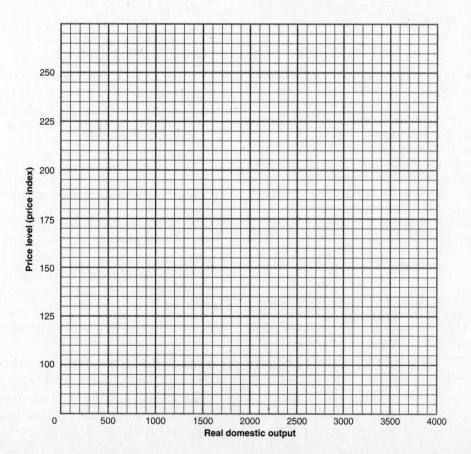

2. In the following list, what most likely will happen as a result of each event to (1) aggregate demand (AD); (2) aggregate supply (AS); (3) the equilibrium price level (**P**); and (4) equilibrium real domestic output (**Q**)? Assume that all other things remain constant when the event occurs and that the economy is operating in the intermediate range of the aggregate supply curve. Use the following symbols to indicate the expected effects: **I** = increase, **D** = decrease, **S** = remains the same, and **U** = uncertain.

a. A decrease in labor productivity.

AD_____   AS_____   **P**_____ **Q**_____

b. A fall in the interest rate for business loans.

AD_____   AS_____   **P**_____ **Q**_____

c. Consumer incomes decline as the economy moves into a recession.

AD_____   AS_____   **P**_____ **Q**_____

d. The price of oil on the world market falls to a low level.

AD_____   AS_____   **P**_____ **Q**_____

e. There is an appreciation in the value of the U.S. dollar.

AD_____   AS_____   **P**_____ **Q**_____

3. Following are hypothetical data showing the relationships between the real domestic output and the quantity of input resources needed to produce each level of output.

Output	Input	Productivity (1)	(2)	Per-unit cost (3)	(4)	(5)
2500	500	___	___	___	___	___
2000	400	___	___	___	___	___
1500	300	___	___	___	___	___

a. In column 1, compute the level of productivity at each level of real domestic output.
b. In column 2, compute the level of productivity if there is a doubling in the quantity of inputs required to produce each level of output.
c. In column 3, compute the per-unit production cost at each level of output if each unit of input costs $15, given the level of productivity in column 1.
d. In column 4, compute the new per-unit production cost at each level of output if each unit of input costs $15, given that there has been a doubling in the required quantity of inputs to produce each level of output as shown in column 2. If this situation occurs, will aggregate supply (decrease, increase, stay the same)?

_____

e. In column 5, compute the new per-unit production cost at each level of output, given that input price is now $10 instead of $15 but the level of productivity stays as it was originally shown in column 1. What will happen to the aggregate supply curve if this situation occurs?

_____

4. Columns 1 and 2 in the table that follows are the aggregate supply schedule of an economy.

(1) Price level	(2) Real GDP	(3) AD$_1$	(4) AD$_2$	(5) AD$_3$	(6) AD$_4$	(7) AD$_5$	(8) AD$_6$
260	2540	940	1140	1900	2000	2090	2390
240	2490	1040	1240	2000	2100	2190	2490
220	2430	1140	1340	2100	2200	2290	2590
200	2390	1240	1440	2200	2300	2390	2690
190	2350	1390	1590	2250	2350	2540	2740
180	2300	1440	1640	2300	2400	2590	2890
160	2200	1540	1740	2400	2500	2690	2990
140	2090	1640	1840	2500	2600	2790	3090
120	1940	1740	1940	2600	2700	2890	3190
100	1840	1840	2040	2700	2800	2990	3290

a. If the aggregate demand in the economy were columns 1 and 3, the equilibrium real GDP would be _____ and the equilibrium price level would be _____, and if aggregate demand increased to that shown in columns 1 and 4, the equilibrium real GDP would increase to _____ and the price level would be _____.
b. Should aggregate demand be that shown in columns 1 and 5, the equilibrium real GDP would be _____ and the equilibrium price would be _____, and if aggregate demand should increase by 100 units to that shown in columns 1 and 6, the equilibrium real GDP would increase to _____ and the price level would rise to _____.
c. If aggregate demand were that shown in columns 1 and 7, the equilibrium real GDP would be _____ and the equilibrium price level would be _____, but if aggregate demand increased to that shown in columns 1 and 8, the equilibrium real GDP would be _____ and the price level would rise to _____.

■ **SHORT ANSWER AND ESSAY QUESTIONS**

1. What is the aggregate demand curve? Draw a graph and explain its features.

2. Use the interest-rate effect, the real-balances effect, and the foreign purchases effect to explain the relationship between the price level and the real domestic output demanded.

3. Explain the wealth effect and its impact on purchasing power. Give an example.

4. What roles do the expectations of consumers and businesses play in influencing aggregate demand?

5. How is aggregate demand changed by changes in net export spending? What factors cause changes in net export spending?

6. Why is the aggregate supply curve in the long run a vertical curve? Why is output not affected by the price level in the long run?

7. Why does the short-run aggregate supply curve slope upward?

8. Why does a change in the degree of market power affect aggregate supply?

9. Describe how changes in the international economy influence aggregate demand or aggregate supply.

10. How does an increase or decrease in per-unit production costs change aggregate supply? Give examples.

11. How does the legal and institutional environment affect aggregate supply? Give examples.

12. Explain how a change in business taxes affects aggregate demand and aggregate supply.

13. What real domestic output is the equilibrium real domestic output? What will happen to real output if the price level is below equilibrium?

14. What are the effects on the real domestic output and the price level when aggregate demand increases along the aggregate supply curve?

15. What is the relationship between the effect of an increase in aggregate demand on real GDP and the rise in the price level that accompanies it? Discuss this in terms of the multiplier effect.

16. If prices were as flexible downward as they are upward, what would be the effects on real domestic output and the price level of a decrease in aggregate demand?

17. Give reasons why prices in the economy tend to be inflexible in a downward direction in the horizontal range of aggregate supply.

18. What are the effects on the real domestic output and the price level of a decrease in aggregate supply?

19. How does an increase in aggregate supply affect the price level and real output?

20. Explain why rises in oil prices lost their strong inflationary effects on the U.S. economy since the mid-1970s (Last Word).

ANSWERS

Chapter 10 Aggregate Demand and Aggregate Supply

FILL-IN QUESTIONS

1. output, price
2. demanded, negative
3. downward, real-balances, interest, foreign
4. decreases, increases
5. movement along, aggregate demand
6. *a.* consumer wealth; *b.* consumer expectations; *c.* household debt; *d.* personal taxes (any order for *a–d*)
7. *a.* interest rates; *b.* expected returns on investment (either order for *a–b*)
8. increase, decrease

9. increase, increase, increase
10. supplied, increases, decreases, positive
11. increase, decrease
12. *a.* (1) domestic resource availability, (2) prices of imported resources, (3) market power (any order for *1–3*); *b.* productivity; *c.* (1) business taxes and subsidies, (2) government regulation (either order for *1–2*)
13. intersection, equal to, accept, pay
14. less than, shortage
15. greater than, surplus
16. increase, increase, demand-pull
17. decrease, recession, rises
18. downward, contracts, efficiency, minimum, costs, price
19. decrease, increase, cost-push
20. increase, decrease, increase, offsets

TRUE–FALSE QUESTIONS

1. F, p. 188	10. F, pp. 188, 190	19. T, pp. 196–197
2. F, pp. 188–189	11. F, p. 190	20. F, pp. 197–197
3. T, p. 189	12. F, pp. 191–192	21. F, pp. 197–198
4. F, p. 189	13. T, p. 192	22. T, pp. 198–199
5. F, p. 189	14. T, p. 193	23. F, p. 199
6. F, p. 189	15. T, p. 195	24. T, pp. 199–200
7. T, p. 189	16. T, p. 195	25. T, pp. 200, 202
8. F, p. 189	17. T, p. 195	
9. T, p. 191	18. T, p. 196	

MULTIPLE-CHOICE QUESTIONS

1. b, p. 188	10. a, p. 195	19. c, pp. 200, 202
2. a, p. 189	11. a, p. 195	20. d, pp. 196–197
3. d, p. 189	12. c, p. 195	21. c, pp. 197–198
4. d, p. 190	13. d, p. 195	22. d, p. 199
5. c, pp. 191–192	14. b, p. 196	23. b, p. 199
6. b, p. 192	15. c, pp. 195–196	24. c, pp. 199–200
7. c, p. 192	16. c, p. 196	25. c, pp. 200, 202
8. b, p. 193	17. b, p. 196	
9. a, pp. 194–195	18. b, pp. 196–197	

PROBLEMS

1. *b.* (1) 1700, 175, (2) 2000, 225, (3) 1000, 125
2. *a.* S, D, I, D; *b.* I, S, I, I; *c.* D, S, D, D; *d.* I, I, U, I; *e.* D, I, D, U
3. *a.* 5, 5, 5; *b.* 2.5, 2.5, 2.5; *c.* $3, $3, $3; *d.* $6, $6, $6, decrease; *e.* $2, $2, $2, it will increase
4. *a.* 1840, 100, 1940, 120; *b.* 2300, 180, 2350, 190; *c.* 2390, 200, 2490, 240

SHORT ANSWER AND ESSAY QUESTIONS

1. p. 188	8. p. 195	15. pp. 196–198
2. pp. 188–189	9. pp. 191, 194	16. pp. 198–199
3. p. 190	10. p. 195	17. p. 199
4. pp. 190–191	11. pp. 195–196	18. pp. 199–200
5. pp. 191–192	12. pp. 195–196	19. pp. 200, 201
6. p. 192	13. p. 196	20. p. 201
7. p. 193	14. pp. 196–197	

The Relationship of the Aggregate Demand Curve to the Aggregate Expenditure Model

This appendix explains how the aggregate expenditures (AE) model that you learned about in Chapter 9 is related to the aggregate demand (AD) curve that was presented in Chapter 10. There are two short sections in this appendix. The first one focuses on the derivation of the aggregate demand curve from the AE model. The second one explains how shifts in aggregate demand are related to shifts in aggregate expenditures.

Although the aggregate expenditures model is a fixed-price-level model and the aggregate demand–aggregate supply model is a variable-price-level model, there is a close relationship between the two models. The important thing to understand is that prices can be fixed or constant at different levels. The AD curve can be derived from the aggregate expenditures model by letting the price level be constant at different levels. For example, the lower (the higher) the level at which prices are constant in the aggregate expenditures model, the larger (the smaller) the equilibrium real GDP in that model of the economy. Various output-price-level combinations can be traced to derive an AD curve that slopes downward, as shown in Figure 1 in the text.

The aggregate demand curve can shift (increase or decrease) because of a change in the nonprice level **determinants of aggregate demand.** Those determinants include changes in factors affecting consumer, investment, government, and net export spending. These determinants are similar to the components of the aggregate expenditures model. It is easy to show the relationship between the shifts in the two models. A change in spending will cause a shift (upward or downward) in the aggregate expenditures schedule, as shown in Figure 2 in the text. The initial change in spending, when multiplied by the multiplier, would be equal to the size of the horizontal shift in AD, assuming a constant price level.

■ CHECKLIST

When you have studied this appendix you should be able to

☐ Contrast the aggregate expenditures and the aggregate demand–aggregate supply models by comparing the variability of the price level and real GDP.
☐ Use a graph to derive the aggregate demand curve from the aggregate expenditures model.
☐ Explain the effect of a change in a determinant of aggregate demand on aggregate expenditures.

☐ Use a graph to show the relationship between a shift in aggregate expenditures and a shift in aggregate demand.
☐ Discuss how the initial change in spending and the multiplier effect influence the size of the shift in aggregate demand.

■ CHAPTER OUTLINE

1. This chapter introduces the **aggregate demand–aggregate supply model** of the economy to explain why real domestic output *and* the price level fluctuate. This model has an advantage over the aggregate expenditures model because it allows the price level to vary (rise and fall) rather than be constant or fixed as in the aggregate expenditures model.

2. The aggregate demand curve can be derived from the intersections of the aggregate expenditures curves and the 45-degree curve. As the price level falls, the aggregate expenditures curve shifts upward and the equilibrium real GDP increases, but as the price level rises, the aggregate expenditures curve shifts downward and the equilibrium real GDP decreases. The inverse relationship between the price level and equilibrium real GDP is the aggregate demand curve. Note that for the aggregate expenditures model,

  a. changes in real balances (wealth) increase or decrease the consumption schedule;
  b. changes in the interest rate increase or decrease the investment schedule; and
  c. changes in imports or exports affect net exports, which can increase or decrease the net export schedule.

3. If the price level is constant, any change in nonprice level determinants of consumption and planned investment that shifts the aggregate expenditures curve upward will increase the equilibrium real GDP and shift the AD curve to the right by an amount equal to the initial increase in aggregate expenditures times the multiplier. Conversely, any change in nonprice level determinants of consumption and planned investment that shifts the aggregate expenditures curve downward will decrease the equilibrium real GDP and shift the AD curve to the left by an amount equal to the initial decrease in aggregate expenditures times the multiplier.

■ HINTS AND TIPS

1. Figure 1 is worth extra study to see the relationship between the quantity (real domestic output) and the price level in both models. The upper panel shows the aggregate expenditures model with aggregate expenditures on the vertical axis and quantity on the horizontal axis. The lower panel shows the aggregate demand model with the price level on the vertical axis and quantity on the horizontal axis. Thus, the horizontal axes in both graphs are the same and are directly related. The connection between the price levels in each graph is more indirect, but they are related nevertheless, as shown in Figure 1.

2. Figure 2 shows how shifts are accounted for in each model. A shift upward in aggregate expenditures is the same as a shift outward in aggregate demand. The magnitude of the change in quantity will depend on the multiplier effect, but in both models quantity increases by the same amount.

■ IMPORTANT TERMS

aggregate demand	aggregate expenditures
determinants of	schedule
aggregate demand	multiplier

SELF-TEST

■ FILL-IN QUESTIONS

1. In the aggregate demand–aggregate supply model, the price level is (fixed, variable) _____, but in the aggregate expenditures model, the price level is

_____.

2. In the aggregate expenditures model, a lower price level would (raise, lower) _____ the consumption, investment, and aggregate expenditures curves, and the equilibrium level of real GDP would (rise, fall) _____.

3. In the aggregate expenditures model, a higher price level would (raise, lower) _____ the consumption, investment, and aggregate expenditures curves, and the equilibrium level of real GDP would (rise, fall) _____.

4. This relationship between the price level and equilibrium real GDP in the aggregate expenditures model is (direct, inverse) _____ and can be used to derive the aggregate (demand, supply) _____ curve.

5. If the price level were constant, an increase in the aggregate expenditures curve would shift the aggregate demand curve to the (right, left) _____ by an amount equal to the upward shift in aggregate expenditures times the (interest rate, multiplier) _____. A decrease in the aggregate expenditures curve would shift the aggregate demand curve to the (right, left) _____ by an amount equal to the (upward, downward) _____ shift in aggregate expenditures times the (interest rate, multiplier) _____.

■ TRUE–FALSE QUESTIONS

Circle T if the statement is true, F if it is false.

1. Both the graph of the aggregate demand curve and that of the aggregate expenditures model show the price level on the vertical axis.   **T F**

2. The higher the price level, the smaller the real balances of consumers and the lower the aggregate expenditures schedule.   **T F**

3. An increase in the price level will shift the aggregate expenditures schedule upward.   **T F**

4. An increase in investment spending will shift the aggregate expenditures curve upward and the aggregate demand curve leftward.   **T F**

5. A shift in the aggregate demand curve is equal to the initial change in spending times the multiplier.   **T F**

■ MULTIPLE-CHOICE QUESTIONS

Circle the letter that corresponds to the best answer.

1. If the price level in the aggregate expenditures model were lower, the consumption and aggregate expenditures curves would be
  (a) lower, and the equilibrium real GDP would be smaller
  (b) lower, and the equilibrium real GDP would be larger
  (c) higher, and the equilibrium real GDP would be larger
  (d) higher, and the equilibrium real GDP would be smaller

2. In the aggregate expenditures model, a decrease in the price level, other things held constant, will shift the
  (a) consumption, investment, and net exports curves downward
  (b) consumption, investment, and net exports curves upward
  (c) consumption and investment curves upward but the net exports curve downward
  (d) consumption and net export curves upward but the investment curve downward

3. An increase in investment spending will
  (a) increase aggregate expenditures and increase aggregate demand
  (b) decrease aggregate expenditures and decrease aggregate demand

(c) increase aggregate expenditures and decrease aggregate demand

(d) decrease aggregate expenditures and increase aggregate demand

4. A decrease in net export spending will shift the

(a) aggregate expenditures schedule upward and the aggregate demand curve rightward

(b) aggregate expenditures schedule upward and the aggregate demand curve leftward

(c) aggregate expenditures schedule downward and the aggregate demand curve rightward

(d) aggregate expenditures schedule downward and the aggregate demand curve leftward

5. An increase in aggregate expenditures shifts the aggregate demand curve to the

(a) right by the amount of the increase in aggregate expenditures

(b) right by the amount of the increase in aggregate expenditures times the multiplier

(c) left by the amount of the increase in aggregate expenditures

(d) left by the amount of the increase in aggregate expenditures times the multiplier

■ **PROBLEMS**

1. Column 1 of the following table shows the real GDP an economy might produce.

(1) Real GDP	(2) AE$_{1.20}$	(3) AE$_{1.00}$	(4) AE$_{0.80}$
$2100	$2110	$2130	$2150
2200	2200	2220	2240
2300	2290	2310	2330
2400	2380	2400	2420
2500	2470	2490	2510
2600	2560	2580	2600

a. If the price level in this economy were $1.20, the aggregate expenditures (AE) at each real GDP would be those shown in column 2 and the equilibrium real GDP would be $_____.

b. If the price level were $1.00, the aggregate expenditures at each real GDP would be those shown in column 3 and the equilibrium real GDP would be $_____.

c. If the price level were $0.80, the aggregate expenditures at each real GDP would be those shown in column 4 and the equilibrium real GDP would be $_____.

d. Show in the following schedule the equilibrium real GDP at each of the three price levels.

Price level	Equilibrium real GDP
$1.20	$_____
1.00	_____
0.80	_____

(1) This schedule is the aggregate (demand, supply) _____ schedule.

(2) The equilibrium real GDP is (directly, inversely) _____ related to the price level.

■ **SHORT ANSWER AND ESSAY QUESTIONS**

1. What do the horizontal axes measure in a graph of the aggregate expenditures model and the aggregate demand curve?

2. Why is there an inverse relationship between aggregate expenditures and the price level? Explain, using real balance, the interest rate, and foreign purchases.

3. Describe how the aggregate demand curve can be derived from the aggregate expenditures model.

4. What is the effect of an increase in aggregate expenditures on the aggregate demand curve? Explain in words and with a graph.

5. What role does the multiplier play in shifting aggregate expenditures and aggregate demand?

ANSWERS

Appendix to Chapter 10 The Relationship of the Aggregate Demand Curve to the Aggregate Expenditures Model

FILL-IN QUESTIONS

1. variable, fixed
2. raise, rise
3. lower, fall
4. inverse, demand
5. right, multiplier, left, downward, multiplier

TRUE–FALSE QUESTIONS

1. F, p. 205   **4.** F, p. 206
2. T, p. 205   **5.** T, p. 206
3. F, p. 206

MULTIPLE-CHOICE QUESTIONS

1. c, p. 205   **4.** d, p. 206
2. b, p. 205   **5.** b, p. 206
3. a, pp. 205–206

PROBLEMS

1. *a.* 2200; *b.* 2400; *c.* 2600; *d.* 2200, 2400, 2600, (1) demand, (2) inversely

SHORT ANSWER AND ESSAY QUESTIONS

1. p. 205   **4.** p. 206
2. p. 205   **5.** p. 206
3. pp. 205–206

CHAPTER 11

Fiscal Policy, Deficits, and Debt

Over the years, the most serious macroeconomic problems have been those resulting from the swings of the business cycle. Learning what determines the equilibrium level of real output and prices in an economy and what causes them to fluctuate makes it possible to find ways to achieve maximum output, full employment, and stable prices. In short, macroeconomic principles can suggest policies to control both recession and inflation in an economy.

As you will discover in Chapter 11, the Federal government may use **fiscal policy**—changes in government spending or taxation—to influence the economy's output, employment, and price level. The chapter first discusses discretionary fiscal policy to show that it affects aggregate demand. **Expansionary fiscal policy** is used to stimulate the economy and pull it out of a slump or recession by increasing government spending, decreasing taxes, or some combination of the two. **Contractionary fiscal policy** is enacted to counter inflationary pressure in the economy by cutting government spending, raising taxes, or both.

Discretionary fiscal policy requires that Congress take action to change tax rates, initiate transfer payment programs, or purchase goods and services. **Nondiscretionary fiscal policy** does not require Congress to take any action and is a **built-in stabilizer** for the economy. The economy has a progressive tax system that provides such automatic or built-in stability. When GDP increases, net tax revenues will increase to reduce inflationary pressure, and when GDP declines, net tax revenues will fall to stimulate the economy.

To evaluate the direction of fiscal policy one must understand the **standardized budget** and the distinction between a **cyclical deficit** and a **standardized deficit**. This budget analysis enables economists to determine whether Federal fiscal policy is expansionary, contractionary, or neutral and determine what policy should be enacted to improve the economy's performance. From this budget analysis you will gain insights into the course of U.S. fiscal policy in recent years.

Fiscal policy is not without its problems, criticisms, or complications. There are timing problems in getting it implemented. There are political considerations in getting it accepted by politicians and voters. If fiscal policy is temporary rather than permanent, it is thought to be less effective. Some economists criticize the borrowing of money by the Federal government for an expansionary fiscal policy because they think it will raise interest rates and crowd out investment spending, thus reducing the

policy's effects. The debate over the value of fiscal policy is an ongoing one, as you will learn from the chapter.

Any budget surplus or deficit from a change in fiscal policy affects the size of the **public debt** (often called the national debt). Over the years the United States accumulated a public debt that now totals about $8 trillion. The debt increased because budget deficits accumulate over time and are not offset by budget surpluses. The size of the public debt is placed into perspective by (1) describing who owns the debt; (2) comparing it (and interest payments on it) to the size of the economy (GDP); and (3) looking at the size of the public debt in other industrial nations.

The last sections of the chapter examine the economic implications or **consequences of the public debt.** These economic problems do not include bankrupting the Federal government because the government can meet its obligations through refinancing and taxation. Nor does the public debt simply shift the economic burden to future generations because the public debt is a public credit for the many people who hold that debt in the form of U.S. securities. Rather, the public debt and payment of interest on the debt contribute to important problems: increased inequality in income, reduced incentives for work and production, a decreased standard of living when part of the debt is paid to foreigners, and the possible crowding out of private investment.

■ CHECKLIST

When you have studied this chapter you should be able to

☐ Distinguish between discretionary and nondiscretionary fiscal policy.

☐ Explain expansionary fiscal policy and the effect of spending and policy decisions on aggregate demand.

☐ Describe contractionary fiscal policy and the effect of spending and tax policy decisions on aggregate demand.

☐ Assess whether it is preferable to use government spending or taxes to counter recession and reduce inflation.

☐ Define automatic or built-in stabilizers.

☐ Indicate how the built-in stabilizers help counter recession and inflation.

☐ Describe how automatic stabilizers are affected by different tax systems (progressive, proportional, and regressive).

☐ Distinguish between the actual budget and the standardized budget for evaluating fiscal policy.

☐ Describe recent U.S. fiscal policy by using the standardized budget.

☐ Describe projections for U.S. budget deficits and surpluses.

☐ Use the standardized budget to evaluate discretionary fiscal policy.

☐ Explain how Social Security affects the size of the federal budget.

☐ Outline three timing problems that may arise with fiscal policy.

☐ Discuss the political considerations that affect fiscal policy.

☐ Explain how expectations of policy reversals in the future change the effectiveness of fiscal policy.

☐ Describe how changes in state and local finances may offset fiscal policy at the federal level.

☐ Use a graph to illustrate the crowding-out effect of fiscal policy.

☐ State the major criticisms of the crowding-out effect.

☐ Discuss current thinking on fiscal policy.

☐ Explain the relationship of budget deficits and surpluses to the public debt.

☐ List the major types of owners of the public debt.

☐ Compare the size of the public debt to GDP.

☐ Compare interest payments on the public debt to GDP.

☐ Compare the U.S. public debt with the debts of other industrial nations.

☐ State two reasons why a large public debt will not bankrupt the federal government.

☐ Discuss whether the public debt imposes a burden on future generations.

☐ State the effect of the public debt on income distribution.

☐ Explain how the public debt affects incentives.

☐ Evaluate the differences between foreign and domestic ownership of the public debt.

☐ Describe the crowding-out effect of a public debt.

☐ State two factors that offset the crowding-out effect of a public debt.

☐ List the 10 items in the index of leading economic indicators (Last Word).

■ **CHAPTER OUTLINE**

1. Fiscal policy consists of the changes made by the Federal government in its budget expenditures and tax revenues to expand or contract the economy. In making these changes, the Federal government may seek to increase the economy's real output and employment or control its rate of inflation.

2. Fiscal policy is *discretionary* when changes in government spending or taxation are designed to change the level of real GDP, employment, incomes, or the price level. The **Council of Economic Advisers (CEA)** advises the U.S. president on such policies. Specific action then needs to be taken by Congress to initiate the discretionary policy, in contrast to *nondiscretionary* fiscal policy, which occurs automatically (see item 3, below).

a. Expansionary fiscal policy generally is used to counteract the negative economic effects of a recession or cyclical downturn in the economy (a decline in real GDP and rising unemployment). The purpose of the policy is to stimulate the economy by increasing aggregate demand. The policy will create a **budget deficit** (government spending greater than tax revenues) if the budget was in balance before the policy was enacted. The stimulative effect on the economy of the initial increase in spending from the policy change will be increased by the multiplier effect. Three policy options are used:
(1) increased government spending;
(2) tax reductions (which increase consumer spending); or
(3) a combination (increased government spending and a tax reduction).

b. Contractionary fiscal policy is a restrictive form of fiscal policy that generally is used to control demand-pull inflation. The purpose of this policy is to reduce aggregate demand pressures that increase the price level. If the government budget is balanced before the policy is enacted, it will create a **budget surplus** (tax revenues are greater than government spending). The contractionary effect on the economy of the initial reduction in spending from the policy will be reinforced by the multiplier effect. Three policy options are used:
(1) decreased government spending;
(2) tax increases (which reduce consumer spending); or
(3) a combination (decreased government spending and tax increases).

c. Whether government purchases or taxes should be altered to reduce recession and inflation depends on whether an expansion or a contraction of the public sector is desired.

3. In the U.S. economy there are automatic or **built-in stabilizers.** Net tax revenues (tax revenues minus government transfer payments) are not a fixed amount or lump sum; they automatically increase as the GDP rises and automatically decrease as the GDP falls.

a. The economic importance of this net tax system is that it serves as a built-in stabilizer of the economy. It reduces purchasing power during periods of rising inflation and expands purchasing during periods of declining output and employment.

b. As GDP increases, the average tax rates will increase in a **progressive tax system,** remain constant in a **proportional tax system,** and decrease in a **regressive tax system;** there is more built-in stability for the economy in progressive tax systems. Built-in stabilizers can reduce but cannot eliminate economic fluctuations, and so discretionary fiscal policy may be needed.

4. To evaluate the direction of discretionary fiscal policy, adjustments need to be made to the actual budget deficits or surpluses.

a. The **standardized budget** is a better index than the actual budget of the direction of government fiscal policy because it indicates what the Federal budget deficit or surplus would be if the economy were operating at full employment. In the case of a budget deficit, the standardized budget

(1) removes the *cyclical deficit* that is produced by swings in the business cycle, and

(2) reveals the size of the **standardized deficit,** indicating how expansionary the fiscal policy was that year.

b. Recent data on *standardized* budget deficits or surpluses show the years in which fiscal policy was expansionary or contractionary. From 1990 to 1993 deficits increased, and so fiscal policy was expansionary. From 1994 to 1998 deficits declined and from 1999 to 2000 there were surpluses, and so fiscal policy was contractionary. From 2002 to 2003 deficits increased, and so fiscal policy was expansionary. From 2004 to 2005 deficits declined, and so fiscal policy was contractionary.

c. Table 11.5 in the text shows past changes in U.S. budget deficits and surpluses. It also shows projections, but these can change with changes in fiscal policy and economic growth.

d. The *Social Security* trust fund currently generates more revenue than expenditures for the federal government. This situation decreases budget deficits and increases budget surpluses.

5. Certain **problems, criticisms, and complications** arise in enacting and applying fiscal policy.

a. There will be problems of *timing* because it requires time to recognize the need for fiscal policy, to take the appropriate steps in Congress, and for the action taken there to affect output, employment, and the rate of inflation in the economy.

b. There may be *political considerations* with fiscal policy that counter the economic effects. Elected officials may cause a **political business cycle** if they lower taxes and increase spending before elections and then do the opposite after elections.

c. Fiscal policy may be less effective if people expect it to be reversed in the future, thus making the policy temporary rather than permanent.

d. The fiscal policies of state and local governments can run counter to Federal fiscal policy and offset it.

e. An expansionary fiscal policy may, by raising the level of interest rates in the economy, reduce investment spending and weaken the effect of the policy on real GDP, but this **crowding-out effect** may be small and can be offset by an expansion in the money supply.

f. Current thinking about discretionary fiscal policy shows differing perspectives. Some economists think that fiscal policy is ineffective because of all the potential problems and complications. They recommend the use of monetary policy to guide the economy. Other economists think that fiscal policy can be useful for directing the economy and that it can reinforce or support monetary policy. There is general agreement that fiscal policy should be designed so that its incentives and investments strengthen long-term economic growth.

6. The **public debt** at any time is the sum of the Federal government's previous annual deficits minus any annual surpluses. In 2005 the total public debt was nearly $8 trillion.

a. The pubic debt is owned by various holders of **U.S. securities** (financial instruments issued by the U.S. government to borrow money, such as U.S. Treasury bills, notes, and bonds). About half (51%) of the public debt is held by Federal government agencies (42%) and the Federal Reserve (9%). The other half (49%) is owned by a "public" that includes U.S. individuals (8%), U.S. banks and financial institutions (8%), foreigners (25%), and others, such as state and local governments (8%).

b. It is better to consider the size of the debt as a percentage of the economy's GDP than as an absolute amount because the percentage shows the capacity of the economy to handle the debt. The percentage in 2005 (31.4%) was well below that of the 1990s.

c. Many industrial nations have public debts as a percentage of GDP that are similar to or much greater than that of the United States.

d. Interest payments as a percentage of the economy's GDP reflect the level of taxation (average tax rate) required to pay interest on the public debt. The percentage in 2005 (1.5%) was down from previous years.

7. The **false contentions** about a large debt are that it will eventually bankrupt the government and that borrowing to finance expenditures passes the cost on to future generations.

a. The debt *cannot bankrupt* the government because the government need not reduce the debt and can refinance it; it also has the constitutional authority to levy taxes to pay the debt.

b. The burden of the debt *cannot be shifted to future generations* because U.S. citizens and institutions hold most of the debt. Repayment of any portion of the principal and the payment of interest on it do not reduce wealth or purchasing power in the United States because the debt would be paid to U.S. citizens and institutions. The only exception is the payment of the part of debt that would go to foreign owners of the debt.

8. The public debt does create **real and potential problems** in the economy.

a. The payment of interest on the debt probably increases *Income inequality* because this payment typically goes to wealthier individuals.

b. The payment of taxes to finance those interest payments may *reduce incentives* to bear risks, to innovate, to invest, and to save and therefore slow growth in the economy.

c. The portion of the debt held by foreign citizens and institutions (the **external public debt**) requires the repayment of principal and the payment of interest to foreign citizens and institutions. This repayment would *transfer to foreigners* a part of the real output of the U.S. economy.

d. An increase in government spending may impose a burden on future generations by *crowding out* private investment spending, thus reducing the future stock of capital goods.

(1) If government spending is financed by increased public debt, the increased borrowing of the Federal government will raise interest rates and reduce private investment spending. Future generations will inherit a smaller stock of capital goods.

(2) The burden imposed on future generations is lessened if the increase in government expenditures is for worthwhile **public investments** that increase the production capacity of the economy. This public investment can also complement and stimulate private investment spending that increases the future capital stock.

9. (Last Word). The index of leading economic indicators consists of 10 economic variables that are used to measure the future direction of economic activities. The 10 variables are the average length of the workweek, initial claims for unemployment insurance, new orders for consumer goods, on-time performance of vendors, new orders for capital goods, building permits for houses, stock prices, the money supply, the spread in interest rates, and consumer expectations.

■ HINTS AND TIPS

1. Fiscal policy is a broad concept that covers several kinds of policies. The main difference is the one between discretionary and nondiscretionary fiscal policies. Discretionary fiscal policy is active and means that Congress has taken specific actions to change taxes or government spending to influence the economy. It can be expansionary or contractionary. Nondiscretionary fiscal policy is passive, or automatic, because changes in tax revenues occur without specific actions by Congress.

2. An increase in government spending that is equal to a cut in taxes will not have an equal effect on real GDP. To understand this point, assume that the MPC is .75, the increase in government spending is $8 billion, and the decrease in taxes is $8 billion. The multiplier would be 4 because it equals $1/(1 - .75)$. The increase in government spending will increase real GDP by $32 billion ($8 billion $\times$ 4). Of the $8 billion decrease in taxes, however, one-quarter of it will be saved ($6 billion $\times$ .25 = $2 billion) and just three-quarters will be spent ($8 billion $\times$ .75 = $6 billion). Thus, the tax cut results in an increase in *initial* spending in the economy of $6 billion, not $8 billion, as was the case with the increase in government spending. The tax cut effect on real GDP is $24 billion ($6 billion $\times$ 4), not $32 billion.

3. Make sure you know the difference between a **budget deficit** (government spending greater than tax revenue for a year) and the **public debt** (the accumulation over time of budget deficits that are offset by any budget surpluses). These two terms are often confused.

4. The best way to gauge the size of budget deficits, the public debt, or interest on the public debt is to calculate each one as a *percentage of real GDP.* The absolute size of these three items is *not* a good indicator of whether each one causes problems for the economy.

5. Try to understand the real rather than the imagined problems caused by the public debt. The debt will not cause the country to go bankrupt, nor will it be a burden on future generations.

■ IMPORTANT TERMS

fiscal policy

Council of Economic
  Advisers (CEA)

expansionary fiscal policy

budget deficit

contractionary fiscal policy

budget surplus

built-in stabilizer

standardized budget

cyclical deficit

political business cycle

crowding-out effect

public debt

U.S. securities

external public debt

public investments

SELF-TEST

■ FILL-IN QUESTIONS

1. Policy actions taken by Congress that are designed to change government spending or taxation are (discretionary, nondiscretionary) _____ fiscal policy, but when the policy takes effect automatically or independently of Congress, it is _____ fiscal policy.

2. Expansionary fiscal policy is generally designed to (increase, decrease) _____ aggregate demand and thus _____ real GDP and employment in the economy. Contractionary fiscal policy is generally used to (increase, decrease) _____ aggregate demand and _____ the level of prices.

3. Expansionary fiscal policy can be achieved with an increase in (government spending, taxes) _____, a decrease in _____, or a combination of the two; contractionary fiscal policy can be achieved by a decrease in (government spending, taxes) _____, an increase in _____, or a combination of the two.

4. An increase in government spending of $5 billion from an expansionary fiscal policy for an economy might ultimately produce an increase in real GDP of $20 billion. This magnified effect occurs because of the (multiplier, crowding-out) _____ effect.

5. Net taxes equal taxes (plus, minus) _____ transfer payments and are called "taxes" in this chapter. In the United States, as GDP increases, tax revenue will (increase, decrease) _____, and as the GDP decreases, tax revenues will _____.

6. Because tax revenues are (directly, indirectly) _____ related to the GDP, the economy has some (artificial, built-in) _____ stability. If the GDP increases, tax revenues will increase, and the budget surplus will (increase, decrease) _____, thus (stimulating, restraining) _____ the economy when that is needed. When GDP decreases, tax revenues decrease and the budget deficit (increases, decreases) _____, thus (stimulating, restraining) _____ the economy when that is needed.

7. As GDP increases, the average tax rates will increase with a (progressive, proportional, regressive) _____ tax system, remain constant with a _____ tax system, and decrease with a _____ tax system. With a progressive tax system, there is (more, less) _____ built-in stability for the economy.

8. If there are growing deficits in the standardized budget, the direction of fiscal policy is (contractionary, expansionary) _____, and if there are growing surpluses in the standardized budget, fiscal policy is _____. A deficit produced by swings in the business cycle is (actual, cyclical) _____. When there is a cyclical deficit, the standardized budget deficit will be (greater, less) _____ than the actual budget deficit.

9. Current contributions to the Social Security system mean that tax revenues are (greater, less) _____ than benefit payouts to retirees. Contributions for Social Security, therefore, create a (deficit, surplus) _____ that (adds to, subtracts from) _____ the size of a Federal budget surplus.

10. There is a problem of timing in the use of discretionary fiscal policy because of the time between the beginning of a recession or inflation and awareness of it, or (an administrative, an operational, a recognition) _____ lag; the time needed for Congress to adjust fiscal policy, or _____ lag; and the time needed for fiscal policy to take effect, or _____ lag.

11. Political problems arise in the application of discretionary fiscal policy to stabilize the economy because government has (one, several) _____ economic goal(s), state and local fiscal policies may (reinforce, counter) _____ Federal fiscal policy, and politicians may use fiscal policies in a way that creates (an international, a political) _____ business cycle.

12. Expectations among households and businesses that fiscal policy will be reversed in the future make fiscal policy (more, less) _____ effective. For example, if taxpayers expect a tax cut to be temporary, they may save (more, less) _____ now to pay for a future increase in the tax rate and spend _____ now. As a result, consumption and aggregate demand (increase, decrease) _____.

13. When the Federal government employs an expansionary fiscal policy to increase real GDP and employment in the economy, it usually has a budget (surplus, deficit) _____ and (lends, borrows) _____ in the money market. These actions may (raise, lower) _____ interest rates in the economy and (stimulate, crowd out) _____ private investment spending.

14. Current thinking on the advisability and effectiveness of discretionary fiscal policy shows general (agreement, disagreement) _____ about the value of fiscal policy in the short run and general _____ about evaluating fiscal policy for its contribution to long-run productivity growth.

15. The public debt is equal to the sum of the Federal government's past budget (deficits, surpluses) _____ minus its budget _____.
   a. Of the public debt, Federal government agencies and the Federal Reserve hold about (49, 51) _____ % and commercial banks, financial institutions, state and local governments, and individuals and institutions here and abroad hold about _____ %.
   b. Most of the public debt is (internal, external) _____ because foreigners hold only about (10, 25) _____ % of it.
   c. The most meaningful way to measure the public debt is relative to (interest rates, GDP) _____.
   d. Compared with the United States, the public debt as a percentage of GDP in Japan was (higher, lower) _____ and the public debt as a percentage of GDP in Poland was _____.

16. The possibility that the Federal government will go bankrupt is a false issue. It does not need to reduce its debt; it can retire maturing U.S. securities by (taxing, refinancing) _____ them. The government can also pay its debts by increasing (interest, tax) _____ rates.

17. If the public debt is held domestically, then for U.S. taxpayers it is (a liability, an asset) _____ and for U.S. citizens and institutions owning the U.S. debt securities it is _____.

18. The public debt and the payment of interest on it may (increase, decrease) _____ income inequality in the economy and _____ the incentives to work, take risks, save, and invest in the economy. The public debt is a burden on an economy if it is held by (foreigners, U.S. citizens) _____.

19. A public debt imposes a burden on future generations if the borrowing done to finance an increase in government expenditures results in (an increase, a decrease) _____ in interest rates, _____ in investment spending, and _____ in the stock of capital goods for future generations.

20. The size of the burden from the crowding out of private investment is lessened if government expenditures are used to finance worthwhile (increases, decreases) _____ in physical and human capital that contribute to the productive capacity of the economy or if they (encourage, discourage) _____ more private investment that complements the public investment.

■ **TRUE–FALSE QUESTIONS**

Circle T if the statement is true, F if it is false.

1. Discretionary fiscal policy is independent of Congress and is left to the discretion of state and local governments. **T F**

2. Expansionary fiscal policy during a recession or depression will create a budget deficit or add to an existing budget deficit. **T F**

3. A decrease in taxes is one of the options that can be used to pursue a contractionary fiscal policy. **T F**

4. To increase initial consumption by a specific amount, government must reduce taxes by more than that amount because some of the tax cut will be saved by households. **T F**

5. A reduction in taxes and an increase in government spending would be characteristic of a contractionary fiscal policy. **T F**

6. Built-in stabilizers are not sufficiently strong to prevent recession or inflation, but they can reduce the severity of a recession or inflation. **T F**

7. The less progressive the tax system, the greater the economy's built-in stability. **T F**

8. The standardized budget indicates how much government must spend and tax if there is to be full employment in the economy. **T F**

9. The key to assessing discretionary fiscal policy is to observe the change in the standardized budget. **T F**

10. In the Federal budget, surpluses obtained from Social Security are treated as an offset to current government spending. **T F**

11. Recognition, administrative, and operational lags in the timing of Federal fiscal policy make fiscal policies more effective in reducing the rate of inflation and decreasing unemployment in the economy. **T F**

12. Economists who see evidence of a political business cycle argue that members of Congress tend to increase taxes and reduce expenditures before elections and reduce taxes and increase expenditures after elections. **T F**

13. If households expect that a tax cut will be temporary, they are likely to spend more and save less, thus reinforcing the intended effect of the tax cut on aggregate demand. **T F**

14. State and local governments' fiscal policies have tended to assist and reinforce the efforts of the Federal government to counter recession and inflation. **T F**

15. The crowding-out effect occurs when an expansionary fiscal policy decreases the interest rate, increases investment spending, and strengthens fiscal policy. **T F**

16. The public debt is the total accumulation of the deficits, minus any surpluses, that the Federal government has incurred over time. **T F**

17. The public debt as a percentage of GDP is higher in the United States than in most other industrial nations. **T F**

18. Interest payments as a percentage of GDP reflect the level of taxation (average tax rate) required to service the public debt. **T F**

19. A large public debt will bankrupt the Federal government because it cannot refinance the debt or increase taxes to pay it. **T F**

20. The public debt is also a public credit. **T F**

21. The payment of interest on the public debt probably increases income inequality. **T F**

22. The additional taxes needed to pay the interest on the public debt increase incentives to work, save, invest, and bear risks. **T F**

23. Selling U.S. securities to foreigners to finance increased expenditures by the Federal government imposes a burden on future generations. **T F**

24. The crowding-out effect increases the investment demand curve and investment in private capital goods. **T F**

25. If government spending is for public investments that increase the capital stock, this spending can increase the future production capacity of the economy. **T F**

■ MULTIPLE-CHOICE QUESTIONS

Circle the letter that corresponds to the best answer.

1. Which combination of policies would be the most expansionary?

(a) an increase in government spending and taxes

(b) a decrease in government spending and taxes

(c) an increase in government spending and a decrease in taxes

(d) a decrease in government spending and an increase in taxes

2. An economy is in a recession, and the government decides to increase spending by \$4 billion. The MPC is .8. What would be the full increase in real GDP from the change in government spending?

(a) \$3.2 billion

(b) \$4 billion

(c) \$16 billion

(d) \$20 billion

3. Which combination of fiscal policies would be the most contractionary?

(a) an increase in government spending and taxes

(b) a decrease in government spending and taxes

(c) an increase in government spending and a decrease in taxes

(d) a decrease in government spending and an increase in taxes

4. When government tax revenues change automatically and in a countercyclical direction over the course of the business cycle, this is an example of

(a) the political business cycle

(b) nondiscretionary fiscal policy

(c) the standardized budget

(d) crowding out

5. If the economy is to have built-in stability, when real GDP falls,

(a) tax revenues and government transfer payments both should fall

(b) tax revenues and government transfer payments both should rise

(c) tax revenues should fall and government transfer payments should rise

(d) tax revenues should rise and government transfer payments should fall

Answer Questions 6, 7, and 8 on the basis of the following diagram.

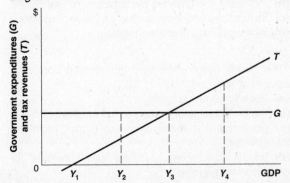

6. If the slope of the line *T* were steeper, there would be

(a) more built-in stability for the economy

(b) less built-in stability for the economy

(c) no change in the built-in stability for the economy

(d) a need for more emphasis on discretionary fiscal policy

7. If the slope of the line *T* were flatter, there would be

(a) larger cyclical deficits produced as GDP moved from Y_3 to Y_2

(b) smaller cyclical deficits produced as GDP moved from Y_3 to Y_2

(c) larger standardized deficits produced as GDP moved from Y_3 to Y_2

(d) smaller standardized deficits produced as GDP moved from Y_3 to Y_2

8. Actions by the Federal government to increase the progressivity of the tax system

(a) flatten the slope of line *T* and increase built-in stability

(b) flatten the slope of line *T* and decrease built-in stability

(c) steepen the slope of line *T* and increase built-in stability

(d) steepen the slope of line *T* and decrease built-in stability

Use the following table to answer question 9. The table shows the standardized budget deficit or surplus as a percentage of GDP over a five-year period.

Year	Deficit (−) Surplus (+)
1	−2.1%
2	−3.0
3	−1.5
4	+0.5
5	+1.0

9. In which year was fiscal policy expansionary?

(a) Year 2

(b) Year 3

(c) Year 4

(d) Year 5

10. If the standardized budget shows a deficit of about \$200 billion and the actual budget shows a deficit of about \$250 billion over a several-year period, it can be concluded that there is a

(a) cyclical deficit

(b) recognition lag

(c) crowding-out effect

(d) political business cycle

11. If the standardized deficit as a percentage of GDP is zero one year and there is a standardized budget surplus the next year, it can be concluded that

(a) fiscal policy is expansionary

(b) fiscal policy is contractionary

(c) the federal government is borrowing money

(d) the federal government is lending money

12. If there is a surplus for the Social Security program in a given year, this Social Security surplus will increase
  (a) a Federal budget deficit that year
  (b) a Federal budget surplus that year
  (c) interest payments on the public debt
  (d) holdings of U.S. securities by foreigners

13. The length of time involved for the fiscal action taken by Congress to affect output, employment, or the price level is referred to as the
  (a) administrative lag
  (b) operational lag
  (c) recognition lag
  (d) fiscal lag

14. The crowding-out effect of an expansionary (deficit) fiscal policy is a result of government borrowing in the money market which
  (a) increases interest rates and net investment spending in the economy
  (b) increases interest rates and decreases net investment spending
  (c) decreases interest rates and increases net investment spending
  (d) decreases interest rates and net investment spending

15. Current thinking about discretionary fiscal policy among mainstream economists is that it should be designed to
  (a) counteract the effects of monetary policy
  (b) contribute to long-run economic growth
  (c) "fine-tune" the economy in the short run but not in the long run
  (d) control inflationary pressure but not be used to fight recession

16. The public debt is the sum of all previous
  (a) expenditures of the Federal government
  (b) budget deficits of the Federal government
  (c) budget deficits minus any budget surpluses of the Federal government
  (d) budget surpluses less the current budget deficit of the Federal government

17. To place the public debt in perspective based on the wealth and productive capacity of the economy, it is more meaningful to
  (a) examine its absolute size
  (b) calculate the interest payments on the debt
  (c) measure it relative to the gross domestic product
  (d) compare it to imports, exports, and the trade deficit

18. According to many economists, the primary burden of the debt is the
  (a) absolute size of the debt for the economy
  (b) annual interest charges from bonds sold to finance the public debt
  (c) deficit arising from a decline in exports and an increase in imports
  (d) government spending that the public debt finances for the economy

19. A major reason why a public debt cannot bankrupt the Federal government is that the Federal government has
  (a) an annually balanced budget
  (b) the Social Security trust fund
  (c) the power to levy taxes
  (d) a strong military defense

20. Incurring an internal debt to finance a war does not pass the cost of the war on to future generations because
  (a) the opportunity cost of the war was borne by the generation that fought it
  (b) the government need not pay interest on internally held debts
  (c) there is never a need for government to refinance the debt
  (d) wartime inflation reduces the relative size of the debt

21. Which would be a consequence of the retirement of the internally held (U.S.-owned) portion of the public debt?
  (a) a reduction in the nation's productive capacity
  (b) a reduction in the nation's standard of living
  (c) a redistribution of the nation's wealth among its citizens
  (d) a decrease in aggregate demand in the economy

22. Which is an important consequence of the public debt of the United States?
  (a) It decreases the need for U.S. securities.
  (b) It transfers a portion of the U.S. output to foreign nations.
  (c) It reduces income inequality in the United States.
  (d) It leads to greater saving at every level of disposable income.

23. Greater interest charges on the public debt can lead to
  (a) fewer purchases of U.S. securities by foreigners
  (b) more private investment spending in the economy
  (c) lower taxes and thus greater incentives to work and invest
  (d) higher taxes and thus reduced incentives to work and invest

24. The crowding-out effect of borrowing to finance an increase in government expenditures
  (a) reduces current spending for private investment
  (b) increases the privately owned stock of real capital
  (c) reduces the economic burden on future generations
  (d) increases incentives to innovate

25. The crowding-out effect from government borrowing is reduced when
  (a) interest rates are rising
  (b) the economy is operating at full employment
  (c) government spending improves human capital in the economy
  (d) private investment spending can substitute for government spending

■ PROBLEMS

1. Columns 1 and 2 in the following table are an aggregate supply schedule. Columns 1 and 3 are aggregate demand schedules.

(1) Price level	(2) Real GDP$_1$	(3) AD$_1$	(4) AD$_2$
220	$2390	$2100	$2200
200	2390	2200	2340
190	2350	2250	2350
180	2300	2300	2400
160	2200	2400	2500

a. The equilibrium real GDP is $_____,

and the price level is _____.

b. Suppose that an expansionary fiscal policy increases aggregate demand from that shown in columns 1 and 3 to that shown in columns 1 and 4. The price level will

increase to _____, and this rise in the price

level will result in real GDP increasing to $_____.

2. The following table shows seven real GDPs and the net tax revenues of government at each real GDP.

Real GDP	Net tax revenues	Government purchases	Government deficit/surplus
$ 850	$170	$____	$____
900	180	____	____
950	190	____	____
1000	200	____	____
1050	210	____	____
1100	220	____	____
1150	230	____	____

a. Looking at the two columns on the left side of the table, it can be seen that
(1) when real GDP increases by $50, net tax revenues

(increase, decrease) _____ by $_____.

(2) when real GDP decreases by $100, net tax revenues (increase, decrease) _____ by

$_____.

(3) the relationship between real GDP and net tax

revenues is (direct, inverse) _____.

b. Assume that the simple multiplier has a value of 10 and that investment spending in the economy decreases by $10.

(1) If net tax revenues remained constant, the equilib-

rium real GDP would decrease by $_____.

(2) But when real GDP decreases, net tax revenues also decrease, and this decrease in net tax revenues

will tend to (increase, decrease) _____ the equilibrium real GDP.

(3) And, therefore, the decrease in real GDP brought about by the $10 decrease in investment spending will

be (more, less) _____ than $100.

(4) The direct relationship between net tax revenues

and real GDP has (lessened, expanded) _____

the impact of the $10 decrease in investment spending on real GDP.

c. Suppose the simple multiplier is also 10 and government wishes to increase the equilibrium real GDP by $50.

(1) If net tax revenues remained constant, government would have to increase its purchases of goods and

services by $_____.

(2) But when real GDP rises, net tax revenues also rise, and this rise in net tax revenues will tend to

(increase, decrease) _____ the equilibrium real GDP.

(3) The effect, therefore, of the $5 increase in government purchases will also be to increase the

equilibrium real GDP by (more, less) _____ than $50.

(4) The direct relationship between net tax revenues

and real GDP has (lessened, expanded) _____

the effect of the $5 increase in government purchases, and to raise the equilibrium real GDP by $50, the government will have to increase its purchases by

(more, less) _____ than $5.

d. Imagine that the full-employment real GDP of the economy is $1150 and that government purchases of goods and services are $200.

(1) Complete the previous table by entering the government purchases and computing the budget deficit or surplus at each of the real GDPs. (Show a government deficit by placing a minus sign in front of the amount by which expenditures exceed net tax revenues.)

(2) The standardized surplus equals $_____.

(3) If the economy were in a recession and producing a real GDP of $900, the budget would show a (surplus,

deficit) _____ of $_____.

(4) This budget deficit or surplus makes it appear that government is pursuing (an expansionary, a

contractionary) _____ fiscal policy; however, this deficit or surplus is not the result of a countercyclical fiscal policy but the result of

the _____.

(5) If government did not change its net tax *rates*, it could increase the equilibrium real GDP from $900 to the full-employment real GDP of $1150 by increasing its purchases by (approximately) $70. At the full-employment real GDP the budget would show a

(surplus, deficit) _____ of $_____.

(6) If government did not change its purchases, it would increase the equilibrium real GDP from $900 to the full-employment real GDP of $1150 by decreasing net tax revenues at all real GDPs by a lump sum of (approximately) $80. The standardized budget

would have a (surplus, deficit) _____ of

$_____.

3. a. Complete the table below by computing the average tax rates, given the net tax revenue data in columns 2, 4, and 6. Calculate the average tax rates in percentages to one decimal place (for example, 5.4%).
b. As real GDP increases in column 1, the average tax rate (increases, decreases, remains the same)

_____ in column 3, _____

in column 5, and _____ in column 7. The tax system is (progressive, proportional,

regressive) _____ in column 2, _____

in column 4, and _____ in column 6.
c. On the graph following the table, plot the real GDP, net tax revenue, and government spending data given in columns 1, 2, 4, 6, and 8. The tax revenue system

with the steepest slope is found in column _____,

and it is (progressive, proportional, regressive) _____,
while the one with the flattest slope is found in column

_____, and it is _____.

4. a. Complete the table on the next page by stating whether the direction of discretionary fiscal policy was contractionary (**C**), expansionary (**E**), or neither (**N**), given the hypothetical budget data for an economy.
b. The best gauge of the direction of fiscal policy is

the (actual, standardized) _____ budget

deficit or surplus because it removes the (cyclical,

actual) _____ component from the discussion of the budget situation.
c. (1) In what years were there cyclical deficits, and what was the amount of the cyclical deficit in each of those years?

_____

(2) In what year was the actual budget surplus greater than the standardized budget surplus, and by what amount was it greater?

_____

5. The following table gives data on interest rates and investment demand (in billions of dollars) in a hypothetical economy.

Interest rate	I_{d1}	I_{d2}
10%	$250	$300
8	300	350
6	350	400
4	400	450
2	450	500

a. Use the I_{d1} schedule. Assume that the government needs to finance a budget deficit and that this public borrowing increases the interest rate from 4% to 6%. How much crowding out of private investment will

occur? _____

(1) Real GDP	(2) Net tax revenue	(3) Average tax rate	(4) Net tax revenue	(5) Average tax rate	(6) Net tax revenue	(7) Average tax rate	(8) Government spending
$1000	$100	_____%	$100	_____%	$100	_____%	$120
1100	120	_____	110	_____	108	_____	120
1200	145	_____	120	_____	115	_____	120
1300	175	_____	130	_____	120	_____	120
1400	210	_____	140	_____	123	_____	120

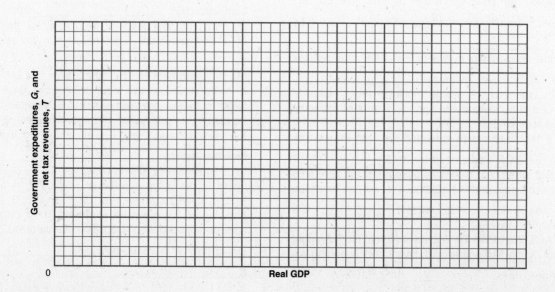

(1) Year	(2) Actual budget deficit (−) or surplus (+)	(3) Standardized budget deficit (−) or surplus (+)	(4) Direction of fiscal policy
1	− $170 billion	− $130 billion	
2	− 120 billion	− 90 billion	_____
3	+ 40 billion	+ 20 billion	_____
4	− 60 billion	− 50 billion	_____
5	− 120 billion	− 100 billion	_____

b. Now assume that the deficit is used to improve the capital stock of the economy and that, as a consequence, the investment demand schedule changes from I_{d1} to I_{d2}. At the same time, the interest rate rises from 4% to 6% as the government borrows money to finance the deficit. How much crowding out of private investment will occur in this case? _____

c. Graph the two investment demand schedules on the next graph and show the difference between the two events. Put the interest rate on the vertical axis and the quantity of investment demanded on the horizontal axis.

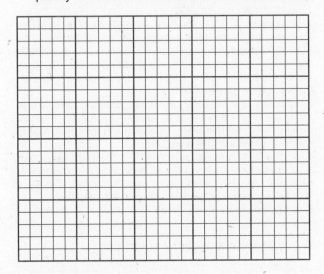

■ **SHORT ANSWER AND ESSAY QUESTIONS**

1. What is the responsibility of the Council of Economic Advisers?

2. What is the difference between discretionary fiscal policy and nondiscretionary fiscal policy?

3. What are the Federal government's three options for conducting expansionary or contractionary fiscal policy?

4. Under what economic conditions would expansionary or contractionary fiscal policy be used? What would be the effect on the Federal budget?

5. Compare and contrast the effect of expansionary and that of contractionary fiscal policy on aggregate demand. Draw a graph to illustrate the likely effects of each one.

6. What is the effect of the multiplier on the initial change in spending from fiscal policy? When the government

wants to increase initial consumption by a specific amount, why must it reduce taxes by more than that amount?

7. In the real world, is the purpose of contractionary fiscal policy to restore a previously lower price level? How do downwardly inflexible prices affect events?

8. Explain the fiscal policies that would be advocated during a recession and during a period of inflation by those who (a) wish to expand the public sector and (b) wish to contract the size of government.

9. What is a built-in stabilizer? How do built-in stabilizers work to reduce rises and falls in the level of nominal GDP?

10. What is the economic importance of the direct relationship between tax receipts and GDP?

11. Supply definitions of progressive, proportional, and regressive tax systems. What are the implications of each type of tax system for the built-in stability of the economy?

12. What is the standardized budget? What problem was the use of the standardized budget designed to solve?

13. Explain the distinction between a cyclical deficit and a standardized deficit. Which type of deficit provides the best indication of the direction of fiscal policy? Why?

14. Explain the three kinds of time lags that make it difficult to use fiscal policy to stabilize the economy.

15. What is the political business cycle? Explain how it works. Evaluate the likelihood of such a cycle.

16. How might the direction of fiscal policy at the Federal level be countered by the actions of state and local governments?

17. How does crowding out reduce the effect of an expansionary (deficit) fiscal policy on real GDP and employment?

18. What is the current thinking about the advisability and effectiveness of discretionary fiscal policy?

19. How are budget deficits and surpluses related to the public debt?

20. How big is the public debt of the United States absolutely and relative to the GDP? How large are the interest payments on this debt absolutely and relative to the GDP?

21. Who owns the public debt? What percentage is held by the two major groups? What percentage of the public debt is held by foreigners?

22. Why can't the public debt result in the bankruptcy of the Federal government? What two actions can the government take to prevent bankruptcy?

23. If most of the public debt was owned by American citizens and institutions and the government decided to pay off the debt, what would happen?

24. Was the increase in the cost of the public debt that resulted from World War II a burden borne by the wartime generation or by future generations? Explain.

25. How do the public debt and the payment of interest on that debt affect the distribution of income?

26. What effects does the public debt have on incentives to work, to save, or to assume risk in the economy?

27. What are the economic implications of the portion of the public debt held by foreigners?

28. How does the public debt crowd out private investment and impose a burden on future generations?

29. Does it matter to future generations whether increases in government spending are financed by taxation or increased public debt?

30. What two qualifications might lessen the crowding-out effect on the size of the economic burden that has shifted to future generations?

ANSWERS

Chapter 11 Fiscal Policy, Deficits, and Debt

FILL-IN QUESTIONS

1. discretionary, nondiscretionary
2. increase, increase, decrease, decrease
3. government spending, taxes, government spending, taxes
4. multiplier
5. minus, increase, decrease
6. directly, built-in, increase, restraining, increases, stimulating
7. progressive, proportional, regressive, more
8. expansionary, contractionary, cyclical, less
9. greater, surplus, adds to
10. a recognition, an administrative, an operational
11. several, counter, a political
12. less, more, less, decrease
13. deficit, borrows, raise, crowd out
14. disagreement, agreement
15. deficits, surpluses; *a.* 51, 49; *b.* internal, 25; *c.* GDP; *d.* higher, lower
16. refinancing, tax
17. a liability, an asset
18. increase, decrease, foreigners
19. an increase, a decrease, a decrease
20. increases, encourage

TRUE–FALSE QUESTIONS

1. F, p. 209	**10.** T, p. 216	**19.** F, p. 220
2. T, p. 209	**11.** F, pp. 216–217	**20.** T, pp. 220–221
3. F, p. 210	**12.** F, p. 217	**21.** T, p. 221
4. T, p. 210	**13.** F, p. 217	**22.** F, p. 221
5. F, pp. 210–211	**14.** F, p. 217	**23.** T, p. 221
6. T, p. 212	**15.** F, pp. 217–218	**24.** F, pp. 221–222
7. F, pp. 212–213	**16.** T, pp. 218–219	**25.** T, p. 222
8. F, p. 213	**17.** F, pp. 219–220	
9. T, pp. 213–215	**18.** T, p. 220	

MULTIPLE-CHOICE QUESTIONS

1. c, pp. 209–210	**10.** a, p. 213	**19.** c, p. 220
2. d, p. 210	**11.** b, pp. 214–215	**20.** a, pp. 220–221
3. d, pp. 210–211	**12.** b, p. 216	**21.** c, pp. 220–221
4. b, p. 212	**13.** b, pp. 216–217	**22.** b, p. 221
5. c, p. 212	**14.** b, pp. 217–218	**23.** d, p. 221
6. a, pp. 212–213	**15.** b, p. 218	**24.** a, pp. 221–222
7. b, pp. 212–213	**16.** c, pp. 218–219	**25.** c, p. 222
8. c, pp. 212–213	**17.** c, p. 219	
9. a, pp. 213–214	**18.** b, p. 220	

PROBLEMS

1. *a.* 2300, 180; *b.* 190, 2350
2. *a.* increase, $10, (2) decrease, $20, (3) direct; *b.* (1) $100, (2) increase, (3) less, (4) lessened; *c.* (1) $5, (2) decrease, (3) less, (4) lessened, more; *d.* (1) government purchases are $200 at all GDPs, government surplus or deficit: −30, −20, −10, 0, 10, 20, 30, (2) $30, (3) deficit, $20, (4) an expansionary, recession, (5) deficit, $40, (6) deficit, $50
3. *a.* column 3: 10.0, 10.9, 12.1, 13.5, 15.0; column 5: 10.0 at each GDP level; column 7: 10.0, 9.8, 9.6, 9.2, 8.8; *b.* increases, remains the same, decreases; progressive, proportional, regressive; *c.* 2, progressive, 6, regressive
4. *a.* (Year 1–2) contractionary, (Year 2–3) contractionary, (Year 3–4) expansionary, (Year 4–5) expansionary; *b.* standardized, cyclical; *c.* (1) year 1 ($40 billion), year 2 ($30 billion), year 4 ($10 billion), year 5 ($20 billion), (2) year 3 ($20 billion)
5. *a.* $50 billion; *b.* none; *c.* graph

SHORT ANSWER AND ESSAY QUESTIONS

1. pp. 209–211	**11.** pp. 217–218	**21.** p. 220
2. pp. 209–211	**12.** p. 218	**22.** p. 221
3. pp. 215–216	**13.** pp. 218–219	**23.** pp. 221–222
4. pp. 209–211	**14.** p. 220	**24.** p. 222
5. p. 212	**15.** pp. 220–221	**25.** p. 222
6. p. 212	**16.** p. 221	**26.** p. 222
7. pp. 212–213	**17.** p. 221	**27.** p. 222
8. pp. 216–217	**18.** p. 221	**28.** pp. 222–223
9. pp. 217	**19.** p. 221	**29.** pp. 222–223
10. p. 217	**20.** pp. 221–222	**30.** p. 223

CHAPTER 12

Money and Banking

Chapter 12 explains how the financial system affects the operation of the economy. The chapter is largely descriptive and factual. Pay particular attention to the following: (1) what the money supply is and the function money performs; (2) what gives value to or "backs" money in the United States; and (3) the principal institutions of the U.S. financial system and their functions.

Several points are worth repeating. First, money is whatever performs the three functions of money (**medium of exchange, unit of account,** and **store of value**). People are willing to accept and trust the use of money for transactions because they are willing to exchange goods and services for it. Thus, money is backed by trust or acceptability *and not by gold*. Money also helps people measure the value of the goods and services they want to buy or sell. In addition, money stores value for people, and so they can use it in the future to make purchases.

Second, the central bank in the United States consists of the 12 **Federal Reserve Banks** and the **Board of Governors** of the **Federal Reserve System** which oversees their operation. These banks, although privately owned by the commercial banks, are operated more or less as public agencies of the Federal government. They operate on a not-for-profit basis but are used primarily to regulate the nation's money supply in the best interests of the economy as a whole and secondarily to perform other services for the banks, the government, and the economy. They are able to perform their primary function because they are bankers' banks in which depository institutions (commercial banks and thrifts) can deposit and borrow money. They do not deal directly with the public.

Third, these depository institutions accept deposits and make loans, but they also are able to create money by lending checkable deposits. Because they are able to do this, they have a strong influence on the size of the money supply and the purchasing power of money. The Federal Reserve Banks exist primarily to regulate the money supply and its value by influencing and controlling the amount of money depository institutions create.

The final section of Chapter 12 discusses recent developments in money and banking. First, there has been a significant shift in financial assets from banks and thrifts to other types of financial services institutions. Second, many banks and thrifts have merged over the years to compete better with other regional or national firms. Third, there has been a convergence in the services provided by the different types of financial institutions.

Fourth, financial markets are now global and more highly integrated than they were in previous decades. Fifth, technological advances have introduced electronic payments and changed the character of money.

■ CHECKLIST

When you have studied this chapter you should be able to

☐ List and explain the three functions of money.
☐ Give an *M*1 definition of money that explains its two major components.
☐ Describe the two major types of institutions that offer checkable deposits.
☐ Give an *M*2 definition of money and its components.
☐ Give an *MZM* definition of money and its components.
☐ Distinguish between credit cards and money.
☐ Explain why money is debt in the U.S. economy and who holds that debt.
☐ State three reasons why currency and checkable deposits are money and have value.
☐ Use an equation to explain the relationship between the purchasing power of money and the price level.
☐ Discuss how inflation affects the acceptability of money.
☐ Explain the role government plays in maintaining or stabilizing the purchasing power of money.
☐ Describe the framework of the Federal Reserve.
☐ Explain the historical background of the Federal Reserve.
☐ Describe the purposes of the Board of Governors of the Federal Reserve.
☐ Explain why the Federal Reserve Banks are central, quasi-public, and bankers' banks.
☐ Discuss the functions of the Federal Open Market Committee (FOMC) of the Federal Reserve.
☐ Discuss the relationship between the Federal Reserve and commercial banks and thrifts.
☐ List and explain the seven major functions of the Federal Reserve System and indicate which one is the most important.
☐ Discuss the reasons for the independence of the Federal Reserve.
☐ Describe the relative decline of banks and thrifts.
☐ Explain the effects of consolidation on banks and thrifts.
☐ Discuss how globalization has changed financial markets.

☐ Explain how electronic payments have transformed banking.

☐ Discuss the reasons why U.S. currency is widely used in other nations (Last Word).

■ CHAPTER OUTLINE

1. Money is whatever performs the three **basic functions of money:** It is a *medium of exchange* for buying and selling goods and services. It serves as a *unit of account* for measuring the monetary cost of goods and services. It is a *store of value* so that people can transfer purchasing power from the present to the future.

2. Money is a stock of items rather than a flow such as income. Any item that is widely accepted as a medium of exchange can serve as money, and many types of such items have done so throughout history.

　a. The narrowly defined money supply is called *M*1 and has two principal components.

　(1) One component is *currency*. It consists of coins that are *token money,* which means the value of the metal in a coin is less than the face value of the coin. It also consists of paper money in the form of *Federal Reserve Notes.*

　(2) The second component is *checkable deposits.* They allow a person to transfer ownership of deposits to others by writing checks; those checks are generally accepted as a medium of exchange.

　(3) The two major types of financial institutions offering checkable deposits are *commercial banks* and *thrift institutions.*

　(4) There are also currency and checkable deposits that are owned by the Federal government, commercial banks and thrift institutions, and the Federal Reserve Banks. They are not included in *M*1 or in the other definitions of the money supply.

　b. *M*2 is a broader definition of money and includes not only the currency and checkable deposits in *M*1 but also *near-monies* that do not function directly or fully as a medium of exchange but can be easily converted to currency or checkable deposits. These near-monies include savings deposits, including *money market deposit accounts (MMDAs),* interest-bearing accounts with short-term securities. It also includes small *time deposits* (less than $100,000) such as CDs and the *money market mutual funds (MMMFs)* of individuals.

　c. *MZM* (money zero maturity) is a definition of money that focuses on money that is immediately available to households and businesses at zero cost. It is calculated by taking *M*2 and subtracting small time deposits and adding money market mutual funds held by businesses. The major advantage of the *MZM* definition of the money supply is that it includes the main items that are used on a daily basis to make transactions: currency, checkable deposits, MMDAs, and MMMFs.

3. The **money supply gets its "backing"** from the ability of the government to keep the purchasing power of money stable.

　a. Money is debt or the promise of a commercial bank, a thrift institution, or a Federal Reserve Bank to pay, but these debts cannot be redeemed for anything tangible.

　b. Money has value only because:

　(1) it is acceptable for the exchange of desirable goods and services;

　(2) it is *legal tender* (legally acceptable for payment of debts); and

　(3) it is relatively scarce because its value depends on supply and demand conditions.

　c. The purchasing power of money is the amount of goods and services a unit of money will buy.

　(1) The purchasing power of the U.S. dollar is inversely related to the price level: Value of the dollar (V) = 1 divided by price level (P) expressed as an index number (in hundredths), or $\$V = 1/P$.

　(2) Rapid inflation can erode the purchasing power of money and public confidence in it. Such situations limit the functions of money as a medium of exchange, measure of value, or store of value.

　d. Money is backed by the confidence the public has that the purchasing power of money will remain stable. U.S. monetary authorities (the Federal Reserve) are responsible for using monetary policy to maintain price-level stability and the purchasing power of money. The actions of the U.S. government are also important because sound fiscal policy supports price-level stability.

4. The monetary and financial sector of the economy is significantly influenced by the *Federal Reserve System* (the *Fed*) and the nation's banks and thrift institutions.

　a. The banking system remains centralized and regulated by government because historical problems in the U.S. economy led to different kinds of money and the mismanagement of the money supply. The U.S. Congress passed the Federal Reserve Act of 1913 to establish the Fed as the nation's central bank and make it responsible for issuing currency and controlling the nation's money supply.

　b. The *Board of Governors* of the Fed exercises control over the supply of money and the banking system. The U.S. president appoints the seven members of the Board of Governors, who serve for 14 years. He also selects the board chair and vice-chair, who serve 4-year terms.

　c. The 12 *Federal Reserve Banks* of the Fed have three main functions.

　(1) They serve as the nation's *central bank* to implement the policies set by the Board of Governors.

　(2) They are *quasi-public banks* that blend private ownership of each Federal Reserve Bank with public control of each bank through the Board of Governors.

　(3) They are *"bankers' banks"* that perform banking services for the member banks in their regions.

　d. The *Federal Open Market Committee (FOMC)* is responsible for acting on the monetary policy set by the Board of Governors. The FOMC includes the seven members of the Board of Governors, the president of the New York Federal Reserve Bank, and four other presidents of Federal Reserve Banks (who serve on a rotating basis). The FOMC conducts open-market operations to buy and sell government securities to control the nation's money supply and influence interest rates.

e. The U.S. banking system contains about 7600 commercial banks. About three-fourths of them are banks charted by states, and about one-fourth are banks chartered by the Federal government. The banking system also includes about 11,400 thrift institutions, such as savings and loans and credit unions. Both banks and thrifts are directly affected by the Fed's decisions concerning the money supply and interest rates.

f. The Fed performs seven functions: issuing currency, setting reserve requirements and holding reserves, lending money to banks and thrifts, collecting and processing checks, serving as the fiscal agent for the Federal government, supervising banks, and controlling the money supply. The last function is the most important.

g. The independence of the Fed protects it from strong political pressure from the U.S. Congress or the president that could lead to poor economic decisions.

5. Recent developments have affected money and banking in the U.S. economy.

a. The U.S. *financial services industry* consists not only of banks and thrifts but also of insurance companies, mutual fund companies, pension funds, and securities firms. Over the last 25 years, the amount of financial assets managed by banks and thrifts fell from nearly 60% to about 24% as households shifted financial assets to these other types of financial services firms.

b. The number of banks and thrift institutions has declined, partly as a result of bank and thrift mergers. These mergers enable banks and thrifts to compete more effectively in the financial services industry on a national or regional basis.

c. There has also been a convergence in the services offered by different types of financial institutions such as banks, thrifts, insurance companies, mutual funds, pension funds, and securities firms.

d. Financial markets are now more integrated and operate worldwide because of advances in communications technologies and greater competition for financial capital assets around the globe.

e. The character of money has changed with the shift to the widespread use of *electronic payments* to make purchases and settle debts and greater use of electronic forms of money.

6. A large amount of U.S. currency is circulating abroad for use by residents of other nations. The "global greenback" is demanded because the dollar does a better job of holding its purchasing power relative to domestic currencies, especially in nations that have experienced high inflation, wars, and political turmoil. The dollar in those nations serves an effective and reliable medium of exchange, store of value, and unit of account compared with domestic currencies.

■ **HINTS AND TIPS**

1. The value of money is largely based on trust or acceptability. You are willing to accept money in exchange for a good or service because you are confident you will be able to use that money to purchase other goods and services or store its value for later use. If you lose trust in money, it no longer functions as a medium of exchange, store of value, or measure of value for you and probably many other people.

2. Most students typically think of money as only currency: coins and paper money in circulation. A key component of the money supply, however, is the checkable deposits held at banks and thrift institutions on which checks can be drawn.

3. There are several definitions of the **money supply** that you must know about, from the narrow *M*1 to the broader *M*2 and *MZM*. The essential relationship among them is that currency and checkable deposits are the main parts of each one.

4. A good portion of the chapter explains the framework of the Federal Reserve. These institutional features are important for understanding how the nation's central bank works, and the Fed will be a major focus of later chapters.

■ **IMPORTANT TERMS**

medium of exchange	time deposits
unit of account	money market mutual fund (MMMF)
store of value	
*M*1	*MZM*
token money	legal tender
Federal Reserve Notes	Federal Reserve System
checkable deposits	
commercial banks	Board of Governors
thrift institutions	Federal Reserve Banks
near-monies	Federal Open Market Committee (FOMC)
*M*2	
savings account	financial services industry
money market deposit account (MMDA)	electronic payments

SELF-TEST

■ **FILL-IN QUESTIONS**

1. When money is usable for buying and selling goods and services, it functions as (a unit of account, a store of value, a medium of exchange) _____, but when money serves as a measure of relative worth, it functions as _____, and when money serves as a liquid asset, it functions as _____.

2. All coins in circulation in the United States are (paper, token) _____ money, which means that their intrinsic value is (less, greater) _____ than the face value of a coin.

3. Paper money and coins are considered (currency, checkable deposits) _____ and are one major component of *M*1; the other major component is (currency, checkable deposits) _____.

4. *M*2 is equal to (*M*1, *MZM*) _____ plus (checkable, noncheckable) _____ deposits, (small, large) _____ time deposits, and money market (deposit accounts, mutual funds) _____ and money market _____.

5. *MZM* is equal to *M*2 (plus, minus) _____ small time deposits and _____ money market mutual funds held by businesses.

6. Credit cards (are, are not) _____ considered money but rather a form of (paper money, loan) _____ from the institutions that issued the cards.

7. Paper money is the circulating debt of (banks and thrifts, the Federal Reserve Banks) _____, while checkable deposits are the debts of _____. In the United States, currency and checkable deposits (are, are not) _____ backed by gold and silver.

8. Money has value because it is (unacceptable, acceptable) _____ in exchange for products and resources, because it is (legal, illegal) _____ tender, and because it is relatively (abundant, scarce) _____.

9. The purchasing power of money varies (directly, inversely) _____ with the price level. To find the value of $1 (multiply, divide) _____ 1 by the price level.

10. Runaway inflation may significantly (increase, decrease) _____ the purchasing power of money and _____ its acceptance as a medium of exchange.

11. Government's responsibility in stabilizing the purchasing power of money calls for effective control over the (demand for, supply of) _____ money and the application by the president and Congress of appropriate (monetary, fiscal) _____ policies.

12. The Federal Reserve System is composed of the Board of (Banks, Governors) _____ and the 12 Federal Reserve _____. These policies of the Federal Reserve are often carried out by the (Federal Deposit Insurance Corporation, Federal Open Market Committee) _____.

13. The Federal Reserve Banks are (private, quasi-public) _____ banks, serve as (consumers', bankers') _____ banks, and are (local, central) _____ banks whose policies are coordinated by the Board of Governors.

14. The Federal Open Market Committee meets regularly to buy and sell government (currency, securities) _____ to control the nation's money supply and influence (productivity, interest rates) _____.

15. The U.S. banking system is composed of about 7600 (thrifts, commercial banks) _____ and about 11,400 _____.

16. The seven major functions of the Fed are

a. _____

b. _____

c. _____

d. _____

e. _____

f. _____

g. _____

Of these, the most important function is _____.

17. Congress established the Fed as a(n) (dependent, independent) _____ agency of government. The objective was to protect it from political pressure so that it could control (taxes, inflation) _____.

18. In the last decade, the number of banks and thrifts (increased, decreased) _____ because competition from other financial institutions _____ and also mainly because of (mergers, bankruptcies) _____ among banks and thrift institutions.

19. Two other recent developments in money and banking are the (convergence, globalization) _____ of services provided by U.S. financial institutions and the _____ of financial markets.

20. Households and businesses are also increasingly using (paper, electronic) _____ payments for transactions such as credit cards, debit cards, Fedwire transfers, and automated clearinghouse transactions (ACHs). New forms of electronic money may include (credit, smart) _____ cards and (stored-value, transfer-value) _____ cards.

■ TRUE–FALSE QUESTIONS

Circle T if the statement is true, F if it is false.

1. When the price of a product is stated in terms of dollars and cents, money is functioning as a unit of account. **T F**

2. The money supply designated *M*1 is the sum of currency and savings deposits. **T F**

3. The currency component of *M*1 includes both coins and paper money. **T F**

4. If a coin is token money, its face value is less than its intrinsic value. **T F**

5. Both commercial banks and thrift institutions accept checkable deposits. **T F**

6. The checkable deposits of the Federal government at the Federal Reserve Banks are a component of *M*1. **T F**

7. *M*2 exceeds *M*1 by the amount of savings deposits (including money market deposit accounts), small time deposits, and the money market mutual funds of individuals. **T F**

8. A *small* time deposit is one that is less than $100,000. **T F**

9. *MZM* is equal to *M*1 minus small time deposits. **T F**

10. The money supply in the United States essentially is "backed" by the government's ability to keep the value of money relatively stable. **T F**

11. The major components of the money supply are debts, or promises to pay. **T F**

12. Currency and checkable deposits are money because they are acceptable to sellers in exchange for goods and services. **T F**

13. If money is to have a fairly stable value, its supply must be limited relative to the demand for it. **T F**

14. The amount a dollar will buy varies directly with the price level. **T F**

15. Price-level stability requires effective management and regulation of the nation's money supply. **T F**

16. Members of the Board of Governors of the Federal Reserve System are appointed by the president of the United States and confirmed by the Senate. **T F**

17. The Federal Reserve Banks are owned and operated by the U.S. government. **T F**

18. Federal Reserve Banks are bankers' banks because they make loans to and accept deposits from depository institutions. **T F**

19. The Federal Open Market Committee (FOMC) is responsible for keeping the stock market open and regulated. **T F**

20. The Federal Reserve Banks are responsible for issuing currency. **T F**

21. At times, the Fed lends money to banks and thrifts, charging them an interest rate called the *bank and thrift rate*. **T F**

22. The Federal Reserve acts as the fiscal agent for the Federal government. **T F**

23. Congress established the Fed as an independent agency to protect it from political pressure so that it can effectively control the money supply and maintain price stability. **T F**

24. In recent years, banks and thrifts have increased their share of the financial services industry and control of financial assets. **T F**

25. Households and businesses are increasingly using electronic payments to buy and sell goods and services. **T F**

■ MULTIPLE-CHOICE QUESTIONS

Circle the letter that corresponds to the best answer.

1. Which one is an economic function of money?
(a) a store of gold
(b) a unit of account
(c) a factor of production
(d) a medium of communications

2. Each month Marti puts a certain percentage of her income in a bank account that she plans to use in the future to purchase a car. For Marti, the money saved in the bank account is primarily functioning as
(a) legal tender
(b) token money
(c) store of value
(d) medium of exchange

3. Which one of the following is included in the *currency* component of *M*1?
(a) gold certificates
(b) silver certificates
(c) checkable deposits
(d) Federal Reserve Notes

4. Checkable deposits are money because they are
(a) legal tender
(b) fiat money
(c) token money
(d) a medium of exchange

5. What type of financial institution accepts deposits from and lends to "members," who are usually a group of people who work for the same company?
(a) credit unions
(b) commercial banks
(c) mutual savings banks
(d) savings and loan associations

6. Which of the following would be excluded from *M*1 and other measures of the money supply?
  (a) coins held by the public
  (b) currency held by banks
  (c) Federal Reserve Notes held by the public
  (d) checkable deposits of individuals at commercial banks

7. Which constitutes the largest element in the *M*2 money supply?
  (a) savings deposits
  (b) small time deposits
  (c) checkable deposits
  (d) money market mutual funds held by individuals

8. The major difference between *M*2 and *MZM* is that in *MZM*
  (a) currency is excluded and checkable deposits are included
  (b) savings deposits are excluded and checkable deposits are included
  (c) savings deposits are excluded and money market mutual funds held by individuals are included
  (d) small time deposits are excluded and money market mutual funds held by businesses are included

Use the following table to answer Questions 9, 10, and 11 about the money supply, given the following hypothetical data for the economy.

Item	Billions of dollars
Savings deposits, including MMDAs	$3452
Small time deposits	997
Currency	721
Checkable deposits	604
Money market mutual funds of individuals	703
Money market mutual funds of businesses	1153

9. The size of the *M*1 money supply is
  (a) $1307
  (b) $1325
  (c) $1719
  (d) $1856

10. The size of the *M*2 money supply is
  (a) $4777
  (b) $5774
  (c) $6477
  (d) $7630

11. The size of the *MZM* money supply is
  (a) $4777
  (b) $5308
  (c) $6633
  (d) $7630

12. The major components of the money supply—paper money and checkable deposits—are
  (a) legal tender
  (b) token money
  (c) debts, or promises to pay
  (d) assets of the Federal Reserve Banks

13. Which *best* describes the backing of money in the United States?
  (a) the gold bullion that is stored in Fort Knox, Kentucky
  (b) the belief of holders of money that it can be exchanged for desirable goods and services
  (c) the willingness of banks and the government to surrender something of value in exchange for money
  (d) the confidence of the public in the ability of government to pay off the national debt

14. If the price level increases 20%, the purchasing power of money decreases
  (a) 14.14%
  (b) 16.67%
  (c) 20%
  (d) 25%

15. High rates of inflation in an economy will
  (a) increase the purchasing power of money
  (b) decrease the conversion of money to gold
  (c) increase the use of money as a measure of value
  (d) decrease the use of money as a medium of exchange

16. To keep the purchasing power of money fairly stable, the Federal Reserve
  (a) buys corporate stock
  (b) employs fiscal policy
  (c) controls the money supply
  (d) uses price and wage controls

17. The members of the Board of Governors of the Federal Reserve System are appointed by
  (a) member banks of the Federal Reserve System
  (b) members of the Federal Open Market Committee
  (c) the U.S. president and confirmed by the Senate
  (d) the presidents of the 12 Federal Reserve Banks

18. The Board of Governors and the 12 Federal Reserve Banks as a system serve as
  (a) a central bank
  (b) a regulator of the stock market
  (c) the printer of U.S. paper money
  (d) the issuer of the nation's gold certificates

19. The 12 Federal Reserve Banks are
  (a) publicly owned and controlled
  (b) privately owned and controlled
  (c) privately owned but publicly controlled
  (d) publicly owned but privately controlled

20. The Federal Reserve Banks perform essentially the same functions for
  (a) the public as do commercial banks and thrifts
  (b) Federal government as does the U.S. Treasury
  (c) commercial banks and thrifts as those institutions do for the public
  (d) commercial banks and thrifts as does the Federal Deposit Insurance Corporation

21. The Federal Open Market Committee (FOMC) of the Federal Reserve System is primarily responsible for
  (a) supervising the operation of banks to make sure they follow regulations and monitoring banks so that they do not engage in fraud

(b) handling the Fed's collection of checks and adjusting legal reserves among banks
(c) setting the Fed's monetary policy and directing the buying and selling of government securities
(d) acting as the fiscal agent for the Federal government and issuing currency

22. The Federal Reserve is responsible for
    (a) supervising all banks and thrifts
    (b) printing currency for banks and thrifts
    (c) collecting Federal taxes from banks and thrifts
    (d) holding the required reserves of banks and thrifts

23. The most important function of the Federal Reserve is
    (a) issuing currency
    (b) controlling the money supply
    (c) supervising banks and thrifts
    (d) lending money to banks and thrifts

24. Which one of the following is a recent development in the financial services industry?
    (a) an increase in the number of banks and thrifts
    (b) increased integration of world financial markets
    (c) increased use of coins and currency as a medium of exchange
    (d) an increase in the separation of services offered by financial institutions

25. Which one of the following would be a recent development in money and banking?
    (a) less reliance on global markets by financial institutions
    (b) less convergence in the types of services offered by financial institutions
    (c) greater use of electronic payments by financial institutions
    (d) a larger percentage of financial assets held by banks and thrifts compared to other financial institutions

■ **PROBLEMS**

1. From the figures in the following table it can be concluded that

Item	Billions of dollars
Small time deposits	$1014
MMMFs held by individuals	743
Checkable deposits	622
Savings deposits, including MMDAs	3649
Currency	730
MMMFs held by businesses	1190

   a. $M1$ is equal to the sum of $_____ and $_____, so it totals $_____ billion.

   b. $M2$ is equal to $M1$ plus $_____ and $_____ and $_____ so it totals $_____ billion.

   c. MZM is equal to $M2$ minus $_____ and plus $_____, so it totals $_____.

2. Complete the following table, which shows the relationship between a percentage change in the price level and the percentage change in the purchasing power of money. Calculate the percentage change in the purchasing power of money to one decimal place.

Change in price level	Change in purchasing power of money
a. *rises* by:	
5%	− _____._____%
10%	− _____._____
15%	− _____._____
20%	− _____._____
25%	− _____._____
b. *falls* by:	
5%	+ _____._____
10%	+ _____._____
15%	+ _____._____

■ **SHORT ANSWER AND ESSAY QUESTIONS**

1. How would you define money based on its three functions?

2. What are the two components of the $M1$ supply of money in the United States?

3. Why are coins token money?

4. What are checkable deposits?

5. Describe the different types of institutions that offer checkable deposits.

6. Are the checkable deposits of government, the Fed, commercial banks, and other financial institutions included in $M1$? Explain.

7. Define $M2$ and explain why it is used.

8. Define MZM and explain why it is used.

9. What is the purpose of having three definitions of the money supply? What is the relationship between the three definitions?

10. What backs the money used in the United States? What determines the purchasing power of money?

11. Explain the relationship between the purchasing power of money and the price level.

12. What must government do if it is to stabilize the purchasing power of money?

13. Describe the purpose and membership of the Board of Governors of the Federal Reserve System.

14. Explain the three major characteristics of the Federal Reserve Banks.

15. What is the Federal Open Market Committee, and how does it operate?

16. Describe the differences in commercial banks and thrifts in terms of numbers, purpose, and regulatory agencies.

17. What are the seven major functions of the Fed, and which function is the most important?

18. What are the basic reasons for the independence of the Federal Reserve System?

19. Describe the decline of and consolidation among banks and thrifts in recent years.

20. Discuss the meaning and effects of increased integration of world financial markets.

ANSWERS

Chapter 12 Money and Banking

FILL-IN QUESTIONS

1. a medium of exchange, a unit of account, a store of value
2. token, less
3. currency, checkable deposits
4. $M1$, noncheckable, small, deposit accounts, mutual funds (either order for the last two)
5. minus, plus
6. are not, loan
7. the Federal Reserve Banks, banks and thrifts, are not
8. acceptable, legal, scarce
9. inversely, divide
10. decrease, decrease
11. supply of, fiscal
12. Governors, Banks, Federal Open Market Committee
13. quasi-public, bankers', central
14. securities, interest rates
15. commercial banks, thrifts
16. *a.* issuing currency; *b.* setting reserve requirements and holding reserves; *c.* lending money to banks and thrifts; *d.* collecting and processing checks; *e.* serving as fiscal agent for the Federal government; *f.* bank supervision; *g.* controlling the money supply (any order *a–g*); controlling the money supply
17. independent, inflation
18. decreased, increased, mergers
19. convergence, globalization
20. electronic, smart, stored-value

TRUE–FALSE QUESTIONS

1. T, p. 229	**10.** F, p. 232	**19.** F, p. 236–237
2. F, pp. 229–230	**11.** T, pp. 232–233	**20.** T, p. 237
3. T, pp. 229–230	**12.** T, p. 233	**21.** F, p. 237
4. F, pp. 229–230	**13.** T, p. 233	**22.** T, p. 237
5. T, pp. 230–231	**14.** F, pp. 233–234	**23.** T, p. 238
6. F, p. 231	**15.** T, p. 234	**24.** F, pp. 238–239
7. T, p. 231	**16.** T, p. 235	**25.** T, pp. 239–240
8. T, p. 231	**17.** F, pp. 235–236	
9. F, pp. 231–232	**18.** T, p. 236	

MULTIPLE-CHOICE QUESTIONS

1. b, p. 229	**10.** c, p. 231	**19.** c, pp. 235–236
2. c, p. 230	**11.** c, p. 232	**20.** c, p. 236
3. d, pp. 233–234	**12.** c, pp. 232–233	**21.** c, p. 235
4. d, p. 230	**13.** b, pp. 232–233	**22.** d, p. 237
5. a, pp. 230–231	**14.** b, pp. 233–234	**23.** b, p. 237
6. b, p. 231	**15.** d, p. 234	**24.** b, p. 237
7. a, p. 231	**16.** c, p. 234	**25.** c, pp. 239–240
8. d, p. 232	**17.** c, p. 235	
9. b, p. 230	**18.** a, p. 235	

PROBLEMS

1. *a.* 730, 622 (either order), 1352; *b.* 3649, 1014, 743 (any order), 6758; *c.* 1014, 1190, 6934
2. *a.* 4.8, 9.1, 13, 16.7, 20; *b.* 5.3, 11.1, 17.6

SHORT ANSWER AND ESSAY QUESTIONS

1. p. 229	**8.** pp. 231–232	**15.** pp. 236–237
2. pp. 229–230	**9.** p. 232	**16.** p. 237
3. pp. 229–230	**10.** p. 232–233	**17.** p. 237
4. p. 230	**11.** pp. 233–234	**18.** p. 238
5. pp. 230–231	**12.** p. 234	**19.** pp. 238–239
6. p. 231	**13.** p. 235	**20.** p. 239
7. p. 231	**14.** pp. 235–236	

CHAPTER 13

Money Creation

Chapter 12 explained the institutional structure of banking in the United States today, the functions which banks and the other depository institutions and money perform, and the composition of the money supply. Chapter 13 explains how banks create money—**checkable deposits**—and the factors that determine and limit the money-creating ability of commercial banks. The other depository institutions, such as thrift institutions, also create checkable deposits, but this chapter focuses on commercial banks to simplify the discussion.

The convenient and simple device used to explain commercial banking operations and money creation is the **balance sheet.** Shown within it are the **assets, liabilities,** and **net worth** of commercial banks. All banking transactions affect this balance sheet. The first step in understanding how money is created is to understand how various simple and typical transactions affect the commercial bank balance sheet.

In reading this chapter, you must analyze for yourself the effect of each and every banking transaction on the balance sheet. The important items in the balance sheet are checkable deposits and reserves because **checkable deposits are money.** The ability of a bank to create new checkable deposits is determined by the amount of reserves that bank has. Expansion of the money supply depends on the possession by commercial banks of excess reserves. Those reserves do not appear explicitly in the balance sheet but do appear there implicitly because **excess reserves** are the difference between the **actual reserves** and the **required reserves** of commercial banks.

Two cases—the single commercial bank and the banking system—are presented to help you build an understanding of banking and money creation. It is important to understand that the money-creating potential of a single commercial bank differs from the money-creating potential of the entire banking system. It is equally important to understand how the money-creating ability of many single commercial banks is **multiplied** and influences the **money-creating ability** of the banking system as a whole.

■ **CHECKLIST**

When you have studied this chapter you should be able to

☐ Recount the story of how goldsmiths came to issue paper money and became bankers who created money and held fractional reserves.

☐ Cite two significant characteristics of the fractional reserve banking system today.

☐ Define the basic items in a bank's balance sheet.

☐ Describe what happens to a bank's balance sheet when the bank is created, buys property and equipment, and accepts deposits.

☐ Explain the effects of the deposit of currency in a checking account on the composition and size of the money supply.

☐ Define the reserve ratio.

☐ Compute a bank's required and excess reserves when you are given the needed balance-sheet figures.

☐ Explain why a commercial bank is required to maintain a reserve and why a required reserve is not sufficient to protect the depositors from losses.

☐ Indicate whether required reserves are assets or liabilities for commercial banks and the Federal Reserve.

☐ Describe how the deposit of a check drawn on one commercial bank and deposited into another will affect the reserves and excess reserves of the two banks.

☐ Show what happens to the money supply when a commercial bank makes a loan.

☐ Show what happens to the money supply when a commercial bank buys government securities.

☐ Describe what would happen to a commercial bank's reserves if it made loans (or bought government securities) in an amount greater than its excess reserves.

☐ State the money-creating potential of a commercial bank (the amount of money a commercial bank can safely create by lending or buying securities).

☐ Explain how a commercial bank's balance sheet reflects a banker's pursuit of the two conflicting goals of profit and liquidity.

☐ Explain how the Federal funds market helps reconcile the goals of profits and liquidity for commercial banks.

☐ State the money-creating potential of the banking system.

☐ Explain how it is possible for the banking system to create an amount of money that is a multiple of its excess reserves when no individual commercial bank ever creates money in an amount greater than its excess reserve.

☐ Compute the size of the monetary multiplier and the money-creating potential of the banking system when you are provided with the necessary data.

☐ Illustrate with an example using the monetary multiplier how money can be destroyed in the banking system.

☐ Discuss how bank panics in the early 1930s led to a contraction of the nation's money supply and worsened economic conditions (Last Word).

■ CHAPTER OUTLINE

1. The United States has a **fractional reserve banking system.** This means that banks keep only a part or a fraction of their checkable deposits backed by cash reserves.

   a. The history of the early goldsmiths illustrates how paper money came into use in the economy and how banks create money. The goldsmiths accepted gold as deposits and began making loans and issuing money in excess of their gold holdings.

   b. The goldsmiths' fractional reserve system is similar to today's fractional reserve banking system, which has two significant characteristics: Banks can create money in such a system, and banks are subject to "panics" or "runs" and thus need government regulation.

2. The **balance sheet** of a single commercial bank is a statement of the *assets, liabilities,* and *net worth* (stock shares) of that bank at a specific time; in the balance sheet, the bank's assets equal its liabilities plus its net worth. This balance sheet changes with various transactions.

   a. *Transaction 1: Creating a bank.* A commercial bank is founded by selling shares of stock and obtaining cash in return. Stock is a liability, and cash is an asset.

   b. *Transaction 2: Acquiring property and equipment.* A commercial bank needs property and equipment to carry on the banking business. They are assets of the bank.

   c. *Transaction 3: Accepting deposits.* When a bank accepts deposits of cash, the cash becomes an asset of the bank, and the checkable deposit accounts that are created are a liability. The deposit of cash in the bank does not affect the total money supply. It only changes its composition by substituting checkable deposits for currency (cash) in circulation.

   d. *Transaction 4: Depositing its reserve in a Federal Reserve Bank.*

   (1) Three reserve concepts are vital to an understanding of the money-creating potential of a commercial bank.

   (a) The **required reserves,** which a bank *must* maintain at its Federal Reserve Bank (or as **vault cash**—which can be ignored), equal the reserve ratio multiplied by the checkable deposit liabilities of a commercial bank.

   (b) The **actual reserves** of a commercial bank are its deposits at the Federal Reserve Bank (plus the vault cash, which is ignored).

   (c) The **excess reserves** are equal to the actual reserves less the required reserve.

   (2) The **reserve ratio** is the ratio of required reserves to a bank's own checkable deposit liabilities. The Fed has the authority to establish and change the ratio within limits set by Congress.

   e. *Transaction 5: Clearing a check drawn against the bank.*
   The writing of a check on the bank and its deposit in a second bank results in a loss of reserves (assets) and checkable deposits (liabilities) for the first bank and a gain in reserves and deposits for the second bank.

3. **A single commercial bank** in a multibank system can create money, as the following two transactions show.

   a. *Transaction 6: Granting a loan.* When a single commercial bank grants a loan to a borrower, its balance sheet changes. Checkable deposit liabilities are increased by the amount of the loan, and the loan value is entered as an asset. In essence, the borrower gives an IOU (a promise to repay the loan) to the bank, and in return the bank creates money by giving the borrower checkable deposits. The bank has "monetized" the IOU and created money. When the borrower writes a check for the amount of the loan to pay for something and that check clears, the checkable deposits are reduced by the amount of that check. A bank lends its funds only in an amount equal to its preloan excess reserves because it fears the loss of reserves to other commercial banks in the economy.

   b. *Transaction 7. Buying government securities.* When a bank buys government securities, it increases its own checkable deposit liabilities and therefore the supply of money by the amount of the securities purchase. The bank's assets increase by the amount of the securities it now holds. The bank buys securities only in an amount equal to its excess reserves because it fears the loss of reserves to other commercial banks in the economy.

   c. An individual commercial bank balances its desire for profits (which result from the making of loans and the purchase of securities) with its desire for liquidity or safety (which it achieves by having excess reserves or vault cash). The Federal funds market allows banks with excess reserves to lend funds overnight to banks that are short of reserves. The interest rate paid on the overnight loans is the **Federal funds rate.**

4. The ability of a **banking system** composed of many individual commercial banks to lend and create money is a multiple (greater than 1) of its excess reserves and is equal to the excess reserves of the banking system multiplied by the checkable-deposit (or monetary) multiplier.

   a. The banking system as a whole can do this even though no single commercial bank ever lends an amount greater than its excess reserves because the banking system, unlike a single commercial bank, does not lose reserves. If a bank receives a deposit of currency, it increases its checkable deposits. This change increases the amount of excess reserves the bank has available for making loans. If a loan is made on those excess reserves, then it creates additional checkable deposits that, when spent, may be deposited in another bank. That other bank now has additional excess reserves and can increase its lending, and so the process continues.

   b. The **monetary multiplier** is equal to the reciprocal of the required reserve ratio for checkable deposits. The maximum expansion of checkable deposits is equal to the initial excess reserves in the banking system times the monetary multiplier.

   c. The money-creating process of the banking system can be reversed. When loans are paid off, money is destroyed.

5. (Last Word). During the early 1930s, more than 6000 banks failed within 3 years. That resulted in a multiple contraction of the nation's money supply that totaled about 25%. The decline in the money supply contributed to the

Great Depression. In 1933, banks were shut for a week for a bank holiday and a deposit insurance program was established to give confidence to depositors and reduce the potential for large withdrawals in the future.

■ **HINTS AND TIPS**

1. Note that several terms are used interchangeably in this chapter: A "commercial bank" (or "bank") is sometimes called a "thrift institution" or "depository institution."

2. A bank's balance sheet must balance. The bank's assets are claimed by owners (net worth) or by nonowners (liabilities). *Assets = liabilities + net worth.*

3. Make a running balance sheet in writing for yourself as you read about each of the eight transactions for the Wahoo Bank in the text. Then determine if you understand the material by telling yourself (or a friend) the story of each transaction without using the text.

4. The **maximum amount of checkable-deposit expansion** is determined by multiplying two factors: the excess reserves by the monetary multiplier. Each factor, however, is affected by the required reserve ratio. The monetary multiplier is calculated by dividing 1 by the required reserve ratio. Excess reserves are determined by multiplying the required reserve ratio by the amount of new deposits. Thus, a change in the required reserve ratio will change the monetary multiplier and the amount of excess reserves. For example, a required reserve ratio of 25% gives a monetary multiplier of 4. For $100 in new money deposited, required reserves are $25 and excess reserves are $75. The maximum checkable-deposit expansion is $300 (4 × $75). If the reserve ratio drops to 20%, the monetary multiplier is 5 and excess reserves are $80, and so the maximum checkable-deposit expansion is $400. Both factors have changed.

5. Be aware that the monetary multiplier can result in **money destruction** as well as money creation in the banking system. You should know how the monetary multiplier reinforces effects in one direction or the other.

■ **IMPORTANT TERMS**

fractional reserve banking
   system
balance sheet
vault cash
required reserves

reserve ratio
excess reserves
actual reserves
Federal funds rate
monetary multiplier

SELF-TEST

■ **FILL-IN QUESTIONS**

1. The banking system used today is a (total, fractional) _____ reserve system, which means that (100%, less than 100%) _____ of the money deposited in a bank is kept on reserve.

2. There are two significant characteristics of today's banking system. Banks can create (reserves, money) _____ depending on the amount of _____ they hold. Banks are susceptible to (panics, regulation) _____, or "runs," and to prevent this situation from happening, banks are subject to government _____.

3. The balance sheet of a commercial bank is a statement of the bank's (gold account, assets) _____, the claims of the owners of the bank [called (net worth, liabilities) _____], and claims of nonowners (called _____). This relationship would be written in equation form as: _____.

4. The coins and paper money that a bank has in its possession are (petty, vault) _____ cash or (till, capital) _____ money.

5. When a person deposits cash in a commercial bank and receives a checkable deposit in return, the size of the money supply has (increased, decreased, not changed) _____.

6. The legal reserve of a commercial bank (ignoring vault cash) must be kept on deposit at (a branch of the U.S. Treasury, its district Federal Reserve Bank) _____.

7. The reserve ratio is equal to a commercial bank's (required, gold) _____ reserves divided by its checkable-deposit (assets, liabilities) _____.

8. The authority to establish and vary the reserve ratio within limits legislated by Congress has been given to the (U.S. Treasury, Fed) _____.

9. If commercial banks are allowed to accept (or create) deposits in excess of their reserves, the banking system is operating under a system of (fractional, currency) _____ reserves.

10. The excess reserves of a commercial bank equal its (actual, required) _____ reserves minus its _____ reserves.

11. The basic purpose of having member banks deposit a legal reserve in the Federal Reserve Bank in their district is to provide (liquidity for, control of) _____ the banking system by the Fed.

12. When a commercial bank deposits a legal reserve in its district Federal Reserve Bank, the reserve is (a liability, an asset) _____ to the commercial bank and _____ to the Federal Reserve Bank.

13. When a check is drawn on Bank X, deposited in Bank Y, and cleared, the reserves of Bank X are (increased, decreased, not changed) _____ and the reserves of Bank Y are _____; deposits in Bank X are (increased, decreased, not changed) _____, and deposits in Bank Y are _____.

14. A single commercial bank in a multibank system can safely make .loans or buy government securities equal in amount to the (required, excess) _____ reserves of that commercial bank.

15. When a commercial bank makes a new loan of $10,000, the supply of money (increases, decreases) _____ by $_____. When a commercial bank buys a $10,000 government bond from a securities dealer, the supply of money (increases, decreases) _____ by $_____.

16. A bank ordinarily pursues two conflicting goals; one goal is the desire to make money, or (profits, liquidity) _____, and the other goal is the need for safety, or _____.

17. When a bank lends temporary excess reserves held at its Federal Reserve Bank to other commercial banks that are temporarily short of legal reserves, it is participating in the (government securities, Federal funds) _____ market. The interest rate paid on these overnight loans is called the (government securities, Federal funds) _____ rate.

18. The monetary multiplier is equal to 1 divided by the (excess, required) _____ reserve ratio. The greater the reserve ratio, the (larger, smaller) _____ the monetary multiplier.

19. The banking system can make loans (or buy government securities) and create money in an amount equal to its (required, excess) _____ reserves multiplied by the (required reserve ratio, monetary multiplier) _____.

20. Assume that the required reserve ratio is 16.67% and the banking system is $6 million short of required reserves. If the banking system is unable to increase its reserves, the banking system must (increase, decrease) _____ the money supply by ($6, $36) _____ million.

■ TRUE–FALSE QUESTIONS

Circle T if the statement is true, F if it is false.

1. Goldsmiths increased the money supply when they accepted deposits of gold and issued paper receipts to the depositors.　　　　**T　F**

2. Modern banking systems use gold as the basis for the fractional reserve system.　　　　**T　F**

3. The balance sheet of a commercial bank shows the transactions in which the bank has engaged during a given period of time.　　　　**T　F**

4. A commercial bank's assets plus its net worth equal the bank's liabilities.　　　　**T　F**

5. Cash held by a bank is sometimes called vault cash.　　　　**T　F**

6. When a bank accepts deposits of cash and puts them into a checking account, there has been a change in the composition of the money supply.　　　　**T　F**

7. A commercial bank may maintain its legal reserve either as a deposit in its Federal Reserve Bank or as government bonds in its own vault.　　　　**T　F**

8. The required reserves that a commercial bank maintains must equal its own checkable-deposit liabilities multiplied by the required reserve ratio.　　　　**T　F**

9. The actual reserves of a commercial bank equal excess reserves plus required reserves.　　　　**T　F**

10. Required reserves are sufficient to meet demands for the return of all funds that are held as checkable deposits at commercial banks.　　　　**T　F**

11. Required reserves help the Fed control the lending ability of commercial banks.　　　　**T　F**

12. The reserve of a commercial bank in the Federal Reserve Bank is an asset of the Federal Reserve Bank.　　　　**T　F**

13. A check for $1000 drawn on Bank X by a depositor and deposited in Bank Y will increase the excess reserves in Bank Y by $1000.　　　　**T　F**

14. A bank that has a check drawn and collected against it will lose to the recipient both reserves and deposits equal to the value of the check.　　　　**T　F**

15. When Manfred Iron and Coal Company borrows $30,000 from a bank, the money supply has increased by $30,000.　　　　**T　F**

16. A single commercial bank can safely lend an amount equal to its excess reserves multiplied by the monetary multiplier ratio.　　　　**T　F**

17. The granting of a $5000 loan and the purchase of a $5000 government bond from a securities dealer by a commercial bank have the same effect on the money supply.　　　　**T　F**

18. The selling of a government bond by a commercial bank will increase the money supply.　　　　**T　F**

19. A commercial bank seeks both profits and liquidity, but these are conflicting goals.　　　　**T　F**

20. The Federal funds rate is the interest rate at which the Federal government lends funds to commercial banks.　　　　**T　F**

21. The reason the banking system can lend by a multiple of its excess reserves but each individual bank can only lend "dollar for dollar" with its excess reserves is that reserves lost by a single bank are not lost to the banking system as a whole. **T F**

22. The monetary multiplier is excess reserves divided by required reserves. **T F**

23. The maximum checkable-deposit expansion is equal to excess reserves divided by the monetary multiplier. **T F**

24. If the banking system has $10 million in excess reserves and the reserve ratio is 25%, the system can increase its loans by $40 million. **T F**

25. When a borrower repays a loan of $500 either in cash or by check, the supply of money is reduced by $500.

  T F

■ MULTIPLE-CHOICE QUESTIONS

Circle the letter that corresponds to the best answer.

1. The fractional reserve system of banking started when goldsmiths began
  (a) accepting deposits of gold for safe storage
  (b) issuing receipts for the gold stored with them
  (c) using deposited gold to produce products for sale to others
  (d) issuing paper money in excess of the amount of gold stored with them

2. The claims of the owners of a bank against the bank's assets is the bank's
  (a) net worth
  (b) liabilities
  (c) balance sheet
  (d) fractional reserves

3. When cash is deposited in a checkable-deposit account in a commercial bank, there is
  (a) a decrease in the money supply
  (b) an increase in the money supply
  (c) no change in the composition of the money supply
  (d) a change in the composition of the money supply

4. A commercial bank has actual reserves of $9000 and liabilities of $30,000, and the required reserve ratio is 20%. The excess reserves of the bank are
  (a) $3000
  (b) $6000
  (c) $7500
  (d) $9000

5. The primary reason commercial banks must keep required reserves on deposit at Federal Reserve Banks is to
  (a) protect the deposits in the commercial bank against losses
  (b) provide the means by which checks drawn on the commercial bank and deposited in other commercial banks can be collected

  (c) add to the liquidity of the commercial bank and protect it against a "run" on the bank
  (d) provide the Fed with a means of controlling the lending ability of the commercial bank

6. Reserves that a commercial bank deposits at a Federal Reserve Bank are
  (a) an asset to the Federal Reserve Bank and a liability of the commercial bank
  (b) an asset of the commercial bank and a liability of the Federal Reserve Bank
  (c) used as insurance funds for the Federal Deposit Insurance Corporation
  (d) used as insurance for the National Credit Union Administration

7. A depositor places $750 in cash in a commercial bank, and the reserve ratio is 33.33%; the bank sends the $750 to the Federal Reserve Bank. As a result, the *actual reserves* and the *excess reserves* of the bank have been increased, respectively, by
  (a) $750 and $250
  (b) $750 and $500
  (c) $750 and $750
  (d) $500 and $500

8. A bank that has a check drawn and collected against it will
  (a) lose to the recipient bank both reserves and deposits
  (b) gain from the recipient bank both reserves and deposits
  (c) lose to the recipient bank reserves but gain deposits
  (d) gain from the recipient bank reserves but lose deposits

9. A commercial bank has no excess reserves until a depositor places $600 in cash in the bank. The bank then adds the $600 to its reserves by sending it to the Federal Reserve Bank. The commercial bank then lends $300 to a borrower. As a consequence of these transactions, the size of the money supply has
  (a) not been affected
  (b) increased by $300
  (c) increased by $600
  (d) increased by $900

10. A commercial bank has excess reserves of $500 and a required reserve ratio of 20%; it grants a loan of $1000 to a borrower. If the borrower writes a check for $1000 that is deposited in another commercial bank, the first bank will be short of reserves, after the check has been cleared, in the amount of
  (a) $200
  (b) $500
  (c) $700
  (d) $1000

11. The buying of government securities by commercial banks is most similar to the
  (a) making of loans by banks because both actions increase the money supply
  (b) making of loans by banks because both actions decrease the money supply

(c) repayment of loans to banks because both actions decrease the money supply

(d) repayment of loans to banks because both actions increase the money supply

12. A commercial bank sells a $1000 government security to a securities dealer. The dealer pays for the bond in cash, which the bank adds to its vault cash. The money supply has

(a) not been affected

(b) decreased by $1000

(c) increased by $1000

(d) increased by $1000 multiplied by the reciprocal of the required reserve ratio

13. A commercial bank has deposit liabilities of $100,000, reserves of $37,000, and a required reserve ratio of 25%. The amount by which a *single commercial bank* and the amount by which the *banking system* can increase loans are, respectively

(a) $12,000 and $48,000

(b) $17,000 and $68,000

(c) $12,000 and $60,000

(d) $17,000 and $85,000

14. If the required reserve ratio were 12.5%, the value of the monetary multiplier would be

(a) 5

(b) 6

(c) 7

(d) 8

15. The commercial banking system has excess reserves of $700, makes new loans of $2100, and is just meeting its reserve requirements. The required reserve ratio is

(a) 20%

(b) 25%

(c) 30%

(d) 33.33%

16. The commercial banking system, because of a recent change in the required reserve ratio from 20% to 30%, finds that it is $60 million short of reserves. If it is unable to obtain any additional reserves, it must decrease the money supply by

(a) $60 million

(b) $180 million

(c) $200 million

(d) $300 million

17. Only one commercial bank in the banking system has an excess reserve, and its excess reserve is $100,000. This bank makes a new loan of $80,000 and keeps an excess reserve of $20,000. If the required reserve ratio for all banks is 20%, the potential expansion of the money supply from this $80,000 loan is

(a) $80,000

(b) $100,000

(c) $400,000

(d) $500,000

Use the following balance sheet for the First National Bank to answer Questions 18, 19, 20, 21, and 22. Assume the required reserve ratio is 20%.

Assets		Liabilities and Net Worth	
Reserves	$ 50,000	Checkable deposits	$150,000
Loans	70,000	Stock shares	100,000
Securities	30,000		
Property	100,000		

18. This commercial bank has excess reserves of

(a) $10,000

(b) $20,000

(c) $30,000

(d) $40,000

19. This bank can safely expand its loans by a maximum of

(a) $50,000

(b) $40,000

(c) $30,000

(d) $20,000

20. Using the original bank balance sheet, assume that the bank makes a loan of $10,000 and has a check cleared against it for the amount of the loan; its reserves and checkable deposits will now be

(a) $40,000 and $140,000

(b) $40,000 and $150,000

(c) $30,000 and $150,000

(d) $60,000 and $140,000

21. Using the original bank balance sheet, assume that the bank makes a loan of $15,000 and has a check cleared against it for the amount of the loan; it will then have excess reserves of

(a) $5000

(b) $10,000

(c) $15,000

(d) $20,000

22. If the original bank balance sheet was for the commercial banking *system* rather than a single bank, loans and deposits could have been expanded by a maximum of

(a) $50,000

(b) $100,000

(c) $150,000

(d) $200,000

Answer Questions 23 and 24 on the basis of the following consolidated balance sheet for the commercial banking system. All figures are in billions. Assume that the required reserve ratio is 12.5%.

Assets		Liabilities and Net Worth	
Reserves	$ 40	Checkable deposits	$200
Loans	80	Stock shares	120
Securities	100		
Property	200		

23. If there is a deposit of $20 billion of new currency into checking accounts in the banking system, excess reserves will increase by

(a) $16.5 billion

(b) $17.0 billion

(c) $17.5 billion

(d) $18.5 billion

24. The maximum amount by which this commercial banking system can expand the supply of money by lending is
  (a) $120 billion
  (b) $240 billion
  (c) $350 billion
  (d) $440 billion

25. If the dollar amount of loans made in some period is less than the dollar amount of loans paid off, checkable deposits will
  (a) expand and the money supply will increase
  (b) expand and the money supply will decrease
  (c) contract and the money supply will decrease
  (d) contract and the money supply will increase

■ PROBLEMS

1. The following table shows the simplified balance sheet of a commercial bank. Assume that the figures given show the bank's assets and checkable-deposit liabilities *prior to each of the following four transactions.* Draw up the balance sheet as it would appear after each of these transactions is completed and place the balance-sheet figures in the appropriate column. Do *not* use the figures you place in columns **a, b,** and **c** when you work the next part of the problem; start all parts of the problem with the printed figures.

		(a)	(b)	(c)	(d)
Assets:					
Cash	$100	$____	$____	$____	$____
Reserves	200	____	____	____	____
Loans	500	____	____	____	____
Securities	200	____	____	____	____
Liabilities and net worth:					
Checkable deposits	900	____	____	____	____
Stock shares	100	100	100	100	100

a. A check for $50 is drawn by one of the depositors of the bank, given to a person who deposits it in another bank, and cleared (column a).
b. A depositor withdraws $50 in cash from the bank, and the bank restores its vault cash by obtaining $50 in additional cash from its Federal Reserve Bank (column b).
c. A check for $60 drawn on another bank is deposited in this bank and cleared (column c).
d. The bank sells $100 in government bonds to the Federal Reserve Bank in its district (column d).

2. Following are five balance sheets for a single commercial bank (columns 1a–5a). The required reserve ratio is 20%.
  a. Compute the required reserves (A), ignoring vault cash, the excess reserves (B) of the bank (if the bank is short of reserves and must reduce its loans or obtain additional reserves, show this by placing a minus sign in front of the amounts by which it is short of reserves), and the amount of new loans it can extend (C).

	(1a)	(2a)	(3a)	(4a)	(5a)
Assets:					
Cash	$ 10	$ 20	$ 20	$ 20	$ 15
Reserves	40	40	25	40	45
Loans	100	100	100	100	150
Securities	50	60	30	70	60
Liabilities and net worth:					
Checkable deposits	175	200	150	180	220
Stock shares	25	20	25	50	50
A. Required reserves	$ ____	$ ____	$ ____	$ ____	$ ____
B. Excess reserves	$ ____	____	____	____	____
C. New loans	____	____	____	____	____

b. In the following table, draw up for the individual bank the five balance sheets as they appear after the bank has made the new loans that it is capable of making.

	(1b)	(2b)	(3b)	(4b)	(5b)
Assets:					
Cash	$ ____	$ ____	$ ____	$ ____	$ ____
Reserves	____	____	____	____	____
Loans	____	____	____	____	____
Securities	____	____	____	____	____
Liabilities and net worth:					
Checkable deposits	____	____	____	____	____
Stock shares	____	____	____	____	____

3. The following table shows several reserve ratios. Compute the monetary multiplier for each reserve ratio and enter the figures in column 2. In column 3 show the maximum amount by which a single commercial bank can increase its loans for each dollar's worth of excess reserves it possesses. In column 4 indicate the maximum amount by which the banking system can increase its loans for each dollar's worth of excess reserves in the system.

(1)	(2)	(3)	(4)
12.50%	$ ____	$ ____	$ ____
16.67	____	____	____
20	____	____	____
25	____	____	____
30	____	____	____
33.33	____	____	____

4. The following table is the simplified consolidated balance sheet for all commercial banks in the economy. Assume that the figures given show the banks' assets and liabilities *prior to each of the following three transactions* and that the reserve ratio is 20%. Do *not* use the figures

		(1)	(2)	(3)	(4)	(5)	(6)
Assets:							
Cash	$ 50	$____	$____	$____	$____	$____	$____
Reserves	100	____	____	____	____	____	____
Loans	200	____	____	____	____	____	____
Securities	200	____	____	____	____	____	____
Liabilities and net worth:							
Checkable deposits	500	____	____	____	____	____	____
Stock shares	50	50	50	50	50	50	50
Loans for Federal Reserve	0	____	____	____	____	____	____
Excess reserves		____	____	____	____	____	____
Maximum possible expansion of the money supply		____	____	____	____	____	____

you placed in columns 2 and 4 when you begin parts **b** and **c** of the problem; start parts **a, b,** and **c** of the problem with the printed figures.

a. The public deposits $5 in cash in the banks, and the banks send the $5 to the Federal Reserve, where it is added to their reserves. Fill in column 1. If the banking system extends the maximum amount of new loans that it is capable of extending, show in column 2 the balance sheet as it will then appear.

b. The banking system sells $8 worth of securities to the Federal Reserve. Complete column 3. Assuming the system extends the maximum amount of credit of which it is capable, fill in column 4.

c. The Federal Reserve lends $10 to the commercial banks; complete column 5. Complete column 6, showing the condition of the banks after the maximum amount of new loans that the banks are capable of making is granted.

■ **SHORT ANSWER AND ESSAY QUESTIONS**

1. How did the early goldsmiths come to issue paper money and then become bankers?

2. Explain the difference between a 100% and a fractional reserve system of banking.

3. What are two significant characteristics of a fractional reserve system of banking?

4. Why does a bank's balance sheet balance?

5. Explain what happens to the money supply when a bank accepts deposits of cash.

6. What are legal reserves? How are they determined? How are legal reserves related to the reserve ratio?

7. Define the meaning of excess reserves. How are they calculated?

8. Explain why bank reserves can be an asset to the depositing commercial bank but a liability to the Federal Reserve Bank receiving them.

9. Do the reserves held by commercial banks satisfactorily protect a bank's depositors? Are the reserves of commercial banks needed? Explain your answers.

10. The owner of a sporting goods store writes a check on her account in a Kent, Ohio, bank and sends it to one of her suppliers, who deposits it in his bank in Cleveland, Ohio. How does the Cleveland bank obtain payment from the Kent bank? If the two banks were in Kent and New York City, how would one bank pay the other? How are the excess reserves of the two banks affected?

11. Explain why the granting of a loan by a commercial bank increases the supply of money.

12. Why is a single commercial bank able to lend safely only an amount equal to its excess reserves?

13. How does the buying or selling of government securities by commercial banks influence the money supply?

14. Commercial banks seek both profits and safety. Explain how the balance sheet of the commercial banks reflects the desires of bankers for profits and for liquidity.

15. What is the Federal funds rate?

16. Discuss how the Federal funds market helps banks reconcile the two goals of profits and liquidity.

17. No single commercial bank ever lends an amount greater than its excess reserves, but the banking system as a whole is able to extend loans and expand the money supply by an amount equal to the system's excess reserves multiplied by the reciprocal of the reserve ratio. Explain why this is possible and how the multiple expansion of deposits and money takes place.

18. What is the monetary multiplier? How does it work?

19. What would happen to maximum checkable-deposit creation if the reserve ratio increased or the reserve ratio decreased? Explain by using numerical examples.

20. Why does the repayment of a loan decrease the supply of money?

ANSWERS

Chapter 13 Money Creation

FILL-IN QUESTIONS

1. fractional, less than 100%
2. money, reserves, panics, regulation
3. assets, net worth, liabilities, assets = liabilities + net worth
4. vault, till

5. not changed
6. its district Federal Reserve Bank
7. required, liabilities
8. Fed
9. fractional
10. actual, required
11. control of
12. an asset, a liability
13. decreased, increased, decreased, increased
14. excess
15. increases, 10,000, increases, 10,000
16. profits, liquidity
17. Federal funds, Federal funds
18. required, smaller
19. excess, monetary multiplier
20. decrease, $36

TRUE–FALSE QUESTIONS

1. F, p. 245	10. F, p. 248	19. T, p. 251
2. F, p. 245	11. T, p. 248	20. F, p. 251
3. F, pp. 245–246	12. F, p. 248	21. T, p. 251
4. F, pp. 245–246	13. F, pp. 248–249	22. F, p. 253
5. T, p. 246	14. T, pp. 248–249	23. F, p. 253
6. F, p. 247	15. T, p. 249	24. T, pp. 253–254
7. F, p. 247	16. F, p. 250	25. T, p. 254
8. T, p. 247	17. T, pp. 249–251	
9. T, p. 247	18. F, p. 251	

MULTIPLE-CHOICE QUESTIONS

1. d, p. 245	10. b, pp. 249–250	19. d, p. 247
2. a, pp. 245–246	11. a, pp. 250–251	20. b, pp. 248–249
3. d, p. 246	12. b, pp. 250–251	21. a, pp. 248–249
4. a, p. 247	13. a, pp. 253–254	22. b, pp. 253–254
5. d, p. 248	14. d, p. 253	23. c, pp. 253–254
6. b, p. 248	15. d, pp. 253–254	24. a, pp. 253–254
7. b, pp. 247–248	16. c, pp. 253–254	25. c, p. 254
8. a, pp. 248–249	17. c, pp. 253–254	
9. b, pp. 249–250	18. b, p. 247	

PROBLEMS

1. Table

	(a)	(b)	(c)	(d)
Assets:				
Cash	$100	$100	$100	$100
Reserves	150	150	260	300
Loans	500	500	500	500
Securities	200	200	200	100
Liabilities and net worth:				
Checkable deposits	850	850	960	900
Stock shares	100	100	100	100

2. *a.* Table (and * below)

	(1a)	(2a)	(3a)	(4a)	(5a)
A. Required reserves	$35	$40	$30	$36	$44
B. Excess reserves	5	0	−5	4	1
C. New loans	5	0	*	4	1

b. Table (and * below)

	(1b)	(2b)	(3b)	(4b)	(5b)
Assets:					
Cash	$ 10	$ 20	$ 20	$ 20	$ 15
Reserves	40	40	25	40	45
Loans	105	100	*	104	151
Securities	50	60	30	70	60
Liabilities and net worth:					
Checkable deposits	180	200	*	184	221
Stock shares	25	20	25	50	50

*If an individual bank is $5 short of reserves, it must either obtain additional reserves of $5 by selling loans, securities, or its own IOUs to the reserve bank or contract its loans by $25.

3. Table

(1)	(2)	(3)	(4)
12.50%	$8	$1	$8
16.67	$6	1	$6
20	$5	1	$5
25	$4	1	$4
30	$3.33	1	$3.33
33.33	$3	1	$3

4. Table

	(1)	(2)	(3)	(4)	(5)	(6)
Assets:						
Cash	$ 50	$ 50	$ 50	$ 50	$ 50	$ 50
Reserves	105	105	110	110	110	110
Loans	200	220	200	250	200	250
Securities	200	200	200	200	200	200
Liabilities and net worth:						
Checkable deposits	505	525	500	550	500	550
Stock shares	50	50	50	50	50	50
Loans from Federal Reserve	0	0	10	10	10	10
Excess reserves	4	0	10	0	10	0
Maximum possible expansion of the money supply	20	0	50	0	50	0

SHORT ANSWER AND ESSAY QUESTIONS

1. p. 245	8. p. 248	15. p. 251
2. p. 245	9. p. 248	16. p. 251
3. p. 245	10. pp. 248–249	17. pp. 251–253
4. pp. 245–246	11. pp. 249–250	18. p. 253
5. p. 246	12. p. 250	19. pp. 253–254
6. pp. 246–247	13. pp. 250–251	20. p. 254
7. pp. 247–248	14. p. 251	

CHAPTER 14

Interest Rates and Monetary Policy

Chapter 14 is the third chapter dealing with money and banking. It explains how the Federal Reserve affects output, income, employment, and the price level of the economy. Central bank policy designed to affect these variables is called **monetary policy,** and its goal is price-level stability, full employment, and economic growth.

The work of the Fed focuses on the interest rate and supply and demand in the market for money. The total **demand for money** is made up of a **transactions demand** and an **asset demand** for money. Because money is used as a medium of exchange, consumers and business firms want to hold money for transaction purposes. The quantity of money they demand for this purpose is directly related to the size of the economy's nominal GDP.

Money is also used as a store of value that creates an asset demand. Consumers and businesses that own assets may choose to have some of their assets in the form of money (rather than in stocks, bonds, goods, or property). Holding money, however, imposes a cost on those who hold it. This cost is the interest they lose when they own money rather than an interest-earning asset such as a bond. Consumers and businesses will demand less money for asset purposes when the rate of interest (the cost of holding money) is high and demand more money when the rate of interest is low; the quantity of money demanded as an asset is inversely related to the interest rate.

The total demand for money is the sum of the transactions demand and the asset demand. It is affected by both nominal GDP and the rate of interest. The total demand for and the supply of money determine interest rates in the market for money. The inverse relationship between bond prices and interest rates helps this market adjust to shortages or surpluses of money.

The chapter explains how the Federal Reserve achieves its basic goal. In this discussion, attention should be paid to the following: (1) the important items on the balance sheet of the Federal Reserve Banks and (2) the three major controls available to the Federal Reserve and how the employment of those controls can affect the reserves, excess reserves, actual money supply, and money-creating potential of the banking system. The most important control is the buying and selling of government securities in the open market.

The Federal Reserve targets the Federal funds rate because it is the interest rate it can best control. This rate is the interest rate that banks charge each other on overnight loans of temporary excess reserves. The Federal Reserve uses open-market operations to sell government securities, and this increases the excess reserves of banks, thus lowering the Federal funds rate. In this case, the Federal

Reserve is pursuing an expansionary monetary policy that increases the money supply and decreases interest rates. Conversely, the Federal Reserve can buy government securities and decrease excess reserves and thus raise the Federal funds rate. In this case, the Federal Reserve is pursuing a restrictive monetary policy that decreases the money supply and increases interest rates.

Professors McConnell and Brue follow the discussion of the Federal funds rate with an explanation of how changes in the money supply ultimately affect the economy. They achieve this objective by describing how the demand for money and the supply of money determine the interest rate (in the market for money) and how the interest rate and the investment demand schedule determine the level of equilibrium GDP. The effects of an expansionary monetary policy or a restrictive monetary policy in this cause-effect chain are illustrated with examples and summarized in Table 14.3. Changes in monetary policy shift aggregate demand across the aggregate supply curve, thus changing real output and the price level.

One of the concluding sections of the chapter evaluates monetary policy. The major strengths of the Federal Reserve are related to its speed and flexibility and isolation from political pressures. The Federal Reserve has had many successes since the 1990s in countering recession by lowering the interest rate and in controlling inflation by raising the interest rate.

Monetary policy, however, is not without its problems or complications. There can be lags between the time actions are taken and the time the monetary policy influences economic activity. Monetary policy can also suffer from cyclical asymmetry by being more influential in controlling inflation than in preventing recession. There have been debates about whether there should be more or less discretion in the conduct of monetary policy and the adoption of inflation targeting.

The final section on the "Big Picture" is short but important. Figure 14.6 gives you an overview of the economic factors and government policies that affect aggregate demand and aggregate supply. It summarizes much of the economic theory and economic policy that have been discussed in this chapter and the eight chapters that preceded it.

■ CHECKLIST

When you have studied this chapter you should be able to

☐ Explain what interest is and why it is important.
☐ Give a definition of the transactions demand for money.

☐ Give a definition of the asset demand for money.

☐ Illustrate graphically how the transactions and asset demands for money combine to form the total demand for money.

☐ Describe the market for money and what determines the equilibrium rate of interest.

☐ Explain how changes in nominal GDP and in the money supply affect the interest rate.

☐ Illustrate with an example how disequilibrium in the market for money is corrected through changes in bond prices.

☐ List the important assets and liabilities of the Federal Reserve Banks.

☐ Identify the three tools of monetary policy.

☐ Explain how the Federal Reserve can expand the money supply by buying government securities from commercial banks and from the public.

☐ Explain how the Federal Reserve can contract the money supply by selling government securities to commercial banks and to the public.

☐ Describe how raising or lowering the reserve ratio can increase or decrease the money supply.

☐ Illustrate how raising or lowering the discount rate can increase or decrease the money supply.

☐ Discuss the relative importance of monetary policy tools.

☐ Explain how the Federal Reserve uses monetary policy to target the Federal funds rate.

☐ Describe the actions the Fed can take to pursue an expansionary monetary policy.

☐ Describe the relationship between the Federal funds rate and the prime interest rate.

☐ Describe the actions the Fed can take to pursue a restrictive monetary policy.

☐ Explain the Taylor rule and its implications for monetary policy.

☐ Draw the demand-for-money and supply-of-money curves and use them to show how a change in the supply of money will affect the interest rate in the market for money.

☐ Draw an investment demand curve to explain the effects of changes in the interest rate on investment spending.

☐ Construct an aggregate supply and aggregate demand graph to show how aggregate demand and the equilibrium level of GDP are affected by changes in interest rates and investment spending.

☐ Use a cause-effect chain to explain the links between a change in the money supply and a change in the equilibrium level of GDP when there is an expansionary monetary policy and when there is a restrictive monetary policy.

☐ List several strengths of monetary policy.

☐ Evaluate recent monetary policy in the United States.

☐ Describe two problems or complications of monetary policy.

☐ Debate whether monetary policy should be conducted largely with discretion or whether there should be inflation targeting.

☐ Summarize the key factors and policies affecting aggregate supply and demand and the level of output, employment, income, and prices in an economy by referring to Figure 14.6.

☐ Describe how the popular press has depicted the Fed (Last Word).

■ **CHAPTER OUTLINE**

1. The fundamental **objective of *monetary policy*** is full employment without inflation. The Federal Reserve can accomplish this by exercising control over the amount of excess reserves held by commercial banks and thereby influencing the size of the money supply and the total level of spending in the economy.

2. Interest is the price paid for the use of money. Although there are many interest rates, the text uses the generic term "interest rate" for the purposes of this chapter. This interest rate is determined by demand and supply in the market for money.

   a. Business firms and households wish to hold and therefore demand money for two reasons.

   (1) Because they use money as a medium of exchange, they have a ***transactions demand*** for money that is directly related to the nominal gross domestic product of the economy.

   (2) Because they also use money as a store of value, they have an ***asset demand*** for money that is inversely related to the rate of interest.

   (3) Their ***total demand for money*** is the sum of the transactions and asset demands.

   b. In the **market for money,** the demand for money and the supply of money determine the equilibrium interest rate. Graphically, the demand for money is a downsloping line and the supply of money is a vertical line, and their intersection determines the equilibrium interest rate.

   c. Disequilibrium in this market is corrected by changes in bond prices and their inverse relationship with interest rates.

   (1) If there is a decrease in the money supply, there will be a shortage of money and bonds will be sold. The increase in the supply of bonds will drive down bond prices, causing interest rates to rise until the shortage is eliminated.

   (2) If there is an increase in the money supply, there will be a surplus of money and bonds will be bought. The increased demand for bonds will drive up bond prices, causing interest rates to fall until the surplus is eliminated.

3. By examining the consolidated **balance sheet** and the principal assets and liabilities of the Federal Reserve Banks, one can obtain an understanding of the ways the Federal Reserve can control and influence the reserves of commercial banks and the money supply.

   a. The principal **assets** of the Federal Reserve Banks are U.S. government securities and loans to commercial banks.

   b. The principal **liabilities** are Federal Reserve Notes, the reserve deposits of commercial banks, and U.S. Treasury deposits.

4. The Federal Reserve Banks use three principal tools (techniques or instruments) to control the reserves of banks and the size of the money supply.

    a. The Federal Reserve can **buy or sell government securities** in the open market to change the lending ability of the banking system.

    (1) Buying government securities in the open market from either banks or the public increases the excess reserves of banks.

    (2) Selling government securities in the open market to either banks or the public decreases the excess reserves of banks.

    b. It can **raise or lower the** *reserve ratio.*

    (1) Raising the reserve ratio decreases the excess reserves of banks and the size of the monetary (checkable-deposit) multiplier.

    (2) Lowering the reserve ratio increases the excess reserves of banks and the size of the monetary multiplier.

    c. It can also **raise or lower the** *discount rate.* Raising the discount rate discourages banks from borrowing reserves from the Fed. Lowering the discount rate encourages banks to borrow from the Fed.

    d. Of the three main monetary tools, the use of open-market operations is the most important because it is the most flexible and direct.

5. The *Federal funds rate,* the interest rate that banks charge each other for overnight loans of excess reserves, is a focus of monetary policy. The Federal Reserve can influence the Federal funds rate by buying or selling government securities. When the Federal Reserve buys bonds, banks have more excess reserves to lend overnight, and so the Federal funds rate falls. Conversely, when the Federal Reserve sells bonds, banks have fewer excess reserves to lend overnight, and so the Federal funds rate rises.

    a. An *expansionary monetary policy* can be implemented by actions of the Federal Reserve to buy government securities in the open market to lower the Federal funds rate. This policy expands the money supply, putting downward pressure on other interest rates, and helps stimulate aggregate demand. The *prime interest rate* is the benchmark rate that banks use to decide on the interest rate for loans to businesses and individuals; it rises and falls with the Federal funds rate.

    b. A *restrictive monetary policy* can be implemented by actions of the Federal Reserve to sell government securities in the open market to raise the Federal funds rate. This policy contracts the money supply, putting upward pressure on other interest rates, and helps reduce aggregate demand to maintain a stable price level.

    c. The Federal Reserve does not target inflation or follow a monetary rule, but it does appear to be guided by the *Taylor rule.* That rule specifies conditions for raising and lowering the Federal funds rate based on the current rate of inflation and the relationship between potential and real GDP.

6. Monetary policy affects the **equilibrium GDP** in many ways.

    a. The cause-effect chain goes from the money market to investment spending to equilibrium GDP (see text Figure 14.5).

    (1) In the market for money, the demand curve for money and the supply curve of money determine the real interest rate.

    (2) This rate of interest in turn determines investment spending.

    (3) Investment spending then affects aggregate demand and the equilibrium levels of real output and prices.

    b. If recession or slow economic growth is a major problem, the Federal Reserve can institute an expansionary monetary policy that increases the money supply, causing the interest rate to fall and investment spending to increase, thereby increasing aggregate demand and increasing real GDP by a multiple of the increase in investment.

    c. If inflation is the problem, the Federal Reserve can adopt a restrictive monetary policy that decreases the money supply, causing the interest rate to rise and investment spending to decrease, thereby reducing aggregate demand and inflation.

7. Monetary policy is considered more important and valuable for stabilizing the national economy because of its several advantages over fiscal policy: it is quicker and more flexible, and it is more protected from political pressure.

    a. Recent monetary policy has been expansionary and restrictive in response to concerns about, respectively, recession and inflation. For example, in the early 1990s, the Federal Reserve reduced the Federal funds rate to counter a recession. The rate was also cut in 2001 and 2002 to offset an economic slowdown and recession during that period. To curtail inflation, the rate was raised during the mid-1990s. The rate was also raised in 2004 and 2005 to contain expected inflation.

    b. There are limitations and complications with monetary policy.

    (1) It is subject to lags between the time when the need for the policy is recognized and the time when the policy influences economic activity.

    (2) There is a *cyclical asymmetry* with monetary policy: A restrictive monetary policy works better than does an expansionary monetary policy.

    c. Debates over the conduct of monetary policy have focused on the use of management discretion or inflation targeting. Although the Federal Reserve has been successful in recent years with its "artful management" of monetary policy, some economists would like it to adopt *inflation targeting,* in which the Federal Reserve must specify and be accountable for achieving an inflation target within a specified range.

8. The **"big picture" of macroeconomics** shows that the equilibrium levels of output, employment, income, and prices are determined by the interaction of aggregate supply and aggregate demand.

a. There are four expenditure components of aggregate demand: consumption, investment, government spending, and net export spending.

b. There are three major components of aggregate supply: the prices of inputs or resources, factors affecting the productivity with which resources are used, and the legal and institutional environment.

c. Fiscal, monetary, or other government policies may have an effect on the components of aggregate demand or supply, which in turn will affect the levels of output, employment, income, and prices.

9. (Last Word). The popular press has used many metaphors to describe the Federal Reserve Board and its chair. The metaphors have included the Fed as a mechanic that works on the economy, the Fed as a warrior that fights inflation and recession, and the Fed as a cosmic force of power and mystery.

■ HINTS AND TIPS

1. Spend extra time learning how the **total demand for money** is determined (see Figure 14.1 in the text). The total demand for money is composed of the transactions and asset demands for money. The **transactions demand** for money is influenced by the level of nominal GDP and is not affected by the interest rate, and so it *is graphed as a vertical line*. The **asset demand** for money is affected by the interest rate, and so it *is graphed as a downsloping curve*. The total demand for money is also graphed as a *downsloping curve* because of the influence of asset demand, but the curve is shifted farther to the right than the asset demand curve because of the influence of the transactions demand.

2. One of the most difficult concepts to understand is the *inverse* relationship between bond prices and interest rates. The simple explanation is that the interest yield from a bond is the ratio of the *fixed* annual interest payment to the bond price. The numerator is fixed, but the denominator (bond price) is variable. If the bond price falls, the interest yield on the bond rises because the fixed annual interest payment is being divided by a smaller denominator.

3. To acquire a thorough knowledge of how Federal Reserve transactions affect required reserves, excess reserves, the actual money supply, and the potential money supply, carefully study the **balance sheets** that are used to explain those transactions. The items to watch are the reserves and checkable deposits. Be sure that you know why a change is made in each balance sheet and be able to make the appropriate balance-sheet entries as you trace the effects of each transaction. Problem 2 in this chapter provides additional practice.

4. You must understand and remember the **cause-effect chain of monetary policy.** The best way to learn it is to draw your own chain (graphs) that shows the links for an expansionary monetary policy and a restrictive monetary policy, as in Figure 14.5. Then check each step for how monetary policy can be used to counter recession or limit inflation, using Table 14.3 in the text.

5. The single most important figure for a "big picture" of the macroeconomics part of the textbook is **Figure 14.6.** It reviews and summarizes the determinants of aggregate supply and demand and identifies the key policy variables that have been discussed in this chapter and in Chapters 7–14.

■ IMPORTANT TERMS

monetary policy	expansionary monetary policy
transactions demand	
asset demand	prime interest rate
total demand for money	restrictive monetary policy
reserve ratio	Taylor rule
discount rate	cyclical asymmetry
Federal funds rate	inflation targeting

SELF-TEST

■ FILL-IN QUESTIONS

1. The goal of monetary policy in the United States is to achieve and maintain stability in the (price level, tax level) _____, a rate of (full, partial) _____ employment in the economy, and economic growth.

2. The transactions demand varies (directly, inversely) _____ with (the rate of interest, nominal GDP) _____, and the asset demand varies (directly, inversely) _____ with (the rate of interest, nominal GDP) _____.

3. The sum of the transactions and asset demands for money is the total (demand for, supply of) _____ money, and the intersection of it with the _____ money determines the equilibrium (interest rate, price level) _____.

4. When the quantity of money demanded exceeds the quantity of money supplied, bond prices (increase, decrease) _____ and interest rates _____. When the quantity of money demanded is less than the quantity of money supplied, bond prices (increase, decrease) _____ and interest rates _____.

5. The two important assets of the Federal Reserve Banks are (Treasury deposits, government securities) _____ and (reserves of, loans to) _____ commercial banks. The three major liabilities are (Treasury deposits, government securities) _____, (reserves of, loans to) _____ commercial banks, and (government securities, Federal Reserve Notes) _____.

6. The three tools the monetary authority uses to control the money supply are (open, closed) _____ -market operations, changing the (loan, reserve) _____ ratio, and changing the (prime interest, discount) _____ rate. The most effective and most frequently used tool of monetary policy is a change in (the reserve ratio, open-market operations) _____.

7. When the Federal Reserve Banks buy government securities in the open market, the reserves of commercial banks will (increase, decrease) _____, and when they sell government securities in the open market, the reserves of commercial banks will _____.

8. If the Federal Reserve Banks were to sell $10 million in government bonds to the *public* and the reserve ratio were 25%, the supply of money would immediately be reduced by $_____, the reserves of commercial banks would be reduced by $_____, and the excess reserves of the banks would be reduced by $_____. But if those bonds were sold to the commercial banks, the supply of money would immediately be reduced by $_____, the reserves of the banks would be reduced by $_____, and the excess reserves of the banks would be reduced by $_____.

9. An increase in the reserve ratio will (increase, decrease) _____ the size of the monetary multiplier and _____ the excess reserves held by commercial banks, thus causing the money supply to (increase, decrease) _____. A decrease in the reserve ratio will (increase, decrease) _____ the size of the monetary multiplier and _____ the excess reserves held by commercial banks, thus causing the money supply to (increase, decrease) _____.

10. If the Federal Reserve Banks were to lower the discount rate, commercial banks would tend to borrow (more, less) _____ from them, and this would (increase, decrease) _____ their excess reserves.

11. The interest rate that banks charge one another for overnight loans is the (prime interest, Federal funds) _____ rate, but the rate banks use as a benchmark for setting interest rates on loans is the _____ rate. The (prime interest, Federal funds) _____ rate is the focus of the monetary policy of the Federal Reserve.

12. An expansionary monetary policy would be characterized by actions of the Federal Reserve to (increase, decrease) _____ the discount rate, _____ reserve ratios, and (buy, sell) _____ government bonds, whereas a restrictive monetary policy would include actions taken to (increase, decrease) _____ the discount rate, _____ reserve ratios, and (buy, sell) _____ government bonds.

13. There is a cause-effect chain of monetary policy.
a. In the market for money, the demand for and the supply of money determine the equilibrium rate of (discount, interest) _____.
b. This rate in turn determines the level of (government, investment) _____ spending based on the _____ demand curve.
c. This spending in turn affects aggregate (demand, supply) _____, and the intersection of aggregate supply and demand determines the equilibrium level of real (interest, GDP) _____ and the (discount, price) _____ level.

14. This cause-effect chain can be illustrated with examples.
a. When there is an *increase* in the money supply curve, the real interest rate will (increase, decrease) _____, investment spending will _____, aggregate demand will (increase, decrease) _____, and real GDP will _____.
b. When there is a *decrease* in the money supply curve, the real interest rate will (increase, decrease) _____, investment spending will _____, aggregate demand will (increase, decrease) _____, and real GDP will _____.

15. To eliminate inflationary pressures in the economy, the traditional view holds that the monetary authority should seek to (increase, decrease) _____ the reserves of commercial banks; this would tend to _____ the money supply and (increase, decrease) _____ the rate of interest, and this in turn would cause investment spending, aggregate demand, and GDP to _____. This action by monetary authorities would be considered (an easy, a tight) _____ money policy.

16. If there were a serious problem with economic growth and unemployment in the economy, the Federal Reserve would typically pursue (an expansionary, a restrictive) _____ monetary policy, in which case the Federal Reserve would (buy, sell) _____ government bonds as a way of (increasing, decreasing) _____ the money supply and thereby _____ interest rates; these events would have the effect of (increasing, decreasing) _____ investment spending and thus _____ real GDP.

17. An increase in the money supply will shift the aggregate (supply, demand) _____ curve to the (right, left) _____. A decrease in the money supply will shift the aggregate (supply, demand) _____ curve to the (right, left) _____. If the marginal propensity to consume is .75, the multiplier will be (3, 4) _____, and an initial increase in investment of $10 billion will (increase, decrease) _____ aggregate demand by ($30, $40) _____ billion.

18. Monetary policy has strengths. Compared to fiscal policy, monetary policy is speedier and (more, less) _____ flexible and _____ isolated from political pressure. Since 1990, the Federal Reserve has been successful in countering recession by (raising, lowering) _____ the Federal funds rate, and it has been successful in limiting inflation by _____ the Federal funds rate.

19. Monetary policy has shortcomings and problems, too. It may be subject to timing (limits, lags) _____ that occur between the time a need is recognized and the time a policy takes effect. It may be more effective in counteracting (recession, inflation) _____ than _____.

20. In recent years, there have been calls for the Federal Reserve to focus primarily on the goal of price-level stability and be more accountable for its actions by using (deflation, inflation) _____ targeting. Critics of such a policy contend that the role that it assigns to the Federal Reserve is too (wide, narrow) _____ and that policymakers at the Federal Reserve should have (more, less)

_____ discretion over the conduct of monetary policy.

■ **TRUE–FALSE QUESTIONS**

Circle T if the statement is true, F if it is false.

1. The goal of monetary policy is to lower interest rates. **T F**

2. There is a transactions demand for money because households and business firms use money as a store of value. **T F**

3. An increase in the price level would increase the transactions demand for money. **T F**

4. An increase in the nominal GDP, other things remaining the same, will increase both the total demand for money and the equilibrium rate of interest in the economy. **T F**

5. Bond prices and interest rates are inversely related. **T F**

6. The securities owned by the Federal Reserve Banks are almost entirely U.S. government bonds. **T F**

7. If the Federal Reserve Banks buy $15 in government securities from the public in the open market, the effect will be to increase the excess reserves of commercial banks by $15. **T F**

8. When the Federal Reserve sells securities in the open market, the price of those securities falls. **T F**

9. A change in the reserve ratio will affect the multiple by which the banking system can create money, but it will not affect the actual or excess reserves of member banks. **T F**

10. When the reserve ratio is lowered, some required reserves are turned into excess reserves. **T F**

11. When commercial banks borrow from the Federal Reserve Banks, they increase their excess reserves and their money-creating potential. **T F**

12. An increase in the required reserve ratio tends to reduce the profits of banks. **T F**

13. The least effective and least used tool of monetary policy is the open-market operation, in which government securities are bought and sold. **T F**

14. The Federal Reserve announces its changes in monetary policy by changing its targets for the Federal funds rate. **T F**

15. To increase the Federal funds interest rate, the Federal Reserve buys bonds in the open market to increase the excess reserves of banks. **T F**

16. The prime interest rate is the rate that banks charge other banks for overnight loans of excess reserves at Federal Reserve banks. **T F**

17. If the monetary authority wished to follow a restrictive monetary policy, it would sell government securities in the open market. **T   F**

18. The equilibrium rate of interest is found at the intersection of the money demand and money supply curves. **T   F**

19. In the cause-effect chain, an expansionary monetary policy increases the money supply, decreases the interest rate, increases investment spending, and increases aggregate demand. **T   F**

20. A restrictive monetary policy is designed to correct the problem of high unemployment and sluggish economic growth. **T   F**

21. It is generally agreed that fiscal policy is more effective than monetary policy in controlling the business cycle because fiscal policy is more flexible. **T   F**

22. Monetary policy is subject to more political pressure than fiscal policy. **T   F**

23. Monetary policy is limited by a time lag that occurs from the time when the problem is recognized to the time when the policy becomes operational. **T   F**

24. An expansionary monetary policy suffers from a "you can lead a horse to water, but you can't make the horse drink" problem. **T   F**

25. Inflation targeting is largely a monetary policy that permits the Federal Reserve to use substantial discretion in managing the economy. **T   F**

■ **MULTIPLE-CHOICE QUESTIONS**

Circle the letter that corresponds to the best answer.

1. The organization directly responsible for monetary policy in the United States is the
 (a) U.S. Treasury
 (b) Federal Reserve
 (c) Internal Revenue Service
 (d) Congress of the United States

2. If the dollars held for transactions purposes are, on the average, spent five times a year for final goods and services, the quantity of money people will wish to hold for transactions is equal to
 (a) five times the nominal GDP
 (b) 20% of the nominal GDP
 (c) five divided by the nominal GDP
 (d) 20% divided by the nominal GDP

3. There is an asset demand for money because money is
 (a) a store of value
 (b) a measure of value
 (c) a medium of exchange
 (d) a standard of deferred payment

4. An increase in the rate of interest would increase
 (a) the opportunity cost of holding money
 (b) the transactions demand for money

 (c) the asset demand for money
 (d) the prices of bonds

Use the table below to answer Questions 5 and 6.

Interest rate	Asset demand (billions)
14%	$100
13	150
12	200
11	250

5. Suppose the transactions demand for money is equal to 10% of the nominal GDP, the supply of money is $450 billion, and the asset demand for money is that shown in the table. If the nominal GDP is $3000 billion, the equilibrium interest rate is
 (a) 14%
 (b) 13%
 (c) 12%
 (d) 11%

6. If the nominal GDP remains constant, an increase in the money supply from $450 billion to $500 billion will cause the equilibrium interest rate to
 (a) rise to 14%
 (b) fall to 11%
 (c) fall to 12%
 (d) remain unchanged

7. The total quantity of money demanded is
 (a) directly related to nominal GDP and the rate of interest
 (b) directly related to nominal GDP and inversely related to the rate of interest
 (c) inversely related to nominal GDP and directly related to the rate of interest
 (d) inversely related to nominal GDP and the rate of interest

8. The stock of money is determined by the Federal Reserve System and does not change when the interest rate changes; therefore, the
 (a) supply of money curve is downward sloping
 (b) demand for money curve is downward sloping
 (c) supply of money curve is upward sloping
 (d) supply of money curve is vertical

9. Which one of the following points is true?
 (a) Bond prices and the interest rate are directly related.
 (b) A lower interest rate raises the opportunity cost of holding money.
 (c) The supply of money is directly related to the interest rate.
 (d) The total demand for money is inversely related to the interest rate.

Answer Questions 10 and 11 on the basis of the following information: Bond price = $10,000; bond fixed annual interest payment = $1000; bond annual rate of interest = 10%.

10. If the price of this bond decreases by $2500, the interest rate in effect will
  (a) decrease by 1.1 percentage points
  (b) decrease by 1.9 percentage points
  (c) increase by 2.6 percentage points
  (d) increase by 3.3 percentage points

11. If the price of this bond increases by $2000, the interest rate in effect will
  (a) decrease by 1.7 percentage points
  (b) decrease by 2.4 percentage points
  (c) increase by 1.1 percentage points
  (d) increase by 2.9 percentage points

12. The largest single asset in the Federal Reserve Banks' consolidated balance sheet is
  (a) securities
  (b) the reserves of commercial banks
  (c) Federal Reserve Notes
  (d) loans to commercial banks

13. The largest single liability of the Federal Reserve Banks is
  (a) securities
  (b) the reserves of commercial banks
  (c) Federal Reserve Notes
  (d) loans to commercial banks

14. Assume that there is a 20% reserve ratio and that the Federal Reserve buys $100 million worth of government securities. If the securities are purchased from the public, this action has the potential to increase bank lending by a maximum of
  (a) $500 million, but only by $400 million if the securities are purchased directly from commercial banks
  (b) $400 million, but by $500 million if the securities are purchased directly from commercial banks
  (c) $500 million, and also by $500 million if the securities are purchased directly from commercial banks
  (d) $400 million, and also by $400 million if the securities are purchased directly from commercial banks

15. Assuming that the Federal Reserve Banks sell $20 million in government securities to commercial banks and the reserve ratio is 20%, the effect will be
  (a) to reduce the actual supply of money by $20 million
  (b) to reduce the actual supply of money by $4 million
  (c) to reduce the potential money supply by $20 million
  (d) to reduce the potential money supply by $100 million

16. Lowering the reserve ratio
  (a) changes required reserves to excess reserves
  (b) increases the amount of excess reserves banks must keep
  (c) increases the discount rate
  (d) decreases the discount rate

17. Commercial bank borrowing from the Federal Reserve
  (a) is not permitted because of the Federal Reserve Act
  (b) is permitted, but only for banks that are bankrupt
  (c) decreases the excess reserves of commercial banks and their ability to offer credit
  (d) increases the excess reserves of commercial banks and their ability to offer credit

18. Which is the most important control used by the Federal Reserve to regulate the money supply?
  (a) changing the reserve ratio
  (b) open-market operations
  (c) changing the discount rate
  (d) changing the Federal funds rate

19. The Federal funds rate is the rate
  (a) that banks charge for overnight use of excess reserves held at the Federal Reserve banks
  (b) that banks charge for loans to the most credit-worthy customers
  (c) that the Federal Reserve charges for short-term loans to commercial banks
  (d) at which government bonds are sold in the open-market operations of the Federal Reserve

20. When the Federal Reserve Banks decide to buy government bonds from banks and the public, the supply of reserves in the Federal fund market
  (a) increases and the Federal funds rate decreases
  (b) decreases and the Federal funds rate decreases
  (c) increases and the Federal funds rate increases
  (d) decreases and the Federal funds rate increases

21. When the Federal Reserve uses open-market operations to reduce the Federal funds rate several times over a year, it is pursuing
  (a) an expansionary monetary policy
  (b) a restrictive monetary policy
  (c) a prime interest rate policy
  (d) a discretionary fiscal policy

22. The economy is experiencing high unemployment and a low rate of economic growth, and the Fed decides to pursue an expansionary monetary policy. Which set of actions by the Fed would be most consistent with this policy?
  (a) buying government securities and raising the reserve ratio
  (b) selling government securities and raising the discount rate
  (c) buying government securities and lowering the reserve ratio
  (d) selling government securities and lowering the discount rate

23. The economy is experiencing inflation, and the Federal Reserve decides to pursue a restrictive monetary policy. Which set of actions by the Fed would be most consistent with this policy?
  (a) buying government securities and lowering the discount rate
  (b) buying government securities and lowering the reserve ratio
  (c) selling government securities and raising the discount rate
  (d) selling government securities and lowering the discount rate

24. In the chain of cause and effect between changes in the excess reserves of commercial banks and the resulting changes in output and employment in the economy,
   (a) an increase in excess reserves will decrease the money supply
   (b) a decrease in the money supply will increase the rate of interest
   (c) an increase in the rate of interest will increase aggregate demand
   (d) an increase in aggregate demand will decrease output and employment

25. Which is most likely to be affected by changes in the rate of interest?
   (a) tax rates
   (b) investment spending
   (c) government spending
   (d) the imports of the economy

Use the following graph to answer Questions 26, 27, and 28.

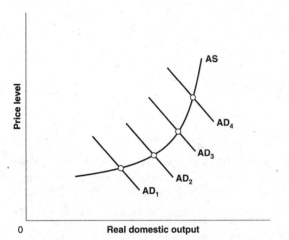

26. A shift from **AD₁** to **AD₂** would be most consistent with
   (a) an increase in the prime interest rate by corporations
   (b) an increase in the discount rate by the Federal Reserve
   (c) the buying of securities by the Federal Reserve
   (d) the selling of securities by the Federal Reserve

27. Assume that the Federal Reserve lowers interest rates to increase investment spending. This monetary policy is most likely to shift
   (a) AD₃ to AD₂
   (b) AD₃ to AD₄
   (c) AD₄ to AD₃
   (d) AD₂ to AD₁

28. A restrictive monetary policy would be most consistent with a shift from
   (a) AD₁ to AD₂
   (b) AD₃ to AD₄
   (c) AD₄ to AD₃
   (d) AD₂ to AD₃

29. Assume that monetary policy increases interest rates and results in a decrease in investment spending of $5 billion. If the marginal propensity to consume is .80, then aggregate demand is most likely to
   (a) increase by $5 billion
   (b) decrease by $25 billion
   (c) increase by $25 billion
   (d) decrease by $25 billion

30. Assume the Fed creates excess reserves, but the policy does not encourage banks to make loans and thus increase the money supply. This situation is a problem of
   (a) a restrictive monetary policy
   (b) cyclical asymmetry
   (c) using a Taylor rule
   (d) targeting the Federal funds rate

■ **PROBLEMS**

1. The total demand for money is equal to the transactions demand plus the asset demand for money.
   a. Assume each dollar held for transactions purposes is spent (on the average) four times per year to buy final goods and services.
   (1) This means that the transactions demand for money will be equal to (what fraction or percent)

   _____ of the nominal GDP, and
   (2) if the nominal GDP is $2000 billion, the trans-

   actions demand will be $_____
   billion.
   b. The following table shows the number of dollars demanded for asset purposes at each rate of interest.
   (1) Given the transactions demand for money in **(a)**, complete the table.

Interest rate	Amount of money demanded (billions)	
	For asset purposes	Total
16%	$ 20	$_____
14	40	_____
12	60	_____
10	80	_____
8	100	_____
6	120	_____
4	140	_____

   (2) On the following graph, plot the total demand for money (**Dₘ**) at each rate of interest.
   c. Assume the money supply (**Sₘ**) is $580 billion.
   (1) Plot this money supply on the graph.
   (2) Using either the graph or the table, the equilibrium

   rate of interest is _____ %.
   d. If the money supply
   (1) increases to $600 billion, the equilibrium interest

   rate will (rise, fall) _____ to _____ %.
   (2) decreases to $540 billion, the equilibrium interest

   rate will _____ to _____ %.

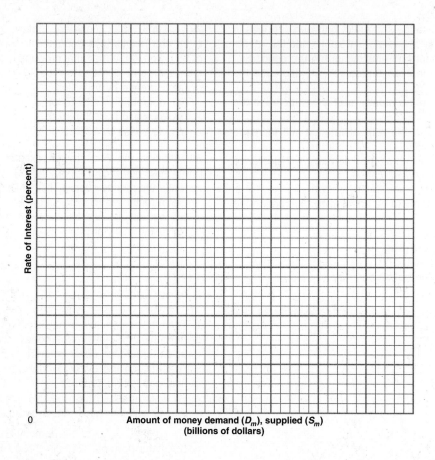

Rate of Interest (percent)

0   Amount of money demand (D_m), supplied (S_m)
(billions of dollars)

e. If the nominal GDP

(1) increased by $80 billion, the total demand for money would (increase, decrease) _____ by $_____ billion at each rate of interest and the equilibrium rate of interest would (rise, fall) _____ by _____ %.

(2) decreased by $120 billion, the total demand for money would _____ by $_____ billion at each rate of interest and the equilibrium interest rate would _____ by _____ %.

2. Suppose a bond with no expiration date pays a fixed $500 annually and sells for its face value of $5000.

a. Complete the following table and calculate the interest rate (to one decimal place) that would be obtained from the bond when the bond price is given or calculate the bond price when the interest rate is given.

Bond price	Interest rate
$4000	___.___%
$_____	11.0
$5000	___.___
$5500	___.___
$_____	8.0

b. Based on the results of the table, as the price increases on a bond with a fixed annual payment, the interest yield on the bond (decreases, increases)

_____, but when the price of a bond decreases, the interest yield _____. Given this situation in an economy, you can conclude that a higher price for bonds (increases, decreases) _____ interest rates and a lower price for bonds _____ interest rates.

3. Assume that the following consolidated balance sheet is for all commercial banks. Assume also that the required reserve ratio is 25% and that cash is *not* a part of the commercial banks' legal reserve.

Assets		Liabilities	
Cash	$ 50	Checkable deposits	$400
Reserves	100	Loans from Federal	
Loans	150	Reserve	25
Securities	200	Net worth	75
	$500		$500

a. To *increase* the supply of money by $100, the Fed could (buy, sell) _____ securities worth $_____ in the open market.

b. To *decrease* the supply of money by $50, the Fed could (buy, sell) _____ securities worth $_____ in the open market.

4. Following are the consolidated balance sheets of the Federal Reserve and of the commercial banks. Assume

	(1)	(2)	(3)	(4)	(5)	(6)
Federal Reserve Banks						
Assets:						
Gold certificates	$ 25	$____	$____	$____	$____	$____
Securities	30	____	____	____	____	____
Loans to commercial banks	10	____	____	____	____	____
Liabilities:						
Reserves of commercial banks	200	____	____	____	____	____
Treasury deposits	5	____	____	____	____	____
Federal Reserve Notes	10	____	____	____	____	____
Commercial Banks						
Assets:						
Reserves	$ 50	$____	$____	$____	$____	$____
Securities	70	____	____	____	____	____
Loans	90	____	____	____	____	____
Liabilities:						
Checkable deposits	200	____	____	____	____	____
Loans from Federal Reserve	10	____	____	____	____	____
A. Required reserves		____	____	____	____	____
B. Excess reserves		____	____	____	____	____
C. How much has the money supply changed?		____	____	____	____	____
D. How much more can the money supply change?		____	____	____	____	____
E. What is the total of C and D?		____	____	____	____	____

that the reserve ratio for commercial banks is 25%, that cash is *not* a part of a bank's legal reserve, and that the figures in column 1 show the balance sheets of the Federal Reserve and the commercial banks *prior to each of the following five transactions*. Place the new balance sheet figures in the appropriate columns and complete A, B, C, D, and E in those columns. Do *not* use the figures you place in columns 2 through 5 when you work the next part of the problem; start all parts of the problem with the printed figures in column 1.

a. The Federal Reserve Banks sell $3 in securities to the public, which pays by check (column 2).

b. The Federal Reserve Banks buy $4 in securities from the commercial banks (column 3).

c. The Federal Reserve Banks lower the required reserve ratio for commercial banks to 20% (column 4).

d. The U.S. Treasury buys $5 worth of goods from U.S. manufacturers and pays the manufacturers by checks drawn on its accounts at the Federal Reserve Banks (column 5).

e. Because the Federal Reserve Banks have raised the discount rate, commercial banks repay $6 which they owe to the Federal Reserve (column 6).

5. On the following graph is the demand-for-money curve that shows the amounts of money consumers and firms wish to hold at various rates of interest (when the nominal GDP in the economy is given).

a. Suppose the supply of money is equal to $300 billion.

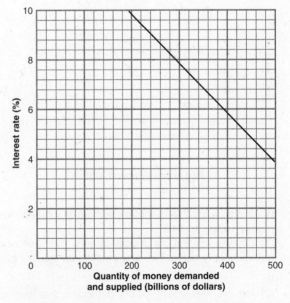

Quantity of money demanded and supplied (billions of dollars)

(1) Draw the supply of money curve on the above graph.

(2) The equilibrium rate of interest in the economy is

_____%.

b. On the next page is a graph of an investment demand curve which shows the amounts of planned investment at various rates of interest. Given your answer to (2) above, how much will investors plan to spend for

capital goods? $_____ billion.

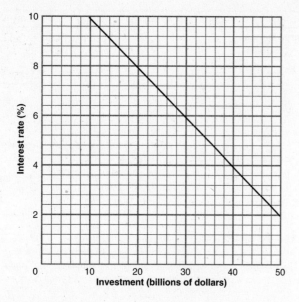

c. The following figure shows the aggregate supply (**AS**) curve in this economy. On the graph, draw an aggregate demand curve (**AD₁**) so that it crosses the **AS** in the middle of the curve. Label the price level (P_1) and output level (Q_1) associated with the intersection of **AD₁** and **AS**.

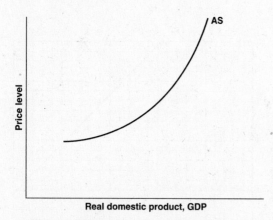

d. Now assume that monetary authorities increase the money supply to $400.
(1) On the market for money graph, plot the new money supply curve. The new equilibrium interest rate

is _____ %.
(2) On the investment graph, determine the level of investment spending that is associated with this new

interest rate: $_____ billion. By how much has investment spending increased as a result of the change

in the interest rate? $_____ billion.
(3) Assume that the marginal propensity to consume

is .75. What is the multiplier? _____ By how much will the new investment spending increase aggregate

demand? $_____ billion.

(4) On the previous figure, indicate how the change in investment spending affects aggregate demand. Draw a new aggregate demand curve (**AD₂**) so that it crosses the **AS** curve. Also label the new price level (P_2) and output level (Q_2) associated with the intersection of **AD₂** and **AS**.

6. Columns 1 and 2 of the following table show the aggregate supply schedule. (The price level is a price index, and real domestic output is measured in billions of dollars.)

(1) Price level	(2) Real output	(3) AD₁	(4) AD₂
110	1600	1800	_____
120	1700	1700	_____
130	1790	1600	_____
140	1800	1500	_____
150	1940	1400	_____
160	2000	1300	_____

a. If the aggregate demand schedule were that shown in columns 1 and 3, the equilibrium real domestic out-

put would be $_____ billion and the price level

would be _____.
b. Now assume that the Federal Reserve took actions to lower the Federal funds rate and that those actions increased investment spending in this economy by $60 billion. Also assume that the marginal propensity to consume in the economy was .8. How much would

aggregate demand increase? $_____ billion
c. In column 4, enter this amount of increase in real domestic output at each price level to define the new **AD** schedule (**AD₂**).
d. What is the new equilibrium real domestic output?

$_____ billion. And the new price level? _____.

■ SHORT ANSWER AND ESSAY QUESTIONS

1. What is the basic goal of monetary policy?

2. What are the two reasons people wish to hold money? How are these two reasons related to the functions of money?

3. Explain the determinant of each of the two demands for money and how a change in the size of those determinants will affect the amount of money people wish to hold.

4. The rate of interest is a price. Of what good or service is it the price? Explain how demand and supply determine this price.

5. Describe how changes in bond prices correct disequilibrium in the market for money. What is the relationship between bond prices and interest rates?

6. What are the important assets and liabilities of the Federal Reserve Banks?

7. Explain how the monetary policy tools of the Federal Reserve Banks would be used to contract the supply of money. How would they be used to expand the supply of money?

8. What is the difference between the effects of the Federal Reserve's buying (selling) government securities in the open market from (to) commercial banks and from (to) the public?

9. Which of the monetary policy tools available to the Federal Reserve is the most effective? Why is it more important than other tools?

10. What happens to the Federal funds rate when the Federal Reserve expands or contracts the money supply through open-market operations?

11. What are the characteristics of an expansionary monetary policy? How does the Federal Reserve implement such policies?

12. What are the characteristics of a restrictive monetary policy? How does the Federal Reserve implement such policies?

13. What is the Taylor rule, and how is it used?

14. Using three graphs, explain what determines (a) the equilibrium interest rate, (b) investment spending, and (c) the equilibrium GDP. Now use those three graphs to show the effects of a decrease in the money supply on the equilibrium GDP.

15. Why are changes in the rate of interest more likely to affect investment spending than consumption and saving?

16. What policies will the Federal Reserve use to counter inflation or unemployment and recession? Describe the effects on bank reserves, the money supply, interest rates, investment spending, aggregate demand, and real GDP from each policy.

17. What are the major strengths of monetary policy?

18. Discuss how monetary policy has been used to counter recession and limit inflation since the 1990s.

19. How do lags affect monetary policy?

20. Should monetary policy be "artful management," or should there be inflation targeting? Discuss the advantages and disadvantages of each approach.

ANSWERS

Chapter 14 Interest Rates and Monetary Policy

FILL-IN QUESTIONS

1. price level, full
2. directly, nominal GDP, inversely, the rate of interest
3. demand for, supply of, interest rate
4. decrease, increase, increase, decrease
5. government securities, loans to, Treasury deposits, reserves of, Federal Reserve Notes
6. open, reserve, discount, open-market operations
7. increase, decrease
8. 10 million, 10 million, 7.5 million, 0, 10 million, 10 million
9. decrease, decrease, decrease, increase, increase, increase
10. more, increase
11. Federal funds, prime interest, Federal funds
12. decrease, decrease, buy, increase, increase, sell
13. a. interest; b. investment, investment; c. demand, GDP, price
14. a. decrease, increase, increase, increase; b. increase, decrease, decrease, decrease
15. decrease, decrease, increase, decrease, a tight
16. an expansionary, buy, increasing, decreasing, increasing, increasing
17. demand, right, demand, left, 4, increase, $40
18. more, more, lowering, raising
19. lags, inflation, recession
20. inflation, narrow, more

TRUE–FALSE QUESTIONS

1. F, p. 258	**11.** T, pp. 266–267	**21.** F, p. 274
2. F, p. 259	**12.** T, pp. 265–266	**22.** F, p. 274
3. T, p. 259	**13.** F, p. 267	**23.** T, pp. 274–275
4. T, pp. 259–260	**14.** T, p. 267	**24.** T, p. 275
5. T, p. 261	**15.** F, pp. 268–269	**25.** F, pp. 275–276
6. T, p. 262	**16.** F, p. 268	
7. F, pp. 263–264	**17.** T, pp. 268–269	
8. T, pp. 264–265	**18.** T, p. 272	
9. F, pp. 265–266	**19.** T, pp. 272–273	
10. T, pp. 265–266	**20.** F, p. 273	

MULTIPLE-CHOICE QUESTIONS

1. b, p. 258	**11.** a, p. 261	**21.** a, pp. 267–269
2. b, p. 259	**12.** a, p. 262	**22.** c, p. 268
3. a, p. 259	**13.** c, p. 262	**23.** c, pp. 268–269
4. a, p. 259	**14.** b, pp. 263–264	**24.** b, pp. 271–273
5. b, pp. 259–260	**15.** d, pp. 264–265	**25.** b, p. 272
6. c, pp. 259–260	**16.** a, pp. 265–266	**26.** c, pp. 271–273
7. b, pp. 259–260	**17.** d, pp. 266–267	**27.** b, pp. 272–273
8. d, pp. 259–260	**18.** b, p. 267	**28.** c, p. 273
9. d, p. 261	**19.** a, pp. 267–268	**29.** d, pp. 272–273
10. d, p. 261	**20.** a, p. 268	**30.** b, p. 275

PROBLEMS

1. a. (1) 1/4 (25%), (2) 500; b. (1) 520, 540, 560, 580, 600, 620, 640; c. (2) 10; d. (1) fall, 8, (2) rise, 14; e. (1) increase, 20, rise, 2, (2) decrease, 30, fall, 3
2. a. 12.5%, $4545, 10.0%, 9.1%, $6250; b. decreases, increases, decreases, increases
3. a. buy, 25; b. sell, 12 1/2
4. See below

	(2)	(3)	(4)	(5)	(6)
			Federal Reserve Banks		
Assets:					
Gold certificates	$ 25	$ 25	$ 25	$ 25	$ 25
Securities	27	34	30	30	30
Loans to commercial banks	10	10	10	10	4
Liabilities:					
Reserves of commercial banks	47	54	50	55	44
Treasury deposits	5	5	5	0	5
Federal Reserve Notes	10	10	10	10	10
			Commercial Banks		
Assets:					
Reserves	$ 47	$ 54	$ 50	$ 55	$ 44
Securities	70	66	70	70	70
Loans	90	90	90	90	90
Liabilities:					
Checkable deposits	197	200	200	205	200
Loans from Federal Reserve	10	10	10	10	4
A. Required reserves	49.25	50	40	51.25	50
B. Excess reserves	−2.25	4	10	3.75	−6
C. How much has the money supply changed?	−3	0	0	+5	0
D. How much more can the money supply change?	−9	+16	+50	+15	−24
E. What is the total of C and D?	−12	+16	+50	+20	−24

5. *a.* (2) 8; *b.* 20; *c.* see Figure 14.2 in text; *d.* (1) 6, (2) 30, 10, (3) 4, 40, (4) see Figure 14.2 in text

6. *a.* 1700, 120; *b.* 300 (multiplier of 5 × $60 billion = $300 billion); *c.* 2100, 2000, 1900, 1800, 1700, 1600; *d.* 1800, 140

SHORT ANSWER AND ESSAY QUESTIONS

1. p. 258	**8.** pp. 263–265	**15.** p. 272
2. p. 259	**9.** p. 267	**16.** pp. 272–273
3. p. 259	**10.** pp. 267–268	**17.** p. 274
4. pp. 259–260	**11.** p. 268	**18.** p. 274
5. p. 261	**12.** pp. 268–269	**19.** pp. 274–275
6. pp. 261–262	**13.** p. 270	**20.** pp. 275–276
7. pp. 263–267	**14.** pp. 270–271	

CHAPTER 14 Web

Financial Economics

Note: This bonus Web chapter is available at the textbook Web site: **www.mcconnell17.com.**

This chapter introduces you to financial economics: the study of investor preferences and the ways they affect the pricing and trading of financial assets such as stocks, bonds, and mutual funds. The chapter begins by making a distinction between **financial investment,** which involves purchases of new or used assets for which there is an expected monetary return, and **economic investment,** which is spending for the production and accumulation of capital goods.

A central idea in financial economics is the concept of **present value.** This concept is important because it gives investors the ability to calculate the price to pay now for assets that will generate expected future payments. This concept is explained with the use of the compound interest formula, which shows how a given amount of money will grow over time if interest is paid on both the amount initially invested and any interest payments. The compound interest formula is then rearranged to determine the present value that a person would have to invest in today's dollars to receive a certain dollar payment in the future. The present value formula has applications to decisions ranging from payouts from lotteries to ways to structure deferred compensation or salary packages.

The chapter also discusses three popular financial assets: **stocks, bonds,** and **mutual funds.** It explains the key differences between these three assets in terms of ownership, risk, and return. A fundamental concept presented in this section is that the rate of return on an investment is inversely related to its price. As the price for a financial asset increases, its rate of return decreases, and vice versa.

One of the peculiar results of financial investments is that the rates of return for assets that are essentially identical also will be equal. The process that produces this result is **arbitrage.** If there are two identical assets and one has a higher rate of return than the other, then investors will purchase more of the asset with the higher rate of return, thus driving up its price and decreasing its rate of return. Investors will sell the asset with the lower rate of return, thus driving down its price and increasing its rate of return. This process will continue until the rates of return for the two assets are equal.

Risk is a major factor affecting financial assets. Some risk can be diversified by purchasing different types of assets with different returns that offset each other. Other risk is nondiversifiable and is measured with the use of beta, as you will learn in the chapter. A general relationship that is found with all types of financial assets is that the riskier the investment, the greater the compensation for bearing the risk that is demanded by investors and thus the higher average return that is expected for such investments. One investment, however, is essentially risk-free: short-term U.S. government bonds. Such an investment is used to measure time preferences for consuming now versus consuming in the future.

The last few sections of the chapter pull together all the previous material to present the **Security Market Line** (SML) and use it to discuss Federal Reserve policy. The SML shows that the average expected return for any investment is composed of two parts: one that compensates for time preference (as measured by a risk-free investment) and one that compensates for nondiversifiable risk (as measured by beta). It can be used to determine an investment's average expected rate of return based on its risk level: The higher the risk level, the higher the average rate of return. The Federal Reserve can shift the SML by changing the short-term interest rate. This action has the effect of changing the average expected return on all assets and changing asset prices, thus influencing the direction of economic activity in the overall economy.

■ CHECKLIST

When you have studied this chapter you should be able to

☐ Distinguish between economic investment and financial investment.

☐ State the compound interest formula.

☐ Calculate compound interest when you are given the interest rate, amount invested, and years of compounding.

☐ State the formula for calculating the present value of a future amount of money.

☐ Apply the present value formula to lottery and salary decisions.

☐ Describe the characteristics of stocks.

☐ Describe bonds and explain how they differ from stocks.

☐ Describe mutual funds and explain how they differ from stocks and bonds.

☐ Define the percentage rate of return for calculating investment returns.

☐ Explain why an investment's rate of return is inversely related to its price.

☐ Describe how the arbitrage process equalizes rates of return for investments with similar characteristics.

☐ Define diversification and its relationship to risk.

☐ Calculate the average expected rate of return when you are given investment data.

☐ Define beta as a measure of risk.

☐ Explain the relationship of risk and average expected returns.

☐ Describe what determines the risk-free rate of return.

☐ Define the two parts of the equation for the average expected rate of return.

☐ Use a graph to illustrate the features of the Security Market Line (SML) model.

☐ Explain how arbitrage affects average expected rates of return in the SML.

☐ Describe the effect of an increase in risk-free interest rates on the SML.

☐ Explain how a change in Federal Reserve policy will affect financial assets and the economy.

☐ Explain why the rates of return on index mutual funds beat the rates of return on actively managed funds over time (Last Word).

■ **CHAPTER OUTLINE**

1. There is a difference between *economic investment* and *financial investment.* Economic investment refers to new additions to the nation's capital stock from building roads, factories, and houses. Financial investment refers to the purchase of an asset (new or used) with the expectation that it will generate a monetary return. In this chapter, the general term "investment" will mean financial investment.

2. *Present value* states the current value or worth of returns or costs that are expected in the future. An investment's current price is equal to the present value of that investment's future returns.

    a. The *compound interest* formula indicates how a given amount of money will increase if interest is paid on the amount initially invested and on any interest payments previously paid. The equation states that if X dollars are invested today at interest rate i and allowed to grow for t years, the original amount will become $(1 + i)^t X$ dollars in t years.

    b. The present value model uses the compound interest formula to calculate the present value that would have to be invested today to receive X dollars in t years. The equation states that an investment of $X/(1 + i)^t$ dollars today at interest rate i will increase to X dollars in t years.

    c. Present value has applications to everyday experiences such as lottery payouts and deferred compensation. For example, the present value formula can be used to calculate how much a person who won the lottery would receive if that person took the winnings as a lump-sum payout instead of receiving equal payments spread over many years.

3. Many financial investments are available to investors. Whatever the type, they share three characteristics. They require that investors pay a market price to obtain them; they give the asset owner the right to receive future payments; and the future payments are typically risky. The three most common and popular investments are stocks, bonds, and mutual funds.

    a. *Stocks* are shares of ownership in corporations. Stocks have value because they give shareholders the right to receive any future profits produced by the corporations that issue them. Because of the *limited liability rule,* the risk of loss for investors is limited to the number of shares they own. Investors can gain from investing in profitable corporations because they can capture *capital gains* (sell their shares at higher prices than they bought them) and can often receive *dividends,* which are payouts of equal shares of corporate profits. Stocks are risky because the future profits are unknown and because it is possible for corporations to go *bankrupt.*

    b. *Bonds* are a type of debt or loan contract. Bonds give the holder the right to a fixed stream of future payments that serve to repay the loan or pay off the debt, and so they are a more predictable investment than stocks. The risks from bonds involve possible *default,* or failure to make the promised payment by the corporations or government agencies that issued the bonds.

    c. *Mutual funds* are a type of financial investment offered by companies that combine the money invested by many investors to buy a portfolio, which typically consists of a large number of stocks and/or bonds. The returns that are generated from the portfolios are owned by the individual investors and are paid to them. The risks from mutual funds are related to the risks of the stocks and bonds they hold in their portfolios. Some funds are *actively managed funds,* with portfolio managers constantly trying to buy and sell stocks to maximize returns, whereas others are *index funds* that are *passively managed funds* that buy or sell assets to closely match a financial index.

    d. The *percentage rate of return* for a financial asset is calculated by determining the change in value of the asset (gain or loss) and dividing it by the purchase price for the asset and expressing the result as a percentage.

    e. The rate of return for an investment is inversely related to its price. This means that the higher the price, the lower the rate of return.

4. *Arbitrage* is the process, carried out through the actions of investors, which results in equalizing the average expected rates of return from assets that are very similar or identical. For example, if two identical assets have different rates of return, investors will buy the asset with the higher rate of return and sell the asset with the lower rate of return. As investors buy the asset with the higher rate of return, its price will increase and its average expected rate of return will decrease. As investors sell the asset with the lower rate of return, its price will decrease and its average expected rate of return will increase. The process continues until the average expected rates of return of the two assets converge and become equal.

5. *Risk* in financial investing means that future payments are uncertain, and many factors affect the degree of risk.

    a. *Diversification* is a strategy designed to decrease investment risk in a portfolio by selecting a group of assets that have risks or returns that compensate for each other so that when returns on one investment are lower, they are offset by higher returns on another investment. Risks that can be eliminated by asset diversification are called *diversifiable risks.* Risks that cannot be eliminated by asset diversification are called *nondiversifiable risks.* An example of a nondiversifiable risk would be a general downturn in the economy that can simultaneously affect the returns of all investments in a similar way so that different assets do not have offsetting returns.

    b. Investment decisions often involve comparing return and risk, especially nondiversifiable risk.

    (1) Investors compare investments by using *average expected rates of return.* This return is a **probability-weighted average** that gives higher weight to outcomes that are more likely to happen.

    (2) *Beta* is a statistic measuring the nondiversifiable risk of an asset relative to the amount of nondiversifiable risk facing the *market portfolio.* This portfolio contains every asset trading in the financial markets, and so it is diversified and consequently has eliminated all of its diversifiable risk and has only nondiversifiable risk.

    c. There is a relationship between risk and average expected returns. Investors demand compensation for bearing risk. The riskier the asset is, the higher its average expected rate of return will be. This relationship applies to all assets.

    d. Rates of return compensate for both risk and time preference. Average expected rates of return must compensate for *time preference* because most people prefer to consume sooner rather than later. The rate of return that compensates *only* for time preference is assumed to be equal to the rate of interest from short-term U.S. government bonds. The returns on these bonds are viewed as the *risk-free interest rate* because the U.S. government is almost 100% guaranteed to make its payments on time. The Federal Reserve has the power to set this interest rate and thereby influence the compensation for time preference across the economy.

6. An asset's average expected rate of return has two components. First, there is the compensation for time preference, which is the risk-free interest rate. Second, there is the compensation for nondiversifiable risk as measured by beta. This risk factor is often referred to by economists as the *risk premium.* The *Security Market Line (SML)* is a straight line that plots how the average expected rates of return on assets and portfolios in the economy must vary with their respective levels of nondiversifiable risk as measured by beta. The slope of the SML indicates how much investors dislike risk: A steeper slope shows that investors demand higher average expected rates of return for bearing increasingly large amounts of nondiversifiable risk, and a flatter slope shows that investors require lower average expected rates of return to compensate them for risk bearing. Because of arbitrage, every asset in the economy should plot onto the SML.

7. The vertical intercept of the SML is determined by the risk-free interest rate, and its slope is determined by the amount of compensation investors need for assuming nondiversifiable risk. The risk-free interest rate is controlled by the **Federal Reserve** through its control over the rate for short-term U.S. government bonds. The Federal Reserve can shift the SML by changing this interest rate and thus the compensation for time preference that must be paid to investors of all assets regardless of risk. The Federal Reserve's power to shift short-run interest rates also gives it the ability to change asset prices and influence economic conditions. For example, when the SML shifts upward, the average expected rate of return on all assets increases and asset prices decline, thus reducing investment, consumption, and eventually aggregate demand.

8. (Last Word). Actively managed mutual funds do much worse than passively managed index funds for several reasons. First, actively managed funds cannot select portfolios that do better than passively managed funds with similar levels of risk because of arbitrage. Second, actively managed funds charge higher fees than do passively managed funds, thus increasing their cost and lowering their return.

■ HINTS AND TIPS

1. Many new terms and concepts are presented in this chapter, so take time to master each one so that you will have the knowledge necessary to comprehend the chapter content. This content is not difficult once you master the basic terms and concepts.

2. The **Security Market Line** may seem more difficult than it actually is. It is simply a graph of the relationship between risk level (measured on the horizontal axis) and the average expected return (measured on the vertical axis). The line is upsloping, reflecting the fact that a greater risk level is associated with a higher average expected return. The average expected return, however, is divided into two parts. One part is compensation for time preference, and it is measured by the risk-free interest rate (the vertical intercept). The other part is a risk premium for a risk level associated with an asset's beta.

3. One purpose of the chapter is to show how the **Federal Reserve** can change the short-term interest rate and influence financial investments and thus the economy. The last section of the chapter makes that important connection.

■ IMPORTANT TERMS

economic investment	present value
financial investment	stocks
compound interest	bankrupt

limited liability rule	diversification
capital gains	diversifiable risk
dividends	nondiversifiable risk
bonds	average expected rate of return
default	
mutual funds	beta
index funds	market portfolio
actively managed funds	time preference
passively managed funds	risk-free interest rate
percentage rate of return	risk premium
arbitrage	Security Market Line (SML)
risk	
portfolios	

SELF-TEST

■ FILL-IN QUESTIONS

1. Paying for new additions to the nation's capital stock would be (financial, economic) _____ investment, whereas buying an asset in the expectation that it will generate a monetary gain would be _____ investment.

2. The compound interest formula defines the rate at which (present, future) _____ amounts of money can be converted to _____ amounts of money and also the rate at which (present, future) _____ amounts of money can be converted into _____ amounts of money.

3. All financial investments share three features: They require that investors pay a (dividend, price) _____ to acquire them; they give the owners the chance to receive (present, future) _____ payments; and such payments are typically (riskless, risky) _____.

4. An investment's proper current price is equal to the sum of the (present, future) _____ values of each of the investment's expected _____ payments.

5. Ownership shares in a corporation are (stocks, bonds) _____, whereas debt contracts issued by corporations are _____.

6. The primary risk for stocks is that future profits are (predictable, unpredictable) _____ and the company may go bankrupt, whereas bonds are risky because of the possibility that the corporate or government issuers (may, may not) _____ make the promised payments.

7. A mutual fund is a company that maintains a portfolio of (stocks and bonds, artworks and antiques) _____. Portfolio managers who constantly buy and sell assets to generate high returns run (passively managed, actively managed) _____ funds, and portfolio managers who buy and sell assets to match whatever assets are contained in an underlying index run _____ funds.

8. Average expected rates of return are (directly, inversely) _____ related to an asset's current price, and so when an asset's price rises, the average expected rate of return (rises, falls) _____.

9. Assume that two assets are nearly identical but one pays a higher rate of return than the other. As investors buy the asset with the higher rate of return, its price will (fall, rise) _____, causing its average expected rate of return to _____. At the same time, as investors sell the asset with the lower rate of return, its price will (fall, rise) _____, causing its average expected rate of return to _____. The process will continue until the two assets have (equal, unequal) _____ average expected rates of return.

10. Risk means that investors are (certain, uncertain) _____ what future payments from assets will be. Risks that can be canceled out by diversification are (diversifiable, nondiversifiable) _____ risks, and risks that cannot be canceled out by diversification are _____ risks.

11. Each investment's average expected rate of return is the probability- (weighted, unweighted) _____ average of the investment's possible future return. This probability weighting means that each of the possible future rates of return is (multiplied, divided) _____ by its probability expressed as a decimal before being added together to obtain the average.

12. Beta is a relative measure of (diversifiable, nondiversifiable) _____ risk and shows how the _____ risk of a given asset or portfolio compares with that of the market portfolio.

13. Since the market portfolio contains every asset trading in the financial markets, it has eliminated all of its (diversifiable, nondiversifiable) _____ risk and has only _____ risk. The market portfolio is the perfect standard against which to measure levels of (diversifiable, nondiversifiable) _____ risk.

14. Investors' dislike of risk and uncertainty causes them to pay higher prices for (more, less) _____ risky assets and lower prices for _____ risky assets. This outcome means that asset prices and expected rates of return are (directly, inversely) _____ related.

15. The compensation for time preference is the risk-free interest rate on (short-term, long-term) _____ U.S. government bonds, and the power to change this interest rate is held by the (U.S. Treasury, Federal Reserve) _____.

16. The Security Market Line shows the relationship between average expected rates of (return, risk) _____ and levels of _____ that hold for every asset or portfolio trading in financial markets. The line's upward slope shows that investors must be compensated for higher levels of risk with (lower, higher) _____ average expected rates of return.

17. If investors dislike risk, then the Security Market Line will be (flatter, steeper) _____; if investors are more comfortable with risk, then the line will be (flatter, steeper) _____. When the line is steeper, it indicates that investors demand (more, less) _____ compensation in terms of higher average expected rates of return for bearing increasingly large amounts of nondiversifiable risk; when the line is flatter, it indicates that investors demand _____ compensation in terms of higher average expected rates of return for bearing higher levels of nondiversifiable risk.

18. Arbitrage will ensure that all investments having an identical level of risk will eventually also have an (equal, unequal) _____ rate of return: the return given by the Security Market Line. If such an investment has a return that is greater than the average for a level of risk, investors will (sell, buy) _____ it, thus (increasing, decreasing) _____ the price and _____ the average expected return. If such an investment has a return that is lower than the average for a level of risk, investors will (sell, buy) _____ it, thus (increasing, decreasing) _____ the price and _____ the average expected return.

19. The Security Market Line's vertical intercept is the (prime, risk-free) _____ interest rate set by the Federal Reserve, and the slope is determined by the amount of compensation investors demand for bearing (diversifiable, nondiversifiable) _____ risk. An increase in the interest rate by the Federal Reserve will shift the line (upward, downward) _____, and a decrease in the interest rate by the Federal Reserve will shift the line _____.

20. An increase in the risk-free interest rate by the Federal Reserve will (increase, decrease) _____

asset prices and can eventually _____ aggregate demand, whereas a decrease in the risk-free interest rate by the Federal Reserve will (increase, decrease) _____ asset prices and can eventually _____ aggregate demand.

■ **TRUE–FALSE QUESTIONS**

Circle T if the statement is true, F if it is false.

1. The purchase of a share of corporate stock would be an example of a financial investment. **T F**

2. The compound interest formula states that if X dollars are invested today at interest rate i and allowed to grow for t years, they will become $(1 + i)^t X$ dollars in t years **T F**

3. The present value formula states that a person would have to invest $X/(1 + i)^t$ dollars today at interest rate i for that investment to become X dollars in t years. **T F**

4. The current price of a financial investment should equal the total present value of all the asset's future payments. **T F**

5. Stocks are ownership shares in corporations and have value because they give shareholders the right to share in any future profits the corporations may generate. **T F**

6. Bonds are risky because of the possibility that the corporations or government bodies that issued them may default on them, or not make the promised payments. **T F**

7. Mutual funds are investment companies that pool the money of many investors in order to buy a portfolio of assets. **T F**

8. Some mutual funds are actively managed, and other mutual funds are passively managed index funds. **T F**

9. A financial investment's percentage rate of return is directly related to its price. **T F**

10. Arbitrage is the process by which investors equalize the average expected rates of return generated by identical or nearly identical assets. **T F**

11. In finance, an asset is risky if its future payments are certain. **T F**

12. Diversification is an investment strategy that seeks to reduce the overall risk facing an investment portfolio by selecting a group of assets whose risks offset each other. **T F**

13. Nondiversifiable risks simultaneously affect all investments in the same direction so that it is not possible to select asset returns that offset each other. **T F**

14. Investors evaluate the possible future returns to risky projects by using average expected rates of return, which give lower weight to outcomes that are more likely to happen. **T F**

15. Beta measures the nondiversifiable risk of an asset or portfolio relative to the amount of nondiversifiable risk facing the market portfolio. **T F**

16. By definition, the market portfolio has a beta of 1.0, so that if an asset has a beta of 0.67, it has a third more nondiversifiable risk than the market portfolio. **T F**

17. The riskier an asset is, the higher its average expected rate of return will be. **T F**

18. The rate of return that compensates for time preference is assumed to be equal to the rate of interest generated by long-term U.S. government bonds. **T F**

19. The Federal Reserve has the power to set the short-term risk-free interest rate and thereby set the economywide compensation for time preference. **T F**

20. An asset's average expected rate of return will be the sum of the rate of return that compensates for time preference plus the rate of return that compensates for the asset's level of nondiversifiable risk as measured by beta. **T F**

21. The Security Market Line (SML) is a straight line that plots how the average expected rates of return on assets and portfolios in the economy must vary with their respective levels of nondiversifiable risk as measured by beta. **T F**

22. The slope of the Security Market Line indicates how much investors dislike risk. **T F**

23. Arbitrage ensures that every asset in the economy will plot onto the Security Market Line. **T F**

24. The Federal Reserve can shift the entire SML by changing risk-free interest rates and the compensation for time preference that must be paid to investors in all assets regardless of their risk level. **T F**

25. The power of the Federal Reserve to shift short-run interest rates also gives it the ability to shift asset prices throughout the economy. **T F**

■ **MULTIPLE-CHOICE QUESTIONS**

Circle the letter that corresponds to the best answer.

1. Which would be an example of an economic investment?
  (a) the sale of a stock
  (b) the building of a new factory
  (c) the buying of a mutual fund
  (d) the purchase of a corporate bond

2. A $100 deposit is placed in a savings account that pays an annual interest rate of 8%. What will its value be after 2 years?
  (a) $116.64
  (b) $125.97
  (c) $136.05
  (d) $146.93

3. The compound interest rate formula defines the rate at which
  (a) a future amount of money can be converted to a present amount of money
  (b) a present amount of money can be converted into present interest rates
  (c) a present amount of money can be divided by the interest rate
  (d) a present amount of money can be multiplied by the interest rate

4. Cecilia has the chance to buy an asset that is guaranteed to return a single payment of exactly $370 in 17 years. Assuming that the interest rate is 8%, the present value of that future payment is equal to
  (a) ($370 − $70) = $300
  (b) ($370 − $29.6) = $340.4
  (c) ($370/(1.08)^{17} = $100
  (d) ($370 × 1.08) + 17 = $416.60

5. Assume that a Ricardo wins a $100 million lottery. Ricardo can be paid the $100 million in 20 payments of $5 million each over 20 years or can be paid a lump sum of the present values of each of the future payments. Assume that the interest rate is 5% a year, what is the lump sum?
  (a) $43.2 million
  (b) $50.4 million
  (c) $62.3 million
  (d) $110.5 million

6. Which of the following is *not* one of the common features of all investments?
  (a) The rate of return on the investments will be positive.
  (b) Investors are given a chance to receive future payments.
  (c) Investors are required to pay a market price to purchase them.
  (d) The future payments from the investments are typically risky.

7. Shares of ownership in a corporation are
  (a) bonds
  (b) stocks
  (c) dividends
  (d) mutual funds

8. Jamie buys 100 shares of General Electric stock for $35 a share one year and then sells the 100 shares for $40 a share the next year. After selling the shares, Jamie will realize a(n)
  (a) depreciation of $500
  (b) capital gain of $500
  (c) dividend increase of $500
  (d) interest payment of $500

9. Which type of investment is a loan contract?
  (a) bonds
  (b) stocks
  (c) actively managed mutual funds
  (d) passively managed mutual funds

10. Sang buys a house for $500,000 and rents it out for a monthly payment of $3500. What is the percentage rate of return on this investment for the year?
  (a) 7.2%
  (b) 8.4%
  (c) 9.1%
  (d) 10.6%

11. Susie wants to buy a $10,000 bond that pays a fixed annual payment of $550. Before she is able to buy the bond, its price rises to $11,000. What happens to the rate of return on the bond because of the change in price?
  (a) It increases from 4.5% to 5.5%.
  (b) It decreases from 5.0% to 4.5%.
  (c) It increases from 5.0% to 5.5%.
  (d) It decreases from 5.5% to 5.0%.

12. The process by which Investors equalize the average expected rates of return generated by identical or nearly identical assets is
  (a) beta
  (b) arbitrage
  (c) diversifiable risk
  (d) nondiversifiable risk

13. In finance, an asset is risky if
  (a) it does not pay dividends
  (b) it does not have capital gains
  (c) its present value is positive
  (d) its future payments are uncertain

14. An investment strategy that seeks to reduce the overall risk facing an investment portfolio by selecting a group of assets whose risks offset each other is called
  (a) indexing
  (b) arbitrage
  (c) diversification
  (d) time preference

15. An investor wants to invest in the beverage industry but does not know which of two major companies, Coca-Cola and Pepsi, will produce the greater return, and so the investor buys shares in both companies to lower the risk. In this case the investor is seeking to lower
  (a) systemic risk
  (b) diversifiable risk
  (c) nondiversifiable risk
  (d) the risk premium

16. The type of risk that pushes the returns from all investments in the same direction at the same time so that there is no possibility of using good effects to offset bad effects is
  (a) constant
  (b) idiosyncratic
  (c) nondiversifiable
  (d) probability-weighted

17. If an investment is 80% likely to return 10% per year and 20% likely to return 12% a year, then its probability-weighted average is
  (a) 8.0%
  (b) 10.4%
  (c) 11.0%
  (d) 12.2%

18. Beta measures how the
  (a) risk premium compares with the time preference
  (b) risk-free interest rate compares with the diversifiable risk of a given asset
  (c) nondiversifiable risk of a given asset compares with that of a market portfolio
  (d) average expected rate of return compares with the probability-weighted average

19. An asset with a beta of 2.0 has
  (a) 2% more risk than the risk-free interest rate
  (b) 100% more risk than the risk-free interest rate
  (c) half the nondiversifiable risk of that in a market portfolio of assets
  (d) twice the nondiversifiable risk of that in a market portfolio of assets

20. Asset prices and average expected returns are inversely related, and so
  (a) more risky assets will have average expected rates of return similar to those of less risky assets
  (b) less risky assets will have higher average expected rates of return than will more risky assets
  (c) more risky assets will have lower average expected rates of return than will less risky assets
  (d) less risky assets will have lower average expected rates of return than will more risky assets

21. The observation that people tend to be impatient and typically prefer to consume things in the present rather than the future is captured in the concept of
  (a) beta
  (b) risk premium
  (c) time preference
  (d) market portfolio

22. The best measure of the risk-free interest rate is the rate of return from
  (a) a portfolio of company stocks
  (b) bonds issued by U.S. corporations
  (c) a passively managed mutual fund
  (d) short-term U.S. government bonds

23. Each investment's average expected rate of return is
  (a) the sum of the risk-free interest rate and the risk premium
  (b) the risk-free interest rate multiplied by the risk premium
  (c) the risk premium divided by the risk-free interest rate
  (d) the risk premium minus the risk-free interest rate

24. The Security Market Line is a straight line that shows how the average expected rates of return on assets and portfolios in the economy must vary with their respective levels of
  (a) diversifiable risk as measured by beta
  (b) nondiversifiable risk as measured by beta
  (c) the risk premium as measured by the risk-free interest rate
  (d) time preference as measured by the risk-free interest rate

25. If the Federal Reserve decides to raise the interest rates on short-term U.S. government bonds, then the vertical intercept for the Security Market Line will shift
- **(a)** upward and asset prices will fall
- **(b)** upward and asset prices will rise
- **(c)** downward and asset prices will fall
- **(d)** downward and asset prices will rise

■ PROBLEMS

1. In the table below, enter the value at year's end of $100 compounded at 5% interest.

Years of compounding	Value at year's end
1	$_____
2	_____
3	_____
4	_____
5	_____

2. In the table below, enter the *present value* of $10,000 that would be paid at the end of different years. Assume the interest rate is 5%. Round the answer to the nearest dollar.

Year period	Value at year's end
1	$_____
2	_____
3	_____
4	_____
5	_____

3. Assume that the investment pays a monthly amount of $2000 but has a different price.
- **a.** Calculate the percentage rate of return for an investment that a person might buy at different prices and enter it into the table.
- **b.** Describe the relationship between the percentage rate of return and the asset price.

Purchase price	Percentage rate of return
$ 50,000	_____
100,000	_____
150,000	_____
200,000	_____

4. The table below shows different probabilities for the rate of return on an investment that might pay 10% a year or 12% a year. Calculate the probability-weighted average for the return on this investment.

	10% return	12% return	Probability-weighted average
a.	50%	50%	_____%
b.	60	40	_____
c.	70	30	_____
d.	80	20	_____

■ SHORT ANSWER AND ESSAY QUESTIONS

1. Explain the difference between financial investment and economic investment and give examples.

2. Explain why the formula for compound interest defines not only the rate at which present amounts of money can be converted to future amounts of money but also the rate at which future amounts of money can be converted to present amounts of money.

3. Assume you are given the choice between being paid $100 million in installments of $5 million per year over 20 years and having it all paid today. Assume the applicable interest rate for the installment payments is 5%. What would the present value be today, and how did you calculate it?

4. Describe how present value can be used to analyze salary caps and deferred compensation.

5. What are the three common features of all financial investments?

6. Compare and contrast stocks, bonds, and mutual funds in terms of ownership, risk, and return.

7. What is the relationship between asset prices and rates of return? What is the cause of this relationship?

8. How does the arbitrage process work? Give an example.

9. Identify the two basic types of risk and explain the difference between them.

10. What is time preference? Give an example to illustrate its meaning.

11. Why are short-term U.S. government bonds considered risk-free investments?

12. What is meant by the term "probability-weighted average" as it applies to the average expected rate of return for investments? Give an example to illustrate the term.

13. Define beta and use it to explain risk. What is the beta for a market portfolio, and why does it have this value?

14. Explain the relationship between risk and average expected return.

15. How can the Federal Reserve influence the risk-free rate of return?

16. Define the components of the average expected rate of return.

17. What is the relationship between beta and the risk premium?

18. Describe the major graphical features (slope, intercept, boxes) of the Security Market Line.

19. Use the Security Market Line to explain how arbitrage will ensure that all investments that have an identical level of risk will also have an identical rate of return.

20. Explain what happens to the Security Market Line and the economy when the Federal Reserve changes policy and uses open-market operations to raise the interest rates of short-term U.S. government bonds.

ANSWERS

Chapter 14 Web Financial Economics

FILL-IN QUESTIONS

1. economic, financial
2. present, future, future, present
3. price, future, risky
4. present, future
5. stocks, bonds
6. unpredictable, may not
7. stocks and bonds, actively managed, passively managed
8. inversely, falls
9. rise, fall, fall, rise, equal
10. uncertain, diversifiable, nondiversifiable
11. weighted, multiplied
12. nondiversifiable, nondiversifiable
13. diversifiable, nondiversifiable, nondiversifiable
14. less, more, inversely
15. short-term, Federal Reserve
16. return, risk, higher
17. steeper, flatter, more, less
18. equal, buy, increasing, decreasing, sell, decreasing, increasing
19. risk-free, nondiversifiable, upward, downward
20. decrease, decrease, increase, increase

Note: Page numbers for True–False, Multiple-Choice, and Short Answer and Essay Questions refer to Bonus Web Chapter 14.

TRUE–FALSE QUESTIONS

1. T, p. 2	10. T, p. 7	19. T, p. 11
2. T, pp. 2–3	11. F, p. 8	20. T, p. 11
3. T, p. 3	12. T, p. 8	21. T, pp. 11–13
4. T, p. 3	13. T, p. 8	22. T, p. 12
5. T, p. 5	14. F, pp. 8–9	23. T, p. 13
6. T, pp. 5–6	15. T, p. 9	24. T, p. 14
7. T, p. 6	16. F, p. 9	25. T, pp. 14, 16
8. T, p. 6	17. T, p. 10	
9. F, p. 7	18. F, pp. 10–11	

MULTIPLE-CHOICE QUESTIONS

1. b, p. 2	10. b, pp. 6–7	19. d, p. 9
2. a, p. 2	11. d, p. 7	20. d, p. 10
3. a, p. 3	12. b, p. 7	21. c, p. 10
4. c, p. 3	13. d, p. 8	22. d, p. 11
5. c, p. 4	14. c, p. 8	23. a, p. 11
6. a, p. 5	15. b, p. 8	24. b, p. 12
7. b, p. 5	16. c, p. 8	25. a, p. 14
8. b, p. 5	17. b, p. 9	
9. a, p. 5	18. c, p. 9	

PROBLEMS

1. See table

Years of compounding	Value at year's end
1	$105.00
2	110.25
3	115.76
4	121.55
5	127.63

2. See table

Year period	Value at year's end
1	$9524
2	9070
3	8638
4	8227
5	7835

3. *a.* See table; *b.* As the asset or purchase price increases, the percentage rate of return decreases

Purchase price	Percentage rate of return
$ 50,000	48
100,000	24
150,000	16
200,000	12

4. See table

	10% return	12% return	Probability-weighted average
a.	50%	50%	11.0%
b.	60	40	10.8
c.	70	30	10.6
d.	80	20	10.4

SHORT ANSWER AND ESSAY QUESTIONS

1. p. 2	8. p. 7	15. p. 11
2. p. 3	9. pp. 8–9	16. p. 11
3. p. 4	10. pp. 10–11	17. p. 11
4. pp. 4–5	11. pp. 8–9	18. pp. 11–12
5. p. 5	12. p. 9	19. p. 13
6. pp. 5–6	13. p. 10	20. pp. 14, 16
7. p. 7	14. pp. 9–10	

CHAPTER 15

Extending the Analysis of Aggregate Supply

Chapter 15 adds to the aggregate demand–aggregate supply (AD–AS) model introduced in Chapter 10. This addition will give you analytical tools to improve your understanding of the short-run and long-run relationships between unemployment and inflation.

The major extension to the AD–AS model is the explanation for the **short-run aggregate supply curve** and the **long-run aggregate supply curve.** In the **short run,** nominal wages do not adjust fully as the price level changes, and so an increase in the price level increases business profits and real output. In the **long run,** nominal wages are fully responsive to previous changes in the price level, and so business profits and employment return to their original levels. Thus, the long-run aggregate supply curve is vertical at the full-employment level of output.

The distinction between the short-run and long-run aggregate supply curves requires a reinterpretation of demand-pull inflation and cost-push inflation. Although **demand-pull inflation** will increase the price level and real output in the short run, once nominal wages increase, the temporary increase in output will be gone, but the price level will be higher at the full-employment level of output. **Cost-push inflation** will increase the price level and decrease real output in the short run, but again, once nominal wages fall, output and the price level will return to their original positions. If government policymakers try to counter cost-push inflation by increasing aggregate demand, they may make matters worse by increasing the price level and causing the short-run aggregate supply curve to decrease, thereby setting off an inflationary spiral.

The relationship between inflation and unemployment has been studied for many years. One influential observation, supported by data from the 1950s and 1960s, was embodied in the **Phillips Curve,** which suggested that there is a stable and predictable tradeoff between the rate of inflation and the unemployment rate. During the 1960s, it was thought that this tradeoff could be used to formulate sound monetary and fiscal policy to manage the economy.

The events of the 1970s and early 1980s, however, called into question the shape and stability of the Phillips Curve because the economy was experiencing higher rates of both inflation and unemployment—**stagflation.** The **aggregate supply shocks** of that period shifted the Phillips Curve rightward. When those shocks dissipated in the 1980s, the Phillips Curve began to shift back to its original position. By the end of the 1990s, points on the Phillips Curve were similar to those of the 1960s.

The conclusion to be drawn from studies of the Phillips Curve is that there is *no long-run tradeoff between inflation and unemployment.* In the long run, the downsloping Phillips Curve is actually a vertical line at the natural rate of unemployment. In the short run, if aggregate demand increases and reduces the unemployment rate below its natural rate, the result will be only temporary. Eventually, the unemployment rate will return to its natural rate, but at a higher rate of inflation.

Aggregate supply can also be affected by taxation. **Supply-side economics** contends that aggregate supply is important for determining levels of inflation, unemployment, and economic growth. Tax cuts are proposed by supply-siders as a way to create more incentives to work, save, and invest, thus increasing productivity and aggregate supply. The relationship between marginal tax rates and tax revenues is expressed in the **Laffer Curve,** which suggests that cuts in tax rates can increase tax revenues if the original tax rates are too high for the economy. Critics contend, however, that the incentive effects are small, are potentially inflationary, and can have positive or negative effects on tax revenues.

■ **CHECKLIST**

When you have studied this chapter you should be able to

☐ Give a definition of the short run and the long run in macroeconomics.
☐ Distinguish between a change in real wages and a change in nominal wages.
☐ Draw the short-run aggregate supply curve and describe its characteristics.
☐ Explain how the long-run aggregate supply curve is determined.
☐ Draw a graph that illustrates equilibrium in the extended AD–AS model.
☐ Explain demand-pull inflation by using the extended AD–AS model and identify its short-run and long-run outcomes.
☐ Describe cost-push inflation by using the extended AD–AS model.
☐ Give two generalizations about the policy dilemma for government in dealing with cost-push inflation.
☐ Explain recession and the process of adjustment by using the extended AD–AS model.
☐ Draw a Phillips Curve and explain the basic tradeoff it presents.
☐ Define stagflation.

☐ Explain why adverse aggregate supply shocks shifted the Phillips Curve over time.

☐ List the events that contributed to the demise of stagflation.

☐ State a generalization about the inflation–unemployment tradeoff in the long run.

☐ Use short-run and long-run Phillips Curves to explain inflation.

☐ Use short-run and long-run Phillips Curves to explain disinflation.

☐ Describe supply-siders' views of the effects of taxation on incentives to work and to save and invest.

☐ Use the Laffer Curve to explain the hypothesized relationship between marginal tax rates and tax revenues.

☐ State three criticisms of the Laffer Curve.

☐ Offer a rebuttal of the criticisms and an evaluation of supply-side economics in the 1980s and 1990s.

☐ Explain why people who pay the highest taxes get the most benefit from a general rate reduction (Last Word).

■ **CHAPTER OUTLINE**

1. The aggregate supply curve has short- and long-run characteristics. The short-run curve also shifts because of a change in nominal wages. These factors make the analysis of aggregate supply and demand more complex.

　a. The *short run* is a period in which nominal wages (and other input prices) are unresponsive to changes in the price level. The *long run* is a period in which nominal wages are fully responsive to changes in the price level.

　b. The *short-run aggregate supply curve* is upward sloping: An increase in the price level increases business revenues and profits because nominal wages do not change; in contrast, when the price level decreases, business revenue and profits decline, and so does real output, but nominal wages do not change.

　c. The *long-run aggregate supply curve* is vertical at the potential level of output. Increases in the price level will increase nominal wages and cause a decrease (a shift to the left) in the short-run aggregate supply curve, and declines in the price level will reduce nominal wages and cause an increase (a shift to the right) in the short-run aggregate supply curve. In either case, although the price level changes, output returns to its potential level, and the long-run aggregate supply curve is vertical at the full-employment level of output.

　d. Equilibrium in the extended AD–AS model occurs at the price level and output where the aggregate demand crosses the long-run aggregate supply curve and also crosses the short-run aggregate supply curve.

2. The extended AD–AS model can be applied to explain conditions of inflation and recession in an economy.

　a. Demand-pull inflation will increase (shift to the right) the aggregate demand curve, which increases the price level and causes a temporary increase in real output. In the long run, workers will realize that their real wages have fallen and will demand an increase in their nominal wages. The short-run aggregate supply curve, which was based on fixed nominal wages, now decreases (shifts to the left), resulting in an even higher price level with real output returning to its initial level.

　b. Cost-push inflation will decrease (shift to the left) the short-run aggregate supply curve. This situation will increase the price level and temporarily decrease real output, causing a recession. This creates a policy dilemma for government.

　(1) If government takes actions to counter the cost-push inflation and recession by increasing aggregate demand, the price level will move to an even higher level, and the government's actions may set off an inflationary spiral.

　(2) If government takes no action, the recession will eventually reduce nominal wages, and eventually the short-run aggregate supply curve will shift back to its original position.

　c. If aggregate demand decreases, it will result in a **recession.** If prices and wages are flexible downward, the price level will fall and increase real wages. Eventually, nominal wages will fall to restore the original real wages. This change will increase short-run aggregate supply and end the recession, but not without a long period of high unemployment and lost output.

3. The short- and long-run relationships between inflation and unemployment are important.

　a. If aggregate supply is constant and the economy is operating in the upsloping range of aggregate supply, the greater the rate of increase in aggregate demand, the higher the rate of inflation (and output) and the lower the rate of unemployment. This inverse relationship between the rate of inflation and unemployment is known as the *Phillips Curve.* In the 1960s, economists thought there was a predictable tradeoff between unemployment and inflation. All society had to do was to choose the combination of inflation and unemployment on the Phillips Curve.

　b. The *aggregate supply shocks* of the 1970s and early 1980s called into question the validity of the Phillips Curve. In that period, the economy experienced *stagflation*—higher rates of both inflation and unemployment. The aggregate supply shocks came from an increase in resource prices (oil), shortages in agricultural production, higher wage demands, and declining productivity. Those shocks decreased the short-run aggregate supply curve, which increased the price level and decreased output (and unemployment). Those shocks shifted the Phillips Curve to the right or showed that there was no dependable tradeoff between inflation and unemployment.

　c. The **demise of stagflation** came in the 1982–1989 period because of such factors as a severe recession in 1981 and 1982 that reduced wage demands, increased foreign competition that restrained price increases, and a decline in OPEC's monopoly power. The short-run aggregate supply curve increased, and the price level and unemployment rate fell. This meant that the Phillips Curve might have shifted back (left). Recent unemployment–inflation data are now similar to the Phillips Curve of the 1960s.

4. In the *long run*, there is no apparent tradeoff between inflation and unemployment. Any rate of inflation is consistent with the natural rate of unemployment at that time. The long-run Phillips Curve is vertical at the natural rate of unemployment. In the *short run*, there can be a tradeoff between inflation and unemployment.

    a. An increase in aggregate demand may temporarily reduce unemployment as the price level increases and profits expand, but these actions also set other events in motion.

    (1) The increase in the price level reduces the real wages of workers, who demand and obtain higher nominal wages; these actions return unemployment to its original level.

    (2) Back at the original level, there are now higher actual and expected rates of inflation for the economy, and so the short-run Phillips Curve has shifted upward.

    (3) The process is repeated if aggregate demand continues to increase. The price level rises as the short-run Phillips Curve shifts upward.

    b. In the long run, the Phillips Curve is stable only as a vertical line at the natural rate of unemployment. After all adjustments in nominal wages to increases and decreases in the rate of inflation, the economy returns to its full-employment level of output and its natural rate of unemployment. There is no tradeoff between unemployment and inflation in the long run.

    c. *Disinflation*—reductions in the inflation rate from year to year—is also explained by the distinction between the short-run and long-run Phillips Curves.

5. *Supply-side economics* views aggregate supply as active rather than passive in explaining changes in the price level and unemployment.

    a. It argues that higher marginal tax rates reduce incentives to work and that high taxes also reduce incentives to save and invest. These policies lead to a misallocation of resources, less productivity, and a decrease in aggregate supply. To counter these effects, supply-side economists call for a cut in marginal tax rates.

    b. The *Laffer Curve* suggests that it is possible to lower tax rates and increase tax revenues, thus avoiding a budget deficit because the policies will result in less tax evasion and avoidance.

    c. Critics of supply-side economics and the Laffer Curve suggest that the policy of cutting tax rates will not work because

    (1) It has only a small and uncertain effect on incentives to work (or on aggregate supply).

    (2) It would increase aggregate demand relative to aggregate supply and thus reinforce inflation when there is full employment.

    (3) The expected tax revenues from tax rate cuts depend on assumptions about the economy's position on the Laffer Curve. If tax cuts reduce tax revenues, that will create budget deficits.

    d. Supply-siders argue that the tax cuts under the Reagan administration in the 1980s worked as would be expected: The cut in tax rates increased tax revenue. Critics contend that the reason that occurred was that aggregate demand increased as the economy came out of recession and not that aggregate supply increased. There is now general recognition that changes in marginal tax rates change people's behavior, although there is continuing debate about the size of the effect.

6. (Last Word). This story illustrates two points about tax cuts: (a) The people who pay the highest taxes get the most benefit from a general rate reduction; (b) redistributing tax reductions at the expense of those paying the largest amount of taxes may have adverse and unintended consequences.

■ HINTS AND TIPS

1. Chapter 15 is a difficult chapter because the AD–AS model is extended to include both short-run and long-run effects. Spend extra time mastering this material but do not try to read everything at once. Break the chapter into its logical sections and practice drawing each graph.

2. Be sure you understand the distinction between the **short-run** and **long-run aggregate supply curves.** Then use these ideas to explain demand-pull inflation, cost-push inflation, and recession. Doing Problem 2 will be especially helpful.

3. Be sure you understand how adverse **aggregate supply shocks** shift and create instability in the Phillips Curve.

4. Use Figure 15.9 in the text to help you understand why there is a difference in the short-run and long-run relationships between unemployment and inflation. Problem 4 will increase your understanding of this complicated graph.

5. The rationales for tax cuts and tax increases have been at the forefront of fiscal policy since the 1980s. This chapter offers a detailed explanation of the supply-side economics that has been used to justify tax cut policies during the last 25 years. The last section of the chapter will help you understand the arguments for and against such tax policies, which have real-world applications.

■ IMPORTANT TERMS

short run	stagflation
long run	aggregate supply shocks
short-run aggregate supply curve	disinflation
long-run aggregate supply curve	supply-side economics
Phillips Curve	Laffer Curve

SELF-TEST

■ **FILL-IN QUESTIONS**

1. In an AD–AS model with a stable aggregate supply curve, when the economy is producing in the upsloping portion of the aggregate supply curve, an increase in aggregate demand will (increase, decrease) _____ real output and employment and a decrease in aggregate supply will _____ real output and employment.

2. In the short run, when the price level changes, nominal wages are (responsive, unresponsive) _____, but in the long run nominal wages are _____. In the short run the aggregate supply curve is (upsloping, vertical) _____, but in the long run the curve is _____.

3. Demand-pull inflation occurs with a shift in the aggregate demand curve to the (right, left) _____, which will (decrease, increase) _____ the price level and temporarily _____ real output. As a consequence, the (short-run, long-run) _____ aggregate supply curve will shift left because of a rise in (real, nominal) _____ wages, producing a (lower, higher) _____ price level at the original level of real output.

4. Cost-push inflation occurs with a shift in the short-run aggregate supply curve to the (right, left) _____; thus, the price level will (increase, decrease) _____ and real output will temporarily _____.

5. If government takes no actions to counter cost-push inflation, the resulting recession will (increase, decrease) _____ nominal wages and shift the short-run aggregate supply curve back to its original position, yet if the government tries to counter the recession with a(n) _____ in aggregate demand, the price level will move even higher.

6. A recession will occur when there is (an increase, a decrease) _____ in aggregate demand. If the controversial assumption is made that prices and wages are flexible downward, the price level (rises, falls) _____. Real wages will then (increase, decrease) _____, but eventually nominal wages will _____ and the aggregate supply curve will (increase, decrease) _____ and end the recession.

7. Along the upsloping portion of the short-run aggregate supply curve, the greater the increase in aggregate demand, the (greater, smaller) _____ the increase in the rate of inflation, the _____ the increase in real output, and the (greater, smaller) _____ the unemployment rate.

8. The original Phillips Curve indicates that there will be (a direct, an inverse) _____ relationship between the rate of inflation and the unemployment rate. This means that high rates of inflation will be associated with a (high, low) _____ unemployment rate or that low rates of inflation will be associated with a _____ unemployment rate.

9. The policy tradeoff based on a stable Phillips Curve was that for the economy to reduce the unemployment rate, the rate of inflation had to (increase, decrease) _____, and to reduce the rate of inflation, the unemployment rate had to _____.

10. During the 1970s and early 1980s, aggregate (demand, supply) _____ shocks made the Phillips Curve (stable, unstable) _____. Those shocks produced (demand-pull, cost-push) _____ inflation that resulted in a simultaneous increase in the inflation rate and the unemployment rate that is called (disinflation, stagflation) _____.

11. Several factors contributed to stagflation's demise during the 1982–1989 period. They included

   a. the 1981–1982 (inflation, recession) _____ largely caused by (a restrictive, an expansionary) _____ money policy. There was also (increased, decreased) _____ foreign competition and the _____ monopoly power of OPEC.

   b. The effect of these factors (increased, decreased) _____ the short-run aggregate supply curve; thus, the inflation rate _____ and the unemployment rate _____.

12. The standard explanation for the Phillips Curve is that during the stagflation of the 1970s, the Phillips Curve shifted (right, left) _____, and during the demise of stagflation of 1982–1989, the Phillips Curve shifted _____. In this view, there is a tradeoff between the unemployment rate and the rate of inflation, but changes in (short-run, long-run) _____ aggregate supply can shift the Phillips Curve.

13. In the long run, the tradeoff between the rate of inflation and the rate of unemployment (does, does not) _____ exist, and the economy is stable at its natural rate of (unemployment, inflation) _____.

14. The Phillips Curve may be downsloping in the (short run, long run) _____, but it is vertical in the _____ at the natural rate of unemployment. A shift in aggregate demand that reduces the unemployment rate in the short run results in the long run in (an increase, a decrease) _____ in the rate of inflation and a return to the natural rate of unemployment.

15. When the actual rate of inflation is higher than the expected rate, profits temporarily (fall, rise) _____ and the unemployment rate temporarily (rises, falls) _____. This would occur during a period of (inflation, disinflation) _____.

16. When the actual rate of inflation is lower than the expected rate, profits temporarily (fall, rise) _____ and the unemployment rate temporarily (rises, falls) _____. This would occur during a period of (inflation, disinflation) _____.

17. It is the view of supply-side economists that high marginal tax rates (increase, decrease) _____ incentives to work, save, invest, and take risks. According to supply-side economists, a stimulus for the economy would be a substantial (increase, decrease) _____ in marginal tax rates that would _____ economic growth through (an increase, a decrease) _____ in aggregate supply.

18. The Laffer Curve depicts the relationship between tax rates and (inflation, tax revenues) _____. It is useful for showing how a (cut, rise) _____ in marginal tax rates will increase aggregate supply.

19. In theory, the Laffer Curve shows that as the tax rates increase from 0%, tax revenues will (increase, decrease) _____ to some maximum level, after which tax revenues will _____ as the tax rates increase; conversely, as tax rates are reduced from 100%, tax revenues will (increase, decrease) _____ to some maximum level, after which tax revenues will _____ as tax rates decrease.

20. Criticisms of the Laffer Curve are that the effects of a cut in tax rates on incentives to work, save, and invest are (large, small) _____; that the tax cuts generate an increase in aggregate (demand, supply) _____ that outweigh any increase in aggregate _____ and may lead to inflation when the economy is at full employment; and that tax cuts can produce a (gain, loss) _____ in tax revenues that only add to a budget deficit.

■ **TRUE–FALSE QUESTIONS**

Circle T if the statement is true, F if it is false.

1. The short run in macroeconomics is a period in which nominal wages are fully responsive to changes in the price level.　　　　**T F**

2. The short-run aggregate supply curve has a negative slope.　　　　**T F**

3. The long-run aggregate supply curve Is vertical because nominal wages eventually change by the same amount as changes in the price level.　　　　**T F**

4. Demand-pull inflation will increase the price level and real output in the short run, but in the long run, only the price level will increase.　　　　**T F**

5. Cost-push inflation results in a simultaneous increase in the price level and real output.　　　　**T F**

6. When the economy is experiencing cost-push inflation, an inflationary spiral is likely to result when the government enacts policies to maintain full employment.　　　　**T F**

7. A recession is the result of an increase in the short-run aggregate supply curve.　　　　**T F**

8. If the economy is in a recession, prices and nominal wages will presumably fall, and the short-run aggregate supply curve will increase, so that real output returns to its full-employment level.　　　　**T F**

9. The Phillips Curve shows an inverse relationship between the rate of inflation and the unemployment rate.　　　　**T F**

10. Stagflation refers to a situation in which both the price level and the unemployment rate are rising.　　　　**T F**

11. Aggregate supply shocks can cause both higher rates of inflation and higher rates of unemployment.　　　　**T F**

12. The data from the 1970s and early 1980s indicated that the aggregate supply curve increased.　　　　**T F**

13. One explanation for the stagflation of the 1970s and early 1980s was an increase in aggregate demand.**T F**

14. Among the factors that contributed to the demise of stagflation during the 1980s was a recession in 1981 and 1982.　　　　**T F**

15. There is no apparent long-run tradeoff between inflation and unemployment.　　　　**T F**

16. When the actual rate of inflation is higher than the expected rate, profits temporarily fall and the unemployment rate temporarily rises.　　　　**T F**

17. The long-run Phillips Curve is essentially a vertical line at the economy's natural rate of unemployment. **T F**

18. Disinflation is the same as mismeasurement of the inflation rate.　　　　**T F**

19. When the actual rate of inflation is lower than the expected rate of inflation, profits temporarily fall and the unemployment rate temporarily rises.　　　　**T F**

20. Most economists reject the idea of a short-run trade-off between the unemployment and inflation rates but accept a long-run tradeoff.   T F

21. Supply-side economists contend that aggregate demand is the only active factor in determining the price level and real output in an economy.   T F

22. One proposition of supply-side economics is that the marginal tax rates on earned income should be reduced to increase incentives to work.   T F

23. Supply-side economists recommend a higher marginal tax rate on interest from saving because no productive work was performed to earn the interest.   T F

24. The Laffer Curve suggests that lower tax rates will increase the rate of inflation.   T F

25. A criticism of supply-side economics is that the incentive effects of tax cuts on working and saving are small and have little influence on aggregate supply.   T F

■ **MULTIPLE-CHOICE QUESTIONS**

Circle the letter that corresponds to the best answer.

1. For macroeconomics, the short run is a period in which nominal wages
   (a) do not fully adjust as the price level stays constant
   (b) change as the price level stays constant
   (c) do not fully adjust as the price level changes
   (d) change as the price level changes

2. Once sufficient time has elapsed for wage contracts to expire and nominal wage adjustments to occur, the economy enters
   (a) the short run
   (b) the long run
   (c) a period of inflation
   (d) a period of unemployment

3. A graph of the short-run aggregate supply curve is
   (a) downsloping, and a graph of the long-run aggregate supply is upsloping
   (b) upsloping, and a graph of the long-run aggregate supply is vertical
   (c) upsloping, and a graph of the long-run aggregate supply is downsloping
   (d) vertical, and a graph of the long-run aggregate supply is upsloping

4. Assume that initially your nominal wage was $10 an hour and the price index was 100. If the price level increases to 110, your
   (a) real wage has increased to $11.00
   (b) real wage has decreased to $9.09
   (c) nominal wage has increased to $11.00
   (d) nominal wage has decreased to $9.09

5. In the extended AD–AS model, demand-pull inflation occurs because of an increase in aggregate demand that will eventually produce
   (a) an increase in real wages, thus a decrease in the short-run aggregate supply curve
   (b) an increase in nominal wages, thus an increase in the short-run aggregate supply curve
   (c) a decrease in nominal wages, thus a decrease in the short-run aggregate supply curve
   (d) an increase in nominal wages, thus a decrease in the short-run aggregate supply curve

6. In the short run, demand-pull inflation increases real
   (a) output and decreases the price level
   (b) wages and increases nominal wages
   (c) output and increases the price level
   (d) wages and decreases nominal wages

7. In the long run, demand-pull inflation
   (a) decreases real wages
   (b) increases the price level
   (c) increases the unemployment rate
   (d) decreases real output

8. A likely result of the government trying to reduce the unemployment associated with cost-push inflation through stimulative fiscal policy or monetary policy is
   (a) an inflationary spiral
   (b) stagflation
   (c) a recession
   (d) disinflation

9. What will occur in the short run if there is cost-push inflation and if the government adopts a hands-off approach to it?
   (a) an increase in real output
   (b) a fall in unemployment
   (c) demand-pull inflation
   (d) a recession

10. If prices and wages are flexible, a recession will increase real wages as the price level falls. Eventually, nominal wages will
   (a) fall to the previous real wages, and the short-run aggregate supply will increase
   (b) rise to the previous real wages, and the short-run aggregate supply will increase
   (c) fall to the previous real wages, and the short-run aggregate supply will decrease
   (d) rise to the previous real wages, and the short-run aggregate supply will decrease

11. The traditional Phillips Curve is based on the idea that with a constant short-run aggregate supply curve, the greater the increase in aggregate demand,
   (a) the greater the unemployment rate
   (b) the greater the rate of inflation
   (c) the greater the increase in real output
   (d) the smaller the increase in nominal wages

12. The traditional Phillips Curve shows the
   (a) inverse relationship between the rate of inflation and the unemployment rate
   (b) inverse relationship between the nominal wage and the real wage
   (c) direct relationship between unemployment and demand-pull inflation
   (d) tradeoff between the short run and the long run

13. As the unemployment rate falls below its natural rate,
 (a) excessive spending produces demand-pull inflation
 (b) productivity rises and creates cost-push inflation
 (c) the expected rate of inflation equals the actual rate
 (d) there is an aggregate supply shock

14. Which would be a factor contributing to stagflation in the 1970s?
 (a) a doubling of stock prices
 (b) a fivefold increase in productivity
 (c) a quadrupling of oil prices by OPEC
 (d) a 10% decline in the rate of inflation

15. If there are adverse aggregate supply shocks, with aggregate demand remaining constant, there will be
 (a) a decrease in the price level
 (b) a decrease in the unemployment rate
 (c) an increase in real output
 (d) an increase in both the price level and the unemployment rate

16. A cause of both higher rates of inflation and higher rates of unemployment would be
 (a) an increase in aggregate demand
 (b) an increase in aggregate supply
 (c) a decrease in aggregate demand
 (d) a decrease in aggregate supply

17. Which would be a factor contributing to the demise of stagflation during the 1982–1989 period?
 (a) a lessening of foreign competition
 (b) a strengthening of the monopoly power of OPEC
 (c) a recession brought on largely by a tight monetary policy
 (d) an increase in regulation of the airline and trucking industries

18. The economy is stable only in the
 (a) short run at a high rate of profit
 (b) short run at the natural rate of inflation
 (c) long run at the natural rate of unemployment
 (d) long run at the natural rate of inflation

19. When the actual inflation rate is higher than expected, profits temporarily
 (a) fall and the unemployment rate temporarily falls
 (b) rise and the unemployment rate temporarily falls
 (c) rise and the unemployment rate temporarily rises
 (d) fall and the unemployment rate temporarily rises

20. When the actual rate of inflation is lower than the expected rate, profits temporarily
 (a) fall and the unemployment rate temporarily rises
 (b) rise and the unemployment rate temporarily falls
 (c) rise and the unemployment rate temporarily rises
 (d) fall and the unemployment rate temporarily falls

21. In a disinflation situation, the
 (a) actual rate of inflation is lower than the expected rate, and so the unemployment rate will rise to bring the expected and actual rates into balance
 (b) expected rate of inflation is lower than the actual rate, and so the unemployment rate will rise to bring the expected and actual rates into balance
 (c) actual rate of inflation is higher than the expected rate, and so the unemployment rate will fall to bring the expected and actual rates into balance
 (d) expected rate of inflation is higher than the actual rate, and so the unemployment rate will fall to bring the expected and actual rates into balance

22. The long-run Phillips Curve is essentially
 (a) horizontal at the natural rate of unemployment
 (b) vertical at the natural rate of unemployment
 (c) vertical at the natural rate of inflation
 (d) horizontal at the natural rate of inflation

23. Supply-side economists contend that the U.S. system of taxation reduces
 (a) unemployment but causes inflation
 (b) incentives to work, save, and invest
 (c) transfer payments to the poor
 (d) the effects of cost-push inflation

24. Based on the Laffer Curve, a cut in the tax rate from 100% to a point before the maximum level of tax revenue will
 (a) increase the price level
 (b) increase tax revenues
 (c) decrease real output
 (d) decrease the real wages

25. A criticism of tax cuts and supply-side economics made by many economists is that
 (a) the demand-side effects exceed the supply-side effects
 (b) the supply-side effects exceed the demand-side effects
 (c) the demand-side and supply-side effects offset each other
 (d) there are only supply-side effects

■ **PROBLEMS**

1. Columns 1 and 2 of the table on the next page show a portion of a short-run aggregate supply schedule. Column 3 shows the number of full-time workers (in millions) who would have to be employed to produce each of the seven real domestic outputs (in billions) in the short-run aggregate supply schedule. The labor force is 80 million workers, and the full-employment output of the economy is $_____.

 a. If the aggregate demand schedule were that shown in columns 1 and 4,

 (1) the price level would be _____ and the real output would be $_____.

 (2) the number of workers employed would be _____ million, the number of workers unemployed would be _____ million, and the unemployment rate would be _____%.

(1) Price level	(2) Real output supplied	(3) Employment (in millions)	(4) Real output demanded	(5) Real output demanded	(6) Real output demanded
130	$ 800	69	$2300	$2600	$1900
140	1300	70	2200	2500	1800
150	1700	72	2100	2400	1700
160	2000	75	2000	2300	1600
170	2200	78	1900	2200	1500
180	2300	80	1800	2100	1400
190	2300	80	1700	2000	1300

b. If aggregate demand were to increase to that shown in columns 1 and 5 and short-run aggregate supply remained constant,

(1) the price level would rise to _____ and the real output would rise to $ _____.

(2) employment would increase by _____ million workers and the unemployment rate would fall to _____%.

(3) the price level would increase by _____ and the rate of inflation would be _____%.

c. If aggregate demand were to decrease to that shown in columns 1 and 6 and short-run aggregate supply remained constant,

(1) the price level would fall to _____ and the real output would fall to $ _____.

(2) employment would decrease by _____ compared with situation **a,** and the unemployment rate would rise to _____%.

(3) the price level would decrease and the rate of inflation would be (positive, negative) _____.

2. The following is an aggregate demand and aggregate supply model. Assume that the economy is initially in equilibrium at **AD₁** and **AS₁**. The price level will be _____, and the real domestic output will be _____.

a. If there is demand-pull inflation, then

(1) in the short run, the new equilibrium is at point _____, with the price level at _____ and real output at _____;

(2) in the long run, nominal wages will rise so that the aggregate supply curve will shift from _____ to _____. The equilibrium will be at point _____ with the price level at _____ and real output at _____, and so the increase in aggregate demand has only moved the economy along its _____ curve.

b. Now assume that the economy is initially in equilibrium at point **W,** where **AD₁** and **AS₁** intersect. If there is cost-push inflation, then

(1) in the short run, the new equilibrium is at point _____, with the price level at _____ and real output at _____.

(2) if the government tries to counter the cost-push inflation with expansionary monetary and fiscal policy, then aggregate demand will shift from _____ to _____, with the price level becoming _____ and real output _____, but this policy has a trap because the price level has shifted from _____ to _____ and the new level of inflation might shift _____ leftward.

(3) if government does not counter the cost-push inflation, the price level will eventually move to _____ and real output to _____ as the recession reduces nominal wages and shifts the aggregate supply curve from _____ to _____.

c. Now assume that the economy is initially in equilibrium at point **Y,** where **AD₂** and **AS₂** intersect. If there is a recession that reduces investment spending, then

(1) aggregate demand decreases and real output shifts from _____ to _____, and assuming that prices and wages are flexible downward, the price level shifts from _____ to _____.

(2) these events cause real wages to (rise, fall) _____, and eventually nominal wages _____ to restore the previous real wages.

(3) when this happens, the short-run aggregate supply curve shifts from _____ to _____ to its new equilibrium at point _____. The equilibrium price level is _____ and the equilibrium level of output is _____ at the long-run aggregate supply curve _____.

3. The following is a traditional Phillips Curve.

a. At full employment (a 4% unemployment rate) the price level would rise by _____% each year.
b. If the price level were stable (increasing by 0% a year), the unemployment rate would be _____%.
c. Which of the combinations along the Phillips Curve would you choose for the economy? _____

Why would you select this combination? _____

_____

4. Following is a model of short- and long-run Phillips Curves.

a. Suppose you begin at point X_1 and an assumption is made that nominal wages are set on the original expectation that a 3% rate of inflation will continue in the economy.
(1) If an increase in aggregate demand reduces the unemployment rate from 6% to 3%, then the actual rate of inflation will move to _____%. The higher product prices will lift the profits of firms, and they will hire more workers; thus, in the short run the economy will temporarily move to point _____.
(2) If workers demand and receive higher wages to compensate for the loss of purchasing power from higher-than-expected inflation, then business profits will fall from previous levels and firms will reduce employment; therefore, the unemployment rate will move from point _____ to point _____ on the graph. The short-run Phillips Curve has shifted from _____ to _____ on the graph.
(3) If aggregate demand continues to increase so that the unemployment rate drops from 6% to 3%, then prices will rise before nominal wages do, and output and employment will increase, so that there will be a move from point _____ to point _____ on the graph.
(4) But when workers get nominal wage increases, profits fall, and the unemployment rate moves from point _____ at _____% to point _____ at _____%. The short-run Phillips Curve has now shifted from _____ to _____ on the graph.
(5) The long-run Phillips Curve is the line _____.
b. Suppose you begin at point X_3, where the expected and actual rate of inflation is 9% and the unemployment rate is 6%.
(1) If there is a decline in aggregate demand because of a recession and if the actual rate of inflation falls to 6%, well below the expected rate of 9%, then business profits will fall and the unemployment rate will decrease to 9%, as shown by the movement from point X_3 to point _____.
(2) If firms and workers adjust their expectation to the 6% rate of inflation, nominal wages will fall, profits will rise, and the economy will move from point _____ to point _____. The short-run Phillips Curve has shifted from _____ to _____.
(3) If this process is repeated, the long-run Phillips Curve will be traced as line _____.

5. The following is a Laffer Curve.

a. The point of maximum tax revenue is _____. As tax rates decrease from 100% to point **B**, tax revenues will (increase, decrease) _____. As tax rates increase from 0% to point **B**, tax revenues will

_____.

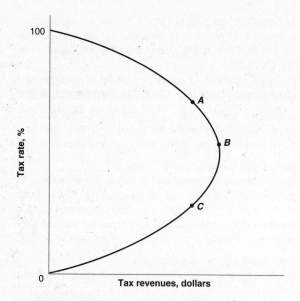

b. Supply-side economists would contend that it would be beneficial for government to cut tax rates if they are (below, above) _____ point **B,** whereas critics of supply-side economics contend that it would be harmful for government to cut tax rates if they are _____ point **B.**

■ **SHORT ANSWER AND ESSAY QUESTIONS**

1. What distinguishes the short run from the long run in macroeconomics?

2. Identify the basic difference between a short-run and a long-run aggregate supply curve.

3. Explain what happens to aggregate supply when an increase in the price level results in an increase in nominal wages.

4. Explain how to find equilibrium in the extended AD–AS model.

5. Describe the process of demand-pull inflation in the short run and in the long run.

6. How does demand-pull inflation influence the aggregate supply curve?

7. Describe cost-push inflation in the extended AD–AS model.

8. What two generalizations emerge from the analysis of cost-push inflation? Describe the two scenarios that provide the basis for those generalizations.

9. Describe recession in the extended AD–AS model.

10. What is a Phillips Curve? What two rates are related?

11. Explain how a Phillips Curve with a negative slope may be derived by holding aggregate supply constant and mentally increasing aggregate demand.

12. Were the rates of inflation and unemployment consistent with the Phillips Curve in the 1960s? What do data on these two rates suggest about the curve since that time?

13. What were the aggregate supply shocks to the U.S. economy during the 1970s and early 1980s? How did those shocks affect interpretation of the Phillips Curve?

14. Describe the factors that contributed to stagflation's demise during the 1982–1989 period. What do many economists contend happened to the aggregate supply curve, unemployment, and inflation during that period?

15. How can there be a short-run tradeoff between inflation and unemployment but no long-run tradeoff? Explain.

16. How can the Phillips Curve be used to explain both inflation and disinflation in the economy.

17. What are the characteristics of the long-run Phillips Curve? How is it related to the natural rate of unemployment?

18. Discuss why supply-side economists contend there are tax disincentives in the economy.

19. Draw and explain a Laffer Curve showing the relationship between tax rates and tax revenues.

20. Outline three criticisms of the ideas expressed in the depiction of the Laffer Curve.

___

ANSWERS

Chapter 15 Extending the Analysis of Aggregate Supply

FILL-IN QUESTIONS

1. increase, decrease
2. unresponsive, responsive, upsloping, vertical
3. right, increase, increase, short-run, nominal, higher
4. left, increase, decrease
5. decrease, increase
6. a decrease, falls, increase, decrease, increase
7. greater, greater, smaller
8. an inverse, low, high
9. increase, increase
10. supply, unstable, cost-push, stagflation
11. *a.* recession, a restrictive, increased, decreased; *b.* increased, decreased, decreased
12. right, left, short-run
13. does not, unemployment
14. short run, long run, an increase
15. rise, falls, inflation
16. fall, rises, disinflation
17. decrease, decrease, increase, an increase
18. tax revenues, cut
19. increase, decrease, increase, decrease
20. small, demand, supply, loss

TRUE–FALSE QUESTIONS

1. F, p. 286	10. T, p. 293	19. T, p. 295
2. F, p. 286	11. T, p. 293	20. F, p. 295
3. T, p. 287	12. F, p. 293	21. F, pp. 295–296
4. T, pp. 288–289	13. F, p. 293	22. T, p. 296
5. F, p. 289	14. T, p. 293	23. F, p. 296
6. T, pp. 289–290	15. T, p. 294	24. F, p. 296
7. F, p. 290	16. F, p. 295	25. T, pp. 297–298
8. T, p. 290	17. T, pp. 294–295	
9. T, p. 291	18. F, p. 295	

MULTIPLE-CHOICE QUESTIONS

1. c, p. 286	**10.** a, p. 290	**19.** b, p. 294
2. b, p. 286	**11.** b, pp. 290–291	**20.** a, p. 294
3. b, p. 287	**12.** a, pp. 290–291	**21.** a, p. 295
4. b, p. 287	**13.** a, p. 292	**22.** b, pp. 294–295
5. d, pp. 288–289	**14.** c, pp. 292–293	**23.** b, pp. 295–296
6. c, pp. 288–289	**15.** d, p. 293	**24.** b, p. 296
7. b, pp. 288–289	**16.** d, p. 293	**25.** a, p. 296
8. a, pp. 289–290	**17.** c, p. 293	
9. d, pp. 289–290	**18.** c, p. 294	

SHORT ANSWER AND ESSAY QUESTIONS

1. p. 286	**8.** pp. 289–290	**15.** pp. 294–295
2. pp. 286–287	**9.** p. 290	**16.** p. 295
3. pp. 286–287	**10.** pp. 291–292	**17.** pp. 294–295
4. pp. 287–288	**11.** pp. 291–292	**18.** pp. 295–296
5. pp. 288–289	**12.** pp. 291–292	**19.** pp. 296–297
6. pp. 288–289	**13.** pp. 292–293	**20.** pp. 297–298
7. p. 289	**14.** pp. 293–294	

PROBLEMS

1. 2300; *a.* (1) 160, 2000, (2) 75, 5, 6.25; *b.* (1) 170, 2200, (2) 3, 2.5, (3) 10, 6.25; *c.* (1) 150, 1700, (2) 3, 10, (3) negative

2. P_1, Q_p; *a.* (1) X, P_2, Q_2, (2) AS_1, AS_2, Y, P_3, Q_p, AS_{LR}; *b.* (1) Z, P_2, Q_1, (2) AD_1, AD_2, P_3, Q_p, P_2, P_3, AS_2, (3) P_1, Q_p, AS_2, AS_1; *c.* (1) Qp, Q_1, P_3, P_2, (2) rise, fall, (3) AS_2, AS_1, W, P_1, Q_p, AS_{LR}

3. *a.* 20; *b.* 9

4. *a.* (1) 6, Y_1, (2) Y_1, X_2, PC_1 PC_2, (3) X_2, Y_2, (4) Y_2, 3, X_3, 6, PC_2, PC_3, (5) PC_{LR}; *b.* (1) Z_2, (2) Z_2, X_2, PC_3, PC_2, (3) PC_{LR}

5. *a.* *B*, increase, decrease; *b.* above, below

CHAPTER 16

Economic Growth

The United States has had an impressive record of economic growth in the last half-century. The purpose of this chapter is to indicate what factors have contributed to this economic growth and the implications for the economy.

The chapter begins by discussing the six main ingredients of economic growth. The four **supply factors** increase the output potential of the economy. Whether the economy actually produces its full potential—that is, whether the economy has both full employment and full production—depends on two other factors: the level of aggregate demand (the **demand factor**) and the efficiency with which the economy allocates resources (the **efficiency factor**).

The next section of the chapter places the factors that contribute to economic growth in graphical perspective with the use of two familiar **economic models.** The production possibilities model was originally presented in Chapter 1 and is now used to discuss how the two major supply factors—labor input and labor productivity—shift the production possibilities curve outward. The second model is the aggregate demand–aggregate supply model that was explained in Chapter 10 and discussed in more detail in Chapter 15. Here you learn how both the short-run and the long-run shifts in aggregate supply combined with shifts in aggregate demand (and the factors underlying those shifts) affect the output and the price level.

The **growth record** of the United States has been impressive in terms of increases in both real GDP and real GDP per capita. What accounts for this long-term economic growth in the United States? First, the size of its labor force has grown. Second and more important, the productivity of the labor force in the United States has increased. The increase in the productivity of labor is the result of technological advances, the expansion of the stock of capital goods in the U.S. economy, the improved education and training of the labor force, economies of scale, the reallocation of resources, and the supportive social, cultural, and political environments.

Increases in productivity have a direct effect on real output, real income, and real wages. A major development in recent years was the doubling in the rate of labor productivity in the period 1995–2005 compared with that in the 1973–1995 period. This change heralded to some observers that the United States had achieved a **New Economy** that is characterized by advances in technology, more entrepreneurship, increasing returns from resource inputs, and greater global competition. The implications for macroeconomics are significant: faster growth with low

inflation, a reduction in the natural rate of unemployment, and an increase in tax revenues. Whether the economy is in fact "new" remains to be seen because the trend may simply be a short-run upturn in labor productivity and not a long-run outcome.

The last section of the chapter raises an important question: Is more economic growth **desirable and sustainable?** This controversy has two sides. The antigrowth view is based on the pollution problems growth creates, its effects on human values, and doubts about whether it can be sustained. The defense of growth is based in part on its contribution to higher standards of living, improvements in worker safety and the environment, and its history of sustainability. After reading this section, you will have to evaluate the advantages and disadvantages of economic growth for the economy.

■ CHECKLIST

When you have studied this chapter you should be able to

☐ Identify four supply factors in economic growth.

☐ Explain the demand factor in economic growth.

☐ Describe the efficiency factor in economic growth.

☐ Show graphically how economic growth shifts the production possibilities curve.

☐ Explain the rationale for an equation for real GDP that is based on labor inputs and labor productivity.

☐ Show that a shift outward in the production possibilities curve is equivalent to a rightward shift in the economy's long-run aggregate supply curve.

☐ Illustrate graphically how economic growth shifts the short-run and long-run aggregate supply curves and the aggregate demand curve.

☐ Describe the average annual growth rates of real GDP and real per capita GDP in the U.S. economy since 1950.

☐ Compare the relative importance of the two major means of increasing real GDP in the United States.

☐ List the sources of growth in the productivity of labor in the United Sates and state their relative importance.

☐ Describe the other factors that affect an economy's growth rate.

☐ Describe the growth of labor productivity in the United States since 1973.

☐ Explain the relationship between productivity growth and the standard of living.

☐ Identify the major characteristics of the New Economy.

☐ Discuss how the microchip and information technology have contributed to the New Economy.
☐ Describe the sources of increasing returns and economies of scale in the New Economy.
☐ Explain how the New Economy increases global competition.
☐ Discuss the implications of the New Economy for economic growth.
☐ Offer a skeptical perspective on the New Economy.
☐ Present several arguments against more economic growth.
☐ Make a case for more economic growth.
☐ Explain the factors that have contributed to China's high rate of economic growth over the last 25 years and the challenges for that economy (Last Word).

■ **CHAPTER OUTLINE**

1. The **ingredients of *economic growth*** depend on supply, demand, and efficiency factors.
  a. *Supply factors* include the quantity and quality of resources (natural, human, and capital) and technology.
  b. The ***demand factor*** influences the level of aggregate demand in the economy, which is important for sustaining full employment of resources.
  c. The ***efficiency factor*** affects the efficient use of resources to obtain maximum production of goods and services (productive efficiency) and allocate them to their highest and best use by society (allocative efficiency).

2. Two familiar **economic models** can be used for the analysis of economic growth.
  a. In the **production possibilities model,** economic growth shifts the production possibilities curve outward because of improvement in supply factors. Whether the economy operates on the frontier of the curve or inside the curve depends on the demand factor and efficiency factors.
  b. Discussions of growth, however, focus primarily on supply factors. From this perspective, economic growth is obtained by increasing *labor inputs* and by increasing labor productivity. This relationship can be expressed in an equation: real GDP = worker-hours × labor productivity.
  (1) The hours of work are determined by the size of the working-age population and the ***labor-force participation rate*** (the percentage of the working-age population in the labor force).
  (2) ***Labor productivity*** (real output per work hour) is determined by many factors, such as technological advance, the quantity of capital goods, the quality of labor, and efficiency in the use of inputs.
  c. In the **aggregate demand–aggregate supply model,** economic growth is illustrated by long-run and short-run shifts.
  (1) A shift outward in the production possibilities curve is equivalent to a shift rightward in the long-run aggregate supply curve for the economy. In either model,

changes in the price level are not important because they do not shift either curve.
  (2) The extended AD–AS model takes into account the supply, demand, and efficiency factors. Supply factors shift the long-run aggregate supply curve to the right, and supply and efficiency factors make that curve vertical at the economy's potential output. If the price level increased over time, it would indicate that the rise in potential output was accompanied by a greater shift in aggregate demand.

3. The **rate of growth in real GDP** has been about 3.5% annually since 1950. The growth rate for real per capita GDP in the United States has been about 2.3% annually since 1950. These rates increased significantly in the period 1996–2000, declined significantly in the recession of 2001, and then returned to their typical levels in recent years.

4. Several factors are important in ***growth accounting.***
  a. The two main factors are increases in quantity of labor (hours of work) and increases in labor productivity. About two-thirds of this growth was the result of increased labor productivity. About one-third of the growth was a result of the increased quantity of labor employed in the economy.
  b. Technological advance is achieved by combining given amounts of resources in new and innovative ways that result in a larger output. It involves the use of new managerial methods and business organizations that improve production. Technological advance is also embodied in new capital investment that adds to the productive capacity of the economy. It accounted for about 40% of the increase in productivity growth.
  c. The **quantity of capital** has expanded with the increase in saving and investment spending for capital goods. This private investment has increased the quantity of each worker's tools, equipment, and machinery. There is also public investment in ***infrastructure*** in the United States. The increase in the quantity of capital goods explains about 30% of productivity growth.
  d. Increased investment in ***human capital*** (the training and education of workers) has expanded the productivity of workers and has accounted for about 15% of productivity growth.
  e. **Improved allocation of resources** (workers shifting to higher-productivity employment) and ***economies of scale*** (reductions in the per-unit cost to firms achieved from larger-sized markets) have also expanded the productivity of workers. Together, these factors have contributed about 15% to productivity growth.
  f. Other factors which are difficult to quantify, such as the **social-cultural-political environment** of the United States, have contributed to economic growth. These factors have fostered growth of the market system under a stable political system and developed positive attitudes toward work, investing, and risk taking.

5. Increases in **productivity growth,** even small ones, can have a substantial effect on average real hourly wages and the standard of living in an economy. In the period

1973–1995, labor productivity grew by an average of 1.4% annually, but in the 1995–2005 period it grew by 2.9% annually. This increase indicates that there may be a *New Economy.*

    a. This New Economy has several characteristics.

    (1) It is based on a dramatic rise in entrepreneurship and innovation based on the microchip and *information technology.*

    (2) The new *start-up firms* often experience *increasing returns,* which means a firm's output increases by a larger percentage than the increase in its resource inputs. These increasing returns have been achieved by means of more specialized inputs, the spreading of development costs, simultaneous consumption, *network effects,* and *learning by doing.*

    (3) The new technology and improvements in communication have increased global competition, thus lowering production costs, restraining price increases, and stimulating innovation to remain competitive.

    b. The New Economy has implications for economic growth. There can be a faster rate of economic growth with low inflation.

    c. Questions remain about whether there is a New Economy or just a short upturn in the business cycle. Skeptics wonder whether the 5-year increase in productivity growth can be sustained over a longer period of time or whether the economy will return to its long-term trend in productivity. Inflationary pressures can increase in economic boom times. More time may be needed to be sure there is a New Economy.

6. There is an ongoing debate about whether economic growth is desirable and sustainable.

    a. The antigrowth view sees several problems: Growth pollutes the environment and may produce more goods and services but does not create a better life; also, doubts remain about whether growth is sustainable at the current rate of resource depletion.

    b. The defense of economic growth is based on several considerations: Growth produces a higher standard of living and reduces the burden of scarcity; the technology it creates improves people's lives and can reduce pollution; and it is sustainable because market incentives encourage the use of substitute resources.

7. (Last Word). China has experienced annual rates of economic growth of almost 9% over the last 25 years. Real income per capita has increased by about 8 percent annually since 1980. The increased output and rising incomes have fueled increases in saving and investment that in turn have contributed to an increase in the stock of capital goods and technological advance. This economic growth is not without economic problems such as trade disputes, rising inflation, unemployment among rural workers, and government inefficiencies.

■ HINTS AND TIPS

1. Chapter 16 contains very little economics that should be new to you. Chapter 1 introduced you to the production

possibilities model that is now discussed in more detail. In Chapters 10 and 15 you learned about the aggregate demand–aggregate supply models that are now used to discuss economic growth. You might review these concepts and models from previous chapters before reading this chapter.

2. Table 16.1 is important if you want to understand the factors that influence economic growth in the United States. The figures in the table indicate the relative importance of each major factor. In the last decade, about two-thirds of U.S. economic growth came from factors affecting increases in labor productivity and about one-third came from increases in the quantity of labor. Five factors affecting the growth of labor productivity are technological advance, quantity of capital, education and training, economies of scale, and resource allocation.

3. The remaining two sections of the chapter focus on major economic issues about which there is some debate. You will want to evaluate the evidence for and against the idea that there is a "New Economy." You will also want to understand the advantages and disadvantages of economic growth.

■ IMPORTANT TERMS

economic growth	human capital
supply factor	economies of scale
demand factor	New Economy
efficiency factor	information technology
labor productivity	start-up firms
labor-force participation rate	increasing returns
growth accounting	network effects
infrastructure	learning by doing

SELF-TEST

■ FILL-IN QUESTIONS

1. Economic growth means that real output in the economy (increases, decreases) _____ and produces a standard of living that is (higher, lower) _____ with (more, less) _____ material abundance.

2. The four supply factors in economic growth are

    a. _____

    b. _____

    c. _____

    d. _____

3. To realize its growing production potential, a nation must fully employ its expanding supplies of resources, which is the (efficiency, demand) _____ factor in economic growth, and it must also achieve productive and allocative _____, the other factor contributing to economic growth.

4. In the production possibilities model, economic growth increases primarily because of (demand, supply) _____ factors that shift the production possibilities curve to the (left, right) _____, but if there is less than full employment and production, the economy (may, may not) _____ realize its potential.

5. The real GDP of any economy in any year is equal to the quantity of labor employed (divided, multiplied) _____ by the productivity of labor. The quantity of labor is measured by the number of (businesses, hours of labor) _____. Productivity is equal to real GDP per (capita, worker-hour) _____.

6. The quantity of labor employed in the economy in any year depends on the size of the (unemployed, employed) _____ labor force and the length of the average workweek. The size element depends on the size of the working-age population and the labor-force (unemployment, participation) _____ rate.

7. In the aggregate demand–aggregate supply framework, economic growth is illustrated by an (increase, decrease) _____ in the long-run aggregate supply curve, which is (vertical, horizontal) _____. When the price level also increases, it indicates that the aggregate demand curve has increased (more, less) _____ rapidly than the long-run aggregate supply.

8. Since 1950, real GDP in the United States has increased at an annual rate of about (2.3, 3.5) _____% and real GDP per capita has increased at an annual rate of about _____%.

9. The economic growth record of the United States shows that the increase in the quantity of labor is (more, less) _____ important than increases in labor productivity in accounting for economic growth.

10. Factors contributing to labor productivity include

   a. technological _____

   b. increases in the quantity of _____ and in the quantity available per _____

   c. the improved _____ and _____ of workers

   d. economies of _____

   e. the improved _____ of resources.

11. An increase in the quantity of the capital stock of a nation is a result of saving and (consumption, investment)

_____. A key determinant of labor productivity is the amount of capital goods available per (consumer, worker) _____.

12. Infrastructure, such as highways and bridges, is a form of (private, public) _____ investment that complements _____ capital goods.

13. The knowledge and skills that make a worker productive are a form of (physical, human) _____ capital. This type of capital is often obtained through (consumption, education) _____.

14. Reductions in per-unit costs that result from an increase in the size of markets and firms are called (improved resource allocation, economies of scale) _____, whereas the movement of a worker from a job with lower productivity to one with higher productivity would be an example of _____.

15. Other factors that have led to economic growth in the United States are its social-cultural-political (parties, environment) _____ and (negative, positive) _____ attitudes toward work and risk taking that increase the supply of willing workers and innovative entrepreneurs.

16. An increase in labor productivity will (increase, decrease) _____ real output, real income, and real wages. Assuming an economy has an increase in labor productivity of 1.5%, it will take (28, 47) _____ years for its standard of living to double, but an increase in labor productivity of 2.5% annually will double its standard of living in _____ years.

17. The characteristics of the New Economy are (advances, declines) _____ in information technology, business firms that experience returns to scale that are (decreasing, increasing) _____, and global competition that is _____.

18. One implication of the New Economy is that the economy can achieve a growth rate that is (faster, slower) _____ and still maintain (high, low) _____ inflation.

19. Those who are skeptical about the New Economy argue that the rapid increase in the rate of productivity growth may be a (short-run, long-run) _____ trend that is not sustainable over a _____ period.

20. Critics of economic growth contend that it (cleans up, pollutes) _____ the environment, (does, does not) _____ solve problems such as poverty and homelessness, and (is, is not) _____ sustainable. Defenders of economic growth say that it creates (less, greater) _____ material abundance, results in a (higher, lower) _____ standard of living, and results in an efficient and sustainable allocation of resources based on price (discounts, incentives) _____ .

■ TRUE–FALSE QUESTIONS

Circle T if the statement is true, F if it is false.

1. Economic growth is measured as either an increase in real GDP or an increase in real per capita GDP.
  T F

2. Changes in the physical and technical agents of production are supply factors for economic growth that enable an economy to expand its potential GDP.   **T F**

3. The demand factor in economic growth refers to the ability of the economy to expand its production as the demand for products grows.   **T F**

4. An increase in the quantity and quality of natural resources is an efficiency factor for economic growth.
  T F

5. A shift outward in the production possibilities curve is a direct result of improvements in supply factors for economic growth.   **T F**

6. The potential output of an economy will not be completely realized unless there is full employment of resources and their efficient use.   **T F**

7. The real GDP of an economy in any year is equal to its input of labor divided by the productivity of labor.
  T F

8. The hours of labor input depend on the size of the employed labor force and the length of the average work-week.   **T F**

9. One determinant of labor productivity is the quantity of capital goods available to workers.   **T F**

10. Supply factors that shift the economy's production possibilities curve outward also cause a leftward shift in its long-run aggregate supply curve.   **T F**

11. An increase in economic growth will increase the long-run aggregate supply curve and the short-run aggregate supply curve but will decrease the aggregate demand curve.   **T F**

12. Since 1950, U.S. data show that the average annual rate of growth has been greater for real GDP per capita than for real GDP.   **T F**

13. Increased labor productivity has been more important than increased labor inputs in the growth of the U.S. economy since 1995.   **T F**

14. The largest factor increasing labor productivity in the U.S. economy has been technological advance.   **T F**

15. Public investment in the form of new infrastructure often complements private capital investment.   **T F**

16. Education and training contribute to a worker's stock of human capital.   **T F**

17. Economies of scale are reductions in per-unit cost that result in a decrease in the size of markets and firms.
  T F

18. The social, cultural, and political environment in the United States has fostered economic growth.   **T F**

19. If the rate of growth in labor productivity averages 2.5% a year, it will take about 50 years for the standard of living to double.   **T F**

20. The idea of a New Economy is based largely on a slower rate of productivity growth and therefore slower economic growth.   **T F**

21. Productivity growth is the basic source of improvements in real wage rates and the standard of living.
  T F

22. More specialized inputs and network effects are two sources of increasing returns and economies of scale in the New Economy.   **T F**

23. From a macroeconomic perspective, a New Economy is likely to achieve a higher rate of economic growth.
  T F

24. Critics of economic growth say that it adds to environmental problems, increases human stress, and exhausts natural resources.   **T F**

25. Defenders of economic growth say it is sustainable in the short run but not in the long run.   **T F**

■ MULTIPLE-CHOICE QUESTIONS

Circle the letter that corresponds to the best answer.

1. What is one major measure of economic growth?
  (a) the supply of money
  (b) the demand for money
  (c) nominal GDP per capita
  (d) real GDP per capita

2. A supply factor in economic growth would be
  (a) an increase in the efficient use of resources
  (b) a decline in the rate of resource depletion
  (c) an improvement in the quality of labor
  (d) an increase in consumption spending

3. Which is a demand factor in economic growth?
  (a) an increase in the purchasing power of the economy
  (b) an increase in the economy's stock of capital goods
  (c) more natural resources
  (d) technological progress

Use the following graph to answer Questions 4 and 5.

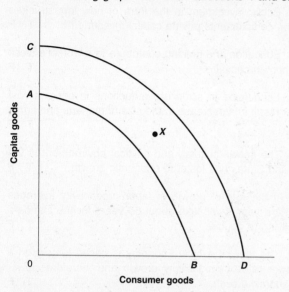

4. If the production possibilities curve of an economy shifts from **AB** to **CD**, it is most likely the result of what factor affecting economic growth?
  (a) a supply factor
  (b) a demand factor
  (c) an efficiency factor
  (d) an allocation factor

5. If the production possibilities curve for an economy is at **CD** but the economy is operating at point **X**, the reasons are most likely to be
  (a) supply and environmental factors
  (b) demand and efficiency factors
  (c) labor inputs and labor productivity
  (d) technological progress

6. Total output or real GDP in any year is equal to
  (a) labor inputs divided by resource outputs
  (b) labor productivity multiplied by real output
  (c) worker-hours multiplied by labor productivity
  (d) worker-hours divided by labor productivity

7. Assume that an economy has 1000 workers, each working 2000 hours per year. If the average real output per worker-hour is $9, total output or real GDP will be
  (a) $2 million
  (b) $9 million
  (c) $18 million
  (d) $24 million

8. A shift outward of the production possibilities curve would be equivalent to a shift
  (a) upward in aggregate demand
  (b) downward in aggregate demand

  (c) rightward in long-run aggregate supply
  (d) leftward in long-run aggregate supply

Use the following graph to answer Questions 9 and 10.

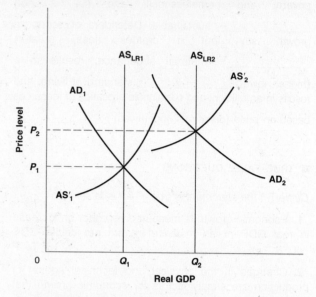

9. A shift from **Q₁** to **Q₂** is caused by a shift in the
  (a) level of prices
  (b) aggregate demand curve
  (c) short-run aggregate supply curve
  (d) long-run aggregate supply curve

10. Which combination would best explain a shift in the price level from **P₁** to **P₂** and an increase in real domestic output from **Q₁** to **Q₂**?
  (a) an increase in long-run aggregate supply (**AS₁** to **AS₂**) and in short-run aggregate supply (**AD₁** to **AD₂**)
  (b) an increase in aggregate demand (**AD₁** to **AD₂**) and a decrease in long-run aggregate supply (**AS₂** to **AS₁**)
  (c) an increase in long-run aggregate supply (**AS₁** to **AS₂**), an increase in aggregate demand (**AD₁** to **AD₂**), and an increase in short-run aggregate supply (**AS′₁** to **AS′₂**)
  (d) a decrease in long-run aggregate supply (**AS₂** to **AS₁**), a decrease in aggregate demand (**AD₂** to **AD₁**), and a decrease in short-run aggregate supply (**AS′₂** to **AS′₁**)

11. The average annual rate of increase in real GDP since 1950 has been about
  (a) 1.1%
  (b) 2.3%
  (c) 3.5%
  (d) 4.5%

12. Real GDP per capita in the United States since 1950 has grown by an average annual rate of about
  (a) 1.1%
  (b) 2.3%
  (c) 3.5%
  (d) 4.6%

13. What is the other major factor that, when combined with the growth of labor productivity, accounts for long-term economic growth in the United States?
(a) an increase in government spending
(b) an increase in the quantity of labor
(c) a decrease in the interest rate
(d) a decrease in personal taxes

14. The factor accounting for the largest increase in the productivity of labor in the United States has been
(a) economies of scale
(b) technological advance
(c) the quantity of capital
(d) the education and training of workers

15. How does a nation typically acquire more capital goods?
(a) by reducing the workweek and increasing leisure
(b) by saving income and using it for capital investment
(c) by increasing government regulation of the capital stock
(d) by reducing the amount of capital goods available per worker

16. An example of U.S. public investment in infrastructure would be
(a) an airline company
(b) a natural gas pipeline
(c) an auto and truck plant
(d) an interstate highway

17. Economists CAll the knowledge and skills that make a worker productive
(a) the labor-force participation rate
(b) learning by doing
(c) human capital
(d) infrastructure

18. What economic concept would be most closely associated with a situation in which a large manufacturer of food products uses extensive assembly lines with computerization and robotics that serve to reduce per-unit costs of production?
(a) economies of scale
(b) sustainability of growth
(c) network effects
(d) simultaneous consumption

19. The decline of discrimination in education and labor markets increased the overall rate of labor productivity in the economy by giving groups freedom to move from jobs with lower productivity to ones with higher productivity. This development would be an example of a(n)
(a) fall in the labor-force participation rate
(b) rise in the natural rate of unemployment
(c) technological advance
(d) improvement in resource allocation

20. If the annual growth in a nation's productivity is 2% rather than 1%, the nation's standard of living will double in
(a) 25 years
(b) 35 years

(c) 50 years
(d) 70 years

21. The New Economy is described as one with
(a) more tax revenues and more government spending
(b) a faster rate of inflation and fewer specialized inputs
(c) more experienced workers but fewer available jobs for them
(d) a faster rate of productivity growth and faster economic growth

22. Increasing returns would be a situation in which a firm
(a) triples its workforce and other inputs and its output doubles
(b) doubles its workforce and other inputs and its output triples
(c) doubles its workforce and other inputs and its output doubles
(d) quadruples its workforce and other inputs and its output triples

23. Which would be a source of increasing returns and economies of scale in the New Economy?
(a) social environment
(b) noninflationary growth
(c) simultaneous consumption
(d) less specialized inputs

24. A person who is skeptical about the New Economy would argue that it
(a) is based on learning by doing instead of infrastructure
(b) raises tax revenues collected by government
(c) lowers the natural rate of unemployment
(d) is based on a short-run trend

25. Defenders of rapid economic growth say that it
(a) produces an equitable distribution of income
(b) creates common property resources
(c) leads to higher living standards
(d) spreads the costs of development

■ **PROBLEMS**

1. The table below shows the quantity of labor (measured in hours) and the productivity of labor (measured in real GDP per hour) in a hypothetical economy in three different years.

Year	Quantity of labor	Productivity of labor	Real GDP
1	1000	$100	$_____
2	1000	105	_____
3	1100	105	_____

a. Compute the economy's real GDP in each of the 3 years and enter them in the table.
b. Between years 1 and 2, the quantity of labor remained constant, but

(1) the productivity of labor increased by _____%, and

(2) as a consequence, real GDP increased by ___%.
c. Between years 2 and 3, the productivity of labor remained constant, but

(1) the quantity of labor increased by _____%, and

(2) as a consequence, real GDP increased by _____%.
d. Between years 1 and 3

(1) real GDP increased by _____%, and
(2) this rate of increase is approximately equal to the

sum of the rates of increase in the _____

and the _____ of labor.

2. In the table below, indicate how many years it will take to double the standard of living (Years) in an economy given different annual rates of growth in labor productivity.

Productivity	Years
1.0%	_____
1.4	_____
1.8	_____
2.2	_____
2.6	_____
3.0	_____

What can you conclude about the importance of small changes in the growth rate of productivity for the standard of living?

3. In the graph below, show an increase in economic growth by using a hypothetical production possibilities curve. In the graph in the next column, show what that increase would mean in terms of the extended aggregate demand and aggregate supply models.

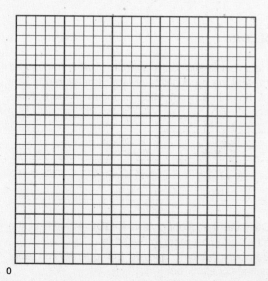

0

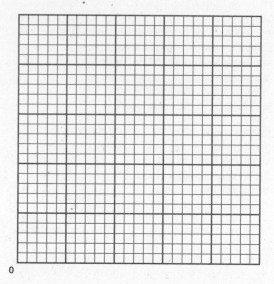

0

■ **SHORT ANSWER AND ESSAY QUESTIONS**

1. What is economic growth, and how is it measured?

2. What are the six basic ingredients of economic growth? What are the essential differences between the supply, demand, and efficiency factors?

3. How does economic growth affect production possibilities? What demand and efficiency assumptions are necessary to achieve maximum productive potential?

4. What is the relationship between the real GDP produced in any year and the quantity of labor employed and labor productivity?

5. What determines the number of hours worked each year?

6. Identify and describe the factors that determine labor productivity.

7. Describe how economic growth can be illustrated in an aggregate demand–aggregate supply framework. What has happened to aggregate demand compared to long-run aggregate supply when the price level and real domestic output both have increased?

8. What has been the growth record of the U.S. economy since 1950?

9. What have been the sources of the growth of the real output in the United States?

10. What changes have occurred in the size of the U.S. population and labor force since 1960? What factor has slowed the rate of growth of the former, and what factor has speeded the growth of the latter?

11. What is technological advance, and why are technological advance and capital formation closely related processes?

12. What is the relationship between investment and the stock of capital? What is the connection between increases in the capital stock and the rate of economic growth?

13. What increases the "quality" or human capital of labor? How is this quality usually measured? What are some of the problems with this path to improving the quality of the labor force?

14. Explain the relationship between productivity growth and the New Economy.

15. Discuss how the microchip and information technology contributed to the New Economy.

16. Describe at least four sources of increasing returns and economies of scale in the New Economy.

17. Identify and explain implications of the New Economy for economic growth.

18. Is the New Economy too good to be true? Present the skeptic's case.

19. What arguments are made against economic growth in the United States?

20. How can economic growth be defended? What are the reasons given to support this type of growth?

ANSWERS

Chapter 16 Economic Growth

FILL-IN QUESTIONS

1. increases, higher, more
2. *a.* quantity and quality of natural resources; *b.* quantity and quality of human resources; *c.* supply or stock of capital goods; *d.* technology (any order for *a–d*)
3. demand, efficiency
4. supply, right, may not
5. multiplied, hours of labor, worker-hour
6. employed, participation
7. increase, vertical, more
8. 3.5, 2.3
9. less
10. *a.* advance; *b.* capital, worker; *c.* education, training (either order); *d.* scale; *e.* allocation
11. investment, worker
12. public, private
13. human, education
14. economies of scale, improved resource allocation
15. environment, positive
16. increase, 47, 28
17. advances, increasing, increasing
18. faster, low
19. short-run, long-run
20. pollutes, does not, is not, greater, higher, incentives

TRUE–FALSE QUESTIONS

1. T, pp. 303–304	10. F, p. 305	19. F, p. 312
2. T, p. 303	11. F, p. 305	20. F, pp. 311–312
3. F, p. 303	12. F, p. 306	21. T, p. 312
4. F, p. 303	13. T, p. 307	22. T, pp. 312–313
5. T, pp. 303–304	14. T, pp. 307–308	23. T, p. 313
6. T, pp. 303–304	15. T, p. 309	24. T, p. 314
7. F, p. 304	16. T, p. 309	25. F, pp. 314–315
8. T, p. 304	17. F, pp. 309–310	
9. T, p. 304	18. T, pp. 310–311	

MULTIPLE-CHOICE QUESTIONS

1. d, p. 303	10. c, p. 306	19. d, pp. 309–310
2. c, p. 303	11. c, pp. 306–307	20. b, p. 312
3. a, p. 303	12. b, pp. 306–307	21. d, p. 312
4. a, p. 304	13. b, p. 308	22. b, p. 312
5. b, p. 304	14. b, pp. 307–308	23. c, pp. 312–314
6. c, p. 304	15. b, p. 309	24. d, p. 314
7. c, p. 304	16. d, p. 309	25. c, pp. 314–315
8. c, p. 305	17. c, p. 309	
9. d, p. 306	18. a, pp. 309–310	

PROBLEMS

1. *a.* 100,000, 105,000, 115,500; *b.* (1) 5, (2) 5; *c.* (1) 10, (2) 10; *d.* (1) 15.5, (2) quantity, productivity
2. 70, 50, 39, 31, 27, 23. Small changes make a large difference in the number of years it takes for the standard of living to double in an economy, especially at very low rates of growth in productivity.
3. See Figure 16.3 and Figure 16.4 in the text.

SHORT ANSWER AND ESSAY QUESTIONS

1. p. 303	8. pp. 306–307	15. p. 312
2. pp. 303	9. pp. 307–308	16. pp. 312–313
3. pp. 303–304	10. pp. 307–308	17. pp. 313–314
4. p. 304	11. pp. 308–309	18. p. 314
5. p. 304	12. p. 309	19. pp. 314–315
6. pp. 305–306	13. p. 309	20. p. 315
7. pp. 305–306	14. p. 311	

The Economics of Developing Countries

Note: This bonus Web chapter is available at the textbook Web site: **www.mcconnell17.com**.

This chapter looks at the critical problem of raising the standards of living in **developing countries** (DVCs) around the world. The development problems in these nations, especially the poorest ones, are extensive: low literacy rates, low levels of industrialization, high dependence on agriculture, rapid rates of population growth, and widespread poverty.

There is also a growing income gap between DVCs and **industrially advanced nations** (IACs). To close that gap, there needs to be more economic growth in the DVCs. Achieving that growth requires that the economic resource bases be expanded and that those resources be used efficiently. As you will discover from the chapter, DVCs trying to apply these principles face **obstacles** quite different from those that limit growth in the United States and other IACs. DVCs have many problems with natural, human, and capital resources and with technology, all of which combine to hinder economic growth. Certain social, cultural, and institutional factors also create a poor environment for economic development.

These obstacles do not mean that it is impossible to increase the living standards of DVCs. What they do indicate is that to encourage growth, DVCs must do things that do not need to be done in the United States or other IACs. Population pressures have to be managed, and there needs to be better use of labor resources. Steps must be taken to encourage capital investment. Governments must take an active role in promoting economic growth and limiting the public sector problems for economic development. Dramatic changes in social practices and institutions are required. If these and other actions are not taken, it may not be possible to reduce the major obstacles to growth and break the **vicious circle of poverty** in the DVCs.

No matter how successful DVCs are in overcoming these obstacles, they still will not be able to grow rapidly without more aid from IACs. This assistance can come in the form of lower trade barriers in IACs that would increase sales of products from DVCs to IACs. There can be more foreign aid in the form of government grants and loans to IACs. The banks, corporations, and other businesses in IACs can provide private capital in the form of loans or direct foreign investment in the building of new factories and businesses.

The final section of the chapter provides a fitting ending to the discussion of economic problems in developing nations. It focuses on specific policies to promote economic growth in DVCs and examines the issue from two sides. One side offers a set of policies from the perspective of DVCs, and the other side lists things IACs can do to foster economic growth in developing nations. You will have to decide after reading the chapter if any of these actions would be worthwhile.

■ **CHECKLIST**

When you have studied this chapter you should be able to

☐ Describe the extent of income inequality among nations.
☐ Give examples of industrially advanced nations (IACs) and developing countries (DVCs).
☐ Classify nations on the basis of three levels of income.
☐ Compare the effects of differences in economic growth in IACs and DVCs.
☐ Discuss the human realities of poverty in DVCs.
☐ Identify two basic paths for economic growth in DVCs.
☐ Describe natural resource problems in DVCs.
☐ Identify the three problems related to human resources that plague the poorest DVCs.
☐ Explain the limitations on economic growth that are created by population growth in DVCs.
☐ Compare the traditional and demographic transition views of population and economic growth in DVCs.
☐ Describe the conditions of unemployment and underemployment in DVCs.
☐ State reasons for low labor productivity in DVCs.
☐ Give three reasons for the emphasis on capital formation in DVCs.
☐ Identify obstacles to domestic capital formation through saving.
☐ List obstacles to domestic capital formation through investment.
☐ Explain why it is difficult to transfer technologies from IACs to DVCs.
☐ Identify three sociocultural factors that can potentially inhibit economic growth.
☐ Describe institutional obstacles to growth.
☐ Explain why poverty in poor nations is a vicious circle.
☐ List five ways in which governments in DVCs can play a positive role in breaking the vicious circle of poverty.

☐ Describe the problems with the public sector in fostering economic development.

☐ Identify the three ways IACs can help DVCs foster economic growth.

☐ Explain how reducing international trade barriers in IACs would help DVCs.

☐ Describe the two sources of foreign aid for DVCs.

☐ Give three criticisms of foreign aid to DVCs.

☐ Explain why foreign aid to DVCs has declined.

☐ Describe what groups in IACs provide private capital to DVCs.

☐ Discuss nine DVC policies for promoting economic growth.

☐ Explain five actions that IACs can take to encourage growth in DVCs.

☐ Discuss the natural and human causes of persistent famine in some African nations (Last Word).

■ **CHAPTER OUTLINE**

1. There is considerable **income inequality among nations.** The richest 20% of the world's population receives more than 80% of the world's income; the poorest 20% receives less than 2%.

a. The World Bank classifies countries into two main groups.

(1) **Industrially advanced countries (IACs)** are characterized by well-developed market economies that are based on large stocks of capital goods, advanced technology for production, and well-educated workers. Among the **high-income** nations are the United States, Japan, Canada, Australia, New Zealand, and most of the nations of western Europe. These countries averaged $32,040 per capita income in 2004.

(2) **Developing countries (DVCs)** are a diverse group of middle-income and low-income nations. **Middle-income** nations (e.g., Brazil, Iran, Poland, Russia, South Africa, and Thailand) have per capita incomes that range from $826 to $1065 and average incomes of about $2190. There are also **low-income** nations with per capita incomes of $825 or less and average incomes of $510. This group is dominated by India, Indonesia, and most of the sub-Saharan nations of Africa. These nations are not highly industrialized, are dependent on agriculture, and often have high rates of population growth and low rates of literacy. The low-income nations account for about 37% of the world's population.

b. There are major differences between the United States and DVCs. The GDP in the United States is more than twice the combined GDPs of all DVCs; the United States produces 31% of the world's output but has only 5% of the world's population.

c. There are disparities in the growth rates of nations, resulting in large income gaps. Some DVCs have been able to improve their economic conditions over time and become IACs. Other DVCs are now showing high rates of economic growth, and still others have experienced a decline in economic growth and standards of living. If growth rates were the same for high- and low-income nations, the gap in per capita income would widen because the income base is higher in high-income nations.

d. The human realities of extreme poverty are important. Compared with IACs, persons in DVCs have not only lower per capita incomes but also lower life expectancies, and DVCs have higher infant mortality, lower literacy rates, more of the labor force in agriculture, and fewer nonhuman sources of energy.

2. The paths to economic development for DVCs require that they (1) use their existing resources more efficiently and (2) expand their available supplies of resources. The physical, human, and socioeconomic conditions in these nations are the reasons why DVCs experience different rates of economic growth.

a. Many DVCs possess inadequate **natural resources.** This limited resource base is an obstacle to growth. The agricultural products that DVCs typically export are also subject to significant price variations on the world market, creating variations in national income.

b. There are problems with **human resources** in DVCs.

(1) DVCs tend to be overpopulated and have high rates of population growth.

(a) Those growing populations reduce DVCs' capacity to save, invest, and increase productivity. They also overuse land and natural resources, and the migration of rural workers to cities creates urban problems.

(b) There is a qualification to the view that a high rate of population growth or population density is a major cause of low incomes in DVCs. The **demographic transition view** holds that rising incomes will reduce birthrates and that large populations are a result of poverty, not a cause of it.

(2) DVCs often experience both unemployment and **underemployment,** which wastes labor resources.

(3) DVCs have low levels of labor productivity because of insufficient physical capital and lack of investment in human capital. There is also a **brain drain** as the more talented and skilled workers from DVCs go to IACs to seek better employment opportunities.

c. DVCs have inadequate amounts of **capital goods** and so find it difficult to accumulate capital.

(1) Domestic capital formation occurs through saving and investing. The potential for saving is low in many DVCs because those nations are too poor to save.

(2) There is also **capital flight** of saving from DVCs to more stable IACs.

(3) The investment obstacles include a lack of investors and entrepreneurs and a lack of incentives to invest in DVC economies.

(4) The **infrastructure** (stock of public capital goods) is also poor in many DVCs.

d. Technological advance is slow in DVCs. Although these nations might adopt the technologies of industrial nations, those technologies are not always appropriate for the resource endowments of DVCs, and so those countries must learn to develop and use their own technologies. Some advances can be achieved with *capital-saving technology* (which requires less use of other capital goods or resources) rather than *capital-using technology.*

    e. The **social, cultural, and institutional** factors in DVCs can be impediments to economic development, and there can be an intangible lack of the *will to develop* among individuals and leaders.

    (1) The sociocultural obstacles to growth include such factors as tribal or ethnic allegiances that reduce national unity, a caste or class system, and a *capricious universe view* that sees little correlation between individual actions and outcomes or results.

    (2) The institutional obstacles include problems with school systems and public services, weak tax systems, lack of control over spending by governments, and the need for *land reform* to reduce the concentration of land holdings among a few wealthy families.

3. In summary, DVCs face a *vicious circle of poverty.* They save little and therefore invest little in real and human capital; because they are poor and because they do not invest, their outputs per capita remain low and they remain poor. Even if the vicious circle were broken, a rapid increase in population would leave the standard of living unchanged.

4. There are differing views about the **role of government** in fostering economic growth in DVCs.

    a. The *positive* view holds that in the initial stages of economic development, government action is needed to help overcome major obstacles to growth by

    (1) providing law and order to achieve political stability;

    (2) stimulating entrepreneurship to encourage business formation;

    (3) improving the infrastructure through the provision of public goods that also make the private sector more productive;

    (4) using policies to force more saving and investment; and

    (5) changing the socioinstitutional climate through land reform and efforts to shift public attitudes.

    b. The *negative* view holds that there are problems and difficulties with using the public sector to promote growth. They include bureaucratic impediments, *corruption,* maladministration, and the importance of political objectives over economic goals. Central planning does not work because it restricts competition and individual incentives, which are important ingredients in the growth process.

5. There are several ways **IACs can help DVCs.**

    a. They can expand trade by lowering the **trade barriers** that prevent DVCs from selling their products in developed countries.

    b. They can provide **foreign aid** in the form of public loans and grants to help improve infrastructure or public goods.

    (1) This foreign aid can come directly from IAC governments.

    (2) The foreign aid can also come from international organizations such as the *World Bank,* which makes grants and loans for basic development projects, offers technical assistance, and serves as a lender of last resort to DVCs.

    (3) This foreign aid has been criticized because it increases dependency on IACs, expands bureaucracy in DVCs, and encourages corruption. For these reasons and because of the end of the cold war, foreign aid to DVCs declined during the 1990s; however, it has rebounded in recent years because of greater interest in reducing global poverty and the spending on the war on terrorism.

    c. DVCs can also receive flows of private capital from IACs. *Direct foreign investment* in new factories and businesses can come from banks, corporations, and financial investment companies, but such investment tends to be highly selective among nations.

6. There are several **policies for promoting growth** that DVCs and IACs might undertake. Both DVC and IAC perspectives are offered in this chapter.

    a. DVC policies for promoting growth include establishing the rule of law, opening economies to international trade, controlling population growth, encouraging direct foreign investment, building human capital, making peace with neighbors, establishing independent central banks, establishing realistic exchange-rate policies, and privatizing state industries.

    b. IAC policies for encouraging economic growth in DVCs include directing foreign aid to the poorest DVCs, reducing tariffs and import quotas, providing debt relief to DVCs, allowing more low-skilled immigration and discouraging brain drain, and limiting arms sales to DVCs.

7. (Last Word). Famines in Africa are caused by natural and human forces. The immediate cause of famine is drought. Other causes are more complex. Civil strife has torn many nations for decades. Population growth has outstripped food production in many nations. Ecological degradation has occurred in nations that use marginal land for crop production. There are also poor public policies such as overspending on armaments, underspending on agriculture, and price controls on agricultural commodities that reduce economic incentives. Some nations also have large external debts to service that require cuts in spending for health care, education, and infrastructure.

■ **HINTS AND TIPS**

1. This chapter offers a comprehensive look at the various factors affecting growth and economic development. Keep in mind that **no single factor** explains why some nations prosper and others remain poor. The chapter should give you insights into how natural, human, and capital resources together with government policies may influence a nation's economic development.

2. Several economic and demographic statistics for comparing rich and poor nations appear in the chapter's tables. You need not memorize the numbers, but you should try to get a sense of the magnitude of the differences between IACs and DVCs on several key indicators. To do this, ask yourself questions calling for **relative comparisons**. For example, how many times larger is average per capita income in IACs than in low-income DVCs? Answer: 63 times greater ($32,040/$510 = 63).

3. The chapter ends with **policies** for increasing economic growth in DVCs. Be sure to look at these policies from the perspective of both DVCs and IACs. Identify those that you think are most important and explain your reasoning.

■ IMPORTANT TERMS

industrially advanced
   countries (IACs)

developing countries
   (DVCs)

demographic
   transition view

underemployment

brain drain

capital flight

infrastructure

capital-saving technology

capital-using technology

will to develop

capricious universe view

land reform

vicious circle of poverty

corruption

World Bank

direct foreign investment

SELF-TEST

■ FILL-IN QUESTIONS

1. There is considerable income inequality among nations. The richest 20% of the world's population receives more than (40, 80) _____% of the world's income, while the poorest 20% of the world's population receives less than (2, 10) _____%. The poorest 60% of nations receives less than (6, 30) _____% of the world's income.

2. High-income nations can be classified as (industrially advanced, developing) _____ countries, or (IACs, DVCs) _____, and middle- or low-income nations as _____ countries, or (DVCs, IACs) _____.

3. IACs have a (higher, lower) _____ starting base for per capita income than DVCs, and so the same percentage growth rate for both IACs and DVCs means (an increase, a decrease) _____ in the absolute income gap.

4. Low per capita income in DVCs means that there are (lower, higher) _____ life expectancies, _____ adult literacy, a (lower, higher) _____ daily calorie supply, _____ energy consumption, and (lower, higher) _____ infant mortality.

5. The process for economic growth is the same for IACs and DVCs. It involves (less, more) _____ efficient use of existing resources and obtaining _____ productive resources.

6. The distribution of natural resources among DVCs is (even, uneven) _____; many DVCs lack vital natural resources. Although oil resources have been used for economic growth in (OPEC nations, DVCs) _____, IACs own or control much of the natural resources in _____. Also, exports of products from DVCs are subject to (small, large) _____ price fluctuations in the world market, and that tends to make DVCs' incomes (more, less) _____ stable.

7. In terms of human resources,

   a. many DVCs are (under-, over-) _____ populated and have (higher, lower) _____ population growth rates than IACs. Rapid population growth can cause per capita income to (increase, decrease) _____.

   b. In DVCs, many people are unable to find jobs, and so there is (underemployment, unemployment) _____, and many people are employed for fewer hours than they desire or work at odd jobs, and so there is _____.

   c. In DVCs, labor productivity is very (high, low) _____, partly because these countries have not been able to invest in (stocks and bonds, human capital) _____; when the best-trained workers leave DVCs to work in IACs, there is a (demographic transition, brain drain) _____ that contributes to the decline in skill levels and productivity.

8. Capital accumulation is critical to the development of DVCs. If there were more capital goods, that would improve (natural resources, labor productivity) _____ and help boost per capita output. An increase in capital goods is necessary because the (demand for, supply of) _____ arable land is limited. The process of capital formation is cumulative, investment increases the (output, natural resources) _____ of the economy, and this in turn makes it possible for the economy to save more and invest more in capital goods.

9. The formation of domestic capital requires that a nation save and invest.

   a. Saving is difficult in DVCs because of (high, low) _____ per capita income, and investment is difficult because of (many, few) _____ investors or entrepreneurs and (strong, weak) _____ incentives to invest. There is also the problem of private savings being transferred to IACs; this transfer is called

(brain drain, capital flight) _____.

b. Many DVCs do not have the infrastructure or

(private, public) _____ capital goods that are

necessary for productive _____ investment by businesses.

c. Nonfinancial (or in-kind) investment involves the transfer of surplus labor from (agriculture, industry)

_____ for the improvement of agricultural facilities or the infrastructure.

10. The technologies used in advanced industrial countries might be borrowed by and used in the DVCs, but

a. the technologies used in advanced countries are based

on a labor force that is (skilled, unskilled) _____,

labor that is relatively (abundant, scarce) _____,

and capital that is relatively _____, and

their technologies tend to be (labor, capital) _____ -using, while

b. the technologies required in developing countries must be based on a labor force that is (skilled, unskilled)

_____, labor that is relatively (abundant,

scarce) _____, and capital that is relatively

_____, and their technologies tend to be

(labor, capital) _____-using.

c. If technological advances make it possible to replace a worn-out plow that cost $10 when new with a new $5 plow, the technological advance is capital (-saving,

-using) _____.

11. Other obstacles to economic growth in DVCs include those dealing with problems of national unity, religion, and

customs, or (institutional, sociocultural) _____ problems, and those dealing with such issues as political corruption, poor school systems, and land reform, or

_____ problems.

12. In most DVCs, there is a vicious circle of poverty. Saving is low because the income per capita is (high, low)

_____, and because saving is low, investment

in real and human capital is _____. For this reason the productivity of labor and output (income) per

capita remain (high, low) _____.

13. List five ways in which government can play a positive role in fostering economic growth in DVCs, especially during the early phases of growth:

a. _____

b. _____

c. _____

d. _____

e. _____

14. Government involvement in the economy of DVCs can create public sector problems because government

bureaucracy can (foster, impede) _____ social and economic change, government planners can place too

much emphasis on (political, economic) _____

objectives, and there can be (good, poor) _____ administration and corruption.

15. Three major ways in which IACs can assist in the economic development of DVCs is by (increasing,

decreasing) _____ international trade barriers,

_____ foreign aid, and _____ the flow of private capital investment.

16. Direct foreign aid for DVCs generally comes from

individual nations in the form of (private, public) _____ loans, grants, and programs. It can also come from the

(Bank of America, World Bank) _____, which is supported by member nations. This organization is a

(first, last) _____ resort lending agency for

DVCs and provides (military, technical) _____ assistance for DVCs.

17. Foreign aid has been criticized in recent years because

it may (increase, decrease) _____ dependency in a nation instead of creating self-sustained growth, may

_____ government bureaucracy and control

over a nation's economy, and may _____ the misuse of funds or corruption. These criticisms and the

end of the cold war have led to a(n) _____ in the amount of foreign aid to DVCs.

18. There can also be private capital flows to DVCs in the

form of direct foreign (aid, investment) _____ from IAC firms, individuals, and commercial banks, and this has increased in recent years. The reason for this change is that many DVCs have reformed their economies

and adopted policies that (limit, encourage) _____

economic growth and _____ direct foreign investment. Nevertheless, the flow of private capital to DVCs is

(selective, widespread) _____ among nations.

19. DVCs can adopt policies to encourage economic

growth. They can (open, close) _____ economies to

international trade, (encourage, discourage) _____ direct foreign investment and the development of human

capital, and (expand, control) _____ population growth.

20. IACs can also adopt policies to help DVCs. They can

(raise, lower) _____ trade barriers, (encour-

age, discourage) _____ immigration of the brightest and best educated, and direct foreign aid to

(middle-income, low-income) _____ DVCs.

■ TRUE–FALSE QUESTIONS

Circle T if the statement is true, F if it is false.

1. The richest 20% of the world's population receives about 50% of the world's income, while the poorest 20% receives only about 20%.　　　　**T F**

2. Low-income developing countries typically have high unemployment, low literacy rates, rapid population growth, and a labor force committed to agricultural production.　　　　**T F**

3. The United States has about 5% of the world's population and produces about 31% of the world's output.　　　　**T F**

4. The absolute income gap between DVCs and industrially advanced countries has decreased over the last 30 years.　　　　**T F**

5. Economic growth in both IACs and DVCs requires using economic resources more efficiently and increasing the supplies of some of these resources.　　　　**T F**

6. It is impossible to achieve a high standard of living with a small supply of natural resources.　　　　**T F**

7. DVCs have low population densities and low population growth relative to IACs.　　　　**T F**

8. The demographic transition view of population growth is that rising incomes must first be achieved, and only then will slower population growth follow.　　　　**T F**

9. A major factor contributing to the high unemployment rates in urban areas of DVCs is the fact that the migration from rural areas to cities has greatly exceeded the growth of urban job opportunities.　　　　**T F**

10. Saving in DVCs accounts for a smaller percentage of domestic output than in IACs, and this is the chief reason total saving in DVCs is small.　　　　**T F**

11. Before private investment can be increased in DVCs, it is necessary to reduce the amount of investment in infrastructure.　　　　**T F**

12. Technological advances in DVCs will be made rapidly because the advances do not require pushing forward the frontiers of technological knowledge, and the technologies used in IACs can be transferred easily to all DVCs. **T F**

13. When technological advances are capital-saving, it is possible for an economy to increase its productivity without any *net* investment in capital goods.　　　　**T F**

14. A critical but intangible ingredient in economic development is the "will to develop."　　　　**T F**

15. The capricious universe view is that there is a strong correlation between individual effort and results.　　**T F**

16. Land reform is one of the institutional obstacles to economic growth in many developing countries.　　**T F**

17. The situation in which poor nations stay poor because they are poor is a description of the vicious circle of poverty.　　　　**T F**

18. The creation of an adequate infrastructure in a nation is primarily the responsibility of the private sector. **T F**

19. Governments always play a positive role in fostering the economic growth of DVCs.　　　　**T F**

20. One effective way in which IACs can help DVCs is to raise trade barriers so that DVCs become more self-sufficient.　　　　**T F**

21. The World Bank provides loans for basic development projects in DVCs.　　　　**T F**

22. Two reasons why foreign aid is viewed as harmful are that it tends to promote dependency and tends to generate government bureaucracy.　　　　**T F**

23. An example of direct foreign investment would be the building of an automobile parts factory by General Motors in Brazil.　　　　**T F**

24. In recent years, the flow of direct foreign investment to DVCs has significantly decreased.　　　　**T F**

25. One policy suggested for promoting economic growth in DVCs is the establishment of independent central banks (where they do not already exist) to keep inflation in check and control the money supply.　　　　**T F**

■ MULTIPLE-CHOICE QUESTIONS

Circle the letter that corresponds to the best answer.

1. Data on per capita income from the nations of the world indicate that there is considerable
  (a) income equality
  (b) income inequality
  (c) stability in the income growth
  (d) deterioration in incomes for most developing nations

2. Which nation would be considered a developing nation?
  (a) India
  (b) Italy
  (c) Japan
  (d) New Zealand

3. If the per capita income is $600 a year in a DVC and $12,000 in an IAC, then a 2% growth rate in each nation will increase the absolute income gap by
  (a) $120
  (b) $228
  (c) $240
  (d) $252

4. The poorest DVCs would probably exhibit high levels of
  (a) literacy
  (b) life expectancy
  (c) infant mortality
  (d) per capita energy consumption

5. The essential paths for economic growth in any nation are expanding the
  (a) size of the population and improving agriculture
  (b) role of government and providing jobs for the unemployed
  (c) supplies of resources and using existing resources more efficiently
  (d) amount of tax subsidies to businesses and tax credits for business investment

6. Based on the rule of 70, if the United States has an annual rate of population increase of 1% and a DVC has one of 2%, how many years will it take for the population to double in each nation?
  (a) 140 years for the United States and 70 years for the DVC
  (b) 35 years for the United States and 70 years for the DVC
  (c) 70 years for the United States and 35 years for the DVC
  (d) 70 years for the United States and 140 years for the DVC

7. Assume the total real output of a developing country increases from $100 billion to $115.5 billion while its population expands from 200 million to 210 million people. Real per capita income has increased by
  (a) $50
  (b) $100
  (c) $150
  (d) $200

8. An increase in the total output of consumer goods in a DVC may not increase the average standard of living because it may increase
  (a) capital flight
  (b) population growth
  (c) disguised unemployment
  (d) the quality of the labor force

9. Which best describes the unemployment found in DVCs?
  (a) the cyclical fluctuations in the nation's economy
  (b) the migration of agricultural workers from rural areas to seek jobs in urban areas
  (c) workers being laid off by large domestic or multinational corporations during periods of economic instability
  (d) the education and training of workers in the wrong types of jobs and for which there is little demand

10. Which is an obstacle to economic growth in DVCs?
  (a) the low demand for natural resources
  (b) the low supply of capital goods
  (c) the decline in the demographic transition
  (d) a fall in population growth

11. Which is a reason for placing special emphasis on capital accumulation in DVCs?
  (a) the flexible supply of arable land in DVCs
  (b) the high productivity of workers in DVCs
  (c) the high marginal benefits of capital goods
  (d) the greater opportunities for capital flight

12. Which is a factor that limits saving in DVCs?
  (a) The output of the economy is too low to permit a large volume of saving.
  (b) Those who do save make their savings available only to their families.
  (c) Governments control the banking system and set low interest rates.
  (d) There is an equal distribution of income in most nations.

13. When citizens of developing countries transfer savings to or invest savings in industrially advanced countries, this is referred to as
  (a) brain drain
  (b) capital flight
  (c) savings potential
  (d) in-kind investment

14. Which is a major obstacle to capital formation in DVCs?
  (a) lack of oil resources
  (b) lack of entrepreneurs
  (c) lack of government price supports for products
  (d) an excess of opportunities for financial investments

15. If it is cheaper to use a new fertilizer that is better adapted to a nation's topography, this is an example of
  (a) a capital-using technology
  (b) a capital-saving technology
  (c) capital consumption
  (d) private capital flows

16. Which is an example of infrastructure?
  (a) a farm
  (b) a steel plant
  (c) an electric power plant
  (d) a deposit in a financial institution

17. Which seems to be the most acute *institutional* problem that needs to be resolved by many DVCs?
  (a) development of strong labor unions
  (b) an increase in natural resources
  (c) the adoption of birth control
  (d) land reform

18. Which is a major positive role for government in the early stage of economic development?
  (a) providing an adequate infrastructure
  (b) conducting central economic planning
  (c) improving the efficiency of tax collection
  (d) creating marketing boards for export products

19. In recent years, many DVCs have come to realize that
  (a) there are few disadvantages from government involvement in economic development
  (b) entrepreneurship and economic incentives for individuals are necessary for economic development
  (c) the World Bank is an institutional barrier to economic growth
  (d) private capital is not essential for economic growth

20. Industrially advanced countries can best help DVCs by
(a) letting them raise tariffs and quotas to protect domestic markets
(b) reducing foreign grant aid but increasing loan aid
(c) increasing the flows of private capital
(d) increasing control over their capital markets

21. The major objective of the World Bank is to
(a) maximize its profits for its worldwide shareholders
(b) assist developing countries in achieving economic growth
(c) provide financial backing for the operation of the United Nations
(d) maintain stable exchange rates in the currencies of developing countries

22. A major criticism of foreign aid to developing nations is that it
(a) provides incentives for capital flight
(b) is capital-using rather than capital-saving
(c) encourages growth in government bureaucracy
(d) gives too much power and control to the World Bank

23. Which would be an example of direct foreign investment in DVCs?
(a) a low-interest loan from the U.S. government to Nigeria
(b) a grant from the World Bank to build a dam in Thailand
(c) the purchase of a computer business in Honduras by a U.S. firm
(d) a payment from a worker in the United States to a family in Iran

24. A suggested policy for DVCs to implement that promotes economic growth is
(a) reducing control of monetary policy by central banks
(b) obtaining more low-interest loans from the World Bank
(c) encouraging more direct foreign investment
(d) expanding state industries

25. Which is a suggested policy for industrially advanced countries to adopt to foster economic growth in DVCs?
(a) increased appreciation of currencies in DVCs
(b) increased debt relief in DVCs
(c) elimination of the International Monetary Fund
(d) elimination of the OPEC oil cartel

■ **PROBLEMS**

1. Suppose that the real per capita income in the average industrially advanced country is $8000 per year and in the average DVC it is $500 per year.
a. The gap between their standards of living is $_____ per year.
b. If GDP per capita were to grow at a rate of 5% during a year in both the industrially advanced country and the DVC,
(1) the standard of living in the IAC would rise to $_____ in a year;

(2) the standard of living in the DVC would rise to $_____ in a year; and
(3) the gap between their standards of living would (narrow, widen) _____ to $_____ in a year.

2. Although economic conditions are not identical in all DVCs, certain conditions are common to or typical of most of them. In the space after each of the following characteristics, indicate briefly the nature of this characteristic in many low-income DVCs.

a. Standard of living (per capita income): _____
b. Average life expectancy: _____
c. Extent of unemployment: _____
d. Literacy: _____
e. Technology: _____
f. Percentage of the population engaged in agriculture:

g. Size of the population relative to the land and capital available: _____
h. Birthrates and death rates: _____
i. Quality of the labor force: _____
j. Amount of capital equipment relative to the labor force: _____
k. Level of saving: _____
l. Incentive to invest: _____
m. Amount of infrastructure: _____
n. Extent of industrialization: _____
o. Size and quality of the entrepreneurial class and the supervisory class: _____
p. Per capita public expenditures for education and per capita energy consumption: _____
q. Per capita consumption of food: _____
r. Disease and malnutrition: _____

3. Suppose it takes a minimum of 5 units of food to keep a person alive for a year, the population can double itself every 10 years, and the food supply can increase every 10 years by an amount equal to what it was in the beginning (year 0).
a. Assume that both the population and the food supply grow at these rates. Complete the following table by computing the size of the population and the food supply in years 10 through 60.

Year	Food supply	Population
0	200	20
10	____	____
20	____	____
30	____	____
40	____	____
50	____	____
60	____	____

b. What happens to the relationship between the food supply and the population in the thirtieth year?

_____

_____

c. What would actually prevent the population from growing at this rate after the thirtieth year?

_____

_____

d. Assuming that the actual population growth in the years after the thirtieth does not outrun the food supply, what would be the size of the population in

(1) Year 40: _____

(2) Year 50: _____

(3) Year 60: _____

e. Explain why the standard of living failed to increase in the years after the thirtieth even though the food supply increased by 75% between years 30 and 60.

_____

_____

■ **SHORT ANSWER AND ESSAY QUESTIONS**

1. What is the degree of income inequality among nations around the world?

2. How do the overall levels of economic growth per capita and the rates of economic growth compare among rich nations and poor countries? Why does the income gap widen?

3. What are the human realities of poverty found in DVCs? (Use the socioeconomic indicators in Table 16W.1 on the Web site to contrast the quality of life in IACs and DVCs.)

4. Describe the basic paths of economic growth. Do these avenues differ for IACs and DVCs?

5. How would you describe the natural resource situation for DVCs? In what ways do price fluctuations affect DVC exports? Is a weak natural resource base an obstacle to economic growth?

6. Describe the implications of the high rate of growth in populations and its effects on the standard of living. Can the standard of living be raised merely by increasing the output of consumer goods in DVCs? What is the meaning of the cliché "the rich get richer and the poor get children," and how does it apply to DVCs?

7. Compare and contrast the traditional view of population and economic growth with the demographic transition view.

8. What is the distinction between unemployment and underemployment? How do these concepts apply to DVCs?

9. What are the reasons for the low level of labor productivity in DVCs?

10. How does the brain drain affect DVCs?

11. What are the reasons for placing special emphasis on capital accumulation as a means of promoting economic growth in DVCs?

12. Why is domestic capital accumulation difficult in DVCs? Answer in terms of both the saving side and the investment side of capital accumulation. Is there capital flight from DVCs?

13. In addition to the obstacles that limit domestic investment, what obstacles tend to limit the flow of foreign capital into DVCs? What role does infrastructure play in capital formation?

14. How might the DVCs improve their technology without engaging in slow and expensive research? Why might this be an inappropriate method of improving the technology used in the DVCs?

15. What is meant by the "will to develop"? How is it related to social and institutional change in DVCs?

16. Explain the vicious circle of poverty in DVCs. How does population growth make an escape from this vicious circle difficult?

17. Why is the role of government expected to be a positive one in the early phases of development in DVCs? What have been the problems with the involvement of government in economic development?

18. What are three ways in which IACs help DVCs?

19. How is it possible for the United States to assist DVCs without spending a penny on foreign aid? Is this type of aid sufficient to ensure rapid and substantial development in DVCs?

20. Discuss the World Bank in terms of its purposes, characteristics, sources of funds, promotion of private capital flows, and success. What are its affiliates and their purposes?

21. Discuss three criticisms of foreign aid to DVCs.

22. Describe the types of private capital flows to encourage economic growth in DVCs.

23. How have DVCs changed to accommodate encouragement of direct foreign investment? What is the problem with the selectivity of this type of investment?

24. Describe the variety of suggested policies that DVCs can adopt to promote economic growth.

25. Explain what IACs can do to assist DVCs in fostering economic growth.

ANSWERS

Chapter 16 Web The Economics of Developing Countries

FILL-IN QUESTIONS

1. 80, 2, 6
2. industrially advanced, IACs, developing, DVCs
3. higher, an increase
4. lower, lower, lower, lower, higher
5. more, more
6. uneven, OPEC nations, DVCs, large, less
7. *a.* over-, higher, decrease; *b.* unemployment, underemployment; *c.* low, human capital, brain drain
8. labor productivity, supply of, output
9. *a.* low, few, weak, capital flight; *b.* public, private; *c.* agriculture
10. *a.* skilled, scarce, abundant, capital; *b.* unskilled, abundant, scarce, labor; *c.* -saving
11. sociocultural, institutional
12. low, low, low
13. *a.* establishing effective law and order; *b.* encouraging entrepreneurship; *c.* improving the infrastructure; *d.* promoting saving and investment; *e.* dealing with the social-institutional obstacles (any order for *a–e*)
14. impede, political, poor
15. decreasing, increasing, increasing
16. public, World Bank, last, technical
17. increase, increase, increase, decrease
18. investment, encourage, encourage, selective
19. open, encourage, control
20. lower, discourage, low-income

Note: Page numbers for True-False, Multiple-Choice, and Short Answer and Essay Questions refer to Bonus Web Chapter 16.

TRUE–FALSE QUESTIONS

1. F, p. 2	10. F, p. 8	19. F, p. 12
2. T, p. 2	11. F, pp. 8–9	20. F, p. 13
3. T, p. 2	12. F, p. 9	21. T, p. 14
4. F, p. 2	13. T, p. 9	22. T, p. 14
5. T, p. 4	14. T, p. 10	23. T, p. 15
6. F, pp. 4–5	15. F, p. 10	24. F, p. 15
7. F, p. 5	16. T, p. 10	25. T, p. 17
8. T, p. 6	17. T, pp. 10–11	
9. T, p. 7	18. F, p. 12	

MULTIPLE-CHOICE QUESTIONS

1. b, pp. 1–2	10. b, pp. 7–8	19. b, p. 12
2. a, p. 2	11. c, p. 8	20. c, p. 14
3. b, p. 2	12. a, p. 8	21. b, p. 14
4. c, pp. 2, 4	13. b, p. 8	22. c, p. 14
5. c, p. 4	14. b, p. 8	23. c, p. 15
6. c, p. 5	15. b, p. 9	24. c, pp. 15–17
7. a, pp. 5–6	16. c, pp. 8–9	25. b, p. 18
8. b, pp. 5–6	17. d, p. 10	
9. b, p. 7	18. a, p. 12	

PROBLEMS

1. *a.* 7500; *b.* (1) 8400, (2) 525, (3) widen, 7875
2. *a.* low; *b.* short; *c.* widespread; *d.* low; *e.* primitive; *f.* large; *g.* large; *h.* high; *i.* poor; *j.* small; *k.* low; *l.* absent; *m.* small; *n.* small; *o.* small and poor; *p.* small; *q.* low; *r.* common
3. *a.* Food supply: 400, 600, 800, 1000, 1200, 1400; Population: 40, 80, 160, 320, 640, 1280; *b.* the food supply is just able to support the population; *c.* the inability of the food supply to support a population growing at this rate; *d.* (1) 200, (2) 240, (3) 280; *e.* the population increased as rapidly as the food supply

SHORT ANSWER AND ESSAY QUESTIONS

1. pp. 1–2	10. p. 7	19. pp. 13–14
2. p. 2	11. pp. 7–9	20. p. 14
3. pp. 2, 4	12. pp. 8–9	21. p. 14
4. p. 4	13. pp. 8–9	22. p. 15
5. pp. 4–5	14. p. 9	23. p. 15
6. pp. 5–6	15. p. 10	24. pp. 15–17
7. pp. 6–7	16. pp. 10–11	25. p. 18
8. p. 7	17. pp. 11–12	
9. p. 7	18. pp. 13–15	

CHAPTER 17

Disputes over Macro Theory and Policy

Now that you understand the basic theory and models of the macro economy, you are ready to learn about different perspectives on how the economy functions and the major disputes in macro theory and policy.

Economics has always been an arena in which conflicting theories and policies oppose each other. This field of intellectual combat, in major engagements, has seen Adam Smith do battle with the defenders of a regulated economy. It witnessed the opposition of Karl Marx to the orthodox economics of his day. In the 1930s, it saw John Maynard Keynes oppose the classical economists. Around the major engagements there have been countless minor skirmishes between opposing viewpoints. Out of these major and minor confrontations have emerged not winners and losers but the advancement of economic theory and the improvement of economic policy.

Chapter 17 sets the foundation for understanding the modern debates by comparing **classical economics** and **Keynesianism** in terms of macroeconomic theory. The now familiar aggregate demand–aggregate supply model is used to illustrate the classical view that aggregate supply is vertical and aggregate demand is relatively stable. Keynesians, however, saw aggregate supply as being horizontal (to full-employment output), viewed aggregate demand as highly unstable, and saw a need for government intervention to stabilize the macro economy.

The chapter then turns to the first of three major questions: **What causes macro instability in the economy?** Four perspectives on the issues are given. First, from the Keynesian-based *mainstream* view, this instability arises primarily from volatility in investment that shifts aggregate demand or from occasional shocks to aggregate supply.

Second, *monetarists* focus on the money supply and assume that the competitive market economy has a high degree of stability except when there is inappropriate monetary policy. The monetarist analysis is based on the equation of exchange and the assumption that the velocity of money is stable. Changes in the money supply therefore directly affect the level of nominal GDP. Third, *real-business-cycle* theorists see instability as coming from the aggregate supply side of the economy and from real factors that affect the long-term growth rather than from monetary factors that affect aggregate demand. Fourth, some economists think that macroeconomic instability is the result of *coordination failures* that do not permit people to act jointly to determine the optimal level of output and that the equilibrium in the economy changes as expectations change.

The next question the chapter discusses is: **Does the economy self-correct its macro instability?** The view of new classical economics is that internal mechanisms in the economy allow it to self-correct. The two variants of this new classical perspective are based on *monetarism* and the *rational expectations theory (RET)*. Monetarists think the economy will self-correct to its long-run level of output, although there can be short-run changes in the price level and real output. Rational expectations theory suggests that the self-correction process is quick and does not change the price level or real output except when there are price-level surprises.

By contrast, mainstream economists contend that the downward inflexibility of wages limits the self-correction mechanisms in the economy. Several explanations are offered for this inflexibility. There can be long-term wage contracts that support wages. Firms may also pay an efficiency wage to encourage work effort, reduce turnover, and prevent shirking. Firms may also be concerned about maintaining the support and teamwork of key workers (insiders), and so they do not cut wages even when other workers (outsiders) might be willing to accept a lower wage.

The different perspectives on macro instability and self-correction set the stage for a discussion of the third and final question: **Should the macro economy be guided by policy rules or discretion?** To restrict monetary policy, monetarists and rational expectations economists call for a monetary rule that would have monetary authorities allow the money supply to grow in proportion to the long-term growth in the productive capacity of the economy. Both monetarists and rational expectations economists also oppose the use of fiscal policy, and a few call for a balanced-budget requirement to limit the use of discretionary fiscal policy.

Mainstream economists see value in discretionary monetary and fiscal policies. They suggest that a monetary rule would be ineffective in achieving growth and would destabilize the economy. A balanced-budget requirement would also have a pro-cyclical effect that would reinforce recessionary or inflationary tendencies in the economy. And since government has taken a more active role in the economy, the historical record shows that discretionary monetary and fiscal actions have reduced macro instability.

As was the case in the past, macroeconomic theory and policy have changed because of the debates among economists. The disputes among mainstream economists, monetarists, rational expectationists, and real-business-cycle theorists have produced new insights into the way the macro economy operates. In particular, it is now recognized that "money matters" and that the money supply has a significant effect on the economy. More attention is also being given to the influence of people's expectations on policy and coordination failures in explaining macroeconomic events. The disputes in macroeconomics in the last half-century have forced economists to reconsider previous conclusions and have led to the incorporation of new ideas about macro theory and policy into mainstream thinking.

■ **CHECKLIST**

When you have studied this chapter you should be able to

☐ Compare and contrast the classical and Keynesian views of the aggregate demand curve and the aggregate supply curve.

☐ Describe the mainstream view of stability in the macro economy and the two potential sources of instability.

☐ Explain the monetarist view of stability in the macro economy.

☐ Write the equation of exchange and define each of the four terms in the equation.

☐ Explain why monetarists think the velocity of money is relatively stable.

☐ Write a brief scenario that explains what monetarists believe will happen to change the nominal GDP and what will happen to *V* (velocity of money) when *M* (money supply) is increased.

☐ Discuss the monetary causes of instability in the macro economy.

☐ Describe the real-business-cycle view of stability in the macro economy.

☐ Give noneconomic and macroeconomic examples of the coordination failures view of stability in the macro economy.

☐ Use a graph to explain the new classical view of self-correction in the macro economy.

☐ Discuss the differences between the monetarist and rational expectations views on the speed of adjustment for self-correction in the macro economy.

☐ State the two basic assumptions of the rational expectations theory (RET).

☐ Use a graph to explain how RET views unanticipated and fully anticipated changes in the price level.

☐ Describe the mainstream view of self-correction in the macro economy.

☐ Give two reasons why there may be downward wage inflexibility.

☐ State three reasons why a higher wage may result in greater efficiency.

☐ Use ideas from the insider–outsider theory to explain the downward inflexibility of wages.

☐ State why monetarists think there should be a monetary rule and illustrate their rationale by using aggregate demand and aggregate supply models.

☐ Describe how monetarists and new classical economists view the effectiveness of fiscal policy.

☐ Offer a mainstream defense of a discretionary stabilization policy and a critique of a monetary rule and balanced-budget requirement.

☐ Describe the possible reasons for increased stability in the macro economy in the last half-century.

☐ Summarize the three alternative views on issues affecting the macro economy.

☐ Explain the purpose and components of the Taylor rule (Last Word).

■ **CHAPTER OUTLINE**

1. Classical economics and **Keynesian economics** can be compared by examining their aggregate demand–aggregate supply models of the economy.

a. In the ***classical view*** (model),

(1) the aggregate supply curve is *vertical* at the economy's full-employment output, and a decrease in aggregate demand will lower the equilibrium price level and have no effect on the real output (or employment) in the economy because of Say's law and flexible, responsive prices and wages.

(2) the aggregate demand curve slopes downward because (with a fixed money supply in the economy) a fall in the price level increases the purchasing power of money and enables consumers and business firms to purchase a larger real output. Aggregate demand will be reasonably stable if the nation's monetary authorities maintain a constant supply of money to accommodate long-term growth.

b. In the ***Keynesian view*** (model),

(1) the aggregate supply curve is *horizontal* at the current price level, and a decrease in aggregate demand will lower the real output (and employment) in the economy and have no effect on the equilibrium price level because of the downward inflexibility of prices and wages.

(2) aggregate demand is viewed as being *unstable* over time, even if the supply of money is held constant, partly because of fluctuations in investment spending. A decline in aggregate demand decreases real domestic output but has no effect on the price level, thus causing output to stay permanently below the full-employment level.

2. There are four different views among economists on **instability** in the macro economy.

a. The **mainstream view** is Keynesian-based and holds that instability in the economy arises from

(1) the volatility in investment spending that makes aggregate demand unstable and

(2) occasional aggregate supply shocks which cause cost-push inflation and recession.

b. ***Monetarism*** focuses on the money supply. Monetarists think markets are highly competitive and that government intervention destabilizes the economy.

(1) In monetarism, the ***equation of exchange*** is $MV = PQ$, where *M* is the money supply, *V* is the ***velocity*** of money, *P* is the price level, and *Q* is the quantity of goods and services produced.

(2) Monetarists think that velocity is relatively stable or that the quantity of money demanded is a stable percentage of GDP (GDP/*M* is constant). If velocity

is stable, there is a predictable relationship between *M* and nominal GDP (= *PQ*). An increase in *M* will leave firms and households with more money than they wish to have, and so they will increase spending and boost aggregate demand. This causes nominal GDP and the amount of money they wish to hold to rise until the demand for money is equal to *M* and nominal GDP/*M* = *V*.

(3) Monetarists view macroeconomic instability as being a result of inappropriate monetary policy. An increase in the money supply will increase aggregate demand, output, and the price level; it will also reduce unemployment. Eventually, nominal wages will rise to restore real wages and real output, and the unemployment rate falls back to its natural level at long-run aggregate supply.

c. *Real-business-cycle theory* sees macroeconomic instability as being caused by real factors that influence aggregate supply instead of monetary factors that cause shifts in aggregate demand. Changes in technology and resources will affect productivity and thus the long-run growth rate of aggregate supply.

d. A fourth view of instability in the macro economy attributes the reasons to *coordination failures.* These failures occur when people are not able to coordinate their actions to achieve an optimal equilibrium. A self-fulfilling prophecy can lead to a recession because if households and firms expect it, they individually cut back on spending and employment. If, however, they were to act jointly, they could take actions to counter the recessionary expectations and achieve an optimal equilibrium.

3. Economists also debate the issue of whether the macro economy self-corrects.

a. *New classical economics,* which is based on monetarism and rational expectations theory, says the economy may deviate from full-employment output, but it eventually returns to that output level because there are self-corrective mechanisms in the economy.

(1) Graphically, if aggregate demand increases, it temporarily raises real output and the price level. Nominal wages rise and productivity falls, and so short-run aggregate supply decreases, thus bringing the economy back to its long-run output level.

(2) There is disagreement about the speed of adjustment. The monetarists adopt the adaptive expectations view that there will be a slower, temporary change in output but that in the long run it will return to its natural level. Other new classical economists adopt the *rational expectations theory* (RET) view that there will be a rapid adjustment with little or no change in output. RET is based on two assumptions: People understand how the economy works so that they quickly anticipate the effect on the economy of an economic event, and all markets in the economy are so competitive that equilibrium prices and quantities quickly adjust to changes in policy.

(3) In RET, unanticipated price-level changes, called *price-level surprises*, cause short-run changes in real output because they cause misperceptions about the economy among workers and firms.

(4) In RET, fully anticipated price-level changes do not change real output even in the short run because workers and firms anticipate and counteract the effects of the changes.

b. The **mainstream view** of self-correction suggests that prices and wages may be inflexible downward in the economy.

(1) Graphically, a decrease in aggregate demand will decrease real output but not the price level because nominal wages will not decline and cause the short-run aggregate supply curve to shift to the right.

(2) Downward wage inflexibility arises primarily because of wage contracts and the legal minimum wage, but it also may result from efficiency wages and insider–outsider relationships, according to new Keynesian economics.

(3) An *efficiency wage* minimizes a firm's labor cost per unit of output but may be higher than the market wage. This higher wage may result in greater efficiency because it stimulates greater work effort, requires lower supervision costs, and reduces job turnover.

(4) *Insider–outsider theory* suggests that relationships may also produce downward wage inflexibility. During a recession, outsiders (who are less essential to the firm) may try to bid down wages to keep their jobs, but the firm may not lower wages because it does not want to alienate insiders (who are more essential to the firm) and disrupt the cooperative environment the firm needs for production.

4. The debates over macro policy also focus on the need for **policy rules or discretion.**

a. Monetarists and new classical economists argue for policy rules to reduce government intervention in the economy. They believe this intervention causes macroeconomic instability.

(1) In regard to monetary policy, monetarists such as Milton Friedman have proposed a *monetary rule* that the money supply be increased at the same annual rate as the potential annual rate of increase in the real GDP. A monetary rule would shift aggregate demand rightward to match a shift in the long-run aggregate supply curve that occurs because of economic growth, thus keeping the price level stable over time. More recently, economists have advocated inflation targeting as an alternative to a Friedman-type monetary rule.

(2) Monetarists and new classical economists question the value of fiscal policy, and some would like to see a balanced Federal budget over time. An expansionist fiscal policy will tend to crowd out investment and cause only a temporary increase in output. RET economists also think that fiscal policy is ineffective and that people will anticipate it and their acts will counteract its intended effects.

b. Mainstream economists think that discretionary fiscal and monetary policy can be effective and are opposed to a monetary rule and a balanced-budget requirement.

(1) They see the velocity of money as relatively unstable and a loose link between changes in the money

supply and aggregate demand. This means that a monetary rule might produce too great a shift in aggregate demand (and demand-pull inflation) or too small a shift (and deflation) to match the shift in aggregate supply. Such a rule would contribute to price instability, not price stability.

(2) They support the use of fiscal policy during a recession or to counter growing inflation. Fiscal policy, however, should be reserved for situations in which monetary policy is relatively ineffective. They also oppose a balanced-budget amendment because its effects would be pro-cyclical rather than countercyclical and would reinforce recessionary or inflationary tendencies.

c. Mainstream economists also note that there has been greater stability in the macro economy since 1946, when discretionary monetary and fiscal policies began to be used more actively to moderate the effects of the business cycle.

5. The **disputes in macroeconomics** have led to the incorporation of several ideas from monetarism and rational expectations theories into mainstream thinking about macroeconomics. First, monetarists have gotten mainstream economists to recognize that changes in the money supply are important in explaining long-lasting and rapid inflation. Second, mainstream economists now recognize that expectations matter because of arguments from the rational expectations theory and theories about coordination failures in the economy. There will be more price stability, full employment, and economic growth if government can create reliable expectations of those outcomes for households and businesses. In short, macroeconomics continues to develop. Table 17.1 summarizes the three alternative views of macroeconomics.

6. (Last Word). The Taylor rule specifies what actions the Fed should take in changing the Federal funds rate given changes in real GDP and inflation. This monetary rule has three parts: (a) If real GDP rises 1% above potential GDP, then the Fed should raise the Federal funds rate .5 percentage point; (b) if inflation rises by 1 percentage point above its target of 2%, then the Fed should raise the Federal funds rate by .5 percentage point; and (c) when real GDP equals potential GDP and inflation is equal to its 2% target, the Federal funds rate should stay at 4% to give a real interest rate of 2%.

■ **HINTS AND TIPS**

1. This chapter may appear complex because many alternative viewpoints are presented. To simplify matters, first focus on the three questions that the chapter addresses: What causes macro instability in the economy? Does the economy self-correct? Should policymakers use rules or discretion? For each question, identify how different types of economists answer it.

2. Review the discussions of aggregate demand and aggregate supply in Chapters 10 and 15 as preparation for the comparison of alternative views of the macro economy presented in this chapter.

3. Monetarist and mainstream views of the macro economy are two ways of looking at the same thing. The similarities can best be seen in equations in nominal form. The monetarist equation of exchange is $MV = PQ$. The Keynesian-based mainstream equation is $C_a + I_g + X_n + G = GDP$. The MV term is the monetarist expression for the mainstream equilibrium $C_a + I_g + X_n + G$. The PQ term is the monetarist expression for GDP. Monetarists place more emphasis on the role of money and assume that velocity is relatively stable. Mainstream economists place more emphasis on the instability caused by investment spending and influences on GDP from consumption, net exports, and government spending.

■ **IMPORTANT TERMS**

classical view	rational expectations theory
Keynesian view	new classical economics
monetarism	price-level surprises
equation of exchange	efficiency wage
velocity	insider–outsider theory
real-business-cycle theory	monetary rule
coordination failures	

SELF-TEST

■ **FILL-IN QUESTIONS**

1. The aggregate supply curve of the classical economists is (horizontal, vertical) _____, and the aggregate supply curve of Keynesian economists is _____ up to the full-employment level of output. Therefore, a decrease in aggregate demand will have no effect on price level and will decrease output and employment in the (classical, Keynesian) _____ model, but a decrease in aggregate demand will decrease the price level and have no effect on output and employment in the _____ model.

2. In the classical way of thinking, changes in the money supply shift the aggregate (demand, supply) _____ curve. If the money supply increases, then the curve will (increase, decrease) _____, and if the money supply decreases, then the curve will _____. If the nation's monetary authorities maintain a constant supply of money, this curve will be (stable, unstable) _____.

3. From the Keynesian perspective, aggregate demand is (stable, unstable) _____ even if there are no changes in the supply of money, largely because of the volatility in (investment, government) _____ spending.

4. The mainstream view is that macro instability is caused by changes in investment spending that shift the aggregate (demand, supply) _____ curve. If it increases too rapidly, then (inflation, recession) _____ can occur, and if it decreases, then the economy can experience _____. Occasionally, adverse aggregate (demand, supply) _____ shocks also cause instability.

5. Monetarists argue that capitalism is inherently (stable, unstable) _____ because most of its markets are (competitive, noncompetitive) _____. They believe that government intervention in the economy has contributed to macroeconomic (stability, instability) _____ and has promoted (flexibility, inflexibility) _____ in wages.

6. The basic equation of the monetarists is _____ _____. Indicate what each of the following four letters in the equation represents:

    a. M: _____

    b. V: _____

    c. P: _____

    d. Q: _____

7. Monetarists believe that V is relatively (stable, unstable) _____ because people have a _____ desire to hold money relative to holding other financial and real assets or for making purchases. The amount of money people will want to hold will depend on the level of (real, nominal) _____ GDP.

8. An increase in M, to the monetarist's way of thinking, will leave the public with (more, less) _____ money than it wishes to have, inducing the public to (increase, decrease) _____ its spending for consumer and capital goods, which will result in a(n) _____ in aggregate demand and nominal GDP until nominal GDP equals MV.

9. Monetarists believe that the most significant cause of macroeconomic instability has been inappropriate (fiscal, monetary) _____ policy. Too rapid increases in M cause (recession, inflation) _____; insufficient growth of M causes _____.

10. The theory that changes in resource availability and technology (real factors), which alter productivity, are the main causes of instability in the macro economy is held by (real-business-cycle, rational expectations) _____ economists. In this theory, shifts in the economy's long-run aggregate (demand, supply) _____ curve change real output. As a consequence, money demand and money supply change, shifting the aggregate demand curve in the (opposite, same) _____ direction as the initial change in long-run aggregate supply. Real output thus can change (with, without) _____ a change in the price level.

11. A coordination failure is said to occur when people (do, do not) _____ reach a mutually beneficial equilibrium because they lack some way to coordinate their actions. In this view, there is (are) (one, a number of) _____ equilibrium position(s) in the economy. Macroeconomic instability is the result of changes in (the money supply, expectations) _____ that result in changing the equilibrium position(s).

12. Monetarists and rational expectations economists view the economy as (capable, incapable) _____ of self-correction when it deviates from the full-employment level of real output. Monetarists suggest that this adjustment occurs (gradually, rapidly) _____, and rational expectations economists argue that it occurs _____.

13. Rational expectations theory assumes that with sufficient information, people's beliefs about future economic outcomes (are, are not) _____ accurate reflections of the likelihood of those outcomes occurring. It also assumes that markets are highly competitive, meaning that prices and wages are (flexible, inflexible) _____.

14. In rational expectations theory, changes in aggregate demand that change the price level and real output are (anticipated, unanticipated) _____, whereas changes in aggregate demand that change only the price level and not real output are _____.

15. The view of mainstream economists is that many prices and wages are (flexible, inflexible) _____ downward for (short, long) _____ periods of time. This situation (increases, decreases) _____ the ability of the economy to self-correct automatically for deviations from full-employment output.

16. A higher wage can result in more efficiency because it results in (greater, less) _____ work effort, supervision costs that are (lower, higher) _____, and (more, less) _____ turnover in jobs. Efficiency wages (increase, decrease) _____ the downward inflexibility of wages because they make firms more reluctant to cut wages when aggregate demand declines.

17. Monetarists and rational expectations economists support a monetary rule because they believe that discretionary monetary policy tends to (stabilize, destabilize) _____ the economy. With this rule the money supply would be increased at a rate (greater than, less than, equal to) _____ the long-run growth of potential GDP; graphically, this can be shown by a shift in aggregate demand that would be _____ the shift in long-run aggregate supply resulting from economic growth.

18. Proponents of the rational expectations theory contend that discretionary monetary policy is (effective, ineffective) _____ and, like monetarists, favor (rules, discretion) _____. When considering discretionary fiscal policy, most monetarists and RET economists (do, do not) _____ advocate its use.

19. Mainstream economists (support, oppose) _____ a monetary rule and a balanced-budget requirement. They view discretionary monetary policy as (effective, ineffective) _____ and think discretionary fiscal policy is _____ but should be held in reserve for when monetary policy works too slowly. They say the use of discretionary monetary and fiscal policies since 1950 has produced (more, less) _____ stability in the macro economy.

20. Many ideas from alternative views of the macro economy have been absorbed into mainstream thinking about macroeconomics. There is more recognition that excessive growth of the money supply is a major cause of (recession, inflation) _____ and that expectations and coordination failures are (important, unimportant) _____ in the formulation of government policies for price stability, unemployment, and economic growth.

■ **TRUE–FALSE QUESTIONS**

Circle T if the statement is true, F if it is false.

1. The classical view is that the aggregate supply curve is vertical. **T F**

2. Classical economists consider the aggregate demand curve to be unstable. **T F**

3. Keynesians think that the aggregate supply curve is horizontal (to full-employment output). **T F**

4. Keynesians suggest that full employment is the norm in the economy. **T F**

5. The mainstream view is that macro instability is caused by the volatility of investment spending, which shifts the aggregate demand curve. **T F**

6. Monetarists argue that the market system would provide for macroeconomic stability if it were not for government interference in the economy. **T F**

7. In the equation of exchange, the left side, *MV,* represents the total amount received by sellers of output, and the right side, *PQ,* represents the total amount spent by purchasers of that output. **T F**

8. Monetarists argue that *V* in the equation of exchange is relatively stable and that a change in *M* will bring about a direct and proportional change in *PQ.* **T F**

9. Most monetarists believe that an increase in the money supply has no effect on real output and employment in the short run. **T F**

10. In the monetarist view, the only cause of the Great Depression was the decline in investment spending. **T F**

11. Real-business-cycle theory views changes in resource availability and technology, which alter productivity, as the main cause of macroeconomic instability. **T F**

12. In the real-business-cycle theory, real output changes only with a change in the price level. **T F**

13. A coordination failure is said to occur when people do not reach a mutually beneficial equilibrium because they lack some way to coordinate their actions to achieve it. **T F**

14. People's expectations have no effect on coordination failures. **T F**

15. New classical economists see the economy as automatically correcting itself when disturbed from its full-employment level of real output. **T F**

16. The rational expectations theory assumes that both product and resource markets are uncompetitive and wages and prices are inflexible. **T F**

17. In the rational expectations theory, a fully anticipated price-level change results in a change in real output. **T F**

18. Mainstream economists contend that many wages and prices are inflexible downward. **T F**

19. An efficiency wage is a below-market wage that spurs greater work effort and gives the firm more profits because of lower wage costs. **T F**

20. Insider–outsider theory offers one explanation for the downward inflexibility of wages in the economy. **T F**

21. Monetarists believe that a monetary rule would reduce instability in the macro economy. **T F**

22. Rational expectations economists argue that monetary policy should be left to the discretion of government.   **T   F**

23. Monetarists support the use of fiscal policy, especially as a means of controlling inflation.   **T   F**

24. Mainstream economists believe that discretionary monetary policy is an effective tool for stabilizing the economy.   **T   F**

25. The mainstream view of the economy since 1950 holds that the economy has become inherently less stable because of the use of fiscal policy.   **T   F**

■ MULTIPLE-CHOICE QUESTIONS

Circle the letter that corresponds to the best answer.

1. Classical economists suggest that full employment is
 (a) best achieved through government interventions
 (b) not possible in an unstable market economy
 (c) inversely related to the price level
 (d) the norm in a market economy

2. The aggregate supply curve of classical economists
 (a) is vertical
 (b) is horizontal
 (c) slopes upward
 (d) slopes downward

3. Classical theory concludes that the production behavior of firms will not change when the price level decreases because input costs will
 (a) rise along with product prices to leave real profits and output unchanged
 (b) fall along with product prices to leave real profits and output unchanged
 (c) fall, but product prices will rise, offsetting any change in real profits or output
 (d) rise, but product prices will rise, offsetting any change in real profits or output

4. In classical economics, a decrease in aggregate demand results in
 (a) a decrease in both the price level and domestic output
 (b) a decrease in the price level and no change in domestic output
 (c) no change in the price level and a decrease in domestic output
 (d) no change in either the price level or domestic output

5. The aggregate supply curve in the Keynesian model is
 (a) vertical at the full-employment output level
 (b) horizontal to the full-employment output level
 (c) positively sloped to the full-employment output level
 (d) negatively sloped to the full-employment output level

6. In the Keynesian model, a decrease in aggregate demand results in
 (a) a decrease in both the price level and domestic output
 (b) a decrease in the price level and no change in domestic output
 (c) no change in the price level and a decrease in domestic output
 (d) no change in either the price level or domestic output

7. The mainstream view of the economy holds that
 (a) government intervention in the economy is not desirable
 (b) product and labor markets are highly competitive and flexible
 (c) changes in investment spending lead to changes in aggregate demand
 (d) economic growth is best achieved through implementation of a monetary rule

8. In the monetarist perspective
 (a) discretionary monetary policy is the most effective way to moderate swings in the business cycle
 (b) government policies have reduced macroeconomic stability
 (c) macroeconomic stability results from adverse aggregate supply shocks
 (d) markets in a capitalistic economy are largely noncompetitive

9. Which is the equation of exchange?
 (a) $PQ/M + V = GDP$
 (b) $V = M + PQ$
 (c) $MV = PQ$
 (d) $V + I_g + M = GDP$

10. In the equation of exchange, if V is stable, an increase in M will necessarily increase
 (a) the demand for money
 (b) government spending
 (c) nominal GDP
 (d) velocity

11. When nominal gross domestic product (GDP) is divided by the money supply (M), you obtain the
 (a) velocity of money
 (b) monetary multiplier
 (c) equation of exchange
 (d) monetary rule

12. Monetarists argue that the amount of money the public will want to hold depends primarily on the level of
 (a) nominal GDP
 (b) investment
 (c) taxes
 (d) prices

13. Real-business-cycle theory suggests that
 (a) velocity changes gradually and predictably; thus, it is able to accommodate the long-run changes in nominal GDP
 (b) the volatility of investment is the main cause of the economy's instability
 (c) inappropriate monetary policy is the single most important cause of macroeconomic instability
 (d) changes in technology and resources affect productivity and thus the long-run growth of aggregate supply

14. In the real-business-cycle theory, if the long-run aggregate supply increased, then aggregate demand would increase by
(a) an equal amount, and so real output and the price level would increase
(b) less than an equal amount, and so real output would increase and the price level would decrease
(c) greater than an equal amount, and so real output and the price level would increase
(d) an equal amount, and so real output would increase and the price level would be unchanged

15. If aggregate demand declined and the economy experienced a recession due to a self-fulfilling prophecy, this would be an example of
(a) real-business-cycle theory
(b) insider–outsider theory
(c) a coordination failure
(d) a change in velocity

16. In the new classical view, when the economy diverges from its full-employment output,
(a) internal mechanisms within the economy automatically return it to its full-employment output
(b) discretionary monetary policy is needed to return it to its full-employment output
(c) discretionary fiscal policy is needed to return it to its full-employment output
(d) the adoption of an efficiency wage in the economy will return it to its full-employment output

17. The differing views about the speed of adjustment for self-correction in the economy suggest that
(a) monetarists think it would be gradual, and rational expectations economists think it would be quick
(b) monetarists think it would be quick, and rational expectations economists think it would be gradual
(c) monetarists and mainstream economists think it would be quick
(d) real-business-cycle theorists and rational expectations economists think it would be gradual

18. Proponents of the rational expectations theory argue that people
(a) are not as rational as monetarists assume them to be
(b) make forecasts that are based on poor information, causing economic policy to be driven by self-fulfilling prophecy
(c) form beliefs about future economic outcomes that accurately reflect the likelihood that those outcomes will occur
(d) do not respond quickly to changes in wages and prices, causing a misallocation of economic resources in the economy

19. In the rational expectations theory, a temporary change in real output would result from a
(a) fully anticipated price-level change
(b) downward wage inflexibility
(c) coordination failure
(d) price-level surprise

20. The conclusion mainstream economists draw about downward price and wage inflexibility is that
(a) the effects can be reversed relatively quickly
(b) efficiency wages do not contribute to the problem
(c) the economy can be mired in recession for long periods
(d) wage and price controls are needed to counteract the situation

21. According to mainstream economists, which of the following contributes to the downward inflexibility of wages?
(a) price-level surprises
(b) insider–outsider relationships
(c) adverse aggregate supply shocks
(d) inadequate investment spending

22. The rule suggested by monetarists is that the money supply should be increased at the same rate as the
(a) price level
(b) interest rate
(c) velocity of money
(d) potential growth in real GDP

23. To stabilize the economy, monetarist and rational expectations economists advocate
(a) the use of price-level surprises and the adoption of an efficiency wage
(b) a monetary rule and a balanced-budget requirement
(c) the use of discretionary fiscal policy instead of discretionary monetary policy
(d) the use of discretionary monetary policy instead of discretionary fiscal policy

24. Mainstream economists support
(a) increasing the money supply at a constant rate
(b) eliminating insider–outsider relationships in business
(c) the use of discretionary monetary and fiscal policies
(d) a balanced-budget requirement and a monetary rule

25. Which of the following would be an idea from monetarism that has been absorbed into mainstream macroeconomics?
(a) how changes in investment spending change aggregate demand
(b) the importance of money and the money supply in the economy
(c) using discretion rather than rules for guiding economic policy
(d) building the macro foundations for microeconomics

■ **PROBLEMS**

1. Assume that you are a monetarist in this problem and that V is stable and equal to 4. In the following table is the aggregate supply schedule: the real output Q which producers will offer for sale at seven different price levels P.

P	Q	PQ	MV
$1.00	100	$_____	$_____
2.00	110	_____	_____
3.00	120	_____	_____
4.00	130	_____	_____
5.00	140	_____	_____
6.00	150	_____	_____
7.00	160	_____	_____

a. Compute and enter in the table the seven values of **PQ**.

b. Assume **M** is $90. Enter the values of **MV** on each of the seven lines in the table. The equilibrium

(1) nominal domestic output (**PQ** or **MV**) is $_____.

(2) price level is $_____.

(3) real domestic output (**Q**) is $_____.

c. When **M** increases to $175, **MV** at each price level

is $_____ and the equilibrium

(1) nominal domestic output is $_____.

(2) price level is $_____.

(3) real domestic output is $_____.

2. Indicate what perspective(s) on economics would be most closely associated with each position. Use the following abbreviations: **MAI** (mainstream economics), **MON** (monetarism), **RET** (rational expectations theory), and **RBC** (real-business-cycle theory).

a. macro instability from investment spending _____

b. macro instability from inappropriate monetary policy _____

c. macro instability from changes in resource availability and technology _____

d. equation of exchange _____

e. fiscal policy can be effective _____

f. unanticipated price-level changes _____

g. downward inflexibility of wages and prices _____

h. monetary rule _____

i. neutral fiscal policy _____

j. economy automatically self-corrects _____

k. monetary policy is effective _____

3. Following are price-level (**PL**) and output (**Q**) combinations to describe aggregate demand and aggregate supply curves: (1) **PL** and **Q₁** is **AD₁**; (2) **PL** and **Q₂** is **AD₂**; (3) **PL** and **Q₃** is **AS_LR1**; (4) **PL** and **Q₄** is **AS_LR2**.

PL	Q₁	Q₂	Q₃	Q₄
250	0	200	400	600
200	200	400	400	600
150	400	600	400	600
100	600	800	400	600
50	800	1000	400	600

a. Use the following to graph **AD₁**, **AD₂**, **AS_LR1**, and **AS_LR2**. Label the vertical axis as the price level and the horizontal axis as real output (**Q**).

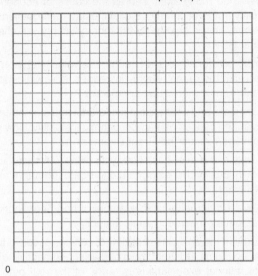

0

b. If the economy is initially in equilibrium where **AD₁** and **AS_LR1** intersect, the price level will be _____ and real output will be _____.

c. If, over time, the economy grows from **AS_LR1** to **AS_LR2**, the equilibrium price level will be _____ and real output will be _____.

d. Assume a monetary rule is adopted that increases the money supply proportionate to the increase in aggregate supply. Aggregate demand will increase from **AD₁** to **AD₂**, making the price level _____ and real output _____.

e. Mainstream economists would argue that velocity is unstable, and so a constant increase in the money supply might not shift **AD₁** all the way to **AD₂**. In this case, the price level would fall below the target of _____. It might also be the case that the constant increase in the money supply would shift **AD₁** beyond **AD₂**, and so the price level would rise above the target of _____.

■ SHORT ANSWER AND ESSAY QUESTIONS

1. What is the difference between the classical and Keynesian aggregate supply curves? Draw a graph showing the difference. What is the justification for each viewpoint?

2. What is the effect of a decrease in aggregate demand on the price level and real domestic output in the classical and Keynesian models? Show the change in a graph.

3. Why did classical economists consider the aggregate demand curve to be stable? What is the response of Keynesians to this position?

4. Why does the classical aggregate demand curve have a negative (downward) slope?

5. Explain the two causes of macroeconomic instability in the view of mainstream economists.

6. What do monetarists see as the cause of economic instability in the economy? Explain, using the equation of exchange, how a change in the money supply will affect nominal GDP.

7. Why do monetarists argue that the velocity of money is stable? If the money supply increases, how will people respond from a monetarist perspective?

8. Compare and contrast the monetarist and mainstream views on the causes of macroeconomic instability. How do monetarists explain the Great Depression?

9. Explain the real-business-cycle view of macroeconomic instability by using an aggregate demand and supply graph.

10. Give a macroeconomic example of how coordination failures cause macroeconomic instability.

11. Explain the new classical view of self-correction in the macro economy. Contrast the monetarist perspective with that of rational expectations in terms of the real output, the price level, and the speed of adjustment.

12. Describe the two assumptions on which rational expectations are based. How realistic is to expect that people will be able to forecast economic outcomes accurately?

13. Use a graph to illustrate and explain the mainstream view of self-correction in the macro economy.

14. Why would an efficiency wage lead to downward inflexibility in prices?

15. Give an example of insider–outsider relationships and explain how they affect wage flexibility.

16. What is the monetary rule? Why do monetarists suggest using this rule to replace discretionary monetary policy?

17. What is the perspective of rational expectations economists on a monetary rule and the conduct of monetary policy?

18. What is the position of some monetarist and rational expectations economists on a requirement for a balanced budget? Why do they adopt such a position?

19. How do mainstream economists defend the use of discretionary monetary and fiscal policies? What interpretation do mainstream economists make of the historical evidence on the relationship between macroeconomic policy and instability?

20. What influences have monetarism and the rational expectations theory had on mainstream macroeconomic theory and policy? Give several examples of ideas that have changed mainstream thinking.

ANSWERS

Chapter 17 Disputes over Macro Theory and Policy

■ **FILL-IN QUESTIONS**

1. vertical, horizontal, Keynesian, classical
2. demand, increase, decrease, stable
3. unstable, investment
4. demand, inflation, recession, supply
5. stable, competitive, instability, inflexibility
6. $MV = PQ$; a. the money supply; b. the velocity of money; c. the average price of each unit of physical output; d. the physical volume of goods and services produced
7. stable, stable, nominal
8. more, increase, increase
9. monetary, inflation, recession
10. real-business-cycle, supply, same, without
11. do not, a number of, expectations
12. capable, gradually, rapidly
13. are, flexible
14. unanticipated, anticipated
15. inflexible, long, decreases
16. greater, lower, less, increase
17. destabilize, equal to, equal to
18. ineffective, rules, do not
19. oppose, effective, effective, more
20. inflation, important

■ **TRUE–FALSE QUESTIONS**

1. T, pp. 319–320	10. F, p. 322	19. F, p. 327
2. F, pp. 319–320	11. T, p. 323	20. T, p. 327
3. T, p. 320	12. F, p. 323	21. T, pp. 328–329
4. F, p. 320	13. T, pp. 324–325	22. F, p. 330
5. T, pp. 320–321	14. F, p. 324	23. F, p. 330
6. T, pp. 321–322	15. T, pp. 324–325	24. T, p. 330
7. F, p. 322	16. F, pp. 325–326	25. F, p. 330
8. T, p. 322	17. F, pp. 325–326	
9. F, p. 322	18. T, p. 327	

■ **MULTIPLE-CHOICE QUESTIONS**

1. d, p. 319	10. c, pp. 321–322	19. d, pp. 325–326
2. a, p. 319	11. a, p. 322	20. c, p. 326
3. b, pp. 319–320	12. a, p. 322	21. b, p. 327
4. b, pp. 319–320	13. d, p. 323	22. d, p. 328
5. b, p. 320	14. d, p. 323	23. b, pp. 328–330
6. c, p. 320	15. c, pp. 323–324	24. c, p. 330
7. c, pp. 320–321	16. a, pp. 324–325	25. b, p. 330
8. b, pp. 321–322	17. a, p. 325	
9. c, pp. 321–322	18. c, pp. 325–326	

■ **PROBLEMS**

1. a. 100, 220, 360, 520, 700, 900, 1120; b. 360, 360, 360, 360, 360, 360, 360, (1) 360, (2) 3.00, (3) 120; c. 700, (1) 700, (2) 5.00, (3) 140
2. a. MAI; b. MON, RET; c. RBC; d. MON; e. MAI; f. RET; g. MAI; h. MON, RET; i. MON, RET; j. MON, RET; k. MAI
3. a. graph similar to Figure 17.4 in the text; b. 150, 400; c. 100, 600; d. 150, 600; e. 150, 150

■ **SHORT ANSWER AND ESSAY QUESTIONS**

1. pp. 319–320	8. p. 322	15. p. 327
2. pp. 319–320	9. p. 323	16. pp. 328–329
3. pp. 319–320	10. pp. 323–324	17. pp. 328–329
4. p. 319	11. pp. 324–325	18. pp. 329–330
5. pp. 320–321	12. pp. 324–325	19. p. 330
6. pp. 321–322	13. p. 326	20. p. 330
7. pp. 321–322	14. pp. 327	

CHAPTER 18

International Trade

In Chapter 5 you learned about the role of the United States in the global economy and the basic principles of international trade. Chapter 18 extends that analysis by giving you a more advanced understanding of comparative advantage. It also uses the tools of supply and demand to explain the equilibrium prices and quantities of imports and exports and the economic effects of tariffs and quotas. It examines the fallacious arguments for trade protectionism and the global efforts to liberalize trade.

After a brief review of the facts of international trade presented in Chapter 5, the text uses graphical analysis to explain why nations trade: to take advantage of the benefits of specialization. Nations specialize in and export those goods and services in the production of which they have a **comparative advantage.** A comparative advantage means that the opportunity cost of producing a particular good or service is lower in that nation than it is in another nation. These nations will avoid producing and will import the goods and services that other nations have a comparative advantage in producing. In this way all nations are able to obtain products that are produced as inexpensively as possible. Put another way, when nations specialize in those products in which they have a comparative advantage, the world as a whole can obtain more goods and services from its resources; each nation in the world can enjoy a standard of living higher than it would have if it did not specialize and export and import.

The principle of comparative advantage explains why nations trade, but what determines the equilibrium prices and quantities of the imports and exports resulting from trade? To answer this question, the text uses the **supply and demand analysis** presented in Chapter 3 to explain equilibrium in the world market for a product. A simplified two-nation and one-product model of trade is used to construct export supply curves and import demand curves for each nation. Equilibrium occurs where one nation's export supply curve intersects another nation's import demand curve.

Regardless of the advantages of specialization and trade among nations, people in the United States and throughout the world for well over 200 years have debated whether **free trade or protection** was the better policy for their nations. Economists took part in that debate and, with few exceptions, argued for free trade and against protection. Those who favor free trade contend that free trade benefits both the nation and the world as a whole. "Free traders" argue that tariffs, import quotas, and other barriers to international trade prevent or reduce specialization and decrease both a nation's and the world's production and standard of living.

Despite the case for trade, nations have erected and continue to erect **trade barriers** against other nations. The latter part of this chapter focuses on (1) what motivates nations to impose tariffs and limit the quantities of goods imported from abroad; (2) the economic effects of protection on a nation's prosperity and the prosperity of the world economy; (3) the kinds of arguments those who favor protection use to support their position (on what grounds do they base their contention that their nation will benefit from the erection of barriers that reduce imports from other nations?); and (4) how the nations of the world have responded to the offshoring of jobs and trade liberalization through the **World Trade Organization** (WTO).

Whether the direction of the international trade policy in the United States will be toward freer trade or more protectionism is a question that gets debated as each new trade issue is presented to the U.S. public. The decision on each issue may well depend on your understanding of the advantages of free trade and the problems with trade protection for the nation and the world economy.

■ CHECKLIST

When you have studied this chapter you should be able to

☐ Cite some key facts about international trade.

☐ State the three economic circumstances that make it desirable for nations to specialize and trade.

☐ Compute the costs of producing two commodities when given the data in a two-nation example.

☐ Determine which nation has the comparative advantage in the production of each commodity by using the cost data you computed for the two-nation example.

☐ Calculate the range in which the terms of trade will occur in the two-nation example.

☐ Explain how nations gain from trade and specialization by referring to the two-nation example.

☐ Discuss how increasing costs affect specialization in the two-nation example.

☐ Restate the case for free trade.

☐ Construct domestic supply and demand curves for two nations that trade a product.

☐ Construct export supply and import demand curves for two nations that trade a product.

☐ Use supply and demand analysis to explain how the equilibrium prices and quantities of exports and imports are determined for two nations that trade a product.

☐ Identify the four principal types of artificial barriers to international trade and the motives for erecting those barriers.

☐ Explain the economic effects of a protective tariff on resource allocation, the price of the commodity, the total production of the commodity, and the outputs of foreign and domestic producers of the commodity.

☐ Analyze the economic effects of an import quota and compare them with the economic effects of a tariff.

☐ Enumerate six arguments used to support the case for protection and find the problems with each argument.

☐ Describe the Trade Adjustment Assistance Act of 2002.

☐ Evaluate reasons for and outcomes from offshoring.

☐ Describe the formation and purpose of the World Trade Organization (WTO).

☐ Evaluate the arguments of critics and defenders of the WTO (Last Word).

■ CHAPTER OUTLINE

1. Some facts on international trade from Chapter 5 are worth reviewing.

a. About 11% of the total output (GDP) of the United States is accounted for by exports of goods and services. Although exports and imports account for a larger share of GDP in other nations, the size of the U.S. economy means that it has the largest combined volume of imports and exports in the world.

b. The United States has a trade deficit in goods, a trade surplus in services, and a trade deficit in goods and services.

c. The major exports of the United States are chemicals, consumer durables, agricultural products, semiconductors, and computers. The major imports are petroleum, automobiles, household appliances, computers, and metals. Most U.S. trade occurs with other industrially advanced nations and members of OPEC. Canada is the largest trading partner of the United States.

d. The major participants in international trade are the United States, Japan, the nations of western Europe, and now China. Other key participants include the Asian economies of South Korea, Singapore, and Taiwan. Russia and the nations of eastern Europe have expanded their international trade.

e. International trade and finance link nations and are the focus of economic policy and debate in the United States and other nations.

2. The **economic basis for trade** is based on several circumstances. Specialization and trade among nations are advantageous because the world's resources are not evenly distributed and the efficient production of different commodities requires different technologies and combinations of resources. Also, products differ in quality and other attributes, and so people may prefer imported to domestic goods in some cases.

3. The **_principle of comparative advantage_**, which was first presented in Chapter 5 to explain the gains from trade, can now be reexamined with the aid of graphical analysis.

a. Suppose the world is composed of only two nations, each of which is capable of producing two different commodities and in which the production possibilities curves are different straight lines (the nations' opportunity cost ratios are constant but different).

b. With different domestic opportunity cost ratios, each nation will have a comparative (cost) advantage in the production of one of the two commodities, and if the world is to use its resources economically, each nation must specialize in the commodity in the production of which it has a comparative advantage.

c. The ratio at which one product is traded for another—the terms of trade—lies between the opportunity cost ratios of the two nations.

d. Each nation gains from this trade because specialization permits a greater total output from the same resources and a better allocation of the world's resources.

e. If opportunity cost ratios in the two nations are not constant (if there is increasing cost), specialization may not be complete.

f. The basic argument for free trade among nations is that it leads to a better allocation of resources and a higher standard of living in the world. Among the several side benefits from trade are that it increases competition and deters monopoly and that it offers consumers a wider array of choices. It also links the interests of nations and can reduce the threat of hostilities or war.

4. Supply and demand analysis of exports and imports can be used to explain how the equilibrium price for and quantity of a product (e.g., aluminum) are determined when there is trade between two nations (e.g., the United States and Canada).

a. For the United States, there will be _domestic_ supply and demand as well as _export_ supply and import demand for aluminum.

(1) The price and quantity of aluminum are determined by the intersection of the domestic demand and supply curves in a world without trade.

(2) In a world with trade, the export supply curve for the United States shows the amount of aluminum that U.S. producers will export at each world price above the domestic equilibrium price. U.S. exports will increase when the world price rises relative to the domestic price.

(3) The import demand curve for the United States shows the amount of aluminum that U.S. citizens will import at each world price below the domestic equilibrium price. U.S. imports will increase when world prices fall relative to the domestic price.

b. For Canada, there will be domestic supply and demand as well as export supply and import demand for aluminum. The description of these supply and demand curves is similar to the account of those of the United States previously described in point **a.**

c. The equilibrium world price and equilibrium world levels of exports and imports can be determined with further supply and demand analysis. The export supply curves of the two nations can be plotted on one graph. The import demand curves of both nations can be plotted on the same graph. In this two-nation model, equilibrium will be achieved when one nation's import demand curve intersects another nation's export supply curve.

5. Nations limit international trade by erecting **trade barriers.** Tariffs, import quotas, a variety of nontariff barriers, and voluntary export restrictions are the principal barriers to trade.

  a. The imposition of a *tariff* on a good imported from abroad has both direct and indirect effects on an economy.

  (1) The tariff increases the domestic price of the good, reduces its domestic consumption, expands its domestic production, decreases its foreign production, and transfers income from domestic consumers to government.

  (2) It also reduces the income of foreign producers and the ability of foreign nations to purchase goods and services in the nation imposing the tariff, causes the contraction of relatively efficient industries in that nation, decreases world trade, and lowers the real output of goods and services.

  b. The imposition of a **quota** on an imported product has the same direct and indirect effects as that of a tariff on that product, with the exception that a tariff generates revenue for government use whereas an *import quota* transfers that revenue to foreign producers.

  c. Special-interest groups benefit from protection and persuade their nations to erect trade barriers, but the costs to consumers of that protection exceed the benefits to the economy.

6. The arguments for **protectionism** are many but are often of questionable validity.

  a. The military self-sufficiency argument can be challenged because it is difficult to determine which industry is "vital" to national defense and must be protected; it would be more efficient economically to provide a direct subsidy to military producers than to impose a tariff.

  b. Using tariff barriers to permit diversification for stability in the economy is not necessary for advanced economies such as the United States, and there may be great economic costs to diversification in developing nations.

  c. It is alleged that infant industries need protection until they are sufficiently large to compete, but that argument may not apply in developed economies: It is difficult to select which industries will prosper; protectionism tends to persist long after it is needed; and direct subsidies may be more economically efficient. For advanced nations, a variant of this argument is *strategic trade policy.* It justifies barriers that protect the investment in high-risk growth industries for a nation, but those policies often lead to retaliation and similar policies in other trading nations.

  d. Sometimes protection is sought against the "dumping" of excess foreign goods on U.S. markets. Dumping is a legitimate concern and is restricted under U.S. trade law, but to use dumping as an excuse for widespread tariff protection is unjustified, and the number of documented cases is few. If foreign companies are more efficient (low-cost) producers, what may appear to be dumping may actually be comparative advantage at work.

  e. Protection sometimes is sought because of the cheap foreign labor argument; it should be realized that nations gain from trade based on comparative advantage and that without trade, living standards will be lower.

  f. Trade barriers do not necessarily increase domestic employment because:

  (1) imports may eliminate some jobs but create others, and so imports may change only the composition of employment, not the overall level of employment;

  (2) the exports of one nation become the imports of another, and so tariff barriers can be viewed as "beggar thy neighbor" policies;

  (3) other nations are likely to retaliate against the imposition of trade barriers that will reduce domestic output and employment; and

  (4) in the long run, barriers create a less efficient allocation of resources by shielding protected domestic industries from the rigors of competition.

  g. The Trade Adjustment Assistance Act of 2002 provides support to qualified workers displaced by imports or plant relocations. It gives cash assistance, education and training benefits, subsides for health care, and wage subsidies (for those age 50 or older). Critics contend that such dislocations are part of a market economy and that workers in the international sector should not get special subsidies for their job losses.

7. *Offshoring* shifts work done in the United States to locations in other nations. Although it has long been used in manufacturing, improvements in communication and technology have made it possible to do offshoring in services. Offshoring, imports, and plant closings account for only about 3% of U.S. job losses, and these losses from international trade are often offset by gains in productivity and growth of other jobs.

8. The *World Trade Organization* (WTO) is an international agency with about 145 participating nations that is charged with overseeing a 1994 trade agreement among nations. That agreement sought trade liberalization by reducing tariffs worldwide; implementing new rules to promote trade in services; cutting domestic subsidies for agricultural products; protecting intellectual property; and phasing out quotas on textiles and apparel. The WTO oversees provisions of the agreement, rules on disputes, and meets on occasion to consider other trade policies.

9. (Last Word). The work of the WTO is not without controversy. Critics claim that it promotes global capitalism at the expense of labor and the environment. Economists argue that trade liberalization increases economic efficiency and output worldwide and that these benefits can then be used to address domestic concerns.

■ HINTS AND TIPS

1. In the discussion of **comparative advantage,** the assumption of a constant-cost ratio means that the production possibilities "curves" for each nation can be drawn as straight lines. The slope of the line in each nation is the opportunity cost of one product (wheat) in terms of the other product (coffee). The reciprocal of the slope of each line is the opportunity cost of the other product (coffee) in terms of the first product (wheat).

2. The **export supply and import demand curves** in Figures 18.3 and 18.4 in the text look different from the typical supply and demand curves you have seen so far, and so you should understand how they are constructed. The export supply and import demand curves for a nation do not intersect. Each curve meets at the price point on the *Y* axis that shows the equilibrium price for domestic supply and demand. At this point there are no exports or imports.

a. The export supply curve is upsloping from that point because as world prices rise above the domestic equilibrium price, there will be increasing domestic surpluses produced by a nation that can be exported. The export supply curve reflects the positive relationship between rising world prices (above the domestic equilibrium price) and the increasing quantity of exports.

b. The import demand curve is downsloping from the domestic equilibrium price because as world prices fall below the domestic equilibrium price, there will be increasing domestic shortages that need to be covered by increasing imports. The import demand curve reflects the inverse relationship between falling world prices (below the domestic price) and the increasing quantity of imports.

3. One of the most interesting sections of the chapter discusses the arguments for and against trade protection. You have probably heard people give one or more of the arguments for trade protection, but now you have a chance to use your economic reasoning to expose the weaknesses in those arguments. Most are half-truths and special pleadings.

■ IMPORTANT TERMS

labor-intensive goods

land-intensive goods

capital-intensive goods

opportunity-cost ratio

principle of comparative
   advantage

terms of trade

trading possibilities line

gains from trade

world price

domestic price

export supply curve

import demand curve

equilibrium world price

tariff

revenue tariff

protective tariff

import quota

nontariff barrier (NTB)

voluntary export restriction
   (VER)

strategic trade policy

dumping

Smoot-Hawley Tariff Act

Trade Adjustment
   Assistance Act

offshoring

World Trade Organization
   (WTO)

SELF-TEST

■ FILL-IN QUESTIONS

1. Exports of goods and services account for about (11, 22) _____% of total output in the United States, and since 1975 this percentage has (doubled, quadrupled) _____.

2. Other industrially advanced nations, such as the Netherlands and Canada, have a (larger, smaller) _____ percentage of exports than the United States. The United States' volume of exports and imports makes it the world's (largest, smallest) _____ trading nation.

3. Nations tend to trade among themselves because the distribution of economic resources among them is (even, uneven) _____, the efficient production of various goods and services necessitates (the same, different) _____ technologies or combinations of resources, and people prefer (more, less) _____ choices in products.

4. The principle of comparative advantage means that total world output will be greatest when each good is produced by the nation that has the (highest, lowest) _____ opportunity cost. The nations of the world tend to specialize in the production of those goods in which they (have, do not have) _____ a comparative advantage and then export them, and they import those goods in which they _____ a comparative advantage in production.

5. If the cost ratio in country X is 4 Panama hats equal 1 pound of bananas and in country Y 3 Panama hats equal 1 pound of bananas, then

a. in country X hats are relatively (expensive, inexpensive) _____ and bananas are relatively _____,

b. in country Y hats are relatively (expensive, inexpensive) _____ and bananas are relatively _____,

c. X has a comparative advantage and should specialize in the production of (bananas, hats) _____, and Y has a comparative advantage and should specialize in the production of _____.

d. when X and Y specialize and trade, the terms of trade will be somewhere between (1, 2, 3, 4) _____ and _____ hats for each pound of bananas and will depend on world demand for and supply of hats and bananas.

e. When the actual terms of trade turn out to be 3 1/2 hats for 1 pound of bananas, the cost of obtaining

(1) 1 Panama hat has been decreased from (2/7, 1/3) _____ to _____ pounds of bananas in Y.

(2) 1 pound of bananas has been decreased from (3 1/2, 4) _____ to _____ Panama hats in X.

f. International specialization will not be complete if the opportunity cost of producing either good (rises, falls) _____ as a nation produces more of it.

6. The basic argument for free trade based on the principle of (bilateral negotiations, comparative advantage) _____ is that it results in a (more, less) _____ efficient allocation of resources and a (lower, higher) _____ standard of living.

7. The world equilibrium price is determined by the interaction of (domestic, world) _____ supply and demand, whereas the domestic equilibrium price is determined by _____ supply and demand.

8. When the world price of a good falls relative to the domestic price in a nation, that nation will (increase, decrease) _____ its imports, and when the world price rises relative to the domestic price, that nation will _____ its exports.

9. In a two-nation model for a product, the equilibrium price and equilibrium quantity of imports and exports occur where one nation's import demand intersects another nation's export (supply, demand) _____ curve. In a highly competitive world market, there can be (multiple, only one) _____ price(s) for a standardized product.

10. Excise taxes on imported products are (quotas, tariffs) _____, whereas limits on the maximum amount of a product that can be imported are import _____. Tariffs applied to a product that is not produced domestically are (protective, revenue) _____ tariffs, and tariffs designed to shield domestic producers from foreign competition are _____ tariffs.

11. There are other types of trade barriers. Imports that are restricted through the use of a licensing requirement or bureaucratic red tape are (tariff, nontariff) _____ barriers. When foreign firms voluntarily limit their exports to another country, that represents a voluntary (import, export) _____ restraint.

12. Nations erect barriers to international trade to benefit the economic positions of (consumers, domestic producers) _____ even though those barriers (increase, decrease) _____ economic

efficiency and trade among nations and the benefits to that nation are (greater, less) _____ than the costs to it.

13. When the United States imposes a tariff on a good that is imported from abroad, the price of that good in the United States will (increase, decrease) _____, the total purchases of the good in the United States will _____, the output of U.S. producers of the good will (increase, decrease) _____, and the output of foreign producers will _____. The ability of foreigners to buy goods and services in the United States will (increase, decrease) _____, and as a result, output and employment in U.S. industries that sell goods and services abroad will _____.

14. In comparing the effects of a tariff with the effects of a quota to restrict U.S. imports of a product, the basic difference is that with a (tariff, quota) _____ the U.S. government will receive revenue and with a _____ foreign producers will receive the revenue.

15. List the six arguments that protectionists use to justify trade barriers.

a. _____

b. _____

c. _____

d. _____

e. _____

f. _____

16. The military self-sufficiency argument can be challenged because it is difficult to determine which industries are (essential, unessential) _____ for national defense and must be protected. Rather than impose a tariff, a direct subsidy to producers would be (more, less) _____ efficient in this case.

17. Using trade barriers to permit diversification for stability in an economy is not necessary for (advanced, developing) _____ economies such as the United States, and there may be great economic costs to forcing diversification in _____ nations; it is also alleged that infant industries need protection until they are sufficiently large to compete, an argument that has been modified to strategic trade policy in _____ economies.

18. Trade barriers do not necessarily increase domestic employment because imports may change only the (level, composition) _____ of employment; trade barriers can be viewed as "beggar thy (customer, neighbor) _____" policies; other nations can (protest, retaliate) _____ against the trade barriers; and in the long run, the barriers create an allocation of resources that is (more, less) _____ efficient by shielding protected domestic industries from competition.

19. The Trade Adjustment Assistance Act of 2002 is designed to help some of the (workers, businesses) _____ hurt by shifts in international trade patterns. Critics contend that such job losses are a (small, large) _____ fraction of the total each year and that such a program is another type of special (tariff, subsidy) _____ that benefits one type worker over another.

20. The shifting of work previously done by U.S. workers to workers in other nations is (dumping, offshoring) _____. It reflects a (growth, decline) _____ in specialization and international trade of services. It may (decrease, increase) _____ some jobs moved to other nations but also _____ jobs and productivity in the United States.

■ **TRUE–FALSE QUESTIONS**

Circle T if the statement is true, F if it is false.

1. A trade deficit occurs when imports are greater than exports. **T F**

2. A factor that serves as the economic basis for world trade is the even distribution of resources among nations. **T F**

3. People trade because they seek products of different quality and other nonprice attributes. **T F**

4. Examples of capital-intensive goods would be automobiles, machinery, and chemicals. **T F**

5. The relative efficiency with which a nation can produce specific goods is fixed over time. **T F**

6. Mutually advantageous specialization and trade are possible between any two nations if they have the same domestic opportunity cost ratios for any two products. **T F**

7. The principle of comparative advantage is that total output will be greatest when each good is produced by that nation which has the higher domestic opportunity cost. **T F**

8. By specializing on the basis of comparative advantage, nations can obtain larger outputs with fixed amounts of resources. **T F**

9. The terms of trade determine how the increase in world output resulting from comparative advantage is shared by trading nations. **T F**

10. Increasing opportunity costs tend to prevent specialization among trading nations from being complete. **T F**

11. Trade among nations tends to bring about a more efficient use of the world's resources and a higher level of material well-being. **T F**

12. Free trade among nations tends to increase monopoly and lessen competition in those nations. **T F**

13. A nation will export a particular product if the world price is less than the domestic price. **T F**

14. In a two-country model, equilibrium in world prices and quantities of exports and imports will occur where one nation's export supply curve intersects the other nation's import demand curve. **T F**

15. A tariff on coffee in the United States is an example of a protective tariff. **T F**

16. The imposition of a tariff on a good imported from abroad will reduce the amount of the imported good that is bought. **T F**

17. A cost of tariffs and quotas imposed by the United States is higher prices that U.S. consumers must pay for protected products. **T F**

18. The major difference between a tariff and a quota on an imported product is that a quota produces revenue for the government. **T F**

19. To advocate tariffs that would protect domestic producers of goods and materials essential to national defense is to substitute a political-military objective for the economic objectives of efficiently allocating resources. **T F**

20. One-crop economies may be able to make themselves more stable and diversified by imposing tariffs on goods imported from abroad, but those tariffs are also apt to lower the standard of living in those economies. **T F**

21. Protection against the "dumping" of foreign goods at low prices on the U.S. market is one good reason for widespread permanent tariffs. **T F**

22. Tariffs and import quotas meant to increase domestic employment achieve short-run domestic goals by making trading partners poorer. **T F**

23. The Trade Adjustment Assistance Act of 2002 provided compensation to U.S. workers who were displaced by shifts in international trade patterns. **T F**

24. Although offshoring decreases some U.S. jobs, it also lowers production costs, expands sales, and may create other U.S. jobs. **T F**

25. The World Trade Organization was established by the United Nations to encourage purchases of products from developing nations. **T F**

■ MULTIPLE-CHOICE QUESTIONS

Circle the letter that corresponds to the best answer.

1. Which nation leads the world in the combined volume of exports and imports?
(a) Japan
(b) Germany
(c) United States
(d) United Kingdom

2. Which nation is the most important trading partner for the United States in terms of the percentage of imports and exports?
(a) India
(b) Russia
(c) Canada
(d) Germany

3. Nations engage in trade because
(a) world resources are evenly distributed among nations
(b) world resources are unevenly distributed among nations
(c) all products are produced from the same technology
(d) all products are produced from the same combinations of resources

Use the following tables to answer Questions 4, 5, 6, and 7.

NEPAL PRODUCTION POSSIBILITIES TABLE

Product	Production alternatives					
	A	B	C	D	E	F
Yak fat	0	4	8	12	16	20
Camel hides	40	32	24	16	7	0

KASHMIR PRODUCTION POSSIBILITIES TABLE

Product	Production alternatives					
	A	B	C	D	E	F
Yak fat	0	3	6	9	12	15
Camel hides	60	48	36	24	12	0

4. The data in the tables show that production in
(a) both Nepal and Kashmir are subject to increasing opportunity costs
(b) both Nepal and Kashmir are subject to constant opportunity costs
(c) Nepal is subject to increasing opportunity costs and Kashmir to constant opportunity costs
(d) Kashmir is subject to increasing opportunity costs and Nepal to constant opportunity costs

5. If Nepal and Kashmir engage in trade, the terms of trade will be
(a) between 2 and 4 camel hides for 1 unit of yak fat
(b) between 1/3 and 1/2 unit of yak fat for 1 camel hide
(c) between 3 and 4 units of yak fat for 1 camel hide
(d) between 2 and 4 units of yak fat for 1 camel hide

6. Assume that prior to specialization and trade Nepal and Kashmir both choose production possibility C. Now if each specializes according to its comparative advantage, the resulting gains from specialization and trade will be
(a) 6 units of yak fat
(b) 8 units of yak fat
(c) 6 units of yak fat and 8 camel hides
(d) 8 units of yak fat and 6 camel hides

7. Each nation produced only one product in accordance with its comparative advantage, and the terms of trade were set at 3 camel hides for 1 unit of yak fat. In this case, Nepal could obtain a maximum combination of 8 units of yak fat and
(a) 12 camel hides
(b) 24 camel hides
(c) 36 camel hides
(d) 48 camel hides

8. What happens to a nation's imports or exports of a product when the world price of that product rises above the domestic price?
(a) Imports of the product increase.
(b) Imports of the product stay the same.
(c) Exports of the product increase.
(d) Exports of the product decrease.

9. What happens to a nation's imports or exports of a product when the world price of the product falls below the domestic price?
(a) Imports of the product increase.
(b) Imports of the product decrease.
(c) Exports of the product increase.
(d) Exports of the product stay the same.

10. Which one of the following is characteristic of tariffs?
(a) They prevent the importation of goods from abroad.
(b) They specify the maximum amounts of specific commodities that may be imported during a given period of time.
(c) They often protect domestic producers from foreign competition.
(d) They enable nations to reduce their exports and increase their imports during periods of recession.

11. The motive for barriers to the importation of goods and services from abroad is to
(a) improve economic efficiency in that nation
(b) protect and benefit domestic producers of those goods and services
(c) reduce the prices of the goods and services produced in that nation
(d) expand exports of goods and services to foreign nations

12. When a tariff is imposed on a good imported from abroad,
(a) the demand for the good increases
(b) the demand for the good decreases
(c) the supply of the good increases
(d) the supply of the good decreases

Answer Questions 13, 14, 15, 16, and 17 on the basis of the following diagram, where S_d and D_d are the domestic supply and demand for a product and P_w is the world price of that product.

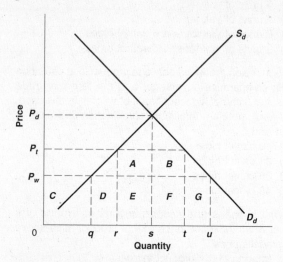

13. In a closed economy (without international trade), the equilibrium price would be

(a) P_d, but in an open economy the equilibrium price would be P_t

(b) P_d, but in an open economy the equilibrium price would be P_w

(c) P_w, but in an open economy the equilibrium price would be P_d

(d) P_w, but in an open economy the equilibrium price would be P_t

14. If there is free trade in this economy and no tariffs, the total revenue going to the foreign producers is represented by

(a) area **C**

(b) areas **A** and **B** combined

(c) areas **A, B, E,** and **F** combined

(d) areas **D, E, F,** and **G** combined

15. If a per-unit tariff were imposed in the amount of P_wP_t, domestic producers would supply

(a) **q** units and foreign producers would supply **qu** units

(b) **s** units and foreign producers would supply **su** units

(c) **r** units and foreign producers would supply **rt** units

(d) **t** units and foreign producers would supply **tu** units

16. Given a per-unit tariff in the amount of P_wP_t, the amount of the tariff revenue paid by consumers of this product is represented by

(a) area **A**

(b) area **B**

(c) areas **A** and **B** combined

(d) areas **D, E, F,** and **G** combined

17. Assume that an import quota of **rt** units is imposed on the foreign nation producing this product. The amount

of *total* revenue going to foreign producers is represented by areas

(a) **A + B**

(b) **E + F**

(c) **A + B + E + F**

(d) **D + E + F + G**

18. Tariffs lead to

(a) the contraction of relatively efficient industries

(b) an overallocation of resources to relatively efficient industries

(c) an increase in the foreign demand for domestically produced goods

(d) an underallocation of resources to relatively inefficient industries

19. Tariffs and quotas are costly to consumers because

(a) the price of the imported good rises

(b) the supply of the imported good increases

(c) import competition increases for domestically produced goods

(d) consumers shift purchases away from domestically produced goods

20. The infant industry argument for tariffs

(a) is especially pertinent for the European Union

(b) generally results in tariffs that are removed after the infant industry has matured

(c) makes it rather easy to determine which infant industries will become mature industries with comparative advantages in producing their goods

(d) might better be replaced by an argument for outright subsidies for infant industries

21. Strategic trade policy is a modified form for advanced economies of which protectionist argument?

(a) the increase-domestic-employment argument

(b) the military self-sufficiency argument

(c) the cheap foreign labor argument

(d) the infant industry argument

22. "The nation needs to protect itself from foreign countries that sell their products in our domestic markets at less than the cost of production." This statement would be most closely associated with which protectionist argument?

(a) diversification for stability

(b) increasing domestic employment

(c) protection against dumping

(d) cheap foreign labor

23. Which is a likely result of imposing tariffs to increase domestic employment?

(a) a short-run increase in domestic employment in import industries

(b) a decrease in the tariff rates of foreign nations

(c) a long-run reallocation of workers from export industries to protected domestic industries

(d) a decrease in consumer prices

24. Which is the likely result of the United States using tariffs to protect its high wages and standard of living from cheap foreign labor?

(a) an increase in U.S. exports

(b) a rise in U.S. real GDP

(c) a decrease in the average productivity of U.S. workers

(d) a decrease in the quantity of labor employed by industries producing the goods on which tariffs have been levied

25. What international agency is charged with overseeing trade liberalization and resolving disputes among nations?

    (a) World Bank
    (b) United Nations
    (c) World Trade Organization
    (d) International Monetary Fund

■ PROBLEMS

1. Shown below are the production possibilities curves for two nations: the United States and Chile. Suppose these two nations do not currently engage in international trade or specialization and suppose that points **A** and **a** show the combinations of wheat and copper they now produce and consume.

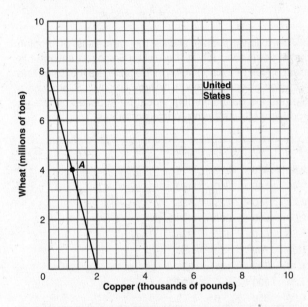

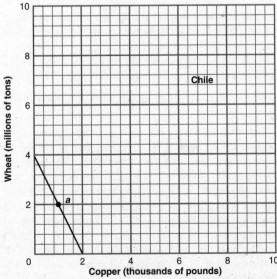

a. The straightness of the two curves indicates that the cost ratios in the two nations are (changing, constant) _____.

b. Examination of the two curves reveals that the cost ratio in

(1) the United States is _____ million tons of wheat for _____ thousand pounds of copper.

(2) Chile is _____ million tons of wheat for _____ thousand pounds of copper.

c. If these two nations were to specialize and trade wheat for copper,

(1) The United States would specialize in the production of wheat because _____

_____.

(2) Chile would specialize in the production of copper

because _____

_____.

d. The terms of trade, if specialization and trade occur, will be greater than 2 million and less than 4 million tons of wheat for 1000 pounds of copper because

_____

_____.

e. Assume the terms of trade turn out to be 3 million tons of wheat for 1000 pounds of copper. Draw in the trading possibilities curve for the United States and Chile.

f. With these trading possibilities curves, suppose the United States decides to consume 5 million tons of wheat and 1000 pounds of copper and Chile decides to consume 3 million tons of wheat and 1000 pounds of copper. The gains from trade to

(1) the United States are _____ million tons of wheat and _____ thousand pounds of copper.

(2) Chile are _____ million tons of wheat and _____ thousand pounds of copper.

2. Following are tables showing the domestic supply and demand schedules and the export supply and import demand schedules for two nations (**A** and **B**).

NATION A

Price	Q_{dd}	Q_{sd}	Q_{di}	Q_{se}
$3.00	100	300	0	200
2.50	150	250	0	100
2.00	200	200	0	0
1.50	250	150	100	0
1.00	300	100	200	0

    a. For nation **A,** the first column of the table is the price of a product. The second column is the quantity demanded domestically (Q_{dd}). The third column is the quantity supplied domestically (Q_{sd}). The fourth column is the quantity demanded for imports (Q_{di}). The fifth column is the quantity of exports supplied (Q_{se}).

(1) At a price of $2.00, there (will, will not) _____ be a surplus or shortage and there _____ be exports or imports.

(2) At a price of $3.00, there will be a domestic (shortage, surplus) _____ of _____ units. This domestic _____ will be eliminated by (exports, imports) _____ of _____ units.

(3) At a price of $1.00, there will be a domestic (shortage, surplus) _____ of _____units. This domestic _____ will be eliminated by (exports, imports) _____ of _____ units.

NATION B

Price	Q_{dd}	Q_{sd}	Q_{di}	Q_{se}
$2.50	100	300	0	200
2.00	150	250	0	100
1.50	200	200	0	0
1.00	250	150	100	0

b. For nation **B**, the first column is the price of a product. The second column is the quantity demanded domestically (Q_{dd}). The third column is the quantity supplied domestically (Q_{sd}). The fourth column is the quantity demanded for imports (Q_{di}). The fifth column is the quantity of exports supplied (Q_{se}).

(1) At a price of $1.50, there (will, will not) _____ be a surplus or shortage and there _____ be exports or imports.

(2) At a price of $2.50, there will be a domestic (shortage, surplus) _____ of _____ units. This domestic _____ will be eliminated by (exports, imports) _____ of _____ units.

(3) At a price of $1.00, there will be a domestic (shortage, surplus) _____ of _____ units. This domestic _____ will be eliminated by (exports, imports) _____ of _____ units.

c. The following table shows a schedule of the import demand in Nation **A** and the export supply in Nation **B** at various prices. The first column is the price of the product. The second column is the quantity demanded for imports (Q_{diA}) in Nation **A**. The third column is the quantity of exports supplied (Q_{seB}) in Nation **B**.

Price	Q_{diA}	Q_{seB}
$2.00	0	100
1.75	50	50
1.50	100	0

(1) If the world price is $2.00, then Nation (**A, B**) _____ will want to import _____ units and Nation _____ will want to export _____ units of the product.

(2) If the world price is $1.75, then Nation (**A, B**) _____ will want to import _____ units and Nation _____ will want to export _____ units of the product.

(3) If the world price is $1.50, then Nation (**A, B**) _____ will want to import _____ units and Nation _____ will want to export _____ units of the product.

3. The following table shows the quantities of woolen gloves demanded (**D**) in the United States at several different prices (**P**). Also shown in the table are the quantities of woolen gloves that would be supplied by U.S. producers (S_a) and the quantities that would be supplied by foreign producers (S_f) at the nine different prices.

P	D	S_a	S_f	S_t	S'_f	S'_t
$2.60	450	275	475	_____	_____	_____
2.40	500	250	450	_____	_____	_____
2.20	550	225	425	_____	_____	_____
2.00	600	200	400	_____	_____	_____
1.80	650	175	375	_____	_____	_____
1.60	700	150	350	_____	_____	_____
1.40	750	125	325	_____	_____	_____
1.20	800	0	300	_____	_____	_____
1.00	850	0	0	_____	_____	_____

a. Compute and enter in the table the total quantities that would be supplied (S_t) by U.S. and foreign producers at each of the prices.

b. If the market for woolen gloves in the United States is a competitive one, the equilibrium price for woolen gloves is $_____ and the equilibrium quantity is _____.

c. Suppose now that the United States government imposes an 80 cent ($.80) tariff per pair of gloves on all gloves imported into the United States from abroad. Compute and enter into the table the quantities that would be supplied (S'_f) by foreign producers at the nine different prices. [*Hint*: If foreign producers were willing to supply 300 pairs at a price of $1.20 when there was no tariff, they are now willing to supply 300 pairs at $2.00 (the $.80 per pair tariff plus the $1.20 they will receive for themselves). The quantities supplied at each of the other prices may be found in a similar fashion.]

d. Compute and enter into the table the total quantities that would be supplied (***S'**$_t$*) by U.S. and foreign producers at each of the nine prices.

e. As a result of the imposition of the tariff, the equilibrium price has risen to $_____ and the equilibrium quantity has fallen to _____.

f. The number of pairs sold by

(1) U.S. producers has (increased, decreased) _____ by _____.

(2) foreign producers has (increased, decreased) _____ by _____.

g. The total revenues (after the payment of the tariff) of

(1) U.S. producers—who do not pay the tariff—have (increased, decreased) _____ by $_____.

(2) foreign producers—who do pay the tariff—have (increased, decreased) _____ by $_____.

h. The total amount spent by U.S. buyers of woolen gloves has _____ by $_____.

i. The total number of dollars earned by foreigners has _____ by $_____, and as a result, the total foreign demand for goods and services produced in the United States has _____ by $_____.

j. The tariff revenue of the U.S. government has _____ by $_____.

k. If an import quota were imposed that had the same effect as the tariff on price and output, the amount of the tariff revenue, $_____, would now be received as revenue by _____ producers.

■ **SHORT ANSWER AND ESSAY QUESTIONS**

1. Describe the quantity of imports and exports for the United States in absolute and relative terms. How has the quantity of imports and exports changed over time?

2. What are the major imports and exports of the United States? With which nations does the United States trade?

3. What role does the United States play in international trade? Who are the other major players in international trade?

4. What three factors—one dealing with the resource distribution, the second with production, and the third with the variety of product—are the basis for trade among nations?

5. Explain
(a) the theory or principle of comparative advantage;
(b) what is meant by and what determines the terms of trade; and
(c) the gains from trade.

6. What is the case for free trade?

7. Explain how the equilibrium prices and quantities of exports and imports are determined.

8. Why will exports in a nation increase when world prices rise relative to domestic prices?

9. What motivates nations to erect barriers to the importation of goods from abroad, and what types of barriers do they erect?

10. Suppose the United States increases the tariff on automobiles imported from Germany (and other foreign countries). What is the effect of this tariff-rate increase on
(a) the price of automobiles in the United States;
(b) the total number of cars sold in the United States during a year;
(c) the number of cars produced by and employment in the German automobile industry;
(d) production by and employment in the U.S. automobile industry;
(e) German income obtained by selling cars in the United States;
(f) the German demand for goods produced in the United States;
(g) the production of and employment in those U.S. industries that now export goods to Germany;
(h) the standards of living in the United States and in Germany;
(i) the allocation of resources in the U.S. economy; and
(j) the allocation of the world's resources?

11. Explain the economic effects of a tariff and show them in a supply and demand graph.

12. Compare and contrast the economic effects of a tariff with the economic effects of an import quota on a product.

13. Critically evaluate the military self-sufficiency argument for protectionism. What industries should be protected?

14. What are four shortcomings of using tariffs or quotas to increase domestic employment in the United States?

15. What is the basis for the infant industry arguments (including strategic trade policy) for protectionism? How can it be countered?

16. Can a strong case for protectionism be made on the basis of defending against the "dumping" of products? How do you determine if a nation is dumping a product? What are the economic effects of dumping on consumers?

17. Does the economy need to shield domestic workers from competition from "cheap" foreign labor? Explain by using the ideas of comparative advantage and standards of living.

18. Discuss the purpose of the Trade Adjustment Assistance Act of 2002 and its advantages and disadvantages.

19. Explain the reasons U.S. businesses have turned to offshoring and evaluate the costs and benefits of such actions.

20. What do critics of the World Trade Organization say about its effects on domestic economies and the global economy, and what is the response from economists?

ANSWERS

Chapter 18 International Trade

FILL-IN QUESTIONS

1. 11, doubled
2. larger, largest
3. uneven, different, more
4. lowest, have, do not have
5. *a.* inexpensive, expensive; *b.* expensive, inexpensive; *c.* hats, bananas; *d.* 3, 4; *e.* (1) 1/3, 2/7, (2) 4, 3 1/2; *f.* rises
6. comparative advantage, more, higher
7. world, domestic
8. increase, increase
9. supply, only one
10. tariffs, quotas, revenue, protective
11. nontariff, export
12. domestic producers, decrease, less
13. increase, decrease, increase, decrease, decrease, decrease
14. tariff, quota
15. *a.* military self-sufficiency; *b.* support of infant industries; *c.* increase in domestic employment; *d.* diversification for stability; *e.* protection against dumping; *f.* cheap foreign labor (any order for *a–f*)
16. essential, more
17. advanced, developing, advanced
18. composition, neighbor, retaliate, less
19. workers, small, subsidy
20. offshoring, growth, decrease, increase

TRUE–FALSE QUESTIONS

1. T, p. 340	10. T, p. 345	19. T, p. 352
2. F, pp. 340–341	11. T, p. 346	20. T, pp. 352–353
3. T, p. 341	12. F, p. 346	21. F, p. 353
4. T, p. 341	13. F, p. 346	22. T, pp. 353–354
5. F, p. 341	14. T, pp. 347–349	23. T, p. 355
6. F, p. 341	15. F, pp. 349–350	24. T, p. 355
7. F, pp. 341–342	16. T, p. 350	25. F, pp. 356–357
8. T, pp. 343–344	17. T, pp. 350–351	
9. T, p. 343	18. F, pp. 350–351	

MULTIPLE-CHOICE QUESTIONS

1. c, p. 340	10. c, pp. 349–350	19. a, pp. 351–352
2. c, p. 340	11. b, pp. 350–351	20. d, p. 353
3. b, pp. 340–341	12. d, pp. 350–351	21. d, p. 353
4. b, pp. 341–342	13. b, pp. 350–351	22. c, p. 353
5. a, p. 343	14. d, pp. 350–351	23. c, p. 353
6. a, pp. 343–345	15. c, pp. 350–351	24. c, p. 354
7. c, pp. 343–345	16. c, pp. 350–351	25. c, p. 356
8. c, pp. 346–349	17. c, p. 351	
9. a, pp. 346–349	18. a, pp. 351–352	

PROBLEMS

1. *a.* constant; *b.* (1) 8, 2, (2) 4, 2; *c.* (1) it has a comparative advantage in producing wheat (its cost of producing wheat is less than Chile's), (2) it has a comparative advantage in producing copper (its cost of producing copper is less than the United States'); *d.* one of the two nations would be unwilling to trade if the terms of trade are outside this range; *f.* (1) 1, 0, (2) 1, 0

2. *a.* (1) will not, will not, (2) surplus, 200, surplus, exports, 200, (3) shortage, 200, shortage, imports, 200; *b.* (1) will not, will not, (2) surplus, 200, surplus, exports, 200, (3) shortage, 100, shortage, imports, 100; *c.* (1) A, 0, B, 100, (2) A, 50, B, 50, (3) A, 100, B, 0

3. *a.* 750, 700, 650, 600, 550, 500, 450, 300, 0; *b.* 2.00, 600; *c.* 375, 350, 325, 300, 0, 0, 0, 0, 0; *d.* 650, 600, 550, 500, 175, 150, 125, 0, 0; *e.* 2.20, 550; *f.* (1) increased, 25, (2) decreased, 75; *g.* (1) increased, 95, (2) decreased, 345; *h.* increased, 10; *i.* decreased, 345, decreased, 345; *j.* increased, 260; *k.* 260, foreign

SHORT ANSWER AND ESSAY QUESTIONS

1. p. 340	8. pp. 346–349	15. p. 353
2. p. 340	9. pp. 349–350	16. p. 353
3. p. 340	10. pp. 350–351	17. p. 354
4. pp. 340–341	11. pp. 350–351	18. pp. 354–355
5. pp. 341–345	12. p. 351	19. p. 355
6. p. 346	13. p. 352	20. pp. 356–357
7. pp. 346–349	14. pp. 353–354	

CHAPTER 19

Exchange Rates, the Balance of Payments, and Trade Deficits

In the last chapter you learned *why* nations engage in international trade and *why* they erect barriers to trade with other nations. In Chapter 19 you will learn *how* nations that use different currencies are able to trade.

The means nations use to overcome the difficulties that result from the use of different currencies are fairly simple. When the residents of a nation (its consumers, business firms, or governments) want to buy goods or services or real or financial assets from, make loans or gifts to, or pay interest and dividends to the residents of other nations, they *buy* some of the currency used in that nation. They pay for the foreign money with some of their own currency. In other words, they exchange their own currency for foreign currency.

When the residents of a nation sell goods or services or real or financial assets to, receive loans or gifts from, or are paid dividends or interest by the residents of foreign nations and obtain foreign currencies, they *sell* that foreign currency—often called foreign exchange—in return for some of their own currency. That is, they exchange foreign currency for their own currency.

The market in which one currency is sold and is paid for with another currency is called the **foreign exchange market.** The price that is paid (in one currency) for a unit of another currency is called the foreign exchange rate. Like most prices, the foreign exchange rate for a foreign currency is determined by the demand for and the supply of that foreign currency.

As you know from Chapter 18, nations buy and sell large quantities of goods and services across national boundaries. But the residents of those nations also buy and sell such financial assets as stocks and bonds and such real assets as land and capital goods in other nations, and the governments and individuals in one nation make gifts (remittances) to other nations. At the end of a year, nations summarize their foreign transactions with the rest of the world. This summary is called a nation's **balance of payments:** a record of how it obtained foreign currency during the year and what it did with that foreign currency.

Of course, all the foreign currency obtained was used for some purpose—it did not evaporate—consequently, the balance of payments *always* balances. The balance of payments is an extremely important and useful device for understanding the amounts and kinds of international transactions in which the residents of a nation engage. It also allows us to understand the meaning of a balance-of-payments deficit or surplus, the causes of those imbalances, and how to deal with them.

Several difficult sections of this chapter are concerned with how **flexible and fixed exchange-rate systems** handle balance-of-payments deficits and surpluses. A balance-of-payments deficit occurs when foreign currency receipts are less than foreign currency payments and the nation must reduce its official reserves to balance its payments. Conversely, a balance-of-payments surplus occurs when foreign currency receipts are greater than foreign currency payments, and the nation must expand its official reserves to balance its payments. In these sections pay particular attention to the ways in which a flexible or floating exchange-rate system and a fixed exchange-rate system will correct balance-of-payments deficits and surpluses and the advantages and disadvantages of these two alternative systems for eliminating imbalances in international accounts.

As examples of these two types of exchange-rate systems, the next section of the chapter examines the **gold standard,** the **Bretton Woods system,** and the **managed floating exchange-rate system.** In the first two systems exchange rates are fixed, and in the third system exchange rates are fixed in the short run (to obtain the advantages of fixed exchange rates) and flexible in the long run (to enable nations to correct balance-of-payments deficits and surpluses).

The final section of the chapter examines U.S. **trade deficits.** As you will learn, these deficits were the result of several factors—differences in national growth rates and a declining saving rate—that contributed to imports rising faster than exports. They also have several implications, including increased current consumption at the expense of future consumption and increased U.S. indebtedness to foreigners.

■ CHECKLIST

When you have studied this chapter you should be able to

☐ Explain how U.S. exports create a foreign demand for dollars that in turn generates a supply of foreign currencies.

☐ Describe how U.S. imports create a domestic demand for foreign currencies that in turn generates a supply of dollars.

☐ Give a definition of a nation's balance of payments.

☐ Use the items in the current account to calculate the balance on goods, the balance on goods and services, and the balance on the current account when given the data.

☐ Describe how balance is achieved in the capital and financial account.

☐ Explain the relationship between the current account and the capital and financial account.

☐ Use a supply and demand graph to illustrate how a flexible exchange-rate system works to establish the price and quantity of a currency.

☐ Discuss the role of official reserves when there is a balance-of-payments deficit or balance-of-payments surplus.

☐ Describe the depreciation and appreciation of a nation's currency under a flexible exchange-rate system.

☐ Identify the five principal determinants of the demand for and supply of a particular foreign currency and explain how they alter exchange rates.

☐ Explain how flexible exchange rates eventually eliminate balance-of-payments deficits or surpluses.

☐ Describe three disadvantages of flexible exchange rates.

☐ Use a supply and demand graph to illustrate how a fixed exchange-rate system functions.

☐ Explain how nations use official reserves to maintain a fixed exchange rate.

☐ Describe how trade policies can be used to maintain a fixed exchange rate.

☐ Discuss the advantages and disadvantages of using exchange controls to maintain a fixed exchange rate.

☐ Explain what domestic macroeconomic adjustments are needed to maintain a fixed exchange rate.

☐ Identify three different exchange-rate systems used by the world's nations in recent years.

☐ List three conditions a nation had to fulfill to be on the gold standard.

☐ Explain how the gold standard worked to maintain fixed exchange rates.

☐ Give reasons for the collapse of the gold standard.

☐ Explain how the Bretton Woods system attempted to stabilize exchange rates and establish orderly changes in exchange rates for correcting balance-of-payments deficits.

☐ State reasons for the demise of the Bretton Woods system.

☐ Describe the current system of managed floating exchange rates.

☐ Discuss the pros and cons of the system of managed floating exchange rates.

☐ Describe the causes of recent trade deficits in the United States.

☐ Explain the economic implications of recent trade deficits in the United States.

☐ Assess the role that speculators play in currency markets (Last Word).

■ **CHAPTER OUTLINE**

1. Trade between two nations differs from domestic trade because the nations use different currencies. This problem is resolved by the existence of **foreign exchange markets** in which the currency used by one nation can be purchased and paid for with the currency of the other nation.

a. U.S. exports create a foreign demand for dollars, and the satisfaction of that demand increases the supply of foreign currencies in the foreign exchange market.

b. U.S. imports create a domestic demand for foreign currencies, and meeting that demand decreases the supplies of foreign currencies in the foreign exchange market.

2. The **balance of payments** for a nation is an annual record of all its transactions with the other nations in the world; it records all the payments received from and made to the rest of the world.

a. The **current account** section of a nation's balance of payments records its trade in currently produced goods and services. Within this section

(1) the balance on goods of the nation is equal to its exports of goods less its imports of goods;

(2) the **balance on goods and services** is equal to its exports of goods and services less its imports of goods and services; and

(3) the **balance on the current account** is equal to its balance on goods and services plus its net investment income (dividends and interest) from other nations and its net private and public transfers to other nations. This balance may produce either a **trade deficit** or a **trade surplus**.

b. The **capital and financial account** of a nation's balance-of-payments record consists of two accounts: a capital account and a financial account.

(1) The *capital account* primarily measures debt forgiveness and is a "net" account. If Americans forgave more debt that was owed to them by foreigners than foreigners forgave debt that was owed to them by Americans, the capital account would be entered as a negative (−).

(2) The financial account shows foreign purchases of real and financial assets in the United States. This item earns the United States some foreign currencies, and so it is entered as a plus (+) in the capital account. U.S. purchases of real and financial assets abroad draw down U.S. holdings of foreign currencies, and so this item is entered as a minus (−) in the capital account. The nation has a surplus in its financial account if foreign purchases of U.S. assets are greater than U.S. purchases of assets abroad. The nation has a deficit in its financial account if foreign purchases of U.S. assets are less than U.S. purchases of assets abroad. The **balance on the capital and financial account** is the difference between the value of the capital account and the value of the financial account.

c. The balance of payments must always sum to zero; sometimes economists refer to a balance-of-payments deficit or surplus. A nation has a **balance-of-payments deficit** when an imbalance in the combined current account and capital and financial account leads to a decrease in **official reserves,** which are central bank holdings of foreign currencies, reserves at the International Monetary Fund, and stock of gold. A **balance-of-payments surplus** arises when imbalances in the combined current account and capital and financial account result in an increase in official reserves.

3. There are both a *flexible or floating exchange-rate system* and a *fixed exchange-rate system* that nations use to correct imbalances in the balance of payments. If nations use a flexible or floating exchange system, the demand for and the supply of foreign currencies determine foreign exchange rates. The exchange rate for any foreign currency is the rate at which the quantity of that currency demanded is equal to the quantity of it supplied.

a. A change in the demand for or the supply of a foreign currency will cause a change in the exchange rate for that currency. When there is an increase in the price paid in dollars for a foreign currency, the dollar has *depreciated* and the foreign currency has *appreciated* in value. Conversely, when there is a decrease in the price paid in dollars for a foreign currency, the dollar has *appreciated* and the foreign currency has *depreciated* in value.

b. Changes in the demand for or supply of a foreign currency are largely the result of changes in tastes, relative incomes, relative price levels, relative interest rates, and speculation.

(1) A change in tastes for foreign goods that leads to an increase in demand for those goods will increase the value of the foreign currency and decrease the value of the U.S. currency.

(2) If the growth of U.S. national income is more rapid than that of other nations, the value of U.S. currency will depreciate because it will expand its imports over its exports.

(3) *Purchasing-power-parity theory* is the idea that exchange rates equate the purchasing power of various currencies. Exchange rates, however, often deviate from this parity. If the domestic price level rises sharply in the United States and remains constant in another nation, the currency of the other nation will appreciate in value and the U.S. currency will depreciate in value.

(4) Changes in the relative interest rate in two nations may change their exchange rate. If real interest rates rise in the United States relative to another major trading partner, the U.S. dollar will appreciate in value because people will want to invest more money in the United States and the value of the other nation's currency will depreciate.

(5) If speculators think the U.S. currency will depreciate, they can sell that currency, and that act will help depreciate its value.

c. Flexible exchange rates can be used to eliminate a balance-of-payments deficit or surplus.

(1) When a nation has a payment deficit, foreign exchange rates will increase, thus making foreign goods and services more expensive and decreasing imports. Those events will make a nation's goods and services less expensive for foreigners to buy, thus increasing exports.

(2) With a payment surplus, the exchange rates will increase, thus making foreign goods and services less expensive and increasing imports. This situation makes a nation's goods and services more expensive for foreigners to buy, thus decreasing exports.

d. Flexible exchange rates have disadvantages because they increase the uncertainties exporters, importers, and investors face, thus reducing international trade. This system also changes the terms of trade and creates instability in domestic economies.

4. If nations use a *fixed exchange-rate system,* they fix (or peg) foreign exchange rates. The governments of those nations must intervene in the foreign exchange markets to prevent shortages and surpluses caused by shifts in demand and supply.

a. One way a nation can stabilize foreign exchange rates is through *currency interventions.* In this case, its government sells its reserves of a foreign currency in exchange for its own currency (or gold) when there is a shortage of the foreign currency. Conversely, a government will buy a foreign currency in exchange for its own currency (or gold) when there is a surplus of the foreign currency; however, currency reserves may be limited and inadequate for handling large and persistent deficits or surpluses, and so it may use other means to maintain fixed exchange rates.

b. A nation may adopt trade policies that discourage imports and encourage exports.

c. A nation may impose *exchange controls* and rationing, but those policies tend to distort trade, lead to government favoritism, restrict consumer choice, and create black markets.

d. Another way a nation can stabilize foreign exchange rates is to use monetary and fiscal policy to reduce its national income and price level and raise interest rates relative to those in other nations. These events would lead to a decrease in the demand for and an increase in the supply of different foreign currencies.

5. In their recent history, the nations of the world have used three different exchange-rate systems.

a. Under the *gold standard,* each nation must define its currency in terms of a quantity of gold, maintain a fixed relationship between its gold and its money supply, and allow gold to be imported or exported without restrictions.

(1) The potential gold flows between nations would ensure that exchange rates remained fixed.

(2) Payment deficits and surpluses would be eliminated through macroeconomic adjustments. For example, if a nation had a balance-of-payments deficit and gold flowing out of the country, its money supply would decrease. That event would increase interest rates and decrease total spending, output, employment, and the price level. The opposite would happen in the other country because it would have a payments surplus. The changes in both nations would eliminate any payments deficit or surplus.

(3) During the worldwide depression of the 1930s nations felt that remaining on the gold standard threatened their recoveries, and the *devaluation* of their currencies to boost exports led to the breakdown and abandonment of the gold standard.

b. From the end of World War II until 1971, under the *Bretton Woods system,* nations were committed to the adjustable-peg system of exchange rates. The ***International Monetary Fund (IMF)*** was created to keep this exchange-rate system feasible and flexible.

(1) The adjustable-peg system required the United States to sell gold to other member nations at a fixed price and required the other members of the IMF to define their monetary units in terms of either gold or dollars (which established fixed exchange rates among the currencies of all member nations). It also required the other member nations to keep the exchange rates for their currencies from rising by selling foreign currencies, selling gold, or borrowing on a short-term basis from the IMF.

(2) The system also provided for orderly changes in exchange rates to correct a fundamental imbalance (persistent and sizable balance-of-payments deficits) by allowing a nation to devalue its currency (increase its defined gold or dollar equivalent).

(3) The other nations of the world used gold and dollars as their international monetary reserves in the Bretton Woods system. For those reserves to grow, the United States had to continue to have balance-of-payments deficits, but to continue the convertibility of dollars into gold, it had to reduce the deficits; faced with that dilemma, in 1971 the United States suspended the convertibility of the dollar, brought an end to the Bretton Woods system, and allowed the exchange rates for the dollar and the other currencies to float.

c. Exchange rates today are allowed to float in the long term to correct balance-of-payments deficits and surpluses, but there can be short-term interventions by governments to stabilize and manage currencies. This new system of ***managed floating exchange rates*** is favored by some and criticized by others.

(1) Its proponents contend that this system has *not* led to any decrease in world trade and has enabled the world to adjust to severe economic shocks throughout its history.

(2) Its critics argue that it has resulted in volatile exchange rates that can hurt developing nations that are dependent on exports, has *not* reduced balance-of-payments deficits and surpluses, and is a "nonsystem" that a nation may use to achieve its own domestic economic goals.

6. The United States had large and persistent ***trade deficits*** in the last decade, and they are likely to continue.

a. Those trade deficits were the result of several factors:

(1) more rapid growth in the domestic economy than in the economies of several major trading partners, which caused imports to rise more than exports;

(2) the emergence of large trade deficits with China;

(3) a rapid rise in the price of oil that must be imported from oil-producing nations; and

(4) a decline in the rate of saving and a capital account surplus, which allowed U.S. citizens to consume more imported goods.

b. The trade deficits of the United States had two principal effects. They increased current domestic consumption (allowing the nation to operate outside its production possibilities frontier). They also increased the indebtedness of U.S. citizens to foreigners. A possible negative implication of these persistent trade deficits is that they will lead to permanent debt and more foreign ownership of domestic assets or lead to large sacrifices of future domestic consumption. However, if foreign lending increases the U.S. capital stock, then it can contribute to long-term U.S. economic growth.

7. (Last Word). Speculators buy foreign currency in hopes of reselling it later at a profit. They also sell foreign currency in hopes of rebuying it later when it is cheaper. Although speculators are often accused of creating severe fluctuations in currency markets, that criticism is overstated because economic conditions rather than speculation are typically the chief source of the problem. One positive function of speculators is that they smooth out temporary fluctuations in the value of foreign currencies. Another positive role speculators play in currency markets is that they bear risks that others do not want to take by delivering the specified amount of foreign exchange at the contract price on the date of delivery.

■ **HINTS AND TIPS**

1. The chapter is filled with many new terms, some of which are just special words used in international economics to mean things with which you are already familiar. Other terms are entirely new to you, and so you must spend time learning them if you are to understand the chapter.

2. The terms **"depreciation"** and **"appreciation"** can be confusing when applied to foreign exchange markets.

a. First, know the related terms. "Depreciate" means decrease or fall, whereas "appreciate" means increase or rise.

b. Second, think of depreciation and appreciation in terms of quantities:

(1) what *decreases* when the currency of Country A *depreciates* is the *quantity* of Country B's currency that can be purchased for *1 unit* of Country A's currency;

(2) what *increases* when the currency of Country A *appreciates* is the *quantity* of Country B's currency that can be purchased for *1 unit* of Country A's currency.

c. Third, consider the effect of changes in **exchange rates:**

(1) when the exchange rate for Country B's currency *rises*, this means that Country A's currency has *depreciated* in value because 1 unit of Country A's currency will now purchase a smaller quantity of Country B's currency;

(2) when the exchange rate for Country B's currency *falls*, this means that Country A's currency has *appreciated* in value because 1 unit of Country A's currency will now purchase a larger quantity of Country B's currency.

3. The meaning of the balance of payments can also be confusing because of the number of accounts in the balance sheet. Remember that the balance of payments must always balance and sum to zero because the current account in the balance of payments can be in deficit, but it will be exactly offset by a surplus in the capital and financial account. When economists speak of a balance-of-payments deficit or surplus, they are referring to adding official reserves to or subtracting official reserves from the capital and financial account so that it equals the current account.

■ **IMPORTANT TERMS**

balance of payments

current account

balance on goods and services

trade deficit

trade surplus

balance on the current account

capital and financial account

balance on the capital and financial account

balance-of-payments deficit

balance-of-payments surplus

official reserves

flexible or floating exchange-rate system

fixed exchange-rate system

purchasing-power-parity theory

currency inventions

exchange controls

gold standard

devaluation

Bretton Woods system

International Monetary Fund (IMF)

managed floating exchange rate

SELF-TEST

■ **FILL-IN QUESTIONS**

1. The rate of exchange for the European euro is the amount in (euros, dollars) _____ that a U.S. citizen must pay to obtain 1 (euro, dollar) _____. The rate of exchange for the U.S. dollar is the amount in (euros, dollars) _____ that a citizen in the euro zone must pay to obtain 1 (euro, dollar) _____. If the rate of exchange for the euro is (1.05 euros, $0.95) _____, the rate of exchange for the U.S. dollar is _____.

2. U.S. exports create a foreign (demand for, supply of) _____ dollars and generate a _____ foreign currencies owned by U.S. banks and available to domestic buyers; U.S. imports create a domestic (demand for, supply of) _____ foreign currencies and reduce the _____ foreign currencies held by U.S. banks and available for domestic consumers.

3. The balance of payments of a nation records all payments (domestic, foreign) _____ residents make to and receive from _____ residents.

Any transaction that *earns* foreign exchange for that nation is a (debit, credit) _____, and any transaction that *uses up* foreign exchange is a _____. A debit is shown with a (+, −) _____ sign, and a credit is shown with a _____ sign.

4. If a nation has a deficit in its balance of goods, its exports of goods are (greater, less) _____ than its imports of goods, and if it has a deficit in its balance on goods and services, its exports of those items are _____ than its imports of them.

5. The current account is equal to the balance on goods and services (plus, minus) _____ net investment income and _____ net transfers.

6. The capital and financial account consists of two types of account.

a. The capital account records measure net (investment, debt forgiveness) _____.

b. The financial account measures the flow of monetary payments from the sale or purchase of real or financial assets. Foreign purchases of real and financial assets in the United States earn foreign currencies, and so they are entered as a (plus, minus) _____ in the financial account, but U.S. purchases of real and financial assets abroad draw down U.S. holding of foreign currencies, and so this item is entered as a _____. If foreign purchases of U.S. assets are greater than U.S. purchases of assets abroad, the nation has a (surplus, deficit) _____ in its financial account, but if foreign purchases of U.S. assets are less than U.S. purchases of assets abroad, it has a _____.

7. A nation may finance a current account deficit by (buying, selling) _____ assets or by (borrowing, lending) _____ abroad and may use a current account surplus to (buy, sell) _____ assets or (borrow, lend) _____ abroad.

8. The sum of the current account and the capital and financial accounts must equal (0, 1) _____ so that the balance of payments always balances. However, when economists speak of a balance-of-payments deficit or surplus, they are referring the use of official reserves, which are the quantities of (foreign currencies, its own money) _____ owned by the central bank. If that nation has a balance-of-payments deficit, its official reserves (increase, decrease) _____ in the capital and financial account, but with a balance-of-payments surplus its official reserves _____ in the capital and financial account.

9. If foreign exchange rates float freely and a nation has a balance-of-payments *deficit,* that nation's currency in the foreign exchange markets will (appreciate, depreciate) _____ and foreign currencies will _____compared to it. As a result of these changes in foreign exchange rates, the nation's imports will (increase, decrease) _____, its exports will _____, and the size of its deficit will (increase, decrease) _____.

10. What effect would each of the following have—the appreciation (**A**) or depreciation (**D**) of the euro compared to the U.S. dollar in the foreign exchange market, *ceteris paribus*?

   a. The increased preference in the United States for domestic wines over wines produced in Europe: _____

   b. A rise in the U.S. national income: _____

   c. An increase in the price level in Europe: _____
   d. A rise in real interest rates in the United States:

   _____

   e. The belief of speculators in Europe that the dollar will appreciate in the foreign exchange market: _____

11. There are three disadvantages of freely floating foreign exchange rates: The risks and uncertainties associated with flexible rates tend to (expand, diminish) _____ trade between nations; when a nation's currency depreciates, its terms of trade with other nations are (worsened, improved) _____; and fluctuating exports and imports can (stabilize, destabilize) _____ an economy.

12. To fix or peg the rate of exchange for the Mexican peso when the exchange rate for the peso is rising, the United States would (buy, sell) _____ pesos in exchange for dollars, and when the exchange rate for the peso is falling, the United States would _____ pesos in exchange for dollars.

13. Under a fixed exchange-rate system, a nation with a balance-of-payments deficit may attempt to eliminate the deficit by (taxing, subsidizing) _____ imports or _____ exports. The nation may use exchange controls and ration foreign exchange among those who wish to (export, import) _____ goods and services and require all those who _____ goods and services to sell the foreign exchange they earn to the (businesses, government) _____.

14. If the United States has a payments deficit with Japan and the exchange rate for the Japanese yen is rising, under a fixed exchange-rate system the United States may adopt (expansionary, contractionary) _____ fiscal and monetary policies to reduce the demand for the yen, but this will bring about (inflation, recession) _____ in the United States.

15. When the nations of the world were on the gold standard exchange, rates were relatively (stable, unstable) _____. When a nation had a payments deficit, gold flowed (into, out of) _____ that nation, its money supply (increased, decreased) _____, its interest rates _____, and output, employment, income, and perhaps prices (increased, decreased) _____; thus, its payments deficit _____.

16. The Bretton Woods system was established to bring about (flexible, fixed) _____ exchange rates. Under the Bretton Woods system, a member nation defined its monetary unit in terms of (oil, gold) _____or dollars. Each member nation stabilized the exchange rate for its currency and prevented it from depreciating by (supplying, saving) _____ its official reserves of foreign currency, by (buying, selling) _____ gold, or by (borrowing from, lending to) _____ the International Monetary Fund. A nation with a deeply rooted payments deficit could (devalue, revalue) _____ its currency. The system was designed so that in the short run exchange rates would be (stable, flexible) _____ enough to promote international trade and in the long run they would be _____ enough to correct balance-of-payments imbalances.

17. The role of the dollar as a component of international monetary reserves under Bretton Woods produced a dilemma. For the dollar to remain an acceptable international monetary reserve, the U.S. payments deficits had to be (eliminated, continued) _____, but for international monetary reserves to grow to accommodate world trade, those payments deficits had to be _____. Those deficits caused an acceptability problem because they resulted in (a decrease, an increase) _____ in the foreign holding of U.S. dollars and _____ in the U.S. reserves of gold, which contributed to (a decrease, an increase) _____ in the ability of the United States to convert dollars into gold and the willingness of foreigners to hold dollars as if they were as good as gold. In 1971, the United States essentially ended this system when it (adopted, suspended) _____ the convertibility of dollars into gold and allowed the value of the dollar to be determined by markets.

18. Since that time the international monetary system has moved to a system of managed (fixed, floating) _____ exchange rates. This means that exchange rates of nations are (restricted from, free to) _____ find their equilibrium market levels, but nations may occasionally (leave, intervene in) _____ the foreign exchange markets to stabilize or alter market exchange rates.

19. The advantages of the current system are that the growth of trade (was, was not) _____ accommodated and that it has survived much economic (stability, turbulence) _____. Its disadvantages are its (equilibrium, volatility) _____ and the lack of guidelines for nations that make it a (bureaucracy, nonsystem) _____.

20. In recent years, the United States had large trade and current account (surpluses, deficits) _____ that were brought about by sharp increases in its (exports, imports) _____ and small increases in its _____. One cause was (stronger, weaker) _____ economic growth in the United States relative to _____ economic growth in Europe and Japan. Another contributing factor was a (rising, falling) _____ saving rate. One effect of the trade deficits of the United States has been (decreased, increased) _____ current domestic consumption that allows the nation to operate outside its production possibility frontier, and another effect has been a (rise, fall) _____ in the indebtedness of U.S. citizens to foreigners.

■ TRUE–FALSE QUESTIONS

Circle T if the statement is true, F if it is false.

1. Imports of goods and services by U.S. citizens from abroad create a supply of dollars in the foreign exchange market. **T F**

2. The balance of payments of the United States records all the payments its residents receive from and make to the residents of foreign nations. **T F**

3. Exports are a debit item and are shown with a minus sign (−), and imports are a credit item and are shown with a plus sign (+) in the balance of payments of a nation. **T F**

4. The current account balance is a nation's exports of goods and services minus its imports of goods and services. **T F**

5. The capital account will be a negative number when Americans forgave more debt that was owed to them by foreigners than foreigners forgave debt that was owed to them by Americans. **T F**

6. The nation's current account balance and the capital and financial account in any year are always equal to zero. **T F**

7. The purchasing-power-parity theory basically explains why there is an inverse relationship between the price of dollars and the quantity demanded. **T F**

8. The expectations of speculators in the United States that the exchange rate for Japanese yen will fall in the future will increase the supply of yen in the foreign exchange market and decrease the exchange rate for the yen. **T F**

9. If a nation has a balance-of-payments deficit and exchange rates are flexible, the price of that nation's currency in the foreign exchange markets will fall; this will reduce its imports and increase its exports. **T F**

10. Were the United States' terms of trade with Nigeria to worsen, Nigeria would obtain a greater quantity of U.S. goods and services for every barrel of oil it exported to the United States. **T F**

11. If a nation wishes to fix (or peg) the foreign exchange rate for the Swiss franc, it must buy Swiss francs with its own currency when the rate of exchange for the Swiss franc rises. **T F**

12. If exchange rates are stable or fixed and a nation has a balance-of- payments surplus, prices and currency incomes in that nation will tend to rise. **T F**

13. A nation using exchange controls to eliminate a balance-of-payments surplus may depreciate its currency. **T F**

14. If country A defined its currency as worth 100 grains of gold and country B defined its currency as worth 20 grains of gold, then, ignoring packing, insuring, and shipping charges, 5 units of country A's currency would be worth 1 unit of country B's currency. **T F**

15. Under the gold standard, the potential free flow of gold among nations would result in exchange rates that are fixed. **T F**

16. In the Bretton Woods system, a nation could not devalue its currency by more than 10% without the permission of the International Monetary Fund. **T F**

17. In the Bretton Woods system, a nation with persistent balance-of-payments surpluses had an undervalued currency and should have increased the pegged value of its currency. **T F**

18. To accommodate expanding world trade in the Bretton Woods system, the U.S. dollar served as a reserve medium of exchange and the United States ran persistent balance-of-payments deficits. **T F**

19. A basic shortcoming of the Bretton Woods system was its inability to bring about the changes in exchange rates needed to correct persistent payments deficits and surpluses. **T F**

20. Using the managed floating system of exchange rates, a nation with a persistent balance-of-payments surplus should allow the value of its currency in foreign exchange markets to decrease. **T F**

21. Two criticisms of the current managed floating exchange-rate system are its potential for volatility and its lack of clear policy rules or guidelines for nations to manage exchange rates.　　　**T　F**

22. The trade deficits of the United States in recent years were caused by sharp increases in U.S. exports and slight increases in U.S. imports.　　　**T　F**

23. Improved economic growth in the economies of the major trading partners of the United States would tend to worsen the trade deficit.　　　**T　F**

24. The decline in the saving rate in the United States contributed to the persistent trade deficit of the past decade.　　　**T　F**

25. The negative net exports of the United States have increased the indebtedness of U.S. citizens to foreigners.　　　**T　F**

■ MULTIPLE-CHOICE QUESTIONS

Circle the letter that corresponds to the best answer.

1. If a U.S. citizen could buy £25,000 for $100,000, the rate of exchange for the pound would be
(a) $40
(b) $25
(c) $4
(d) $.25

2. U.S. residents demand foreign currencies to
(a) produce goods and services exported to foreign countries
(b) pay for goods and services imported from foreign countries
(c) receive interest payments on investments in the United States
(d) have foreigners make real and financial investments in the United States

3. Which of the following would be a credit in the current account?
(a) U.S. imports of goods
(b) U.S. exports of services
(c) U.S. purchases of assets abroad
(d) U.S. interest payments for foreign capital invested in the United States

4. A nation's balance on the current account is equal to its exports less its imports of
(a) goods and services
(b) goods and services, plus U.S. purchases of assets abroad
(c) goods and services, plus net investment income and net transfers
(d) goods and services, minus foreign purchases of assets in the United States

5. The net investment income of the United States in its international balance of payments is the
(a) interest income it receives from foreign residents
(b) dividends it receives from foreign residents

(c) excess of interest and dividends it receives from foreign residents over what it paid to them
(d) excess of public and private transfer payments it receives from foreign residents over what it paid to them

6. In a flexible or floating exchange-rate system, when the U.S. dollar price of a British pound rises, this means that the dollar has
(a) appreciated relative to the pound and the pound has appreciated relative to the dollar
(b) appreciated relative to the pound and the pound has depreciated relative to the dollar
(c) depreciated relative to the pound and the pound has appreciated relative to the dollar
(d) depreciated relative to the pound and the pound has depreciated relative to the dollar

7. Which statement is correct about a factor that causes a nation's currency to appreciate or depreciate in value?
(a) If the supply of a nation's currency decreases, all else equal, that currency will depreciate.
(b) If the supply of a nation's currency increases, all else equal, that currency will depreciate.
(c) If the demand for a nation's currency increases, all else equal, that currency will depreciate.
(d) If the demand for a nation's currency decreases, all else equal, that currency will appreciate.

8. Assuming exchange rates are flexible, which of the following should increase the dollar price of the Swedish krona?
(a) a rate of inflation greater in Sweden than in the United States
(b) real interest rate increases more in Sweden than in the United States
(c) national income increases more in Sweden than in the United States
(d) the increased preference of Swedish citizens for U.S. automobiles over Swedish automobiles

9. Under a flexible exchange-rate system, a nation may be able to correct or eliminate a persistent (long-term) balance-of-payments deficit by
(a) lowering the barriers on imported goods
(b) reducing the international value of its currency
(c) expanding its national income
(d) reducing its official reserves

10. If a nation had a balance-of-payments surplus and exchange rates floated freely, the foreign exchange rate for its currency would
(a) rise, its exports would increase, and its imports would decrease
(b) rise, its exports would decrease, and its imports would increase
(c) fall, its exports would increase, and its imports would decrease
(d) fall, its exports would decrease, and its imports would increase

11. Which would be a result associated with the use of freely floating foreign exchange rates to correct a nation's balance-of-payments surplus?

(a) The nation's terms of trade with other nations would be worsened.

(b) Importers in the nation who had made contracts for the future delivery of goods would find that they had to pay a higher price than expected for the goods.

(c) If the nation were at full employment, the decrease in exports and the increase in imports would be inflationary.

(d) Exporters in the nation would find their sales abroad had decreased.

12. The use of exchange controls to eliminate a nation's balance-of-payments deficit results in decreasing that nation's

(a) imports

(b) exports

(c) price level

(d) income

13. Which of these conditions did a nation have to fulfill to be under the gold standard?

(a) use only gold as a medium of exchange

(b) maintain a flexible relationship between its gold stock and its currency supply

(c) allow gold to be freely exported from and imported into the nation

(d) define its monetary unit in terms of a fixed quantity of dollars

14. If the nations of the world were on the gold standard and one nation had a balance-of-payments surplus,

(a) foreign exchange rates in that nation would rise

(b) gold would tend to be imported into that country

(c) the level of prices in that country would fall

(d) employment and output in that country would fall

15. Which was the principal disadvantage of the gold standard?

(a) unstable foreign exchange rates

(b) persistent payments imbalances

(c) the uncertainties and decreased trade that resulted from the depreciation of gold

(d) the domestic macroeconomic adjustments experienced by a nation with a payments deficit or surplus

16. The objective of the adjustable-peg or Bretton Woods system was exchange rates that were

(a) adjustable in the short run and fixed in the long run

(b) adjustable in both the short run and the long run

(c) fixed in both the short run and the long run

(d) fixed in the short run and adjustable in the long run

17. Which is the best definition of international monetary reserves in the Bretton Woods system?

(a) gold

(b) dollars

(c) gold and dollars

(d) gold, dollars, and British pounds

18. The major dilemma created by the persistent U.S. payments deficits under the Bretton Woods system was that in order to maintain the status of the dollar as an acceptable international monetary reserve, the deficits had to

(a) decrease, but to expand reserves to accommodate world trade, the deficits had to continue

(b) continue, but to expand reserves to accommodate world trade, the deficits had to be eliminated

(c) increase, but to expand reserves to accommodate world trade, the deficits had to be reduced

(d) decrease, but to expand reserves to accommodate world trade, the deficits had to be eliminated

19. "Floating" the dollar means

(a) the value of the dollar is determined by the demand for and the supply of the dollar

(b) the dollar price of gold has been increased

(c) the price of the dollar has been allowed to crawl upward at the rate of one-fourth of 1% a month

(d) the IMF decreased the value of the dollar by 10%

20. A system of managed floating exchange rates

(a) allows nations to stabilize exchange rates in the short term

(b) requires nations to stabilize exchange rates in the long term

(c) entails stable exchange rates in both the short term and the long term

(d) fixes exchange rates at market levels

21. Floating exchange rates

(a) tend to correct balance-of-payments imbalances

(b) reduce the uncertainties and risks associated with international trade

(c) increase the world's need for international monetary reserves

(d) tend to have no effect on the volume of trade

22. The trade problem that faced the United States in recent years was a

(a) deficit in its capital account

(b) surplus in its balance on goods

(c) deficit in its current account

(d) surplus in its current account

23. Which was a cause of the growth of U.S. trade deficits in recent years?

(a) protective tariffs imposed by the United States

(b) slower economic growth in the United States

(c) direct foreign investment in the United States

(d) a declining saving rate in the United States

24. What would be the effect on U.S. imports and exports when the United States experiences strong economic growth but its major trading partners experience sluggish economic growth?

(a) U.S. imports will increase more than U.S. exports.

(b) U.S. exports will increase more than U.S. imports.

(c) U.S. imports will decrease, but U.S. exports will increase.

(d) There will be no effect on U.S. imports and exports.

25. Two major outcomes from the trade deficits of recent years were

(a) decreased domestic consumption and U.S. indebtedness

(b) increased domestic consumption and U.S. indebtedness

(c) increased domestic consumption but decreased U.S. indebtedness

(d) decreased domestic consumption but increased U.S. indebtedness

■ **PROBLEMS**

1. Assume a U.S. exporter sells $3 million worth of wheat to an importer in Colombia. If the rate of exchange for the Colombian peso is $.02 (2 cents), the wheat has a total value of 150 million pesos.

    a. There are two ways the importer in Colombia may pay for the wheat. It might write a check for 150 million pesos drawn on its bank in Bogotá and send it to the U.S. exporter.

    (1) The American exporter would then sell the check to its bank in New Orleans, and its demand deposit there would increase by $_____ million.

    (2) This New Orleans bank now sells the check for 150 million pesos to a correspondent bank (a U.S. commercial bank that keeps an account in the Bogotá bank).

    (a) The New Orleans bank's account in the correspondent bank increases by _____ million (dollars, pesos) _____; and

    (b) the correspondent bank's account in the Bogotá bank increases by _____ million (pesos, dollars) _____.

    b. The second way for the importer to pay for the wheat is to buy from its bank in Bogotá a draft on a U.S. bank for $3 million, pay for the draft by writing a check for 150 million pesos drawn on the Bogotá bank, and send the draft to the U.S. exporter.

    (1) The U.S. exporter would then deposit the draft in its account in the New Orleans bank, and its demand deposit account there would increase by $_____ million.

    (2) The New Orleans bank collects the amount of the draft from the U.S. bank on which it is drawn through the Federal Reserve Banks.

    (a) Its account at the Fed increases by $_____ million; and

    (b) the account of the bank on which the draft was drawn decreases by $_____ million.

    c. Regardless of the method used by the Colombian importer to pay for the wheat,

    (1) the export of the wheat created a (demand for, supply of) _____ dollars and a _____ pesos.

    (2) The number of dollars owned by the U.S. exporter has (increased, decreased) _____, and the number of pesos owned by the Colombian importer has _____.

2. The following table contains hypothetical balance-of-payments data for the United States. All figures are in billions. Compute with the appropriate sign (+ or −) and enter in the table the six missing items.

Current Account

(1)	U.S. goods exports	$+150
(2)	U.S. goods imports	−200
(3)	*Balance on goods*	_____
(4)	U.S. exports of services	+75
(5)	U.S. imports of services	−60
(6)	*Balance on services*	_____
(7)	*Balance on goods and services*	_____
(8)	Net investment income	+12
(9)	Net transfers	−7
(10)	**Balance on current account**	_____

Capital Account and Financial Account

(11)	Capital Account	−5

Financial Account:

(12)	Foreign purchases of assets in the U.S.	+90
(13)	U.S. purchases of assets abroad	−55
(14)	*Balance on financial account*	_____
(15)	**Balance on capital and financial account**	_____
		$ 0

3. The following table shows supply and demand schedules for the British pound.

Quantity of pounds supplied	Price	Quantity of pounds demanded
400	$5.00	100
360	4.50	200
300	4.00	300
236	3.50	400
267	3.00	500
240	2.50	620
200	2.00	788

    a. If the exchange rates are flexible,

    (1) what will be the rate of exchange for the pound?

    $_____

    (2) what will be the rate of exchange for the dollar?

    £_____

    (3) how many pounds will be purchased in the market?

    _____

    (4) how many dollars will be purchased in the market?

    _____

    b. If the U.S. government wished to fix or peg the price of the pound at $5.00, it would have to (buy, sell) _____ (how many) _____ pounds for $_____.

    c. And if the British government wished to fix the price of the dollar at £ 2/5, it would have to (buy, sell) _____ (how many) _____ pounds for $_____

■ **SHORT ANSWER AND ESSAY QUESTIONS**

1. What is the foreign exchange rate? Who are the demanders and suppliers of a particular foreign exchange, say, the British pound? Why is a buyer (demander) in the foreign exchange markets also always a seller (supplier)?

2. What is meant when it is said that "a nation's exports pay for its imports"? Do nations pay for all their imports with exports?

3. What is a balance of payments? What are the principal sections in a nation's balance of payments, and what are the principal "balances" to be found in it?

4. How can a nation finance a current account deficit, and what can it do with a current account surplus?

5. How does a nation finance a balance-of-payments deficit, and what does it do with a balance-of-payments surplus?

6. What types of events cause the exchange rate for a foreign currency to appreciate or depreciate? How will each event affect the exchange rate for a foreign currency and for a nation's own currency?

7. How can flexible foreign exchange rates eliminate balance-of-payments deficits and surpluses? What are the problems associated with this method of correcting payments imbalances?

8. How may a nation use its international monetary reserves to fix or peg foreign exchange rates? Be precise. How does a nation obtain or acquire those monetary reserves?

9. What kinds of trade policies may nations with payments deficits use to eliminate their deficits?

10. How can foreign exchange controls be used to restore international equilibrium? Why do such exchange controls necessarily involve the rationing of foreign exchange? What effect do these controls have on prices, output, and employment in the nations that use them?

11. If foreign exchange rates are fixed, what kind of domestic macroeconomic adjustments are required to eliminate a payments deficit? To eliminate a payments surplus?

12. What is the gold standard? How did the international gold standard correct payments imbalances?

13. What were the disadvantages of the gold standard for eliminating payments deficits and surpluses?

14. What did nations use as international monetary reserves under the Bretton Woods system? Why was the dollar used by nations as international money, and how could they acquire additional dollars?

15. Explain the dilemma created by the need for expanding international monetary reserves and for maintaining the status of the dollar under the Bretton Woods system.

16. Why and how did the United States shatter the Bretton Woods system in 1971?

17. Explain what is meant by a managed floating system of foreign exchange rates. When are exchange rates managed, and when are they allowed to float?

18. Explain the arguments of the proponents and the critics of the managed floating system.

19. What were the causes of the trade deficits of the United States in recent years?

20. What were the effects of the trade deficits of recent years on the U.S. economy?

ANSWERS

Chapter 19 Exchange Rates, the Balance of Payments, and Trade Deficits

FILL-IN QUESTIONS

1. dollars, euro, euros, dollar, $0.95, 1.05 euros
2. demand for, supply of, demand for, supply of
3. domestic, foreign, credit, debit, −, +
4. less, less
5. plus, plus
6. *a.* debt forgiveness; *b.* plus, minus, surplus, deficit
7. selling, borrowing, buy, lend
8. 0, foreign currencies, decrease, increase
9. depreciate, appreciate, decrease, increase, decrease
10. *a.* D; *b.* A; *c.* D; *d.* D; *e.* D
11. diminish, worsened, destabilize
12. sell, buy
13. taxing, subsidizing, import, export, government
14. contractionary, recession
15. stable, out of, decreased, increased, decreased, decreased
16. fixed, gold, supplying, selling, borrowing from, devalue, stable, flexible
17. eliminated, continued, an increase, a decrease, a decrease, suspended
18. floating, free to, intervene in
19. was, turbulence, volatility, nonsystem
20. deficits, imports, exports, stronger, weaker, falling, increased, rise

TRUE–FALSE QUESTIONS

1. T, p. 361	**10.** T, p. 369	**19.** T, p. 373
2. T, p. 361	**11.** F, pp. 369–370	**20.** F, pp. 373–374
3. F, p. 362	**12.** T, pp. 365–366	**21.** T, p. 374
4. F, pp. 362–363	**13.** F, p. 370	**22.** F, pp. 375–376
5. T, p. 363	**14.** F, pp. 371–372	**23.** F, p. 375
6. T, p. 364	**15.** T, pp. 371–372	**24.** T, p. 376
7. F, pp. 366–367	**16.** T, p. 373	**25.** T, p. 376
8. T, p. 367	**17.** T, p. 373	
9. T, pp. 367–369	**18.** T, pp. 372–373	

MULTIPLE-CHOICE QUESTIONS

1. c, p. 361
2. b, p. 361
3. b, p. 362
4. c, pp. 362–363
5. c, p. 363
6. c, p. 364
7. b, p. 365
8. b, p. 367
9. b, pp. 368–369

10. b, pp. 368–369
11. d, p. 369
12. a, p. 370
13. c, p. 371
14. b, pp. 371–372
15. d, p. 372
16. d, pp. 372–373
17. c, p. 373
18. a, p. 373

19. a, pp. 373–374
20. a, pp. 373–374
21. a, pp. 373–374
22. c, p. 375
23. d, pp. 375–376
24. a, p. 375
25. b, p. 376

SHORT ANSWER AND ESSAY QUESTIONS

1. p. 361
2. p. 361
3. pp. 362–363
4. pp. 362–364
5. p. 364
6. pp. 365–367
7. pp. 367–368

8. pp. 369–370
9. p. 370
10. p. 370
11. p. 371
12. p. 371
13. p. 372
14. pp. 372–373

15. p. 373
16. p. 373
17. pp. 373–374
18. p. 374
19. pp. 375–376
20. p. 376

PROBLEMS

1. *a.* (1) 3, (2) (a) 3, dollars, (b) 150, pesos; *b.* (1) 3, (2) (a) 3, (b) 3; *c.* (1) demand for, supply of, (2) increased, decreased
2. −50, +15, −35, −30, +35, +30
3. *a.* (1) 4.00, (2) 1/4, (3) 300, (4) 1200; *b.* buy, 300, 1500; *c.* sell, 380, 950

Glossary

Note: Terms set in *italic* type are defined separately in this glossary.

actual investment The amount that *firms* invest; equal to *planned investment* plus *unplanned investment*.

actual reserves The funds that a bank has on deposit at the *Federal Reserve Bank* of its district (plus its *vault cash*).

adjustable pegs The device used in the *Bretton Woods system* to alter *exchange rates* in an orderly way to eliminate persistent payments deficits and surpluses. Each nation defined its monetary unit in terms of (pegged it to) gold or the dollar, kept the *rate of exchange* for its money stable in the short run, and adjusted its rate in the long run when faced with international payments disequilibrium.

aggregate A collection of specific economic units treated as if they were one. For example, all prices of individual goods and services are combined into a *price level,* or all units of output are aggregated into *gross domestic product*.

Aggregate demand A schedule or curve that shows the total quantity of goods and services demanded (purchased) at different *price levels*.

aggregate demand–aggregate supply (AD-AS) model The macroeconomic model that uses *aggregate demand* and *aggregate supply* to determine and explain the *price level* and the real *domestic output*.

aggregate expenditures The total amount spent for final goods and services in an economy.

aggregate expenditures–domestic output approach - Determination of the equilibrium *gross domestic product* by finding the real GDP at which *aggregate expenditures* equal *domestic output*.

aggregate expenditures schedule A schedule or curve showing the total amount spent for final goods and services at different levels of *real GDP*.

aggregate supply A schedule or curve showing the total quantity of goods and services supplied (produced) at different *price levels*.

aggregate supply shocks Sudden, large changes in resource costs that shift an economy's aggregate supply curve.

allocative efficiency The apportionment of resources among firms and industries to obtain the production of the products most wanted by society (consumers); the output of each product at which its *marginal cost* and price or *marginal benefit* are equal.

anticipated inflation Increases in the price level *(inflation)* that occur at the expected rate.

appreciation (of the dollar) An increase in the value of the dollar relative to the currency of another nation, so a dollar buys a larger amount of the foreign currency and thus of foreign goods.

asset Anything of monetary value owned by a firm or individual.

asset demand for money The amount of *money* people want to hold as a *store of value;* this amount varies inversely with the *interest rate*.

average propensity to consume Fraction (or percentage) of *disposable income* that households plan to spend for consumer goods and services; consumption divided by *disposable income*.

average propensity to save (APS) Fraction (or percentage) of *disposable income* that households save; *saving* divided by *disposable income*.

average tax rate Total tax paid divided by total (taxable) income, as a percentage.

balance of payments (See *international balance of payments*.)

balance-of- payments deficit The amount by which *in-payments* from a nation's stock of *official reserves* are required to balance that nation's *capital and financial account* with its *current account* (in its *balance of payments*).

balance-of- payments surplus The amount by which *outpayments* to a nation's stock of *official reserves* are required to balance that nation's *capital and financial account* with its *current account* (in its *international balance of payments*).

balance on current account The exports of goods and services of a nation less its imports of goods and services plus its *net investment income* and *net transfers* in a year.

balance on goods and services The exports of goods and services of a nation less its imports of goods and services in a year.

balance sheet A statement of the *assets, liabilities,* and *net worth* of a firm or individual at some given time.

bank deposits The deposits that individuals or firms have at banks (or thrifts) or that banks have at the *Federal Reserve Banks*.

bankers' bank A bank that accepts the deposits of and makes loans to *depository institutions;* in the United States, a *Federal Reserve Bank*.

bank reserves The deposits of commercial banks and thrifts at *Federal Reserve Banks* plus bank and thrift *vault cash*.

barter The exchange of one good or service for another good or service.

base year The year with which other years are compared when an index is constructed; for example, the base year for a *price index*.

Board of Governors The seven-member group that supervises and controls the money and banking system of the United States; the Board of Governors of the Federal Reserve System; the Federal Reserve Board.

bond A financial device through which a borrower (a firm or government) is obligated to pay the principal and interest on a loan at a specific date in the future.

break-even income The level of *disposable income* at which *households* plan to consume (spend) all their income and to save none of it; also, in an income transfer program, the level of earned income at which subsidy payments become zero.

Bretton Woods system The international monetary system developed after the Second World War in which *adjustable pegs* were employed, the *International Monetary Fund* helped stabilize foreign exchange rates, and gold and the dollar were used as *international monetary reserves*.

budget deficit The amount by which the expenditures of the Federal government exceed its revenues in any year.

budget surplus The amount by which the revenues of the Federal government exceed its expenditures in any year.

built-in stabilizer A mechanism that increases government's budget deficit (or reduces its surplus) during a recession and increases government's budget surplus (or reduces its deficit) during an expansion without any action by policymakers. The tax system is one such mechanism.

Bureau of Economic Analysis (BEA) An agency of the U.S. Department of Commerce that compiles the national income and product accounts.

business cycle Recurring increases and decreases in the level of economic activity over periods of years; consists of peak, recession, trough, and expansion phases.

business firm (See *firm*.)

capital Human-made resources (buildings, machinery, and equipment) used to produce goods and services; goods that do not directly satisfy human wants; also called capital goods.

capital and financial account The section of a nation's *international balance of payments* that records (1) debt forgiveness by and to foreigners and (2) foreign purchases of assets in the United States and U.S. purchases of assets abroad.

capital and financial account deficit A negative balance on its *capital and financial account* in a country's *international balance of payments*.

capital and financial account surplus A positive balance on its *capital and financial account* in a country's *international balance of payments*.

capital gain The gain realized when securities or properties are sold for a price greater than the price paid for them.

capital goods (See *capital*.)

capital-intensive commodity A product that requires a relatively large amount of *capital* to be produced.

capitalism An economic system in which property resources are privately owned and markets and prices are used to direct and coordinate economic activities.

capital stock The total available *capital* in a nation.

cartel A formal agreement among firms (or countries) in an industry to set the price of a product and establish the outputs of the individual firms (or countries) or to divide the market for the product geographically.

causation A relationship in which the occurrence of one or more events brings about another event.

CEA (See *Council of Economic Advisers*.)

central bank A bank whose chief function is the control of the nation's *money supply*; in the United States, the Federal Reserve System.

central economic planning Government determination of the objectives of the economy and how resources will be directed to attain those goals.

***ceteris paribus* assumption** (See *other-things-equal assumption*.)

change in demand A change in the *quantity demanded* of a good or service at every price; a shift of the *demand curve* to the left or right.

change in quantity demanded A change in the amount of a product that consumers are willing and able to purchase because of a change in the product's price.

change in quantity supplied A change in the amount of a product that producers offer for sale because of a change in the product's price.

change in supply A change in the *quantity supplied* of a good or service at every price; a shift of the *supply curve* to the left or right.

checkable deposit Any deposit in a *commercial bank* or *thrift institution* against which a check may be written.

checkable-deposit multiplier (See *monetary multiplier*.)

check clearing The process by which funds are transferred from the checking accounts of the writers of checks to the checking accounts of the recipients of the checks.

checking account A *checkable deposit* in a *commercial bank* or *thrift institution*.

circular flow diagram An illustration showing the flow of resources from *households* to *firms* and of products from firms to households. These flows are accompanied by reverse flows of money from firms to households and from households to firms.

classical economics The macroeconomic generalizations accepted by most economists before the 1930s that led to the conclusion that a capitalistic economy was self-regulating and therefore would usually employ its resources fully.

closed economy An economy that neither exports nor imports goods and services.

coincidence of wants A situation in which the good or service that one trader desires to obtain is the same as that which another trader desires to give up and an item that the second trader wishes to acquire is the same as that which the first trader desires to surrender.

COLA (See *cost-of-living adjustment*.)

command system A method of organizing an economy in which property resources are publicly owned and government uses *central economic planning* to direct and coordinate economic activities; command economy; communism.

commercial bank A firm that engages in the business of banking (accepts deposits, offers checking accounts, and makes loans).

commercial banking system All *commercial banks* and *thrift institutions* as a group.

communism (See *command system*.)

comparative advantage A lower relative opportunity cost than that of another producer or country.

compensation to employees *Wages* and salaries plus wage and salary supplements paid by employers to workers.

competition The presence in a market of independent buyers and sellers competing with one another along with the freedom of buyers and sellers to enter and leave the market.

complementary goods Products and services that are used together. When the price of one falls, the demand for the other increases (and conversely).

conglomerates Firms that produce goods and services in two or more separate industries.

constant opportunity cost An *opportunity cost* that remains the same for each additional unit as a consumer (or society) shifts purchases (production) from one product to another along a straight-line *budget line* (*production possibilities curve*).

consumer goods Products and services that satisfy human wants directly.

Consumer Price Index (CPI) An index that measures the prices of a fixed "market basket" of some 300 goods and services bought by a "typical" consumer.

consumer sovereignty Determination by consumers of the types and quantities of goods and services that will be produced with the scarce resources of the economy; consumers' direction of production through their dollar votes.

consumer surplus The difference between the maximum price a consumer is (or consumers are) willing to pay for an additional unit of a product and its market price; the triangular area below the demand curve and above the market price.

consumption of fixed capital An estimate of the amount of *capital* worn out or used up (consumed) in producing the *gross domestic product;* also called depreciation.

consumption schedule A schedule showing the amounts *households* plan to spend for *consumer goods* at different levels of *disposable income.*

contractionary fiscal policy A decrease in *government purchases* for goods and services, an increase in *net taxes,* or some combination of the two, for the purpose of decreasing *aggregate demand* and thus controlling inflation.

coordination failure A situation in which people do not reach a mutually beneficial outcome because they lack some way to jointly coordinate their actions; a possible cause of macroeconomic instability.

corporate income tax A tax levied on the net income (accounting profit) of corporations.

corporation A legal entity ("person") chartered by a state or the Federal government that is distinct and separate from the individuals who own it.

correlation A systematic and dependable association between two sets of data (two kinds of events); does not necessarily indicate causation.

cost-of-living adjustment (COLA) An automatic increase in the incomes (wages) of workers when inflation occurs; guaranteed by a collective bargaining contract between firms and workers.

cost-push inflation Increases in the price level (inflation) resulting from an increase in resource costs (for example, raw-material prices) and hence in *per-unit production costs;* inflation caused by reductions in *aggregate supply.*

Council of Economic Advisers (CEA) A group of three persons that advises and assists the president of the United States on economic matters (including the preparation of the annual *Economic Report of the President*).

creative destruction The hypothesis that the creation of new products and production methods simultaneously destroys the market power of existing monopolies.

credit An accounting item that increases the value of an asset (such as the foreign money owned by the residents of a nation).

credit union An association of persons who have a common tie (such as being employees of the same firm or members of the same labor union) that sells shares to (accepts deposits from) its members and makes loans to them.

crowding-out effect A rise in interest rates and a resulting decrease in *planned investment* caused by the Federal government's increased borrowing to finance budget deficits and refinance debt.

currency Coins and paper money.

currency appreciation (See *exchange-rate appreciation*.)

currency depreciation (See *exchange-rate depreciation*.)

currency intervention A government's buying and selling of its own currency or foreign currencies to alter international exchange rates.

current account The section in a nation's *international balance of payments* that records its exports and imports of goods and services, its net *investment income,* and its *net transfers.*

cyclical asymmetry The idea that *monetary policy* may be more successful in slowing expansions and controlling *inflation* than in extracting the economy from severe recession.

cyclical deficit A Federal *budget deficit* that is caused by a recession and the consequent decline in tax revenues.

cyclical unemployment A type of *unemployment* caused by insufficient total spending (or by insufficient *aggregate demand*).

debit An accounting item that decreases the value of an asset (such as the foreign money owned by the residents of a nation).

deflating Finding the *real gross domestic product* by decreasing the dollar value of the GDP for a year in which prices were higher than in the *base year*.

deflation A decline in the economy's *price level*.

demand A schedule showing the amounts of a good or service that buyers (or a buyer) wish to purchase at various prices during some time period.

demand curve A curve illustrating *demand*.

demand factor (in growth) The increase in the level of *aggregate demand* that brings about the *economic growth* made possible by an increase in the production potential of the economy.

demand management The use of *fiscal policy* and *monetary policy* to increase or decrease *aggregate demand*.

demand-pull inflation Increases in the price level (inflation) resulting from an excess of demand over output at the existing price level, caused by an increase in *aggregate demand*.

demand schedule (See *demand*.)

dependent variable A variable that changes as a consequence of a change in some other (independent) variable; the "effect" or outcome.

depository institutions Firms that accept deposits of *money* from the public (businesses and persons); *commercial banks, savings and loan associations, mutual savings banks,* and *credit unions*.

depreciation (See *consumption of fixed capital*.)

depreciation (of the dollar) A decrease in the value of the dollar relative to another currency, so a dollar buys a smaller amount of the foreign currency and therefore of foreign goods.

derived demand The demand for a resource that depends on the demand for the products it helps to produce.

determinants of aggregate demand Factors such as consumption spending, *investment,* government spending, and *net exports* that, if they change, shift the aggregate demand curve.

determinants of aggregate supply Factors such as input prices, *productivity,* and the legal-institutional environment that, if they change, shift the aggregate supply curve.

determinants of demand Factors other than price that determine the quantities demanded of a good or service.

determinants of supply Factors other than price that determine the quantities supplied of a good or service.

devaluation A decrease in the governmentally defined value of a currency.

developing countries Many countries of Africa, Asia, and Latin America that are characterized by lack of capital goods, use of nonadvanced technologies, low literacy rates, high unemployment, rapid population growth, and labor forces heavily committed to agriculture.

direct foreign investment The building of new factories (or the purchase of existing capital) in a particular nation by corporations of other nations.

direct relationship The relationship between two variables that change in the same direction, for example, product price and quantity supplied; positive relationship.

discount rate The interest rate that the *Federal Reserve Banks* charge on the loans they make to *commercial banks* and *thrift institutions*.

discouraged workers Employees who have left the *labor force* because they have not been able to find employment.

discretionary fiscal policy Deliberate changes in taxes (tax rates) and government spending by Congress to promote full employment, price stability, and economic growth.

discrimination The practice of according individuals or groups inferior treatment in hiring, occupational access, education and training, promotion, wage rates, or working conditions even though they have the same abilities, education, skills, and work experience as other workers.

disinflation A reduction in the rate of *inflation*.

disposable income (DI) *Personal income* less personal taxes; income available for *personal consumption expenditures* and *personal saving*.

dissaving Spending for consumer goods and services in excess of *disposable income;* the amount by which *personal consumption expenditures* exceed disposable income.

dividends Payments by a corporation of all or part of its profit to its stockholders (the corporate owners).

division of labor The separation of the work required to produce a product into a number of different tasks that are performed by different workers; *specialization* of workers.

Doha Round The latest, uncompleted (as of fall 2006) sequence of trade negotiations by members of the *World Trade Organization;* named after Doha, Qatar, where the set of negotiations began.

dollar votes The "votes" that consumers and entrepreneurs cast for the production of consumer and capital goods, respectively, when they purchase those goods in product and resource markets.

domestic capital formation The process of adding to a nation's stock of *capital* by saving and investing part of its own domestic output.

domestic output *Gross* (or net) *domestic product;* the total output of final goods and services produced in the economy.

domestic price The price of a good or service within a country, determined by domestic demand and supply.

dumping The sale of a product in a foreign country at prices either below cost or below the prices commonly charged at home.

durable good A consumer good with an expected life (use) of 3 or more years.

earnings The money income received by a worker; equal to the *wage* (rate) multiplied by the amount of time worked.

economic cost A payment that must be made to obtain and retain the services of a *resource;* the income a firm must provide to a resource supplier to attract the resource away from an alternative use; equal to the quantity of other products that cannot be produced when resources are instead used to make a particular product.

economic efficiency The use of the minimum necessary resources to obtain the socially optimal amounts of goods and services; entails both *productive efficiency* and *allocative efficiency.*

economic growth (1) An outward shift in the *production possibilities curve* that results from an increase in resource supplies or quality or an improvement in *technology;* (2) an increase of real output *(gross domestic product)* or real output per capita.

economic law An *economic principle* that has been tested and retested and has stood the test of time.

economic model A simplified picture of economic reality; an abstract generalization.

economic perspective A viewpoint that envisions individuals and institutions making rational decisions by comparing the marginal benefits and marginal costs associated with their actions.

economic policy A course of action intended to correct or avoid a problem.

economic principle A widely accepted generalization about the economic behavior of individuals or institutions.

economic profit The *total revenue* of a firm less its *economic costs* (which include both *explicit costs* and *implicit costs*); also called "pure profit" and "above-normal profit."

economic resources The *land, labor, capital,* and *entrepreneurial ability* that are used in the production of goods and services; productive agents; factors of production.

economics The social science concerned with how individuals, institutions, and society make optimal (best) choices under conditions of scarcity.

economic system A particular set of institutional arrangements and a coordinating mechanism for solving the economizing problem; a method of organizing an economy, of which the *market system* and the *command system* are the two general types.

economic theory A statement of a cause-effect relationship; when accepted by all or nearly all economists, an *economic principle.*

economies of scale Reductions in the *average total cost* of producing a product as the firm expands the size of plant (its output) in the *long run;* the economies of mass production.

economizing problem The choices necessitated because society's economic wants for goods and services are unlimited but the resources available to satisfy these wants are limited (scarce).

efficiency factors (in growth) The capacity of an economy to combine resources effectively to achieve growth of real output that the *supply factors* (of growth) make possible.

efficiency loss Reductions in combined consumer and producer surplus caused by an underallocation or overallocation of resources to the production of a good or service. Also called deadweight loss.

efficiency wage A wage that minimizes wage costs per unit of output by encouraging greater effort or reducing turnover.

efficient allocation of resources That allocation of an economy's resources among the production of different products that leads to the maximum satisfaction of consumers' wants, thus producing the socially optimal mix of output with society's scarce resources.

electronic payments Purchases made by transferring funds electronically. Examples: Fedwire transfers, automated clearinghouse transactions (ACHs), payments via the PayPal system, and payments made through stored-value cards.

employment rate The percentage of the *labor force* employed at any time.

entrepreneurial ability The human resource that combines the other resources to produce a product, makes nonroutine decisions, innovates, and bears risks.

equation of exchange $MV = PQ$, in which M is the supply of money, V is the *velocity* of money, P is the *price level,* and Q is the physical volume of *final goods and services* produced.

equilibrium GDP (See *equilibrium real domestic output.*)

equilibrium price The *price* in a competitive market at which the *quantity demanded* and the *quantity supplied* are equal, there is neither a shortage nor a surplus, and there is no tendency for price to rise or fall.

equilibrium price level The price level at which the aggregate demand curve intersects the aggregate supply curve.

equilibrium quantity (1) The quantity demanded and supplied at the equilibrium price in a competitive market; (2) the profit-maximizing output of a firm.

equilibrium real domestic output The *gross domestic product* at which the total quantity of final goods and services purchased *(aggregate expenditures)* is equal to the total quantity of final goods and services produced (the real domestic output); the real domestic output at which the aggregate demand curve intersects the aggregate supply curve.

equilibrium real output (See *equilibrium real domestic output*)

euro The common currency unit used by 12 European nations (as of 2006) in the Euro zone, which consists of Austria, Belgium, Finland, France, Germany, Greece, Ireland, Italy, Luxembourg, the Netherlands, Portugal, and Spain.

European Union (EU) An association of 25 European nations that has eliminated tariffs and quotas among them, established common tariffs for imported goods from outside the member nations, eliminated barriers to the free movement of capital, and created other common economic policies.

excess reserves The amount by which a bank's or thrift's *actual reserves* exceed its *required reserves;* actual reserves minus required reserves.

exchange control (See *foreign exchange control.*)

exchange rate The *rate of exchange* of one nation's currency for another nation's currency.

exchange-rate appreciation An increase in the value of a nation's currency in foreign exchange markets; an increase in the *rate of exchange* for foreign currencies.

exchange-rate depreciation A decrease in the value of a nation's currency in foreign exchange markets; a decrease in the *rate of exchange* for foreign currencies.

exchange-rate determinant Any factor other than the *rate of exchange* that determines a currency's demand and supply in the *foreign exchange market.*

excise tax A tax levied on the production of a specific product or on the quantity of the product purchased.

exhaustive expenditure An expenditure by government resulting directly in the employment of *economic resources* and in the absorption by government of the goods and services those resources produce; a *government purchase.*

expansion A phase of the *business cycle* in which *real GDP, income,* and employment rise.

expansionary fiscal policy An increase in *government purchases* of goods and services, a decrease in *net taxes,* or some combination of the two for the purpose of increasing *aggregate demand* and expanding real output.

expansionary monetary policy Federal Reserve system actions to increase the *money supply,* lower *interest rates,* and expand *real GDP;* an easy money policy.

expectations The anticipations of consumers, firms, and others about future economic conditions.

expected rate of return The increase in profit a firm anticipates it will obtain by purchasing capital (or engaging in research and development); expressed as a percentage of the total cost of the investment (or R&D) activity.

expenditures approach The method that adds all expenditures made for *final goods and services* to measure the *gross domestic product.*

expenditures-output approach (See *aggregate expenditures–domestic output approach.*)

exports Goods and services produced in a nation and sold to buyers in other nations.

export subsidies Government payments to domestic producers to enable them to reduce the *price* of a good or service to foreign buyers.

export supply curve An upward-sloping curve that shows the amount of a product that domestic firms will export at each *world price* that is above the *domestic price.*

export transaction A sale of a good or service that increases the amount of foreign currency flowing to a nation's citizens, firms, and government.

external benefit (See *positive externality.*)

external cost (See *negative externality.*)

external debt Private or public debt owed to foreign citizens, firms, and institutions.

externality A cost or benefit from production or consumption, accruing without compensation to someone other than the buyers and sellers of the product (see *negative externality* and *positive externality*) .

external public debt The portion of the public debt owed to foreign citizens, firms, and institutions.

face value The dollar or cents value placed on a U.S. coin or piece of paper money.

factors of production *Economic resources: land, capital, labor,* and *entrepreneurial ability.*

fallacy of composition The false notion that what is true for the individual (or part) is necessarily true for the group (or whole).

FDIC (See *Federal Deposit Insurance Corporation.*)

Federal Deposit Insurance Corporation (FDIC) The federally chartered corporation that insures deposit liabilities (up to $100,000 per account) of *commercial banks* and *thrift institutions* (excluding *credit unions,* whose deposits are insured by the *National Credit Union Administration*).

Federal funds rate The interest rate banks and other depository institutions charge one another on overnight loans made out of their *excess reserves.*

Federal government The government of the United States, as distinct from the state and local governments.

Federal Open Market Committee (FOMC) The 12-member group that determines the purchase and sale policies of the *Federal Reserve Banks* in the market for U.S. government securities.

Federal Reserve Banks The 12 banks chartered by the U.S. government to control the *money supply* and perform other functions. (See *central bank, quasi-public bank,* and *bankers' bank.*)

Federal Reserve Note Paper money issued by the *Federal Reserve Banks.*

Federal Reserve System The U.S. central bank, consisting of the *Board of Governors* of the Federal Reserve and the 12 *Federal Reserve Banks,* which controls the lending activity of the nation's banks and thrifts and thus the *money supply;* commonly referred to as the "Fed."

fiat money Anything that is *money* because government has decreed it to be money.

final goods and services Goods and services that have been purchased for final use and not for resale or further processing or manufacturing.

financial capital (See *money capital.*)

financial services industry The broad category of firms that provide financial products and services to help households and businesses earn *interest*, receive *dividends*, obtain *capital gains*, insure against losses, and plan for retirement. The industry includes *commercial banks*, *thrift institutions*, insurance companies, mutual fund companies, pension funds, and securities firms.

firm An organization that employs resources to produce a good or service for profit and owns and operates one or more *plants*.

fiscal policy Changes in government spending and tax collections designed to achieve a full-employment and noninflationary domestic output; also called *discretionary fiscal policy*.

fixed exchange rate A *rate of exchange* that is set in some way and therefore prevented from rising or falling with changes in currency supply and demand.

flexible exchange rate A *rate of exchange* determined by the international demand for and supply of a nation's money; a rate free to rise or fall (to float).

floating exchange rate (See *flexible exchange rate*.)

foreign competition (See *import competition*.)

foreign exchange control The control a government may exercise over the quantity of foreign currency demanded by its citizens and firms and over the *rates of exchange* in order to limit its *outpayments* to its *inpayments* (to eliminate a *payments deficit*).

foreign exchange market A market in which the money (currency) of one nation can be used to purchase (can be exchanged for) the money of another nation; currency market.

foreign exchange rate (See *rate of exchange*.)

foreign purchase effect The inverse relationship between the *net exports* of an economy and its price level relative to foreign price levels.

45° line A line along which the value of *GDP* (measured horizontally) is equal to the value of *aggregate expenditures* (measured vertically).

fractional reserve banking system A *reserve requirement* that is less than 100 percent of the checkable-deposit liabilities of a *commercial bank* or *thrift institution*.

freedom of choice The freedom of owners of property resources to employ or dispose of them as they see fit, of workers to enter any line of work for which they are qualified, and of consumers to spend their incomes in a manner that they think is appropriate.

freedom of enterprise The freedom of *firms* to obtain economic resources, to use those resources to produce products of the firm's own choosing, and to sell their products in markets of their choice.

free-rider problem The inability of potential providers of an economically desirable good or service to obtain payment from those who benefit, because of *nonexcludability*.

free trade The absence of artificial (government-imposed) barriers to trade among individuals and firms in different nations.

frictional unemployment A type of unemployment caused by workers voluntarily changing jobs and by temporary layoffs; unemployed workers between jobs.

full employment (1) The use of all available resources to produce want-satisfying goods and services; (2) the situation in which the *unemployment rate* is equal to the *full-employment unemployment rate* and there is *frictional* and *structural* but no *cyclical unemployment* (and the *real GDP* of the economy equals *potential output*).

full-employment unemployment rate The *unemployment rate* at which there is no *cyclical unemployment* of the *labor force;* equal to between 4 and 5 percent in the United States because some *frictional* and *structural unemployment* is unavoidable.

functional distribution of income The manner in which *national income* is divided among the functions performed to earn it (or the kinds of resources provided to earn it); the division of national income into wages and salaries, proprietors' income, corporate profits, interest, and rent.

gains from trade The extra output that trading partners obtain through specialization of production and exchange of goods and services.

GDP (See *gross domestic product*.)

GDP gap Actual *gross domestic product* minus potential output; may be either a positive amount (a *positive GDP gap*) or a negative amount (a *negative GDP gap*).

GDP price index A *price index* for all the goods and services that make up the *gross domestic product;* the price index used to adjust *nominal gross domestic product* to *real gross domestic product*.

G8 nations A group of eight major nations (Canada, France, Germany, Italy, Japan, Russia, United Kingdom, and United States) whose leaders meet regularly to discuss common economic problems and try to coordinate economic policies.

General Agreement on Tariffs and Trade (GATT) The international agreement reached in 1947 in which 23 nations agreed to give equal and nondiscriminatory treatment to one another, to reduce tariff rates by multinational negotiations, and to eliminate *import quotas*. It now includes most nations and has become the *World Trade Organization*.

generalization Statement of the nature of the relationship between two or more sets of facts.

gold standard A historical system of fixed exchange rates in which nations defined their currencies in terms of gold, maintained a fixed relationship between their stocks of gold and their money supplies, and allowed gold to be freely exported and imported.

government purchases (G) Expenditures by government for goods and services that government consumes in providing public goods and for public (or social) capital that has a long lifetime; the expenditures of all governments in the economy for those *final goods and services*.

government transfer payment The disbursement of money (or goods and services) by government for which government receives no currently produced good or service in return.

gross domestic product (GDP) The total market value of all *final goods and services* produced annually within the boundaries of the United States, whether by U.S.- or foreign-supplied resources.

gross private domestic investment (Ig) Expenditures for newly produced *capital goods* (such as machinery, equipment, tools, and buildings) and for additions to inventories.

growth accounting The bookkeeping of the supply-side elements such as productivity and labor inputs that contribute to changes in *real GDP* over some specific time period.

guiding function of prices The ability of price changes to bring about changes in the quantities of products and resources demanded and supplied.

horizontal axis The "left-right" or "west-east" measurement line on graph or grid.

household An economic unit (of one or more persons) that provides the economy with resources and uses the income received to purchase goods and services that satisfy economic wants.

human capital The knowledge and skills that make a person productive.

human capital investment Any expenditure undertaken to improve the education, skills, health, or mobility of workers, with an expectation of greater productivity and thus a positive return on the investment.

hyperinflation A very rapid rise in the price level; an extremely high rate of inflation.

hypothesis A tentative explanation of cause and effect that requires testing.

IMF (See *International Monetary Fund*.)

import competition The competition that domestic firms encounter from the products and services of foreign producers.

import demand curve A downsloping curve showing the amount of a product that an economy will import at each *world price* below the *domestic price*.

import quota A limit imposed by a nation on the quantity (or total value) of a good that may be imported during some period of time.

imports Spending by individuals, *firms,* and governments for goods and services produced in foreign nations.

import transaction The purchase of a good or service that decreases the amount of foreign money held by citizens, firms, and governments of a nation.

income A flow of dollars (or purchasing power) per unit of time derived from the use of human or property resources.

income approach The method that adds all the income generated by the production of *final goods and services* to measure the *gross domestic product*.

income effect A change in the quantity demanded of a product that results from the change in *real income (purchasing power)* caused by a change in the product's price.

income inequality The unequal distribution of an economy's total income among households or families.

increase in demand An increase in the *quantity demanded* of a good or service at every price; a shift of the *demand curve* to the right.

increase in supply An increase in the *quantity supplied* of a good or service at every price; a shift of the *supply curve* to the right.

increasing returns An increase in a firm's output by a larger percentage than the percentage increase in its inputs.

independent goods Products or services for which there is little or no relationship between the price of one and the demand for the other. When the price of one rises or falls, the demand for the other tends to remain constant.

independent variable The variable causing a change in some other (dependent) variable.

individual demand The demand schedule or *demand curve* of a single buyer.

individual supply The supply schedule or *supply curve* of a single seller.

industrially advanced countries High-income countries such as the United States, Canada, Japan, and the nations of western Europe that have highly developed *market economies* based on large stocks of technologically advanced capital goods and skilled labor forces.

industry A group of (one or more) *firms* that produce identical or similar products.

inferior good A good or service whose consumption declines as income rises (and conversely), price remaining constant.

inflating Determining *real gross domestic product* by increasing the dollar value of the *nominal gross domestic product* produced in a year in which prices are lower than those in a *base year*.

inflation A rise in the general level of prices in an economy.

inflationary expectations The belief of workers, firms, and consumers that substantial inflation will occur in the future.

inflationary expenditure gap The amount by which the *aggregate expenditures schedule* must shift downward to decrease the *nominal GDP* to its full-employment noninflationary level.

inflation premium The component of the *nominal interest rate* that reflects anticipated inflation.

inflation targeting The annual statement by a *central bank* of a goal for a specific range of inflation in a future year, coupled with monetary policy designed to achieve the goal.

information technology New and more efficient methods of delivering and receiving information through use of computers, fax machines, wireless phones, and the Internet.

infrastructure The capital goods usually provided by the *public sector* for the use of its citizens and firms (for example, highways, bridges, transit systems, wastewater treatment facilities, municipal water systems, and airports).

injection An addition of spending to the income-expenditure stream: *investment, government purchases,* and *net exports.*

innovation The first commercially successful introduction of a new product, the use of a new method of production, or the creation of a new form of business organization.

inpayments The receipts of domestic or foreign money that individuals, firms, and governments of one nation obtain from the sale of goods and services abroad, as investment income and remittances, and from foreign purchases of its assets.

insider-outsider theory The hypothesis that nominal wages are inflexible downward because firms are aware that workers ("insiders") who retain employment during recession may refuse to work cooperatively with previously unemployed workers ("outsiders") who offer to work for less than the current wage.

interest The payment made for the use of money (of borrowed funds).

interest income Payments of income to those who supply the economy with *capital*.

interest rate The annual rate at which interest is paid; a percentage of the borrowed amount.

interest-rate effect The tendency for increases in the *price level* to increase the demand for money, raise interest rates, and, as a result, reduce total spending and real output in the economy (and the reverse for price-level decreases).

intermediate goods Products that are purchased for resale or further processing or manufacturing.

internally held public debt *Public debt* owed to citizens, firms, and institutions of the same nation that issued the debt.

international balance of payments A summary of all the transactions that took place between the individuals, firms, and government units of one nation and those of all other nations during a year.

international balance-of-payments deficit (See *balance-of-payments deficit.*)

international balance-of-payments surplus (See *balance-of-payments surplus.*)

international gold standard (See *gold standard.*)

International Monetary Fund (IMF) The international association of nations that was formed after the Second World War to make loans of foreign monies to nations with temporary *payments deficits* and, until the early 1970s, to administer the *adjustable pegs*. It now mainly makes loans to nations facing possible defaults on private and government loans.

international monetary reserves The foreign currencies and other assets such as gold that a nation can use to settle a *balance-of-payments deficit.*

international value of the dollar The price that must be paid in foreign currency (money) to obtain one U.S. dollar.

intrinsic value The market value of the metal within a coin.

inventories Goods that have been produced but remain unsold.

inverse relationship The relationship between two variables that change in opposite directions, for example, product price and quantity demanded; negative relationship.

investment Spending for the production and accumulation of *capital* and additions to inventories.

investment demand curve A curve that shows the amounts of *investment* demanded by an economy at a series of *real interest rates.*

investment goods Same as *capital* or capital goods.

investment in human capital (See *human capital investment.*)

investment schedule A curve or schedule that shows the amounts firms plan to invest at various possible values of *real gross domestic product.*

"invisible hand" The tendency of firms and resource suppliers that seek to further their own self-interests in competitive markets to also promote the interest of society.

Joint Economic Committee (JEC) Committee of senators and representatives that investigates economic problems of national interest.

Keynesian economics The macroeconomic generalizations that lead to the conclusion that a capitalistic economy is characterized by macroeconomic instability and that *fiscal policy* and *monetary policy* can be used to promote *full employment, price-level stability,* and *economic growth.*

Keynesianism The philosophical, ideological, and analytical views pertaining to *Keynesian economics.*

labor People's physical and mental talents and efforts that are used to help produce goods and services.

labor force Persons 16 years of age and older who are not in institutions and who are employed or are unemployed and seeking work.

labor-force participation rate The percentage of the working-age population that is actually in the *labor force.*

labor-intensive commodity A product requiring a relatively large amount of *labor* to be produced.

labor market discrimination (See *discrimination.*)

labor productivity Total output divided by the quantity of labor employed to produce it; the *average product* of labor or output per hour of work.

labor union A group of workers organized to advance the interests of the group (to increase wages, shorten the hours worked, improve working conditions, and so on).

Laffer Curve A curve relating government tax rates and tax revenues and on which a particular tax rate (between zero and 100 percent) maximizes tax revenues.

laissez-faire capitalism (See *capitalism.*)

land Natural resources ("free gifts of nature") used to produce goods and services.

land-intensive commodity A product requiring a relatively large amount of *land* to be produced.

law of demand The principle that, other things equal, an increase in a product's price will reduce the quantity of it demanded, and conversely for a decrease in price.

law of increasing opportunity costs The principle that as the production of a good increases, the *opportunity cost* of producing an additional unit rises.

law of supply The principle that, other things equal, an increase in the price of a product will increase the quantity of it supplied, and conversely for a price decrease.

leakage (1) A withdrawal of potential spending from the income-expenditures stream via *saving,* tax payments, or *imports;* (2) a withdrawal that reduces the lending potential of the banking system.

learning by doing Achieving greater *productivity* and lower *average total cost* through gains in knowledge and skill that accompany repetition of a task; a source of *economies of scale.*

legal tender A legal designation of a nation's official currency (bills and coins). Payment of debts must be accepted in this monetary unit, but creditors can specify the form of payment, for example, "cash only" or "check or credit card only."

lending potential of an individual commercial bank The amount by which a single bank can safely increase the *money supply* by making new loans to (or buying securities from) the public; equal to the bank's excess reserves.

lending potential of the banking system The amount by which the banking system can increase the *money supply* by making new loans to (or buying securities from) the public; equal to the *excess reserves* of the banking system multiplied by the *monetary multiplier.*

liability A debt with a monetary value; an amount owed by a firm or an individual.

limited liability Restriction of the maximum loss to a predetermined amount for the owners (stockholders) of a *corporation.* The maximum loss is the amount they paid for their shares of stock.

liquidity The ease with which an asset can be converted quickly into cash with little or no loss of purchasing power. Money is said to be perfectly liquid, whereas other assets have a lesser degree of liquidity.

long run (1) In *microeconomics,* a period of time long enough to enable producers of a product to change the quantities of all the resources they employ; period in which all resources and costs are variable and no resources or costs are fixed. (2) In *macroeconomics,* a period sufficiently long for *nominal wages* and other input prices to change in response to a change in the nation's *price level.*

long-run aggregate supply curve The aggregate supply curve associated with a time period in which input prices (especially *nominal wages*) are fully responsive to changes in the *price level.*

long-run vertical Phillips Curve The *Phillips Curve* after all nominal wages have adjusted to changes in the rate of inflation; a line emanating straight upward at the economy's *natural rate of unemployment.*

lump-sum tax A tax that is a constant amount (the tax revenue of government is the same) at all levels of GDP.

M1 The most narrowly defined *money supply,* equal to *currency* in the hands of the public and the *checkable deposits* of commercial banks and thrift institutions.

M2 A more broadly defined *money supply,* equal to *M1* plus *noncheckable savings accounts* (including *money*

market deposit accounts), small *time deposits* (deposits of less than $100,000), and individual *money market mutual fund* balances.

macroeconomics The part of economics concerned with the economy as a whole; with such major aggregates as the household, business, and government sectors; and with measures of the total economy.

managed floating exchange rate An *exchange rate* that is allowed to change (float) as a result of changes in currency supply and demand but at times is altered (managed) by governments via their buying and selling of particular currencies.

marginal analysis The comparison of marginal ("extra" or "additional") benefits and marginal costs, usually for decision making.

marginal benefit The extra (additional) benefit of consuming 1 more unit of some good or service; the change in total benefit when 1 more unit is consumed.

marginal cost (MC) The extra (additional) cost of producing 1 more unit of output; equal to the change in *total cost* divided by the change in output (and, in the short run, to the change in total *variable cost* divided by the change in output).

marginal propensity to consume (MPC) The fraction of any change in *disposable income* spent for *consumer goods;* equal to the change in consumption divided by the change in disposable income.

marginal propensity to save (MPS) The fraction of any change in *disposable income* that households save; equal to the change in *saving* divided by the change in disposable income.

marginal tax rate The tax rate paid on each additional dollar of income.

marginal utility The extra *utility* a consumer obtains from the consumption of 1 additional unit of a good or service; equal to the change in total utility divided by the change in the quantity consumed.

market Any institution or mechanism that brings together buyers (demanders) and sellers (suppliers) of a particular good or service.

market demand (See *total demand.*)

market economy An economy in which the private decisions of consumers, resource suppliers, and firms determine how resources are allocated; the *market system.*

market failure The inability of a market to bring about the allocation of resources that best satisfies the wants of society; in particular, the overallocation or underallocation of resources to the production of a particular good or service because of *externalities* or informational problems or because markets do not provide desired *public goods.*

market system All the product and resource markets of a *market economy* and the relationships among them; a method that allows the prices determined in those markets to allocate the economy's scarce resources and to communicate and coordinate the decisions made by consumers, firms, and resource suppliers.

Medicaid A Federal program that helps finance the medical expenses of individuals covered by the *Supplemental*

Security Income (SSI) and *Temporary Assistance for Needy Families (TANF)* programs.

Medicare A Federal program that is financed by *payroll taxes* and provides for (1) compulsory hospital insurance for senior citizens, (2) low-cost voluntary insurance to help older Americans pay physicians' fees, and (3) subsidized insurance to buy prescription drugs.

medium of exchange Any item sellers generally accept and buyers generally use to pay for a good or service; *money;* a convenient means of exchanging goods and services without engaging in *barter.*

menu costs The reluctance of firms to cut prices during recessions (that they think will be short lived) because of the costs of altering and communicating their price reductions; named after the cost associated with printing new menus at restaurants.

microeconomics The part of economics concerned with decision making by individual units such as a *household,* a *firm,* or an *industry* and with individual markets, specific goods and services, and product and resource prices.

minimum wage The lowest *wage* that employers may legally pay for an hour of work.

monetarism The macroeconomic view that the main cause of changes in aggregate output and price level is fluctuations in the *money supply;* espoused by advocates of a *monetary rule.*

monetary multiplier The multiple of its *excess reserves* by which the banking system can expand *checkable deposits* and thus the *money supply* by making new loans (or buying securities); equal to 1 divided by the *reserve requirement.*

monetary policy A central bank's changing of the *money supply* to influence interest rates and assist the economy in achieving price stability, full employment, and economic growth.

monetary rule The rule suggested by *monetarism.* As traditionally formulated, the rule says that the *money supply* should be expanded each year at the same annual rate as the potential rate of growth of the *real gross domestic product;* the supply of money should be increased steadily between 3 and 5 percent per year. (Also see *Taylor rule.*)

money Any item that is generally acceptable to sellers in exchange for goods and services.

money capital Money available to purchase *capital;* simply *money,* as defined by economists.

money income (See *nominal income.*)

money market The market in which the demand for and the supply of money determine the *interest rate* (or the level of interest rates) in the economy.

money market deposit accounts (MMDAs) Bank- and thrift-provided interest-bearing accounts that contain a variety of short-term securities; such accounts have minimum balance requirements and limits on the frequency of withdrawals.

money market mutual funds (MMMFs) Interest-bearing accounts offered by investment companies, which pool depositors' funds for the purchase of short-term securities. Depositors can write checks in minimum amounts or more against their accounts.

money supply Narrowly defined, *M*1; more broadly defined, *M*2 and *MZM.* (See each.)

monopoly A market structure in which the number of sellers is so small that each seller is able to influence the total supply and the price of the good or service. (Also see *pure monopoly.*)

most-favored-nation (MFN) status An agreement by the United States to allow some other nation's *exports* into the United States at the lowest tariff level levied by the United States.

multinational corporations Firms that own production facilities in two or more countries and produce and sell their products globally.

multiple counting Wrongly including the value of *intermediate goods* in the *gross domestic product;* counting the same good or service more than once.

multiplier The ratio of a change in the equilibrium GDP to the change in *investment* or in any other component of *aggregate expenditures* or *aggregate demand;* the number by which a change in any such component must be multiplied to find the resulting change in the equilibrium GDP.

multiplier effect The effect on equilibrium GDP of a change in *aggregate expenditures* or *aggregate demand* (caused by a change in the *consumption schedule, investment,* government expenditures, or *net exports*).

MZM A definition of the *money supply* that includes monetary balances immediately available at zero cost to households and businesses for making transactions. *MZM* (money zero maturity) equals *M*2 minus small *time deposits* plus *money market mutual fund* balances owned by businesses.

national bank A *commercial bank* authorized to operate by the U.S. government.

National Credit Union Administration (NCUA) The federally chartered agency that insures deposit liabilities (up to $100,000 per account) in *credit unions.*

national income Total income earned by resource suppliers for their contributions to *gross domestic product* plus *taxes on production and imports*; the sum of wages and salaries, *rent, interest, profit, proprietors' income,* and such taxes.

national income accounting The techniques used to measure the overall production of the economy and other related variables for the nation as a whole.

natural monopoly An industry in which *economies of scale* are so great that a single firm can produce the product at a lower average total cost than would be possible if more than one firm produced the product.

natural rate of unemployment (NRU) The *full-employment unemployment rate;* the unemployment rate occurring when there is no cyclical unemployment and the economy is achieving its potential output; the unemployment rate at which actual inflation equals expected inflation.

near-money Financial assets, the most important of which are *noncheckable savings accounts, time deposits,* and U.S. short-term securities and savings bonds, which are not a medium of exchange but can be readily converted into money.

negative externality A cost imposed without compensation on third parties by the production or consumption of sellers or buyers. Example: A manufacturer dumps toxic chemicals into a river, killing the fish sought by sports fishers; an external cost or a spillover cost.

negative GDP gap A situation in which actual *gross domestic product* is less than *potential output.*

negative relationship (See *inverse relationship.*)

net domestic product *Gross domestic product* less the part of the year's output that is needed to replace the *capital goods* worn out in producing the output; the nation's total output available for consumption or additions to the *capital stock.*

net exports (X_n) *Exports* minus *imports.*

net foreign factor income Receipts of resource income from the rest of the world minus payments of resource income to the rest of the world.

net investment income The interest and dividend income received by the residents of a nation from residents of other nations less the interest and dividend payments made by the residents of that nation to the residents of other nations.

net private domestic investment *Gross private domestic investment* less *consumption of fixed capital;* the addition to the nation's stock of *capital* during a year.

net taxes The taxes collected by government less *government transfer payments.*

net transfers The personal and government transfer payments made by one nation to residents of foreign nations less the personal and government transfer payments received from residents of foreign nations.

network effects Increases in the value of a product to each user, including existing users, as the total number of users rises.

net worth The total *assets* less the total *liabilities* of a firm or an individual; for a firm, the claims of the owners against the firm's total assets; for an individual, his or her wealth.

new classical economics The theory that, although unanticipated price-level changes may create macroeconomic instability in the short run, the economy is stable at the full-employment level of domestic output in the long run because prices and wages adjust automatically to correct movements away from the full-employment, non-inflationary output.

New Economy The label attached by some economists and the popular press to the U.S. economy since 1995. The main characteristics are accelerated *productivity growth* and *economic growth,* caused by rapid technological advance and the emergence of the global economy.

nominal gross domestic product (GDP) The *GDP* measured in terms of the price level at the time of measurement (unadjusted for *inflation*).

nominal income The number of dollars received by an individual or group for its resources during some period of time.

nominal interest rate The interest rate expressed in terms of annual amounts currently charged for interest and not adjusted for inflation.

nominal wage The amount of money received by a worker per unit of time (hour, day, etc.); money wage.

nondiscretionary fiscal policy (See *built-in stabilizer.*)

nondurable good A *consumer good* with an expected life (use) of less than 3 years.

nonexcludability The inability to keep nonpayers (free riders) from obtaining benefits from a certain good; a *public good* characteristic.

nonexhaustive expenditure An expenditure by government that does not result directly in the employment of economic resources or the production of goods and services; see *government transfer payment.*

nonincome determinants of consumption and saving All influences on consumption and saving other than the level of *GDP.*

noninterest determinants of investment All influences on the level of investment spending other than the *interest rate.*

noninvestment transaction An expenditure for stocks, bonds, or secondhand *capital goods.*

nonmarket transactions The production of goods and services excluded in the measurement of the *gross domestic product* because they are not bought and sold.

nonproduction transaction The purchase and sale of any item that is not a currently produced good or service.

nonrivalry The idea that one person's benefit from a certain good does not reduce the benefit available to others; a *public good* characteristic.

nontariff barriers (NTBs) All barriers other than *protective tariffs* that nations erect to impede international trade, including *import quotas,* licensing requirements, unreasonable product-quality standards, unnecessary bureaucratic detail in customs procedures, and so on.

normal good A good or service whose consumption increases when income increases and falls when income decreases, price remaining constant.

normal profit The payment made by a firm to obtain and retain *entrepreneurial ability;* the minimum income entrepreneurial ability must receive to induce it to perform entrepreneurial functions for a firm.

normative economics The part of economics involving value judgments about what the economy should be like; focused on which economic goals and policies should be implemented; policy economics.

North American Free Trade Agreement (NAFTA) A 1993 agreement establishing, over a 15-year period, a free-trade zone composed of Canada, Mexico, and the United States.

official reserves Foreign currencies owned by the central bank of a nation.

offshoring The practice of shifting work previously done by American workers to workers located abroad.

Okun's law The generalization that any 1-percentage-point rise in the *unemployment rate* above the *full-employment unemployment rate* will increase the GDP gap by 2 percent of the *potential output* (GDP) of the economy.

OPEC (See *Organization of Petroleum Exporting Countries.*)

open economy An economy that exports and imports goods and services.

open-market operations The buying and selling of U.S. government securities by the *Federal Reserve Banks* for purposes of carrying out *monetary policy.*

opportunity cost The amount of other products that must be forgone or sacrificed to produce a unit of a product.

opportunity-cost ratio An equivalency showing the number of units of two products that can be produced with the same resources; the cost 1 corn ≡ 3 olives show that the resources required to produce 3 units of olives must be shifted to corn production to produce 1 unit of corn.

Organization of Petroleum Exporting Countries (OPEC) A cartel of 11 oil-producing countries (Algeria, Indonesia, Iran, Iraq, Kuwait, Libya, Nigeria, Qatar, Saudi Arabia, Venezuela, and the UAE) that controls the quantity and price of crude oil exported by its members and that accounts for a large percentage of the world's export of oil.

other-things-equal assumption The assumption that factors other than those being considered are held constant; *ceteris paribus* assumption.

outpayments The expenditures of domestic or foreign currency that the individuals, firms, and governments of one nation make to purchase goods and services, for remittances, to pay investment income, and for purchases of foreign assets.

paper money Pieces of paper used as a *medium of exchange;* in the United States, *Federal Reserve Notes.*

partnership An unincorporated firm owned and operated by two or more persons.

patent An exclusive right given to inventors to produce and sell a new product or machine for 20 years from the time of patent application.

payments deficit (See *balance-of-payments deficit.*)

payments surplus (See *balance-of-payments surplus.*)

payroll tax A tax levied on employers of labor equal to a percentage of all or part of the wages and salaries paid by them and on employees equal to a percentage of all or part of the wages and salaries received by them.

peak The point in a business cycle at which business activity has reached a temporary maximum; the economy is near or at full employment and the level of real output is at or very close to the economy's capacity.

per capita GDP *Gross domestic product* (GDP) per person; the average GDP of a population.

per capita income A nation's total income per person; the average income of a population.

personal consumption expenditures The expenditures of *households* for *durable* and *nondurable consumer goods* and *services.*

personal distribution of income The manner in which the economy's *personal* or *disposable income* is divided among different income classes or different households or families.

personal income (PI) The earned and unearned income available to resource suppliers and others before the payment of personal taxes.

personal income tax A tax levied on the taxable income of individuals, households, and unincorporated firms.

personal saving The *personal income* of households less personal taxes and *personal consumption expenditures; disposable income* not spent for *consumer goods.*

per-unit production cost The average production cost of a particular level of output; total input cost divided by units of output.

Phillips Curve A curve showing the relationship between the *unemployment rate* (on the horizontal axis) and the annual rate of increase in the *price level* (on the vertical axis).

planned investment The amount that *firms* plan or intend to invest.

plant A physical establishment that performs one or more functions in the production, fabrication, and distribution of goods and services.

policy economics The formulation of courses of action to bring about desired economic outcomes or to prevent undesired occurrences.

political business cycle The alleged tendency of Congress to destabilize the economy by reducing taxes and increasing government expenditures before elections and to raise taxes and lower expenditures after elections.

positive economics The analysis of facts or data to establish scientific generalizations about economic behavior.

positive externality A benefit obtained without compensation by third parties from the production or consumption of sellers or buyers. Example: A beekeeper benefits when a neighboring farmer plants clover. An *external benefit* or a spillover benefit.

positive GDP gap A situation in which actual *gross domestic product* exceeds *potential output.*

positive relationship (See *direct relationship.*)

post hoc, ergo propter hoc fallacy The false belief that when one event precedes another, the first event must have caused the second event.

potential output The real output *(GDP)* an economy can produce when it fully employs its available resources.

poverty A situation in which the basic needs of an individual or family exceed the means to satisfy them.

poverty rate The percentage of the population with incomes below the official poverty income levels that are established by the Federal government.

price The amount of money needed to buy a particular good, service, or resource.

price index An index number that shows how the weighted-average price of a "market basket" of goods changes over time.

price level The weighted average of the prices of all the final goods and services produced in an economy.

price-level stability A steadiness of the price level from one period to the next; zero or low annual inflation; also called "price stability."

price-level surprises Unanticipated changes in the price level.

price war Successive and continued decreases in the prices charged by firms in an oligopolistic industry. Each firm lowers its price below rivals' prices, hoping to increase its sales and revenues at its rivals' expense.

prime interest rate The benchmark *interest rate* that banks use as a reference point for a wide range of loans to businesses and individuals.

principal-agent problem A conflict of interest that occurs when agents (workers or managers) pursue their own objectives to the detriment of the principals' (stockholders') goals.

private good A good or service that is individually consumed and that can be profitably provided by privately owned firms because they can exclude nonpayers from receiving the benefits.

private property The right of private persons and firms to obtain, own, control, employ, dispose of, and bequeath *land, capital,* and other property.

private sector The *households* and business *firms* of the economy.

producer surplus The difference between the actual price a producer receives (or producers receive) and the minimum acceptable price; the triangular area above the supply curve and below the market price.

production possibilities curve A curve showing the different combinations of two goods or services that can be produced in a *full-employment, full-production* economy where the available supplies of resources and technology are fixed.

productive efficiency The production of a good in the least costly way; occurs when production takes place at the output at which *average total cost* is a minimum and *marginal product* per dollar's worth of input is the same for all inputs.

productivity A measure of average output or real output per unit of input. For example, the productivity of labor is determined by dividing real output by hours of work.

productivity growth The percentage increase in *productivity* from one period to another.

product market A market in which products are sold by *firms* and bought by *households.*

profit The return to the resource *entrepreneurial ability* (see *normal profit*); *total revenue* minus *total cost* (see *economic profit*).

progressive tax A tax whose *average tax rate* increases as the taxpayer's income increases and decreases as the taxpayer's income decreases.

property tax A tax on the value of property (*capital, land, stocks* and *bonds,* and other *assets*) owned by *firms* and *households.*

proportional tax A tax whose *average tax rate* remains constant as the taxpayer's income increases or decreases.

protective tariff A *tariff* designed to shield domestic producers of a good or service from the competition of foreign producers.

public debt The total amount owed by the Federal government to the owners of government securities; equal to the sum of past government *budget deficits* less government *budget surpluses.*

public good A good or service that is characterized by *nonrivalry* and *nonexcludability;* a good or service with these characteristics provided by government.

public investments Government expenditures on public capital (such as roads, highways, bridges, mass-transit systems, and electric power facilities) and on *human capital* (such as education, training, and health).

public sector The part of the economy that contains all government entities; government.

purchasing power The amount of goods and services that a monetary unit of income can buy.

purchasing power parity The idea that exchange rates between nations equate the purchasing power of various currencies. Exchange rates between any two nations adjust to reflect the price-level differences between the countries.

pure rate of interest An essentially risk-free, long-term interest rate that is free of the influence of market imperfections.

quantity demanded The amount of a good or service that buyers (or a buyer) desire to purchase at a particular price during some period.

quantity supplied The amount of a good or service that producers (or a producer) offer to sell at a particular price during some period.

quasi-public bank A bank that is privately owned but governmentally (publicly) controlled; each of the U.S. *Federal Reserve Banks.*

quasi-public good A good or service to which excludability could apply but that has such a large *positive externality* that government sponsors its production to prevent an underallocation of resources.

R&D Research and development activities undertaken to bring about *technological advance.*

rate of exchange The price paid in one's own money to acquire 1 unit of a foreign currency; the rate at which the money of one nation is exchanged for the money of another nation.

rate of return The gain in net revenue divided by the cost of an investment or an *R&D* expenditure; expressed as a percentage.

rational behavior Human behavior based on comparison of marginal costs and marginal benefits; behavior designed to maximize total utility.

rational expectations theory The hypothesis that firms and households expect monetary and fiscal policies to have certain effects on the economy and (in pursuit of their own self-interests) take actions that make these policies ineffective.

rationing function of prices The ability of market forces in competitive markets to equalize *quantity demanded* and *quantity supplied* and to eliminate shortages and surpluses via changes in prices.

real-balances effect The tendency for increases in the *price level* to lower the real value (or purchasing power) of financial assets with fixed money value and, as a result, to reduce total spending and real output, and conversely for decreases in the price level.

real-business-cycle theory A theory that *business cycles* result from changes in technology and resource availability, which affect *productivity* and thus increase or decrease long-run aggregate supply.

real capital (See *capital*.)

real GDP (See *real gross domestic product*.)

real GDP per capita *Inflation*-adjusted output per person; *real GDP*/population.

real gross domestic product (GDP) *Gross domestic product* adjusted for inflation; gross domestic product in a year divided by the GDP *price index* for that year, the index expressed as a decimal.

real income The amount of goods and services that can be purchased with *nominal income* during some period of time; nominal income adjusted for inflation.

real interest rate The interest rate expressed in dollars of constant value (adjusted for *inflation*) and equal to the *nominal interest rate* less the expected rate of inflation.

real wage The amount of goods and services a worker can purchase with his or her *nominal wage;* the purchasing power of the nominal wage.

recession A period of declining real GDP, accompanied by lower real income and higher unemployment.

recessionary expenditure gap The amount by which the *aggregate expenditures schedule* must shift upward to increase the real *GDP* to its full-employment, noninflationary level.

Reciprocal Trade Agreements Act A 1934 Federal law that authorized the president to negotiate up to 50 percent lower tariffs with foreign nations that agreed to reduce their tariffs on U.S. goods. (Such agreements incorporated the *most-favored-nation* clause.)

refinancing the public debt Paying owners of maturing government securities with money obtained by selling new securities or with new securities.

regressive tax A tax whose *average tax rate* decreases as the taxpayer's income increases and increases as the taxpayer's income decreases.

rental income The payments (income) received by those who supply *land* to the economy.

required reserves The funds that banks and thrifts must deposit with the *Federal Reserve Bank* (or hold as *vault cash*) to meet the legal *reserve requirement;* a fixed percentage of the bank's or thrift's checkable deposits.

reserve requirement The specified minimum percentage of its checkable deposits that a bank or thrift must keep on deposit at the Federal Reserve Bank in its district or hold as *vault cash*.

resource A natural, human, or manufactured item that helps produce goods and services; a productive agent or factor of production.

resource market A market in which *households* sell and *firms* buy resources or the services of resources.

restrictive monetary policy Federal Reserve system actions to reduce the *money supply*, increase *interest rates,* and reduce *inflation*; a tight money policy.

revenue tariff A *tariff* designed to produce income for the Federal government.

rule of 70 A method for determining the number of years it will take for some measure to double, given its annual percentage increase. Example: To determine the number of years it will take for the *price level* to double, divide 70 by the annual rate of *inflation*.

sales tax A tax levied on the cost (at retail) of a broad group of products.

saving Disposable income not spent for consumer goods; equal to *disposable income* minus *personal consumption expenditures*.

savings account A deposit in a *commercial bank* or *thrift institution* on which interest payments are received; generally used for saving rather than daily transactions; a component of the *M*2 money supply.

savings and loan association (S&L) A firm that accepts deposits primarily from small individual savers and lends primarily to individuals to finance purchases such as autos and homes; now nearly indistinguishable from a *commercial bank*.

saving schedule A schedule that shows the amounts *households* plan to save (plan not to spend for *consumer goods*), at different levels of *disposable income*.

savings deposit A deposit that is interest-bearing and that the depositor can normally withdraw at any time.

savings institution (See *thrift institution*.)

Say's law The largely discredited macroeconomic generalization that the production of goods and services (supply) creates an equal *demand* for those goods and services.

scarce resources The limited quantities of *land, capital, labor,* and *entrepreneurial ability* that are never sufficient to satisfy people's virtually unlimited economic wants.

scientific method The procedure for the systematic pursuit of knowledge involving the observation of facts and the formulation and testing of hypotheses to obtain theories, principles, and laws.

seasonal variations Increases and decreases in the level of economic activity within a single year, caused by a change in the season.

secular trend A long-term tendency; a change in some variable over a very long period of years.

self-interest That which each firm, property owner, worker, and consumer believes is best for itself and seeks to obtain.

seniority The length of time a worker has been employed absolutely or relative to other workers; may be used to determine which workers will be laid off when there is insufficient work for them all and who will be rehired when more work becomes available.

separation of ownership and control The fact that different groups of people own a *corporation* (the stockholders) and manage it (the directors and officers).

service An (intangible) act or use for which a consumer, firm, or government is willing to pay.

shirking Workers' neglecting or evading work to increase their *utility* or well-being.

shortage The amount by which the *quantity demanded* of a product exceeds the *quantity supplied* at a particular (below-equilibrium) price.

short run (1) In microeconomics, a period of time in which producers are able to change the quantities of some but not all of the resources they employ; a period in which some resources (usually plant) are fixed and some are variable. (2) In macroeconomics, a period in which nominal wages and other input prices do not change in response to a change in the price level.

short-run aggregate supply curve An aggregate supply curve relevant to a time period in which input prices (particularly *nominal wages*) do not change in response to changes in the *price level*.

simple multiplier The *multiplier* in any economy in which government collects no *net taxes,* there are no *imports,* and *investment* is independent of the level of income; equal to 1 divided by the *marginal propensity to save.*

simultaneous consumption The same-time derivation of *utility* from some product by a large number of consumers.

slope of a line The ratio of the vertical change (the rise or fall) to the horizontal change (the run) between any two points on a line. The slope of an upward-sloping line is positive, reflecting a direct relationship between two variables; the slope of a downward-sloping line is negative, reflecting an inverse relationship between two variables.

Smoot-Hawley Tariff Act Legislation passed in 1930 that established very high tariffs. Its objective was to reduce imports and stimulate the domestic economy, but it resulted only in retaliatory tariffs by other nations.

Social Security The social insurance program in the United States financed by Federal payroll taxes on employers and employees and designed to replace a portion of the earnings lost when workers become disabled, retire, or die.

Social Security trust fund A Federal fund that saves excessive Social Security tax revenues received in one year to meet Social Security benefit obligations that exceed Social Security tax revenues in some subsequent year.

sole proprietorship An unincorporated *firm* owned and operated by one person.

specialization The use of the resources of an individual, a firm, a region, or a nation to concentrate production on one or a small number of goods and services.

speculation The activity of buying or selling with the motive of later reselling or rebuying for profit.

SSI (See *Supplemental Security Income.*)

stagflation Inflation accompanied by stagnation in the rate of growth of output and an increase in unemployment in the economy; simultaneous increases in the *inflation rate* and the *unemployment rate*.

standardized budget A comparison of the government expenditures and tax collections that would occur if the economy operated at *full employment* throughout the year; the full-employment budget.

start-up (firm) A new firm focused on creating and introducing a particular new product or employing a specific new production or distribution method.

stock (corporate) An ownership share in a corporation.

store of value An *asset* set aside for future use; one of the three functions of *money*.

strategic trade policy The use of trade barriers to reduce the risk inherent in product development by domestic firms, particularly that involving advanced technology.

structural unemployment Unemployment of workers whose skills are not demanded by employers, who lack sufficient skill to obtain employment, or who cannot easily move to locations where jobs are available.

subsidy A payment of funds (or goods and services) by a government, firm, or household for which it receives no good or service in return. When made by a government, it is a *government transfer payment*.

substitute goods Products or services that can be used in place of each other. When the price of one falls, the demand for the other product falls; conversely, when the price of one product rises, the demand for the other product rises.

substitution effect (1) A change in the quantity demanded of a *consumer good* that results from a change in its relative expensiveness caused by a change in the product's price; (2) the effect of a change in the price of a *resource* on the quantity of the resource employed by a firm, assuming no change in its output.

supply A schedule showing the amounts of a good or service that sellers (or a seller) will offer at various prices during some period.

supply curve A curve illustrating *supply*.

supply factor (in growth) An increase in the availability of a resource, an improvement in its quality, or an expansion of technological knowledge that makes it possible for an economy to produce a greater output of goods and services.

supply schedule (See *supply.*)

supply-side economics A view of macroeconomics that emphasizes the role of costs and *aggregate supply* in explaining *inflation, unemployment,* and *economic growth*.

surplus The amount by which the *quantity supplied* of a product exceeds the *quantity demanded* at a specific (above-equilibrium) price.

tariff A tax imposed by a nation on an imported good.

tax An involuntary payment of money (or goods and services) to a government by a *household* or *firm* for which the household or firm receives no good or service directly in return.

taxes on production and imports A *national income accounting* category that includes such taxes as *sales*, *excise*, business property taxes, and *tariffs* which firms treat as costs of producing a product and pass on (in whole or in part) to buyers by charging a higher price.

tax incidence The person or group that ends up paying a tax.

tax-transfer disincentives Decreases in the incentives to work, save, invest, innovate, and take risks that allegedly result from high *marginal tax rates* and *transfer payments*.

Taylor rule A modern monetary rule proposed by economist John Taylor that would stipulate exactly how much the Federal Reserve should change interest rates in response to divergences of real GDP from potential GDP and divergences of actual rates of inflation from a target rate of inflation.

technological advance New and better goods and services and new and better ways of producing or distributing them.

technology The body of knowledge and techniques that can be used to combine *economic resources* to produce goods and services.

terms of trade The rate at which units of one product can be exchanged for units of another product; the price of a good or service; the amount of one good or service that must be given up to obtain 1 unit of another good or service.

theoretical economics The process of deriving and applying economic theories and principles.

thrift institution A *savings and loan association, mutual savings bank,* or *credit union.*

till money (See *vault cash.*)

time deposit An interest-earning deposit in a *commercial bank* or *thrift institution* that the depositor can withdraw without penalty after the end of a specified period.

total demand The demand schedule or the *demand curve* of all buyers of a good or service; also called market demand.

total demand for money The sum of the *transactions demand for money* and the *asset demand for money.*

total product (TP) The total output of a particular good or service produced by a firm (or a group of firms or the entire economy).

total revenue (TR) The total number of dollars received by a firm (or firms) from the sale of a product; equal to the total expenditures for the product produced by the firm (or firms); equal to the quantity sold (demanded) multiplied by the price at which it is sold.

total spending The total amount that buyers of goods and services spend or plan to spend; also called *aggregate expenditures.*

total supply The supply schedule or the *supply curve* of all sellers of a good or service; also called market supply.

Trade Adjustment Assistance Act A U.S. law passed in 2002 that provides cash assistance, education and training benefits, health care subsidies, and wage subsidies (for persons age 50 or older) to workers displaced by imports or relocations of U.S. plants to other countries.

trade balance The export of goods (or goods and services) of a nation less its imports of goods (or goods and services).

trade bloc A group of nations that lower or abolish trade barriers among members. Examples include the *European Union* and the nations of the *North American Free Trade Agreement.*

trade controls *Tariffs, export subsidies, import quotas,* and other means a nation may employ to reduce *imports* and expand *exports.*

trade deficit The amount by which a nation's *imports* of goods (or goods and services) exceed its *exports* of goods (or goods and services).

tradeoff The sacrifice of some or all of one economic goal, good, or service to achieve some other goal, good, or service.

trade surplus The amount by which a nation's *exports* of goods (or goods and services) exceed its *imports* of goods (or goods and services).

trading possibilities line A line that shows the different combinations of two products that an economy is able to obtain (consume) when it specializes in the production of one product and trades (exports) it to obtain the other product.

transactions demand for money The amount of money people want to hold for use as a *medium of exchange* (to make payments); varies directly with the *nominal GDP.*

transfer payment A payment of *money* (or goods and services) by a government to a *household* or *firm* for which the payer receives no good or service directly in return.

unanticipated inflation Increases in the price level (*inflation*) at a rate greater than expected.

underemployment A situation in which workers are employed in positions requiring less education and skill than they have.

undistributed corporate profits After-tax corporate profits not distributed as dividends to stockholders; corporate or business saving; also called retained earnings.

unemployment The failure to use all available *economic resources* to produce desired goods and services; the failure of the economy to fully employ its *labor force.*

unemployment compensation (See *unemployment insurance*).

unemployment insurance The social insurance program that in the United States is financed by state *payroll taxes* on employers and makes income available to workers who become unemployed and are unable to find jobs.

unemployment rate The percentage of the *labor force* unemployed at any time.

unit labor cost Labor cost per unit of output; total labor cost divided by total output; also equal to the *nominal wage* rate divided by the *average product* of labor.

unit of account A standard unit in which prices can be stated and the value of goods and services can be compared; one of the three functions of *money*.

unlimited liability Absence of any limits on the maximum amount that an individual (usually a business owner) may become legally required to pay.

unlimited wants The insatiable desire of consumers for goods and services that will give them satisfaction or *utility*.

unplanned changes in inventories Changes in inventories that firms did not anticipate; changes in inventories that occur because of unexpected increases or decreases of aggregate spending (of *aggregate expenditures*).

unplanned investment Actual investment less *planned investment;* increases or decreases in the *inventories* of firms resulting from production greater than sales.

Uruguay Round A 1995 trade agreement (fully implemented in 2005) that established the *World Trade Organization (WTO)*, liberalized trade in goods and services, provided added protection to intellectual property (for example, *patents* and *copyrights*), and reduced farm subsidies.

U.S. securities U.S. Treasury bills, notes, and bonds used to finance *budget deficits;* the components of the *public debt.*

utility The want-satisfying power of a good or service; the satisfaction or pleasure a consumer obtains from the consumption of a good or service (or from the consumption of a collection of goods and services).

value added The value of the product sold by a *firm* less the value of the products (materials) purchased and used by the firm to produce the product.

value judgment Opinion of what is desirable or undesirable; belief regarding what ought or ought not to be (regarding what is right or just and wrong or unjust).

value of money The quantity of goods and services for which a unit of money (a dollar) can be exchanged; the purchasing power of a unit of money; the reciprocal of the *price index.*

vault cash The *currency* a bank has in its vault and cash drawers.

velocity The number of times per year that the average dollar in the *money supply* is spent for *final goods and services;* nominal GDP divided by the money supply.

vertical axis The "up-down" or "north-south" measurement line on a graph or grid.

vertical intercept The point at which a line meets the vertical axis of a graph.

very long run A period in which *technology* can change and in which *firms* can introduce new products.

voluntary export restrictions (VER) Voluntary limitations by countries or firms of their exports to a particular foreign nation to avoid enactment of formal trade barriers by that nation.

wage The price paid for the use or services of *labor* per unit of time (per hour, per day, and so on).

wage rate (See *wage.*)

wages The income of those who supply the economy with *labor.*

wealth Anything that has value because it produces income or could produce income. Wealth is a stock; income is a flow. Assets less liabilities; net worth.

wealth effect The tendency for people to increase their consumption spending when the value of their financial and real assets rises and to decrease their consumption spending when the value of those assets falls.

world price The international market price of a good or service, determined by world demand and supply.

World Trade Organization (WTO) An organization of 149 nations (as of fall 2006) that oversees the provisions of the current world trade agreement, resolves trade disputes stemming from it, and holds forums for further rounds of trade negotiations.

WTO (See *World Trade Organization.*)